Get the eBooks FREE!

(PDF, ePub, Kindle, and liveBook all included)

We believe that once you buy a book from us, you should be able to read it in any format we have available. To get electronic versions of this book at no additional cost to you, purchase and then register this book at the Manning website.

Go to https://www.manning.com/freebook and follow the instructions to complete your pBook registration.

That's it!
Thanks from Manning!

Entity Framework Core in Action

Entity Framework Core
in Action

JON P SMITH

MANNING
SHELTER ISLAND

For online information and ordering of this and other Manning books, please visit www.manning.com. The publisher offers discounts on this book when ordered in quantity.

For more information, please contact

Special Sales Department
Manning Publications Co.
20 Baldwin Road
PO Box 761
Shelter Island, NY 11964
Email: orders@manning.com

Manning Publications Co.	Development editor:	Marina Michaels
20 Baldwin Road	Technical development editor:	Mike Shepard
PO Box 761	Copy editor:	Sharon Wilkey
Shelter Island, NY 11964	Proofreader:	Elizabeth Martin
	Technical proofreader:	Julien Pohie
	Typesetter:	Happenstance Type-O-Rama
	Cover designer:	Marija Tudor

ISBN 9781617294563
Printed in the United States of America
1 2 3 4 5 6 7 8 9 10 – DP – 23 22 21 20 19 18

brief contents

contents

5 Using EF Core in ASP.NET Core web applications   115

preface

Any software developer should be used to having to learn new libraries or languages, but for me, it's been a bit extreme. I stopped coding in 1988 when I went into technical management, and I didn't come back to coding until 2009—that's a 21-year gap. To say that the landscape had changed is an understatement; I felt like a child on Christmas morning with so many lovely presents I couldn't take it all in.

I made all the rookie mistakes at the beginning, like thinking object-oriented programming was about using inheritance, which it isn't. But I learned the new syntax, new tools (wow!), and reveled in the amount of information I could get online. I chose to focus on Microsoft's stack, mainly because of the wealth of documentation available. That was a good choice at the time, but now with .NET Core and its open source, multi-platform approach, it turns out to be an excellent choice.

The first applications I worked on in 2009 were ones that optimized and displayed healthcare needs geographically, especially around where to locate treatment centers. That required complex math (which my wife provided) and serious database work. I went through ADO.NET, LINQ to SQL, and then in 2013 I swapped to Entity Framework (EF), when EF 5 supported SQL's spatial (geographical) types.

Over the intervening years, I used EF a lot and have come to know EF6.x well. I've written extensively on EF in my own blog (www.thereformedprogrammer.net/) and on the Simple Talk site (www.simple-talk.com/author/jon-smith/). It turns out I like taking complex software ideas and trying to make them easy for other people to understand. So, when Manning Publications approached me to write a book on Entity Framework Core (EF Core), I said yes.

Entity Framework Core in Action covers all the features of EF Core 2.0, with plenty of examples and lots of code you can run. I've also included numerous patterns and practices to help you build robust and refactorable code. The book ends with an entire section, "Using Entity Framework Core in real-world applications," which shows my focus on building and shipping real applications. And I have not one, but two, chapters on performance tuning EF Core because your users/clients won't accept a slow application.

Some of the most pleasurable chapters to write were ones where I solved a technical problem, such as the best way to handle business logic (chapter 4), or performance tuning an application (chapters 13 and 14). These needed a combination of technical knowledge and insight into what business/development problem I was trying to solve. I also present the pros and cons of each approach I use, as I don't believe there is "silver bullet" answer in software—just a range of compromises that we as developers need to consider when choosing how to implement something.

acknowledgments

While I did most of the work on the book, I had a lot of help along the way and I want to say thank you to all those who helped.

My wife, Dr. Honora Smith, is not only my first line of proofreading but is the person who got me back into programming. I love her to bits. A special mention to my great friend JC for his help and support too.

Manning Publications has been magnificent, with a robust and comprehensive process that is thorough (and hard work), but results in an excellent end product. The team is great, and I'm going to list the significant people in chronological order, starting with Nicole Butterfield, Brian Sawyer, Marjan Bace, Rebecca Rinehart, Bert Bates, Marina Michaels, Candace Gillhoolley, Ivan Martinović, Christopher Kaufmann, Ana Romac, and many others who helped with production of the book.

I want to single out Marina Michaels and Mike Shepard, who were my development editor and technical development editor, respectively. Both Marina and Mike reviewed each chapter as I wrote them; their quick feedback helped me to refine my approach early on and made the book much more readable. Thanks also to Andrew Lock, author of *ASP.NET Core in Action* ; it was great to compare notes with another author who was writing a book at the same time as I.

I would also like to thank Julien Pohie, technical proofreader, and the reviewers of the book: Alberto Acerbis, Anne Epstein, Ernesto Cardenas, Evan Wallace, Foster Haines, Jeffrey Smith, Mauro Quercioli, Philip Taffet, Rahul Rai, Rami Abdelwahed, Raushan Jha, Ronald Tischliar, Sebastian Rogers, Stephen Byrne, Tanya Wilke, and Thomas Overby Hansen. Special thanks to the Microsoft people who reviewed the book: Rowan Miller, Diego Vega, Arthur Vickers, and Tom Dykstra; plus Paul Middleton and Erik Ejlskov Jensen, who are both open source providers to the EF Core project.

Finally, to the whole EF Core team for their work on a great library, plus putting up with the issues I kept posting in the EF Core's GitHub issues page. And a thank you to Rick Anderson at Microsoft for his input over the years and help on getting my articles out to a wider audience.

about this book

Entity Framework Core in Action is about how to write EF Core database code quickly, correctly, and ultimately, for fast performance. To help with the "quick, correct, fast" aspects, I include a lot of examples with plenty of tips and techniques. And along the way, I throw in quite a bit on how EF Core works on the inside, because that will help you when things don't work the way you think they should.

The Microsoft documentation is good but doesn't have room for detailed examples. In this book, I try to give you at least one example of each feature I cover, and you'll often find unit tests in the Git repo (see the "About the code" section for links) that test a feature in multiple ways. Sometimes reading a unit test can convey what's happening much more quickly than reading the text in the book can, so consider the unit tests as a useful resource.

Who should read this book

Entity Framework Core in Action is aimed at both software developers who've never before used EF and seasoned EF6.x developers, plus anyone else who wants to know what EF Core is capable of. I assume you're familiar with .NET development with C# and that you have at least some idea of what a relational database is. You don't need to be a C# expert, but if you're new to C#, you might find some of the code hard to read, as I don't explain C#. But I do provide an appendix on LINQ (Language Integrated Query) in case you haven't seen LINQ before.

How this book is organized

I've tried to build a path that starts with the basics (part 1), goes deep into the details (part 2), and ends with useful tools and techniques (part 3). I try not to assume you'll read the book cover to cover, especially the reference section in part 2, but at least skim-reading the first five chapters will help you understand the basics that I use later in the book.

Part 1: Getting started

- Chapter 1 introduces EF Core with a super-simple console application so you can see all the parts of EF Core in action. I also provide an overview of how EF Core works and why you might like to use it.
- Chapter 2 looks at querying (reading data from) the database. I cover the relationships between data stored in the database and how you can load that related data by using EF Core.
- Chapter 3 moves on to changing the data in a database: adding new data, updating existing data, and deleting data from a database.
- Chapter 4 looks at how to build robust business logic that uses EF Core to access the database. *Business logic* is the name given to code that implements business rules or workflow that's specific to the business problem your application solves.
- Chapter 5 is about building an ASP.NET Core application that uses EF Core. It pulls together the code developed in chapters 2 to 4 to make a web application. I also talk about deploying the web application and accessing the hosted database.

Part 2: Entity Framework Core in Depth

- Chapter 6 covers the configuration of nonrelational properties—properties that hold a value, such as int, string, DateTime, and so on.
- Chapter 7 covers the configuration of relationships—the links between classes, such as a Book class linking to one or more Author classes. It also includes special mapping techniques, such as mapping multiple classes to one table.
- Chapter 8 looks at advanced mapping features and the whole area of detecting and handling concurrency conflicts.
- Chapter 9 digs deep into how EF Core's DbContext works, with a blow-by-blow view of what the various methods and properties do inside your application's DbContext.

Part 3: Using Entity Framework Core in real-world applications

- Chapter 10 is a compendium of tools, patterns and techniques that can make your EF Core quicker to develop and/or more robust. I also look at using EF Core in a domain-driven design approach.
- Chapter 11 covers all the ways you can change the database structure when using EF Core. It also looks at the issues that arise when you need to change the structure of a database that's being used by a live application.
- Chapter 12 lists all the issues that could affect the performance of your database accesses, and what to do about them.

- Chapter 13 is a worked example of performance tuning an EF Core application. I take the book app, developed in part 1, and apply three levels of performance tuning.
- Chapter 14 starts with what happens if you change the database type. It then looks at another application architecture that can help performance of some business applications. It ends with accessing and modifying EF Core's internal services.
- Chapter 15 is all about unit-testing applications that use EF Core. I've also created a NuGet package that you can use to help in your own unit testing.

Appendixes

- Appendix A introduces the LINQ language that EF Core uses. This is useful for those who are unfamiliar with LINQ, or anybody who wants a quick refresh on LINQ.
- Appendix B provides preliminary information on the EF Core 2.1 release, with links to Microsoft's documentation.

NOTE I have added notes about EF Core 2.1 features to chapters throughout the book. These point out areas where the 2.1 release offers new options over what EF Core 2.0 has.

About the code

I feel I really know something only if I've written code to use that function or feature, which is why every chapter has its own Git branch, or sometimes a branch per chapter section, in the repo found at https://github.com/JonPSmith/EfCoreInAction. See the "Where's the code" section of the Readme file in the Git repo for more information at https://github.com/JonPSmith/EfCoreInAction/blob/master/README .md#wheres-the-code.

Chapters 1 and 2 include sidebars on how to download and run the sample code locally. As you look at each chapter, you can select a different Git branch to access the code specifically for that chapter. Also, look out for the associated unit tests, grouped by chapter and feature.

NOTE Chapter 15, which is about unit testing, has its own Git repo at https:// github.com/JonPSmith/EfCore.TestSupport. I made this separate because it contains tools and features that will help you with unit testing. You can also install the NuGet package called EfCore.TestSupport into your test project to use the features I describe in chapter 15.

To write your own code, or run the code from the Git repo, you will need the following:

1 A development environment
- Visual Studio 2017 (VS 2017) is the recommended version of Visual Studio for .NET Core development. A community version of Visual Studio 2017 is available that's free for individuals or small companies; see www.visualstudio.com/vs/ compare/. You should ensure that you have VS 2017 version 15.7.1 or above to

pick up the latest version of NuGet. Older versions of NuGet have a problem; see https://stackoverflow.com/a/45946273/1434764.

- Visual Studio Code, which is a newer, lighter, open source development environment that runs on Windows, Mac, and Linux, and is free is another possibility. See http://code.visualstudio.com/. I've set up the .vscode directory in each branch to correctly build, test, and run the code.

2 The .NET Core SDK

NOTE The Git repo assumes .NET Core 2.0, but I have updated a few branches to .NET Core 2.1—see https://github.com/JonPSmith/EfCoreInAction#net -core-21-examples.

- If you install VS 2017 and include the .NET Core Cross-Platform Development feature, found under the Other Toolsets section, during the install workloads stage, then that will install the .NET Core.
- Alternatively, if you're using Visual Studio Code, you need to download and install the .NET Core SDK for your development environment. See www.microsoft .com/net/download/core.

If you're in a hurry to see the example book-selling site (referred to in the book as the *book app*), a live version is at http://efcoreinaction.com/ (chapter 13 version) and http://cqrsravendb.efcoreinaction.com/ (chapter 14 CQRS version). These sites don't allow changes to the data other than you "buying a book" (no money changes hands, but then again, I don't send you a book!). But if you download the code and run the book app locally, various add, update, or delete commands will become available to you.

Code conventions

The code samples in this book, and their output, appear in a `fixed-width font` and are often accompanied by annotations. The code samples are deliberately kept as simple as possible, because they aren't intended to be reusable parts that can be plugged into your code. Instead, the code samples are stripped down so that you can focus on the principle being illustrated.

This book contains many examples of source code, both in numbered listings and in line with normal text. In both cases, source code is formatted in a `fixed-width font` `like this` to separate it from ordinary text. Sometimes code is also **in bold** to highlight code that has changed from previous steps in the chapter, such as when a new feature adds to an existing line of code.

In many cases, the original source code has been reformatted; we've added line breaks and reworked indentation to accommodate the available page space in the book. In rare cases, even this was not enough, and listings include line-continuation markers (➥). Additionally, comments in the source code have often been removed from the listings when the code is described in the text. Code annotations accompany many of the listings, highlighting important concepts.

Source code for the examples in this book is available for download from the Git repo at https://github.com/JonPSmith/EfCoreInAction.

Book forum

The purchase of *Entity Framework Core in Action* includes free access to a private web forum run by Manning Publications, where you can make comments about the book, ask technical questions, and receive help from the author and from other users. To access the forum and subscribe to it, point your web browser to https://www.manning.com/books/entity-framework-core-in-action. This page provides information about how to get on the forum when you're registered and what kind of help is available. You can learn more about Manning's forums and the rules of conduct at https://forums.manning.com/forums/about.

Manning's commitment to our readers is to provide a venue where a meaningful dialogue between individual readers and between readers and the author can take place. It's not a commitment to any specific amount of participation on the part of the author, whose contribution to the book's forum remains voluntary (and unpaid). We suggest that you try asking him some challenging questions, lest his interest strays! The book forum and the archives of previous discussions will be accessible from the publisher's website as long as the book is in print.

Online resources

Here are useful links to the Microsoft documentation and code:

- Microsoft's EF Core documentation: https://docs.microsoft.com/en-us/ef/core/index
- The EF Core roadmap: https://github.com/aspnet/EntityFrameworkCore/wiki/roadmap
- The EF Core code: https://github.com/aspnet/EntityFrameworkCore
- ASP.NET Core, working with EF Core: https://docs.microsoft.com/en-us/aspnet/core/data/
- Stack Overflow EF Core tag: [entity-framework-core] https://stackoverflow.com

about the author

Jon P Smith is a full-stack developer focused on the .NET stack covering the full range of features from database access, web/mobile applications, and front-end JavaScript libraries. Jon has designed and built several web applications, all with him as the lead developer. Jon writes articles on a range of topics, mainly about EF, ASP.NET, and React.js. He works as an independent principal developer/consultant.

about the cover illustration

The figure on the cover of *Entity Framework Core in Action* is captioned "The Wife of a Franc Merchant." The illustration is taken from Thomas Jefferys' *A Collection of the Dresses of Different Nations, Ancient and Modern* (four volumes), London, published between 1757 and 1772. The title page states that these are hand-colored copperplate engravings, heightened with gum arabic.

Thomas Jefferys (1719–1771) was called "Geographer to King George III." He was an English cartographer who was the leading map supplier of his day. He engraved and printed maps for government and other official entities and produced a wide range of commercial maps and atlases, especially of North America. His work as a map maker sparked an interest in local dress customs of the lands he surveyed and mapped, which are brilliantly displayed in this collection. Fascination with faraway lands and travel for pleasure were relatively new phenomena in the late 18th century, and collections such as this one were popular, introducing both the tourist as well as the armchair traveler to the inhabitants of other countries.

The diversity of the drawings in Jefferys' volumes speaks vividly of the uniqueness and individuality of the world's nations some 200 years ago. Dress codes have changed since then, and the diversity by region and country, so rich at the time, has faded away. It's now often hard to tell the inhabitants of one continent from another. Perhaps, trying to view it optimistically, we've traded a cultural and visual diversity for a more varied personal life—or a more varied and interesting intellectual and technical life.

At a time when it's difficult to tell one computer book from another, Manning celebrates the inventiveness and initiative of the computer business with book covers based on the rich diversity of regional life of two centuries ago, brought back to life by Jeffreys' pictures.

Part 1

Getting started

Data is everywhere, growing by petabytes per year, and a lot of it is stored in databases. Millions of applications are also out there—half a million new mobile applications in 2016 alone—and most of them need to access data in databases. And I haven't started on the Internet of Things yet. So it shouldn't be a surprise that Gartner says, "Global IT Spending to Reach $3.5 Trillion in 2017" (www .gartner.com/newsroom/id/3482917).

The good news for you is that your skills will be in demand. But the bad news is that the pressure to develop applications quickly is unrelenting. This book is about one tool that you can use to write database access code quickly: Microsoft's Entity Framework Core (EF Core). EF Core provides an object-oriented way to access relational databases, and in EF Core 2 nonrelational (NoSQL) databases, in the .NET environment. The cool thing about EF Core, and the other .NET Core libraries, is that they can run on Windows, Linux, and Apple platforms.

In part 1, I get you into the code straightaway. In chapter 1, you'll build a super-simple console application, and by the end of chapter 5, we'll have covered enough for you to build a web application that accesses a database. Chapters 2 and 3 explain the reading and writing of data to a relational database, respectively, and chapter 4 covers writing business logic, the business rules specific to each application. In chapter 5, you'll pull it all together by using Microsoft's ASP.NET Core web framework to build an example book-selling site, which you can try on a live site at http://efcoreinaction.com/.

You'll have a lot of learning in part 1, even though I skip over a few topics, mainly by relying on a lot of EF Core's default settings. Nevertheless, part 1 should give you a good understanding of what EF Core can do, with later parts growing your knowledge with extra EF Core features, more detail on how you can configure EF Core, and chapters devoted to specific areas such as performance tuning.

Introduction to Entity FrameworkCore

Entity Framework Core, or *EF Core*, is a library that allows software developers to access databases. There are many ways to build such a library, but EF Core is designed as an *object-relational mapper* (*O/RM*). O/RMs work by mapping between the two worlds: the relational database with its own API, and the object-oriented software world of classes and software code. EF Core's main strength is allowing software developers to write database access code quickly.

EF Core, which Microsoft released in 2016, is multiplatform-capable: it can run on Windows, Linux, and Apple. It does this as part of the .NET Core initiative, hence the *Core* part of the EF Core name. (But EF Core can be used with the existing .NET Framework too—see the note in section 1.10.5.) EF Core, ASP.NET Core (a web server-side application), and .NET Core are also all open source, each with an active issues page for interacting with development teams.

EF Core isn't the first version of Entity Framework; an existing, non-Core, Entity Framework library is known as *EF6.x*. EF Core starts with years of experience built into it via feedback from these previous versions, 4 to 6.x. It has kept the same type of interface as EF6.x but has major changes underneath, such as the ability to handle nonrelational databases, which EF6.x wasn't designed to do. As a previous user of EF5 and EF6.x, I can see where EF Core has been improved, as well as where it's still missing features of the old EF6.x library that I liked (although those features are on the roadmap).

This book is intended for both software developers who've never used Entity Framework and seasoned EF6.x developers, plus anyone who wants to know what EF Core is capable of. I do assume that you're familiar with .NET development with C# and that you have at least some idea of what relational databases are. I don't assume you know how to write Structured Query Language (SQL), the language used by a majority of relational databases, because EF Core can do most of that for you. But I do show the SQL that EF Core produces, because it helps you understand what's going on; using some of the EF Core advanced features requires you to have SQL knowledge, but the book provides plenty of diagrams to help you along the way.

> **TIP** If you don't know a lot about SQL and want to learn more, I suggest the W3Schools online resource: www.w3schools.com/sql/sql_intro.asp. The SQL set of commands is vast, and EF Core queries use only a small subset (for example, SELECT, WHERE, and INNER JOIN), so that's a good place to start.

This chapter introduces you to EF Core through the use of a small application that calls into the EF Core library. You'll look under the hood to see how EF Core interprets software commands and accesses the database. Having an overview of what's happening inside EF Core will help you as you read through the rest of the book.

1.1 *What you'll learn from this book*

The book is split into three parts. In addition to this chapter, part 1 has four other chapters that cover:

- Querying the database with EF Core
- Updating the database with EF Core (creating, updating, and deleting data)
- Using EF Core in business logic
- Building an ASP.NET Core web application that uses EF Core

By the end of part 1, you should be able to build a .NET application that uses a relational database. But the way the database is organized is left to EF Core; for instance, EF Core's default configuration sets the type and size of the database columns, which can be a bit wasteful on space.

Part 2 covers how and why you can change the defaults, and looks deeper into some of the EF Core commands. After part 2, you'll be able to use EF Core to create a database in exactly the way you want it, or link to an existing database that has a specific schema, or design. In addition, by using some of EF Core's advanced features, you can change the way the database data is exposed inside your .NET application—for instance, controlling software access to data more carefully or building code to automatically track database changes.

Part 3 is all about improving your skills and making you a better developer, and debugger, of EF Core applications. I present real-world applications of EF Core, starting with a range of known patterns and practices that you can use. You'll read chapters on unit testing EF Core applications, extending EF Core, and most important, finding and fixing EF Core performance issues.

1.2　*My "lightbulb moment" with Entity Framework*

Before we get into the nitty-gritty, let me tell you one defining moment I had when using Entity Framework that put me on the road to embracing EF. It was my wife who got me back into programming after a 21-year gap (that's a story in itself!).

My wife, Dr. Honora Smith, is a lecturer in mathematics at the University of Southampton who specializes in the modeling of healthcare systems, especially focusing on where to locate health facilities. I had worked with her to build several applications to do geographic modeling and visualization for the UK National Health Service and work for South Africa on optimizing HIV/AIDS testing.

At the start of 2013, I decided to build a web application specifically for healthcare modeling. I used ASP.NET MVC4 and EF5, which had just come out and supported SQL spatial types that handle geographic data. The project went okay, but it was hard work. I knew the frontend was going to be hard; it was a single-page application using Backbone.js, but I was surprised at how long it took me to do the server-side work.

I had applied good software practices and made sure the database and business logic were matched to the problem space—that of modeling and optimizing the location of health facilities. That was fine, but I spent an inordinate amount of time writing code to convert the database entries and business logic into a form suitable to show to the user. Also, I was using a Repository/Unit of Work pattern to hide EF5 code, and I was continually having to tweak areas to make the repository work properly.

At the end of a project, I always look back and ask, "Could I have done that better?" As a software architect, I'm always looking for parts that (a) worked well, (b) were repetitious and should be automated, or (c) had ongoing problems. This time, the list was as follows:

- *Worked well*—The ServiceLayer, a layer in my application that isolated/adapted the lower layers of the application from the ASP.NET MVC4 frontend, worked well. (I introduce this layered architecture in chapter 2.)
- *Was repetitious*—I used ViewModel classes, also known as *data transfer objects* (DTOs), to represent the data I needed to show to the user. Using a ViewModel/DTO worked well, but writing the code to copy the database tables to

the ViewModel/DTO was repetitious and boring. (I also talk about ViewModels/ DTOs in chapter 2.)

- *Had ongoing problems*—The Repository/Unit of Work pattern didn't work for me. Ongoing problems occurred throughout the project. (I cover the Repository pattern and alternatives in chapter 10.)

As a result of my review, I built a library called GenericServices (https://github.com/ JonPSmith/GenericServices) to use with EF6.x. This automated the copying of data between database classes and ViewModels/DTOs and removed the need for a Repository/Unit of Work pattern. It seemed to be working well, but to stress-test GenericServices, I decided to build a frontend over one of Microsoft's example databases, the AdventureWorks 2012 Light database. I built the whole application with the help of a frontend UI library in 10 days!

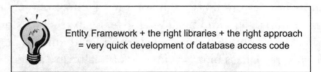

Entity Framework + the right libraries + the right approach
= very quick development of database access code

The site isn't that pretty, but that wasn't the point. My GenericServices library allowed me to quickly implement a whole range of database Create, Read, Update, and Delete (CRUD) commands. Definitely a "lightbulb moment," and I was hooked on EF. You can find the site at http://complex.samplemvcwebapp.net/.

Since then, I've built other libraries, some open source and some private, and used them on several projects. These libraries significantly speed up the development of 90% of database accesses, leaving me to concentrate on the harder topics, such as building great frontend interfaces, writing custom business logic to meet the client's specific requirements, and performance tuning where necessary.

1.3 Some words for existing EF6.x developers

TIME-SAVER If you're new to Entity Framework, you can skip this section.

If you're a reader who knows EF6.x, much of EF Core will be familiar to you. To help you navigate quickly through this book, I've added EF6 notes.

EF6 Watch for notes like this throughout the book. They point out the places where EF Core is different from EF6.x. Also, be sure to look at the summaries at the end of each chapter. They point out the biggest changes between EF6 and EF Core in the chapter.

I'll also give you one tip from my journey of learning EF Core. I know EF6.x well, but that became a bit of a problem at the start of using EF Core. I was using an EF6.x approach to problems and didn't notice that EF Core had new ways to solve them. In most cases, the approach is similar, but in some areas, it isn't.

My advice to you as an existing EF6.x developer is to approach EF Core as a new library that someone has written to mimic EF6.x, but understand that it works in a different way. That way, you'll keep your eyes open for the new and different ways of doing things in EF Core.

1.4 An overview of EF Core

EF Core can be used as an O/RM that maps between the relational database and the .NET world of classes and software code. Table 1.1 shows how EF Core maps the two worlds of the relational database and .NET software.

Table 1.1   EF Core mapping between a database and .NET software

Relational database	.NET software
Table	.NET class
Table columns	Class properties/fields
Rows	Elements in .NET collections—for instance, `List`
Primary keys: unique row	A unique class instance
Foreign keys: define a relationship	Reference to another class
SQL—for instance, `WHERE`	.NET LINQ—for instance, `Where(p => ...`

1.4.1 The downsides of O/RMs

Making a good O/RM is complex. Although EF6.x or EF Core can seem easy to use, at times the EF Core "magic" can catch you by surprise. Let me mention two issues to be aware of before we dive into how EF Core works.

The first issue is *object-relational impedance mismatch*. Database servers and object-oriented software use different principles: databases use primary keys to define that a row is unique, whereas .NET class instances are, by default, considered unique by their reference. EF Core handles most of this for you, but your nice .NET classes get "polluted" by these keys, and their values matter. In most cases, EF Core is going to work fine, but sometimes you need to do things a little differently to a software-only solution to suit the database. One example you'll see in chapter 2 is a many-to-many relationship: easy in C#, but a bit more work in a database.

The second issue is that an O/RM—and especially an O/RM as comprehensive as EF Core—hides the database so well that you can sometimes forget about what's going on underneath. This problem can cause you to write code that works great in your test application, but performs terribly in the real world when the database is complex and has many simultaneous users.

That's why I spend time in this chapter showing how EF Core works on the inside, and the SQL it produces. The more you understand about what EF Core is doing, the better equipped you'll be to write good EF Core code, and more important, know what to do when it doesn't work.

> **NOTE**   Throughout this book, I use a "get it working, but be ready to make it faster if I need to" approach to using EF Core. EF Core allows me to develop quickly, but I'm aware that because of EF Core, or my poor use of it, the performance of my database access code might not be good enough for a particular business need. Chapter 5 covers how to isolate your EF Core so you can tune it with minimal side effects, and chapter 13 shows how to find and improve database code that isn't fast enough.

1.5   *What about NoSQL?*

We can't talk about relational databases without mentioning nonrelational databases, also known colloquially as NoSQL (see http://mng.bz/DW63). Both relational and nonrelational databases have a role in modern applications. I've used both SQL Server (relational database) and Azure Tables (nonrelational database) in the same application to handle two business needs.

EF Core is designed to handle both relational and nonrelational databases—a departure from EF6.x, which was designed around relational databases only. Many of the principles covered in this book apply to both types of databases, but because relational databases are inherently much more complex than nonrelational databases, more commands are needed to use relational databases. You'll see whole chapters dedicated to commands that are used only in a relational database. Chapter 7, for instance, is all about modeling database relationships.

EF Core 2.0 will contain a preview database provider for the Azure NoSQL database, Cosmos DB. The aim is to use this as a learning exercise for handling NoSQL databases, with a robust solution coming out in EF Core 2.2. More NoSQL database providers are likely to be written for EF Core over time, either by Microsoft or the writers of NoSQL databases.

> **NOTE**   In section 14.2, you'll build an application using both an SQL/relational database and a NoSQL database in a Command Query Responsibility Segregation (CQRS) architectural pattern to get a higher-performing application.

1.6   *Your first EF Core application*

In this chapter, you'll start with a simple example so that we can focus on what EF Core is doing, rather than what the code is doing. For this, you're going to use a small console application called MyFirstEfCoreApp, which accesses a simple database. The MyFirstEfCoreApp application's job is to list and update books in a supplied database. Figure 1.1 shows the console output.

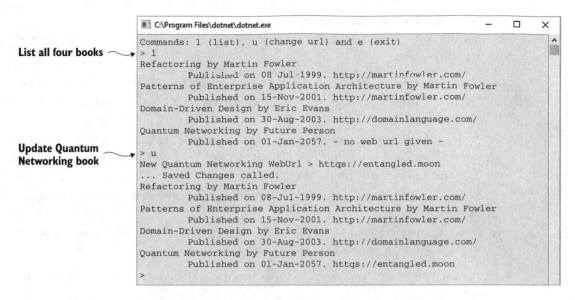

List all four books

Update Quantum
Networking book

Figure 1.1   The output from the console application you'll use to look at how EF Core works

This application isn't going to win any prizes for its interface or complexity, but it's a good place to start, especially because I want to show you how EF Core works internally in order to help you understand what's going on later in this book.

You can download this example application from the Chapter01 branch of the Git repo at http://mng.bz/KTjz. You can look at the code and run the application. To do this, you need software development tools.

1.6.1   *What you need to install*

You can use two main development tools to develop a .NET Core application: Visual Studio 2017 (VS 2017) or Visual Studio Code (VS Code). I describe using VS 2017 for your first application, because it's slightly easier to use for newcomers to .NET development.

You need to install Visual Studio 2017 (VS 2017) from www.visualstudio.com. Numerous versions exist, including a free community version, but you need to read the license to make sure you qualify; see www.visualstudio.com/vs/community/.

When you install VS 2017, make sure you include the .NET Core Cross-Platform Development feature, which is under the Other Toolsets section during the Install Workloads stage. This installs .NET Core on your system. Then you're ready to build a .NET Core application. See http://mng.bz/2x0T for more information.

1.6.2   *Creating your own .NET Core console app with EF Core*

I know many developers like to create their own applications, because building the code yourself means that you know exactly what's involved. This section details how to create the .NET Core console application MyFirstEfCoreApp by using Visual Studio 2017.

CREATING A .NET CORE CONSOLE APPLICATION

The first thing you need to do is create a .NET Core console application. Using VS 2017, here are the steps:

1 In the top menu of VS 2017, click File > New > Project to open the New Project form.

2 From the installed templates, select Visual C# > .NET Core > Console App (.NET Core).

3 Type in the name of your program (in this case, `MyFirstEfCoreApp`) and make sure the location is sensible. By default, VS 2017 will put your application in a directory ending with \Source\Repos.

4 Make sure the Create Directory for Solution box is ticked so that your application has its own folder.

5 If you want to create a Git repo for this project, make sure the Create New Git Repository box is selected too. Then click OK.

At this point, you've created a console application, and the editor should be in the file called Program.cs.

> **TIP**   You can find out which level of .NET Core your application is using by choosing Project > MyFirstEfCoreApp Properties from the main menu; the Application tab shows the Target Framework.

ADDING THE EF CORE LIBRARY TO YOUR APPLICATION

You need to install the correct EF Core NuGet library for the database you're going to use. For local development, Microsoft.EntityFrameworkCore.SqlServer is the best choice, because it'll use the development SQL Server that was installed when you installed VS 2017.

You can install the NuGet library in various ways. The more visual way is to use the NuGet Package Manager. The steps are as follows:

1 In the Solution Explorer, typically on the right-hand side of VS 2017, right-click the Dependencies line in your console application and select the Manage NuGet Packages option.

2 At the top right of the NuGet Package Manager page that appears, click the Browse link.

3 In the Search box below the Browse link, type `Microsoft.EntityFramework-Core.SqlServer` and then select the NuGet package with that name.

4 A box appears to the right of the list of NuGet packages with the name Microsoft.EntityFrameworkCore.SqlServer at the top and an Install button below it, showing which version will install.

5 Click the Install button and then accept the license agreements. The package installs. Installation could take a little while, depending on your internet connection speed.

Downloading and running the example application from the Git repo

You have two options for downloading and running the MyFirstEfCoreApp console application found in the Git repo: either VS 2017 or VS Code. I describe both.

Using Visual Studio 2017, version 15.3.3 or above (VS 2017), follow these steps:

1 *Clone the Git repo.* First you need to select the Team Explorer view and select the Manage Connections tab. In the Local Git Repositories section, click the Clone button. This opens a form containing an input line saying "Enter the URL of a Git repo to clone" in which you should input the URL https://github.com/JonPSmith/ EfCoreInAction. The local directory path shown below the URL should update to end with EfCoreInAction. Now click the Clone button at the bottom of the form.

2 *Select the right branch.* After the clone has finished, the list of local Git repositories should have a new entry called EfCoreInAction. Double-click this, and the Home tab appears. Currently, the Git repo will be on the master branch, which doesn't have any code. You need to select the remotes/origin > Chapter01 branch: click the Branches button, click the Remotes/Origin drop-down, and select Chapter01. Next, click the Home button. You'll see a Solution called EfCoreInAction.sln, which you need to click. That loads the local solution, and you're ready to run the application.

3 *Run the application.* Go to the Solutions Explorer window, which shows you the code. Click any of the classes to see the code. If you press F5 (Start Debugging), the console application will start in a new command-line window. The first line shows you the commands you can type. Have fun!

Using Visual Studio Code (VS Code), follow these steps:

Note: I assume that you've set up VS Code to support C# development.

1 *Clone the Git repo.* In the command palette (Ctrl-Shift-P), type `Git: Clone`. This presents you with a Repository Url input line, in which you should place the https:// github.com/JonPSmith/EfCoreInAction URL and then press the Return key. You'll then see a Parent Directory input line; indicate the directory that will contain the Git repo and then press the Return key. This clones the Git repo to your local storage, in a directory called EfCoreInAction.

2 *Select the right branch.* After the clone, you'll see a message asking, "Would you like to open the cloned repository?" Click the Open Repository button to do that. You should see just a few files in the master branch, but no code. Select the Chapter01 branch by typing `Git: Checkout to` in the command palette (Ctrl-Shift-P) and selecting the origin/Chapter01 branch. The files change, and you'll now have the code for the MyFirstEfCoreApp console application.

3 *Run the application.* I've already set up the tasks.json and launch.json files for this project, so you can press F5 to start debugging. The console application starts in a new command-line window. The first line shows the commands you can type. Have fun!

1.7   *The database that MyFirstEfCoreApp will access*

EF Core is about accessing databases, but where does that database come from? EF Core gives you two options: EF Core can create it for you, known as *code-first*, or you can provide an existing database you built outside EF Core, known as *database-first*.

> **EF6**   In EF6, you could use an EDMX/database designer to visually design your database, an option known as *design-first*. EF Core doesn't support the design-first approach, and there are no plans to add it.

In this chapter, we're going to skip over how I created the database for the MyFirstEf-CoreApp application and simply assume it exists.

> **NOTE**   In my code, I use a basic EF Core command meant for unit testing to create the database, because it's simple and quick. Chapter 2 covers how to get EF Core to create a database properly, and chapter 11 presents the whole issue of creating and changing databases.

For this MyFirstEfCoreApp application example, I created a simple database, shown in figure 1.2, with only two tables:

- A Books table holding the book information
- An Author table holding the author of each book

> **NOTE**   The Books table name comes from the `DbSet<Book>` property name of `Books` in the application's DbContext, which I show in figure 1.5. The Author table name doesn't have a `DbSet<T>` property in the application's DbContext, so the table defaults to the class name, `Author`. Section 6.10.1 covers these configuration rules in more detail.

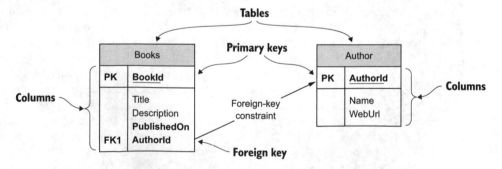

Figure 1.2   Our example relational database with two tables: Books and Author

Figure 1.3 shows the content of the database. It holds only four books, the first two of which have the same author, Martin Fowler.

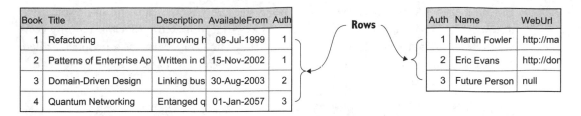

Book	Title	Description	AvailableFrom	Auth
1	Refactoring	Improving h	08-Jul-1999	1
2	Patterns of Enterprise Ap	Written in d	15-Nov-2002	1
3	Domain-Driven Design	Linking bus	30-Aug-2003	2
4	Quantum Networking	Entanged q	01-Jan-2057	3

Auth	Name	WebUrl
1	Martin Fowler	http://ma
2	Eric Evans	http://dor
3	Future Person	null

Figure 1.3   The content of the database, showing four books, two of which have the same author

1.8   Setting up the MyFirstEfCoreApp application

Having created and set up a .NET Core console application, you can now start writing EF Core code. You need to write two fundamental parts before creating any database access code:

1 The classes that you want EF Core to map to the tables in your database

2 The application's DbContext, which is the primary class that you'll use to config-ure and access the database

1.8.1   The classes that map to the database—Book and Author

EF Core maps classes to database tables. Therefore, you need to create a class that will define the database table, or match a database table if you already have a database. Lots of rules and configurations exist (covered later in the book), but figure 1.4 gives the typical format of a class that's mapped to a database table.

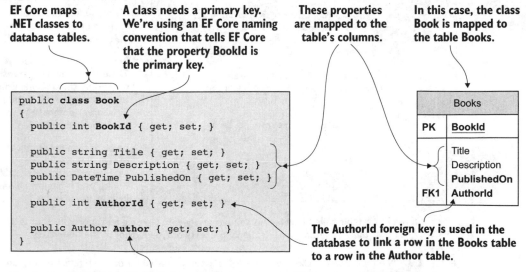

EF Core maps .NET classes to database tables.

A class needs a primary key. We're using an EF Core naming convention that tells EF Core that the property BookId is the primary key.

These properties are mapped to the table's columns.

In this case, the class Book is mapped to the table Books.

```
public class Book
{
    public int BookId { get; set; }

    public string Title { get; set; }
    public string Description { get; set; }
    public DateTime PublishedOn { get; set; }

    public int AuthorId { get; set; }

    public Author Author { get; set; }
}
```

Books	
PK	BookId
	Title
	Description
	PublishedOn
FK1	AuthorId

The AuthorId foreign key is used in the database to link a row in the Books table to a row in the Author table.

The Author property is an EF Core navigational property. EF Core uses this on a save to see whether the Book has an Author class attached—if so, it sets the foreign key, AuthorId.

Figure 1.4   The .NET class Book, on the left, maps to a database table called Books, on the right. This is a typical way to build your application, with multiple classes that map to database tables.

Listing 1.1 shows the other class you'll be using: `Author`. This has the same structure as the `Book` class in figure 1.4, with a primary key that follows the EF Core naming conventions of `<ClassName>Id` (see section 6.3.15). The `Book` class has a property called `AuthorId`, which EF Core knows is a foreign key because it has the same name as the `Author` primary key.

Listing 1.1   The `Author` class from MyFirstEfCoreApp

```
public class Author
{
    public int AuthorId { get; set; }        ◄──   Holds the primary key of the Author row
    public string Name { get; set; }                in the DB. Note that the foreign key in
    public string WebUrl { get; set; }              the Book class has the same name.
}
```

1.8.2   *The application's DbContext*

The other important part of the application is its DbContext. This is a class that you create that inherits from EF Core's `DbContext` class. This holds the information EF Core needs to configure that database mapping, and is also the class you use in your code to access the database (see section 1.9.2). Figure 1.5 shows the application's DbContext, called `AppDbContext`, that the MyFirstEfCoreApp console application uses.

You must have a class that inherits from the EF Core class DbContext. This class holds the information and configuration for accessing your database.

```
public class AppDbContext : DbContext
{
    private const string ConnectionString =
      @" Server = (local db)\nssql local dv;
        Database=MyFirstEfCoreDb;
        Trusted_Connection=True";

    protected override void OnConfiguring(
        DbContextOptionsBuilder optionsBuilder)
    {
        optionsBuilder
            .UseSqlServer(connectionString);
    }

    public DbSet<Book> Books { get; set; }

}
```

The database connection string holds information about the database:
- **How to find the database server**
- **The name of the database**
- **Authorization to access the database**

In a console application, you configure EF Core's database options by overriding the OnConfiguring method. In this case you tell it you're using an SQL Server database by using the UseSqlServer method.

By creating a property called Books of type DbSet<Book>, you tell EF Core that there's a database table named Books, and it has the columns and keys as found in the Book class.

Our database has a table called Author, but you purposely didn't create a property for that table. EF Core finds that table by finding a navigational property of type Author in the Book class.

Figure 1.5   Two main parts of the application's DbContext created for the MyFirstEfCoreApp console application. First, the setting of the database options to define what type of database to use and where it can be found. Second, the DbSet<T> property(s) that tell EF Core what classes should be mapped to the database.

In our small example application, all the decisions on the modeling are done by EF Core, which works things out by using a set of conventions. You have loads of extra ways to tell EF Core what the database model is, and these commands can get complex. It takes both chapter 6 and chapter 7 to cover all the options available to you as a developer.

Also, you're using a standard approach to define the database access in a console application: overriding the OnConfiguring method inside the application's DbContext and providing all the information EF Core needs to define the type and location of the database. The disadvantage of this approach is that it has a fixed connection string, which makes development and unit testing difficult.

For ASP.NET Core web applications, this is a bigger problem, because you want to access a local database for testing, and a different hosted database when running in production. In chapter 2, as you start building an ASP.NET Core web application, you'll use a different approach that allows you to change the database string (see section 2.2.2).

1.9　*Looking under the hood of EF Core*

Having built your MyFirstEfCoreApp application, you can now use it to see how an EF Core library works. The focus isn't on the application code but on what happens inside the EF Core library when you read and write data to the database. My aim is to provide you with a mental model of what happens when a database access code uses EF Core. This should help as you dig into myriad commands described throughout the rest of this book.

> ### Do you really need to know how EF Core works inside to use it?
>
> You can use the EF Core library without bothering to learn how it works. But knowing what's happening inside EF Core will help you understand why the various commands work the way they do. You'll also be better armed when you need to debug your database access code.
>
> The following pages include lots of explanations and diagrams to show you what happens inside EF Core. EF Core "hides" the database so that you as a developer can write database access code easily—which does work well in practice. But, as I stated earlier, knowing how EF Core works can help you if you want to do something more complex, or things don't work the way you expect.

1.9.1　*Modeling the database*

Before you can do anything with the database, EF Core must go through a process that I refer to as *modeling the database*. This modeling is EF Core's way of working out what the database looks like by looking at the classes and other EF Core configuration data. The resulting model is then used by EF Core in all database accesses.

The modeling process is kicked off the first time you create the application's DbContext, in this case called AppDbContext (shown in figure 1.5). This has one property, DbSet<Book>, which is the way that the code accesses the database.

Figure 1.6 provides an overview of the modeling process, which will help you understand the process EF Core uses to model the database. Later chapters introduce you to a range of commands that allow you to more precisely configure your database, but for now you'll use the default configurations.

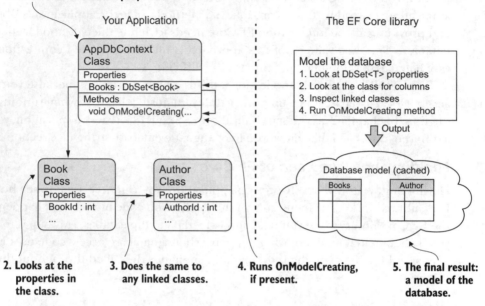

Figure 1.6   How EF Core models the database

Figure 1.6 shows the modeling steps that EF Core uses on our `AppDbContext`. The following text gives a more detailed description of the process:

1 EF Core looks at the application's DbContext and finds all the public `DbSet<T>` properties. From this, it defines the initial name for the one table it finds, Books.

2 EF Core looks through all the classes referred to in `DbSet<T>` and looks at its properties to work out the column names, types, and so forth. It also looks for special attributes on the class and/or properties that provide extra modeling information.

3 EF Core looks for any classes that the `DbSet<T>` classes refer to. In our case, the `Book` class has a reference to the `Author` class, so EF Core scans that too. It carries out the same search on the properties of the `Author` class as it did on the `Book` class in step 2. It also takes the class name, `Author`, as the table name.

4 For the last input to the modeling process, EF Core runs the virtual method `OnModelCreating` inside the application's DbContext. In this simple application, you don't override the `OnModelCreating` method, but if you did, you could provide extra information via a fluent API to do more configuration of the modeling.

5 EF Core creates an internal model of the database based on all the information it gathered. This database model is cached so that later accesses will be quicker. This model is then used when performing all database accesses.

You might have noticed that figure 1.6 shows no database. This is because when EF Core is building its internal model, it doesn't look at the database. I emphasize that to show how important it is to build a good model of the database you want; otherwise, problems could occur if a mismatch exists between what EF Core thinks the database looks like and what the actual database is like.

In your application, you may use EF Core to create the database, in which case there's no chance of a mismatch. Even so, if you want a good and efficient database, it's worth taking care to build a good representation of the database you want in your code so that the created database performs well. The options for creating, updating, and managing the database structure are a big topic, which are detailed in chapter 11.

1.9.2 Reading data from the database

You're now at the point where you can access the database. Let's use the list (1) command, which reads the database and prints the information on the terminal. Figure 1.7 shows the result.

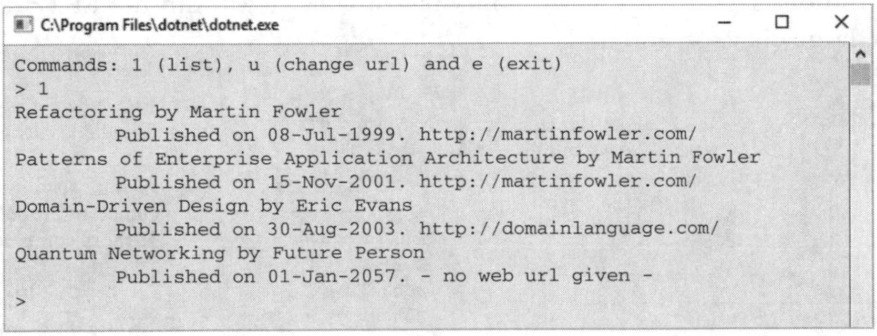

```
C:\Program Files\dotnet\dotnet.exe                               —   □   ×

Commands: 1 (list), u (change url) and e (exit)
> 1
Refactoring by Martin Fowler
        Published on 08-Jul-1999. http://martinfowler.com/
Patterns of Enterprise Application Architecture by Martin Fowler
        Published on 15-Nov-2001. http://martinfowler.com/
Domain-Driven Design by Eric Evans
        Published on 30-Aug-2003. http://domainlanguage.com/
Quantum Networking by Future Person
        Published on 01-Jan-2057. - no web url given -
>
```

Figure 1.7 Output of the console application when listing the content of the database

The following listing shows the code that's called to list all the books, with each author, out to the console.

Listing 1.2 The code to read all the books and output them to the console

```
public static void ListAll()
{
    using (var db = new AppDbContext())
    {
        foreach (var book in
            db.Books.AsNoTracking()

            .Include(a => a.Author))
        {
            var webUrl = book.Author.WebUrl == null
```

You create the application's DbContext through which all database accesses are done.

Reads all the books. AsNoTracking indicates this is a read-only access.

The "include" causes the author information to be eagerly loaded with each book. See chapter 2 for more on this.

```
       ? "- no web URL given -"
       : book.Author.WebUrl;
   Console.WriteLine(
       $"{book.Title} by {book.Author.Name}");
   Console.WriteLine("        " +
       "Published on " +
       $"{book.PublishedOn:dd-MMM-yyyy}" +
       $". {webUrl}");
   }
   }
}
```

EF Core uses Microsoft's .NET's Language Integrated Query (LINQ) to carry the commands it wants done, and normal .NET classes to hold the data. Listing 1.2 includes minimal use of LINQ, but later in the book you'll see much more complex examples.

NOTE If you're not familiar with LINQ, you'll be at a disadvantage in reading this book. Appendix A provides a brief introduction to LINQ. Plenty of online resources are also available; see https://msdn.microsoft.com/en-us/library/bb308959.aspx.

Two lines of code in bold in listing 1.2 cause the database access. Now let's see how EF Core uses that LINQ code to access the database and return the required books with their authors. Figure 1.8 follows those lines of code down into the EF Core library, through the database, and back.

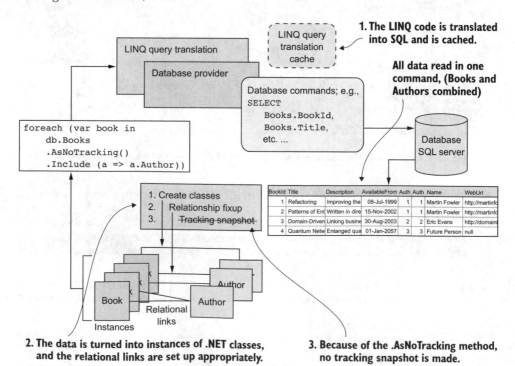

Figure 1.8   A look inside EF Core as it executes a database query

The process to read data from the database is as follows:

1 The LINQ query `db.Books.AsNoTracking().Include(a => a.Author)` accesses the `DbSet<Book>` property in the application's DbContext and adds a `.Include (a => a.Author)` at the end to ask that the Author parts of the relationship are loaded too. This is converted by the database provider into an SQL command to access the database. The resulting SQL is cached to avoid the cost of retranslation if the same database access is used again.

 EF Core tries to be as efficient as possible on database accesses. In this case, it combines the two tables it needs to read, Books and Author, into one big table so that it can do the job in one database access. The following listing shows the SQL created by EF Core and the database provider.

> **Listing 1.3 SQL command produced to read Books and Author**

```
SELECT [b].[BookId],
[b].[AuthorId],
[b].[Description],
[b].[PublishedOn],
[b].[Title],
[a].[AuthorId],
[a].[Name],
[a].[WebUrl]
FROM [Books] AS [b]
INNER JOIN [Author] AS [a] ON
[b].[AuthorId] = [a].[AuthorId]
```

2 After the database provider has read the data, EF Core puts the data through a process that (a) creates instances of the .NET classes and (b) uses the database relational links, called *foreign keys*, to correctly link the .NET classes together by reference—called a *relationship fixup*. The result is a set of .NET class instances linked in the correct way. In this example, two books have the same author, Martin Fowler, so the `Author` property of those two books points to one `Author` class.

3 Because the code includes the command `AsNoTracking`, EF Core knows to suppress the creation of a *tracking snapshot*. Tracking snapshots are used for spotting changes to data; you'll see this in the example of editing the WebUrl. Because this is a read-only query, suppressing the tracking snapshot makes the command faster.

1.9.3 Updating the database

Now you want to use the second command, update (u), in MyFirstEfCoreApp to update the WebUrl column in the Author table of the book *Quantum Networking*. As shown in figure 1.9, you first list all the books to show that the last book has no author URL set. You then run the command u, which asks for a new author URL for the last book, *Quantum Networking*. You input a new URL of `httqs://entangled.moon` (it's a fictitious future book, so why not a fictitious URL), and after the update, the command lists all the books again, showing that the author's URL has changed (the two ovals show you the before and after URLs).

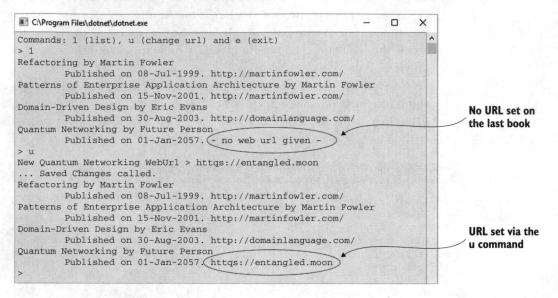

Figure 1.9   The book information before and after the WebUrl of the last book's author is updated

The code for updating the WebUrl of the last book, *Quantum Networking*, is shown here.

Listing 1.4   The code to update the author's WebUrl of the book *Quantum Networking*

```
public static void ChangeWebUrl()
{
    Console.Write("New Quantum Networking WebUrl > ");
    var newWebUrl = Console.ReadLine();                    ◄───────┤ Reads in from the console the new URL

    using (var db = new AppDbContext())          Makes sure the author information
    {                                            is eager loaded with the book
        var book = db.Books
            .Include(a => a.Author)                                          Selects only the book
            .Single(b => b.Title == "Quantum Networking");   ◄──────────    with the title Quantum
                                                                            Networking
        book.Author.WebUrl = newWebUrl;
        db.SaveChanges();                                   SaveChanges tells EF Core to check
        Console.WriteLine("... SavedChanges called.");      for any changes to the data that has
    }                                                       been read in and write out those
                                                            changes to the database.
    ListAll();          ◄───────┤ Lists all the book information
}
```

To update the database, you change the data that was read in.

Figure 1.10 shows what is happening inside the EF Core library and follows its progress. This is a lot more complicated than the previous read example, so let me give you some pointers on what to look for.

First, the read stage, at the top of the diagram, is similar to the read example and so should be familiar. In this case, the query loads a specific book, using the book's title as the filter. The important change is point 2: that a tracking snapshot is taken of the data.

This change occurs in the update stage, in the bottom half of the diagram. Here you can see how EF Core compares the loaded data with the tracking snapshot to find the changes. From this, it sees that only the WebUrl has been updated, and from that it can create an SQL command to update only that column in the right row.

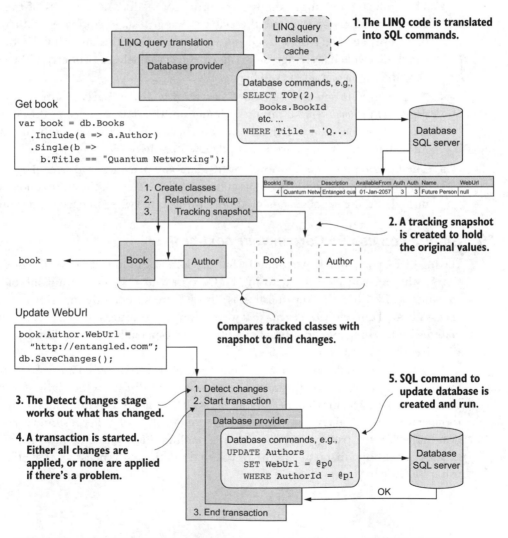

Figure 1.10   A look inside EF Core as it executes and reads, followed by a database update

I've described most of the steps, but here is a blow-by-blow account of how the author's WebUrl column is updated:

1 The application uses a LINQ query to find a single book with its author information. EF Core turns the LINQ query into an SQL command to read the rows where the Title is *Quantum Networking*, returning an instance of both the Book and the Author classes, and checks that only one row was found.

2 The LINQ query doesn't include the .AsNoTracking method you had in the previous read versions, so the query is considered to be a *tracked query*. Therefore, EF Core creates a tracking snapshot of the data loaded.

3 The code then changes the WebUrl property in the Author class of the book. When SaveChanges is called, the Detect Changes stage compares all the classes that were returned from a tracked query with the tracking snapshot. From this, it can detect what has changed—in this case, just the WebUrl property of the Author class that has a primary key of 3.

4 As a change is detected, EF Core starts a *transaction*. Every database update is done as an *atomic unit*: if multiple changes to the database occur, they either all succeed, or they all fail. This is important, because a relational database could get into a bad state if only part of an update was applied.

5 The update request is converted by the database provider into an SQL command that does the update. If the SQL command is successful, the transaction is committed and the SaveChanges method returns; otherwise, an exception is raised.

1.10 *Should you use EF Core in your next project?*

Having given you a quick overview of what EF Core is and how it works, the next question is whether you should start using EF Core in your project. For anyone planning to switch to EF Core, the key question is, "Is EF Core sufficiently superior to the data access library I currently use to make it worth using for our next project?" A cost is associated with learning and adopting any new library, especially complex libraries such as EF Core, so it's a valid question.

I'll give you a detailed answer, but as you can see, I think visually. Figure 1.11 captures my view of EF Core's strengths and weaknesses: good things to the right, and not-so-good to the left. The width of each block shows the time period over which I think that topic will improve—the wider the block, the longer this will take. It's only my view, so don't take it as the truth, especially if you're reading this book some time after I wrote this section. I hope that it at least helps you to think through the issues that affect your using EF Core in your project.

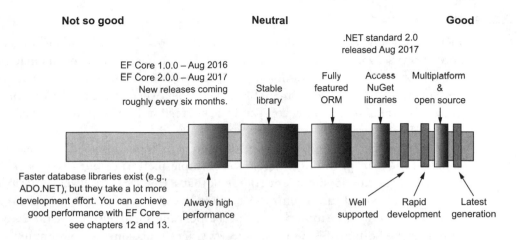

Figure 1.11 My view of the strengths and weaknesses of EF Core

Let me give you more details about each of the blocks in figure 1.11, starting with the good stuff on the right.

1.10.1 *Latest generation*

I swapped from Microsoft's LINQ to SQL O/RM, which I liked, to EF4 because EF was the future, and no further effort was being put into LINQ to SQL. It's the same now for EF Core. It's where Microsoft is putting its effort, and it's going to be extended and well supported for many years. EF Core is much more lightweight and generally faster than EF6.x, and I think the improvements in its API are good.

If you're starting a new project, and .NET Core and EF Core have the necessary features your project needs, then moving to EF Core means you won't be left behind.

1.10.2 *Multiplatform and open source*

As I said at the start of the chapter, EF Core is multiplatform-capable: you can develop and run EF Core applications on Windows, Linux, and Apple. EF Core is also open source, so you have access to the source code and an open list of issues and defects— see https://github.com/aspnet/EntityFramework/issues.

1.10.3 *Rapid development*

In a typical data-driven application, I write a lot of database access code, some of it complex. I've found that EF6.x, and now EF Core, allow me to write data access code quickly, and in a way that's easy to understand and refactor. This is one of the main reasons I use EF.

EF Core also is developer-friendly, and tends to create working queries even if I didn't write the most efficient code. Most properly formed LINQ queries work, though maybe they won't produce the best-performing SQL—and having a query that works is a great start. Chapter 12 covers the whole area of performance tuning.

1.10.4 *Well supported*

EF Core has good documentation (https://docs.microsoft.com/en-us/ef/core/index) and, of course, you now have this book, which brings together the documentation with deeper explanations and examples, plus patterns and practices to make you a great developer. Because a large group of EF6.x developers will migrate to EF Core, the internet will be full of blogs on EF Core, and Stack Overflow is likely to have the answers to your problems already.

The other part of support is the development tools. Microsoft seems to have changed focus by providing support for multiple platforms, but also has created a cross-platform development environment that's free—called Visual Studio Code (https://code.visualstudio.com/). Microsoft has also made its main development tool, Visual Studio, free for individual developers and small businesses; the Usage section near the bottom of its web page at www.visualstudio.com/vs/community/ details the terms. That's a compelling offer.

1.10.5 *Access to NuGet libraries*

Although some early difficulties arose with .NET Core 1, the introduction of .NET Standard 2.0 in August 2017, with its *.NET Framework compatibility mode*, overcame much of this, which is what EF Core 2.0 is built on. .NET Standard 2.0 allows (most) existing NuGet libraries that use earlier .NET versions to be used. The only problem occurs if the NuGet package uses an incompatible .NET feature, such as `System.Reflection`. .NET Standard 2.0 also supports a much bigger range of system methods, which makes it easier to convert a package to .NET Standard 2.0.

> **NOTE** If you want to stay on .NET 4.x, you can still use EF Core if you upgrade to .NET 4.6.1 or higher. For more information, see http://mng.bz/sB0y.

1.10.6 *Fully featured O/RM*

Entity Framework in general is a feature-rich implementation of an O/RM, and EF Core continues this trend. It allows you to write complex data access code covering most of the database features you'll want to use. As I have moved through ADO.NET, LINQ to SQL, EF 4 to 6, and now EF Core, I believe this is already a great O/RM.

But, at the time of writing this book, EF Core (version 2.0) still has some features yet to be added. That's why the block is so wide in figure 1.11. If you're a user of EF6.x, you'll notice that some features available in EF6.x aren't yet available in EF Core, but as time goes on, these will appear. I suggest you look at the Feature Comparison page on the EF Core docs site, http://mng.bz/ek4D, for the latest on what has been implemented.

1.10.7 *Stable library*

When I started writing this book, EF Core wasn't stable. It had bugs and missing features. I found an error on using the year part of a `DateTime` in the version 1.0.0 release, along with a whole load of other LINQ translation issues that were fixed in 1.1.0.

By the time you read this, EF Core will be much better, but still changing, albeit at a much slower rate. If you want something stable, EF6.x is a good O/RM, or there are other database access technologies. The choice is yours.

1.10.8 *Always high-performance*

Ah, the database performance issue. Look, I'm not going to say that EF Core is going to, out of the box, produce blistering database access performance with beautiful SQL and fast data ingest. That's the cost you pay for quick development of your data access code: all that "magic" inside EF Core can't be as good as hand-coded SQL, but you might be surprised how good it can be–see chapter 13

But you can do something about it. In my applications, I find only about 5% to 10% of my queries are the key ones that need hand-tuning. Chapters 12 and 13 are dedicated to performance tuning, plus part of chapter 14. These show that there's a lot you can do to improve the performance of EF Core database accesses.

If you're worried about EF Core's performance, I recommend you skim through chapter 13, where you'll progressively improve the performance of an application. You'll see that you can make an EF Core application perform well with little extra effort. I also have two live demo sites, http://efcoreinaction.com/ and http://cqrsravendb.efcoreinaction .com/; click the About menu to see how big the databases are.

1.11 *When should you not use EF Core?*

I'm obviously pro EF Core, but I won't use it on a client project unless it makes sense. So, let's look at a few blockers that might suggest you don't use EF Core.

The first one is obvious: Does it support the database you want to use? You can find a list of supported databases at https://docs.microsoft.com/en-us/ef/core/providers/.

The second factor is the level of performance you need. If you're writing, say, a small, RESTful service that needs to be quick and has a small number of database accesses, then EF Core isn't a good fit; you could use a fast, but development-time-hungry library because there isn't much to write. But if you have a large application, with lots of boring admin accesses and a few important customer-facing accesses, then a hybrid approach could work for you (see chapter 13 for an example of a mixed EF Core/Dapper application).

Summary

- EF Core is an object-relational mapper (O/RM) that uses Microsoft's Language Integrated Query (LINQ) to define database queries and return data into linked instances of .NET classes.
- EF Core is designed to make writing code for accessing a database quick and intuitive. This O/RM has plenty of features to match many requirements.
- You've seen various examples of what's happening inside EF Core. This will help you understand what the EF Core commands described in later chapters can do.

- There are many good reasons to consider using EF Core: it's built on a lot of experience, is well supported, and runs on multiple platforms.
- At the time this book was written, EF Core was at version 2.0 with added notes about the next release, EF Core 2.1. Some features that you might want may not be out yet, so check the online documentation for the latest state (https://docs. microsoft.com/en-us/ef/core/index).

For readers who are familiar with EF6.x:

- Look for EF6 notes throughout the book. They mark differences between the EF Core approach and EF6.x's approach. Also check the summaries at the end of each chapter, which will point you to the major EF Core changes in that chapter.
- Think of EF Core as a new library that someone has written to mimic EF6.x, but that works in a different way. That will help you spot the EF Core improvements that change the way you access a database.
- EF Core no longer supports the EDMX/database designer approach that earlier forms of EF used.

Querying the database

> **This chapter covers**
>
> - Modeling three main types of database relationships
> - Creating and changing a database via migration
> - Defining and creating an application DbContext
> - Loading related data
> - Splitting complex queries into subqueries

This chapter is all about using EF Core for reading, called *querying*, the database. You'll create a database that contains the three main types of database relationships found in EF Core. Along the way, you'll learn to create and change a database's structure via EF Core.

Next you'll learn how to access a database via EF Core, reading data from the database tables. You'll explore the basic format of EF Core queries before looking at various approaches to loading related data with the main data; for instance, loading the author with the book from chapter 1.

After learning the ways to load related data, you'll start to build the more complex queries needed to make a book-selling site work. This covers sorting, filtering, and paging, plus approaches to combine each of these separate query commands to create one composite database query.

2.1 Setting the scene—our book-selling site

In this chapter, you'll start building the example book-selling site, referred to as the *book app* from now on. This example application provides a good vehicle for looking at relationships in queries. This section introduces the database, the various classes, and EF Core parts that the book app needs to access the database.

> **NOTE** You can see a live site of the book app at http://efcoreinaction.com/.

2.1.1 The book app's relational database

Although we could have created a database with all the data about a book, its author(s), and its reviews in one table, that wouldn't have worked well in a relational database, especially because the reviews are variable in length. The norm for relational databases is to split out any repeated data (for instance, the authors).

We could have arranged the various parts of the book data in the database in several ways, but for this example the database has one of each of the main types of relationships you can have in EF Core. These three types are:

- One-to-one relationship: PriceOffer to a Book
- One-to-many relationship: Reviews to a Book
- Many-to-many relationship: Books to Authors

ONE-TO-ONE RELATIONSHIP: PRICEOFFER TO A BOOK

A book can have a promotional price applied to it. This is done with an optional row in the PriceOffer, which is an example of a one-to-one (technically, it's a one-to-zero-or-one relationship, but EF Core handles this the same way); see figure 2.1.

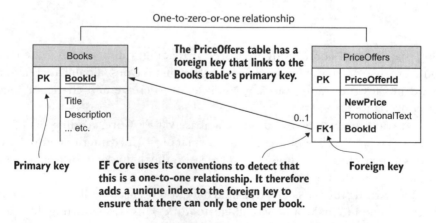

Figure 2.1   The one-to-one relationship between a Book and an optional PriceOffer

To calculate the final price of the book, you need to check for a row in the PriceOffer table that's linked via a foreign key to the book. If such a row is found, the NewPrice would supersede the price for the original book, and the PromotionalText will be shown onscreen; for instance:

　$40 $30 Our summertime price special, for this week only!

ONE-TO-MANY RELATIONSHIP: REVIEWS TO A BOOK

You want to allow customers to review a book; they can give a book a star rating and optionally leave a comment. Because a book may have no reviews or many (unlimited) reviews, you need to create a table to hold that data. In this example, you'll call the table Review. The Books table has a one-to-many relationship to the Review table, as shown in figure 2.2.

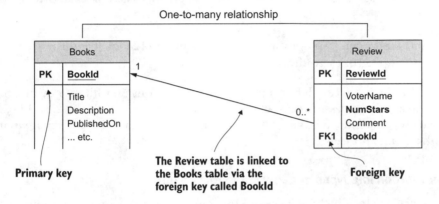

Figure 2.2　The one-to-many relationship between a book and its zero-to-many reviews

In the Summary display, you need to count the number of reviews and work out the average star rating, to show a summary. For instance, here's a typical onscreen display you might produce from this one-to-many relationship:

　　Votes 4.5 by 2 customers

MANY-TO-MANY RELATIONSHIP: BOOKS TO AUTHORS

Books can be written by one or more authors, and an author may write one or more books. You therefore need a table called Books holding the books data, and another table called Authors holding the authors. The link between the Books and Authors tables is called a many-to-many relationship, which needs a linking table (see figure 2.3).

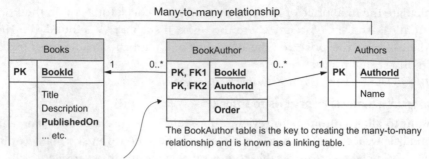

The BookAuthor table is the key to creating the many-to-many relationship and is known as a linking table.

This table uses the foreign keys as the primary keys. Because primary keys must be unique, this ensures that only one link can exist between a book and an author.

Figure 2.3   The three tables involved in creating the many-to-many relationship between the Books table and the Authors table

The typical onscreen display from this relationship would look like this:

by Dino Esposito, Andrea Saltarello

> **EF6**   In EF6.x you can define a many-to-many relationship without needing to define a linking class (for instance, the `BookAuthor` class in figure 2.3). EF6.x then creates a hidden linking table for you. In EF Core, you have to create that linking table yourself.

2.1.2   *Other relationship types not covered in this chapter*

In EF Core, you can include a class in the application's DbContext that inherits from another class in the application's DbContext. For instance, you could've defined the `PriceOffer` class as inheriting the `Book` class. That would have achieved a similar result to the one-to-one relationship shown previously. EF Core can provide this via the table-per-hierarchy (TPH) configuration, covered in chapter 7.

Another relationship type is *hierarchical*: a set of data items that are related to each other by hierarchical relationships. A typical example is an `Employee` class that has a relationship pointing to the employee's manager, who in turn is an employee. EF Core uses the same approaches as one-to-one and one-to-many to provide hierarchical relationships, and I talk more about this type of relationship in chapter 7, where I explain how to configure them.

2.1.3   *The final database showing all the tables*

Figure 2.4 shows the book app's database that you'll be using for the examples in this chapter and in chapter 3. It contains all the tables already described, including the full definition of all the columns in the Books table.

> **NOTE**   The database diagram uses the same layout and terms as in the first chapter, where *PK* means *primary key*, and *FK* means *foreign key*.

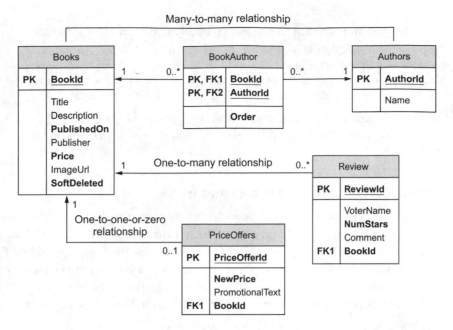

Figure 2.4 The complete relational database schema for the book app, showing all the tables and their columns

To help you make sense of this database, figure 2.5 shows the onscreen output of the list of books, but focusing on just one book. As you can see, the book app needs to access every table in the database to build the book list. Later, I show you this same book display, but with the query that supplies each element.

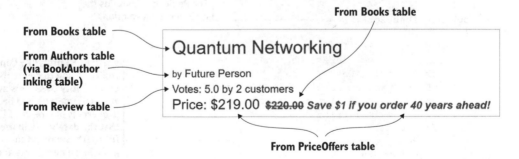

Figure 2.5 A listing of a single book showing which database table provides each part of the information

TIP You can see a live site running the book app code at http://efcoreinaction .com/. This might help you understand the rest of this chapter.

Downloading and running the example application from the Git repo

If you want to download the book app code and run it locally, follow the steps defined in the sidebar with the same name as this in section 1.6.2. The only change you need to make is to use the Chapter02 branch instead of Chapter01. The book app is ready to compile and run either from Visual Studio 2017 or in Visual Studio Code.

Each chapter has its own branch, so you as you go through the book, you can switch branches to get the appropriate code of the book app at each stage of the development.

2.1.4   *The classes that EF Core maps to the database*

I've created five .NET classes to map onto the five tables in the database. They're called `Book`, `PriceOffer`, `Review`, `Author`, and `BookAuthor` for the many-to-many-linking table.

These classes are referred to as *entity classes* to show that they're mapped by EF Core to the database. From the software point of view, there's nothing special about entity classes. They're normal .NET classes, sometimes referred to as *plain old CLR objects* (POCOs). The term *entity class* identifies the class as one that EF Core has mapped to the database.

The primary entity class is the `Book` class, shown in the following listing. You can see it refers to a single `PriceOffer` class, a collection of `Review` classes, and finally a collection of `BookAuthor` classes, which link the book data to one or more `Author` classes that contain the author's name.

Listing 2.1   The `Book` class, which is mapped to the Books table in the database

```csharp
public class Book              ◄—————  The Book class contains the
{                                      main book information.
    public int BookId { get; set; }    ◄—
    public string Title { get; set; }
    public string Description { get; set; }
    public DateTime PublishedOn { get; set; }
    public string Publisher { get; set; }
    public decimal Price { get; set; }
    /// <summary>
    /// Holds the url to get the image of the book
    /// </summary>
    public string ImageUrl { get; set; }

    //--------------------------------------------------
    //relationships

    public PriceOffer Promotion { get; set; }         ◄—
    public ICollection<Review> Reviews { get; set; }  ◄—
    public ICollection<BookAuthor>
        AuthorsLink { get; set; }    ◄—
}
```

We use EF Core's "By Convention" configuration to define the primary key of this entity class. This means we use `<ClassName>Id`, and because the property is of type int, EF Core assumes that the database will use the SQL IDENTITY command to create a unique key when a new row is added.

Link to the optional one-to-one PriceOffer relationship

There can be zero to many reviews of the book.

Provides a link to the many-to-many linking table that links the Book to its Author classes

For simplicity, we use EF Core's *By Convention* configuration approach to model the database. We use EF Core By Convention naming for the properties that hold the primary key and foreign keys in each for the entity classes. In addition, the .NET type of the navigational properties, such as ICollection<Review> Reviews, defines what sort of relationship I want. For instance, because the Reviews property is of the .NET type ICollection<Review>, the relationship is a one-to-many relationship. Chapters 6 and 7 describe the other approaches for configuring the EF Core database model.

What happens if you have an existing database that you want to access?

The examples in this book show how to define and create a database via EF Core. I do that because that's the most complex situation—where you need to understand all the configuration options.

But if you have an existing database that you want to access, that's much easier, because EF Core can build your application's DbContext class and all your entity classes for you. EF Core does this using a feature called *reverse-engineering* a database, which is covered in section 11.3.

The other possibility is you don't want EF Core changing the database structure, but you want to look after that yourself, via an SQL change script or a database deployment tool, for instance. I cover that approach in section 11.4.

2.2 Creating the application's DbContext

To access the database, you need to do the following:

1. Define your application's DbContext, which you do by creating a class and inheriting from EF Core's DbContext class.
2. Create an instance of that class every time you want to access the database.

All the database queries you'll see later in this chapter use these steps, which I now describe in more detail.

2.2.1 Defining the application's DbContext: EfCoreContext

The key class you need in order to use EF Core is the application's DbContext. This is a class you define by inheriting EF Core's DbContext and adding various properties to allow your software to access the database tables. It also contains methods you can override to access other features in EF Core, such as configuring the database modeling, and so on. Figure 2.6 gives you an overview of an application DbContext, pointing out all the important parts.

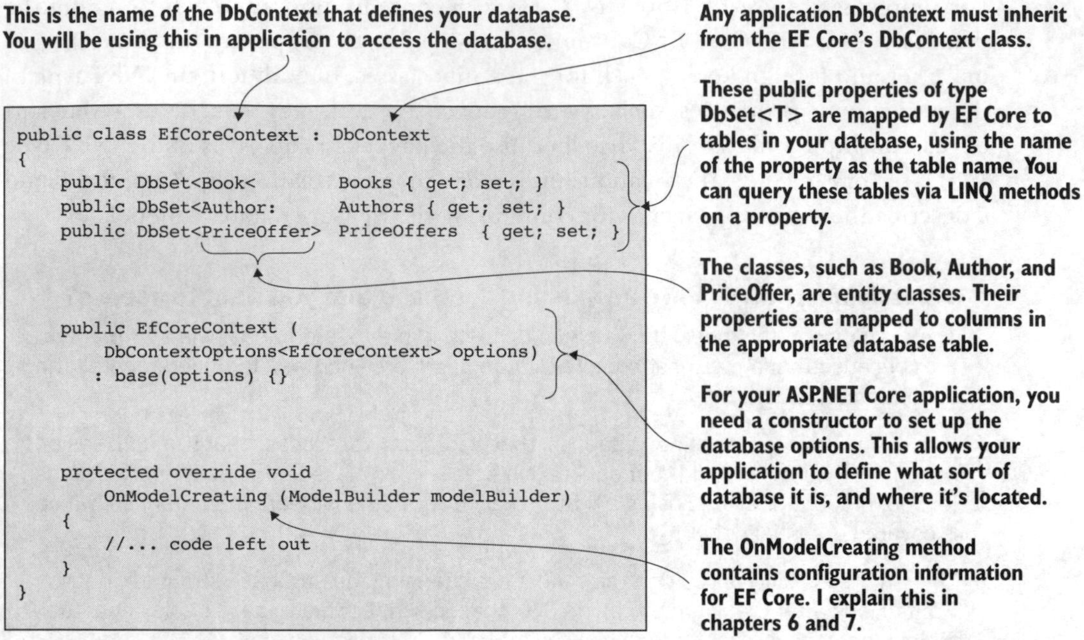

This is the name of the **DbContext** that defines your database. You will be using this in application to access the database.

Any application DbContext must inherit from the EF Core's DbContext class.

These public properties of type **DbSet<T>** are mapped by EF Core to tables in your datebase, using the name of the property as the table name. You can query these tables via LINQ methods on a property.

```
public class EfCoreContext : DbContext
{
    public DbSet<Book<         Books { get; set; }
    public DbSet<Author:       Authors { get; set; }
    public DbSet<PriceOffer>  PriceOffers { get; set; }


    public EfCoreContext (
        DbContextOptions<EfCoreContext> options)
       : base(options) {}



    protected override void
        OnModelCreating (ModelBuilder modelBuilder)
    {
        //... code left out
    }
}
```

The classes, such as Book, Author, and PriceOffer, are entity classes. Their properties are mapped to columns in the appropriate database table.

For your ASP.NET Core application, you need a constructor to set up the database options. This allows your application to define what sort of database it is, and where it's located.

The OnModelCreating method contains configuration information for EF Core. I explain this in chapters 6 and 7.

Figure 2.6   The main parts of an application's DbContext

One point to note about figure 2.6 is that your application's DbContext doesn't include DbSet<T> properties for your Review entity class and the BookAuthor linking entity class. This is because both entity classes are accessed only via the Book class, as you'll see later.

> **NOTE** I skip over configuring the database modeling, done in the OnModel-Creating method in the application's DbContext. Chapters 6 and 7 cover how to model the database in detail.

2.2.2   *Creating an instance of the application's DbContext*

Chapter 1 showed you how to set up the application's DbContext by overriding its OnConfiguring method. The downside of that approach is that the connection string is fixed. In this chapter, you'll use another approach, because we want to use a different database for development and unit testing. You'll use a method that provides that via the application's DbContext constructor.

> **NOTE** Chapter 15 covers unit testing of an application that uses EF Core.

Listing 2.2 provides the options for the database at the time you create the application DbContext, called EfCoreContext. To be honest, this listing is based on what I use in my unit testing, because it has the benefit of showing you the component parts. Chapter 5, which is about using EF Core in an ASP.NET Core application, presents a more powerful way to create the application's DbContext, by using a feature called *dependency injection.*

Listing 2.2   Creating an instance of the application's DbContext to access the database

```
const string connection =
    "Data Source=(localdb)\\mssqllocaldb;"+
    "Database=EfCoreInActionDb.Chapter02;"+
    "Integrated Security=True;";
var optionsBuilder =
    new DbContextOptionsBuilder
        <EfCoreContext>();

optionsBuilder.UseSqlServer(connection);
var options = optionsBuilder.Options;

using (var context = new EfCoreContext(options))
{

    var bookCount = context.Books.Count();
    //... etc.
```

The connection string, with its format dictated by the sort of database provider and hosting you're using

You need an EF Core DbContextOptionsBuilder<> instance to be able to set the options you need.

You're accessing an SQL Server database and using the UseSqlServer method from the Microsoft .EntityFrameworkCore .SqlServer library, and this method needs the database connection string.

This creates the all-important EfCoreContext using the options you've set up. You use a using statement because the DbContext is disposable.

Uses the DbContext to find out the number of books in the database

---

At the end of this listing, you create an instance of `EfCoreContext` inside a using statement. That's because DbContext has an `IDisposable` interface and therefore should be disposed after you've used it. So, from now on, if you see a variable called `context`, it was created using the code in listing 2.2 or a similar approach.

2.2.3   *Creating a database for your own application*

There are a few ways to create a database using EF Core, but the normal way is to use EF Core's migrations feature. This uses your application's DbContext and the entity classes, like the ones I've just described, as the model for the database structure. The `Add-Migration` command first models your database and then, using that model, builds commands to create a database that fits that model.

> **TIP**   If you're running this example application downloaded from the Git repo that goes with this book, you don't need to use the `Migrate` commands that follow. The code uses the `context.Database.EnsureCreated` command to create the database. This is less flexible than `Migrate`, but it doesn't require you to type any commands.

Besides handling creating the database, the great thing about migrations is that they can update the database with any changes you make in the software. If you change your entity classes or any of your application's DbContext configuration, the `Add-Migration` command will build a set of commands to update the existing database.

To use the migration feature, you need to install one extra EF Core NuGet library called Microsoft.EntityFrameworkCore.Tools to your application startup project. This allows you to use the `Migrate` commands in the Visual Studio Package Manager Console (PMC). Here are the ones you need:

- `Add-Migration MyMigrationName`—This creates a set of commands that will migrate the database from its current state to a state that matches your application's DbContext and the entity classes at the time that you run your command. The `MyMigrationName` shown in the command is the name that will be used for the migration.
- `Update-Database`—This applies the commands created by the `Add-Migration` command to your database. If no database exists, `Update-Database` will create one. If a database already exists, the command checks to see whether that database has this database migration applied to it; if any database migrations are missing, this command will apply them to the database.

NOTE   You can also use EF Core's command-line interface (CLI) to run these commands (see http://mng.bz/454w). Chapter 11 lists both the VS 2017 and CLI versions of the migration commands. In addition, .NET 2.1 will introduce global tools, which will allow you to call these commands via normal command line functions.

An alternative to using the `Update-Database` command is to call the `context.Database.Migrate` method in the startup code of your application. This approach is especially useful for an ASP.NET Core web application that's hosted; chapter 5 covers this option, including some of its limitations.

NOTE   Although EF Core's migrate feature is useful, it doesn't cover all types of database structure changes. Also, for some projects, the database will be defined and managed outside EF Core, which means you can't use EF Core's migrate feature. Chapter 11 explores options available for database migration, as well as their pros and cons.

WHAT TO DO IF YOUR APPLICATION USES MULTIPLE PROJECTS

If your application has a separate project for the application's DbContext from the main startup application (as the book app does), the `Add-Migration` command is a little more complex.

In the book app, the application's DbContext is in a project called DataLayer, and the ASP.NET Core application is in a project called EfCoreInAction (I describe why later in this chapter). To add an EF Core migration, the `Add-Migration` commands would be as follows:

```
Add-Migration Chapter02 -Project DataLayer -StartupProject
➥ EfCoreInAction
```

You also need to provide a way for the migrations to create a correcting configured instance of your application's DbContext. The book app's DbContext, called

EfCoreContext, has no parameterless constructor, so the Add-Migration command will fail. To deal with this potential problem, the Add-Migration command looks for a class that implements the IDesignTimeDbContextFactory<T> interface. This allows you to provide a class that will create a correctly configured instance of your application's DbContext so that the Add-Migration command will work, which is what we did in the example application. See http://mng.bz/7tYR for more details.

2.3 Understanding database queries

Now you can start looking at how to query a database by using EF Core. Figure 2.7 shows an example EF Core database query, with the three main parts of the query highlighted.

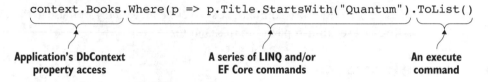

Figure 2.7   The three parts of an EF Core database query, with example code

> **TIME-SAVER**   If you're familiar with EF and/or LINQ, you can skip this section.

The command shown in figure 2.7 consists of several methods, one after the other. This is known as a *fluent interface*. Fluent interfaces like this flow logically and intuitively, making them easy to read. The three parts of this command are described next, in turn.

2.3.1 Application's DbContext property access

The first part of the command is something that's connected, via EF Core, to the database. The most common way to refer to a database table is via a DbSet<T> property in the application's DbContext, shown in figure 2.7.

You'll use this DbContext property access throughout this chapter, but later chapters introduce other ways to get to a class or property. The basic idea is the same: you need to start with something that's connected to the database via EF Core.

2.3.2 A series of LINQ/EF Core commands

The major part of the command is a set of LINQ and/or EF Core methods that create the type of query you need. The LINQ query can range from nothing to very complicated. This chapter starts with simple examples of queries, but by the end of this chapter, you'll be learning how to build complex queries.

> **NOTE**   If you're not familiar with LINQ, you'll be at a disadvantage in reading this book. Appendix A gives you a brief overview of LINQ. Plenty of online resources also are available; see https://msdn.microsoft.com/en-us/library/bb308959.aspx.

2.3.3   *The execute command*

The last part of the command reveals something about LINQ. Until a final execute command is applied at the end of the sequence of LINQ commands, the LINQ is held as a series of commands; it hasn't been executed on the data yet. EF Core can translate each command in the LINQ query into the correct commands to use for the database you're using. In EF Core, a query is executed against the database when

- It's enumerated by a `foreach` statement.
- It's enumerated by a collection operation such as `ToArray`, `ToDictionary`, `ToList`, `ToListAsync`, and so forth.
- LINQ operators such as `First` or `Any` are specified in the outermost part of the query.
- You use certain EF Core commands, such as `Load`, which you'll use in the explicit loading of a relationship later in this chapter.

2.4   Loading related data

I've shown you the `Book` entity class, which has links to three other entity classes: `PriceOffer`, `Review`, and `BookAuthor`. I now want to explain how you, as a developer, can access the data behind these relationships. You can load data in three ways: *eager loading, explicit loading, select loading,* and *lazy loading* (in EF Core 2.1).

But before I cover these approaches, you need to be aware that EF Core won't load any relationships in an entity class unless you ask it to. If you load a `Book` class, each of the relationship properties in the `Book` entity class (`Promotion`, `Reviews`, and `AuthorsLink`) will be `null` by default.

This default behavior of not loading relationships is correct, because it means that EF Core minimizes the database accesses. If you want to load a relationship, you need to add code to tell EF Core to do that. The next sections describe the three approaches, with their pros and cons, to get EF Core to load a relationship.

2.4.1   *Eager loading: loading relationships with the primary entity class*

The first approach to loading related data is eager loading. *Eager loading* entails telling EF Core to load the relationship in the same query that loads the primary entity class. Eager loading is specified via two fluent methods, `Include` and `ThenInclude`. The next listing shows the loading of the first row of the Books table as an instance of the `Book` entity class, and the eager loading of the single relationship, `Reviews`.

> **Listing 2.3   Eager loading of first book with the corresponding `Reviews` relationship**

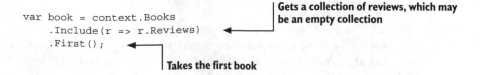

```
var book = context.Books
    .Include(r => r.Reviews)          ◄─── Gets a collection of reviews, which may
    .First();   ◄─────                         be an empty collection
                                       Takes the first book
```

If you look at the SQL command that this EF Core query creates, shown in the following snippet, you'll see two SQL commands. The first loads the first row in the Books table. The second loads the reviews, where the foreign key, BookId, has the same value as the first Books row primary key.

```
-- First SQL command to get the first row in the Books table
SELECT TOP(1)
    [r].[BookId], [r].[Description], [r].[ImageUrl],
    [r].[Price], [r].[PublishedOn], [r].[Publisher],
    [r].[Title]
FROM [Books] AS [r]
ORDER BY [r].[BookId]
-- Second SQL command to get the reviews for this book
SELECT [r0].[ReviewId], [r0].[BookId],
       [r0].[Comment], [r0].[NumStars], [r0].[VoterName]
FROM [Review] AS [r0]
INNER JOIN (
    SELECT DISTINCT TOP(1) [r].[BookId]
    FROM [Books] AS [r]
    ORDER BY [r].[BookId]
) AS [r1] ON [r0].[BookId] = [r1].[BookId]
ORDER BY [r1].[BookId]
```

EF6 Eager loading in EF Core is similar to that in EF6.x, but with improved syntax and a different SQL implementation. First, syntax: EF6.x doesn't have a Then-Include method, so you have to use Select (for example, Books.Include(p => p.AuthorLink.Select(q => q.Author). Second, SQL implementation: EF6.x would try to load all the data in one query, including collections. This can be inefficient. EF Core loads collections in a separate query; you can see this in the preceding SQL snippet.

Now let's look at a more complex example. The following listing shows a query to get the first book, with eager loading of all its relationships—in this case, AuthorsLink and the second-level Author table, the Reviews, and the optional Promotion table.

Listing 2.4 Eager loading of the Book class and all of the related data

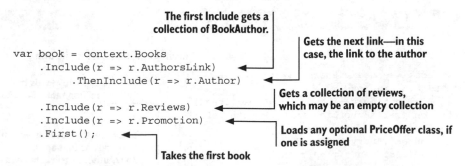

The listing shows the use of the eager-loading method Include to get the AuthorsLink relationship. This is a first-level relationship, a relationship referred to directly from the entity class you're loading. That Include is followed by ThenInclude to load the

second-level relationship, in this case the Author table at the other end of the linking table, BookAuthor. This pattern, Include followed by a ThenInclude, is the standard way of accessing relationships that go deeper than a first-level relationship. You can go to any depth with multiple ThenIncludes, one after the other.

If the relationship doesn't exist (for example, the optional PriceOffer class pointed to by the Promotion property in the Book class), Include doesn't fail; it simply doesn't load anything, or in the case of collections, it returns an empty collection (a valid collection but with zero entries). This applies to ThenInclude as well. If the previous Include or ThenInclude was empty, subsequent ThenIncludes are ignored.

Eager loading has the advantage that EF Core will load all the data referred to by the Include and ThenInclude in an efficient manner, using a minimum of database accesses, called *database round-trips*. I find this type of loading useful in relational updates in which I need to update an existing relationship; chapter 3 covers this topic. I also find eager loading useful in business logic, and chapter 4 covers this in much more detail.

The downside is that eager loading loads *all* the data, when sometimes you don't need part of it. For instance, the book list display doesn't need the book description, which could be quite large.

> **NOTE** In EF Core 2.0, a warning is logged if you use an Include method in a query and it's not needed. For instance, you don't need the Include because only the BookId is returned: context.Books.Include(b => b.Promotion). Where(b => b.Promotion.NewPrice > 10).Select(b => b.BookId). The EF Core team has added this warning because unnecessary use of the Include method is common, and the warning helps people understand where the method is and isn't needed.

2.4.2   *Explicit loading: loading relationships after the primary entity class*

The second approach to loading data is *explicit loading*; after you've loaded the primary entity class, you can explicitly load any other relationships you want. This listing shows a series of commands that first load the book and then use explicit-loading commands to read all the relationships.

Listing 2.5   Explicit loading of the Book class and related data

```
var book = context.Books.First();          ◄── Reads in the first book on its own
context.Entry(book)
    .Collection(c => c.AuthorsLink).Load();    ◄── Explicitly loads the linking table, BookAuthor
foreach (var authorLink in book.AuthorsLink)
{
    context.Entry(authorLink)
        .Reference(r => r.Author).Load();
}
```

To load all the possible authors, the code has to loop through all the BookAuthor entries and load each linked Author class.

```
context.Entry(book)
    .Collection(c => c.Reviews).Load();
```
Loads all the reviews
```
context.Entry(book)
    .Reference(r => r.Promotion).Load();
```
Loads the optional PriceOffer class

Explicit loading has an extra command that allows a query to be applied to the relationship, rather than just loading it. Listing 2.6 shows use of the explicit-loading method `Query` to obtain the count of the number of reviews and to load all the star ratings of each review. You can use any standard LINQ command after the `Query` method; for instance, `Where`, `OrderBy`, and so forth.

Listing 2.6 Explicit loading of the `Book` class with refined set of related data

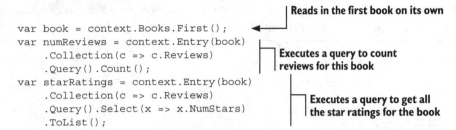

```
var book = context.Books.First();
var numReviews = context.Entry(book)
    .Collection(c => c.Reviews)
    .Query().Count();
var starRatings = context.Entry(book)
    .Collection(c => c.Reviews)
    .Query().Select(x => x.NumStars)
    .ToList();
```

Reads in the first book on its own

Executes a query to count reviews for this book

Executes a query to get all the star ratings for the book

The advantage of explicit loading is that you can load a relationship of an entity class later. I've found this useful when using a library that loads only the primary entity class and I need one of its relationships. Explicit loading can also be useful if you need that related data only in some circumstances. You might also find explicit loading useful in complex business logic, because you can leave the job of loading the specific relationships to the parts of the business logic that need it.

The downside of explicit loading is more database round-trips, which can be inefficient. If you know up front the data you need, eager loading the data is usually more efficient because it takes fewer database round-trips to load the relationships.

2.4.3 Select loading: loading specific parts of primary entity class and any relationships

The third approach to loading data is to use the LINQ `Select` method to specifically pick out the data you want, which I call *select loading*. Listing 2.7 shows the use of the `Select` method to select a few standard properties from the `Book` class and execute specific code inside the query to get the count of customer reviews for this book.

Listing 2.7   Select of the Book class picking specific properties and one calculation

```
var result = context.Books
    .Select(p => new
        {
            p.Title,
            p.Price,
            NumReviews
                = p.Reviews.Count,
        }
    ).First();
```

Simple copies of a couple of properties

Uses the LINQ Select keyword and creates an anonymous type to hold the results

Runs a query that counts the number of reviews

The advantage of the select query approach is that only the data you need is loaded, which can be more efficient if you don't need all the data. For listing 2.7, only one SQL SELECT command is required to get all that data, which is also efficient in terms of database round-trips. EF Core turns the p.Reviews.Count part of the query into an SQL command, so that count is done inside the database, as you can see in the following snippet of the SQL created by EF Core:

```
SELECT TOP(1) [p].[Title], [p].[Price], (
    SELECT COUNT(*)
    FROM [Review] AS [r0]
    WHERE [p].[BookId] = [r0].[BookId]
)
FROM [Books] AS [p]
```

The downside to the select-loading approach is that you need to write code for each property/calculation you want. In section 10.3 I show a way you can automate this.

NOTE   You'll see a much more complex select-loading example later in this chapter, as you'll use this type of loading to build the book list query for the book app.

Lazy loading: coming in EF Core version 2.1

I can't write this section without mentioning lazy loading. This EF6.x feature allows you to mark a property as virtual, and the database access occurs only when you read that property. Lazy loading will be added to EF Core in version 2.1, and you can find the early information available on lazy loading in appendix B, which covers all the major changes planned for the EF Core 2.1 release.

The proponents of lazy loading say that it's easy to use because you don't need the application's DbContext when you read the property. The downside of lazy loading is that it requires more database accesses to lazy load data, which can make your queries slow. The approach described in this chapter for building queries removes the need for lazy loading and can therefore produce better-performing database access.

2.5 Using client vs. server evaluation: moving part of your query into software

All the queries you've seen so far are ones that EF Core can convert to commands that can be run on the database server. But EF Core has a feature called *client vs. server evaluation*, which allows you to include methods in your query that can't be run on the database—for example, on relational databases, methods that EF Core can't convert to SQL commands. EF Core runs these non-server-runnable commands after the data has come back from the database. Let me show you an example of where client vs. server evaluation is useful and then a diagram to illustrate what's happening inside EF Core to make client vs. server evaluation work.

> **EF6:** Client vs. server evaluation is a new feature in EF Core, and a useful one too.

2.5.1 Creating the display string of a book's authors

For the list display of the books on the book app, you need to (a) extract all the author's names, in order, from the Authors table and (b) turn them into one string with commas between each name. Here's an example that loads two properties, `BookId` and `Title`, in the normal manner, and a third property, `AuthorsString`, which uses client vs. server evaluation.

Listing 2.8 Select query that includes a non-SQL command, `string.Join`

string.Join is executed on the client in software.

```
var book = context.Books
    .Select(p => new
    {
        p.BookId,
        p.Title,
        AuthorsString = string.Join(", ",
            p.AuthorsLink
            .OrderBy(q => q.Order)
            .Select(q => q.Author.Name)),
    }
    ).First();
```

These parts of the select can be converted to SQL and run on the server.

Running this code on a book that has two authors, Jack and Jill, would cause `AuthorsString` to contain Jack, Jill, and the `BookId`; and `Title` would be set to the value of the corresponding columns in the Books table.

Figure 2.8 shows how listing 2.8 would be processed through four stages. I want to focus on stage 3, where EF Core runs the client-side code that it couldn't convert into SQL.

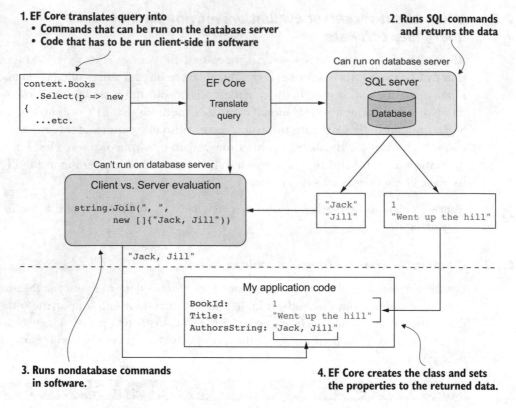

1. EF Core translates query into
- **Commands that can be run on the database server**
- **Code that has to be run client-side in software**

2. Runs SQL commands and returns the data

Can run on database server

```
context.Books
  .Select(p => new
{
  ...etc.
```

EF Core

Translate query

SQL server

Database

Can't run on database server

Client vs. Server evaluation

```
string.Join(", ",
      new []{"Jack, Jill"))
```

```
"Jack"
"Jill"
```

```
1
"Went up the hill"
```

```
"Jack, Jill"
```

My application code

```
BookId:        1
Title:         "Went up the hill"
AuthorsString: "Jack, Jill"
```

3. Runs nondatabase commands in software.

4. EF Core creates the class and sets the properties to the returned data.

Figure 2.8   Some parts of the query are converted to SQL and run in the SQL server, and another part, in this case `string.Join`, has to be done client-side by EF Core before the combined result is handed back to the application code.

The client vs. server evaluation feature allows you, as a developer, to create complex queries, and EF Core will optimize the query to run as much as it can on the database server. But if a method in your query can't be run on the database server, the query won't fail. Instead, EF Core will apply that method after SQL Server has done its part.

The example in listing 2.8 is fairly simple, and the possibilities are endless. But there are a few things to watch out for.

2.5.2   *Understanding the limitations of client vs. server evaluation*

The client vs. server evaluation feature is a useful addition to EF. But, as with all powerful features, it's best to understand what's going on so you can use it in the right way.

First, the obvious thing is that the method you provide is run on every entity (row) you read from the database. If you have 10,000 rows in the database and don't filter/limit what's loaded, then, in addition to having an SQL command that takes a long time, your processor will spend a long time running your method 10,000 times.

The second point is subtler: the client vs. server evaluation feature blurs the lines between what's run in the database and what's run in the client. It's possible to create a query that works, but it's slower than it could be because it has to use client-side evaluation. To give you some context, in EF6.x this form of mixed client/server query would have failed because EF6.x didn't support it. Therefore, you were forced to change your code—often by changing the query to better suit the database. Now your query may work, but perform worse than one that EF Core can directly convert into SQL commands.

One extreme example of the problem is that client vs. server evaluation allows you to sort on a client-side evaluated property, which means the sorting is done in the client rather than in the database server. I tried this by replacing the `First` command with `.Sort(p => p. AuthorsString)` in listing 2.8 and returning a list of books. In that case, EF Core produces SQL code that reads all the books, then reads each row individually, twice, which is definitely not optimal.

Even so, my experiments with client vs. server evaluation showed that EF Core is quite intelligent and builds an optimal SQL query for all the sensible cases I gave it, so maybe this isn't such a big worry. I suggest you use it and performance-tune later (see chapters 12 and 13 on finding issues and improving database performance).

> **TIP** You can use EF Core's logging to identify possible bad-performing client vs. server queries. EF Core will log a warning on the first use of a client vs. server query that could have an adverse effect on performance of the SQL commands it produces. Also, you can configure logging to throw an exception on client vs. server query warnings; for more information, see http://mng.bz/0644.

2.6 Building complex queries

Having covered the basics of querying the database, let's look at examples that are more common in real applications. You're going to build a query to list all the books in the book app, with a range of features including sorting, filtering, and paging.

2.6.1 Building the book list query by using select loading

You could build the book display by using eager loading: you'd load all the data, and then in the code you'd combine the authors, calculate the price, calculate the average votes, and so on. The problem with that approach is that the book list query includes sorting options (such as on price) and filtering options (for instance, showing only books with four or more customer star ratings).

With eager loading, you could load *all* the books into memory, and then sort or filter them. For this chapter's book app, which has 50-ish books, that would work, but I don't think that approach would work for Amazon! The better solution is for the values to be calculated inside SQL Server so that sorting and filtering can be done before the data is returned to the application.

Although you could add sorting and filtering methods in front of eager loading (or explicit loading), in this example, you'll use a *select-loading* approach, combining all the individual queries into one big select query. This select precedes the sorting, filtering, and paging parts of the query. That way, EF Core knows, via the select query, how to load each part of the query and can therefore use any property in the LINQ select in an SQL `ORDER BY` (sort) or SQL `WHERE` (filter) clause as it needs to.

NOTE You'll use client vs. server evaluation to get the string containing the author(s) of the book. That excludes, for performance reasons, that property from being used in an SQL sort or filter command.

Before I show you the select query that loads the book data, let's go back to the book list display of *Quantum Networking* from the beginning of this chapter. But this time, figure 2.9 shows each individual LINQ query needed to get each piece of data.

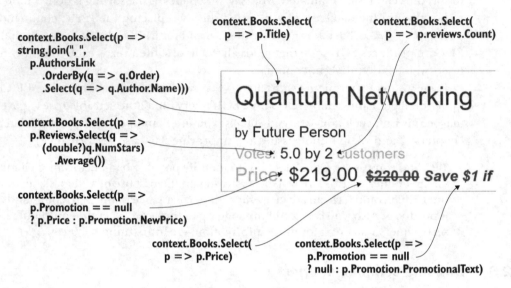

Figure 2.9   Each individual query needed to build the book list display, with each part of the query that's used to provide the value needed for that part of the book display

This diagram is complicated because the queries needed to get all the data are complicated. With this diagram in mind, let's look at how to build the book select query.

You start with the class you're going to put the data in. This type of class, which exists only to bring together the exact data you want, is referred to in various ways. In ASP.NET, it is referred to as a *ViewModel*, but that term also has other connotations and uses. I therefore refer to this type of class as a DTO. Listing 2.9 shows you the DTO class, `BookListDto`.

DEFINITION *Data transfer object* (DTO) describes "an object that carries data between processes" (Wikipedia) or an "object that is used to encapsulate data, and send it from one subsystem of an application to another" (Stack Overflow answer). This book's use of the term is closer to the Stack Overflow answer.

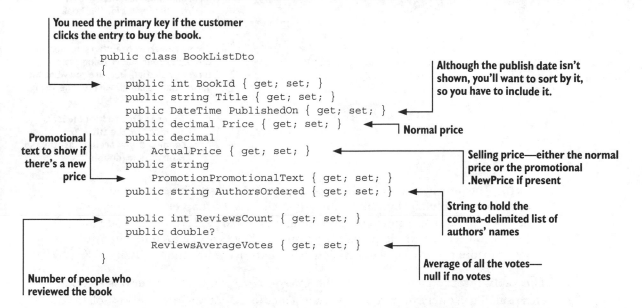

Listing 2.9 The DTO `BookListDto`

You need the primary key if the customer clicks the entry to buy the book.

Although the publish date isn't shown, you'll want to sort by it, so you have to include it.

Normal price

Promotional text to show if there's a new price

Selling price—either the normal price or the promotional .NewPrice if present

String to hold the comma-delimited list of authors' names

Average of all the votes—null if no votes

Number of people who reviewed the book

```
public class BookListDto
{
    public int BookId { get; set; }
    public string Title { get; set; }
    public DateTime PublishedOn { get; set; }
    public decimal Price { get; set; }
    public decimal
        ActualPrice { get; set; }
    public string
        PromotionPromotionalText { get; set; }
    public string AuthorsOrdered { get; set; }

    public int ReviewsCount { get; set; }
    public double?
        ReviewsAverageVotes { get; set; }
}
```

To work with EF Core's select loading, the class that's going to receive the data must have a default constructor (it can be created without needing to provide any properties to the constructor), the class must not be static, and the properties must have public setters.

Next, you'll build a select query that fills in every property in `BoolListDto`. Because you want to use this with other query parts, such as sort, filter, and paging, you'll use the `IQueryable<T>` type to create a method called `MapBookToDto` that takes in `IQueryable<Book>` and returns `IQueryable<BookListDto>`. The following listing shows this method and, as you can see, the LINQ `Select` pulls together all the individual queries you saw in figure 2.9.

Listing 2.10 The `Select` query to fill `BookListDto`

```
public static IQueryable<BookListDto>
    MapBookToDto(this IQueryable<Book> books)
{
    return books.Select(p => new BookListDto
        {
            BookId = p.BookId,
            Title = p.Title,
            Price = p.Price,
            PublishedOn = p.PublishedOn,
            ActualPrice = p.Promotion == null
                ? p.Price
                : p.Promotion.NewPrice,
```

Takes in IQueryable<Book> and returns IQueryable<BookListDto>

Simple copies of existing columns in the Books table

Calculates the selling price, which is the normal price, or the promotion price if that relationship exists

```
        PromotionPromotionalText =
            p.Promotion == null
              ? null
              : p.Promotion.PromotionalText,
        AuthorsOrdered = string.Join(", ",
            p.AuthorsLink
            .OrderBy(q => q.Order)
            .Select(q => q.Author.Name)),
        ReviewsCount = p.Reviews.Count,
        ReviewsAverageVotes =
            p.Reviews.Select(y =>
                (double?)y.NumStars).Average()
    });
}
```

PromotionalText depends on whether a PriceOffer exists for this book

Obtains an array of authors' names, in the right order. You're using client vs. server evaluation, because you want the author names combined into one string.

You need to calculate the number of reviews.

To get EF Core to turn the LINQ average into the SQL AVG command, you need to cast the NumStars to (double?).

NOTE The individual parts of the Select query in listing 2.10 are the repetitive code I mention in my lightbulb moment in chapter 1. Chapter 10 introduces mappers to automate much of this coding, but in part 1, I list all the code in full so you see the whole picture. Be assured, there's a way to automate the select-loading approach of querying that will improve your productivity.

The MapBookToDto method is using the *Query Object pattern.* This pattern is all about encapsulating a query, or part of a query, in a method. That way, the query is isolated in one place, which makes it easier to find, debug, and performance-tune. You'll use the Query Object pattern for the sort, filter, and paging parts of the query too.

NOTE *Query objects* are useful for building queries such as the book list in this example, but alternative approaches exist, such as the Repository pattern. Chapter 10, which covers patterns that can be used with EF Core, provides more details.

The MapBookToDto method is also what .NET calls an *extension method.* Extension methods allow you to chain query objects together. You'll see this chaining used later, when you combine each part of the book list query to create the final, composite query.

NOTE A method can become an extension method if (a) it's declared in a static class, (b) the method is static, and (c) the first parameter has the keyword this in front of it.

Because the MapBookToDto method uses IQueryable<T> for both input and output, the LINQ commands inside the method aren't executed. The input can be the DbSet<Books> property in the application's DbContext, or another source of type IQueryable<Book>. Also, the MapBookToDto method's output can be fed into a method that takes IQueryable<BookListDto> and returns IQueryable<BookListDto>, in which case the LINQ commands are still not executed.

EF Core turns this into a reasonably efficient query. In chapter 13, you'll work through a series of performance tuning to make the book list query even faster.

NOTE You can see the results of this query by cloning the code from the Git repo, selecting the Chapter02 branch, and then running the EfCoreInAction web application locally. A Logs menu feature will show you the SQL used to load the book list with the specific sorting, filtering, and paging setting you've selected.

2.6.2 Introducing the architecture of the book app

I've waited until this point to talk about the design of the book app, because it should make more sense now that you've created the BookListDto class. At this stage, you have the entity classes (Book, Author, and so on) that map to the database via EF Core. You also have a BookListDto class, which holds the data in the form that the presentation side needs—in this case, an ASP.NET Core web server.

In a simple example application, you might put the entity classes in one folder and the DTOs in another, and so on. But even in a small application, such as the book app, this can be confusing because the approach you use with the database is different from the approach you use when displaying data to the customer. It's all about *separation of concerns* (https://en.wikipedia.org/wiki/Separation_of_concerns).

You could split up the parts of the book app in numerous ways, but we'll use a common design called *layered architecture*. This approach works well for small-to-medium .NET web applications. Figure 2.10 shows the architecture of the book app for this chapter.

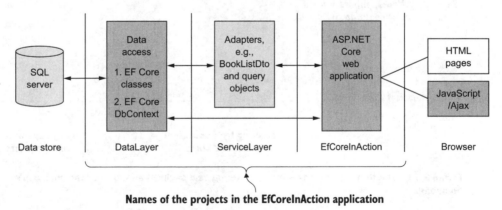

Names of the projects in the EfCoreInAction application

Figure 2.10 The layered architectural approach for the book app. Separating each part of the code into discrete projects makes the code easier to find and refactor.

The three large rectangles are .NET projects, with their names at the bottom of the figure. The classes and code between these three projects are split in the following way:

- *DataLayer*—This layer's focus is the database access. The entity classes and the application's DbContext are in this project. This layer doesn't know anything about the layers above it.

- *ServiceLayer*—This layer acts as an adapter between the DataLayer and the ASP .NET Core web application. It does this by using DTOs, query objects, and various classes to run the commands. The idea is that the frontend ASP.NET Core layer has so much to do that the ServiceLayer hands it premade data for display.

- *EfCoreInAction*—The focus of this layer, called the *presentation layer*, is on presenting data in a way that's convenient and applicable to the user. That in itself is a challenge, which is why we move as much of the database and data adapting out of the presentation layer. In the book app, you'll use an ASP.NET Core web application mainly serving HTML pages, with a small amount of JavaScript running in the browser.

Using a layered architecture makes the book app a little more complex to understand, but it's one way to build real applications. Using layers also enables you to more easily know what each bit of the code is supposed to be doing in the associated Git repo, because the code isn't all tangled up together.

2.7 Adding sorting, filtering, and paging

With the project structure out of the way, you can now push on more quickly and build the remaining query objects to create the final book list display. I'll start by showing you a screenshot (figure 2.11) of the book app's sort, filter, and page controls to give you an idea of what you're implementing.

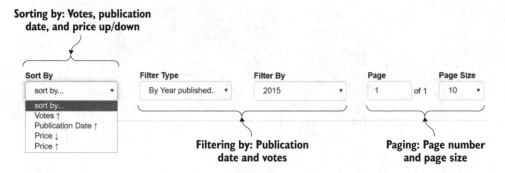

Figure 2.11   The three commands—sorting, filtering, and paging—as shown on the book app's homepage

2.7.1 Sorting books by price, publication date, and customer ratings

Sorting in LINQ is done by the methods `OrderBy` and `OrderByDescending`. You create a query object called `OrderBooksBy` as an extension method, as shown in listing 2.11. You'll see that in addition to the `IQueryable<BookListDto>` parameter, this method takes in an enum parameter. This enum defines the type of sort the user wants.

Listing 2.11 The `OrderBooksBy` query object method

```
public static IQueryable<BookListDto> OrderBooksBy
    (this IQueryable<BookListDto> books,
     OrderByOptions orderByOptions)
{
    switch (orderByOptions)
    {
        case OrderByOptions.SimpleOrder:
            return books.OrderByDescending(
                x => x.BookId);
        case OrderByOptions.ByVotes:
            return books.OrderByDescending(x =>
                x.ReviewsAverageVotes);
        case OrderByOptions.ByPublicationDate:
            return books.OrderByDescending(
                x => x.PublishedOn);
        case OrderByOptions.ByPriceLowestFirst:
            return books.OrderBy(x => x.ActualPrice);
        case OrderByOptions.ByPriceHigestFirst:
            return books.OrderByDescending(
                x => x.ActualPrice);
        default:
            throw new ArgumentOutOfRangeException(
                nameof(orderByOptions), orderByOptions, null);
    }
}
```

Because of paging, you always need to sort. You default sort on the primary key, which is fast.

This orders the book by votes. Books without any votes (null return) go at the bottom.

Orders by publication date—latest books at the top

Orders by actual price, which takes into account any promotional price—both lowest first and highest first

Calling the `OrderBooksBy` method returns the original query with the appropriate LINQ sort command added to the end. You then pass this on to the next query object, or, if you've finished, you call a command to execute the code, such as `ToList`.

NOTE Even if the user doesn't select a sort, you'll still sort (see the `SimpleOrder` switch statement). This is because you'll be using paging, providing only a page at a time rather than all the data, and SQL requires the data to be sorted to handle paging. The most efficient sort is on the primary key, so you sort on that.

2.7.2 *Filtering books by publication year and customer ratings*

The filtering created for the book app is a bit more complex than the sorting we just covered. That's because you get the customer to first select the type of filter they want and then select the actual filter value. The filter value for Votes is easy: it's a set of fixed values (4 or above, 3 or above, and so on). But to filter by Date, you need to find the dates of the publications to put into the drop-down list.

It's instructive to look at the code for working out the years that have books, because it's a nice example of combining LINQ commands to create the final drop-down list. Here's a snippet of code taken from the `GetFilterDropDownValues` method.

Listing 2.12   The code to produce a list of the years that books are published

Gets the next year so you can
filter out all future publications

Returns true if a book in the
list isn't yet published

```
var comingSoon = _db.Books.
    Any(x => x.PublishedOn > DateTime.UtcNow);
var nextYear = DateTime.UtcNow.AddYears(1).Year;
var result = _db.Books
    .Select(x => x.PublishedOn.Year)
    .Distinct()
    .Where(x => x < nextYear)
    .OrderByDescending(x => x)
    .Select(x => new DropdownTuple
    {
        Value = x.ToString(),
        Text = x.ToString()
    }).ToList();
if (comingSoon)
    result.Insert(0, new DropdownTuple
    {
        Value = BookListDtoFilter.AllBooksNotPublishedString,
        Text = BookListDtoFilter.AllBooksNotPublishedString
    });

return result;
```

Gets the year of publication, uses distinct
to have only one of each year, filters out
the future books, and orders with newest
year at the top.

Uses two client/server evaluations
to turn the values into strings

Adds a coming soon filter for all the
future books

The result of this code is a list of Value/Text pairs holding each year that books are
published, plus a Coming Soon section for books yet to be published. This is turned
into an HTML drop-down list by ASP.NET Core and sent to the browser.

The following listing shows the filter query object called `FilterBooksBy`. This takes
as an input the Value part of the drop-down list created in listing 2.12, plus whatever
type of filtering the customer has asked for.

Listing 2.13   The `FilterBooksBy` query object method

```
public static IQueryable<BookListDto> FilterBooksBy(
    this IQueryable<BookListDto> books,
    BooksFilterBy filterBy, string filterValue)
{
    if (string.IsNullOrEmpty(filterValue))
        return books;

    switch (filterBy)
    {
        case BooksFilterBy.NoFilter:
            return books;
        case BooksFilterBy.ByVotes:
            var filterVote = int.Parse(filterValue);
            return books.Where(x =>
                x.ReviewsAverageVotes > filterVote);
        case BooksFilterBy.ByPublicationYear:
```

The method is given both the type of
filter and the user-selected filter value.

If the filter value isn't set, it
returns IQueryable with no change.

Same for no filter selected—it returns
IQueryable with no change.

The filter by votes is a value
and above; if there are no
reviews for a book, the
ReviewsAverageVotes property
will be null, and the test
always returns false.

```
              if (filterValue == AllBooksNotPublishedString)
                  return books.Where(
                      x => x.PublishedOn > DateTime.UtcNow);

              var filterYear = int.Parse(filterValue);
              return books.Where(
                  x => x.PublishedOn.Year == filterYear
                      && x.PublishedOn <= DateTime.UtcNow);
          default:
              throw new ArgumentOutOfRangeException
                  (nameof(filterBy), filterBy, null);
      }
  }
```

> If coming soon was picked, you return only books not yet published.

> If you have a specific year, you filter on that. You also remove future books (in case the user chose this year's date).

OTHER FILTERING OPTIONS—SEARCHING TEXT FOR A SPECIFIC STRING

We could've created loads of other types of filters/searches of books, and searching by title is an obvious one. But you want to make sure that the LINQ commands you use to search a string are executed in the database, because then they'll perform much better than loading all the data and filtering in software. The string search commands that EF Core converts into SQL that can run on the database are shown in table 2.1. Other string commands will work, but will run in software and therefore will be slow.

Table 2.1. .NET string comparison commands that EF Core can translate into SQL to run on the database

String command	Example: these will find a title with the string "The Cat sat on the mat."
StartsWith	```var books = context.Books` ` .Where(p => p.Title.StartsWith("The"))` ` .ToList();```
EndsWith	```var books = context.Books` ` .Where(p => p.Title.EndsWith("mat."))` ` .ToList();```
Contains	```var books = context.Books` ` .Where(p => p.Title.Contains("Cat"))` ` .ToList();```

NOTE These are the only string commands that get translated to SQL. Commands such as IndexOf, Substring, and Regex commands would work, but would use client vs. server evaluation and be run as software.

You can access another SQL command, called LIKE, through the EF.Function.Like method. This provides a simple pattern-matching approach using _ (underscore) to match any letter, and % to match zero-to-many characters. The following code snippet would match `The Cat sat on the mat.` and `The dog sat on the step.`, but not `The rabbit sat on the hutch.` because `rabbit` isn't three letters long:

```
var books = context.Books
    .Where(p => EF.Functions.Like(p.Title, "The ___ sat on the %."))
    .ToList();
```

The other important thing to know is that the case sensitivity of a string search executed by SQL commands depends on a setting in the database called *collation*. If you create an SQL Server database via EF Core, for instance, the collation will be set to case-insensitive searches, so searching for `Cat` would find `cat` and `Cat`.

2.7.3 *Paging the books in the list*

If you've used Google search, you've used paging. Google presents the first dozen or so results, and you can *page* through the rest. Our book app uses paging, which is simple to implement by using the LINQ commands' `Skip` and `Take` methods.

Although the other query objects were tied to the `BookListDto` class because the LINQ paging commands are so simple, you can create a generic paging query object that will work with any `IQueryable<T>` query. This query object is shown in the following listing. The object does rely on getting a page number in the right range, but another part of the application has to do that anyway in order to show the correct paging information onscreen.

> **Listing 2.14   A generic `Page` query object method**

```
public static IQueryable<T> Page<T>(
    this IQueryable<T> query,
    int pageNumZeroStart, int pageSize)
{
    if (pageSize == 0)
        throw new ArgumentOutOfRangeException
            (nameof(pageSize), "pageSize cannot be zero.");

    if (pageNumZeroStart != 0)
        query = query
            .Skip(pageNumZeroStart * pageSize);      ◀─── Skips the correct number of pages

    return query.Take(pageSize);      ◀─── Takes the number for this page size
}
```

As I said earlier, paging works only if the data is ordered. Otherwise, SQL Server will throw an exception. That's because relational databases don't guarantee the order in which data is handed back; there's no default row order in a relational database.

2.8   *Putting it all together: combining query objects*

We've covered each query object you need to build a book list for the book app. Now it's time to see how to combine each of these query objects to create a composite query to work with the website. The benefit of building a complex query as separate parts is that it makes writing and testing the overall query simpler, because you can test each part on its own.

Listing 2.15 shows a class called ListBooksService, which has one method, Sort-FilterPage, which uses all the query objects (select, sort, filter, and page) to build the composite query. It also needs the application's DbContext to access the Books property, which you provide via the constructor.

TIP Listing 2.15 highlights in bold the AsNoTracking method. This stops EF Core from taking a tracking snapshot (see figure 1.6), which makes the query slightly quicker. You should use the AsNoTracking method in any read-only queries (queries in which you only read the data, but don't ever update the data).

Listing 2.15   The ListBookService class provides a sorted, filtered, and paged list

**Because this is a read-only
query, you add .AsNoTracking.**

```
public class ListBooksService
{
    private readonly EfCoreContext _context;

    public ListBooksService(EfCoreContext context)
    {
        _context = context;
    }

    public IQueryable<BookListDto> SortFilterPage
        (SortFilterPageOptions options)
    {
        var booksQuery = _context.Books
            .AsNoTracking()
            .MapBookToDto()
            .OrderBooksBy(options.OrderByOptions)
            .FilterBooksBy(options.FilterBy,
                           options.FilterValue);

        options.SetupRestOfDto(booksQuery);

        return booksQuery.Page(options.PageNum-1,
                               options.PageSize);
    }
}
```

**Starts by selecting the Books
property in the Application's
DbContext**

**Uses the Select query object, which will
pick out/calculate the data it needs**

**Adds the commands
to filter the data**

**This stage sets up the number
of pages and makes sure
PageNum is in the right range.**

**Applies the paging
commands**

**Adds the commands to order the
data by using the given options**

At you can see, the four query objects—select, sort, filter, and page—are added in turn (called *chaining*) to form the final composite query. Note that the options .SetupRestOfDto(booksQuery) code just before the Page query object sorts out things such as how many pages there are, ensures that the `PageNum` is in the right range, and performs a few other housekeeping items.

Chapter 5 shows how the `ListBooksService` is called in our ASP.NET Core web application.

Summary

- To access a database in any way via EF Core, you need to define an application DbContext.
- An EF Core query consists of three parts: the application's DbContext property, a series of LINQ/EF Core commands, and a command to execute the query.
- Using EF Core, you can model three primary database relationships: one-to-one, one-to-many, and many-to-many. Another is hierarchical, covered in chapter 7.
- The classes that EF Core maps to the database are referred to as *entity classes.* I use this term to highlight that the class I'm referring to is mapped by EF Core to the database.
- If you load an entity class, it won't load any of its relationships by default. For example, querying the `Book` entity class won't load its relationship properties (`Reviews`, `AuthorsLink`, and `Promotion`), but leave them as `null`.
- You can load related data that's attached to an entity class in four ways: eager loading, explicit loading, select loading, and lazy loading (which is available in only EF Core 2.1 onward).
- The EF Core feature called *client vs. server evaluation* allows you to include commands that can't be converted to SQL commands in your database query. EF Core extracts these non-SQL commands and executes them after the database access has finished.
- I've used the term *query object* to refer to an encapsulated query, or a section of a query. These query objects are often built as .NET extension methods, which means they can easily be chained together, similar to the way LINQ is written.

For readers who are familiar with EF6.x:

- Many of the concepts in this chapter are the same as in EF6.x. In some cases (for instance, *eager loading*), the EF Core commands have changed slightly, but often for the better.
- Some features in EF6.x, such as automatic many-to-many relationship setup, are missing from EF Core. Alternatives exist, but you'll need to write your code slightly differently than in EF6.x.
- EF Core's client vs. server evaluation feature is new and allows you to write queries that would've previously thrown an exception in EF6.x.

Changing the
database content

This chapter covers

- Creating a new row in a database table

- Updating existing rows in a database table for
  two types of applications

- Updating entities with one-to-one, one-to-many,
  and many-to-many relationships

- Deleting single entities, and entities with
  relationships, from a database

Chapter 2 covered querying a database. This chapter moves on to changing the content of a database. Changing data has three distinct parts: creating new rows in a database table, updating existing rows in a database table, and deleting rows in a database table, which I cover in that order. *Create*, *update*, and *delete*, along with *read* (which is *query* in EF Core terms) are database terms for what's happening, and the foursome is often shortened to *CRUD*.

You'll use the same database as in chapter 2, which has the Book, PriceOffer, Review, BookAuthor, and Author entity classes. These provide a good selection of property types and relationships that you can use to learn the various issues and approaches to changing data in a database via EF Core.

3.1 Introducing EF Core's entity State

Before I start describing the methods to add, update, or delete entities, I want to introduce you to EF Core's entity property, called `State`. This provides another look under the hood at the way EF Core does things. You can skip this section, but it can help you understand what's going on when you add, update, or delete entities.

When you read in an entity, it's tracked by EF Core by default. This is known as a *tracked entity,* and EF Core holds extra information on the entity.

> **DEFINITION** *Tracked entities* are entity instances that have been read in from the database by using a query that didn't include the `AsNoTracking` method. Alternatively, after an entity instance has been used as a parameter to EF Core methods (such as `Add`, `Update`, or `Delete`), it becomes tracked.

For all the tracked entities—all entity instances that EF Core has loaded from the database without the `AsNoTracking` method, or all entities to which you've applied an EF Core command such as `Add`, `Update`, or `Delete`—EF Core holds a property called `State`. The `State` of an entity can be obtained using the following EF command:

```
context.Entry(someEntityInstance).State
```

Here's a list of the possible states and what happens if `SaveChanges` is called:

- `Added`—The entity doesn't yet exist in the database. `SaveChanges` inserts it.
- `Unchanged`—The entity exists in the database and hasn't been modified on the client. `SaveChanges` ignores it.
- `Modified`—The entity exists in the database and has been modified on the client. `SaveChanges` updates it.
- `Deleted`—The entity exists in the database but should be deleted. `SaveChanges` deletes it.
- `Detached`—The entity you provided isn't tracked. `SaveChanges` doesn't see it.

Normally, you don't look at or alter the `State` directly. You use the various commands listed in this chapter to add, update, or delete entities. These commands make sure the `State` is set in all the entities involved so that the action you want is done correctly. I refer to the entity's `State` in the rest of the chapter to show you how EF Core decides what type of change to apply to the database.

3.2 Creating new rows in a table

Creating new data in a database is about adding (via SQL `INSERT`) a new row to a table. For instance, if you want to add a new author to our book app, that would be referred to as a create operation on the database.

In EF Core terms, creating new data in a database is the simplest of the update operations. This is because EF Core can take a set of linked entity classes, save them to the database, and sort out the foreign keys needed to link things together. In this section, you'll start with a simple example and then build up to more complex creates.

3.2.1 Creating a single entity on its own

Let's start with an entity class that has no links, which is rare but shows the two steps in a create operation:

1 Adding the entity to the application's DbContext
2 Calling the application's DbContext's `SaveChanges` method

This listing creates an `ExampleEntity` entity class and adds a new row to the table that the entity is mapped to, in this case the ExampleEntities table.

Listing 3.1 An example of creating a single entity

```
var itemToAdd = new ExampleEntity
{
    MyMessage = "Hello World"
};

context.Add(itemToAdd);
context.SaveChanges();
```

Uses the Add method to add SingleEntity to the application's DbContext. The DbContext determines the table to add it to, based on its parameter type.

Calls the SaveChanges method from the application's DbContext to update the database

Because you add the entity instance `itemToAdd` that wasn't originally tracked, EF Core starts to track it and sets its `State` to `Added`. After `SaveChanges` is called, EF Core finds a tracked entity of type `ExampleEntity` with a `State` of `Added`, so it's added as a new row in the database table associated with the `ExampleEntity` class.

EF6 In EF6.x, you'd need to add the `ExampleEntity` to a `DbSet<ExampleEntity>` property in the application's DbContext. That approach is still valid, but EF Core has introduced the shorthand shown in listing 3.1. This applies to the Add, Remove, Update, and Attach methods (see chapter 9 for more on these last two commands). EF Core works out which entity you're altering by looking at the type of the instance you provide.

EF Core creates the SQL command to update an SQL Server–based database.

Listing 3.2 SQL commands created to insert a new row into the SingleEntities table

```
SET NOCOUNT ON;
INSERT INTO ExampleEntities]
    ([MyMessage]) VALUES (@p0);

SELECT [ExampleEntityId]
FROM [ExampleEntities]
WHERE @@ROWCOUNT = 1 AND
    [ExampleEntityId] = scope_identity();
```

Inserts (creates) a new row in the ExampleEntities table

Reads back the primary key in the newly created row

The second SQL command produced by EF Core reads back the primary key of the row that was created by the database server. This ensures that the original instance is updated with the primary key so that the in-memory version of the entity is the same as the version in the database. That can be useful if you need the primary key in your code, or in case the same entity will be updated again later.

> **EF6** In EF6.x, when you call SaveChanges, EF6.x by default will validate the data by using the standard .NET validation approach: EF6.x looks for data validation attributes and, if present, runs IValidatableObject.Validate on entity classes. EF Core doesn't include this feature. Chapter 4 shows you how to implement this feature yourself.

3.2.2   *Creating a book with a review*

Next, you'll look at a create that includes relationships—in this case, adding a new book with a review. Although the code is a bit more complex, the process has the same steps as our earlier, nonrelational create:

1 It adds the entity class(es) in some way to EF Core's tracked entities with the State of Add.
2 It calls SaveChanges, which looks at the State of all the tracked entities and runs the SQL INSERT command for all entities with the State set to Added.

This example uses the book app database with its Books and Review tables. Figure 3.1 shows a partial database diagram of these tables.

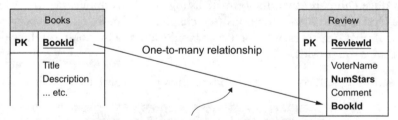

A Book entity with one Review

When EF Core writes this new book entity and its related Review entity to the database, it copies the Book's database-generated primary key into the foreign key in the Review entity.

Figure 3.1   The Books and Review tables. The Review row has a foreign key that EF Core fills with the primary key value from the new Books row that's created.

In listing 3.3, you create a new `Book` entity and fill the `Reviews` collection property with a single `Review` entity. You then call the `context.Add` method, followed by the `SaveChanges` method, which writes both entities to the database.

Listing 3.3   Adding a `Book` entity class also adds any linked entity classes

```
var book = new Book
{
    Title = "Test Book",
    PublishedOn = DateTime.Today,
    Reviews = new List<Review>()
    {
        new Review
        {
            NumStars = 5,
            Comment = "Great test book!",
            VoterName = "Mr U Test"
        }
    }
};

context.Add(book);
context.SaveChanges();
```

Creates the book with the title "Test Book"

Creates a new collection of reviews

Adds one review with its content

Calls the SaveChanges method from the application's DbContext to update the database. It finds a new Book, which has a collection containing one new Review, and it then adds both to the database.

Uses the Add method to add the book to the application's DbContext property, Books

The thing to note from this is that you add only the `Book` entity class to the application's DbContext property `Books`, but the related `Review` entity class is also written to the database. This is because EF Core follows all the relational links and finds the other entity classes.

As you saw in the simple example in listing 3.1, EF Core works out what to do with the linked entity classes by accessing their EF Core `State` values. If the linked instances are new (not already known to EF Core), EF Core will track them and set their `State` to `New`. In all other cases, EF Core will obey the `State` linked to the entity instance. In listing 3.3, the `Review` entity instance isn't already known to EF Core, so its `State` is set to `Added`. That instance will be `INSERTed` into the database as a new row.

WHAT HAPPENS WHEN SAVECHANGES RETURNS SUCCESSFULLY

After `SaveChanges` has successfully updated the database, a few things happen. First, the instances that have been inserted into the database are now tracked by EF Core, and their `State` is set to `Unchanged`.

NOTE   Chapter 1 described EF Core's internal tracking snapshot copy that EF Core creates when you don't include the AsNoTracking method in your query. Entities loaded this way are known as tracked entities, and EF Core knows their State.

In this example, because these two entity classes, Book and Review, have primary keys that are of type int, EF Core by default expects the database to create the primary keys by using the SQL IDENTITY keyword. Therefore, the SQL commands created by EF Core return the primary keys, which are copied into the properties mapped to the database primary key.

Also, EF Core knows about the relationships by the navigational properties in the entity classes. In listing 3.3, the Book entity's Reviews collection property has a new Review entity instance in it. As part of the SaveChanges process, any foreign key will be set by copying the primary keys into the foreign keys in each of the new relationships. The entity instance then matches the database. That's useful in case you want to read the primary or foreign keys, and EF Core can detect any change you make to the primary or foreign keys if you call SaveChanges again.

NOTE   Some primary keys, such as GUIDs (globally unique identifiers), are generated by what EF Core calls a ValueGenerator. These are filled in by the software and copied to any related foreign keys before the write to the database. Chapter 8 covers the ValueGenerator feature, which allows you to define key values via software.

EXAMPLE THAT HAS ONE INSTANCE ALREADY IN THE DATABASE

The other situation you may need to deal with is creating a new entity containing a navigational property that uses another entity already in the database. If you want to create a new Book entity that has an Author that already exists in the database, you need to obtain a tracked instance of the Author entity you want to add to your new Book entity. Here's one example.

Listing 3.4   Adding a book with an existing author

```
var oneBook =
    EfTestData.CreateDummyBookOneAuthor();
context.Add(oneBook);
context.SaveChanges();

var book = new Book
{
    Title = "Test Book",
    PublishedOn = DateTime.Today
};
```

Creates dummy books for testing. You create one dummy book with one Author and add it to the empty database.

Creates a book in the same way as the previous example, but sets up its Author

```
book.AuthorsLink = new List<BookAuthor>
{
    new BookAuthor
    {
        Book = book,
        Author = oneBook.AuthorsLink
            .First().Author
    }
};
```

Adds an AuthorBook linking entity, but reads in an existing Author from the first book

```
context.Add(book);
context.SaveChanges();
```

The same process: adds the new book to the DbContext Books property and calls SaveChanges

The first four lines use a method to create a Book entity with one Author, linked to the Book entity via a BookAuthor linking entity. You then create a new Book entity and add a new BookAuthor linking entity, but instead of creating a new Author entity instance, you use the Author entity from the first book. The instance assigned to the Author link has already been written to the database, so it's tracked. This means EF Core won't try to add it again to the database when SaveChanges is called again at the end of listing 3.4.

To be clear: in this example, you write the first book, with its BookAuthor and Authors entity classes, by calling SaveChanges (line 4). If you leave out SaveChanges in line 4, you'd have the same result: only one author would be written to the database. That's because the author had already been tracked by EF Core because of the Add of the first book.

3.3 Updating database rows

Updating a database row is achieved in three stages:

1 Read the data (database row), possibly with some relationships.
2 Change one or more properties (database columns).
3 Write the changes back to the database (update the row).

In this section, you'll ignore any relationships and focus on the three stages. In the next section, you'll learn how to update relationships by adding more commands into each stage.

Listing 3.5 changes the publication date of an existing book. Through this code, you can see the standard flow of an update:

1 You load the entity class(es) you want to change as a tracked entity.
2 You change the property/properties in your entity class(es).
3 You call SaveChanges to update the database.

Listing 3.5   Updating *Quantum Networking*'s publication date

Finds the specific book you want to update—our special book on Quantum Networking

Changes the expected publication date to year 2058 (it was 2057)

```
var book = context.Books
    .Single(p => p.Title == "Quantum Networking");
book.PublishedOn = new DateTime(2058, 1, 1);
context.SaveChanges();
```

Calls SaveChanges, which includes running a method called DetectChanges. This spots that the PublishedOn property has been changed.

When the SaveChanges method is called, it runs a method called DetectChanges, which compares the tracking snapshot copy with the copy that it handed to the application when the query was originally executed. From this, it decides that only the PublishedOn property has been changed, and EF Core builds the SQL to update that.

> **NOTE** Using the tracking snapshot is the normal way that DetectChanges finds the changed properties. But chapter 8 describes an alternative to the tracking snapshot, called INotifyPropertyChanging. This is an advanced topic, so I use the tracked entities approach throughout part 1 of this book.

The following listing shows the two SQL commands that EF Core produces for the code in listing 3.5. One SQL command finds and loads the Book entity class, and a second command updates the PublishedOn column.

Listing 3.6   SQL generated by EF Core for the query and update in listing 3.5

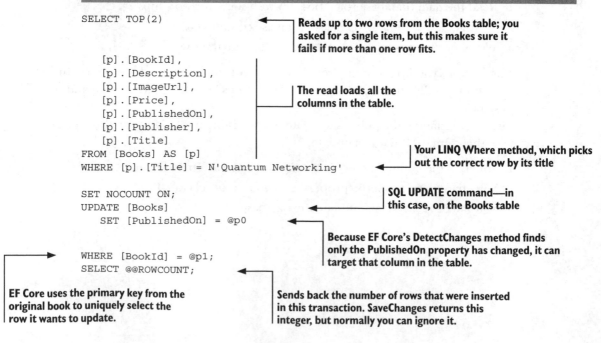

```
SELECT TOP(2)



    [p].[BookId],
    [p].[Description],
    [p].[ImageUrl],
    [p].[Price],
    [p].[PublishedOn],
    [p].[Publisher],
    [p].[Title]
FROM [Books] AS [p]
WHERE [p].[Title] = N'Quantum Networking'

SET NOCOUNT ON;
UPDATE [Books]
    SET [PublishedOn] = @p0


WHERE [BookId] = @p1;
SELECT @@ROWCOUNT;
```

Reads up to two rows from the Books table; you asked for a single item, but this makes sure it fails if more than one row fits.

The read loads all the columns in the table.

Your LINQ Where method, which picks out the correct row by its title

SQL UPDATE command—in this case, on the Books table

Because EF Core's DetectChanges method finds only the PublishedOn property has changed, it can target that column in the table.

EF Core uses the primary key from the original book to uniquely select the row it wants to update.

Sends back the number of rows that were inserted in this transaction. SaveChanges returns this integer, but normally you can ignore it.

3.3.1 *Handling disconnected updates in a web application*

As you learned in the previous section, an update is a three-stage process, needing a read, an update, and a `SaveChanges` call to all be executed using the same instance of the application's DbContext. The problem is that for certain applications, such as websites and RESTful APIs, using the same instance of the application's DbContext isn't possible. In these types of applications an update consists of two stages:

1 The first stage is an initial read, done in one instance of the application's DbContext.
2 The second stage then applies the update using a new instance of the application's DbContext.

In EF Core, this is called a *disconnected* update, whereas the update example in listing 3.5 is known as a *connected* update. You can handle a disconnected update in several ways. The method you should use depends a lot on your application. Here are the two main ways of handling disconnected updates:

1 *You send only the data you need to update back from the first stage.* If you were updating the published date for a book you would only send back the `BookId` and the `PublishedOn` properties. In the second stage, you use the primary key to reload the original entity with tracking and update the specific properties you want to change. In this example, the primary key is the `BookId` and the property to update is `PublishedOn` property of the `Book` entity (see figure 3.2). When you call `SaveChanges`, EF Core can work out which properties you've changed and update only those columns in the database.
2 *You send all the data needed to re-create the entity class back from the first stage.* In the second stage, you rebuild the entity class, and maybe relationships, by using the data from the first stage and tell EF Core to update the whole entity (see figure 3.3). When you call `SaveChanges`, EF Core will know, because you told it, that it must update all the columns in the table row(s) affected with the substitute data that the first stage provided.

> **NOTE** Another way of handling the partial update of an entity described in option 1 is by creating a new entity instance and manipulating the `State` of each property. Chapter 9 covers this option, when we look at how to alter the entity's `State` in more detail.

That's a lot of words! Now I'll give you an example of each approach for handling disconnected updates.

DISCONNECTED UPDATE, WITH RELOAD

Figure 3.2 shows an example of a disconnected update in a web application. In this case, you're providing a feature to allow an admin user to update the publication date of a book. The figure shows that you send only the `BookId` and the `PublicationDate` back from the first stage.

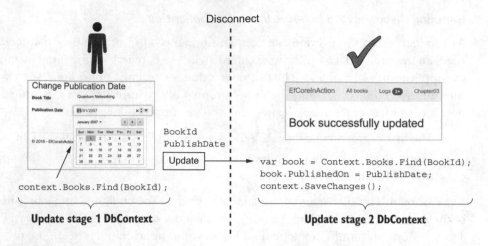

Figure 3.2   The two stages in a disconnected update on a website using EF Core. The thick, dashed line in the middle represents the point where the data held in the application in the first stage is lost, and the second stage starts with no knowledge of what stage 1 did. Only the `BookId` and `PublishDate` information are returned when the user clicks the Update button that bridges the gap.

For web applications, the approach of returning only a limited amount of data back to the web server is a common way of handling EF Core updates. There are several ways of controlling what data is returned/accepted by the web server. In ASP.NET Core, you have two attributes, `BindRequired` and `BindNever`, that you can apply to properties in a class to require or stop, respectively, the data being input to the second stage.

A more general approach, and one I prefer, is to use a special class that contains only properties that should be sent/received. This class is referred to as a DTO or View-Model. It's similar in nature to the DTO used in the select-loading query in chapter 2, but in this case is used not only in the query, but also to receive the specific data you need back from the user, via a browser.

For our example that updates the publication date, you need three parts. The first part, a DTO to send/receive the data to/from the user, is shown here.

Listing 3.7   `ChangePubDateDto` sends data to and receives it from the user

```
public class ChangePubDateDto
{
    public int BookId { get; set; }

    public string Title { get; set; }

    [DataType(DataType.Date)]
    public DateTime PublishedOn { get; set; }
}
```

Holds the primary key of the row you want to update. This makes finding the right row quick and accurate.

You send over the title to show the user, so that they can be clear about altering the right book.

The property you want to alter. You send out the current publication date and get back the changed publication date.

> ## The Find command
>
> When you want to update a specific entity and you have its primary key, the Find command is a quick way of loading the entity. This command has two forms:
>
> - DbSet's `Find(key(s))`; for instance, `context.Book.Find(key)`
> - DbContext's `Find<T>(key(s))`; for instance, `context.Find<Book>(key)`
>
> Both Find methods take one key (see listing 3.8) or multiple keys, known as *composite keys* (the `BookAuthor` entity has a composite key, consisting of the `BookId` and the `AuthorId`). The key parameters must be in the same order that the composite key is defined in. Find returns `null` if no matching entity with that key is found.
>
> Also, Find checks the current application's DbContext to see whether the required entity instance has already been loaded, which can save an access to the database. This makes the Find methods efficient to use when you want to load only a specific entity.

Second, you need a method to get the initial data for stage 1. Third, you need a method to receive the data back from the browser and then reload/update the book. This listing shows the ChangePubDateService class that contains two methods to handle these stages.

Listing 3.8   The `ChangePubDateService` class to handle the disconnected update

```
public class ChangePubDateService
{
    private readonly EfCoreContext _context;

    public ChangePubDateService(EfCoreContext context)
    {
        _context = context;
    }

    public ChangePubDateDto GetOriginal(int id)
    {
        return _context.Books
            .Select(p => new ChangePubDateDto
            {
                BookId = p.BookId,
                Title = p.Title,
                PublishedOn = p.PublishedOn
            })
            .Single(k => k.BookId == id);
    }

    public Book UpdateBook(ChangePubDateDto dto)
    {
        var book = _context.Find<Book>(dto.BookId);
        book.PublishedOn = dto.PublishedOn;
```

Handles the first part of the update by getting the data from the chosen book to show to the user

A select load query, which returns only three properties

Uses the primary key to select the exact row you want to update

Handles the second part of the update, performing a selective update of the chosen book

Loads the book. The EF Core Find method is an efficient way of loading a row by its primary key.

Selective update of just the PublishedOn property of the loaded book

```
                    _context.SaveChanges();
                    return book;
            }
    }
```

Returns the updated book

SaveChanges uses its DetectChanges method to find out what has changed, and then updates the database.

The advantages of this reload update approach is it's more secure (in our example, sending/returning the price of the book over HTTP would allow someone to alter it) and it's faster because of less data. The downside is you have to write code to copy over the specific properties you want to update. A few tricks to automate this are covered in chapter 10.

> **NOTE**   You can see this code and try updating the publication date on the example book app. If you download the code from the Git repo and run it locally, you'll see an Admin button on each book. This contains an action called Change Pub Date, which will step you through this process. You can also see the SQL commands that EF Core uses to carry out this update via the Logs menu item.

DISCONNECTED UPDATE, SENDING ALL THE DATA

In some cases, all the data may be sent back, so there's no reason to reload the original data. This can happen for simple entity classes, in some RESTful APIs, or process-to-process communication. A lot depends on how closely the given API format matches the database format and how much you trust the other system.

Figure 3.3 shows an example of a RESTful API in which an external system first queries the system for books with a given title. In the update stage, the external system sends back an update on the author of the book it received.

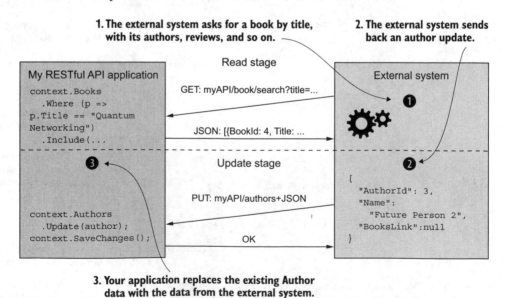

Figure 3.3   An example of a disconnected update, in which you replace all of the database information with the new data. Unlike the previous example, this process doesn't need to reload the original data before performing the update.

Listing 3.9 simulates the RESTful API by having a first stage that reads in the `Author` entity class you wish to update and then serializes it into a JSON string (see figure 3.3, step 2 for what that JSON looks like). You then decode that JSON and use the EF Core `Update` command, which replaces all the information in the row defined by the primary key; in this case, the `AuthorId`.

Listing 3.9 Simulating an update/replace request from an external system

> Simulates an external system returning a modified Author entity class as a JSON string

```
string json;
using (var context = new EfCoreContext(options))
{
    var author = context.Books
        .Where(p => p.Title == "Quantum Networking")
        .Select(p => p.AuthorsLink.First().Author)
        .Single();
    author.Name = "Future Person 2";
    json = JsonConvert.SerializeObject(author);
}

using (var context = new EfCoreContext(options))
{
    var author = JsonConvert
        .DeserializeObject<Author>(json);
```

> Simulates receiving a JSON string from an external system and decoding it into an Author class

```
    context.Authors.Update(author);
    context.SaveChanges();
```

> Provides a link to the many-to-many linking table that links to the authors of this book

> Update command, which replaces all the row data for the given primary key—in this case, AuthorId

---

You call the EF Core `Update` command with the `Author` entity instance as a parameter, which marks as modified all the properties of the `Author` entity. When the `SaveChanges` command is called, it'll update all the columns in the row that have the same primary key as the entity class.

> **EF6** The `Update` command is new in EF Core. In EF6.x, you need to manipulate the entity object state directly; for instance, using the command `DbContext`
> `.Entry(object).State = EntityState.Modified`. Subtle changes in how EF
> Core sets the entity state are covered in chapter 9.

The plus side of this approach is that the database update is quicker, because you don't have the extra read of the original data. You also don't have to write code to copy over the specific properties you want to update, which you did need to do in the previous approach.

The downside is that more data can be transferred and, unless the API is carefully designed, it can be difficult to reconcile the data you receive to the data already in the database. Also, you're trusting the external system to correctly remember all the data, especially the primary keys of your system.

NOTE   Listing 3.9 covers only a single class with no relationship, but in many RESTful APIs and process-to-process communication, a lot of linked data might be sent over. In the example, the API might expect the whole book with all its relationships to be sent back only for an update of the author's name. This gets complicated, so I cover that in chapter 9, which shows how to manage the state of each property and introduces EF Core's `TrackGraph` method, which helps handle partial updates of classes with relationships.

3.4   *Handling relationships in updates*

Now that we've established the three basic steps to updating the database, it's time to look at updating relationships between entity classes—for example, adding a new review to a book. Updating relationships adds another level of complexity to the code, especially in the disconnected state, which is why I put this content in a separate section.

This section covers updates for the three types of relational linking that EF Core uses and gives examples of both connected and disconnected updates. In all cases, you'll use the Book entity class, which has three relationship links. The following listing shows the Book entity class, but with the focus on the relationships at the end. (I've removed some nonrelational properties to keep the focus on the relationships.)

Listing 3.10   The `Book` entity class, showing the relationships to update

Link to the optional PriceOffer

```
public class Book          ◄───────   Book class contains the
{                                      main book information
    public int BookId { get; set; }
    //… other nonrelational properties removed for clarity

    //------------------------------------------------
    //relationships

    public PriceOffer Promotion { get; set; }          Can be zero to many
    public ICollection<Review> Reviews { get; set; } ◄─ reviews of the book
    public ICollection<BookAuthor>
        AuthorsLink { get; set; }         Provides a link to the many-to-many
}                                         linking table that links to the authors
                                          of this book
```

3.4.1   *Principal and dependent relationships*

The terms *principal* and *dependent* are used in EF to define parts of a relationship:

- *Principal entity*—Contains the key property(s) that the dependent relationship refers to via a foreign key(s)
- *Dependent entity*—Contains the foreign key property(s) that refers to the principal entity

In the book app example, the `Book` entity class is the principal entity. The `PriceOffer`, `Review`, and `BookAuthor` entity classes are the dependent entities. I find the terms *principal* and *dependent* helpful, because they define who's in charge—the principal entity. I use these terms throughout the book, where applicable.

> **NOTE** An entity class can be both a principal and a dependent entity at the same time. For instance, in a hierarchical relationship of, say, libraries having books having reviews, the book would be a dependent relationship on the library entity class.

CAN THE DEPENDENT PART OF A RELATIONSHIP EXIST WITHOUT THE PRINCIPAL?

The other aspect of a dependent relationship is whether it can exist on its own. If the principal relationship is deleted, is there a business case for the dependent relationship to still exist? In many cases, the dependent part of a relationship doesn't make sense without the principal relationship. For instance, a book review has no meaning if the book it links to is deleted.

In a few cases, a dependent relationship should exist even if the principal part is deleted. Say you want to have a log of all the changes that happen to a book in its lifetime. If you delete a book, you wouldn't want that set of logs to be deleted too.

The way this is handled in databases is by handling the nullability of the foreign key. If the foreign key in the dependent relationship is non-nullable, the dependent relationship can't exist without the principal. In the example book app database, the `PriceOffer`, `Review`, and `BookAuthor` entities are all dependent on the principal, `Book` entity, so their foreign keys are of type `int`. If the book is deleted or the link to the book is removed, the dependent entities will be deleted.

But if you define a class for logging—let's call it `BookLog`—you want this to exist even if the book is deleted. To make this happen, you'd make its `BookId` foreign key of type `Nullable<int>`. Then, if you delete the book that the `BookLog` entity is linked to, you could configure that the `BookLog`'s `BookId` foreign key would be set to `null`.

> **NOTE** In the preceding `BookLog` example, if you delete a `Book` entity that a `BookLog` is linked to, the default action is to set the `BookLog`'s foreign key to null. This is because EF Core defaults to a `ClientSetNull` setting for the `OnDelete` property of optional relationships. Section 7.4.4 covers this in more detail.

I mention this now because as we go through updating the relationships, in some cases a dependent relationship is removed from its principal. I'll give an example of replacing all the dependent relationships with new ones, and what happens to the old relationships we remove depends on the nullability of its foreign key: if the foreign key is non-nullable, the dependent relationships are deleted, and if the foreign key is nullable, it's set to `null`.

I talk more about this and how EF Core handles deletion in section 3.5.

3.4.2   *Updating one-to-one relationships—adding a PriceOffer to a book*

In our example book app database, we have an optional, dependent relationship property called `Promotion` from the `Book` entity class to the `PriceOffer` entity class. This subsection covers how to add a `PriceOffer` class to an existing book. This listing shows you the content of the `PriceOffer` entity class, which links to the `Books` table via the foreign key called `BookId`.

Listing 3.11   `PriceOffer` entity class, showing the foreign key back to the `Book` entity

```
public class PriceOffer                          ◄─────  PriceOffer, if present, is designed
{                                                        to override the normal price.
    public int PriceOfferId { get; set; }
    public decimal NewPrice { get; set; }
    public string PromotionalText { get; set; }

    //------------------------------------------------
    //Relationships
                                                         Foreign key back to the book
    public int BookId { get; set; }          ◄─────      it should be applied to

}
```
You could provide a backward navigational link from this entity to the Book entity, but you don't because there's no business reason for having this link. I explain why in section 7.2.

CONNECTED STATE UPDATE

The connected state update assumes you're using the same context for both the read and the update. Listing 3.12 shows an example of the code, which has three stages:

1 Load the `Book` entity with any existing `PriceOffer` relationship.
2 Set the relationship to the new `PriceOffer` entity you want to apply to this book.
3 Call `SaveChanges` to update the database.

Listing 3.12   Adding a new promotional price to an existing book

Although the include isn't needed because you're loading something without a Promotion, using the include is good practice, as you should load any relationships if you're going to change a relationship.

```
var book = context.Books                         ◄─────  Finds the first book that doesn't
    .Include(p => p.Promotion)                           have an existing promotion
    .First(p => p.Promotion == null);

book.Promotion = new PriceOffer
{                                                        The SaveChanges method calls
    NewPrice = book.Price / 2,                           DetectChanges, which finds that
    PromotionalText = "Half price today!"                the Promotion property has
};                                                       changed, so it adds that entity to
context.SaveChanges();                           ◄─────  the PriceOffers table.
```
Adds a new **PriceOffer** to this book

As you can see, the update of the relationship is just like the basic update you made to change the book's published date. In this case, EF Core has to do extra work because it's a relationship. In this case, EF Core creates a new row in the PriceOffers table, which you can see in the SQL snippet that EF Core produces for the code in listing 3.12:

```
INSERT INTO [PriceOffers]
    ([BookId], [NewPrice], [PromotionalText])
     VALUES (@p0, @p1, @p2);
```

Now, what happens if there's an existing promotion on the book (the Promotion property in the Book entity class isn't null)? That's why the Include(p => p.Promotion) command in the query that loaded the Book entity class is so important. Because of that Include method, EF Core will know there's an existing PriceOffer assigned to this book and will delete that before adding the new version.

To be clear, in this case you must use some form of loading of the relationship—either *eager, explicit, select,* or *lazy* loading of the relationship—so EF Core knows about it before the update. If you don't and there's an existing relationship, EF Core in this case will throw an exception on a duplicate key on the BookId, which EF Core has placed a unique index on, and another row in the PriceOffers table will have the same value.

DISCONNECTED STATE UPDATE

In the disconnected state, the information to define which book to update and what to put in the PriceOffer entity class would be passed back from stage 1 to stage 2. That's what happened in the update of the book's publication date (figure 3.2), where the BookId and the PublishedOn values were fed back.

In the case of adding a promotion to a book, you need to pass in the BookId, which uniquely defines the book you want, plus the NewPrice and the PromotionalText values that make up the PriceOffer entity class. The next listing shows you the Change-PriceOfferService class, which contains the two methods to show the data to the user and update the promotion on the Book entity class when the user submits a request.

Listing 3.13 **ChangePriceOfferService class with a method to handle each stage**

```
public class ChangePriceOfferService
{
    private readonly EfCoreContext _context;

    public Book OrgBook { get; private set; }

    public ChangePriceOfferService(EfCoreContext context)
    {
        _context = context;
    }

    public PriceOffer GetOriginal(int id)          ◄─── Gets a PriceOffer class to
    {                                                   send to the user to update
        OrgBook = _context.Books
            .Include(r => r.Promotion)             ┐─── Loads the book with any
            .Single(k => k.BookId == id);          ┘    existing Promotion
```

You return either the existing Promotion for editing, or create a new one. The important point is to set the BookId, as you need to pass that through to the second stage.

```
return OrgBook?.Promotion
    ?? new PriceOffer
        {
            BookId = id,
            NewPrice = OrgBook.Price
        };
}

public Book UpdateBook(PriceOffer promotion)
{
    var book = _context.Books
        .Include(r => r.Promotion)
        .Single(k => k.BookId
            == promotion.BookId);
    if (book.Promotion == null)
```

Handles the second part of the update, performing a selective update of the chosen book

Loads the book with any existing promotion, which is important because otherwise your new PriceOffer will clash and throw an error

Checks whether this is an update of an existing PriceOffer or adds a new PriceOffer

You need to add a new PriceOffer, so you assign the promotion to the relational link. EF Core will see this and add a new row in the PriceOffer table.

```
    {
        book.Promotion = promotion;
    }
    else
    {
        book.Promotion.NewPrice
            = promotion.NewPrice;
        book.Promotion.PromotionalText
            = promotion.PromotionalText;
    }
    _context.SaveChanges();
    return book;
}
}
```

You need to do an update, so you copy over just the parts that you want to change. EF Core will see this update and produce code to update just these two columns.

Returns the updated book

SaveChanges uses its DetectChanges method, which sees what changes— either adding a new PriceOffer or updating an existing one

This code either updates an existing PriceOffer, or adds a new PriceOffer if none exists. When SaveChanges is called, it can work out, via EF Core's DetectChanges method, what type of update is needed and creates the correct SQL to update the database.

ALTERNATIVE WAY OF UPDATING THE RELATIONSHIP—CREATING A NEW ROW DIRECTLY

We've approached this update as changing a relationship in the Book entity class, but you can also approach it as creating/deleting a row in the PriceOffers table. This listing creates a PriceOffer entity (section 3.5 covers deletion).

Listing 3.14 Creating a PriceOffer row to go with an existing book

```
var book = context.Books
    .First(p => p.Promotion == null);

//ATTEMPT
context.Add( new PriceOffer
{
    BookId = book.BookId,
    NewPrice = book.Price / 2,
    PromotionalText = "Half price today!"
});
context.SaveChanges();
```

You find the book that you want to add the new PriceOffer to. It must not be an existing PriceOffer.

Adds the new PriceOffer to the PriceOffers table

Defines the PriceOffer. You must include the BookId (previously, EF Core filled that in).

SaveChanges adds the PriceOffer to the PriceOffers table.

You should note that previously you didn't have to set the `BookId` property in the `PriceOffer` entity class, because EF Core did that for you. But when creating a relationship this way, you do need to set the foreign key. Having done that, if you load the `Book` entity class with its `Promotion` relationship after the previous create code, you'll find that the `Book` has gained a `Promotion` relationship.

> **NOTE** The `PriceOffer` entity class doesn't have a relational property link back to the `Book` class (`public Book BookLink {get; set;}`). If it did, you could set the `BookLink` to the book entity class instead of setting the foreign key. Either setting the foreign key(s) or setting a relational link back to the principal entity will tell EF Core to set up the relationship.

The advantage of creating the dependent entity class is that it saves you from needing to reload the principal entity class (in this case, `Book`) in a disconnected state. The downside is that EF Core doesn't help you with the relationships. For instance, in this case, if there was an existing `PriceOffer` on the book and you added another, `SaveChanges` would fail because you'd have two `PriceOffer` rows with the same key.

When EF Core can't help you with the relationships, you need to use the create/delete approach with care. Sometimes it can make handling a complex relationship easier, so it's worth keeping in mind, but I prefer updating the principal entity class's relationship in most one-to-one cases.

> **NOTE** Later in this section, you'll learn another way of updating relationships by changing foreign keys.

3.4.3 *Updating one-to-many relationships—adding a review to a book*

You've learned the basic steps in updating a relationship by looking at a one-to-one relationship. I'll move a bit quicker with the remaining relationships, as you've seen the basic pattern. But I'll also point out some differences around the *many* side of a relationship.

The one-to-many relationship in the book app database is represented by book reviews: a user of the site can add a review to a book. There can be any number of reviews, from none to a lot. This listing shows the `Review`-dependent entity class, which links to the Books table via the foreign key called `BookId`.

Listing 3.15   The `Review` class, showing the foreign key back to the `Book` entity class

```
public class Review              ◄──┤ Holds customer reviews with their ratings
{
    public int ReviewId { get; set; }
    public string VoterName { get; set; }
    public int NumStars { get; set; }
    public string Comment { get; set; }

    //----------------------------------------
    //Relationships
                                        Foreign key holds the key of the
    public int BookId { get; set; }  ◄──┘ book this review belongs to
}
```

CONNECTED STATE UPDATE

Listing 3.16 adds a new review to a book. This code follows the same pattern as the one-to-one connected update: load the `Book` entity class, and the `Reviews` relationship via the `Include` method, but in this case you add the review to the collection. Because you used the `Include` method, the `Reviews` property will either be an empty collection if there are no reviews, or a collection of the reviews linked to this book.

Listing 3.16   Adding a review to a book in the connected state

```
var book = context.Books
    .Include(p => p.Reviews)      │ Finds the first book and loads it
    .First();                     │ with any reviews it might have

book.Reviews.Add(new Review
{
    VoterName = "Unit Test",      │ Adds a new review to this book
    NumStars = 5,
    Comment = "Great book!"
});
context.SaveChanges();  ◄──── SaveChanges calls DetectChanges, which finds that the
                              Reviews property has changed, and from there finds
                              the new Review, which it adds to the Review table
```

As with the `PriceOffer` example, you don't fill in the foreign key (the `BookId` property) in the review, because EF Core knows the review is being added to a `Book` entity class and sets up the foreign key to the right value.

ALTERING/REPLACING ALL THE ONE-TO-MANY RELATIONSHIPS

Before moving on to the disconnected state update, I want to consider the case where you want to alter or replace the whole collection, rather than just add to the collection as you did with the review.

For instance, if the books had categories (say, Software Design, Software Languages, and so forth), you might allow an admin user to change the categories. One way to implement this would be to show the current categories in a multiselect list, allow the admin user to change them, and then replace *all* the categories on the book with the new selection.

EF Core makes replacing the whole collection easy. If you assign a new collection to a one-to-many relationship that has been loaded with tracking (for instance, by using the `Include` method), EF Core will replace the whole collection with the new one. If the items in the collection can be linked to only the principal class (the dependent class has a non-nullable foreign key), then, by default, EF Core will delete the items that were in the collection that have been removed.

Next is an example of replacing the whole collection of existing book reviews with a new collection. The effect is to remove the original reviews and replace them with the one new review.

Listing 3.17 Replacing a whole collection of reviews with another collection

```
                                        This include is important; otherwise, EF
                                        Core won't know about the old reviews.
var book = context.Books  ◄─────────
    .Include(p => p.Reviews)
    .Single(p => p.BookId == twoReviewBookId);
                                                     This book you're loading
                                                     has two reviews.
book.Reviews = new List<Review>
{
                                        You completely replace
    new Review                          the whole collection.
    {
        VoterName = "Unit Test",
        NumStars = 5,
    }
};
context.SaveChanges();
```

SaveChanges, via DetectChanges, knows that the
old collection should be deleted, and the new
collection should be written to the database.

Because you're using test data in the example, you know that the book with primary key `twoReviewBookId` has two reviews, and that the book is the only one with reviews; hence there are only two reviews in the whole database. After the `SaveChanges` method is called, the book has only one review, and the two old reviews have been deleted, meaning that the database now has only one review in it.

Removing a single row is as simple as removing the entity from the list. EF Core will see the change and delete the row that's linked to that entity. Similarly, altering the content of an entity would be found by EF Core, and an update action would be applied to the database.

The loading of the existing collection is important for these changes: if you don't load them, EF Core can't remove, update, or replace them. The old versions will still be in the database after the update, because EF Core didn't know about them at the time of the update.

DISCONNECTED STATE UPDATE

In the disconnected state, you create an empty `Review` entity class, but fill in its foreign key, `BookId`, with the book the user wants to provide a review for. The user then votes on the book, and you add that review to the book that they referred to.

The following listing shows the `AddReviewService` class, which has methods for the setup and update of the book, to add a new review from a user.

Listing 3.18 Adding a new review to a book in the example book app

```
public class AddReviewService
{
    private readonly EfCoreContext _context;

    public string BookTitle { get; private set; }

    public AddReviewService(EfCoreContext context)
    {
        _context = context;
    }

    public Review GetBlankReview(int id)
    {
        BookTitle = _context.Books
            .Where(p => p.BookId == id)
            .Select(p => p.Title)
            .Single();
        return new Review
        {
            BookId = id
        };
    }

    public Book AddReviewToBook(Review review)
    {
        var book = _context.Books
            .Include(r => r.Reviews)
            .Single(k => k.BookId
                    == review.BookId);
        book.Reviews.Add(review);
        _context.SaveChanges();
        return book;
    }
}
```

Forms a review to be filled in by the user

You read the book title to show to the user when they're filling in their review.

Creates a review with the BookId foreign key filled in

Updates the book with the new review

Loads the correct book by using the value in the review's foreign key, and includes any existing reviews (or empty collection if no reviews yet)

Adds the new review to the Reviews collection

Returns the updated book

SaveChanges uses its DetectChanges method, which sees that the Book Review property has changed. It then creates a new row in the Review table.

This code has a simpler first part than the previous disconnected state examples because you're adding a new review, so you don't have to load the existing data for the user. But overall, it takes the same approach that the `ChangePriceOfferService` class used.

ALTERNATIVE WAY OF UPDATING THE RELATIONSHIP—CREATING A NEW ROW DIRECTLY

As with the `PriceOffer`, you can add a one-to-many relationship directly to the database. But again, this means you take on the role of managing the relationship. If you want to totally replace the reviews collection, for instance, you'd have to delete all the rows that the reviews linked to the book in question before adding your new collection.

Adding a row directly to the database has some advantages, because loading all the one-to-many relationships might turn out to be a lot of data if you have lots of items and/or they're big. Therefore, keep this approach in mind if you have performance issues.

> **NOTE** My experiments show that not loading the relationship, and then assigning a new collection to a one-to-many relationship, is equivalent to creating a new row directly. But I don't recommend doing this because it's not the normal update pattern, and someone else (or even yourself) might come back later and misread your intentions.

3.4.4 *Updating many-to-many relationships—changing a book's authors*

In EF Core, we talk about many-to-many relationships, but a relational database doesn't directly implement many-to-many relationships. Instead, we're dealing with two one-to-many relationships, as shown in figure 3.4.

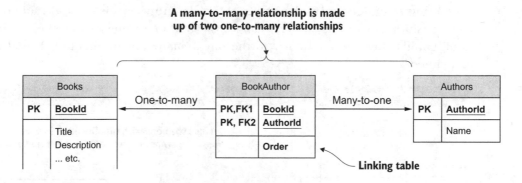

Figure 3.4 The Book to its Authors many-to-many relationship, which uses a BookAuthor linking table

If you look at the `BookAuthor` entity class, shown in listing 3.19, you'll see it has two properties, `BookId` and `AuthorId`. These are foreign keys to the Books table and the Authors table, respectively. Together they also form the primary key (known as a *composite key*, because it has more than one part to it) for the BookAuthor row. This has the effect of ensuring that there's only one link between the Book and the Author. Chapter 6 covers composite keys in more detail.

Listing 3.19   The BookAuthor entity class that links books to their authors

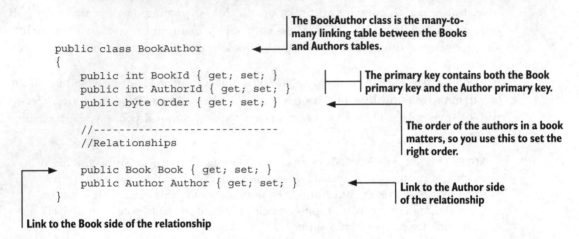

The BookAuthor class is the many-to-many linking table between the Books and Authors tables.

```
public class BookAuthor
{
    public int BookId { get; set; }
    public int AuthorId { get; set; }
    public byte Order { get; set; }

    //----------------------------
    //Relationships

    public Book Book { get; set; }
    public Author Author { get; set; }
}
```

The primary key contains both the Book primary key and the Author primary key.

The order of the authors in a book matters, so you use this to set the right order.

Link to the Author side of the relationship

Link to the Book side of the relationship

EF6   In EF6.x, you can define a many-to-many relationship, and EF6.x will create a hidden linking table for you and handle all the creation/deletion of the rows in that table. At the time of writing this book, EF Core doesn't support automatic many-to-many relationships. See http://mng.bz/9nD5 to follow the work on implementing automatic many-to-many linking tables.

The thing to understand is that the BookAuthor entity class is the *many* side of the relationship. This listing, which changes the author of one of the books, should look familiar because it's similar to the one-to-many update methods I've already explained.

Listing 3.20   Changing the author of *Quantum Networking*

Finds the book with title Quantum Networking, whose current author is Future Person

```
var book = context.Books
    .Include(p => p.AuthorsLink)
    .Single(p => p.Title == "Quantum Networking");

var newAuthor = context.Authors
    .Single(p => p.Name == "Martin Fowler");
```

You then find an existing author, in this case Martin Fowler.

```
book.AuthorsLink = new List<BookAuthor>
{
    new BookAuthor
    {
        Book = book,
        Author = newAuthor,
        Order = 0
    }
};

context.SaveChanges();
```

You replace the list of authors, so Quantum Networking's author is Martin Fowler.

SaveChanges calls DetectChanges, which finds that the AuthorsLink has changed and so deletes the old ones and replaces them with the new link.

One thing to note is that you load the Book's AuthorsLink, but you don't load the corresponding BooksLink in the Author entity class. That's because you're updating the AuthorsLink, but not touching the BooksLink. The BooksLink property is dynamically filled in by EF Core when it's loaded, so the next time someone loads the Author entity class and its BooksLink relationship, they'll see a link to the *Quantum Networking* book in that collection.

The change from the other examples is that the original author of *Quantum Networking*, Future Person, *isn't* deleted when the link to him is removed (Future Person has, in my test data, written only *Quantum Networking*). That's because it's the *one* end of a one-to-many relationship, and these aren't dependent on the book directly; in fact, the Author class is a *principal entity*, with the BookAuthor classes being dependent on it.

What's deleted is the BookAuthor row that used to link the *Quantum Networking* book to its author, Future Person, and a new BookAuthor row is added to link Martin Fowler to *Quantum Networking*. (I'm sure Martin Fowler would love to write this book if he's around when quantum networking is perfected.)

Alternatively, you could've added Martin Fowler as a second author by using the Add method on the AuthorsLink property in the Book entity class, and adding a new Book-Author entity class to set up the link between the book and its second author.

ALTERNATIVE WAY OF UPDATING THE RELATIONSHIP—CREATING A NEW ROW DIRECTLY

Again, you could create/delete a BookAuthor entity class directly, but you'd still need a tracked instance of both the Book and Author entity classes so it won't save on database access. Another simpler approach to building/finding the linking class (for instance, BookAuthor) is to use the primary keys of the Books and Authors rows, which I explain next as it's a useful approach to any disconnected update.

> **TIP** I've written an article about updating many-to-many relationships on my technical blog site. The article includes an example of updating the relationship by adding a BookAuthor entity. See http://mng.bz/HCp9.

3.4.5   *Advanced feature—updating relationships via foreign keys*

Up to this point, I've shown you how to update relationships by using the entity classes themselves; for instance, when you added a review to a book, you loaded the Book entity with all its Reviews. That's fine, but in a disconnected state, you have to load the Book and all its Reviews from the book's primary key that came back from the browser/RESTful API. In many situations, you can cut out the loading of the entity classes and set the foreign keys instead.

This applies to most of the disconnected updates I've shown before, but let me give you an example of moving a review from one book to another (I know, not a likely scenario in the real world, but it makes a simple example). The following listing carries out the update after the user has typed in the request. The code assumes that the ReviewId of the Review the user wants to change, and new BookId that they want to attach the review to, are returned in a variable called dto.

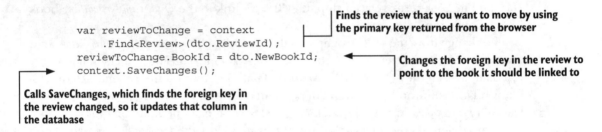

Listing 3.21   Updating the foreign key to change a relationship

```
var reviewToChange = context         Finds the review that you want to move by using
    .Find<Review>(dto.ReviewId);     the primary key returned from the browser
reviewToChange.BookId = dto.NewBookId;    Changes the foreign key in the review to
context.SaveChanges();                    point to the book it should be linked to
```

Calls SaveChanges, which finds the foreign key in the review changed, so it updates that column in the database

The benefit of this technique is that you don't have to load the Book entity class, nor use an Include command to load all the Reviews associated with this book. In our example book app, these entities aren't that big, but in a real application, the principal and dependent entities could be quite large. In disconnected systems, where we often send just the primary keys over the disconnect, this can be a useful approach to cut down on database accesses and hence improve performance.

> **NOTE** When updating relationships via foreign keys, you may need to access entities that don't have a DbSet<T> property in the application's DbContext, so how can you read in the data? Listing 3.21 uses the Find<T> method, but if you need a more complex query, you can access any entity via the Set<T> method; for instance, context.Set<Review>().Where(p => p.NumVotes > 5).

3.5   *Deleting entities*

The final way to change the data in the database is to delete a row from a table. Deleting data is easier than the updates we looked at, but it does have a few points to be aware of. Before I describe how to delete entities from the database, I want to introduce an approach called *soft delete,* in which an entity is hidden instead of deleted.

3.5.1 *Using a soft delete—using model-level query filters to "hide" entities*

One school of thought says that you shouldn't delete anything from a database, but use a status to hide it, known as a soft delete. (See Udi Dahan's post, "Don't Delete—Just Don't" at http://udidahan.com/2009/09/01/dont-delete-just-dont/). I think this is a sensible approach, and EF Core provides a feature called model-level query filters that allow a soft delete to be simply implemented.

The thinking behind a soft delete is that in real-world applications, data doesn't stop being data: it transforms into another state. In the case of our books example, a book may not still be on sale, but the fact that the book existed isn't in doubt, so why delete it? Instead, you set a flag to say the entity is to be hidden in normal queries.

To show you how this works, you'll add the soft-delete feature to the list of Book entities. To do so, you need to do two things:

1 *Add a boolean property called SoftDeleted to the Book entity class.* If that property is true, the Book entity instance is *soft deleted*; it shouldn't be found in a normal query.

2 *Add a model-level query filter via EF Core fluent configuration commands.* The effect of this is to apply an extra Where filter to any access to the Books table.

Adding the SoftDeleted property in a Book entity instance is straightforward. This code snippet shows the Book entity class with the SoftDeleted property:

```
public class Book
{
    //… other properties left out for clarity
    public bool SoftDeleted { get; set; }
}
```

Adding the model-level query filter to the DbSet<Book>Books property means adding a fluent configuration command to the application's DbContext. Chapter 6 covers this command, but it's shown in bold in the following listing so you have an idea of what's going on.

Listing 3.22 Adding a model-level query filter to the DbSet<Book>Books property

```
public class EfCoreContext : DbContext
{
    //… Other parts removed for clarity

    protected override void
        OnModelCreating(ModelBuilder modelBuilder)
    {
        //… other configration parts removed for clarity

        modelBuilder.Entity<Book>()
            .HasQueryFilter(p => !p.SoftDeleted);      ⟵ Adds a filter to all accesses to
    }                                                      the Book entities. You can
}                                                          bypass this filter by using the
                                                           IgnoreQueryFilters operator.
```

To soft delete a Book entity, you need to set the SoftDeleted property to true and call SaveChanges. Then any query on the Book entities will exclude the Book entities that have the SoftDeleted property set to true.

> **NOTE** If you want to access all the entities that have a model-level filter, you add the IgnoreQueryFilters method to the query—or instance, context.Books .IgnoreQueryFilters(). This bypasses any model-level filter on an entity. Also, the Find method isn't affected by a model-level filter.

Now that we've covered the soft-delete approach, let's cover the ways to delete an entity from the database. We'll start with a straightforward example and work up to deleting an entity that has relationships.

3.5.2   *Deleting a dependent-only entity—no relationships*

I've chosen the PriceOffer entity class to show a basic delete because it's a dependent entity. You can therefore delete it without it affecting other entities. This listing finds a PriceOffer and then deletes it.

Listing 3.23   Removing (deleting) an entity from the database

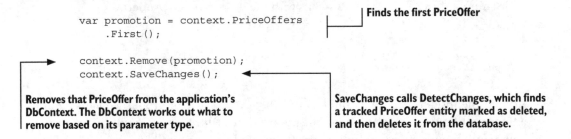

```
var promotion = context.PriceOffers          Finds the first PriceOffer
    .First();

context.Remove(promotion);
context.SaveChanges();
```

Removes that PriceOffer from the application's DbContext. The DbContext works out what to remove based on its parameter type.

SaveChanges calls DetectChanges, which finds a tracked PriceOffer entity marked as deleted, and then deletes it from the database.

Calling the Remove method sets the State of the entity provided as the parameter to Deleted. Then when you call SaveChanges, EF Core finds the entity marked as Deleted and creates the correct database commands to delete the appropriate row from the table the entity referred to (in this case, a row in the PriceOffers table).

The SQL command that EF Core produces for SQL Server is shown in the following snippet:

```
SET NOCOUNT ON;
DELETE FROM [PriceOffers]
WHERE [BookId] = @p0;
SELECT @@ROWCOUNT;
```

3.5.3   *Deleting a principal entity that has relationships*

Section 3.3.1 discussed principal and dependent relationships and the nullability of the foreign key. Relational databases need to keep *referential integrity*, so if you delete a row in a table that other rows are pointing to via a foreign key, something has to happen to stop referential integrity from being lost.

DEFINITION   *Referential integrity* is a relational database concept indicating that table relationships must always be consistent. Any foreign-key field must agree with the primary key referenced by the foreign key (Techopedia).

The following are three ways that you can set a database to keep referential integrity when you delete a principal entity with dependent entities:

- You can tell the database server to delete the dependent entities that rely on the principal entity. This is known as *cascade deletes*.
- You can tell the database server to set the foreign keys of the dependent entities to `null`, if the column allows that.
- If neither of those rules are set up, the database server will raise an error if you try to delete a principal entity with dependent entities.

DELETING A BOOK WITH ITS DEPENDENT RELATIONSHIPS

Here you're going to delete a `Book` entity, which is a principal entity with three dependent relationships: `Promotion`, `Reviews`, and `AuthorsLink`. These three dependent entities can't exist without the `Book` entity; they have a foreign key that's non-nullable that points to a specific `Book` row.

By default, EF Core uses cascade deletes for dependent relationships with non-nullable foreign keys. Cascade deletes make deleting principal entities easier from the developer's point of view, because the other two rules need extra code to handle deleting the dependent entities. But in many business applications, this may not be the appropriate approach. This chapter uses the cascade delete approach because it's EF Core's default.

With that in mind, let's see this in action by deleting a book that has relationships using the default cascade delete setting. This listing loads the `Promotion` (`PriceOffer` entity class) and `Reviews` relationships with the `Book` entity class before deleting that `Book`.

Listing 3.24   Deleting a book that has three dependent entity classes

```
var book = context.Books
    .Include(p => p.Promotion)
    .Include(p => p.Reviews)
    .Include(p => p.AuthorsLink)
    .Single(p => p.Title
        == "Quantum Networking");

context.Books.Remove(book);
context.SaveChanges();
```

The three Includes make sure that the three dependent relationships are loaded with the Book.

Deletes that book.

SaveChanges calls DetectChanges, which finds a tracked Book entity marked as deleted, and then deletes its dependent relationships and deletes the book.

Finds the Quantum Networking book, which you know has a promotion, two reviews, and one BookAuthor link

My test data contains a book with the title *Quantum Networking*, which has one PriceOffer, two Reviews, and a BookAuthor entity associated with it. The foreign keys of all those dependent entities I mentioned point to the *Quantum Networking* book. After the code in listing 3.24 has run the Book, EF Core deletes the PriceOffer, the two Reviews, and the single BookAuthor link.

That last statement, indicating that all are deleted by EF Core, is an important point. Because you put in the three Includes, EF Core knew about the dependent entities and performed the delete. If you didn't incorporate the Includes in your code, EF Core wouldn't know about the dependent entities and couldn't delete the three dependent entities. In that case, the problem of keeping referential integrity would fall to the database server, and its response would depend on how the DELETE ON part of the foreign-key constraint was set up. Databases created by EF Core would, by default, be set to use cascade deletes.

Section 7.7.1 shows how to configure the way EF Core handles the deletion of a dependent entity in a relationship. Sometimes it's useful to stop a principal entity from being deleted if a certain dependent entity is linked to it. For instance, in our example book app, if a customer orders a book, you want to keep that order information even if the book is no longer for sale. In this case, you change the EF Core's on-delete action to Restrict, and remove the ON DELETE CASCADE from the foreign-key constraint in the database, so that an error will be raised if an attempt is made to delete the book.

NOTE   When deleting a principal entity with a dependent entity that has a nullable foreign key (known as an *optional dependent relationship*), subtle differences exist between the way EF Core handles the delete and the way the database handles the delete. I explain this in section 7.7.1, with a useful table 7.1.

Summary

- Entity instances that are tracked have a State, which can be Added, Unchanged, Modified, or Deleted. This State defines what happens to the entity when SaveChanges is called.

- If you Add an entity that isn't currently tracked, it will be tracked, and its State will be set to Added.

- You can update a property, or properties, in an entity class by loading the entity class as a tracked entity, changing the property/properties, and calling SaveChanges.

- Real-world applications use two types of update scenarios—connected and disconnected state—that affect the way you perform the update.

- EF Core has an Update method, which marks the whole of the entity class as updated. You can use this when you want to update the entity class and have all the data already available to you.

- When you're updating a relationship, you have two options, with different advantages and disadvantages:
  - You can load the existing relationship with the primary entity and update that relationship in the primary entity. EF Core will sort things out from there.
  - You can create, update, or delete the dependent entity directly.
- To delete an entity from the database, you use the `Remove` method, followed by calling the `SaveChanges` method.

For EF6.x readers:

- The `Update` method is a welcome new command in EF Core. In EF6.x, you have to use `DbContext.Entry(object).State` to achieve that feature.
- EF Core provides shorthand for `Add`, `Update`, and `Remove`. You can apply any of these commands to the context itself; for instance, `context.Add(book)`.
- In EF6.x, by default, `SaveChanges` validates the data before adding or updating an entity to the database. EF Core doesn't run any validation on `SaveChanges`, but it's easy to add back (see chapter 4).
- EF6.x allows you to define many-to-many relationships directly, and looks after creating the linking table and managing the rows to make that work. At the time of writing this book, EF Core doesn't have that feature, so you need to create the linking table and manage the adding/removing of rows in that table to implement a many-to-many relationship.

Using EF Core in business logic

4

This chapter covers

- Understanding business logic and its use of EF Core

- Using a pattern for building business logic

- Working through a business logic example

- Adding validation of data before it's written to the database

- Using transactions to daisy-chain code sequences

Real-world applications are built to supply a set of services, ranging from holding a simple list of things on your computer to managing a nuclear reactor. Every real-world problem has a set of rules, often referred to as *business rules*, or by the more generic name *domain rules* (this book uses *business rules*).

The code you write to implement a business rule is known as *business logic* or *domain logic*. Because business rules can be complex, the business logic you write can also be complex. Just think about all the checks and steps that should be done when you order something online.

Business logic can range from a simple check of status to massive artificial intelligence (AI) code, but in nearly all cases, business logic needs access to a database. Although the approaches in chapters 2 and 3 all come into play, the way you apply those EF Core commands in business logic can be a little different, which is why I've written this chapter.

This chapter describes a pattern for handling business logic that compartmentalizes some of the complexity in order to reduce the load on you, the developer. You'll also learn several techniques for writing business logic that uses EF Core to access the database. These techniques range from using software classes for validation to standardizing your business logic's interface in order to make frontend code simpler. The overall aim is to help you quickly write accurate, understandable, and well-performing business logic.

4.1 Why is business logic so different from other code?

Our CRUD code in chapters 2 and 3 adapted and transformed data as it moved into and out of the database. Some of that code got a little complex, and I showed you the Query Object pattern to make a large query more manageable. Convesely, business logic can reach a whole new level of complexity. Here's a quote from one of the leading books on writing business logic:

> *The heart of software is its ability to solve domain (business)-related problems for its users. All other features, vital though they may be, support this basic purpose. When the domain is complex, this is a difficult task, calling for the concentrated effort of talented and skilled people.*

> *Eric Evans, Domain-Driven Design[1]*

Over the years, I've written quite a bit of complex business logic, and I've found Eric Evan's comment "this is a difficult task" to be true. When I came back to software development after a long gap, the first applications I wrote were for geographic modeling and optimization, which have complex business rules. The business code I wrote ended up being hundreds of lines long, all intertwined. The code worked, but it was hard to understand, debug, and maintain.

So, yes, you can write business logic just like any other bit of code, but there's a case for a more thought-through approach. Here are a few of the questions you should ask when writing business logic:

- Do you fully understand the business rule you're implementing?
- Are there any edge cases or exceptions that you need to cover?
- How can you prove that your implementation is correct?
- How easy will it be to change your code if the business rules change?
- Will you, or someone else, understand the code if it needs changing later?

---

[1] *Domain-Driven Design: Tackling Complexity in the Heart of Software* was published in 2003 by Addison-Wesley Professional.

4.2   *Our business need—processing an order for books*

Let's start by describing the business issue that we want to implement. The example you'll use is handling a user's order for books. Figure 4.1 shows the checkout page of our book app. You're going to implement the code that runs when the user clicks the Purchase button.

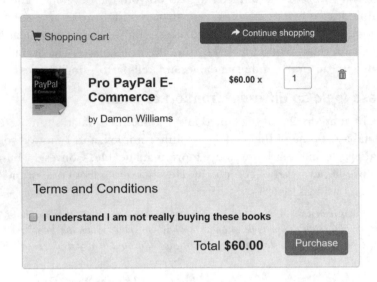

Figure 4.1   The checkout page of the book app. Clicking Purchase calls the business logic to create the order.

NOTE   You can try the checkout process on the live site at http://efcoreinaction .com/. The site uses an HTTP cookie to hold your basket and your identity (which saves you from having to log in). No money needed—as the Terms and Conditions says, you aren't actually going to buy a book.

4.2.1   *The business rules that you need to implement*

The following list gives the rules set for this business need. As I'm sure you can imagine, a real order-processing piece of business logic would have a lot more steps, especially on payment and shipping, but these six rules are enough for this example:

1. The Terms and Conditions box must be ticked.
2. An order must include at least one book.
3. A book must be available for sale, as defined by the price being positive in value.
4. The price of the book must be copied to the order, because the price could change later.
5. The order must remember the person who ordered the books.
6. Good feedback must be provided to the user so they can fix any problems in the order.

The quality and quantity of the business rules will change with the project. The preceding rules aren't bad, but they don't cover things such as what to do if the book selected by the user has been removed (unlikely, but possible), nor how to weed out malicious input. This is where you, as a developer, need to think through the problem and try to anticipate issues.

4.3 Using a design pattern to help implement business logic

Before you start writing code to process an order, you should describe a pattern that you're going to follow. This pattern helps you to write, test, and performance-tune your business logic. The pattern is based on the domain-driven design (DDD) concepts expounded by Eric Evans, but where the business logic code isn't inside the entity classes. This is known as a *transactions script* or *procedural* pattern of business logic because the code is contained in a standalone method.

This procedural pattern is easier to understand and uses the basic EF Core commands you have already seen. But many see the procedural approach as a DDD antipattern, known as an *anemic domain model* (see www.martinfowler.com/bliki/AnemicDomainModel.html). After you have learned about EF Core's *backing field* feature and the DDD entity pattern, you will extend this approach to a fully DDD design in section 10.4.2.

This section, and section 10.4, present my interpretation of Eric Evans' DDD approach, and plenty of other ways for applying DDD with EF. Although I offer my approach, which I hope will help some of you, don't be afraid to look for other approaches.

4.3.1 Five guidelines for building business logic that uses EF Core

The following list explains the five guidelines that make up the business logic pattern you'll be using in this chapter. Most of the pattern comes from DDD concepts, but some are the result of writing lots of complex business logic and seeing areas to improve.

1 *The business logic has first call on how the database structure is defined.* Because the problem you're trying to solve (called the *domain model* by Eric Evans) is the heart of the problem, it should define the way the whole application is designed. Therefore, you try to make the database structure, and the entity classes, match your business logic data needs as much as you can.

2 *The business logic should have no distractions.* Writing the business logic is difficult enough in itself, so you isolate it from all the other application layers, other than the entity classes. When you write the business logic, you must think only about the business problem you're trying to fix. You leave the task of adapting the data for presentation to the service layer in your application.

3 *Business logic should think it's working on in-memory data.* This is something Eric Evans taught me: write your business logic as if the data is in-memory. Of course, you need to have some *load* and *save* parts, but for the core of your business logic, treat the data, as much as is practical, as if it's a normal, in-memory class or collection.

4 *Isolate the database access code into a separate project.* This fairly new rule came out of writing an e-commerce application with complex pricing and delivery rules. Before this, I used EF directly in my business logic, but I found that it was hard to maintain and difficult to performance-tune. Instead, you should use another project, which is a companion to the business logic, to hold all the database access code.

5 *The business logic shouldn't call EF Core's SaveChanges directly.* You should have a class in the service layer (or a custom library) whose job it is to run the business logic. If there are no errors, this class calls SaveChanges. The main reason for this rule is to have control of whether to write out the data, but there are other benefits I'll describe later.

Figure 4.2 shows the application structure you'll create to help you apply these guidelines when implementing business logic. In this case, you'll add two new projects to the original book app structure described in chapter 2:

- The pure business logic project, which holds the business logic classes that work on the in-memory data provided by its companion business database access methods.

- The business database access project, which provides a companion class for each pure business logic class that needs database access. Each companion class makes the pure business logic class think it's working on an in-memory set of data.

Figure 4.2 has five numbers, with comments, that match the five guidelines listed previously.

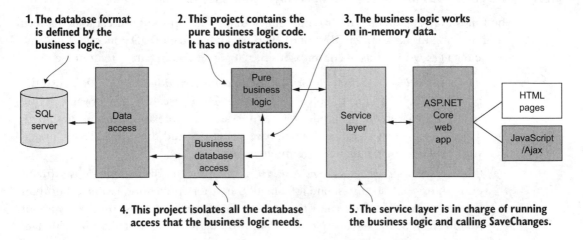

Figure 4.2   The projects inside our book app, with two new projects for handling business logic

Does all business logic in an application live in the BizLogic layer?

In real-world applications, especially ones that interact with a human being, you want the user experience to be as great as possible. As a result, the business logic may move outside the BizLogic layer into other layers, especially the presentation layer. So, no, all business logic in an application doesn't live in the BizLogic layer.

As a developer, I find it useful to separate the distinct parts of the business rules that my clients present into three types:

- *Manipulation of a state or data*—For instance, creating an order
- *Validation rules*—For instance, checking that a book is available to buy
- *A sequence or flow*—For instance, the steps in processing an order

The manipulation of a state or data is the core business logic. The code for this manipulation can be complicated and may require a lot of design and programming effort to write. This chapter focuses on server-side business logic, but with sophisticated frontend JavaScript libraries, some data or state manipulation may move out to the frontend.

Validation of data is ubiquitous, so you find validation code cropping up in every layer of your application. In human-facing applications, I generally move the validation as far forward as possible so that the user gets feedback quickly. But, as you'll see in the examples, plenty of extra validation can exist in the business logic.

A sequence or flow is often shown to a human user as a sequence of pages or steps in a wizard, but backed up by the data manipulations that each stage needs done by some sort of CRUD and/or business logic.

None of this invalidates the approach of having a specific area in your server-side application dedicated to business logic. There's plenty of complex code to write, and having a zone where business rules are the number one focus helps you to write better code.

4.4 *Implementing the business logic for processing an order*

Now that I've described the business need, with its business rules, and the pattern you're going to use, you're ready to write code. The aim is to break the implementation into smaller steps that focus on specific parts of the problem at hand. You'll see how this business logic pattern helps you to focus on each part of the implementation in turn.

You're going to implement the code in sections that match the five guidelines listed in section 4.3.1. At the end, you'll see how this combined code is called from the ASP .NET Core application that the book app is using.

4.4.1 Guideline 1: Business logic has first call on defining the database structure

This guideline says that the design of the database should follow the business needs—in this case, represented by six business rules. The three rules that are relevant to the database design are as follows:

- An order must include at least one book (implying there can be more).
- The price of the book must be copied to the order, because the price could change later.
- The order must remember the person who ordered the books.

From this, you come up with a fairly standard design for an order, with an Order entity class that has a collection of LineItem entity classes—a one-to-many relationship. The Order entity class holds the information about the person placing the order, while each LineItem entity class holds a reference to the book order, how many, and at what price.

Figure 4.3 shows what these two tables, LineItem and Orders, look like in the database. To make the image more understandable, I show the Books table (in gray) that each LineItem row references.

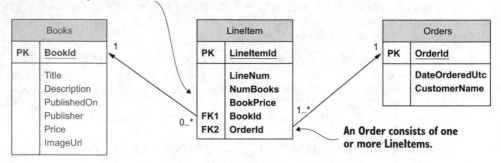

Figure 4.3   The new LineItem and Orders tables added to allow orders for books to be taken

> **NOTE** The Orders table name is plural because you added a DbSet<Order> Orders property to the application's DbContext, and EF Core, by default, uses the property name, Orders, as the table name. You haven't added a property for the LineItem entity class because it's accessed via the Order's relational link. In that case, EF Core, by default, uses the class name, LineItem, as the table name.

4.4.2 Guideline 2: Business logic should have no distractions

Now you're at the heart of the business logic code, and the code here will do most of the work. It's going to be the hardest part of the implementation that you write, but you want to help yourself by cutting off any distractions. That way, you can stay focused on the problem.

You do this by writing the pure business code with reference to only two other parts of the system: the entity classes shown in figure 4.3, Order, LineItem, and Book, and your companion class that will handle all the database accesses. Even with this minimization of scope, you're still going to break the job into a few parts.

CHECKING FOR ERRORS AND FEEDING THEM BACK TO THE USER—VALIDATION

The business rules contain several checks, such as "The Terms and Conditions box must be ticked." And they also say you need to give good feedback to the person, so that they can fix any problems and complete their purchase. These sorts of checks, called *validation*, are common throughout an application.

To help, you'll create a small abstract class called BizActionErrors, shown in listing 4.1. This provides a common error-handling interface for all your business logic. This class contains a C# method called AddError that the business logic can call to add an error, and an immutable list (a list that can't be changed) called Errors, which holds all the validation errors found while running the business logic.

You'll use a class called ValidationResult for storing each error because it's the standard way of returning errors with optional, additional information on what exact property the error was related to. Using the ValidationResult class instead of a simple string fits in with another validation method you'll add later in this chapter.

> **NOTE** You have two main approaches to handling the passing of errors back up to higher levels. One is to throw an exception when an error occurs, and the other is to pass back the errors to the caller. Each has its own advantages and disadvantages; this example uses the second approach—passing the errors back for the higher level to check.

Listing 4.1 Abstract base class providing error handling for your business logic

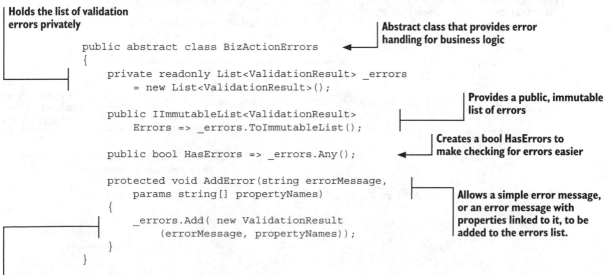

Holds the list of validation errors privately

Abstract class that provides error handling for business logic

```
public abstract class BizActionErrors
{
    private readonly List<ValidationResult> _errors
        = new List<ValidationResult>();

    public IImmutableList<ValidationResult>
        Errors => _errors.ToImmutableList();

    public bool HasErrors => _errors.Any();

    protected void AddError(string errorMessage,
        params string[] propertyNames)
    {
        _errors.Add( new ValidationResult
            (errorMessage, propertyNames));
    }
}
```

Provides a public, immutable list of errors

Creates a bool HasErrors to make checking for errors easier

Allows a simple error message, or an error message with properties linked to it, to be added to the errors list.

Validation result has an error message and a possibly empty list of properties it's linked to.

Using this abstract class means your business logic is easier to write and all your business logic has a consistent way of handling errors. The other advantage is that you can change the way errors are handled internally without having to change any of your business logic code.

Your business logic for handling an order does a lot of validation; that's typical for an order, because it often involves money. Other business logic may not do any tests, but the base class `BizActionErrors` will automatically return a `HasErrors` of `false`, which means all business logic can be dealt with in the same way.

4.4.3   Guideline 3: Business logic should think it's working on in-memory data

Now you'll start on the main class, `PlaceOrderAction`, that contains the pure business logic. It relies on the companion class, `PlaceOrderDbAccess`, to present the data as an in-memory set (in this case, a dictionary) and to take the created order and write it to the database. Although you're not trying to hide the database from the pure business logic, you do want it to work as if the data were normal .NET classes.

Listing 4.2 shows the `PlaceOrderAction` class, which inherits the abstract class `BizActionErrors` to handle returning error messages to the user. It also uses two methods that the companion `PlaceOrderDbAccess` class provides:

- `FindBooksByIdsWithPriceOffers`—Takes the list of `BookIds` and returns a dictionary with the `BookId` as the key and the `Book` entity class as the value (`null` if no book found), and any associated `PriceOffers`
- `Add`—Adds the `Order` entity class with its `LineItem` collection to the database

Listing 4.2   `PlaceOrderAction` class contains build-a-new-order business logic

Makes the business logic conform to a standard interface for business logic that has an input and an output

Provides all the error handling required for the business logic

Needs the companion PlaceOrderDbAccess class to handle all the database accesses

The method called by BizRunner to execute this business logic.

You start with basic validation.

```
public class PlaceOrderAction :
    BizActionErrors,
    IBizAction<PlaceOrderInDto,Order>
{
    private readonly IPlaceOrderDbAccess _dbAccess;

    public PlaceOrderAction(IPlaceOrderDbAccess dbAccess)
    {
        _dbAccess = dbAccess;
    }

    public Order Action(PlaceOrderInDto dto)
    {
        if (!dto.AcceptTAndCs)
        {
            AddError(
"You must accept the T&Cs to place an order.");
            return null;
        }
```

```
if (!dto.LineItems.Any())
{
    AddError("No items in your basket.");
    return null;
}
```

You start with basic validation.

You ask the PlaceOrderDbAccess class to find all the books you need, with any optional PriceOffers.

Creates the Order entity class. Calls the private method FormLineItemsWithErrorChecking, which creates the LineItems.

```
var booksDict =
    _dbAccess.FindBooksByIdsWithPriceOffers
        (dto.LineItems.Select(x => x.BookId));
var order = new Order
{
    CustomerName = dto.UserId,
    LineItems =
        FormLineItemsWithErrorChecking
            (dto.LineItems, booksDict)
};

if (!HasErrors)
    _dbAccess.Add(order);

return HasErrors ? null : order;
}

private List<LineItem>  FormLineItemsWithErrorChecking
    (IEnumerable<OrderLineItem> lineItems,
     IDictionary<int,Book> booksDict)


{
    var result = new List<LineItem>();
    var i = 1;

    foreach (var lineItem in lineItems)
    {
        if (!booksDict.
            ContainsKey(lineItem.BookId))
                throw new InvalidOperationException
("An order failed because book, " +
$"id = {lineItem.BookId} was missing.");

        var book = booksDict[lineItem.BookId];
        var bookPrice =
            book.Promotion?.NewPrice ?? book.Price;
        if (bookPrice <= 0)
            AddError(
$"Sorry, the book '{book.Title}' is not for sale.");
        else
        {
            //Valid, so add to the order
```

Adds the order to the database only if there are no errors

If there are errors, you return null; otherwise, you return the order.

Private method handles the creation of each LineItem entity class for each book ordered.

Goes through each book type that the person has ordered

Treats a book being missing as a system error and throws an exception.

Calculates the price at the time of the order

More validation where you check that the book can be sold

```
                result.Add(new LineItem
                {
                    BookPrice = bookPrice,
                    ChosenBook = book,
                    LineNum = (byte)(i++),
                    NumBooks = lineItem.NumBooks
                });
            }
        }
        return result;
    }
}
```

> All is OK, so now you can create the LineItem entity class with the details.

> Returns all the LineItems for this order

You'll notice that you add another check that the book selected by the person is still in the database. This wasn't in the business rules, but this could occur, especially if malicious inputs were provided. In this case, you make a distinction between errors that the user can correct, which are returned by the Errors property, and system errors (in this case, a book being missing), for which you throw an exception that the system should log.

You may have seen at the top of the class that you apply an interface in the form of IBizAction<PlaceOrderInDto,Order>. This ensures that this business logic class conforms to a standard interface you use across all your business logic. You'll see this later when you create a generic class to run and check the business logic.

4.4.4 Guideline 4: Isolate the database access code into a separate project

Our guideline says to put all the database access code that the business logic needs into a separate, companion class. This ensures that the database accesses are all in one place, which makes testing, refactoring, and performance tuning much easier.

Another benefit that a reader of my blog noted is that this guideline can help if you're working with an existing, older database. In this case, the database entities may not be a good match for the business logic you want to write. If so, you can use the BizDbAccess methods as an *Adapter pattern* that converts the older database structure to a form more easily processed by your business logic.

> **DEFINITION**　The *Adapter pattern* converts the interface of a class into another interface that the client expects. This pattern lets classes work together that couldn't otherwise do so because of incompatible interfaces. See https://sourcemaking.com/design_patterns/adapter.

You make sure that your pure business logic, class PlaceOrderAction, and your business database access class PlaceOrderDbAccess are in separate projects. That allows you to exclude any EF Core libraries from the pure business logic project, which ensures that all database access is done via the companion class, PlaceOrderDbAccess. In my own projects, I split the entity classes into a separate project from the EF code. Then my business logic accesses only the project containing the entity classes, and not the project that contains EF Core. For simplicity, the example code holds the entity classes in the same project as the application's DbContext. Listing 4.3 shows our `PlaceOrderDbAccess` class, which implements two methods to provide the database accesses that the pure business logic needs:

1 `FindBooksByIdsWithPriceOffers` method, which finds and loads the `Book` entity class, with any optional `PriceOffer`.

2 `Add` method, which adds the finished `Order` entity class to the application's DbContext property, `Orders`, so it can be saved to the database after EF Core's `SaveChanges` method is called.

Listing 4.3 `PlaceOrderDbAccess`, which handles all the database accesses

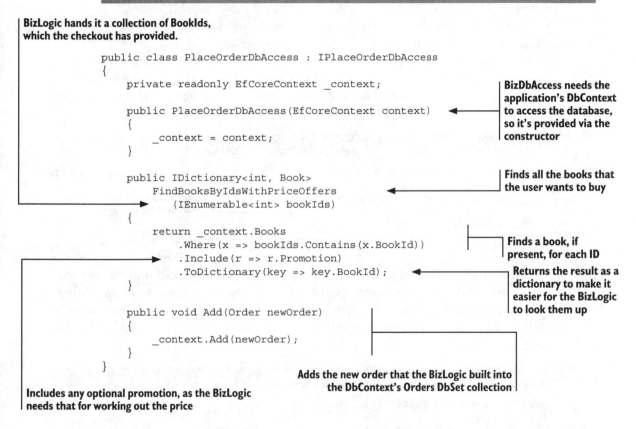

BizLogic hands it a collection of BookIds, which the checkout has provided.

```
public class PlaceOrderDbAccess : IPlaceOrderDbAccess
{
    private readonly EfCoreContext _context;

    public PlaceOrderDbAccess(EfCoreContext context)
    {
        _context = context;
    }

    public IDictionary<int, Book>
        FindBooksByIdsWithPriceOffers
            (IEnumerable<int> bookIds)
    {
        return _context.Books
            .Where(x => bookIds.Contains(x.BookId))
            .Include(r => r.Promotion)
            .ToDictionary(key => key.BookId);
    }

    public void Add(Order newOrder)
    {
        _context.Add(newOrder);
    }
}
```

BizDbAccess needs the application's DbContext to access the database, so it's provided via the constructor

Finds all the books that the user wants to buy

Finds a book, if present, for each ID

Returns the result as a dictionary to make it easier for the BizLogic to look them up

Includes any optional promotion, as the BizLogic needs that for working out the price

Adds the new order that the BizLogic built into the DbContext's Orders DbSet collection

The `PlaceOrderDbAccess` class implements an interface called `IPlaceOrderDbAccess`, which is how the `PlaceOrderAction` class accesses this class. In addition to helping with dependency injection, which is covered in chapter 5, using an interface allows you to replace the `PlaceOrderDbAccess` class with a test version, a process called *mocking*, when you're unit testing the `PlaceOrderAction` class. Section 15.8 covers this in more detail.

4.4.5   *Guideline 5: Business logic shouldn't call EF Core's SaveChanges*

The final rule says that the business logic doesn't call EF Core's SaveChanges, which would update the database directly. There are a few reasons for this. First, you consider the service layer as the main orchestrator of database accesses: it's in command of what gets written to the database. Second, the service layer calls SaveChanges only if the business logic returns no errors.

To help you run your business logic, I've built a series of simple classes that I use to run any business logic; I call these *BizRunners*. They're generic classes, able to run business logic with different input and output types. Different variants of the BizRunner can handle different input/output combinations and async methods (chapter 5 covers async/await with EF Core), plus some with extra features, which are covered later in this chapter.

Each BizRunner works by defining a generic interface that the business logic must implement. Your PlaceOrderAction class in the BizLogic project runs an action that expects a single input parameter of type PlaceOrderInDto and returns an object of type Order. Therefore, the PlaceOrderAction class implements the interface as shown in the following listing, but with its input and output types (IBizAction<PlaceOrderInDto,Order>).

> **Listing 4.4   The interface that allows the BizRunner to execute business logic**

```
public interface IBizAction<in TIn, out TOut>          ◄────┤ BizAction has both a TIn and a TOut
{
    IImmutableList<ValidationResult>                         ┐ Returns the error information
        Errors { get; }                                      ┘ from the business logic
    bool HasErrors { get; }
    TOut Action(TIn dto);                              ◄────┤ The action that the
}                                                             BizRunner will call
```

By having the business logic class implement this interface, the BizRunner knows how to run that code. The BizRunner itself is small, as you'll see in the following listing, which shows that it called RunnerWriteDb<TIn, TOut>. This BizRunner variant is designed to work with business logic that has an input, provides an output, and writes to the database.

> **Listing 4.5   The BizRunner that runs the business logic and returns a result or errors**

```
public class RunnerWriteDb<TIn, TOut>
{
    private readonly IBizAction<TIn, TOut> _actionClass;
    private readonly EfCoreContext _context;

    public IImmutableList<ValidationResult>
        Errors => _actionClass.Errors;                          ┐
    public bool HasErrors => _actionClass.HasErrors;            ┘
```

Error information from the business logic is passed back to the user of the BizRunner

```
                  public RunnerWriteDb(
                      IBizAction<TIn, TOut> actionClass,        ┐   Handles business logic that conforms to
                      EfCoreContext context)                    │   the IBizAction<TIn, TOut> interface.
                  {
                      _context = context;                       ┐   Calls RunAction in your service layer, or
                      _actionClass = actionClass;               │   in your presentation layer if the data
                  }                                             │   comes back in the right form

Runs the business    public TOut RunAction(TIn dataIn)
logic you gave it    {
        ┌───────►        var result = _actionClass.Action(dataIn);
                         if (!HasErrors)
                             _context.SaveChanges();            ┐   If there are no errors, it calls
                                                                │   SaveChanges to execute any add,
                                                                │   update, or delete methods.
                         return result;                ◄───┐   Returns the result that the
                  }                                         │   business logic returned
                  }
```

The BizRunner pattern hides the business logic and presents a common interface/ API that other classes can use. The caller of the BizRunner doesn't need to worry about EF Core, because all the calls to EF Core are in the BizDbAccess code or in the Biz-Runner. That in itself is reason enough to use it, but, as you'll see later, this BizRunner pattern allows you to create other forms of BizRunner that add extra features.

> **NOTE** You may want to check out an open source library I created, called EfCore.GenericBizRunner. This library, which is available as a NuGet package, provides a more sophisticated version of the BizRunner described in this chapter; see https://github.com/JonPSmith/EfCore.GenericBizRunner for more information.

One important point about the BizRunner is that it should be the only method allowed to call SaveChanges during the lifetime of the application's DbContext. Why? Because some business logic might add/update an entity class before an error is found. To stop these changes from being written to the database, you're relying on SaveChanges *not* being called at all during the lifetime of the application's DbContext.

In an ASP.NET application, controlling the lifetime of the application's DbContext is fairly easy to manage, because a new instance of the application's DbContext is created for each HTTP request. In longer-running applications, this is a problem. In the past, I've avoided this by making the BizRunner create a new, hidden instance of the application's DbContext so that I can be sure no other code is going to call SaveChanges on that DbContext instance.

4.4.6 *Putting it all together—calling the order-processing business logic*

Now that you've learned all the parts of the business logic pattern, you're ready to see how to call this code. Listing 4.6 shows the PlaceOrderService class in the service layer, which calls the BizRunner to execute the PlaceOrderAction that does the order processing. If the business logic is successful, the code clears the checkout cookie and returns the Order entity class key, so that a confirmation page can be shown to the user. If the order fails, it doesn't clear the checkout cookie, and the checkout page is shown again, with the error messages, so that the user can correct any problems and retry.

Listing 4.6   The `PlaceOrderService` class that calls the business logic

Handles the checkout cookie. This is a cookie, but with a specific name and expiry time.

```
public class PlaceOrderService
{
    private readonly CheckoutCookie _checkoutCookie;
    private readonly
        RunnerWriteDb<PlaceOrderInDto, Order> _runner;

    public IImmutableList<ValidationResult>
    Errors => _runner.Errors;

    public PlaceOrderService(
        IRequestCookieCollection cookiesIn,
        IResponseCookies cookiesOut,
        EfCoreContext context)
    {
        _checkoutCookie = new CheckoutCookie(
            cookiesIn, cookiesOut);
        _runner =
            new RunnerWriteDb<PlaceOrderInDto, Order>(
                new PlaceOrderAction(
                    new PlaceOrderDbAccess(context)),
                context);
    }

    public int PlaceOrder(bool acceptTAndCs)
    {
        var checkoutService = new CheckoutCookieService(
            _checkoutCookie.GetValue());

        var order = _runner.RunAction(
            new PlaceOrderInDto(acceptTAndCs,
            checkoutService.UserId,
            checkoutService.LineItems));

        if (_runner.HasErrors) return 0;
```

The BizRunner you'll use to execute the business logic. It's of type **RunnerWriteDb<TIn, TOut>.**

Holds any errors sent back from the business logic. The caller can use these to redisplay the page and show the errors that need fixing.

The constructor needs access to the cookies, both in and out, and the application's DbContext.

Creates a CheckoutCookie using the cookie in/out access parts from ASP.NET Core

Creates the BizRunner with the business logic, PlaceOrderAction, that you want to run. PlaceOrderAction needs PlaceOrderDbAccess when it's created.

The method you call from the ASP.NET action that's called when the user clicks the Purchase button

Encodes/decodes the checkout data into a string that goes inside the checkout cookie.

You're ready to run the business logic, handing it the checkout information in the format that it needs.

If the business logic has any errors, you return immediately. The checkout cookie hasn't been cleared, so the user can try again.

```
                //successful, so clear the cookie line items
                checkoutService.ClearAllLineItems();
                _checkoutCookie.AddOrUpdateCookie(
                    checkoutService.EncodeForCookie());

            return order.OrderId;
        }
    }
```

The order was placed successfully. You therefore clear the checkout cookie of the order parts.

Returns the OrderId, the primary key of the order, which ASP.NET uses to show a confirmation page that includes the order details

In addition to running the business logic, this class acts as an Adapter pattern: it transforms the data from the checkout cookie into a form that the business logic accepts, and on a successful completion, it extracts the Order primary key, OrderId, to send back to the ASP.NET Core presentation layer.

This Adapter pattern role is typical of the code that calls the business logic, because a mismatch often occurs between the presentation layer format and the business logic format. This mismatch can be small, as in this example, but you're likely to need to do some form of adaptation in all but the simplest calls to your business logic. That's why my more sophisticated EfCore.GenericBizRunner library has a built-in Adapter pattern feature.

4.4.7 Any disadvantages of this business logic pattern?

I find the business logic pattern I've described useful, yet I'm aware of a few downsides, especially for developers who are new to a DDD approach. This section presents some thoughts to help you evaluate whether this approach is for you.

The first disadvantage is that the pattern is more complicated than just writing a class with a method that you call to get the job done. This business logic pattern relies on interfaces and code/libraries such as the BizRunners, and at least four projects in your solution. For small applications, this can be overkill.

The second disadvantage is, even in medium-sized projects, you can have simple business logic that may be only 10 lines long. In this case, is it worth creating both the pure business logic class and the companion data access class? For small business logic jobs, maybe you should create one class that combines the pure business logic and the EF Core calls. But be aware: if you do this to cut corners, it can come back and bite you when you need to refactor.

There's also a development cost inherent in the business logic pattern's guideline 2, the "no distraction" rule. The data that the business logic takes in and returns can be different from what the caller of the business logic needs. For instance, in our example, the checkout data was held in an HTTP cookie; the business logic has no concept of what a cookie is (nor should it), so the calling method had to convert the cookie content into the format that the business logic wanted. Therefore, the Adapter pattern is used a lot in the service layer to transform data between the business logic and the presentation layer—which is why I included an Adapter pattern feature in the EfCore .GenericBizRunner library.

Having listed all these disadvantages, I still find this approach far superior to my earlier approach of considering business logic as "just another piece of code." In chapter 10 I further enhance this business logic pattern once you have learned how to apply the DDD principals to the entity classes themselves. DDD-styled entity classes are "locked down"; that is, their properties have private setters and all creates/updates are done via methods inside the entity class. These methods can contain some of your business logic, which improves the overall robustness of your solution because no one can bypass your business logic by simply altering properties in the entity class. After you have learned about the features needed to truly lock down an entity class, I recommend you read about the business logic enhancements in section 10.4.2.

4.5   *Placing an order on the book app*

Now that we've covered the business logic for processing an order, the BizRunner, and the `PlaceOrderService` that executes the business logic, let's see how to use these in the context of the book app. Figure 4.4 shows the process, from the user clicking the Purchase button through running the business logic and returning a result.

I don't go into the presentation code in detail here, as this chapter is about using EF Core in business logic, but I do cover some of this in the next chapter, which is about using EF Core in ASP.NET Core applications.

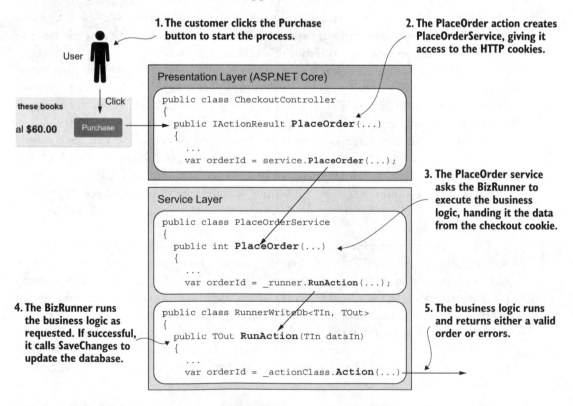

Figure 4.4   The series of steps, from the user clicking the Purchase button, to the service layer, where the BizRunner executes the business logic to process the order

From the click of the Purchase button in figure 4.4, the ASP.NET Core action, `PlaceOrder`, in the `CheckoutController` is executed. This creates a class called `PlaceOrderService` in the service layer, which holds most of the Adapter pattern logic. The caller provides that class with read/write access to the cookies, as the checkout data is held in an HTTP cookie on the user's device.

You've already seen the `PlaceOrderService` class in listing 4.6. Its `PlaceOrder` method extracts the checkout data from the HTTP cookie and creates a DTO in the form that the business logic needs. It then calls the generic BizRunner to run the business logic that it needs to execute. When the BizRunner has returned from the business logic, two routes are possible:

- *The order was successfully placed—no errors.* In this case, the `PlaceOrder` method clears the checkout cookie and returns the `OrderId` of the placed order, so that the ASP.NET Core code can show a confirmation page with a summary of the order.
- *The order was unsuccessful—errors present.* In this case, the `PlaceOrder` method returns immediately to the ASP.NET Core code. That detects that errors occurred and redisplays the checkout page, and adds the error messages so that the user can rectify them and try again.

NOTE You can try the checkout process on the live book app at http://efcore-inaction.com/ and see the results. To try the error path, don't tick the Terms and Conditions (T&C) box.

4.6 Adding extra features to your business logic handling

This pattern for handling business logic makes it easier to add extra features to your business logic handling. In this section, you'll add two features:

- Entity class validation to `SaveChanges`
- Transactions that daisy-chain a series of business logic code

These features use EF Core commands that aren't limited to business logic. Both could be used in other areas, so you might want to keep these features in mind when you're working on your application.

4.6.1 Validating the data that you write to the database

.NET contains a whole ecosystem to *validate* data, to check the value of a property against certain rules (for example, checking that an integer is within the range of 1 to 10, or that a string isn't longer than 20 characters).

EF6 If you're scanning for EF6.x changes, read the next paragraph. EF Core's `SaveChanges` doesn't validate the data before writing to the database, but this section shows how to add this back.

In the previous version of EF (EF6.x), data that was being added or updated was validated by default before writing it out to the database. In EF Core, which is aimed at being lightweight and faster, no validation occurs when adding or updating the database. The idea is that the validation is often done at the frontend, so why repeat the validation?

As you've seen, the business logic contains lots of validation code, and it's often useful to move this into the entity classes as validation checks, especially if the error is related to a specific property in the entity class. This is another case of breaking a complex set of rules into several component parts.

Listing 4.7 moves the test to check that the book is for sale into the validation code, rather than having to do it in the business logic. The listing also adds two new validation checks to show you the various forms that validation checks can take, so that the example is comprehensive.

Figure 4.5 shows the `LineItem` entity class with two types of validation added. The first is a `[Range(min,max)]` attribute, known as `DataAnnotation`, which is added to the `LineNum` property. The second validation method to apply is the `IValidatableObject` interface. This requires you to add a method called `IValidatableObject.Validate`, in which you can write your own validation rules and return errors if those rules are violated.

Listing 4.7   Validation rules applied to the `LineNum` entity class

By applying the IValidatableObject interface, the validation will call the method the interface defines.

```
public class LineItem : IValidatableObject
{
    public int LineItemId { get; set; }

    [Range(1,5, ErrorMessage =
        "This order is over the limit of 5 books.")]
    public byte LineNum { get; set; }

    public short NumBooks { get; set; }

    public decimal BookPrice { get; set; }

    // relationships

    public int OrderId { get; set; }
    public int BookId { get; set; }

    public Book ChosenBook { get; set; }

    IEnumerable<ValidationResult> IValidatableObject.Validate
        (ValidationContext validationContext)
    {
        var currContext =
            validationContext.GetService(typeof(DbContext));

        if (ChosenBook.Price < 0)
            yield return new ValidationResult(
        $"Sorry, the book '{ChosenBook.Title}' is not for sale.");
```

A validation DataAnnotation. Shows your error message if the LineNum property isn't in range.

The method that the IValidatableObject interface requires you to create

Moves the Price check out of the business logic

Uses the ChosenBook link to look at the date the book was published. You can also format your own error message.

You can access the current DbContext that this database access is using. In this case, you don't use it, but you could, to get better error feedback information for the user.

```
            if (NumBooks > 100)
                yield return new ValidationResult(
    If you want to order a 100 or more books"+
    please phone us on 01234-5678-90",
                new[] { nameof(NumBooks) });
        }
    }
```

Tests a property in this class
so you can return that
property with the error

I should point out that in the `IValidatableObject.Validate` method you access a property outside the `LineNum` class: the `Title` of the `ChosenBook`. You need to be careful when doing this, because you can't be sure that the relationship isn't `null`. Microsoft says that EF Core will run the internal *relationship fixup* (see figure 1.6) when `DetectChanges` is called, so this is fine when using the validation code in listing 4.8.

> **NOTE** In addition to using the extensive list of built-in validation attributes, you can create your own validation attributes by inheriting the `Validation-Attribute` class on your own class. See http://mng.bz/9ec for more on the standard validation attributes that are available and how to use the `Valida-tionAttribute` class.

After adding the validation rule code to your `LineItem` entity class, you need to add a validation stage to EF Core's `SaveChanges` method, called `SaveChangesWithValidation`. Although the obvious place to put this is inside the application's DbContext, you'll create an extension method instead. This will allow `SaveChangesWithValidation` to be used on any DbContext, which means you can copy this class and use it in your application.

The following listing shows this `SaveChangesWithValidation` extension method, and listing 4.9 shows the private method `ExecuteValidation` that `SaveChangesWith-Validation` calls to handle the validation.

Listing 4.8 `SaveChangesWithValidation` **added to the application's DbContext**

If there are errors, you return them
immediately and don't call SaveChanges.

Returns a list of ValidationResults. If it's an empty
collection, the data was saved. If it has errors, the
data wasn't saved.

```
public static ImmutableList<ValidationResult>
```

Defined as an extension method, which means you
can call it in the same way you call SaveChanges.

```
    SaveChangesWithValidation(this DbContext context)
{
    var result = context.ExecuteValidation();
```

Creates a private method to do the
validation, as you need to apply this
in SaveChangesWithValidation and
SaveChangesWithValidationAsync

```
    if (result.Any()) return result;

    context.SaveChanges();
```

No errors exist, so you're
going to call SaveChanges.

```
    return result;
}
```

Returns the empty set of errors, which
tells the caller that everything is OK

Listing 4.9   `SaveChangesWithValidation` **calls** `ExecuteValidation` **method**

```
private static ImmutableList<ValidationResult>
   ExecuteValidation(this DbContext context)
{
    var result = new List<ValidationResult>();        ⟵ Calls ChangeTracker.DetectChanges,
    foreach (var entry in                               which makes sure all your changes to
       context.ChangeTracker.Entries()    ⟵            the tracked entity classes are found.
          .Where(e =>
             (e.State == EntityState.Added) ||
             (e.State == EntityState.Modified)))
                                                     Filters out only those that need to be
                                                     added to, or updates the database
    {
       var entity = entry.Entity;
       var valProvider = new
          ValidationDbContextServiceProvider(context);  ⟵

                                       Creates an instance of the  class that implements the
                                       IServiceProvider interface, which makes the current
                                       DbContext available in the IValidatableObject.Validate method

       var valContext = new
          ValidationContext(entity, valProvider, null);
       var entityErrors = new List<ValidationResult>();   Calls method to find
       if (!Validator.TryValidateObject(                  any validation errors
          entity, valContext, entityErrors, true))
       {
          result.AddRange(entityErrors);        ⟵  If there are errors, you
       }                                            add them to the list.
    }
    return result.ToImmutableList();    ⟵  Returns the list of
}                                           all the errors found
```

The main code is in the `ExecuteValidation` method, because you need to use it in sync and async versions of `SaveChangesWithValidation`. The call to `context.ChangeTracker` `.Entries` calls the DbContext's `DetectChanges` to ensure that all the changes you've made are found before the validation is run. It then looks at all the entities that have been added or modified (updated) and validates them all.

One piece of code I want to point out is that when you create `ValidationContext`, you provide your own class called `ValidationDbContextServiceProvider` (which can be found in the Git repo) that implements the `IServiceProvider` interface. This allows any entity classes that have the `IValidatableObject` interface to access the current DbContext in its `Validate` method, which could be used to gather better error feedback information or do deeper testing.

You design the `SaveChangesWithValidation` method to return the errors rather than throw an exception, which is what EF6.x did. You do this to fit in with the business logic, which returns errors as a list, not an exception. You can create a new BizRunner variant, `RunnerWriteDbWithValidation`, that uses `SaveChangesWithValidation` instead of the normal `SaveChanges`, and returns errors from the business logic or any validation errors found when writing to the database. Listing 4.10 shows the BizRunner class `RunnerWriteDbWithValidation`.

Listing 4.10 BizRunner variant, `RunnerWriteDbWithValidation`

```
public class RunnerWriteDbWithValidation<TIn, TOut>
{
    private readonly IBizAction<TIn, TOut> _actionClass;
    private readonly EfCoreContext _context;

    public IImmutableList<ValidationResult>
        Errors { get; private set; }
    public bool HasErrors => Errors.Any();

    public RunnerWriteDbWithValidation(
        IBizAction<TIn, TOut> actionClass,
        EfCoreContext context)
    {
        _context = context;
        _actionClass = actionClass;
    }

    public TOut RunAction(TIn dataIn)
    {
        var result = _actionClass.Action(dataIn);

        Errors = _actionClass.Errors;

        if (!HasErrors)
        {

            Errors =
                _context.SaveChangesWithValidation()
                    .ToImmutableList();
        }
        return result;
    }
}
```

In this version, you need your own Errors and HasErrors properties, because errors can come from two sources.

Handles business logic that conforms to the IBizAction<TIn, TOut> interface.

Calls RunAction in your service layer, or in your presentation layer if the data comes back in the right form

Runs the business logic you gave it

If there are no errors, you call SaveChangesWithValidation to execute any add, update, or delete methods.

Assigns any errors from the business logic to your local errors list

Extracts the error message part of the ValidationResults and assigns the list to your Errors

Returns the result that the business logic returned

The nice thing about this new variant of the BizRunner pattern is that it has exactly the same interface as the original, nonvalidating BizRunner. You can substitute RunnerWriteDbWithValidation<TIn, TOut> for the original BizRunner without needing to change the business logic or the way that the calling method executes the BizRunner.

In the next section, you'll produce yet another variant of the BizRunner that can run multiple business logic classes in such a way that, from the database write point of view, look like one single business logic method, known as a database *atomic unit*. This is possible because of the business logic pattern described at the start of this chapter.

4.6.2 *Using transactions to daisy-chain a sequence of business logic code*

As I said earlier, business logic can get complex. When it comes to designing and implementing a large or complex piece of business logic, you have three options:

- *Option 1*—Write one big method that does everything.

- *Option 2*—Write a few smaller methods, with one overarching method to run them in sequence.
- *Option 3*—Write a few smaller methods and get the system to run them as one unit.

Option 1 isn't normally a good idea because the method will be so hard to understand and refactor. It also has problems if parts of the business logic are used elsewhere, because you could break the DRY (don't repeat yourself) software principle.

Option 2 can work, but can have problems if later stages rely on database items written by earlier stages, because this could break the *atomic unit* rule mentioned in chapter 1: with multiple changes to the database, either they all succeed, or they all fail.

This leaves option 3, which is possible because of a feature in EF Core (and most relational databases) called *transactions*. When EF Core starts a relational database transaction, the database creates an explicit, local transaction. This has two effects. First, any writes to the database are hidden from other database users until you call the transaction Commit command. Second, if you decide you don't want the database writes (say, because the business logic has an error), you can discard all database writes done in the transaction by calling the transaction RollBack command.

Figure 4.5 shows three separate pieces of business logic being run by a class called the *transactional BizRunner*. After each piece of business logic has run, the BizRunner calls SaveChanges, which means anything it writes is now available for subsequent business logic stages via the local transaction. On the final stage, the business logic, Biz 3, returns errors, which causes the BizRunner to call the RollBack command. This has the effect of removing any database writes that Biz 1 and Biz 2 did.

1. A special BizRunner runs each business logic class in turn. Each business logic stage uses an application DbContext that has an EF Core's BeginTransaction applied to it.

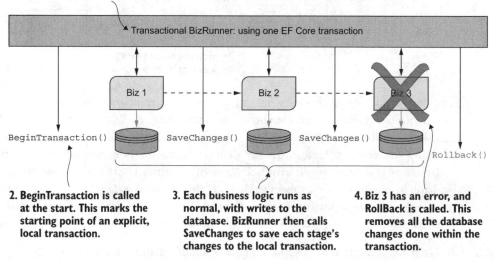

2. BeginTransaction is called at the start. This marks the starting point of an explicit, local transaction.

3. Each business logic runs as normal, with writes to the database. BizRunner then calls SaveChanges to save each stage's changes to the local transaction.

4. Biz 3 has an error, and RollBack is called. This removes all the database changes done within the transaction.

Figure 4.5   An example of executing three separate business logic stages under one transaction. When the last business logic stage returns an error, the other database changes applied by the first two business logic stages are rolled back.

Here's the code for the new transactional BizRunner, which starts a transaction on the application's DbContext before calling any of the business logic.

Listing 4.11 `RunnerTransact2WriteDb` **runs two business logic stages in series**

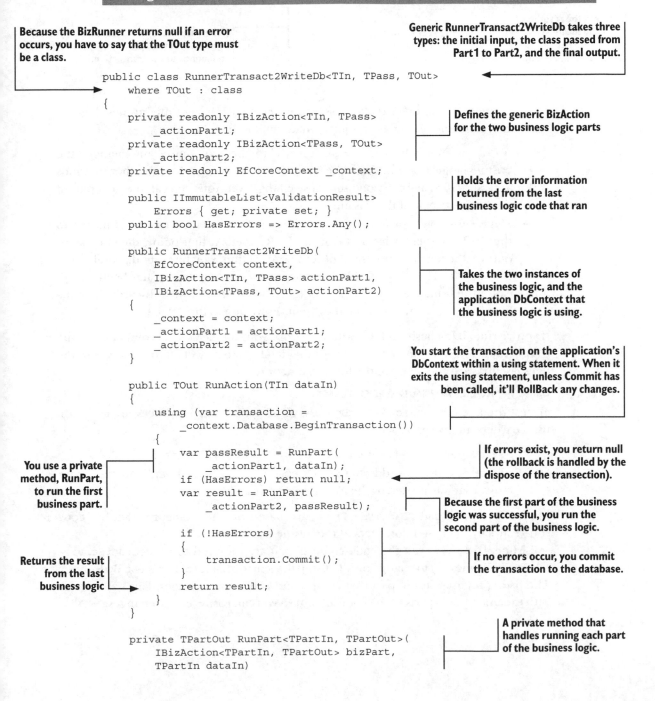

Because the BizRunner returns null if an error occurs, you have to say that the TOut type must be a class.

Generic RunnerTransact2WriteDb takes three types: the initial input, the class passed from Part1 to Part2, and the final output.

```
public class RunnerTransact2WriteDb<TIn, TPass, TOut>
    where TOut : class
{
    private readonly IBizAction<TIn, TPass>
        _actionPart1;
    private readonly IBizAction<TPass, TOut>
        _actionPart2;
    private readonly EfCoreContext _context;

    public IImmutableList<ValidationResult>
        Errors { get; private set; }
    public bool HasErrors => Errors.Any();

    public RunnerTransact2WriteDb(
        EfCoreContext context,
        IBizAction<TIn, TPass> actionPart1,
        IBizAction<TPass, TOut> actionPart2)
    {
        _context = context;
        _actionPart1 = actionPart1;
        _actionPart2 = actionPart2;
    }

    public TOut RunAction(TIn dataIn)
    {
        using (var transaction =
            _context.Database.BeginTransaction())
        {
            var passResult = RunPart(
                _actionPart1, dataIn);
            if (HasErrors) return null;
            var result = RunPart(
                _actionPart2, passResult);

            if (!HasErrors)
            {
                transaction.Commit();
            }
            return result;
        }
    }

    private TPartOut RunPart<TPartIn, TPartOut>(
        IBizAction<TPartIn, TPartOut> bizPart,
        TPartIn dataIn)
```

Defines the generic BizAction for the two business logic parts

Holds the error information returned from the last business logic code that ran

Takes the two instances of the business logic, and the application DbContext that the business logic is using.

You start the transaction on the application's DbContext within a using statement. When it exits the using statement, unless Commit has been called, it'll RollBack any changes.

You use a private method, RunPart, to run the first business part.

If errors exist, you return null (the rollback is handled by the dispose of the transection).

Because the first part of the business logic was successful, you run the second part of the business logic.

If no errors occur, you commit the transaction to the database.

Returns the result from the last business logic

A private method that handles running each part of the business logic.

```
        where TPartOut : class
    {
        var result = bizPart.Action(dataIn);
        Errors = bizPart.Errors;
        if (!HasErrors)
        {
            _context.SaveChanges();
        }
        return result;
    }
}
```

Runs the business logic and copies the business logic's Errors property to the local Errors property

Returns the result that the business logic returned

If the business logic was successful, you call SaveChanges to apply any add/update/delete commands to the transaction.

In your `RunnerTransact2WriteDb` class, you execute each part of the business logic in turn, and at the end of each execution, you do one of the following:

- *No errors*—You call `SaveChanges` to save to the transaction any changes the business logic has run. That save is within a local transaction, so other methods accessing the database won't see those changes yet. You then call the next part of the business logic, if there is one.

- *Has errors*—You copy the errors found by the business logic that just finished to the BizRunner error list and exit the BizRunner. At that point, the code steps outside the `using` clause that holds the transaction, which causes disposal of the transaction. The disposal will, because no transaction `Commit` has been called, cause the transaction to execute its `RollBack` method, which discards the database writes to the transaction; they're never written to the database.

If you've run all the business logic with no errors, you call the `Commit` command on the transaction. This does an *atomic update* of the database to reflect all the changes to the database that are contained in the local transaction.

USING THE RUNNERTRANSACT2WRITEDB CLASS

To test the `RunnerTransact2WriteDb` class, you'll split the order-processing code you used earlier into two parts:

- `PlaceOrderPart1`—Creates the `Order` entity, with no `LineItems`
- `PlaceOrderPart2`—Adds the `LineItems` for each book bought to the `Order` entity that was created by the `PlaceOrderPart1` class

`PlaceOrderPart1` and `PlaceOrderPart2` are based on the `PlaceOrderAction` code you've already seen, so I don't repeat the business code here.

Listing 4.12 shows you the code changes that are required to `PlaceOrderService` (shown in listing 4.6) to change over to using the `RunnerTransact2WriteDb` BizRunner. The listing focuses on the part that creates and runs the two stages, Part1 and Part2, with the unchanged parts of the code left out so you can easily see the changes.

Listing 4.12 The `PlaceOrderServiceTransact` class showing the changed parts

```
public class PlaceOrderServiceTransact
{
    //… code removed as the same as in listing 4.5

    public PlaceOrderServiceTransact(
        IRequestCookieCollection cookiesIn,
        IResponseCookies cookiesOut,
        EfCoreContext context)
    {
        _checkoutCookie = new CheckoutCookie(
            cookiesIn, cookiesOut);
        _runner = new RunnerTransact2WriteDb

            <PlaceOrderInDto, Part1ToPart2Dto, Order>(
            context,
            new PlaceOrderPart1(
                new PlaceOrderDbAccess(context)),
            new PlaceOrderPart2(
                new PlaceOrderDbAccess(context)));
    }

    public int PlaceOrder(bool tsAndCsAccepted)
    {
        //… code removed as the same as in listing 4.6
    }
}
```

A version of **PlaceOrderService**, but using transactions to execute the business logic in two parts

Creates the BizRunner variant called **RunnerTransact2WriteDb**, which runs the two business logic parts inside a transaction

The BizRunner needs to know the data types used for input, passing from part 1 to part 2, and output.

The BizRunner needs the application's DbContext.

Provides an instance of the first part of the business logic

Provides an instance of the second part of the business logic

The important thing to note is that the business logic has no idea whether it's running in a transaction. You can use a piece of business logic on its own or as part of a transaction. Similarly, listing 4.12 shows that only the caller of transaction-based business logic, what I call the BizRunner, needs to change. This makes it easy to combine multiple business logic classes under one transaction without the need to change any of your business logic code at all.

The advantage of using transactions like this is that you can split up and/or reuse parts of your business logic while still making these multiple business logic calls look to your application, especially its database, like one call. I've used this approach when I needed to create and then immediately update a complex, multipart entity. Because I needed the Update business logic for other cases, I used a transaction to call the Create business logic followed by the Update business logic. That saved me development effort and kept my code DRY.

The disadvantage of this approach is that it adds complexity to the database access. That might make debugging a little more difficult, or the use of database transactions could cause a performance issue. These are normally small issues, but you should be aware of them if you use this approach.

Summary

- The term *business logic* describes code written to implement real-world business rules. This type of code can be complex and difficult to write.
- Various approaches and patterns can make business logic easier to write, test, and performance-tune.
- Isolating the database access part of your business logic into another class/project can make the pure business logic simpler to write, and helps when performance tuning.
- Creating a standardized interface for your business logic makes calling and running the business logic much simpler for the frontend.
- Sometimes it's easier to move some of the validation logic into the entity classes and run the checks when that data is being written to the database.
- For business logic that's complex or being reused, it might be simpler to use a database transaction to allow a sequence of business logic parts to be run in sequence, but, from the database point of view, look like one atomic unit.

For readers who are familiar with EF6.x:

- Unlike EF6.x, EF Core's SaveChanges method doesn't validate data before it's written to the database. But it's easy to implement a method that provides this feature.

Using EF Core in ASP.NET Core web applications

This chapter covers

- Introduction to using EF Core in ASP.NET Core

- Using dependency injection in ASP.NET Core

- Accessing the database in ASP.NET Core MVC actions

- Using EF Core migrations to update a database

- Using async/await to improve scalability

In this last chapter of part 1, you'll pull everything together by using ASP.NET Core to build a real web application. Using ASP.NET Core brings in issues that are outside EF Core, such as dependency injection, which I describe later. But they're necessary if you're going to use EF Core in this type of application.

This chapter assumes you've read chapters 2 to 4, and know about querying and updating the database and what business logic is. This chapter is about where to place your database access code and how to call it in a real application. It also covers the specific issues of using EF Core in an ASP.NET Core application. For that reason, this chapter includes quite a bit about ASP.NET Core, but it's all focused on using EF Core well in this type of application. I end with more general information on the various ways to obtain an instance of the application's DbContext for cases such as running parallel tasks.

5.1   *Introducing ASP.NET Core*

> **TIME-SAVER**   If you're familiar with ASP.NET MVC5, you have a good idea of what ASP.NET Core is, so you can skip this section.

The ASP.NET Core website, https://docs.microsoft.com/aspnet/core/, states "ASP.NET Core is a lean and composable framework for building web and cloud applications. ASP.NET Core is fully open source and available on GitHub. ASP.NET Core is available on Windows, Mac, and Linux." This is a good description. I'd add that ASP.NET Core is mainly about the server-side of web/mobile services: your ASP.NET Core runs on a server somewhere that's accessed via HTTP requests.

I've been using the precursor of ASP.NET Core, ASP.NET MVC5, for years. I still have a book on my shelf for MVC3, and I think it's a good framework, if a bit slow in performance. Like EF Core, ASP.NET Core is another total rewrite to make it more modular, multiplatform-capable, and faster (hooray).

> **TIP**   When I first tried ASP.NET Core, I was a bit disappointed with the performance. To me, it didn't feel that much faster than the existing ASP.NET MVC5. But when I replaced the default logging with my slimmer, in-memory logging, the book list page was three times faster! So watch out for too much logging slowing down your application.

As I stated earlier, ASP.NET Core is a web server; its code runs on a host of some kind and responds to HTTP requests. In general, the handling of an HTTP request splits into two types:

- A request from a browser, where HTML is returned. This is known in ASP.NET Core as *Web UI*.
- A request from software, where data is returned. This is known in ASP.NET Core as *Web API*, or *web services*.

5.2   *Understanding the architecture of the book app*

Chapter 2 presented a diagram of the book app, and chapter 4 extended it with two more projects to handle the business logic. Figure 5.1 shows you the combined architecture after chapter 4, with all the projects in the application. As you go through this chapter, you'll learn how, and why, we split the database access code across the various projects. One reason is to make your web application easier to write, change, and test.

This layered architecture, which creates a single executable containing all the code, works well with many cloud providers that can *spin up more instances* of the web application if it's under a heavy load; your host will run multiple copies of a web application and place a load balancer to spread the load over all the copies. This is known as *scale out* on Microsoft Azure and *auto scaling* on Amazon Web Services (AWS).

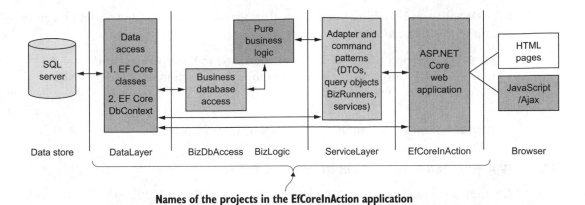

Names of the projects in the EfCoreInAction application

Figure 5.1 All the projects in the book app. The arrows show the main routes by which EF Core data moves up and down the layers.

5.3 Understanding dependency injection

ASP.NET Core uses *dependency injection* (DI) extensively, as does .NET Core in general. You need to understand DI because it's the method used in ASP.NET Core to get an instance of the application's DbContext.

> **DEFINITION** *Dependency injection* (DI) is a way to dynamically link together your application. Normally, you'd write `var myClass = new MyClass()` to create a new instance of `MyClass`. That works, but you've hardcoded the creation of that class, and you can change it only by changing your code. With DI, you can *register* your `MyClass` with a DI provider, using, say, an interface such as `IMyClass`. Then, when you need the class, you use `IMyClass myClass`, and the DI provider will dynamically create an instance and *inject* it into the `IMyClass myClass` parameter/property.

Using DI has lots of benefits, and here are the main ones:

- DI allows your application to dynamically link itself. The DI provider will work out what classes you need and create them in the right order. For example, if one of your classes needs the application's DbContext, the DI can provide it.
- Using interfaces and DI together means your application is more *loosely coupled*; you can replace a class with another class that matches the same interface. This is especially useful in unit testing: you can provide a replacement version of the service with another, simpler class that implements the interface (called *mocking* or *faking* in unit tests).
- Other, more advanced features exist, such as using DI to select which class to return based on certain settings. For instance, if you're building an e-commerce application, in development mode you might want to use a dummy credit card handler instead of the normal credit card system.

I use DI a lot and I wouldn't build any real application without it, but I admit it can be confusing the first time you see it.

> **NOTE** This section gives you a quick introduction to DI so that you understand how to use DI with EF Core. If you want more information on DI in ASP.NET Core, see http://mng.bz/Kv16.

> **TIME-SAVER** If you're familiar with DI, you can skip this section.

5.3.1 *Why you need to learn about DI in ASP.NET Core*

Chapter 2 showed you how to create an instance of the application's DbContext by using the following snippet of code:

```
const string connection =
    "Data Source=(localdb)\\mssqllocaldb;" +
    "Database=EfCoreInActionDb.Chapter02;" +
    "Integrated Security=True;";
var optionsBuilder =
    new DbContextOptionsBuilder
        <EfCoreContext>();

optionsBuilder.UseSqlServer(connection);
var options = optionsBuilder.Options;

using (var context = new EfCoreContext(options))
{…
```

That works, but has a few problems. First, you're going to have to repeat this code for each database access you make. Second, this code uses a fixed database access string, which isn't going to work when you want to deploy your site to a host, because the database location for the hosted database will be different from the database you use for development.

You can work around these two problems in several ways, such as overriding the OnConfiguration method in the application's DbContext (covered in section 5.11.1). But DI is a better way of handling this, and that's what ASP.NET Core uses. Using a slightly different set of commands, you can tell the DI provider how to create your application's DbContext, a process called *registering a service,* and then ask the DI for an instance of your application's DbContext anywhere in ASP.NET Core's system that supports DI.

5.3.2 *A basic example of dependency injection in ASP.NET Core*

Setting up the code to configure the application's DbContext is a little complicated and can hide the DI part. My first example of DI in ASP.NET Core, shown in figure 5.2, uses a simple class called Demo, which you'll use in an ASP.NET controller. This example is useful later, when I show you how to use DI to make your code simpler to call.

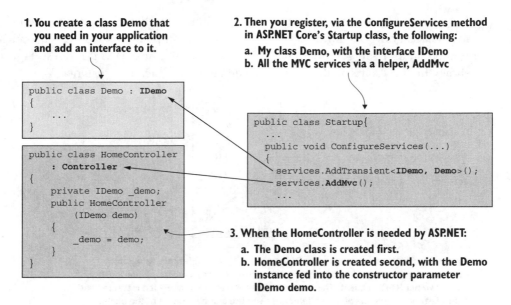

1. You create a class Demo that you need in your application and add an interface to it.

2. Then you register, via the ConfigureServices method in ASP.NET Core's Startup class, the following:
   a. My class Demo, with the interface IDemo
   b. All the MVC services via a helper, AddMvc

```
public class Demo : IDemo
{
    ...
}
```

```
public class HomeController
    : Controller
{
    private IDemo _demo;
    public HomeController
        (IDemo demo)
    {
        _demo = demo;
    }
}
```

```
public class Startup{
    ...
    public void ConfigureServices(...)
    {
        services.AddTransient<IDemo, Demo>();
        services.AddMvc();
        ...
```

3. When the HomeController is needed by ASP.NET:
   a. The Demo class is created first.
   b. HomeController is created second, with the Demo instance fed into the constructor parameter IDemo demo.

Figure 5.2   An example of a class called `Demo` being inserted via DI into a controller's constructor

Figure 5.2 shows that by registering your `IDemo`/`Demo` class with ASP.NET Core's DI, you can then access it in your `HomeController` class. Classes that are registered are referred to as *services*.

The rules are that any DI service can be referenced, or *injected*, in any other DI service. In figure 5.2, you register your `IDemo`/`Demo` class and call the `AddMvc` method to register the ASP.NET Core's classes—specifically, in this example, the `HomeController` class. This allows you to use the `IDemo` interface in the `HomeController`'s constructor, and the DI provides an instance on the `Demo` class. In DI terms, you use *constructor injection* to create an instance of the class that you've registered.

You'll use DI in various ways in this chapter, but the rules and terms just defined will help you make sense of these later examples.

5.3.3   *The lifetime of a service created by DI*

One feature of DI that's important when talking about EF Core is the *lifetime* of an instance created by DI—how long the instance exists before being lost or disposed of. In our `IDemo`/`Demo` example, you registered the instance as *transient*; every time you ask for an instance of `Demo`, it creates a new one. If you want to use your own classes with DI, you most likely declare them a *transient* lifetime or, for simple, value-like classes, you may declare them as *singleton* (you get the same instance every time).

The application's DbContext is different. It has its lifetime set to *scoped*, which means that however many instances of the application's DbContext you ask for during one

HTTP request, you get the same instance. But after that HTTP request ends, that instance is gone (technically, because DbContext implements `IDisposable`, it's disposed of), and you get a new, scoped instance in the next HTTP request. Figure 5.3 shows the three sorts of lifetimes, with a new letter for each new instance.

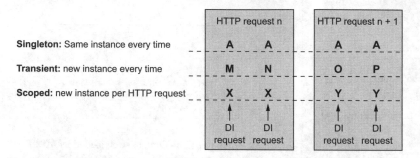

Figure 5.3   Instances produced by DI have three types of lifetimes: singleton, transient, and scoped. This figure shows those three types with four *injections* for each, two per HTTP request. The letters represent each instance—if a letter is used multiple times, it means all those *injections* are the same instance of the class.

Using a scoped lifetime for the application's DbContext is critical if you use something like AJAX with EF Core database accesses (AJAX allows multiple requests within one HTTP request). For example, if you update a book's information by using separate AJAX requests, you want all the AJAX requests to use the same instances of the Book entities. That way, each AJAX request could apply its changes to the Book entity separately, and when the user clicks the Update button, the call to `SaveChanges` will save all the changes as one update.

The AJAX example works only because the application's DbContext has a *scoped* lifetime, and each AJAX request will get the same application's DbContext instance, which holds the *tracked entity* of the Book instance. Conversely, each HTTP request must have its own instance of the application's DbContext, because EF Core's DbContext isn't *thread safe* (see section 5.11). This is why the application's DbContext has a *scoped* lifetime for each HTTP request, and is one reason why DI is so useful.

5.4   *Making the application's DbContext available via DI*

Now that you understand DI, you're ready to set up your application's DbContext as a service so that you can access it later via DI. This is done at the startup of the ASP.NET Core web application by registering the application's DbContext with the DI provider, using information that tells EF Core what sort of database you're accessing and where it's located.

5.4.1   *Providing information on the database's location*

When developing your application, you'll want to run it on your development machine, and access a local database for testing. The type of the database will be defined by the business need, but the location of the database on your development machine is up to you and whatever database server you're using.

For web applications, the location of the database isn't normally hardcoded into the application because it'll change when the web application is moved to its host, where real users can access it. Therefore, the location and various database configuration settings are typically stored as a *connection string*. This string is stored in an application setting file that ASP.NET reads when it starts.

ASP.NET Core has a range of application setting files, but for now you'll concentrate on the three standard ones:

- *appsetting.json*—Holds the settings that are common to development and production
- *appsettings.Development.json*—Holds the settings for the development build
- *appsettings.Production.json*—Holds the settings for the production build (when the web application is deployed to a host for users to access it)

NOTE There's a lot more to application setting files in ASP.NET Core that we haven't covered. Please look at the APS.NET Core documentation for a more complete description.

Typically, the development connection string is stored in the appsettings.Development.json file. Listing 5.1 shows a connection string suitable for running an SQL database locally on a windows PC.

NOTE The Visual Studio 2017 installation includes a feature called *SQL Server Express*, which allows you to use SQL Server for development.

Listing 5.1 appsettings.Development.json file with the database connection string

```
{
  "ConnectionStrings": {
    "DefaultConnection":
"Server=(localdb)\\mssqllocaldb;Database=EfCoreInActionDb
➥;Trusted_Connection=True"
  },
  … other parts removed as not relevant to database access
}
```

You need to edit your appsettings.Development.json file to add the connection string for your local, development database. This file may or may not have a `Connection-Strings` section, depending on whether you set Authentication to Individual User Accounts. (The Individual User Accounts option needs its own database, so a connection string for the authorization database is added by Visual Studio to the appsetting.json file.) You can call your connection string anything you like; this example uses the name `DefaultConnection` in our application.

5.4.2 *Registering your application's DbContext with the DI provider*

The next step is to register your application's DbContext with the DI provider at startup. Any configuration to be done when ASP.NET Core starts up is done in the aptly named `Startup` class. This class is executed when the ASP.NET Core application starts, and contains several methods to set up/configure the web application.

The application's DbContext for ASP.NET Core has a constructor that takes a `DbContextOptions<T>` parameter defining the database options. That way, the database connection string can change when you deploy your web application (see section 5.8). Just to remind you, here's what the book app's DbContext constructor looks like, as shown in bold in this code snippet:

```
public class EfCoreContext : DbContext
{
    //… properties removed for clarity

    public EfCoreContext(
        DbContextOptions<EfCoreContext> options)
        : base(options) {}

    //… other code removed for clarity
}
```

The following listing shows how the application's DbContext is registered as a service in an ASP.NET Core application. This is done in the `ConfigureServices` method in the `Startup` class of your ASP.NET Core application, along with all the DI services you need to register.

Listing 5.2 The `ConfigureServices` method in the `Startup` class of ASP.NET Core

The method in ASP.NET to set up services

```
public void ConfigureServices(IServiceCollection services)
{
    // Add framework services.
    services.AddMvc();
    var connection = Configuration
        .GetConnectionString("DefaultConnection");
    services.AddDbContext<EfCoreContext>(
        options => options.UseSqlServer(connection,
        b => b.MigrationsAssembly("DataLayer")));

    //… other service defintions removed
}
```

Sets up a series of services to use controllers, etc.

Configures the application's DbContext to use SQL Server and provide the connection

You're using EF Core's Add-Migrations command, so you need to indicate which project your application's DbContext is in.

You get the connection string from the appsettings.json file, which can be changed when you deploy.

Your first step is to get the connection string from the application's `Configuration` class. In ASP.NET Core, the `Configuration` class is set up during the `Startup` class constructor, which reads the `appsetting` files. Getting the connection string that way allows you to change the database connection string when you deploy the code to a host. Section 5.8.1, which is about deploying an ASP.NET Core application that uses a database, covers how this works.

The second step, making the application's DbContext available via DI, is done by the `AddDbContext` method, which registers the application's DbContext, `EfCoreContext`, as a service. When you use the type `EfCoreContext` in places where DI intercepts, the DI provider will run the code inside the `AddDbContext` method, which creates an instance of the application's DbContext; or, if you ask for multiple instances in the same HTTP request, the DI provider will return the same instance.

You'll see this in action when you start using the application's DbContext to do database queries and updates in section 5.6.

5.5   Calling your database access code from ASP.NET Core

Having configured the application DbContext and registered it as a DI service, you're ready to access the database. In these examples, you're going to run a query to display the books, and do a database update. You'll focus on how to execute these methods from ASP.NET Core; I assume you've already grasped how to query and update the database from the previous chapters.

5.5.1   A summary of how ASP.NET Core works and the terms it uses

First, a quick summary of how to use ASP.NET Core to implement our book app. To display the various HTML pages, you'll use an ASP.NET Core *controller*, which is the class that handles delivering HTML pages and Web API (for instance, RESTful data access). To do this, you'll create a class called `HomeController`, which inherits from ASP.NET Core's `Controller` class. This controller provides several HTML pages via methods, which in ASP.NET Core are known as *action methods*.

Our book app's `HomeController` has an action method called `Index`, which shows the book list, and one called `About`, which gives a summary page about the site. You then have other controllers to handle checkout, existing orders, admin actions, and so on.

Although you could put all your database access code inside each action method of each controller, I rarely do that. This is because I use a software design principle called *separation of concerns* (SoC), which the next subsection explains.

5.5.2   Where does the EF Core code live in the book app?

As you learned in section 5.2, our book app is built using a layered architecture, which is meant to represent an architecture that could be used in a real-world application. In this section, you'll see where to place the various pieces of EF Core's database access code, and why.

DEFINITION   *Separation of concerns* (SoC) is the idea that a software system must be decomposed into parts that overlap in functionality as little as possible. It's linked to two other principles: coupling and cohesion. With *coupling,* you want each project in your application to be as self-contained as possible, and with *cohesion,* each project in your application should have code that provides similar or strongly related functions. See http://mng.bz/wHJS for more information.

Figure 5.4 maps where the database access code is located in your application, using the earlier architecture diagram, figure 5.1. The size of the bubbles relates to the amount of code you'll find in each layer. Notice that the ASP.NET Core project and the pure business logic (BizLogic) project have no EF Core query/update code in them at all.

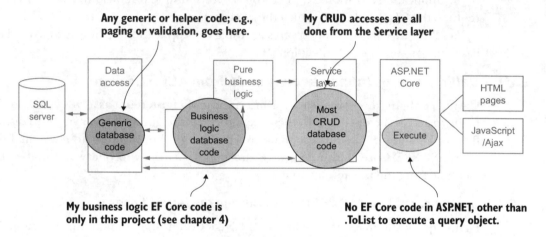

Figure 5.4   Locations of the database access code (the EF Core code) in the book app. Separating the EF Core code in this way makes it easier to find, understand, refactor, and test.

Applying SoC principles has benefits throughout the application. For instance, you learned about the reason for splitting out the business logic in chapter 4. But in this chapter, you'll see the benefits for the ASP.NET Core project.

First, the ASP.NET Core frontend is all about displaying data, and to do that well is a big task that needs lots of concentration. You'll therefore use the service layer to handle both the EF Core commands and the transformation of the database data into a form that the ASP.NET Core frontend can easily use—often via DTOs, also known as View-Models in ASP.NET. You can then concentrate on making the best user experience, rather than thinking about whether you have the database query right.

Second, ASP.NET controllers often have multiple pages/actions (say, one to list items, one to add a new item, one to edit an item, and so on), each of which would need its own database code. By moving the database code out to the service layer, you can create individual classes for each database access rather than have the code spread throughout a controller.

Finally, it's much easier to unit test your database code if it's in the service layer than when it's in an ASP.NET Core controller. You can test ASP.NET Core controllers, but testing can get complicated if your code accesses properties such as `HtppRequest` (which it does), because it's hard to replicate some of these features to get your unit test to work.

5.6   *Implementing the book list query page*

Having set the scene, now you're going to implement the ASP.NET Core part of the list of books in our book app. To remind you of what the site looks like, figure 5.5 shows a screenshot of the book app, with the list of books and the local admin update features.

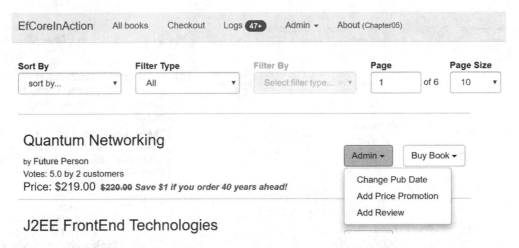

Figure 5.5   The homepage of the book app showing the list of books and the admin features, including the Change Pub(lication) Date of a book

In chapter 2, you wrote a class called `ListBooksService` that handled the complexities of transforming, sorting, filtering, and paging the books to display. You'll want to use this class in an ASP.NET Core action called `Index` in the controller `HomeController`. The main issue is that to create an instance of the `ListBooksService` class, you need an instance of the application's DbContext.

The standard way of providing an instance of the application's DbContext is to add a constructor in the controller that has the application's DbContext class as a parameter. You saw this type of constructor injection in section 5.3.2.

Listing 5.3 shows the start of the ASP.NET Core `HomeController`, where you've added a constructor and copied the injected `EfCoreContext` class into a local field that can be used to create an instance of the `BookListService` class that you need to list the books. This uses the same DI approach from section 5.3.2 and figure 5.2, but replaces the `Demo` class with the application's DbContext class, `EfCoreContext`.

Listing 5.3   The `Index` action in the `HomeController` displays the list of books

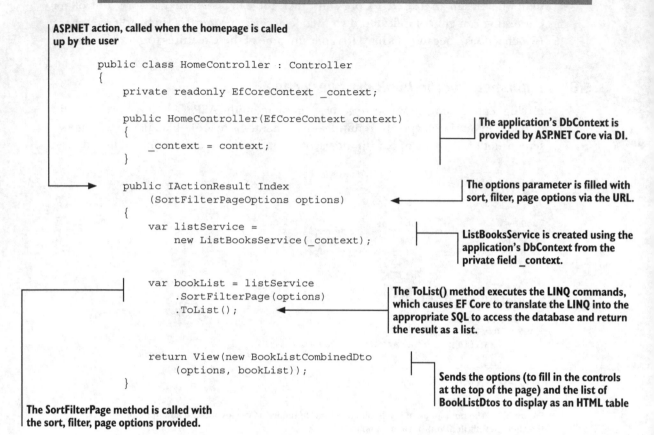

ASP.NET action, called when the homepage is called
up by the user

```
public class HomeController : Controller
{
    private readonly EfCoreContext _context;

    public HomeController(EfCoreContext context)
    {
        _context = context;
    }

    public IActionResult Index
        (SortFilterPageOptions options)
    {
        var listService =
            new ListBooksService(_context);

        var bookList = listService
            .SortFilterPage(options)
            .ToList();

        return View(new BookListCombinedDto
            (options, bookList));
    }
}
```

The application's DbContext is provided by ASP.NET Core via DI.

The options parameter is filled with sort, filter, page options via the URL.

ListBooksService is created using the application's DbContext from the private field _context.

The ToList() method executes the LINQ commands, which causes EF Core to translate the LINQ into the appropriate SQL to access the database and return the result as a list.

Sends the options (to fill in the controls at the top of the page) and the list of BookListDtos to display as an HTML table

The SortFilterPage method is called with the sort, filter, page options provided.

After you've used the local copy of the application's DbContext to create your `ListBooksService`, you can call its `SortFilterPage` method. This takes the parameters returned from the various controls on the list page and returns an `IQueryable<BookListDto>` result. You then add the `ToList` method to the end of the result, which causes EF Core to execute that `IQueryable` result against the database and return the list of book information the user has asked for. This is then given to an ASP. NET Core view to display.

You could've had the `SortFilterPage` method return a `List<BookListDto>` result, but that would've limited you to using a synchronous database access. As you'll see in section 5.10 on async/await, by returning an `IQueryable<BookListDto>` result, you can choose to use a normal (synchronous) or an async version of the final command that executes the query.

5.7 Implementing your database methods as a DI service

Although the constructor injection approach you just used works, there's another way to use DI that provides better isolation of the database access code: *parameter injection*. In ASP.NET Core, you can arrange for a service to be injected into an *action* method via a parameter marked with the attribute [FromServices]. You can provide a specific service that each action method in your controller needs; this is both more efficient and simpler to unit test.

To illustrate this, you're going to use a class called ChangePubDateService that's in your service layer to update the publication date of a book. This allows the admin user to change the publication date of a book, as shown in figure 5.6.

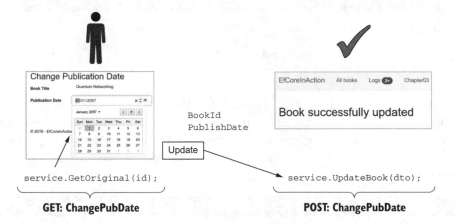

Figure 5.6   The two stages in changing the publication date of a book. The GET stage calls the GetOriginal method to show the user the book and its current publication date. The POST stage then calls the UpdateBook method with the user set date.

You can see that there are two stages to the process. First, you show the admin user the current publication date and allow them to change it. Second, the update is applied to the database, and you tell the user that it was successful.

To use parameter injection of your ChangePubDateService class, you need to do two things:

1 Register your class, ChangePubDateService, with the DI so it becomes a service that you can inject by using DI.

2 Use parameter injection to inject the class instance, ChangePubDate, into the two ASP.NET action methods that need it (GET and POST).

This approach works well for building ASP.NET Core applications, and I've used it in all my ASP.NET MVC projects for many years. In addition to providing good isolation and making testing easier, this approach also makes the ASP.NET Core controller action methods much easier to write. You'll see in section 5.7.2 that the code inside the ChangePubDate action method is simple and short.

5.7.1   *Registering your class as a DI service*

You can register a class with DI in ASP.NET in numerous ways. The standard way is to add an `IChangePubDateService` interface to the class. Technically, you don't need an interface, but it's good practice and can be helpful when unit testing. You also use the interface in section 5.7.3 to make registering your classes simpler.

The following listing shows the `IChangePubDateService` interface. Don't forget that the ASP.NET Core controller will be dealing with something of type `IChangePubDate-Service`, so you need to make sure all the public methods and properties are available in the interface.

> **Listing 5.4   The `IChangePubDateService` interface needed to register the class in DI**

```
public interface IChangePubDateService
{
    ChangePubDateDto GetOriginal(int id);
    Book UpdateBook(ChangePubDateDto dto);
}
```

You then register this interface/class with the DI service. The default way to do this in ASP.NET Core is to add a line to the `ConfigureServices` method in the `Startup` class. This listing shows the updated method, with the new code in bold. You add the `ChangePubDateService` as a transient, because you want a new version created every time you ask for it.

> **Listing 5.5   The ASP.NET Core `ConfigureService` method in the `Startup` class**

```
public void ConfigureServices
    (IServiceCollection services)
{
    // Add framework services.
    services.AddMvc();
    var connection = Configuration
        .GetConnectionString("DefaultConnection");
    services.AddDbContext<EfCoreContext>(
        options => options.UseSqlServer(connection,
        b => b.MigrationsAssembly("DataLayer")));

    services.AddTransient
        <IChangePubDateService, ChangePubDateService>();
}
```

Registers the ChangePubDateService class as a service, with the IChangePubDateService interface as the way to access it

5.7.2   *Injecting ChangePubDateService into the ASP.NET action method*

Having set up the `ChangePubDateService` class as a service that can be injected via DI, you now need to create an instance in your ASP.NET Core `AdminController`. The two GET ASP.NET Core action methods, both called `ChangePubDate`, need an instance of the `ChangePubDateService` class.

You could provide an instance of the `ChangePubDateService` class via constructor injection, as you did with the application's DbContext, but that approach has a downside. `AdminController` contains several other database update commands, such as adding a review to a book and adding a promotion to a book, and so on. That would mean you were needlessly creating an instance of `ChangePubDateService` class when one of these other commands is being called. The way around this is to use DI parameter injection into the two specific action methods that need it, `ChangePubDate` (GET and POST), so it's created only if that method is called.

This listing shows the `ChangePubDate` ASP.NET GET action that's called when someone clicks the Admin > Change Pub Date link. This is when the user wants to change the publication date.

Listing 5.6 The `ChangePubDate` action method in `AdminController`

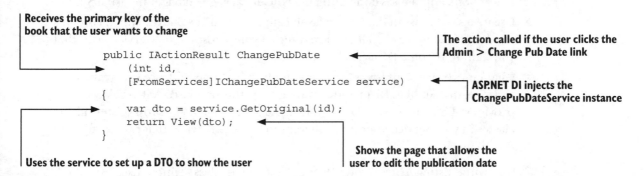

Receives the primary key of the book that the user wants to change

The action called if the user clicks the Admin > Change Pub Date link

```
public IActionResult ChangePubDate
    (int id,
    [FromServices]IChangePubDateService service)
{
    var dto = service.GetOriginal(id);
    return View(dto);
}
```

ASP.NET DI injects the ChangePubDateService instance

Uses the service to set up a DTO to show the user

Shows the page that allows the user to edit the publication date

Line 3 in this listing is the important one. You've used parameter injection to inject, via DI, an instance of the `ChangePubDateService` class. The same line is also in the POST version of the `ChangePubDate` action.

Note that the `ChangePubDateService` class needs the `EfCoreContext` class that's the application's DbContext, in its constructor. That's fine because DI is recursive; it'll keep filling in parameters, or other DI injections, as long as each class that's needed has been registered.

> **NOTE** I've changed the `AdminController` in the Git repo for branch Chapter05 to use parameter injection for every command in that controller. You can compare this with the same code in the Chapter04 branch, which uses constructor injection.

5.7.3 *Improving registering your database access classes as services*

Before leaving the topic of DI, I want to introduce a better way of registering your classes as services via DI. The previous example, in which you made your `ChangePubDateService` class into a service, needed you to add code to register that class as a service in ASP.NET

Core's `ConfigureServices`. This works, but it's time-consuming and error-prone, as you need to add a line of code to register each class that you want to use as a service.

You can use a more comprehensive DI library, called Autofac (http://docs.autofac.org), which can enhance ASP.NET Core's DI feature. I've used Autofac for years, and one command makes my life easier: Autofac's `RegisterAssemblyTypes` method. This command will look through a project, which in .NET is known as an *assembly*, and register each class against its interface.

HOW TO UPGRADE ASP.NET CORE'S DI FEATURE WITH THE AUTOFAC NUGET PACKAGE

Upgrading ASP.NET Core's DI to Autofac and swapping over to automatic registration of your classes as services requires three steps:

1 Install the NuGet package Autofac.Extensions.DependencyInjection in both the ASP.NET Core project, called EfCoreInAction, and into the ServiceLayer project in our book app. This is done using the NuGet Package Manager in Visual Studio.

2 Create a small class in the service layer, called `MyAutoFacModule`, which contains the Autofac commands. This will register all your classes in the service layer that you want to become DI accessible services.

3 Change over the `ConfigureServices` method in ASP.NET Core's `Startup` class to using the Autofac DI provider rather than the standard, ASP.NET Core, DI provider. That allows you to use your `MyAutoFacModule` class to register all the classes in your service layer that you want to become services that can be injected via DI.

The following listing shows your `MyAutoFacModule` class, which uses Autofac's `RegisterAssemblyTypes` method to scan the service layer assembly and register every class whose name ends with `Service` and has an interface.

Listing 5.7   `AutoFacModule` class tells Autofac how to find the classes to register

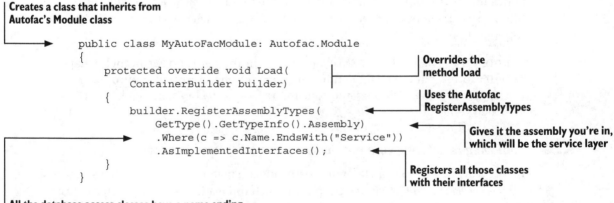

Creates a class that inherits from
Autofac's Module class

```
public class MyAutoFacModule: Autofac.Module
{
    protected override void Load(                      // Overrides the
        ContainerBuilder builder)                      //   method load
    {
        builder.RegisterAssemblyTypes(                 // Uses the Autofac
            GetType().GetTypeInfo().Assembly)          //   RegisterAssemblyTypes
            .Where(c => c.Name.EndsWith("Service"))    // Gives it the assembly you're in,
            .AsImplementedInterfaces();                //   which will be the service layer
    }                                                  // Registers all those classes
}                                                      //   with their interfaces
```

All the database access classes have a name ending
in "Service", so you only pick those

The third step is to replace ASP.NET Core's built-in DI container with the Autofac DI provider. This allows you to use Autofac's more powerful registering services, such as its `RegisterAssemblyTypes` method shown in listing 5.7. The following listing shows the updated class, with code changes in bold. Note that you can remove your hand-coded registration of your `ChangePubDateService`, shown in listing 5.5, because Autofac now finds and registers that service via your `MyAutoFacModule` class.

> **Listing 5.8** `ConfigureServices` **method that uses Autofac to register your classes**

Uses your **MyAutoFacModule** class
to register everything that you want
as a service in the ServiceLayer

```
public IServiceProvider ConfigureServices
    (IServiceCollection services)
{
    // Add framework services.
    services.AddMvc();
    var connection = Configuration
        .GetConnectionString("DefaultConnection");
    services.AddDbContext<EfCoreContext>(
        options => options.UseSqlServer(connection,
        b => b.MigrationsAssembly("DataLayer")));

    // Add Autofac
    var containerBuilder = new ContainerBuilder();
    containerBuilder.RegisterModule
        <ServiceLayer.Utils.MyAutoFacModule>();
    containerBuilder.Populate(services);
    var container = containerBuilder.Build();
    return new AutofacServiceProvider(container);
}
```

You needed to change the method's return type from void to IServiceProvider.

Creates an Autofac container builder, which you use to add all the services to

Builds an Autofac IContainer, which holds all the services to be available via DI

Needed to add services that were added using a normal ASP.NET Core service-registering approach, such as AddMVC and AddDbContext

Uses this IContainer to create an alternative DI provider via Autofac

The result of making these changes is that the classes you wanted to create via DI are now automatically found, rather than needing to hand-code each registration. This is another way to make development quicker and less error-prone.

5.8 *Deploying an ASP.NET Core application with a database*

After developing your ASP.NET Core application with a database, at some point you'll want to copy it to a web server so others can use it. This is called *deploying* your application to a *host*. This section shows how to do this.

NOTE For more information on ASP.NET Core deployment, I recommend *ASP.NET Core in Action* by Andrew Lock (Manning, 2018), or Microsoft's online documentation at https://docs.microsoft.com/en-us/aspnet/core/publishing/.

5.8.1   *Knowing where the database is on the web server*

When you run your ASP.NET Core application locally during development, it accesses a database server on your development computer. This example uses Visual Studio, which runs on a Windows computer, and it comes with a local SQL server for development that's available via the reference (localdb)\mssqllocaldb. As explained in section 5.4.1, the connection string for that database is held in the appsettings.Development.json file.

When you deploy your application to a web server, Visual Studio will by default rebuild your application with the ASPNETCORE_ENVIRONMENT variable set to Production. This causes your application to try to load the appsetting.json file, followed by the appsettings.Production.json file. The appsettings.Production.json file is the place where you, or the publishing system, put the connection string for your host database.

> **TIP**   At startup, appsettings.Production.json is read last, and will override any setting with the same name in the appsetting.json file. Therefore, you can put your development connection string setting in the appsetting.json file if you want to, but best practice is to put it in the appsettings.Development.json file.

You'll use Visual Studio's Publish feature (right-click the ASP.NET Core project in the Solution Explorer view and select Publish), which allows you to manually set the connection string of your hosted database. When you publish your application, Visual Studio creates/updates the appsettings.Production.json file with that connection string you provided, and deploys that file with the application. On startup, the constructor of the ASP.NET Core's Startup class will read both files, and the appsettings.Production.json connection string will be used.

Most Windows hosting systems will provide you with a Visual Studio publish profile that you can import to the Publish feature. That makes setting up deployment much easier, as it not only details where the ASP.NET Core application should be written to, but also provides the connection string for the hosted database.

5.8.2   *Creating and migrating the database*

When your application and its database are running on a web server, the control over the database changes. On your development machine, you can do pretty much anything to the database, but after you deploy to a web server, the rules can change. Depending on the host, or your company's business rules, what you can do to the database will vary.

For example, the live version of our book app is hosted on a cost-effective (cheap!) shared hosting platform (WebWiz in the UK), and our application can't create or delete the database. I've also used Microsoft's Azure cloud system, on which I can delete and create a database, but creating a database takes a long time.

The simplest approach, which works on all the systems I've come across, is to get the hosting system to create an empty database and then apply the commands to alter the database structure. The easiest way to do that is via EF Core migrations, which I'm about to describe, but there are other ways.

Before I start, I need to warn you that changing the database structure of a website needs to be approached carefully, especially for 24/7 websites that need to keep working during a database change. Lots of things can go wrong, and the effect could be lost data or a broken website. This chapter describes EF Core migrations, which is a good system but has its limitations. Chapter 11 presents ways of handling database migrations, including more sophisticated techniques, and the pros and cons of each approach.

5.9 Using EF Core's Migrate to change the database structure

This section describes how to use EF Core's migration feature to update a database. You can use migrations on both your development machine and your host, but, as explained in the preceding section, the one that's the challenge is the database on your web host.

5.9.1 Updating your production database

As you may remember from chapter 2, which briefly introduced EF Core migrations, you can type two commands into Visual Studio's Package Manager Console (PMC):

- `Add-Migration`—Creates migration code in your application to create/update your database structure
- `Update-Database`—Applies the migration code to the database referred to by the application's DbContext

The first command is fine, but the second command will update only the default database, which is likely to be on your development machine, not your production database. What happens when you want to deploy your web application to some sort of web host, and the database isn't at the right level to match the code? There are three ways to update your production database if you're using EF Core's migration feature:

- You can have your application check and migrate the database during startup.
- You can have a standalone application migrate your database.
- You can extract the SQL commands needed to update your database and then use a tool to apply those SQL commands to your production database.

The simplest is the first option, which I'm going to describe here. It does have limitations—such as it's not designed to work in multiple-instance web hosting (called *scaling out* on Azure). But having the application do the migration is simple and is a good first step in using EF Core's migrations in an ASP.NET Core application.

> **WARNING** Microsoft recommends that you update a production database by using SQL commands, because that's the most robust approach. But that approach requires quite a few steps and tools you may not have on hand, so I cover the simpler `Database.Migrate` approach. Chapter 11 covers every aspect of database migrations, including the advantages and limitations of each approach.

5.9.2 *Having your application migrate your database on startup*

The advantage of having your application apply any outstanding database migrations at startup is you can't forget to do it: deploying a new application will stop the old application and then start the new application. By adding code that's run when the application starts, you can call the `context.Database.Migrate` method, which applies any missing migrations to the database. Simple, until it goes wrong, which is why I have a whole chapter dedicated to database migrations that discusses all these issues. But for now, let's keep to the simple approach.

Having decided to apply the migration on startup, you need to decide where to call your migration code. The recommended approach to adding any startup code to an ASP.NET Core application is to append your code to the end of the `BuildWebHost` method in ASP.NET Core's `Program` class. By appending your code after the ASP.NET Core setup has run, you have access to all the services that have been configured.

> **NOTE** The `Program` class file, with its `public static void Main(string[] args)` method, is the standard way of starting a .NET application.

The best way to do this is to build an extension method holding the EF Core code you want to run and appending it after the `Build` method call. The following listing shows the ASP.NET Core's `Program` class with one new line (in bold) added to call your extension method called `MigrateDatabase`.

Listing 5.9   ASP.NET Core `Program` class, including a method to migrate the database

```
public class Program
{

    public static void Main(string[] args)
    {
        BuildWebHost(args).Run();
    }

    public static IWebHost BuildWebHost(string[] args) =>
        WebHost.CreateDefaultBuilder(args)
            .UseStartup<Startup>()          The recommended way to run startup code
            .Build()                        is to add it to the end of the BuildWebHost
            .MigrateDatabase();             in the ASP.NET Core Program file.
}
```

The `MigrateDatabase` method should contain all the code you want to run at startup in order to migrate, and possibly seed, your database. This listing shows one example of how you might use this method to migrate your database.

Listing 5.10   The `MigrateDatabase` extension method to migrate the database

Creates an extension method that takes in
IWebHost and returns IWebHost. You can chain
multiple startup code blocks, each of which can
access the services set up by ASP.NET Core.

Creates a scoped service provider. After the using
block is left, all the services will be unavailable. This
is the recommended way to obtain services outside
an HTTP request.

```
public static IWebHost MigrateDatabase
    (this IWebHost webHost)
{
    using (var scope = webHost.Services.CreateScope())
    {
        var services = scope.ServiceProvider;
        using (var context = services
            .GetRequiredService<EfCoreContext>())
        {
            try
            {
                context.Database.Migrate();
                //Possible seed database here
            }
            catch (Exception ex)
            {
                var logger = services
                    .GetRequiredService<ILogger<Program>>();
                logger.LogError(ex,
                "An error occurred while migrating the database.");

                throw;
            }
        }
    }

    return webHost;
}
```

Creates an instance of the
application's DbContext that
has a lifetime of only the outer
using statement

Calls EF Core's Migrate command to apply
any outstanding migrations at startup

You can add a method here to
seed the database if required

If an exception occurs,
you log the information
so you can diagnose it.

Rethrows the exception because you don't want
the application to carry on if a problem occurs
with migrating the database

Returns the IWebHost so that if there's additional
code to run at startup, it can be chained behind this
extension

The series of calls at the start of the listing is the recommended way to get a copy of the application's DbContext inside the `Configure` method in the ASP.NET Core `Startup` class. This code creates a *scoped* lifetime instance (see section 5.3.3) of the DbContext that can be safely used to access the database.

The key commands in listing 5.10, inside the `try` block (in bold), call EF Core's `Migrate` command. This applies any database migration that exists but hasn't already been applied to the database. Optionally, you may want to follow the migration code with any code to seed the database, which I cover next.

EF6 The EF Core approach to database setup is different from that of EF6.x. On first use of the DbContext, EF6.x runs various checks by using *database initializers,* whereas EF Core does nothing at all to the database. Therefore, you need to add your own code to handle migrations. The downside is you need to write some code, but that gives you total control of what happens.

SETTING UP INITIAL DATABASE CONTENT DURING STARTUP

In addition to migrating the database, you may want to add default data to the database at the same time, especially if it's empty. This is called *seeding* the database and covers adding initial data to the database, or maybe updating data in an existing database. In EF Core 2.1 and above you'll be able to seed via the database migrations route, but for now you're going seed via code you call at startup.

In our book app, you want to add a default set of books if there aren't books already in the database. To do this, you create an extension method, SeedDatabase, which is shown in the following listing. This code is added after the call to the Database.Migrate method in listing 5.10.

> **Listing 5.11   Our example `MigrateAndSeed` extension method**

```
public static void SeedDatabase
    (this EfCoreContext context)
{
    if (context.Books.Any()) return;

    context.Books.AddRange(
        EfTestData.CreateFourBooks());
    context.SaveChanges();
}
```

Extension method that takes in the application's DbContext

If there are existing books, you return, as you don't need to add any.

Database has no books, so you seed it; in this case, you add the default books.

In this example SeedDatabase method, you check whether any books are in the database and then add them only if it's empty (for instance, if the database has just been created). You can do more-complex checks and updates.

If you want to run your seed database method only when a new migration has been applied, you can use the DbContext method Database.GetPendingMigrations to get the list of migrations that are about to be applied. You must call GetPendingMigrations before you execute the Database.Migrate method, because the pending migration is empty after the Migrate method has finished.

EF6 In EF6.x, the Add-Migration command adds a class called Configuration, which contains a method called Seed that's run every time the application starts. EF Core doesn't have that class, and you can either use the procedure described in the preceding text or, when EF Core 2.1 is out, use its new data-seeding feature.

5.10   Using async/await for better scalability

Async/await is a feature that allows a developer to easily use *asynchronous programming,* running tasks in parallel. Async/await is a big topic, but in this section, you'll look only at how using async/await can benefit an ASP.NET Core's application scalability. It does this by releasing resources while waiting for the database server to carry out the command(s) that EF Core has asked it to do.

> **NOTE**   If you want to find out more about async/await's other features, such as running tasks in parallel, have a look at the Microsoft documentation at https://msdn.microsoft.com/en-gb/library/mt674882.aspx.

5.10.1   Why async/await is useful in a web application using EF Core

When EF Core accesses the database, it needs to wait for the database server to run the commands and return the result. For large datasets and/or complex queries, this can take hundreds of milliseconds. During that time, a web application is holding onto a *thread* from the application's *thread pool.* Each access to the web application needs a thread from the thread pool, and there's an upper limit.

Using an async/await form of an EF Core command means that during the time that EF Core is waiting for the database server to respond, it releases its thread for someone else to use. Figure 5.7 shows two cases. In case A, two users are simultaneously accessing the website by using normal synchronous accesses and they clash, so two threads are needed from the thread pool. In case B, user 1's access is a long-running database access that uses an async command to release the thread while it's waiting for the database. This allows user 2 to reuse the thread that the async command has released while user 2 is waiting for the database.

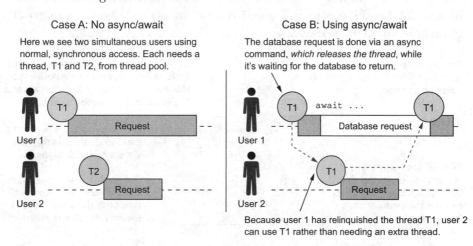

Case A: No async/await

Here we see two simultaneous users using normal, synchronous access. Each needs a thread, T1 and T2, from thread pool.

Case B: Using async/await

The database request is done via an async command, *which releases the thread,* while it's waiting for the database to return.

Because user 1 has relinquished the thread T1, user 2 can use T1 rather than needing an extra thread.

Figure 5.7   Differences in database access. In the normal, synchronous database access in case A, two threads are needed to handle the two users. In case B, user 1's database access is accomplished with an async command, which frees up the thread, T1, making it available for user 2.

> **NOTE**   You can read a more in-depth explanation of what async/await does in an ASP.NET web application at https://msdn.microsoft.com/en-gb/magazine/dn802603.aspx.

The use of async/await improves the scalability of your website: your web server will be able to handle more concurrent users. The downside is that async/await commands take longer to execute, because they run more code. A bit of analysis is needed here to get the right balance of scalability and performance.

5.10.2 Where should you use async/await with database accesses?

The general advice from Microsoft is to use async methods wherever possible in a web application because that gives you better scalability. That's good advice, but you should be aware that, in general, async EF Core commands take slightly longer than the equivalent synchronous (sync) commands because of the extra code to handle the threading.

In summary, the speed difference is small, so sticking to Microsoft's "always use async commands in ASP.NET applications" is a good rule. But if your application is lacking in speed on some commands, you may have a case for swapping to normal, synchronous database access methods. Chapter 12 covers the trade-off between the scalability and speed of using async database methods (see section 12.7).

> **NOTE**   I wrote an article some time ago covering, in more detail, async/await and its features, scalability, and speed issues. You can find it at http://mng.bz/13b6.

5.10.3 Changing over to async/await versions of EF Core commands

Let me start by showing you a method that calls an async version of an EF Core command, and then I'll explain it. Figure 5.8 shows an async method that returns the total number of books in the database.

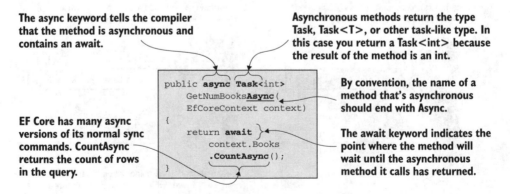

The async keyword tells the compiler that the method is asynchronous and contains an await.

Asynchronous methods return the type Task, Task<T>, or other task-like type. In this case you return a Task<int> because the result of the method is an int.

By convention, the name of a method that's asynchronous should end with Async.

EF Core has many async versions of its normal sync commands. CountAsync returns the count of rows in the query.

The await keyword indicates the point where the method will wait until the asynchronous method it calls has returned.

```
public async Task<int>
    GetNumBooksAsync(
    EfCoreContext context)
{
    return await
        context.Books
    .CountAsync();
}
```

Figure 5.8   The anatomy of an asynchronous method, highlighting the parts of the code that are different from a normal synchronous method

EF Core contains an async version of most of its commands, which all have a method name that ends with the string `Async`. As you saw in the preceding async method example, you then need to carry the "async-ness" to the method in which you call the async EF Core command.

The rule is, after you use an async command, every caller must either be an async method or should pass on the task directly until it gets to the top-level caller, which must handle it asynchronously. ASP.NET Core supports async for all the main commands, such as controller actions, so this isn't a problem in such an application.

The next listing shows an async version of your `Index` action method from your `HomeController`, with the parts you have to change to make this command use an async database access, with the async parts in bold.

> **Listing 5.12   The async `Index` action method from the `HomeController`**

```
public async Task<IActionResult> Index
    (SortFilterPageOptions options)
{
    var listService =
        new ListBooksService(_context);

    var bookList = await listService
        .SortFilterPage(options)
        .ToListAsync();

    return View(new BookListCombinedDto
        (options, bookList));
}
```

You have to make the Index action method async by using the async keyword, and the returned type has to be wrapped in a generic task.

You have to await the result of the ToListAsync method, which is an async command.

You can change SortFilterPage to async by replacing .ToList() with .ToListAsync().

Because you design your `SortFilterPage` method to return `IQueryable<T>`, it's simple to change database access to async by replacing the `ToList` method with the `ToListAsync` method.

> **TIP**   Business logic code is often a good candidate for using async databases' access methods because their database accesses often contain complex read/ write commands. I've created async versions of the BizRunners in case you need them. You can find them in the service layer in the BizRunners directory (see http://mng.bz/53Dw).

5.11   Running parallel tasks: how to provide the DbContext

In some situations, running more than one thread of code is useful. By this, I mean running a separate *task*—a parallel set of code that runs "at the same time" as the main application. I put "at the same time" in quotes because if there's only one CPU, the two tasks need to share it.

Parallel tasks are useful in various scenarios. Say you're accessing multiple, external sources that you need to wait for before they return a result. By using multiple tasks running in parallel, you gain performance improvements. In another scenario, you might have a long-running task, such as processing an order fulfillment. You use parallel tasks to avoid blocking the normal flow and making your website look slow and unresponsive. Figure 5.9 shows this background task example.

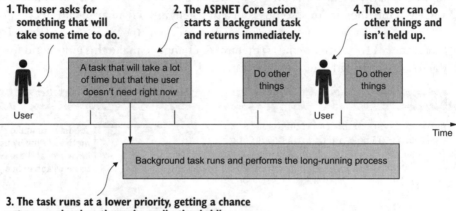

Figure 5.9   Moving long-running processes to a background task that runs in parallel to the main website. This makes the website feel more responsive.

Running parallel tasks isn't specific to ASP.NET Core; it can occur in any application. But larger web applications often use this feature, so I explain it in this chapter. The solution I show, which uses DI, might not be relevant in all applications, so I also show other approaches at the end of this section.

There're lots of options and features around running tasks that I don't cover here. What we're interested in is, if your background task wants to use EF Core to access the database, how do you get an instance of the application's DbContext? DbContext isn't thread-safe—you can't use the same instance in multiple tasks. EF Core will throw an exception if it finds that the same DbContext instance is used in two tasks. You therefore need to create unique instances of the application's DbContext for each task.

In ASP.NET Core, the correct way to get a DbContext is by using a DI scoped service. This scoped service allows you to create, via DI, a DbContext that's unique to the task that you're running. To do this, you need to do four things:

1 Get a copy of the DI service provider.
2 Use the DI service provider to produce a *service scope factory*.
3 Use the service scope factory to create a *scoped DI service*, which you pass to your task.
4 Inside your task, you use the scoped DI service that was passed to get an instance of the application's DbContext.

The following listing covers step 1. You get the DI service provider via constructor injection into your `AdminController`, which is where you want to run two tasks in parallel.

Listing 5.13   Getting an instance of the DI service provider via constructor injection

```
private readonly IServiceProvider _serviceProvider;
```
← Holds a local reference of the DI service provider

```
public AdminController(
    IServiceProvider serviceProvider)
```
← Uses constructor injection to get the service provider

```
{
    _serviceProvider = serviceProvider;
}
```
← Copies the instance provided by DI into your private field

In this example, you're going to run two tasks in parallel. I use this example because this is something that you may want to do if you were trying to access multiple RESTful services at the same time: doing that in parallel means it takes only as long as the longest one, rather than the sum of all the accesses. The following listing shows a simple example of running two tasks from an ASP.NET Core action method in the `AdminController`, where it can get access to the `serviceProvider` field.

Listing 5.14   How to run two tasks in parallel that need to access the database

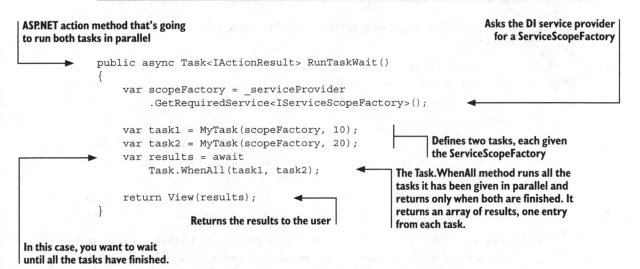

ASP.NET action method that's going to run both tasks in parallel

Asks the DI service provider for a ServiceScopeFactory

```
public async Task<IActionResult> RunTaskWait()
{
    var scopeFactory = _serviceProvider
        .GetRequiredService<IServiceScopeFactory>();

    var task1 = MyTask(scopeFactory, 10);
    var task2 = MyTask(scopeFactory, 20);
    var results = await
        Task.WhenAll(task1, task2);

    return View(results);
}
```

Defines two tasks, each given the ServiceScopeFactory

The Task.WhenAll method runs all the tasks it has been given in parallel and returns only when both are finished. It returns an array of results, one entry from each task.

Returns the results to the user

In this case, you want to wait until all the tasks have finished.

The important point from the code is that you provide `ServiceScopeFactory` to each task, so that it can use DI to get an instance of the DbContext (and any other service that has been registered).

The following listing shows the `MyTask` method that needs an instance of the application's DbContext because it accesses the database to count the number of books.

Listing 5.15   An example of a task needing an instance of the application's DbContext

```
private async Task<int> MyTask
    (IServiceScopeFactory scopeFactory,          Passes in the service scope factory, which
    int waitMilliseconds)                         allows you to create a private scope
{
    using (var serviceScope =
        scopeFactory.CreateScope())               You've created your own service scope. Services will
    using (var context =                          last only until the disposal of your service scope.
        serviceScope.ServiceProvider
        .GetService<EfCoreContext>())             Now you can ask the service provider to create
    {                                             a local instance of the application's DbContext.

                    await Task.Delay(waitMilliseconds);
                    await context.Books.CountAsync();     Uses the local application's
    }                                                      DbContext to read the database
}
```

Calls a delay to simulate work

Here you first create a *scoped service*, a way to called the DI such that it creates instances that exist only until the scoped service is disposed of. Once you have the scoped service, you can call the service provider, which handles the creation of DI services, to get the service you want—in this case, the application's DbContext. After you have that, you can get on with your code—in this case, asking the database for the number of books by using an async method, CountAsync, but you could've used the synchronous method Count.

5.11.1 Other ways of obtaining a new instance of the application's DbContext

Although DI is the recommended method to get the application's DbContext, in some cases, such as a console application, DI may not be configured or available. In these cases, you have two other options that allow you to obtain an instance of the application's DbContext:

- Move your configuration of the application's DbContext by overriding the OnConfiguring method in the DbContext and placing the code to set up the DbContext there.
- Use the same constructor used for ASP.NET Core and manually inject the database options and connection string. This is what you do in unit tests (see chapter 15).

The downside of both approaches is that they use a fixed connection string, so it always accesses the same database, which could make deployment to another system difficult if the database name or options change. The second option, manually providing the database options, allows you to read in a connection string from a file inside your code.

Another issue to be aware of is that each call will give you a new instance of the application's DbContext. From the discussions of lifetime scopes in section 5.3.3, at times you might want to have the same instance of the application's DbContext to ensure that tracking changes works. You can work around this issue by designing your application so that one instance of the application's DbContext is passed between all the code that needs to collaborate on database updates.

Summary

- ASP.NET Core uses dependency injection (DI) to provide the application's DbContext. DI is a feature that allows you to dynamically link parts of your application by letting DI create class instances as required.

- The `ConfigureServices` method ASP.NET Core `Startup` class is the place to configure and register your version of the application's DbContext by using a connection string that you place in an ASP.NET Core application setting file.

- To get an instance of the application's DbContext to use with your code via DI, you can use constructor injection. DI will look at the type of each of the constructor's parameters and attempt to find a service for which it can provide an instance.

- Your database access code can be built as a service and registered with the DI. You can then inject your services into the ASP.NET Core action methods via parameter injection: the DI will find a service that finds the type of an ASP.NET Core action method's parameter that's marked with the attribute `[FromServices]`.

- Deploying an ASP.NET Core application that uses a database requires you to define a database connection string that has the location and name of the database on the host.

- EF Core's migration feature provides one way to change your database if your entity classes and/or the EF Core configuration changes. The `Migrate` method has some limitations when used on cloud hosting sites that run multiple instances of your web application.

- Async/await tasking methods on database access code can make your website handle more simultaneous users, but performance could suffer, especially on simple database accesses.

- If you want to use parallel tasks, you need to provide a unique, scoped instance of the application's DbContext.

For readers who are familiar with EF6.x:

- The way you obtain an instance of the application's DbContext in ASP.NET Core is via DI.

- As compared to EF6.x, EF Core has a different approach to creating the first instance of a DbContext. EF6.x has database initializers and can run a `Seed` method. EF Core has none of these, but leaves you to write the specific code you want to run at startup.

- EF Core migrations don't create a `Configuration` class with a `Seed` method. If you want to seed the database, you write your own `Seed` code and call it in the `Configure` method in ASP.NET Core's `Startup` class, or manually via an admin page.

Part 2

Entity Framework in depth

Part 1 showed how you might build an application by using EF Core. Part 2 covers how to configure EF Core exactly the way you need it, and introduces you to advanced features that can make your software more efficient in both development and performance terms. Part 2 is more of a reference section that covers each part of EF Core in detail, but hopefully not in a boring way.

Chapter 6 introduces the way that EF Core configures itself when it's first used so that you know where and how to apply any of your own EF Core configurations. The chapter focuses on nonrelational properties, with types such as `int`, `string`, and `DateTime`. If you need to link to an existing database, this chapter tells you how to set specific table and column names.

Chapter 7 shows how EF Core finds and configures relationships. EF Core does a good job of configuring most relationships for you, but it does need help on some, and you'll want to configure others because EF Core's default settings don't suit your needs. You'll also look at handling groups of classes that inherit from each other and learn useful features of EF Core implementations.

Chapter 8 covers more-advanced configurable features, such as defining computed columns in your database and catching and handling concurrent updates of the database. You'll use these features in only certain circumstances, but you should know they're there in case you need them.

Chapter 9 looks at methods inside the EF Core's `DbContext` class, especially how `SaveChanges` works out what to write to the database and how you can influence that. This chapter covers other diverse topics such as raw SQL access to the database, database connection resiliency, and the DbContext's `Model` property.

Configuring nonrelational properties

This chapter covers

- Configuring EF Core
- Focusing on nonrelational properties
- Defining the database structure
- Using shadow properties and backing fields

This chapter is the first of three that look at configuring EF Core, and it concentrates on configuring the nonrelational properties in an entity class, known as *scalar properties*. Chapter 7 covers configuring relational properties, and chapter 8 covers configuring more advanced features, such as DbFunctions, computed columns, and so on.

This chapter starts with an overview of the configuration process that EF Core runs when the application's DbContext is used for the first time. You'll then learn how to configure the mapping between the .NET classes and their associated database tables, with features such as setting the name, SQL type, and nullability of the columns in a table.

This chapter also introduces two EF Core features—*shadow properties* and *backing fields*—that enable you to control how the data is exposed to the rest of your non-EF Core code. For instance, these features allow you to "hide," or control access to, data linked to your database. These two features can help you write better, less fragile applications through better control of the developer's access to the data held in the entity class.

6.1 *Three ways of configuring EF Core*

Chapter 1 covered how EF Core models the database and presented a figure to show what EF Core is doing, with the focus on the database. Figure 6.1 has a more detailed depiction of the configuration process that happens the first time you use the application's DbContext. This figure shows the entire process, with the three configuration approaches: By Convention, Data Annotation, and the Fluent API. This example focuses on the configuration of scalar properties, but the process is the same for all configurations of EF Core.

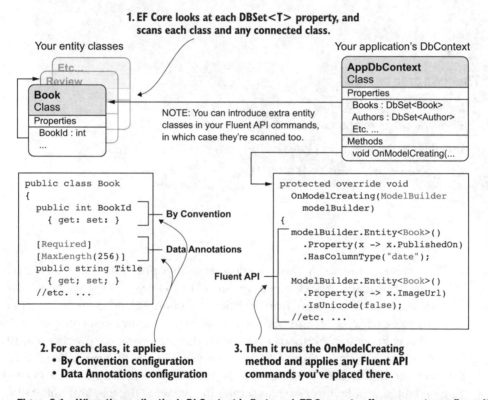

Figure 6.1   When the application's DbContext is first used, EF Core sets off a process to configure itself and build a model of the database it's supposed to access. You can use three approaches to configure EF Core: By Convention, Data Annotations, and Fluent API. Most real applications need a mixture of all three approaches to configure EF Core in exactly the way your application needs.

This list summarizes the three approaches to configuring EF Core:

- *By Convention*—When you follow simple rules on property types and names, EF Core will autoconfigure many of the software and database features. Using the By Convention approach is quick and easy, but it can't handle every eventuality.
- *Data Annotations*—A range of .NET attributes, known as *Data Annotations*, can be added to entity classes and/or properties to provide extra configuration information. These can also be useful for data validation, covered in chapter 4.
- *Fluent API*—EF Core has a method called `OnModelCreating` that's run when the EF context is first used. You can override this method and add commands, known as the Fluent API, to provide extra information to EF Core in its modeling stage. The Fluent API is the most comprehensive form of configuration information, and some features are available only via the Fluent API.

NOTE Most real applications need to use all three approaches to configure EF Core and the database in exactly the way they need. Some configuration features are available via two or even all three approaches (for instance, defining the primary key in an entity class). Section 6.12 gives you my recommendations on which approach to use for certain features.

6.2 A worked example of configuring EF Core

For anything beyond a Hello World version of using EF Core, you're likely to need some form of Data Annotations or Fluent API configuration. In part 1, you needed to set up the key for the many-to-many link table. In this chapter, you'll see an example of applying the three configuration approaches introduced in section 6.1 to better match the database to the needs of our book app.

In this example, you're going to remodel the `Book` entity class used in chapters 2 to 5 and change the size and type of some of the columns from the defaults that EF Core uses. These changes make your database smaller, make sorting or searching on some columns faster, and check that some columns aren't `null`. It's always good practice to define the correct size, type, and nullability for your database columns based on the business needs.

To do this, you'll use a combination of all three configuration approaches. The By Convention configuration has a major part to play, as it defines the table and column names, but you'll add specific Data Annotations and Fluent API configuration methods to change a few of the columns from the default By Convention settings. Figure 6.2 shows how each configuration approach affects the database table structure. Because of space limitations, the figure doesn't show all the Data Annotations and Fluent API configuration methods applied to the table, but you can see these in listings 6.1 and 6.2, respectively.

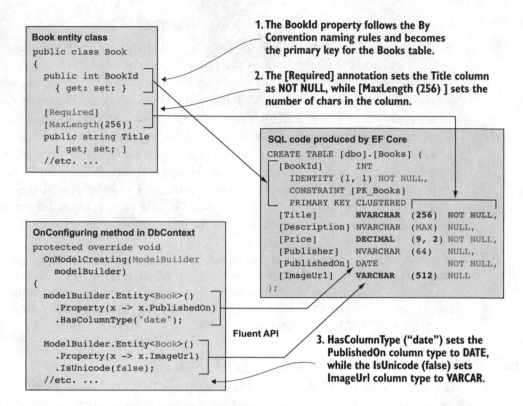

Figure 6.2   **To configure the Books table in the exact format you want, you must use all three configuration approaches. A large part is done by convention (all the parts not in bold), but you then use Data Annotations to set the size and nullability of the Title column, and the Fluent API to change the type of the `PublishedOn` and `ImageUrl` columns.**

These changes to the database table are ones you'd want to make in a real project. Here's why they're useful:

- Telling EF Core that the `Title` can't be null means the database will return an error if you try to insert/update a book with a null title.
- Having fixed-length strings of the right type, 2-byte Unicode or 1-byte ASCII, makes the database access slightly more efficient and allows an *SQL index* to be applied to these fixed-size columns.

DEFINITION   An *SQL index* is a feature that improves the performance of sorting and searching. Section 6.10 covers this in more detail.

- You don't need a book `Price` that could go up to 10^{16} dollars (the default size), so you set a precision of 10^7, which reduces the size of the `Price` from 8 bytes to its smallest storage size of 5 bytes.

- The same goes for the PublishedOn property: making it hold only the date, which is all you need, rather than the default datetime2. This reduces the column size from 8 bytes to 3 bytes, and makes searching and sorting on the PublishedOn column faster.

This listing shows you the updated Book entity class code, with the new Data Annotations in bold (the Fluent API commands are shown later in the chapter).

Listing 6.1   The Book entity class with added Data Annotations

```
public class Book
{
    public int BookId { get; set; }

    [Required]
    [MaxLength(256)]
    public string Title { get; set; }
    public string Description { get; set; }
    public DateTime PublishedOn { get; set; }
    [MaxLength(64)]
    public string Publisher { get; set; }
    public decimal Price { get; set; }

    [MaxLength(512)]
    public string ImageUrl { get; set; }
    public bool SoftDeleted { get; set; }

    //-----------------------------------------------
    //relationships

    public PriceOffer Promotion { get; set; }
    public ICollection<Review> Reviews { get; set; }
    public ICollection<BookAuthor>
        AuthorsLink { get; set; }
}
```

Tells EF Core that the string is non-nullable

Defines the size of the string column in the database

TIP You'd normally set the size parameter in the [MaxLength(nn)] attribute by using a constant so that if you create a DTO, it will use the same constant. If you change the size of one property, that changes all the associated properties.

Now that you've seen an example that uses all three configuration approaches, let's explore each approach in detail.

6.3   *Configuring By Convention*

By Convention is the default configuration and can be overridden by the other two approaches, Data Annotations and the Fluent API. The By Convention approach relies on the developer using the By Convention naming standards and type mappings, which then allow EF Core to find and configure entity classes and their relationships as well as define much of the database model. This approach provides a quick way to configure much of your database mapping, so it's worth learning.

6.3.1 Conventions for entity classes

Classes that EF Core maps to the database are called *entity classes*. As stated in chapter 2, entity classes are normal .NET classes, sometimes referred to as POCOS (plain old CLR objects). EF Core requires entity classes to have the following features:

- The class must be of public access: the keyword `public` should be before the class.
- The class can't be a `static` class, as EF Core must be able to create a new instance of the class.
- The class should have no constructor or should have a parameterless constructor, which can have any accessibly level of access, including private. The class can be created without any parameters being required.

NOTE EF Core 2.1 adds a new feature in which an entity class's constructor can have parameters. Another EF Core 2.1 new feature, lazy loading, needs a method provided via the entity class's constructor. In addition, having a constructor with parameters allows you to provide value properties and inject services into an entity being read in. Please see appendix B for more information.

6.3.2 Conventions for parameters in an entity class

By convention, EF Core will look for properties in an entity class that have a `public` access, a `public` getter, and a setter of any access mode (`public`, `internal`, `protected`, or `private`). The typical, all-public property is

```
public int MyProp { get; set; }
```

Although the all-`public` property is the norm, in some places having a property with a more localized access setting (for instance, `public int MyProp { get; private set; }`) allows you more control (see section 10.4 for more on this). You can control how it's set, via a method in the entity class that also does some checks before setting the property.

6.3.3 Conventions for name, type, and size

The rules for name, type, and size of a relational column are the following:

- The name of the property is used as the name of the column in the table.
- The .NET type is translated by the database provider to the corresponding SQL type. Many basic .NET types have a one-to-one mapping to a corresponding database type. These basic .NET types are mostly .NET *primitive* types (for example, `int`, `bool`, and so on), with some special cases (for example, `string`, `DateTime`, `Guid`).

EF6 One change in the default mapping conventions is that EF Core maps a .NET `DateTime` type to SQL `datetime2(7)`, whereas EF6 maps .NET `DateTime` to SQL `datetime`.

6.3.4   By Convention, the nullability of a property is based on .NET type

In relational databases, NULL represents missing or unknown data. Whether a column can be NULL is defined by the .NET type:

- If the type is string, the column can be NULL, because a string can be null.
- Primitive types (for instance, int) or struct types (for instance, DateTime) are, by default, non-null.
- Primitive or struct types can be made nullable by using either the ? suffix (for instance, int?) or the generic Nullable<T> (for instance, Nullable<int>). In these cases, the column can be NULL.

Figure 6.3 shows the application of the name, type, size, and nullability conventions applied to a property.

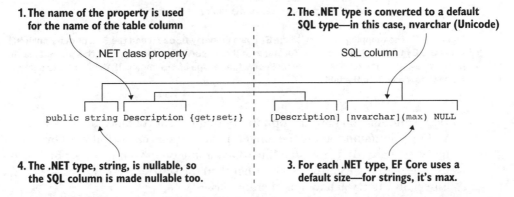

1. The name of the property is used for the name of the table column

2. The .NET type is converted to a default SQL type—in this case, nvarchar (Unicode)

.NET class property

SQL column

```
public string Description {get;set;}     [Description] [nvarchar](max) NULL
```

4. The .NET type, string, is nullable, so the SQL column is made nullable too.

3. For each .NET type, EF Core uses a default size—for strings, it's max.

Figure 6.3   The application of the By Convention rules to define an SQL column. The type of the property is converted by the database provider to the equivalent SQL type, whereas the name of the property is used for the name of the column.

6.3.5   An EF Core naming convention identifies primary keys

The other rule is about defining the database table's primary key. The EF Core conventions for designating a primary key are as follows:

- EF Core expects one primary-key property (the By Convention approach doesn't handle keys made up of multiple properties/columns, called *composite keys*).
- The property is called Id or <class name>id (for instance, BookId).
- The type of the property defines what assigns a unique value to the key. Chapter 8 covers key generation. Figure 6.4 is an example of a database-generated primary key.

This shows the primary-key By Convention mapping between the .NET class and the SQL column.

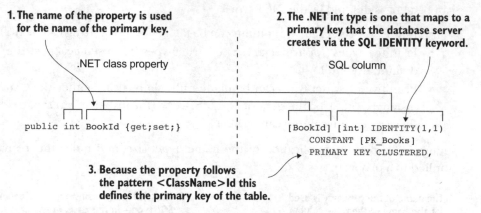

Figure 6.4   The mapping between the .NET class property `BookId` and the SQL primary column `BookId` using the By Convention approach. The name of the property tells EF Core that this property is the primary key. Also, the database provider knows that a type of `int` means it should create a unique value for each row added to the table.

TIP   Although you have the option of using the short name, `Id`, for a primary key, I recommend you use the longer name: `<class name>` followed by `Id` (for instance, `BookId`). Understanding what's going on in your code is easier if you use `Where(p => BookId == 1)` rather than the shorter `Where(p => Id == 1)`, especially when you have lots of entity classes.

6.4   *Configuring via Data Annotations*

Data Annotations are a specific type of .NET attribute used for validation and database features. These attributes can be applied to an entity class or property and provide configuration information to EF Core. This section introduces where you can find them and how they're typically applied. The Data Annotation attributes that are relevant to EF Core configuration come from two namespaces.

6.4.1   *System.ComponentModel.DataAnnotations*

The attributes in the `System.ComponentModel.DataAnnotations` namespace are mainly used for data validation at the frontend, such as ASP.NET, but EF Core uses some of them for creating the mapping model. Attributes such as `[Required]` and `[MaxLength]` are the main ones, with many of the other Data Annotations having no effect on EF Core. Figure 6.5 shows how the main attributes, `[Required]` and `[MaxLength]`, affect the database column definition.

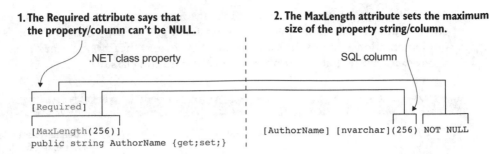

Figure 6.5 The `[Required]` and `[MaxLength]` attributes affect the mapping to a database column. The `[Required]` attribute indicates that the column shouldn't be `null`, and the `[MaxLength]` attribute sets the size of the `nvarchar`.

6.4.2 *System.ComponentModel.DataAnnotations.Schema*

The attributes in the `System.ComponentModel.DataAnnotations.Schema` namespace are more specific to database configuration, with attributes such as `[Table]`, `[Column]`, and so on, that set the table name and column name/type, as described in section 6.11. Other attributes are in this namespace, such as `[DatabaseGenerated]`, which I cover in chapter 9.

6.5 *Configuring via the Fluent API*

The third approach to configuring EF Core, called the *Fluent API*, is a set of methods that works on the `ModelBuilder` class that's available in the `OnModelCreating` method inside your application's DbContext. The Fluent API provides the most comprehensive list of configuration commands, with many configurations available only via the Fluent API.

But before defining the Fluent API relationship commands, I want to introduce a different way of applying the Fluent API to your application's DbContext.

6.5.1 *A better way to structure your Fluent API commands*

You can place all the Fluent API commands inside the `OnModelCreating` method (as shown in figure 2.6). But as your application grows, and you need to add more Fluent API configuration code, this can become unwieldy. The answer is to move the Fluent API for an entity class into a separate configuration class that's then called from the `OnModelCreating` method. The benefit of this approach is that the Fluent API for an entity class is all in one place, and not mixed in with Fluent API commands for other entity classes.

EF Core provides a method to facilitate this in the shape of the `IEntityType-Configuration<T>` interface. Listing 6.2 shows your new application DbContext, `EfCoreContext`, where you move the Fluent API setup of the various classes into separate configuration classes.

EF6 EF6.x has an `EntityTypeConfiguration<T>` class you can inherit to encapsulate the Fluent API configuration for a given entity class. EF Core's implementation achieves the same result, but uses an `IEntityTypeConfigura-tion<T>` interface that you apply to your configuration class.

Listing 6.2   Application's DbContext for database with relationships

```
public class EfCoreContext : DbContext
{
    public DbSet<Book> Books { get; set; }
    public DbSet<Author> Authors { get; set; }
    public DbSet<PriceOffer> PriceOffers { get; set; }
    public DbSet<Order> Orders { get; set; }

    public EfCoreContext(
        DbContextOptions<EfCoreContext> options)
        : base(options) {}

    protected override void
        OnModelCreating(ModelBuilder modelBuilder)
    {
        modelBuilder.ApplyConfiguration(new BookConfig());
        modelBuilder.ApplyConfiguration(new BookAuthorConfig());
        modelBuilder.ApplyConfiguration(new PriceOfferConfig());
        modelBuilder.ApplyConfiguration(new LineItemConfig());
    }
}
```

> **Defines four tables in the database: Books, Authors, PriceOffers, and Orders. The Review and BookAuthor tables are found via navigational links from the other tables.**

> **Moves the Fluent API configuration of various entity classes to separate configuration classes that implement the IEntityTypeConfiguration<T> interface**

The following listing shows an example of a configuration class that implements the `IEntityTypeConfiguration<T>` interface. In this example, the configuration class `BookConfig` contains the Fluent API methods for the `Book` entity class.

Listing 6.3   `BookConfig` extension class configures `Book` entity class

```
internal class BookConfig : IEntityTypeConfiguration<Book>
{
    public void Configure
        (EntityTypeBuilder<Book> entity)
    {
        entity.Property(p => p.PublishedOn)
            .HasColumnType("date");

        entity.Property(p => p.Price)
            .HasColumnType("decimal(9,2)");

        entity.Property(x => x.ImageUrl)
            .IsUnicode(false);

        entity.HasIndex(x => x.PublishedOn);
```

> **Convention-based mapping for .NET DateTime is SQL datetime2. This command changes the SQL column type to date, which holds only the date, not the time.**

> **The convention-based mapping for .NET string is SQL nvarchar (16 bit Unicode). This command changes the SQL column type to varchar (8-bit ASCII).**

> **Adds an index to the PublishedOn property because you sort and filter on this property**

> **Sets a smaller precision and scale of (9,2) for the price instead of the default (18,2)**

```
        //Model-level query filter
        entity
            .HasQueryFilter(p => !p.SoftDeleted);
    }
}
```

> **Sets a model-level query filter on the Book entity. By default, a query will exclude Book entities when the SoftDeleted property is true.**

The examples show a typical use of the Fluent API, but please remember that the fluent nature of the API allows chaining of multiple commands, as shown in this code snippet:

```
modelBuilder.Entity<Book>()
    .Property(x => x.ImageUrl)
    .IsUnicode(false)
    .HasColumnName("DifferentName")
    .HasMaxLength(123)
    .IsRequired(false);
```

EF6　　The Fluent API works the same in EF6.x, but with substantial changes in setting up relationships (covered in the next chapter) and subtle changes in data types, which I mention in the next section. There are also some new commands, described in sections 6.13 and 6.14.

OnModelCreating is called when the application first accesses the application's DbContext. At that stage, EF Core configures itself by using all three approaches: By Convention, Data Annotations, and any Fluent API you've added in the OnModelCreating method.

What if Data Annotations and the Fluent API say different things?

The Data Annotations and the Fluent API modeling methods always override convention-based modeling. But what happens if a data annotation and the Fluent API both provide a mapping of the same property and setting?

I tried setting the SQL type and length of the WebUrl property to different values via Data Annotations and via the Fluent API. The Fluent API values were used. That isn't a definitive test, but it makes sense that the Fluent API is the final arbitrator.

Now that you've learned about the Data Annotations and Fluent API configuration approaches, let's detail the configuration of specific parts of the database model.

6.6　*Excluding properties and classes from the database*

Section 6.3.2 describes how EF Core finds properties. But at times you'll want to exclude data that you have in your entity classes from being in the database. You might want to have local data for a calculation used during the lifetime of the class instance, but you don't want it saved to the database. You can exclude a class or a property in two ways: via Data Annotations or via the Fluent API.

6.6.1   *Excluding a class or property via Data Annotations*

EF Core will exclude a property, or a class, that has a [NotMapped] data attribute applied to it. This shows the application of the [NotMapped] data attribute to both a property and a class.

Listing 6.4   Excluding three properties, two by using [NotMapped]

```
public class MyEntityClass
{
    public int MyEntityClassId { get; set; }

    public string NormalProp{ get; set; }

    [NotMapped]
    public string LocalString { get; set; }

    public ExcludeClass LocalClass { get; set; }
}
[NotMapped]
public class ExcludeClass
{
    public int LocalInt { get; set; }
}
```

Included: A normal public property, with public getter and setter

Excluded: Placing a [NotMapped] attribute tells EF Core to not map this property to a column in the database.

Excluded: This class won't be included in the database because the class definition has a [NotMapped] attribute on it.

Excluded: This class will be excluded because the class definition has a [NotMapped] attribute on it.

6.6.2   *Excluding a class or property via the Fluent API*

In addition, you can exclude properties and classes by using the Fluent API configuration command Ignore, as shown in listing 6.5.

NOTE For simplicity, I show the Fluent API inside the OnModelCreating method rather than in a separate configuration class.

Listing 6.5   Excluding a property and a class by using the Fluent API

```
public class ExcludeDbContext : DbContext
{
    public DbSet<MyEntityClass> MyEntities { get; set; }

    protected override void OnModelCreating
        (ModelBuilder modelBuilder)
    {
        modelBuilder.Entity<MyEntityClass>()
            .Ignore(b => b.LocalString);

        modelBuilder.Ignore<ExcludeClass>();
    }
}
```

The Ignore method is used to exclude the LocalString property in the entity class, MyEntityClass, from being added to the database.

A different Ignore method can exclude a class such that if you have a property in an entity class of the Ignored type, that property isn't added to the database.

6.7 Configuring model-level query filters

Section 3.5.1 used a *model-level query filter* to provide a *soft-delete* feature to the Book entity class: instead of deleting a book, a model-level query filter allows you to "hide" soft-deleted books. That's a typical use of model-level query filters, but other uses exist, such as filtering data based on the user or company ID. The configuration was shown in chapter 3, but the following listing repeats it (in bold) in case you missed it.

Listing 6.6   Adding a model-level query filter to the `DbSet<Book>Books` property

```
public class EfCoreContext : DbContext
{
    //... Other parts removed for clarity

    protected override void
        OnModelCreating(ModelBuilder modelBuilder)
    {
        //... other configration parts removed for clarity

        modelBuilder.Entity<Book>()
            .HasQueryFilter(p => !p.SoftDeleted);
    }
}
```

> Adds a filter to all accesses to the Book entities. All book queries will exclude books where the SoftDeleted property is true.

6.8 Setting database column type, size, and nullability

As just described, the convention-based modeling uses default values for the SQL type, size/precision, and nullability, based on the .NET type. A common requirement is to manually set one or more of these attributes, either because you're using an existing database or for performance or business reasons.

In the introduction to configuring (section 6.3), you worked through an example that changed the type and size of various columns. Table 6.1 provides a full list of the commands that are available to do this.

Table 6.1   Setting nullability and SQL type/size for a column

Setting	Data annotations	Fluent API
Set not null (Default is nullable)	`[Required]` `public string MyProp` `    { get; set; }`	`modelBuilder.Entity<MyClass>()` `.Property(p => p.MyProp)` `    .IsRequired();`
Set size (string) (Default is MAX length)	`[MaxLength(123)]` `public string MyProp` `    { get; set; }`	`modelBuilder.Entity<MyClass>()` `.Property(p => p.MyProp)` `    .HasMaxLength(123);`
Set string type varchar (Default is nvarchar)	Not available (other than setting the column data type to `varchar(nnn)`—see the following EF6 note)	`modelBuilder.Entity<MyClass>()` `.Property(p => p.MyProp)` `    .IsUnicode(false);`
Set SQL type/size (Each type has a default precision and size)	`[Column(DataType =` `"decimal(9,2)")]` `public decimal Price` `    { get; set; }`	`modelBuilder.Entity<MyClass>()` `.Property(p => p.Price)` `    .HasColumnType` `        ("decimal(9,2)");`

EF6   EF Core has a slightly different approach to setting the SQL data type of a column. If you provide the data type, you need to give the whole definition, both type and length/precision—for instance: [Column(DataType = "varchar(nnn)")], where nnn is an integer number. In EF6, you can use [Column(DataType = "varchar")] and then define the length by using [Max-Length(nnn)], but that doesn't work in EF Core. See https://github.com/aspnet/EntityFramework/issues/3985 for more information.

TIP   I recommend using the IsUnicode(false) Fluent API if you wish to make a string property containing only the single-byte ASCII format (SQL Server varchar), because using the IsUnicode method allows you to set the string size separately.

6.9   *The different ways of configuring the primary key*

You've already seen the By Convention approach of setting up the primary key of an entity. This covers the normal primary-key setting, one key where the .NET property defines the name and type. You need to explicitly configure the primary key in two situations:

- When the key name doesn't fit the By Convention naming schema
- When the primary key is made up of more than one property/column, called a *composite key*

A many-to-many relationship-linking table is an example of where the By Convention approach doesn't work. There are the two alternative approaches to defining primary keys.

NOTE   Chapter 7 deals with configuring foreign keys, because they define relationships even though they're of a scalar type.

6.9.1   *Configuring a primary key via Data Annotations*

Listing 6.7 shows the BookAuthor linking entity class with the primary composite key being defined using Data Annotations. Because there's more than one key, you need to include the [Column(Order = nn)] attribute to define the order that the properties appear in the composite primary key.

> **Listing 6.7   The BookAuthor entity class using Data Annotations to define the key**

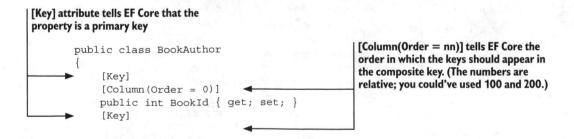

[Key] attribute tells EF Core that the property is a primary key

```
public class BookAuthor
{
    [Key]
    [Column(Order = 0)]
    public int BookId { get; set; }
    [Key]
```

[Column(Order = nn)] tells EF Core the order in which the keys should appear in the composite key. (The numbers are relative; you could've used 100 and 200.)

```
[Column(Order = 1)]
public int AuthorId { get; set; }
public byte Order { get; set; }

//----------------------------
//Relationships

public Book Book { get; set; }
public Author Author { get; set; }
}
```

The [Key] attribute is needed because the By Convention approach can't handle composite keys. This attribute tells EF Core that property is the primary key, or part of a composite primary key. The [Column(Order = nn)] attribute is needed to define the order of the keys in a composite key: in this case, it's BookId followed by AuthorId. You need the [Column(Order = nn)] attribute only when you have a composite primary key.

6.9.2 *Configuring a primary key via the Fluent API*

The following listing shows two ways of configuring a key via the Fluent API methods. The first is a single primary key in the Book entity class and then the composite primary key, consisting of two columns, in the BookAuthor linking table.

Listing 6.8 Using the Fluent API to configure primary keys on two entity classes

```
protected override void
    OnModelCreating(ModelBuilder modelBuilder)
{
    modelBuilder.Entity<Book>()              Defines a normal,
        .HasKey(x => x.BookId);    ◄───────  single-column primary key

    modelBuilder.Entity<BookAuthor>()
        .HasKey(x => new {x.BookId, x.AuthorId}); ◄──── Uses an anonymous object to define
                                                          two (or more) properties to form a
    //... other configuration settings removed           composite key. The order in which the
}                                                         properties appear in the anonymous
                                                          object defines their order.
```

Setting the key to BookId in the Book entity class isn't needed because that's the By Convention default. The second composite key can't be configured By Convention, so the Fluent API's HasKey method is used.

6.10 *Adding indexes to database columns*

Relational databases have a feature called an *index*, which provides quicker searching and sorting of rows based on the column, or columns, in the index. In addition, an index may have a constraint, which ensures that each entry in the index is unique. For instance, a primary key is given a unique index to ensure that the primary key is different for each row in the table.

You can add an index to a column only via the Fluent API, as shown in table 6.2. An index will speed up the quick searching and sorting, and adding the unique constraint will ensure that the column value in each row will be different.

Table 6.2   Adding an index to a column

Action	Fluent API
Add index	```modelBuilder.Entity<MyClass>()``` ``` .HasIndex(p => p.MyProp);```
Add index, multiple columns	```modelBuilder.Entity<Person>()``` ``` .HasIndex(p => new {p.First, p.Surname});```

Add named index	```modelBuilder.Entity<MyClass>()```
	 ``` .HasIndex(p => p.MyProp)```
	 ``` .HasName("Index_MyProp");```

Add unique index	```modelBuilder.Entity<MyClass>()```
	 ``` .HasIndex(p => p.BookISBN)```
	 ``` .IsUnique();```

> **TIP**   Don't forget, you can chain the Fluent API commands together so you can mix and match these methods.

6.11   Configuring the naming on the database side

If you're building a new database, using the default names for the various parts of the database is fine. But if you have an existing database, or your database needs to be accessed by an existing system you can't change, then you most likely need to use specific names for the *schema* name, the table names, and the column names of the database.

> **DEFINITION**   *Schema* refers to the organization of data inside a database—the way the data is organized as tables, columns, constraints, and so on. In some databases, such as SQL Server, *schema* is also used to give a namespace to a particular grouping of data that the database designer uses to partition the database into logical groups.

6.11.1   Configuring table names

By convention, the name of a table is set either by the name of the `DbSet<T>` property in the application's DbContext, or, if no `DbSet<T>` property is defined, the table uses the class name. For example, in the application's DbContext of our book app, you defined a `DbSet<Book>` Books property, so the database table name is set to Books. Conversely, you haven't defined a `DbSet<T>` property for the `Review` entity class in the application's DbContext, so its table name used the class name, and is therefore Review.

If your database has specific table names that don't fit the By Convention naming rules—for instance, if the table name can't be converted to a valid .NET variable name because it has a space in it—then you can use either Data Annotations or the Fluent API to specifically set the table name. Table 6.3 summarizes the two approaches to setting the table name.

Table 6.3 Two ways to explicitly configure a table name for an entity class

Configuring method	Example: Setting the table name of the `Book` class to "XXX"
Data Annotations	`[Table("XXX")]` `public class Book … etc.`
Fluent API	`modelBuilder.Entity<Book>().ToTable("XXX");`

6.11.2 Configuring the schema name, and schema groupings

By convention, the schema name is set by the database provider. This is done because some databases, such as SQLite and MySQL, don't support schemas.

In the case of SQL Server, which does support schemas, the default schema name is dbo. You can change the default schema name only via the Fluent API, using the following snippet in the `OnModelCreating` method of your application's DbContext:

`modelBuilder.HasDefaultSchema("NewSchemaName");`

Table 6.4 shows how to set the schema name for a table. You use this if your database is split into logical groups such as sales, production, accounts, and so on, and a table needs to be specifically assigned to a schema.

Table 6.4 Setting the schema name on a specific table

Configuring method	Example: Setting the schema name `"sales"` on a table
Data Annotations	`[Table("SpecialOrder", Schema = "sales")]` `class MyClass … etc.`
Fluent API	`modelBuilder.Entity<MyClass>()` `    .ToTable("SpecialOrder", schema: "sales");`

6.11.3 Configuring the database column names in a table

By convention, the column in a table has the same name as the property name. If your database has a name that either can't be represented as a valid .NET variable name or doesn't fit the software usage, you can set the column names by using Data Annotations or the Fluent API. Table 6.5 shows the two approaches to doing that.

Table 6.5 The two ways to configure a column name

Configuring method	Example: Setting the column name of the `BookId` property to `SpecialCol`
Data Annotations	`[Column("SpecialCol")]` `public int BookId { get; set; }`

Fluent API	`modelBuilder.Entity<MyClass>()`
	`    .Property(b => b.BookId)`
	`    .HasColumnName("SpecialCol");`

6.12 *Using specific database-provider Fluent API commands*

The Fluent API commands, such as the `HasColumnName` method, apply to any relational database provider. But what happens when you want a column name, or a table name, to have a different name based on the type of database it's in? The answer is that each database provider has an extension method that will return `true` if the database is of that specific type, which you can use in your Fluent API commands. The SQL Server database provider, for instance, has a method called `IsSqlServer`, the SQLite database provider has a method called `IsSqlite`, and so on.

The following listing will set the name of the column on the property `NormalColumn` to `SqliteDatabaseCol` if the database is an SQLite one; otherwise, the column will be set to `GenericDatabaseCol`.

Listing 6.9 Using database-provider commands to set a column name

You're setting a column name, but the same would work for ToTable.

```
protected override void OnModelCreating
    (ModelBuilder modelBuilder)
{
    modelBuilder.Entity<MyEntityClass>()
        .Property(p => p.NormalProp)
        .HasColumnName(
            Database.IsSqlite()
                ? "SqliteDatabaseCol"
                : "GenericDatabaseCol");
    //… other configuration left out
```

Each database provider has an extension called Is<DatabaseName> that returns true if the database is of that type.

Using the tests, you pick a specific name for the column if it's an SQLite database; otherwise, a generic name for any other database type.

You can use `Database.Is<DatabaseName>` freely in your Fluent API to affect how the database is configured. For instance, SQLite doesn't support computed columns (see chapter 8 for more on computed columns), so you could "turn off" the computed column configuration with a simple `if (!Database.IsSqlite())` around the Fluent API that will configure it.

One of the extension methods you'll find is `ForSqlServerIsMemoryOptimized`, which enables an SQL Server 2016 feature that holds an entire table and all its content in memory to provide better performance. This is an example of a feature unique to one database server being made available to EF Core via a database provider's specific extension method.

6.13　Recommendations for using EF Core's configuration

With so many ways to configure EF Core, some of which duplicate each other, it isn't always obvious which of the three approaches should be used for each part of the configuration. Here are suggestions on which of the approaches to use for each part of the configuration of EF Core:

1 Start by using the By Convention approach wherever possible, because it's quick and easy.
2 Use the validation attributes, for instance `MaxLength` and `Required` and so on, from the Data Annotations approach, as they're useful for validation.
3 For everything else, use the Fluent API approach, because it has the most comprehensive set of commands.

The following is a more detailed explanation of my recommendations for configuring EF Core.

6.13.1　Use By Convention configuration first—its quick and easy

EF Core does a respectable job of configuring most standard properties, so always start with that. In part 1, you built the whole of this initial database by using the By Convention approach, apart from the composite key in the `BookAuthor` many-to-many linking entity class.

　　The By Convention approach is quick and easy. You'll see in the next chapter that most relationships can be set up purely by using the By Convention naming rules. That can save you a lot of time.

6.13.2　Use validation Data Annotations wherever possible

Although you can do things such as limit the size of a string property with either Data Annotations or the Fluent API, I recommend using Data Annotations for the following reasons:

- *Frontend validation can use them.* Although EF Core doesn't validate the entity class before saving it to the database, other parts of the system may use Data Annotations for validation. For instance, ASP.NET Core uses Data Annotations to validate input, so if you input directly into an entity class, the validation attributes will be useful. Or if you use separate ASP.NET ViewModel or DTO classes, you can cut and paste the properties with their validation attributes.
- *You may want to add validation into EF Core's SaveChanges.* Using data validation to move checks out of your business logic can make your business logic simpler.

Chapter 4 showed you how to add validation of entity classes when `SaveChanges` is called.

- *Data annotations make great comments.* Attributes, what Data Annotations are, are compile-time constants. They're easy to see and easy to understand.

6.13.3 *Use the Fluent API for anything else*

Typically, I use the Fluent API for setting up the database column mapping (column name, column data type, and so on) when it differs from the conventional values. You could use the schema Data Annotations to do that, but I try to hide things like this inside the `OnModelCreating` method because they're a database implementation issue rather than a software structure issue. That's more a preference than a rule, so make your own decision on that.

6.14 *Shadow properties—hide column data inside EF Core*

> **EF6** EF6.x had the concept of shadow properties, but they were only used internally to handle missing foreign keys. In EF Core, shadow properties become a proper feature that you can use yourself.

Shadow properties are a way to access database columns, but without having them appear in the entity class as a property. Shadow properties allow you to "hide" data that you consider not part of the normal use of the entity class. This is all about good software practice, where you let upper layers access only the data they need, and you hide anything they don't need to know about. Let me give you two examples of where you might use shadow properties.

First, a common need is to track by whom and when data was changed. Maybe it's for auditing purposes, or it's to understand customer behavior. The tracking data you receive is separate from the primary use of the class, so you may decide to implement that data by using shadow properties, which can then be picked up outside the entity class.

Second, when setting up relationships in which you don't define the foreign-key properties in your entity class, EF Core must add them to make the relationship work, and it will do this via shadow properties. The next chapter covers this topic.

6.14.1 *Configuring shadow properties*

There's a By Convention approach to configuring shadow properties, but because this relates only to relationships, I explain that in the next chapter.

The other method is via the Fluent API. You can introduce a new property by using the Fluent API method `Property<T>`. Because you're setting up a shadow property, there won't be a property of that name in the entity class, so you need to use the Fluent API `Property<T>` method, which takes a .NET `Type` and the name of the shadow property. The following listing shows the setup of a shadow property called `UpdatedOn` that's of type `DateTime`.

Listing 6.10 Creating the `UpdatedOn` shadow property by using the Fluent API

```
public class Chapter06DbContext : DbContext
{
    ...

    protected override void
        OnModelCreating(ModelBuilder modelBuilder)
    {
        modelBuilder.Entity<MyEntityClass>()
            .Property<DateTime>("UpdatedOn");
    ...
    }
}
```

> Uses the Property<T> method to define the shadow property type

The name of the table column it's mapped to by convention is the same as the name of the shadow property. You can override this by adding the `HasColumnName` method on the end of the `property` method.

> **WARNING** If a property of that name already exists in the entity class, the configuration will use that property instead of creating a shadow property.

6.14.2 Accessing shadow properties

Because the shadow properties don't map to a class property, you need to access them directly via EF Core. For this, you have to use the EF Core commands `Entity(myEntity).Property("MyPropertyName").CurrentValue`, which is a read/write property, as shown here.

Listing 6.11 Using `Entity(inst).Property(name)` to set the shadow property

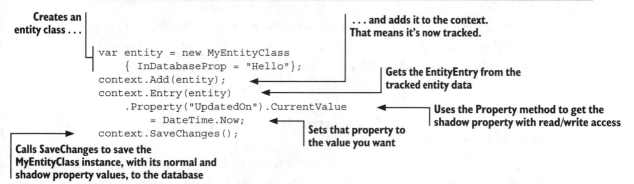

Creates an entity class . . .

... and adds it to the context. That means it's now tracked.

```
var entity = new MyEntityClass
    { InDatabaseProp = "Hello"};
context.Add(entity);
context.Entry(entity)
    .Property("UpdatedOn").CurrentValue
        = DateTime.Now;
context.SaveChanges();
```

Gets the EntityEntry from the tracked entity data

Uses the Property method to get the shadow property with read/write access

Sets that property to the value you want

Calls SaveChanges to save the MyEntityClass instance, with its normal and shadow property values, to the database

If you want to read a shadow property in an entity that has been loaded, use the `Entity(entityInstance).Property("propertyName").CurrentValue` command. But you *must* read the entity as a tracked entity: you should read the entity without the `AsNoTracking` method being used in the query. This is because the `Entity(<entityInstance>).Property` method uses the tracked entity data inside EF Core to hold the value, as it's not held in the entity class instance.

In LINQ queries, you use another way to access a shadow property by using the `EF.Property` command. For instance, you could sort by the `UpdatedOn` shadow property by using the following query snippet, with the `EF.Property` method in bold:

```
context.MyEntities
    .OrderBy(b => EF.Property<DateTime>(b, "UpdatedOn"))
    .ToList();
```

6.15   Backing fields—controlling access to data in an entity class

EF6   Backing fields are new in EF Core. They provide a level of control over access to data that EF6.x users have been after for some time.

As you saw earlier, columns in a database table are normally mapped to an entity class property with normal getters and setters—`public int MyProp { get ; set; }`. But you can also map a private field to your database; this feature is called a *backing field*, and it gives you more control over the way database data is read or set by the software.

For instance, if you want to save data to the database in JSON format (`json` is a string that holds data in a structured format), but you want higher-level application code to access only the decoded JSON data, using a backing field with two methods to set/get the decoded data is an appropriate solution.

As you'll see, backing fields provide nice ways to control and format your data. This section introduces backing fields, but we'll cover other uses in section 8.1 (hiding collection relationships), section 10.4 (DDD pattern), and section 13.4 (worked example of performance tuning). But before you learn how to configure backing fields, it's worth seeing a few ways you can use them for scalar (nonrelational) properties. Here are examples:

1   Using a simple backing field to show the basics of how a backing field works.
2   Using a backing field to provide a read-only view of a database column.
3   Using a backing field to hide sensitive data from other layers of the software.
4   Using a backing field to allow data to be transformed on read or write.

6.15.1   Creating a simple backing field accessed by a read/write property

Let's start with the simplest form of backing fields, in which a property getter/setter accesses the field. By convention, the column that the backing field is mapped to still uses the property name, but the data is placed in the private field. The following code snippet shows you what this looks like:

```
public class MyClass
{
    private string _myProperty;
    public string MyProperty
```

```
    {
        get { return _myProperty; }
        set { _myProperty = value; }
    }
}
```

This form of backing field doesn't bring anything particularly different from using a normal property, but this example shows the concept of a property linked to a private field.

CREATING A READ-ONLY COLUMN

Creating a read-only column is the most obvious use, although it can also be implemented via a private setting property (see section 6.3.2). If you have a column in the database that you need to read but you don't want the software to write, a backing field is a great solution. In this case, you can create a private field and use a public property, with a getter only, to retrieve the value. The following code snippet gives you an example:

```
public class MyClass
{
    private string _readOnlyCol;
    public string ReadOnlyCol => _readOnlyCol;
}
```

Something must set the column property, but as you'll see later, that can be done via other EF Core features, such as setting a default value in the database column (covered in chapter 8) or through some sort of internal database method.

TO HIDE DATA OUTSIDE EF CORE

Say you want to hide data in a private field and not allow a developer to access it outside EF Core. For this example, you've deemed for security reasons that a person's date of birth can be set, but only their age can be read from the entity class. The following listing shows how to do this in the `Person` class by using a private `_dateOfBirth` field and then providing a method to set it, and a property to calculate the person's age.

Listing 6.12   Using a backing field to hide sensitive data from normal access

```
public class Person                          The private backing field, which can't be
{                                            directly accessed via normal .NET software
    private DateTime _dateOfBirth;  ◄─────

    public void SetDateOfBirth(DateTime dateOfBirth)  ◄───
    {                                                       Allows the backing
        _dateOfBirth = dateOfBirth;                         field to be set
    }
                                    You can access the person's age,
                                    but not their exact date of birth.
    public int AgeYears =>  ◄─────
        Years(_dateOfBirth, DateTime.Today);

    //Thanks to dana on stackoverflow
    //see http://stackoverflow.com/a/4127477/1434764
```

```
      private static int Years(DateTime start, DateTime end)
      {
          return (end.Year - start.Year - 1) +
                  (((end.Month > start.Month) ||
                  ((end.Month == start.Month)
                  && (end.Day >= start.Day)))
                    ? 1 : 0);
      }}
```

NOTE   In the preceding example, you'd need to use the Fluent API to create a backing-field-only variable, covered in section 6.15.2.

From the class point of view, the _dateOfBirth field is hidden, but you can still access the table column via various EF Core commands in the same way that you accessed the shadow properties—by using the EF.Property method.

The backing field, _dateOfBirth, isn't totally secure from the developer, but that's not the aim. The idea is to remove the data of birth data from the normal properties so that it doesn't unintentionally get displayed in any user-visible view.

WHERE YOU NEED TO TRANSFORM THE DATA LOADED

At times you need to change/reformat data coming from or going to the database. For me, a common problem is that when you store a DateTime in a database, it loses the DateTime's Kind property, which defines whether the time is based on local time or UTC (Coordinated Universal Time). This matters because some libraries use the Kind property in their calculations/formatting, Newtonsoft.Json being one of them. Backing fields provide a way around this problem, as the following code shows:

```
public class Person
{
    private DateTime _updatedOn ;
    public DateTime UpdatedOn
    {
        get
        {
            return DateTime.SpecifyKind(
                _updatedOn, DateTimeKind.Utc);
        }
        set { _updatedOn = value; }
    }
}
```

The type of the backing field and the property must be the same, which limits the transformations that can be done on the data.

WARNING: Running a unit test on the previous code shows that if you use the UpdatedOn property in a LINQ query, EF Core will use the original column, not the transformed column. That's helpful in this case, as the performance won't be hampered by applying a transform, but in other cases the query might not yield what you expected. This type of use of backing fields should be used with caution.

6.15.2 Configuring backing fields

Having seen backing fields in action, you can configure them By Convention or by using the Fluent API, but not via Data Annotations. While the By Convention approach is easy to use, it relies on having a valid property with a matching name, which isn't the norm, so you'll rarely find the By Convention approach useful (other than in EF Core's 2.1.0 new lazy loading of relationships feature). Therefore, you'll find that most of your backing fields will be configured by using the Fluent API. I describe both approaches for completeness.

CONFIGURING BACKING FIELDS BY CONVENTION

If your backing field is linked to a valid property (see section 6.3.2), the field can be configured by convention. The rules for By Convention configuration are that the private field must have one of the following names that match a property in the same class:

- `_<property name>` (for example, `_MyProperty`)
- `_<camel-cased property name >` (for example, `_myProperty`)
- `m_<property name>` (for example, `m_MyProperty`)
- `m_<camel-cased property name>` (for example, `m_myProperty`)

DEFINITION *Camel case* is a convention in which a variable name starts with a lowercase letter but uses an uppercase letter to start each subsequent word in the name—for instance, `thisIsCamelCase`.

CONFIGURING BACKING FIELDS VIA THE FLUENT API

You have several ways of configuring backing fields via the Fluent API. We'll start with the simplest and work up to the more complex. Each example shows you the `OnModelCreating` method inside the application's DbContext, with only the field part being configured.

- *Setting the name of the backing field*—If your backing field name doesn't follow EF Core's conventions, you need to specify the field name via the Fluent API. Here's an example:

```
protected override void OnModelCreating
    (ModelBuilder modelBuilder)
{
    modelBuilder.Entity<Person>()
        .Property(b => b.UpdatedOn)
        .HasField("_differentName");
    …
}
```

- *Supplying just the field name*—You can provide just the field name. In this case, if there's a property with the correct name, by convention EF Core will refer to the property, and the property name will be used for the database column. Here's an example:

```
protected override void OnModelCreating
    (ModelBuilder modelBuilder)
{
    modelBuilder.Entity<Person>()
        .Property("_dateOfBirth");
    ...
}
```

If no property getter or setter is found, the field will still be mapped to the column, using its name, which in this example is _dateOfBirth, but that's most likely not the name you want for the column. You can set the column name with the HasColumnName Fluent API method, as shown in section 6.11.3. But the downside is that you'd still need to refer to the data in a query by its field name (in this case, _dateOfBirth), which isn't that friendly or obvious.

EF Core provides a better method that overcomes this for backing fields that aren't attached to a property: you can create a *notional* property (a named property), but it refers to the field instead of a property. The benefit is that you can use the actual name of the table column (in this case, DateOfBirth), and if you need to refer to it in a query, you can use the same name (in this case, DateOfBirth). The following listing shows how to set this up. Note that you need to define the type because there's no property called DateOfBirth, so the configuration process can't refer to that property to get the type.

Listing 6.13   Creating a notional property `DateOfBirth` so it's easier to access

```
protected override void
    OnModelCreating(ModelBuilder modelBuilder)
{
    modelBuilder.Entity<Person>()
        .Property<DateTime>("DateOfBirth")      ◄── Creates a notional property called
        .HasField("_dateOfBirth");      ◄──           DateOfBirth, by which you can access
    ...                                                this property via EF Core. This also sets
}                                                      the column name in the database.

                                         Links it to a backing field _dateOfBirth
```

- *Controlling how the data is loaded*—By default, EF will place data in the field when constructing instances of your entity during a query. But if the entity instance already exists and EF Core wants to refresh the value (say, when using a command such as Reload, covered in chapter 9), it uses the property setter if it exists, or the field if the property doesn't exist or has no setter.

The `UsePropertyAccessMode` Fluent API method allows you to change which route EF Core will use to set new data into the backing field/property. In this next example, you've forced all EF Core accesses to always use the field:

```
protected override void
    OnModelCreating(ModelBuilder modelBuilder)
{
    modelBuilder.Entity<Person>()
        .Property(b => b.UpdatedOn)
        .HasField("_updatedOn")
        .UsePropertyAccessMode(PropertyAccessMode.Field);
    ...
}
```

Setting the access mode to `Field` tells EF Core to use the field only to get/set data for the database. This might be useful if you did some form of transformation in your getters or setters.

Other options are `PropertyAccessMode.Property`, which always goes through the property and will throw an exception if it can't read or write the property, and `PropertyAccessMode.FieldDuringConstruction`, which is the default setting described at the beginning of this subsection.

Summary

- The first time you create the application's DbContext, EF Core configures itself by using a combination of three approaches: By Convention, Data Annotations, and the Fluent API.
- Use the By Convention approach to set up as much as you can, because it's simple and quicker to code.
- When the By Convention approach doesn't fit your needs, data attributes and/or EF Core's Fluent API provide extra commands to configure both the way EF Core maps the entity classes to the database and the way EF Core will handle that data.
- Two EF Core features, shadow properties and backing fields, allow you to hide data from higher levels of your code and/or control access to data in an entity class.

For readers who are familiar with EF6:

- The basic process of configuring EF Core is, on the surface, similar to the way EF6 works. But a significant number of changed or new commands exist.
- EF Core can use configuration classes to hold the Fluent API commands for a given entity class. This provides a similar feature to the EF6.x `EntityType-Configuration<T>` class, but EF Core uses an `IEntityTypeConfiguration<T>` interface instead.
- The main configuration commands related to scalar properties are generally the same, but you should watch out for a few small changes.
- EF Core has introduced many extra features not available in EF6. Two new features covered in this chapter are shadow properties and backing fields, both of which are welcome additions to EF.

Configuring relationships

7

This chapter covers

- Configuring relationships using By Convention
- Configuring relationships using Data Annotations
- Configuring relationships using Fluent API
- Other ways to map entities to database tables

Chapter 6 described how to configure scalar, or nonrelational, properties. This chapter covers how to configure database relationships. I assume you've read at least the first part of chapter 6, because configuring relationships uses the same three approaches, By Convention and Data Annotations and the Fluent API, to map the database relationships.

This chapter covers how EF Core finds and configures relationships between entity classes, with pointers on how to configure each type of relationship—one-to-one, one-to-many, and many-to-many—and examples of each. EF Core's By Convention relationship rules can quickly configure many relationships, but you'll also learn about all the Data Annotations and Fluent API configuration options, which allow you to precisely define the way you want a relationship to behave. You'll also look at features that allow you to enhance your relationships with extra keys and alternative table-mapping approaches.

7.1 Defining some relationship terms

This chapter refers to the various parts of a relationship, and you need clear terms so you know exactly what part of the relationship we're talking about. Figure 7.1 shows those terms, using the Book and Review entity classes from our book app. I follow this figure with a more detailed description so the terms will make sense to you when I use them in this chapter.

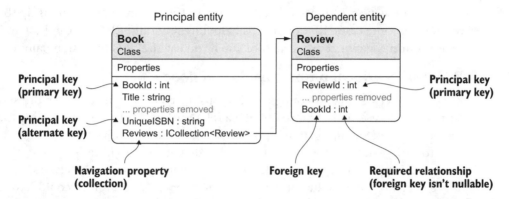

Figure 7.1 The Book and Review entity classes show six of the terms used in this chapter to discuss relationships: principal entity, dependent entity, principal key, navigational property, foreign key, and required relationship. Not shown is the optional relationship, which is described in section 2.4.4.

To ensure that these terms are clear, here are detailed descriptions:

- *Principal key*—A new term, taken from EF Core's documentation, that refers to either the primary key, defined in part 1, or the new *alternate key*, which has a unique value per row and isn't the primary key (see section 7.7.3).

NOTE Figure 7.1 provides an example of an alternate key called UniqueISBN, which represents a unique value per entity. (*ISBN* stands for *International Standard Book Number*, which is unique for every book.)

- *Principal entity*—The entity that contains the principal-key property(s), which the dependent relationship refers to via a foreign key(s) (covered in chapter 3).
- *Dependent entity*—The entity that contains the foreign-key property(s) that refers to the principal entity (covered in chapter 3).
- *Navigational property*—A new term taken from EF Core's documentation that refers to the property containing a single entity class, or collection of entity classes, which EF Core uses to link entity classes.
- *Foreign key*—Defined in section 2.1.3, this holds the principal-key value(s) of the database row it's linked to (or could be null).

- *Required relationship*—A relationship in which the foreign key is non-nullable; the principal entity must exist.
- *Optional relationship*—A relationship in which the foreign key is nullable; the principal entity can be missing.

NOTE A principal key and a foreign key can consist of more than one property/column. These are called *composite keys*. You've already seen one in section 3.4.4, as the BookAuthor many-to-many linking entity class has a composite primary key consisting of the BookId and the AuthorId.

You'll see in section 7.4 that EF Core can find and configure most relationships by convention. In some cases, EF Core needs help, but generally, EF Core can find and configure your navigational properties for you if you use the By Convention naming rules.

7.2   *What navigational properties do you need?*

Before I describe how to configure relationship types, I want to cover the software design decisions around how you model a relationship. This is about selecting the best arrangement of the navigational properties between the entity classes—what do you want to expose at the software level, and what do you want to hide?

In our book app, the Book entity class has many Review entity classes, and each Review class is linked, via a foreign key, to one Book. You therefore could have a navigational property of type ICollection<Review> in the Book class, and a navigational property of type Book in the Review class. In that case, you'd have a *fully defined relationship*: a relationship with navigational properties at both ends.

But do you need a fully defined relationship? From the software design point of view, there are two questions about the Book/Review navigational relationships. The answers to these questions will define which of the navigational relationships you need to include:

- Does the Book entity class need to know about the Review entity classes? I say yes, because we want to calculate the average review score.
- Does the Review entity class need to know about the Book entity class? I say no, because in this example application we don't do anything with that relationship.

Our solution is therefore to have only the ICollection<Review> navigational property in the Book class, which is what figure 7.1 portrays.

7.3   *Configuring relationships*

In the same way as in chapter 6, which covered configuring nonrelational properties, EF Core has three ways to configure relationships. Here are the three approaches for configuring properties, but focused on relationships:

- *By Convention*—EF Core finds and configures relationships by looking for references to classes that have a primary key in them.

- *Data Annotations*—These can be used to mark foreign keys and relationship references.
- *Fluent API*—This provides the richest set of commands to fully configure any relationship.

The next three sections detail each of these in turn. As you'll see, the By Convention approach can autoconfigure many relationships for you, if you follow its naming standards. At the other end of the scale, the Fluent API allows you to manually define every part of a relationship, which can be useful if you have a relationship that falls outside the By Convention approach.

7.4 *Configuring relationships By Convention*

The By Convention approach is a real time-saver when it comes to configuring relationships. In EF6.x, I used to laboriously define my relationships because I hadn't fully understood the power of the By Convention approach when it comes to relationships. Now that I understand the conventions, I let EF Core set up most of my relationships, other than the few cases where By Convention doesn't work (section 7.4.6 lists those exceptions).

The rules are straightforward, but the ways the property name, type, and nullability all work together to define a relationship takes a bit of time to absorb. Hopefully, reading this section will save you time when you're developing your next application that uses EF Core.

7.4.1 *What makes a class an entity class?*

Chapter 2 defined the term *entity class* as a normal .NET class that has been mapped by EF Core to the database. Here I want to define how EF Core finds and identifies a class as an entity class by using the By Convention approach.

Figure 6.1 showed the three ways that EF Core configures itself. The following is a recap of that process, but now focused on finding the relationships and navigational properties:

1. EF Core scans the application's DbContext, looking for any public `DbSet<T>` properties. It assumes the classes, `T`, in the `DbSet<T>` properties are entity classes.
2. EF Core also looks at every public property in the classes found in step 1, and looks at properties that could be navigational properties. These are all classes that aren't defined as being scalar properties by the current database provider (`string` is a class, but it's defined as a scalar property). These classes may appear as a single link (for instance, `public PriceOffer Promotion ( get; set; })` or a type that implements the `IEnumerable<T>` interface (for instance, `public ICollection<Review> Reviews { get; set; }`).

NOTE   Backing fields and the Fluent API, covered later in this chapter, can also add entity classes. Section 6.6 shows how you can exclude a class from EF Core's mapping.

3   EF Core then checks that each of these entity classes has a primary key (chapter 6 shows how a primary key is defined). If the class doesn't have a primary key, and the class isn't excluded, then EF Core will throw an exception.

7.4.2   *An example of an entity class with navigational properties*

Listing 7.1 shows the entity class `Book`, which is defined in the application's DbContext. In this case, you have a public property of type `DbSet<Book>`, which passed the "must have a valid primary key" test in that it has a public property called `BookId`.

What you're interested in is how EF Core's By Convention configuration handles the three navigational properties at the bottom of the class. As you'll see in this section, EF Core can work out which sort of relationship it is by the type of the navigational property and the foreign key in the class that the navigational property refers to.

> **Listing 7.1   The `Book` entity class, with the relationships at the bottom**

```
public class Book
{
    public int BookId { get; set; }
    //other scalar properties removed as not relevant…            Link to an optional
                                                                   PriceOffer: one-to-zero-
                                                                   or-one relationship
    public PriceOffer Promotion { get; set; }  ◄─────

    public ICollection<BookAuthor>          Link to one side of the many-to-many
        AuthorsLink { get; set; }           relationship of authors

    public ICollection<Review> Reviews { get; set; }  ◄──  Link to any reviews for
}                                                           this book: one-to-many
                                                            relationship
```

If two navigational properties exist between the two entity classes, the relationship is known as *fully defined,* and EF Core can work out By Convention whether it's a one-to-one or a one-to-many relationship. If only one navigational property exists, EF Core can't be sure, and assumes a one-to-many relationship.

Certain one-to-one relationships may need configuration via the Fluent API if you have only one navigational property, or you want to change the default By Convention setting—for example, when deleting an entity class with a relationship.

7.4.3   *How EF Core finds foreign keys By Convention*

A foreign key must match the *principal key* (defined in section 7.1) in type and in name, but to handle a few scenarios, the foreign-key name matching has three options, shown in figure 7.2. The figure shows an example of all three options for a foreign-key name using the entity class `Review` that reference the primary key, `BookId`, in the entity class `Book`.

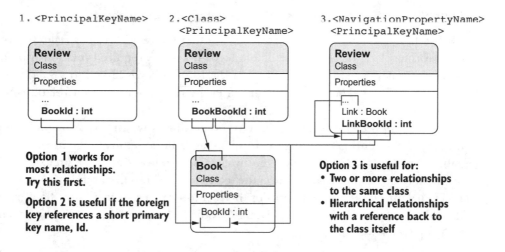

Figure 7.2   Three options for a foreign key referring to the `Book` entity class's primary key. These allow you to use a unique name for your foreign key, from which EF Core can work out which primary key this relationship refers to.

Option 1 is used the most; I showed this in figure 7.1. Option 2 is for developers who use the short, By Convention primary-key name, `Id`, as it makes the foreign key unique to the class it's linking to.

Option 3 helps with specific cases in which you'd get duplicate named properties if you used option 1. The following listing shows an example of using option 3 to handle a hierarchical relationship.

Listing 7.2   A hierarchical relationship with an option 3 foreign key

```
public class Employee
{
    public int EmployeeId { get; set; }

    public string Name { get; set; }

    //------------------------------
    //Relationships

    public int? ManagerEmployeeId { get; set; }
    public Employee Manager { get; set; }
}
/**************************************************
```

Foreign key uses the <navigationalPropertyName> <PrimaryKeyName> pattern.

The entity class called `Employee` has a navigational property called `Manager` that links to the employee's manager, who is an employee as well. You can't use a foreign key of `EmployerId` (option 1) because that's already used for the primary key. You therefore use option 3, and call the foreign key `ManagerEmployeeId` by using the navigational property name at the start.

7.4.4   *Nullability of foreign keys—required or optional relationships*

The nullability of the foreign key defines whether the relationship is *required* (non-nullable foreign key) or *optional* (nullable foreign key). A required relationship ensures that relationships exist by ensuring that the foreign key is linked to a valid principal key. Section 7.6.1 describes an `Attendee` entity that has a required relationship to a `Ticket` entity class.

An *optional relationship* allows there to be no link between the principal entity and the dependent entity, by having the foreign-key value(s) set to `null`. The `Manager` navigational property in the `Employee` entity class, shown in listing 7.2, is an example of an optional relationship, as someone at the top of the business hierarchy won't have a boss.

The required or optional status of the relationship also affects what happens when the principal entity is deleted. The default setting of the `OnDelete` action for each relationship type is as follows:

- For a *required relationship,* EF Core sets the `OnDelete` action to `Cascade`. If the principal entity is deleted, the dependent entity will be deleted too.
- For an *optional relationship,* EF Core sets the `OnDelete` action to `ClientSetNull`. If the dependent entity is being tracked, the foreign key will be set to `null` when the principal entity is deleted. But if the dependent entity *isn't* being tracked, the database settings take over, and the entity is set to `Restrict`, so the delete will fail in the database, and an exception will be thrown.

> **NOTE**   The `ClientSetNull` delete behavior is rather unusual, and section 7.7.1 explains why. That section also describes how to configure the delete behavior of a relationship.

7.4.5   *Foreign keys—what happens if you leave them out?*

If EF Core finds a relationship via a navigational property, or through a relationship you configured via the Fluent API, it needs a foreign key to set up the relationship in the relational database. Including foreign keys in your entity classes is good practice. This gives you better control over the nullability of the foreign key, and access to foreign keys can be useful when handling relationships in a disconnected update (see section 3.3.1).

But if you do leave out a foreign key (on purpose or by accident), EF Core configuration will add a foreign key as a shadow property. Chapter 6 introduced shadow properties, hidden properties that can be accessed only via specific EF Core commands.

Figure 7.3 shows the By Convention naming of shadow foreign-key properties if added by EF Core. It's useful to know the default names, as you can access the shadow foreign-key properties by using the `EF.Property<T>(string)` method if you need to (see section 6.11.2 for more details on accessing shadow properties).

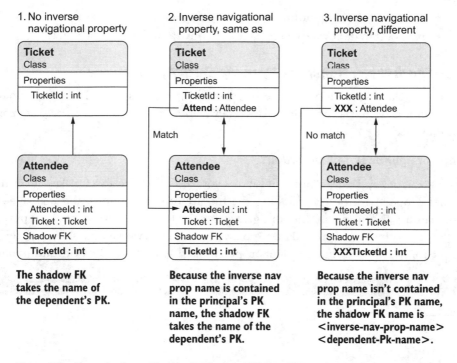

Figure 7.3 If you don't provide a foreign key and EF Core deems that one is needed, EF Core will create a shadow foreign key and use the preceding rules to decide what name to give it. If you want to access the shadow foreign key yourself, you can find which rule applies and then use it in an `EF.Property<T>` method.

The important point to note is that the shadow foreign-key property will be nullable, which has the effect described in section 7.4.4 on nullability of foreign keys. If this isn't what you want, you can alter the shadow property's nullability by using the Fluent API `IsRequired` method, as described in section 7.7.2.

> **EF6** EF6.x uses a similar approach of adding foreign keys if you left them out of your entity classes, but in EF6.x you can't configure the nullability or access the content. EF Core's shadow properties make the approach of leaving out foreign keys more controllable.

7.4.6 When does By Convention configuration not work?

If you're going to use the By Convention configuration approach, you need to know when it's not going to work, so you can use other means to configure your relationship. Here's my list of scenarios that won't work, with the most common listed first:

- You have composite foreign keys (see section 7.6 or section 7.5.1).
- You want to create a one-to-one relationship without navigational links going both ways (see section 7.6.1).
- You want to override the default delete behavior setting (see section 7.7.1).

- You have two navigational properties going to the same class (see section 7.5.2).
- You want to define a specific database constraint (see section 7.7.4).

7.5   *Configuring relationships by using Data Annotations*

Only two Data Annotations relate to relationships, as most of the navigational configuration is done via the Fluent API. They're the ForeignKey and InverseProperty annotations.

7.5.1   *The ForeignKey Data Annotation*

The ForeignKey Data Annotation allows you to define the foreign key for a navigational property in the class. Taking the hierarchical example of the Employee class, you can use this to define the foreign key for the Manager navigational property. The following listing shows an updated Employee entity class with a new, shorter foreign-key name for the Manager navigational property that doesn't fit the By Convention naming.

> **Listing 7.3   Using the `ForeignKey` data annotation to set the foreign-key name**

```
public class Employee
{
    public int EmployeeId { get; set; }

    public string Name { get; set; }

    //-----------------------------
    //Relationships

    public int? ManagerId { get; set; }
    [ForeignKey(nameof(ManagerId))]          ◄── Defines which property is the
    public Employee Manager { get; set; }        foreign key for the Manager
}                                                navigational property
```

NOTE You've applied the ForeignKey data annotation to the Manager navigational property, giving the name of the foreign key, ManagerId. But the ForeignKey data annotation also works the other way around. You could've applied the ForeignKey data annotation to the foreign-key property, ManagerId, giving the name of navigational property, Manager—for instance, [ForeignKey(nameof(Manager))].

The ForeignKey data annotation takes one parameter, which is a string. This should hold the name of the foreign-key property. If the foreign key is a composite key (it has more than one property), these should be comma delimited—for instance, [ForeignKey("Property1, Property2")].

TIP I suggest you use the nameof keyword to provide the property name string. That's safer, because if you change the name of the foreign-key property, nameof will either be updated at the same time, or throw a compile error if you forgot to change all the references.

7.5.2 *The InverseProperty Data Annotation*

The `InverseProperty` Data Annotation is a rather specialized Data Annotation for use when you have two navigational properties going to the same class. At that point, EF Core can't work out which foreign keys relate to which navigational property. This is best shown by code, and the following listing gives you an example of the `Person` entity class having two lists: one for books owned by the librarian and one for `Books` out on loan to a specific person.

Listing 7.4 `LibraryBook` entity class with two relationships to `Person` class

```
public class LibraryBook
{
    public int LibraryBookId { get; set; }

    public string Title { get; set; }

    //----------------------------------
    //Relationships

    public int LibrarianPersonId { get; set; }
    public Person Librarian { get; set; }

    public int? OnLoanToPersonId { get; set; }
    public Person OnLoanTo { get; set; }
}
```

The `Librarian` and the borrower of the book (`OnLoanTo` navigational property) are both represented by the `Person` entity class. The `Librarian` navigational property and the `OnLoanTo` navigational property both link to the same class, and EF Core can't set up the navigational linking without help. The `InverseProperty` Data Annotation shown in the following listing provides the information to EF Core when it's configuring the navigational links.

Listing 7.5 The `Person` entity class, which uses the `InverseProperty` annotation

```
public class Person
{
    public int PersonId { get; set; }

    public string Name { get; set; }

    //-----------------------------
    //relationships

    [InverseProperty("Librarian")]        ◄── Links LibrarianBooks to the
    public ICollection<LibraryBook>            Librarian navigational property in
        LibrarianBooks { get; set; }           the LibraryBook class

    [InverseProperty("OnLoanTo")]         ◄── Links the BooksBorrowedByMe list to the
    public ICollection<LibraryBook>            OnLoanTo navigational property in the
        BooksBorrowedByMe { get; set; }        LibraryBook class
}
```

This is one of those configuration options that you rarely use, but if you have this situation, you must use this, or define the relationship using the Fluent API. Otherwise, EF Core will throw an exception when it starts, as it can't work out how to configure the relationships.

7.6   *Fluent API relationship configuration commands*

As I said in section 7.4, you can configure most of your relationships by using EF Core's By Convention approach. But if you want to configure a relationship, the Fluent API has a well-designed set of commands that cover all the possible combinations of relationships. It also has extra commands to allow you to define other database constraints. The format for defining a relationship with the Fluent API is shown in figure 7.4. All Fluent API relationship configuration commands follow this pattern.

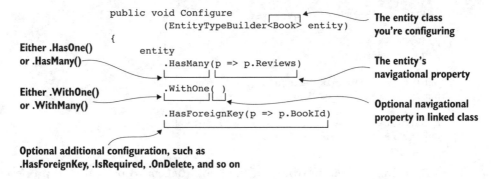

Figure 7.4   The Fluent API allows you to define a relationship between two entity classes. `HasOne/` `HasMany` and `WithOne/WithMany` **are the two main parts, followed by other commands to specify other parts or set certain features.**

> **EF6**   EF Core's Fluent API command names have changed from EF6 and, for me, they're much clearer. Personally I found EF6's `WithRequired` and `WithRe-` `quiredPrincipal/WithRequiredDependent` commands a bit confusing, whereas the EF Core Fluent API commands have a clearer `HasOne/HasMany` followed by `WithOne/WithMany` syntax.

We'll now define a one-to-one, one-to-many, and many-to-many relationship to illustrate the use of these Fluent API relationships.

7.6.1   *Creating a one-to-one relationship*

One-to-one relationships can get a little complicated because there are three ways to build them in a relational database. To understand these options, you'll look at an example in which you have attendees (entity class `Attendee`) at a software convention, and each attendee has a unique ticket (entity class `Ticket`).

Chapter 3 showed how to create, update, and delete relationships. To recap, here's a code snippet showing how to create a one-to-one relationship:

```
var attendee = new Attendee
{
    Name = "Person1",
    Ticket = new Ticket{ TicketType = TicketTypes.VIP}
};
context.Add(attendee);
context.SaveChanges();
```

Figure 7.5 shows the three options for building this sort of one-to-one relationship. The principal entities are at the top of the diagram, and the dependent entities are at the bottom. Note that option 1 has the `Attendee` as the dependent entity, whereas options 2 and 3 have the `Ticket` at the dependent entity.

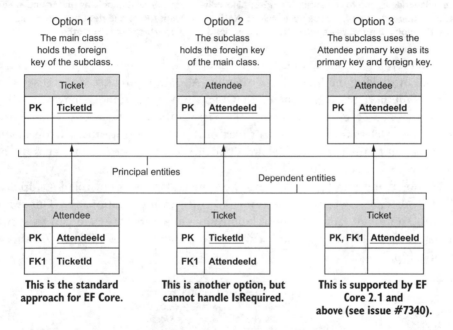

Figure 7.5 The three ways of defining a one-to-one relationship in a relational database; comments at the bottom indicate EF Core's handling of each approach. The difference between option 1 and option 2 (and 3) is that the order of the two ends of the one-to-one relationship are swapped, which changes which part can be forced to exist. In option 1, the `Attendee` must have a `Ticket`, whereas in options 2 and 3, the `Ticket` is optional for the `Attendee`.

Each option has its own advantages and disadvantages. You should use the one that's right for your business need.

Option 1 is the standard approach to building one-to-one relationships, because it allows you to define that the one-to-one dependent entity is required (it must be present). In our example, an exception will be thrown if you try to save an `Attendee` entity instance without a unique `Ticket` attached to it. Figure 7.6 shows option 1 in more detail.

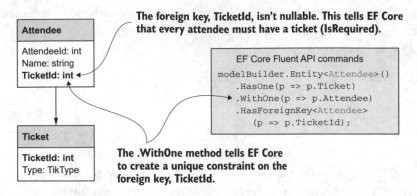

Figure 7.6   The non-nullable foreign key ensures that the principal entity (in this case, `Attendee`) must have a dependent, one-to-one entity, `Ticket`. Also, configuring the relationship as one-to-one ensures that each dependent entity, `Ticket`, is unique. Notice the Fluent API on the right has navigational properties going both ways—each entity has a navigational property going to the other.

With the option 1 one-to-one arrangement, you can make the dependent entity optional by making the foreign key nullable. Also, in figure 7.6, you can see that the `WithOne` method has a parameter that picks out the `Attendee` navigational property in the `Ticket` entity class that links back to the `Attendee` entity class. Because the `Attendee` class is the dependent part of the relationship, then if you delete the `Attendee` entity, the linked `Ticket` won't be deleted, because the `Ticket` is the principal entity in the relationship.

Options 2 and 3 in figure 7.5 turn the principal/dependent relationship around, with the `Attendee` becoming the principal entity in the relationship. This swaps the required/optional nature of the relationship—now the `Attendee` can exist without the `Ticket`, but the `Ticket` can't exist without the `Attendee`. Figure 7.7 shows this relationship.

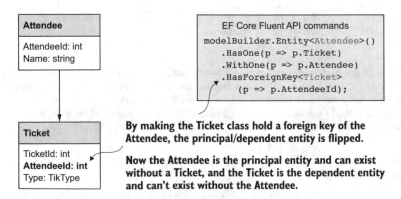

Figure 7.7   Option 2: The `Ticket` entity holds the foreign key of the `Attendee` entity. This changes which entity is the principal and dependent entity. In this case, the `Attendee` is now the principal entity, and the `Ticket` is the dependent entity.

Option 2 can be useful because optional one-to-one relationships, often referred to as *one-to-zero-or-one relationships*, are more common. All you've done here is think of the relationship in a different order.

Option 3 is another, more efficient, way to define option 2, with the primary key and the foreign key combined. I would've used this for the `PriceOffer` entity class in the book app, but some limitations exist in EF Core 2.0 (see https://github.com/aspnet/EntityFramework/issues/7340). EF Core 2.1 has fixed those limitations.

7.6.2 Creating a one-to-many relationship

One-to-many relationships are simpler, because there's one format: the "many" entities contain the foreign-key value. Most one-to-many relationships can be defined using the By Convention approach, but figure 7.8 shows the Fluent API code to create a "one `Book` has many `Reviews`" relationship in the book app.

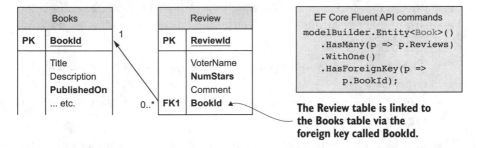

Figure 7.8 A one-to-many relationship, in which the foreign key must be in the dependent entity; in this case, the `Review` entity class. You can see in the Fluent API on the right that the `Book` has a collection navigational property, `Reviews`, linked to the `Review` entity classes, but `Review` doesn't have a navigational property back to `Book`.

In this case, the `Review` entity class doesn't have a navigational link back to the `Book`, so the `WithOne` method has no parameter.

> **NOTE** Listing 3.16 shows how to add a `Review` to the `Book`'s one-to-many collection navigational property, `Reviews`.

Collections have a couple of features that are worth knowing about. First, you can use any generic type for a collection that implements the `IEnumerable<T>` interface, such as `ICollection<T>`, `Collection<T>`, `HashSet<T>`, `List<T>`, and so on. `IEnumerable<T>` on its own is a special case, as you can't add to that collection (but see section 8.1 for one place where this is useful). The point is, for performance reasons, you should use the simplest generic collection type so that EF Core can instantiate the collection quickly when using the `Include` method. That's why I tend to use `ICollection<T>`.

> **NOTE** Internally, EF Core uses `HashSet<T>` to hold a collection. In some specific cases with noninitialized backing field collections, you may need to use the `HashSet<T>` type as the collection type.

Second, although you typically define a collection navigational property with a getter and a setter (for instance, `public ICollection<Review> Reviews { get; set; }`), that isn't totally necessary. You can provide a getter only if you initialize the backing field with an empty collection. The following is also valid:

```
public ICollection<Review> Reviews { get; } = new List<Review>();
```

Personally, I don't initialize a collection to an empty list, because the collection will be `null` if you load an entity with a collection navigational property without an `Include` method to load that collection. Then your code is likely to fail rather than deliver an empty list when you forget the `Include` (this is defensive programming). The downside of doing this is you need to manually initialize a collection navigational property in a new entity before you can add entries to it.

7.6.3 *Creating a many-to-many relationship*

In EF Core, a many-to-many relationship is made up of two one-to-many relationships. The many-to-many relationship between a `Book` entity class and its `Author` entity classes consists of the following:

- A one-to-many relationship from the `Book` entity class to the `BookAuthor` linking entity class
- A one-to-many relationship from the `Author` entity class to the `BookAuthor` linking entity class

This listing shows the Fluent API that configures the primary key and then the two one-to-many relationships for this many-to-many relationship.

> **Listing 7.6   Configuring a many-to-many relationship via two one-to-many relationships**

```
public static void Configure
    (this EntityTypeBuilder<BookAuthor> entity)
{
    entity.HasKey(p =>
        new { p.BookId, p.AuthorId });        ◄─── Uses the names of the Book and
                                                   Author primary keys to form its
                                                   own composite key

    //-----------------------------
    //Relationships

    entity.HasOne(pt => pt.Book)
        .WithMany(p => p.AuthorsLink)              Configures the one-to-many
        .HasForeignKey(pt => pt.BookId);           relationship from the Book to
                                                   BookAuthor entity class
    entity.HasOne(pt => pt.Author)
        .WithMany(t => t.BooksLink)                Configures the one-to-many
        .HasForeignKey(pt => pt.AuthorId);         relationship from the Author to
}                                                  the BookAuthor entity class
```

Note that you don't need to add the Fluent API to configure the two one-to-many relationships because they follow the By Convention naming and therefore don't need the

Fluent API. The key, however, does need configuring because it doesn't follow the By Convention naming.

> **EF6**   EF6.x users need to do a bit more work in EF Core to handle many-to-many relationships. EF6.x automatically creates the linking table and automates the adding or removal of entries in the linking table. EF Core may gain the same many-to-many features that EF6.x has, but there's no timescale on that.

7.7   Additional methods available in Fluent API relationships

In addition to the Fluent API relationship commands, other methods can be added to the end of the Fluent API methods that define a relationship. In summary, they're as follows:

- OnDelete—Changes the delete action of a dependent entity (section 7.7.1)
- IsRequired—Defines the nullability of the foreign key (section 7.7.2)
- HasPrincipalKey—Uses an alternate unique key (section 7.7.3)
- HasConstraintName—Sets the foreign-key constraint name and MetaData access to the relationship data (section 7.7.4)

7.7.1   OnDelete—changing the delete action of a dependent entity

Section 7.4.4 described the default action on the deletion of a principal entity, which is based on the nullability of the dependent's foreign key(s). The OnDelete Fluent API method allows you to alter what EF Core does when a deletion that affects a dependent entity happens.

You can add the OnDelete method to the end of a Fluent API relationship configuration. This listing shows the code added in chapter 4 to stop a Book entity from being deleted if it was referred to in a customer order, via the LineItem entity class.

> **Listing 7.7   Changing the default OnDelete action on a dependent entity**

```
public static void Configure
    (this EntityTypeBuilder<LineItem> entity)
{
    entity.HasOne(p => p.ChosenBook)
        .WithMany()
        .OnDelete(DeleteBehavior.Restrict);   ◄─┐
}
```

Adds the OnDelete method onto the end of defining a relationship. Setting it to Restrict stops the LineItem from being deleted, hence EF Core will throw an exception if a Book entity class is deleted and a LineItem is linked to that specific book.

This code causes an exception to be thrown if someone tries to delete a Book entity that a LineItem's foreign key links to that Book. You do this because you want a customer's order to not be changed. Table 7.1 explains the possible DeleteBehavior settings.

Table 7.1   Delete behaviors available in EF Core. The middle column highlights the delete behavior that will be used if you don't apply the `OnDelete` option.

Name	Effect the delete behavior has on the dependent entity	Default for
`Restrict`	The delete operation isn't applied to dependent entities. The dependent entities remain unchanged. This may cause the delete to fail, either in EF Core or in the relational database.	
`SetNull`	The dependent entity isn't deleted, but its foreign-key property is set to `null`. If any of the dependent entity foreign-key properties aren't nullable, an exception is thrown when `SaveChanges` is called.	
`ClientSetNull`	If EF Core is tracking the dependent entity, its foreign key is set to `null` and the dependent entity isn't deleted. But if EF Core isn't tracking the dependent entity, the database rules will apply; in a database created by EF Core, this will be set to `Restrict`, which will cause the delete to fail with an exception.	Optional relationships
`Cascade`	The dependent entity is deleted.	Required relationships

The `ClientSetNull` delete behavior is unusual, because it's the only one in which the action EF Core takes in software is different from the foreign-key constraint EF Core sets in the database. Here are the two dissimilar actions that EF Core and the database take on deleting a principal entity with an optional dependent entity and a delete behavior of `ClientSetNull`:

- EF Core sets the optional dependent-entity foreign key to `null`, but only if the optional dependent entity is loaded and being tracked.
- The database, if created by EF Core, has a foreign-key constraint of ON DELETE NO ACTION (SQL Server). If the optional dependent entity isn't loaded and EF Core hasn't set its foreign key to `null`, the database will return a foreign-key constraint error.

EF Core sets a dissimilar database setting because the "correct" setting of ON DELETE SET NULL (SQL Server) can cause a database error when EF Core tries to create the database (typically, when the database server spots possible cyclic delete paths).

Having a default setting causing an exception on database creation/migration isn't that friendly for the developer, so, in EF Core 2.0, the team added the new `ClientSetNull` delete behavior. With this behavior, you won't get an unexpected exception when EF Core creates/migrates the database for you, but you need to be a bit more careful when you delete a principal entity that has an optional dependent entity. Listing 7.8 shows the correct way to delete a principal entity that has an optional dependent entity: by ensuring that the optional dependent entity is tracked.

Listing 7.8   Deleting a principal entity with an optional dependent entity

Reads in the principal entity

```
var entity = context.DeletePrincipals
    .Include(p => p.DependentDefault)
    .Single(p => p.DeletePrincipalId == 1);
context.Remove(entity);
context.SaveChanges();
```

Includes the dependent entity that has the default delete behavior of ClientSetNull

Sets the principal entity for deletion

Calls SaveChanges, which, because the dependent entity is tracked, then sets its foreign key to null

Note that if you don't include the `Include` method or another way of loading the optional dependent entity, `SaveChanges` would throw a `DbUpdateException` because the database server will have reported a foreign-key constraint violation.

One way to align EF Core's approach to an optional relationship with the database server's approach is to set the delete behavior to `SetNull` instead of the default `Client-SetNull`. This sets the foreign-key constraint in the database to `ON DELETE SET NULL` (SQL Server), which is in line with what EF Core does. Whether or not you load the optional dependent entity, the outcome of the called `SaveChanges` will be the same; the foreign key on the optional dependent entity will be set to `null`. Be aware that some database servers may return an error on database creation in some circumstances, such as an optional hierarchical relationship, as shown in listing 7.2. All the other delete behaviors (`Restrict`, `SetNull`, and `Cascade`) produce a foreign-key constraint that has the same behavior as EF Core's software.

> **NOTE** If you're managing the database creation/migration outside EF Core, it's important to ensure that the relational database foreign-key constraint is in line with EF Core's `OnDelete` setting. Otherwise, you'll get inconsistent behavior, depending on whether the dependent entity is being tracked.

7.7.2   *IsRequired—defining the nullability of the foreign key*

Chapter 6 describes how the Fluent API method `IsRequired` allows you to set the nullability of a scalar property, such as a string. In a relationship, the same command sets the nullability of the foreign key, which, as I've already said, defines whether the relationship is required or optional.

The `IsRequired` method is most useful in shadow properties because EF Core, by default, makes shadow properties nullable, and the `IsRequired` method can change them to non-nullable. Listing 7.9 shows you the `Attendee` entity class used previously to show a one-to-one relationship, but showing two other one-to-one relationships that are using shadow properties for their foreign keys.

Listing 7.9   The `Attendee` entity class showing all its relationships

```
public class Attendee
{
    public int AttendeeId { get; set; }
    public string Name { get; set; }

    public int TicketId { get; set; }
    public Ticket Ticket { get; set; }

    public OptionalTrack Optional { get; set; }
    public RequiredTrack Required { get; set; }
}
```

Foreign key for the one-to-one relationship, Ticket

One-to-one navigational property that accesses the Ticket entity

One-to-one navigational property using a shadow property for the foreign key. By default, the foreign key is nullable, so the relationship is optional.

One-to-one navigational property using a shadow property for the foreign key. You use Fluent API commands to say that the foreign key isn't nullable, so the relationship is required.

The `Optional` navigational property, which uses a shadow property for its foreign key, is configured by convention, which means the shadow property is left as a nullable value. Therefore, it's optional, and if the `Attendee` entity is deleted, the `Optional-Track` entity isn't deleted.

For the `Required` navigational property, the following listing presents the Fluent API configuration. Here you use the `IsRequired` method to make the `Required` one-to-one navigational property as required; each `Attendee` entity must have a `RequiredTrack` entity assigned to the `Required` property.

Listing 7.10   The Fluent API configuration of the `Attendee` entity class

```
public void Configure
    (EntityTypeBuilder<Attendee> entity)
{
    entity.HasOne(p => p.Ticket)
        .WithOne(p => p.Attendee)
        .HasForeignKey<Attendee>
            (p => p.TicketId)
        .IsRequired();

    entity.HasOne(p => p.Required)
        .WithOne(p => p.Attend)
        .HasForeignKey<Attendee>(
            "MyShadowFk")
        .IsRequired();
}
```

Sets up the one-to-one navigational relationship, Ticket, which has a foreign key defined in the Attendee class

Specifies the property that's the foreign key. You need to provide the class type, as the foreign key could be in the principal or dependent entity class.

Sets up the one-to-one navigational relationship, Required, which doesn't have a foreign key defined

Uses IsRequired to say the foreign key should not be nullable

Uses the HasForeignKey<T> method that takes a string, because it's a shadow property and can be referred to only via a name. Note that you use your own name.

You could've left out the configuration of the `Ticket` navigational property, as this would be correctly configured with the By Convention rules. You leave it in so you can compare it with the configuration of the `Required` navigational property, which uses a shadow property for its foreign key.

The configuration of the `Required` navigational property is necessary, because the `IsRequired` method changes the shadow foreign-key property from nullable to non-nullable, which in turn makes the relationship as required.

TYPE AND NAMING CONVENTIONS FOR SHADOW PROPERTY FOREIGN KEYS

Notice how listing 7.10 refers to the shadow foreign-key property: you need to use the `HasForeignKey<T>(string)` method. The `<T>` class tells EF Core where to place the shadow foreign-key property, which can be either end of the relationship for one-to-one relationships, or the "many" entity class of a one-to-many relationship.

The string parameter of the `HasForeignKey<T>(string)` method allows you to define the shadow foreign-key property name. You can use any name; you don't need to stick with the By Convention name listed in figure 7.3. But you need to be careful not to use a name of any existing property in the entity class you're targeting, because that can lead to strange behaviors. (There's no warning if you do select an existing property, as you might be trying to define a nonshadow foreign key.)

7.7.3 *HasPrincipalKey—using an alternate unique key*

I mentioned the term *alternate key* at the beginning of this chapter, and said it was a unique value but isn't the primary key. I gave an example of an alternate key called `UniqueISBN`, which represents a unique key that isn't the primary key. (Remember, *ISBN* stands for *International Standard Book Number*, which is a unique number for every book.)

Now let's look at a different example. You may be aware that the ASP.NET authorization library uses the user's email address as its `UserId`, which is unique for each user. The following listing creates a `Person` entity class, which uses a normal `int` primary key, but you'll use the `UserId` as an alternate key when linking to the person's contact information, shown in listing 7.12.

> Listing 7.11 `Person` class, with `UserId` taken from ASP.NET authorization

```
public class Person
{
    public int PersonId { get; set; }

    public string Name { get; set; }

    [MaxLength(256)]
    [Required]
    public string UserId { get; set; }          ◀—  The UserId holds the ASP.NET
}                                                     authorization UserId, which is the
                                                      person's email address and is unique.
```

Listing 7.12   `ContactInfo` class with `EmailAddress` as a foreign key

```
public class ContactInfo
{
    public int ContactInfoId { get; set; }

    public string MobileNumber { get; set; }
    public string LandlineNumber { get; set; }

    [MaxLength(256)]
    [Required]
    public string EmailAddress { get; set; }
}
```

> The email address is used as a foreign key for the Person entity to link to this contact info.

Figure 7.9 shows the Fluent API configuration commands, which use the alternate key in the `Person` entity class as a foreign key in the `ContactInfo` entity class.

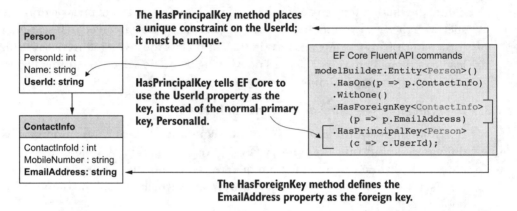

Figure 7.9   The Fluent API sets up a one-to-one relationship by using the `UserId` property, which contains the person's email address and is unique, as the foreign key to link to the `ContactInfo`. The command `HasPrincipalKey` both defines the `UserId` property as an alternate key and makes the foreign-key constraint link between the `EmailAddress` property in the `ContactInfo` entity and the `UserId` in the `Person` entity.

Here are a few notes on alternate keys:

- You can have composite alternate keys—an *alternate key* made up of two or more properties. This is handled in the same way as composite keys, by using an anonymous class. For example, `HasPrincipalKey<MyClass>(c => new {c.Part1, c.Part2})`.

- Unique keys (see section 6.6) and alternate keys are different, and you should choose the correct one for your business case. Here are some of the differences:

  - Unique keys ensure that each entry is unique; they can't be used in a foreign key.

  - Unique keys can be `null`, but alternate keys can't.

  - Unique key values can be updated, but alternate keys can't. (See EF Core issue #4073 at https://github.com/aspnet/EntityFramework/issues/4073.)

- You can define a property as a standalone alternate key by using the Fluent API command `modelBuilder.Entity<Car>().HasAlternateKey(c => c.LicensePlate)`, but there isn't any need to do that, because using the `HasPrincipalKey` method to set up a relationship automatically registers the property as an alternate key.

7.7.4 Less-used options in Fluent API relationships

This section briefly mentions but doesn't cover in detail two Fluent API commands that can be used when setting up relationships.

HasConstraintName—setting the foreign-key constraint name

The method `HasConstraintName` allows you to set the name of the foreign-key constraint. This can be useful if you want to catch the exception on foreign-key errors and use the constraint name to form a more user-friendly error message. Section 10.7.3 shows an example of setting the constraint name so that you can produce user-friendly error messages out of SQL errors.

MetaData—access to the relationship information

The `MetaData` property provides access to the relationship data, some of which is read/write. Much of what the `MetaData` property exposes can be accessed via specific commands, such as `IsRequired`, but some parts can be useful. I recommend an article by an EF Core team member Arthur Vickers on `MetaData`: http://mng.bz/YfiT.

7.8 Alternative ways of mapping entities to database tables

Sometimes it's useful to not have a one-to-one mapping from an entity class to a database table. Instead of having a relationship between two classes, you might want to combine both classes into one table. This allows you to load only part of the table when you use one of the entities, which will improve the query's performance. EF Core provides three alternative ways to map classes to the database, each with its own features:

- *Owned types*—This allows a class to be merged into the entity class's table. Useful for using normal classes to group data.
- *Table per hierarchy*—This allows a set of inherited classes to be saved into one table; for instance, classes called `Dog`, `Cat`, and `Rabbit` that inherit from the `Animal` class.
- *Table splitting*—This allows multiple entity classes to be mapped to the same table. Useful when some columns in a table are read more often than all the table columns.

7.8.1 Owned types—adding a normal class into an entity class

EF Core has *owned types*, which allow you to define a class that holds a common grouping of data, such as an address or audit data, that you want to use in multiple places in your database. The owned type class doesn't have a primary key, so doesn't have an identity of its own, but relies on the entity class that "owns" it for its identity. In DDD terms, owned types are known as *value objects*.

> **EF6**   EF Core's owned types are similar to EF6.x's complex types. The biggest change is you must specifically configure an owned type, whereas EF6.x considers any class without a primary key to be a complex type (which could cause bugs). EF Core's owned types have an extra feature over EF6.x's implementation: the data in an owned type can be configured to be saved into a separate, hidden table.

Here are two ways of using owned types:

- The owned type data is held in the same table that the entity class is mapped to.
- The owned type data is held in a separate table from the entity class.

OWNED TYPE DATA IS HELD IN THE SAME TABLE AS THE ENTITY CLASS

As an example of an owned type, you'll create an entity class called `OrderInfo` that needs two addresses: `BillingAddress` and `DeliveryAddress`. These are provided by the `Address` class, as shown in this listing. The `Address` class is an owned type with no primary key, as shown at the bottom of the listing.

> **Listing 7.13   The `Address` owned type, followed by the `OrderInfo` entity class**

```
public class OrderInfo          ◄─────    The entity class OrderInfo, with a
{                                         primary key and two addresses
    public int OrderInfoId { get; set; }
    public string OrderNumber { get; set; }

    public Address BillingAddress { get; set; }       Two distinct Address classes. The data for
    public Address DeliveryAddress { get; set; }      each Address class will be included in the
}                                                     table that the OrderInfo is mapped to.

public class Address          ◄─────
{                                        An owned type has no primary key and
    public string NumberAndStreet { get; set; }   relies on its "owner" for its identity. This
    public string City { get; set; }              type of class is referred to as a value
    public string ZipPostCode { get; set; }       object in DDD.
    public string CountryCodeIso2 { get; set; }
}
```

You tell EF Core that the `BillingAddress` and the `DeliveryAddress` properties in the `OrderInfo` entity class aren't relationships, but owned types, through the Fluent API. Listing 7.14 shows the configuration commands to do that.

Listing 7.14 The Fluent API to configure the owned types within `OrderInfo`

Selects the owner of the owned type

```
public class SplitOwnDbContext: DbContext
{
    public DbSet<OrderInfo> Orders { get; set; }
    //… other code removed for clarity

    protected override void OnModelCreating
        (ModelBuilder modelBuilder)
    {
        modelBuilder.Entity<OrderInfo>()
           .OwnsOne(p => p.BillingAddress);
        modelBuilder.Entity<OrderInfo>()
           .OwnsOne(p => p.DeliveryAddress);
    }
}
```

Uses the OwnsOne method to tell EF Core that property BillingAddress is an owned type and the data should be added to the columns in the table that the OrderInfo maps to

Repeats the process for the second property, DeliveryAddress

The result is a table containing the two scalar properties in the `OrderInfo` entity class, followed by two sets for `Address` class properties, one prefixed by `BillingAddress_` and another prefixed by `DeliveryAddress_`. The following listing shows part of the SQL Server `CREATE TABLE` command that EF Core produces for the `OrderInfo` entity class with the naming convention.

Listing 7.15 The `SQL CREATE TABLE` command showing the column names

```
CREATE TABLE [Orders] (
    [OrderInfoId] int NOT NULL IDENTITY,
    [OrderNumber] nvarchar(max) NULL,
    [BillingAddress_City] nvarchar(max) NULL,
    [BillingAddress_CountryCodeIso2] nvarchar(max) NULL,
    [BillingAddress_NumberAndStreet] nvarchar(max) NULL,
    [BillingAddress_ZipPostCode] nvarchar(max) NULL,
    [DeliveryAddress_City] nvarchar(max) NULL,
    [DeliveryAddress_CountryCodeIso2] nvarchar(max) NULL,
    [DeliveryAddress_NumberAndStreet] nvarchar(max) NULL,
    [DeliveryAddress_ZipPostCode] nvarchar(max) NULL,
    CONSTRAINT [PK_Orders] PRIMARY KEY ([OrderInfoId])
);
```

Using owned types like this can help organize your database. Any common groups of data can be turned into owned types and added to entity classes. Here are two final points on owned types held in an entity class:

- You must provide all the owned class instances when you create a new instance to write to the database (for instance, `BillingAddress = new Address{…etc.}`. If you don't, `SaveChanges` will throw an exception.
- The owned type properties, such as `BillingAddress`, are automatically created and filled with data when you read the entity. There's no need for an `Include` method or any other form of relationship loading.

OWNED TYPE DATA IS HELD IN A SEPARATE TABLE FROM THE ENTITY CLASS

The other way that EF Core can save the data inside an owned type is into a separate table, rather than the entity class. In this example, you'll create a `User` entity class that has a property called `HomeAddress` of type `Address`. In this case, you add a `ToTable` method after the `OwnsOne` method in your configuration code.

Listing 7.16   Configuring the owned table data to be stored in a separate table

```
public class SplitOwnDbContext: DbContext
{
    public DbSet<OrderInfo> Orders { get; set; }
    //… other code removed for clarity

    protected override void OnModelCreating
        (ModelBuilder modelBuilder)
    {
        modelBulder.Entity<User>()
            .OwnsOne(p => p.HomeAddress);
            .ToTable("Addresses");
    }
}
```

Adding ToTable to OwnsOne tells EF Core to store the owned type, Address, in a separate table, with a primary key equal to the primary key of the User entity that was saved to the database.

EF Core sets up a one-to-one relationship, in which the primary key is also the foreign key (see section 7.6.1, option 3). And the `OnDelete` state is set to `Cascade` so that the owned type entry of the primary entity, `User`, is deleted. The database therefore has two tables, the Users table and the Addresses table.

Listing 7.17   The two tables, Users and Addresses, in the database

```
CREATE TABLE [Users] (
    [UserId] int NOT NULL IDENTITY,
    [Name] nvarchar(max) NULL,
    CONSTRAINT [PK_Orders] PRIMARY KEY ([UserId])
);
CREATE TABLE [Addresses] (
    [UserId] int NOT NULL IDENTITY,
    [City] nvarchar(max) NULL,
    [CountryCodeIso2] nvarchar(max) NULL,
    [NumberAndStreet] nvarchar(max) NULL,
    [ZipPostCode] nvarchar(max) NULL,
    CONSTRAINT [PK_Orders] PRIMARY KEY ([UserId]),
    CONSTRAINT "FK_Addresses_Users_UserId" FOREIGN KEY ("UserId")
        REFERENCES "Users" ("UserId") ON DELETE CASCADE
);
```

This use of owned types differs from the first usage, in which the data is stored in the entity class table, because you can save a `User` entity instance without an address. But the same rules apply on querying—the `HomeAddress` property will be read in on a query of the `User` entity, without the need for an `Include` method.

The Addresses table used to hold the `HomeAddress` data is hidden; you can't access it via EF Core. This could be a good thing or a bad thing, depending on your business needs. But if you want to access the `Address` part, you can implement the same feature by using two entity classes with a one-to-one relationship between them.

7.8.2 *Table per hierarchy—placing inherited classes into one table*

Table per hierarchy (TPH) stores all the classes that inherit from each other in a single database table. For instance, if you want to save a payment in a shop, it could be cash (`PaymentCash`) or credit card (`PaymentCard`). Both contain the amount (say, $10), but the credit card option has extra information; an online transaction receipt for instance. In this case, TPH uses a single table to store all the versions of the inherited classes and return the correct entity type, `PaymentCash` or `PaymentCard`, depending on what was saved.

TPH can be configured by convention, which will then combine all the versions of the inherited classes into one table. This has the benefit of keeping common data in one table, but accessing that data is a little cumbersome because each inherited type has its own `DbSet<T>` property. But by adding the Fluent API, all the inherited classes can be accessed via one `DbSet<T>` property, which in our example makes the `Payment-Cash`/ `PaymentCard` example much more useful.

CONFIGURING TPH BY CONVENTION

To apply the By Convention approach to the `PaymentCash`/`PaymentCard` example, you create a class called `PaymentCash` and then another class, `PaymentCard`, which inherits from `PaymentCash` classes, as shown in this listing. As you can see, `PaymentCard` inherits from `PaymentCash` and adds an extra `ReceiptCode` property.

> **Listing 7.18 The two classes: `PaymentCash` and `PaymentCard`**

```
public class PaymentCash
{
    [Key]
    public int PaymentId { get; set; }
    public decimal Amount { get; set; }
}

//PaymentCredit - inherits from PaymentCash
public class PaymentCard : PaymentCash
{
    public string ReceiptCode { get; set; }
}
```

Listing 7.19, which uses the By Convention approach, shows your application's DbContext with two `DbSet<T>` properties, one for each of the two classes. Because you include both classes, and `PaymentCard` inherits from `PaymentCash`, EF Core will store both classes in one table.

Listing 7.19   The updated application's DbContext with the two `DbSet<T>` properties

```csharp
public class Chapter07DbContext : DbContext
{
    //… other DbSet<T> properties removed

    //Table-per-hierarchy
    public DbSet<PaymentCash> CashPayments { get; set; }
    public DbSet<PaymentCard> CreditPayments { get; set; }

    public Chapter07DbContext(
        DbContextOptions<Chapter07DbContext> options)
        : base(options)
    { }

    protected override void OnModelCreating
        (ModelBuilder modelBuilder)
    {
        //no configuration needed for PaymentCash or PaymentCard
    }
}
```

Finally, this listing shows the code that EF Core produces to create the table that will store both the PaymentCash and PaymentCard entity classes.

Listing 7.20   The SQL produced by EF Core to build the `CashPayment` table

```sql
CREATE TABLE [CashPayments] (
    [PaymentId] int NOT NULL IDENTITY,
    [Amount] decimal(18, 2) NOT NULL,
    [Discriminator] nvarchar(max) NOT NULL,
    [ReceiptCode] nvarchar(max),
    CONSTRAINT [PK_CashPayments]
        PRIMARY KEY ([PaymentId])
);
```

> The Discriminator column holds the name of the class; EF Core uses this to define what sort of data is saved. When set by convention, this column holds the name of the class as a string.

> The ReceiptCode column is used only if it's a PaymentCredit.

As you can see, EF Core has added a Discriminator column, which it uses when returning data to create the correct type of class, PaymentCash or PaymentCard, based on what was saved. Also, the ReceiptCode column is filled/read only if the class type is PaymentCard.

USING THE FLUENT API TO IMPROVE OUR TPH EXAMPLE

Although the By Convention approach reduces the number of tables in the database, you have two separate DbSet<T> properties, and you need to use the right one to find the payment that was used. Also, you don't have a common Payment class that you can use in any other entity classes. But by a bit of rearranging and adding some Fluent API configuration, you can make this solution much more useful.

Figure 7.10 shows the new arrangement. You create a common base class by having an abstract class called `Payment` that the `PaymentCash` and `PaymentCard` inherit from. This allows you to use the `Payment` class in another entity class called `SoldIt`.

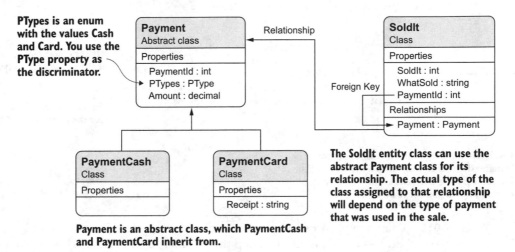

PTypes is an enum with the values Cash and Card. You use the PType property as the discriminator.

Payment is an abstract class, which PaymentCash and PaymentCard inherit from.

The SoldIt entity class can use the abstract Payment class for its relationship. The actual type of the class assigned to that relationship will depend on the type of payment that was used in the sale.

Figure 7.10   By using the Fluent API, you can create a more useful form of the TPH. Here an abstract class called `Payment` is used as the base, and this class can be used inside another entity class. The actual class type placed in the `SoldIt` payment property will be either `PaymentCash` or `PaymentCard`, depending on what was used when the `SoldIt` class was created.

This approach is much more useful because you can now place a `Payment` abstract class in the `SoldIt` entity class and get the amount and type of payment, regardless of whether it's cash or a card. The `PType` property tells you the type (the `PType` property is of type `PTypes`, which is an enum with values `Cash` or `Card`), and if you need the `Receipt` property in the `PaymentCard`, you can cast the `Payment` class to the type `PaymentCard`.

In addition to creating the entity classes shown in figure 7.10, you also need to change the application's DbContext and add some Fluent API configuration to tell EF Core about your TPH classes, as they no longer fit the By Convention approach. This listing shows the application's DbContext, with the configuration of the Discrimination column.

Listing 7.21   Changed application's DbContext with Fluent API configuration added

```
public class Chapter07DbContext : DbContext
{
    //… other DbSet<T> properties removed
    public DbSet<Payment> Payments { get; set; }

    public DbSet<SoldIt> SoldThings { get; set; }

    public Chapter07DbContext(
```

Defines the property through which you can access all the payments, both PaymentCash and PaymentCard

List of sold items, with a required link to Payment

```
        DbContextOptions<Chapter07DbContext> options)
        : base(options)
    { }

    protected override void OnModelCreating
        (ModelBuilder modelBuilder)
    {
        //… other configuretions removed
        modelBuilder.Entity<Payment>()
            .HasDiscriminator(b => b.PType)
            .HasValue<PaymentCash>(PTypes.Cash)
            .HasValue<PaymentCard>(PTypes.Card);
    }
}
```

Sets the discriminator value for the PaymentCash type

Sets the discriminator value for the PaymentCard type

The HasDiscriminator method identifies the entity as a TPH and then selects the property PType as the discriminator for the different types. In this case, it's an enum, which you set to be bytes in size.

> **NOTE**   This example uses an abstract class as the base class, but you don't have to do that. You could just as well keep the original PaymentCash, with the PaymentCard inheriting from that. I wanted to show you that EF Core can handle an abstract base class.

ACCESSING TPH ENTITIES

Now that you've configured a TPH set of classes, let's cover any differences in CRUD operations. Most EF database access commands are the same, but a few changes access the TPH parts of the entities. EF Core does a nice job (as EF6.x did) of handling TPH.

First, the creation of TPH entities is straightforward. You create an instance of the specific type you need. For instance, the following code snippet creates a PaymentCash type entity to go with a sale:

```
var sold = new SoldIt()
{
    WhatSold = "A hat",
    Payment = new PaymentCash {Amount = 12}
};
context.Add(sold);
context.SaveChanges();
```

EF Core then saves the correct version of data for that type, and sets the discriminator so it knows the TPH class type of the instance. When you read back the SoldIt entity you just saved, with an Include to load the Payment navigational property, the type of the loaded Payment instance will be the correct type (PaymentCash or PaymentCard), depending on what was used when you wrote it to the database. Also, in this example the Payment's property PType, which you set as the discriminator, tells you the type of payment, Cash or Card.

When querying TPH data, the EF Core `OfType<T>` method allows you to filter TPH data to find a specific class. The query `context.Payments.OfType<PaymentCard>()` would return only the payments that used a card, for example.

Updating the data inside a TPH entity uses all the normal conventions. But changing the type of the entity (from `PaymentCard` to `PaymentCash`) is possible but difficult. You need to set the discriminator value in your code and configure the discriminator value's `AfterSaveBehavior` to `PropertySaveBehavior.Save`.

Listing 7.22 The updated application's DbContext with the two `DbSet<T>` properties

```
public class Chapter07DbContext : DbContext
{
    //... other code removed

    protected override void OnModelCreating
        (ModelBuilder modelBuilder)
    {
        //... other configuretions removed
        modelBuilder.Entity<Payment>()
            .HasDiscriminator(b => b.PType)
            .HasValue<PaymentCash>(PTypes.Cash)
            .HasValue<PaymentCard>(PTypes.Card);

        entity.Property(p => p.PType)
            .Metadata.AfterSaveBehavior =
                PropertySaveBehavior.Save;
    }
}
```

> To change the type of a TPH entry, you need to configure the discriminator to be saved, so your change is saved to the database.

NOTE EF Core 2.1 adds a further small, but useful improvement to THP handling. I list this in section B.2.4.

7.8.3 Table splitting—mapping multiple entity classes to the same table

The final feature, called *table splitting*, allows you to map multiple entities to the same table. This is useful if you have a large amount of data to store for one entity, but your normal queries to this entity need only a few columns. It's like building a `Select` query into an entity class; the query will be quicker because you're loading only a subsection of the whole entity's data.

This example has two entity classes, `BookSummary` and `BookDetail`, that both map to a database table called Books. Figure 7.11 shows the result of configuring these two entity classes as a table split.

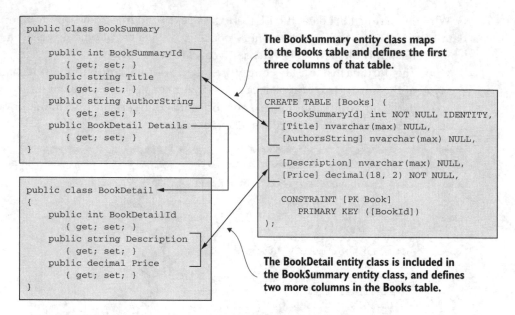

```
public class BookSummary
{
    public int BookSummaryId
        { get; set; }
    public string Title
        { get; set; }
    public string AuthorString
        { get; set; }
    public BookDetail Details
        { get; set; }
}
```

The **BookSummary** entity class maps to the Books table and defines the first three columns of that table.

```
CREATE TABLE [Books] (
    [BookSummaryId] int NOT NULL IDENTITY,
    [Title] nvarchar(max) NULL,
    [AuthorsString] nvarchar(max) NULL,

    [Description] nvarchar(max) NULL,
    [Price] decimal(18, 2) NOT NULL,

    CONSTRAINT [PK Book]
        PRIMARY KEY ([BookId])
);
```

```
public class BookDetail
{
    public int BookDetailId
        { get; set; }
    public string Description
        { get; set; }
    public decimal Price
        { get; set; }
}
```

The **BookDetail** entity class is included in the BookSummary entity class, and defines two more columns in the Books table.

Figure 7.11 **The result of using the table-splitting feature in EF Core to map two entity classes,** `BookSummary` **and** `BookDetail`**, to one table, Books. You do this because a book needs a lot of information, but most queries need only the** `BookSummary` **part. The effect is to build a preselected set of columns for faster querying.**

Here's the configuration code to achieve this.

Listing 7.23   Configuring a table split between `BookSummary` **and** `BookDetail`

```
public class SplitOwnDbContext : DbContext
{
    //… other code removed

    protected override void OnModelCreating
        (ModelBuilder modelBuilder)
    {
        modelBuilder.Entity<BookSummary>()
            .HasOne(e => e.Details)
            .WithOne()
            .HasForeignKey<BookDetail>
                (e => e.BookDetailId);
        modelBuilder.Entity<BookSummary>()
            .ToTable("Books");

        modelBuilder.Entity<BookDetail>()
            .ToTable("Books");
    }
}
```

Defines the two books as having a relationship in the same way that you'd set up a one-to-one relationship

In this case, the HasForeignKey method must reference the primary key in the BookDetail entity.

You must map both entity classes to the Books table. That triggers the table splitting.

After you've configured the two entities as a table split, you can query the BookSummary entity on its own and get the summary parts. To get the BookDetails part, you can either query the BookSummary entity and load the Details relationship property at the same time (say, with an `Include` method) or read just the `BookDetails` part straight from the database.

A few points before leaving this topic:

- When you create a new entity that's table-split to be added into the database, you must define all the parts of the table split. For example, in the case of the `BookSummary` and the `BookDetails` case, `BookSummary` must have an instance of the `BookDetails` entity class assigned to its `Details` property before you call `SaveChanges`.
- You can update an individual entity class in a table split individually; you don't have to load all the entities involved in a table split to do an update.
- You've seen a table split to two entity classes, but you can table-split any number of entity classes.

Summary

- If you follow the By Convention naming rules for foreign keys, EF Core can find and configure most normal relationships.
- Two Data Annotations provide a solution to a couple of specific issues around foreign keys with names that don't fit the By Convention naming rules.
- The Fluent API is the most comprehensive way to configure relationships, and some features, such as setting the action on deletion of the dependent entity, are available only via the Fluent API.
- EF Core provides three alternative ways to map entity classes to a database table: owned types, table per hierarchy, and table splitting.

For readers who are familiar with EF6:

- The basic process of configuring relationships in EF Core is the same as in EF6.x, but the Fluent API commands have changed significantly.
- EF6.x adds foreign keys if you forget to add them yourself, but they aren't accessible via normal EF6.x commands. EF Core allows you to access them via shadow properties.
- EF6.x provides a many-to-many relationship directly, but EF Core doesn't. You need to use two one-to-many relationships with a linking table in the middle.
- EF Core has introduced new features, such as access to shadow properties, alternate keys, and backing fields.
- EF Core's feature called *owned types* provides similar features to EF6.x's complex types.
- EF Core's table-per-hierarchy feature is similar to EF6.x's table-per-hierarchy feature.
- EF Core's table-splitting feature is similar to EF6.x's table-splitting feature.

Configuring advanced features and handling concurrency conflicts

8

This chapter covers

- Using backing fields with relationships
- Using an SQL user-defined function in EF Core
- Configuring SQL column properties
- Handling concurrency conflicts

This chapter starts with more-advanced approaches to working with a database. These include a method to "hide" a relationship from outside changes, and various ways to move calculations into the database. Then we'll cover several configuration features that aren't the normal, run-of-the-mill features, but provide access or control of columns in the database. Although you won't use these features every day, they can be useful in specific circumstances.

The second half of this chapter is about handling multiple, near-simultaneous updates of the same piece of data in the database; these updates can cause problems known as *concurrency conflicts*. By default, EF Core uses an *Optimistic Concurrency pattern*, meaning it'll take the last value that was written to the database. You'll learn how to configure just one property/column or a whole entity/table to catch concurrency conflicts, and how to capture and then write code to correct the concurrency conflict.

206

8.1 Advanced feature—using backing fields with relationships

Chapter 6 introduced backing fields. In summary, with backing fields you can save/load a private field to the database, which allows you to control access to that value. You can do the same to a navigational property, which is especially useful for controlling access to collection navigational properties—the adding or removing of entries to one-to-many relationships. It's difficult to describe the benefits of this in a few words, so I'll describe a problem and then we'll solve it with a navigational relationship backing field.

> **EF6**   Using a backing field for a navigational property is new in EF Core. Backing fields provide a feature that developers who apply DDD principles to the database will find useful for locking down access to what DDD calls *aggregates*.

8.1.1 The problem—the book app performance is too slow

In our book app, the average of the review votes for a Book is found, obviously, by averaging the individual votes in all the reviews associated with the book, referred to as *average votes*. This calculation takes time and significantly slows the performance of the site. You therefore want to precalculate the average vote value for each book.

The problem is, if you precalculate the average votes, you must ensure that no changes to the database could invalidate the precalculated value. You therefore must intercept every conceivable way in which the average votes value could be changed. In this example, you'll change the Book's Reviews collection navigational property so that the developer can't update it directly, but has to go through your code, which recalculates the average votes value on every Review addition/removal.

> **NOTE**   This is an example of a *navigational backing field* and as such doesn't cover all the other ways in which the average votes value could be changed, such as someone changing the rating in a Review entity. In section 13.4.2, which uses precalculated values to improve performance, you'll handle all the possible ways in which the average votes value could become out-of-date.

8.1.2 Our solution—IEnumerable<Review> property and a backing field

In this example, our solution is to change the existing Book's Reviews property from an ICollection<Review> to an IEnumerable<Review> collection, and "hide" the real Reviews collection in an EF Core navigational backing field. You'll then provide two new methods, AddReview and RemoveReview, to your Book entity class, which a developer must use to change the Reviews linked to a Book.

The first change is to the Reviews collection:

1   Change the type of the Reviews collection navigational property from ICollection<Review> to IEnumerable<Review>. Because IEnumerable<T> doesn't support Add/Remove, the developer can't change this collection directly.

2 Create a backing field of type List<Review> called _reviews, which EF Core will automatically configure by convention.

3 With that done, you can add the following parts to the Book entity class:

a An AddReview method to add a Review entity to the _reviews backing field.

b A RemoveReview method to remove a Review entity from the _reviews backing field.

c Finally, both methods, AddReview and RemoveReview, will recalculate the average vote and place it in a property called CachedVotes.

The following listing shows the altered Book entity class with all the changes.

Listing 8.1   The Book entity class showing the backing field properties

```
public class Ch07Book
{
    private readonly List<Review> _reviews =
        new List<Review>();

    public int BookId { get; set; }
    public string Title { get; set; }

    public double? CachedVotes { get; private set; }

    public IEnumerable<Review> Reviews => _reviews.ToList();

    public void AddReview(Review review)
    {
        _reviews.Add(review);
        CachedVotes =
            _reviews.Average(x => x.NumStars);
    }

    public void RemoveReview(Review review)
    {
        _reviews.Remove(review);
        CachedVotes = _reviews.Any()
            ? _reviews.Average(x => x.NumStars)
            : (double?)null;
    }
}
```

Adds a backing field, which is a list, and tells EF Core to use this for all reads and writes

Holds a recalculated average of the reviews. It's read-only, so it can't be changed outside this class.

Returns a copy of the reviews that were loaded. By taking a copy, no one can alter the list by casting IEnumerable<T> to List<T>.

Adds a method to allow a new Review to be added to the _reviews collection

Recalculates the average votes for the book

Adds a method to remove a review from the _reviews collection

Removes the review from the list. This updates the database on the call to SaveChanges.

If there are no reviews, you set the value to null.

If there are reviews, you recalculate the average votes for the book.

Adds the new review to the backing field _reviews. This updates the database on the call to SaveChanges.

You do need to add some Fluent API configuration to tell EF Core to always read and write to the _reviews field. (I explain this configration in section 6.14.2.)

Listing 8.2 Configuring the backing field to read/write only to the `_reviews` field

Using MetaData for this entity class, you can access some of the deeper features of the entity class.

Finds the navigation property by using the name of the property

```
public static void Configure
    (this EntityTypeBuilder<Ch07Book> entity)
{
    entity.HasKey(p => p.BookId);

    //see https://github.com/aspnet/EntityFramework/issues/6674
    entity.Metadata
        .FindNavigation(nameof(Ch07Book.Reviews))
        .SetPropertyAccessMode
            (PropertyAccessMode.Field);
}
```

Sets the access mode so EF Core will read/write only to the backing field

The solution is good, but not foolproof in its current form, with issues around concurrent updates and other ways the developer can change NumStars. But the aim of this example is to show you how backing fields can be used to control access to navigational properties.

8.2 DbFunction—using user-defined functions with EF Core

SQL has a useful feature called *user-defined functions* (UDFs) that allow you to write SQL code that will be run in the database server. UDFs are useful because you can move a calculation from your software into the database, which can be more efficient because it can access the database directly. EF Core provides a feature called *database scalar function mapping*, DbFunction for short, which allows you to reference a UDF in your database as if it were a local method.

> **DEFINITION** An SQL *user-defined function* (UDF) is a routine that accepts parameters, performs an action (such as a complex calculation), and returns the result of that action as a value. The return value can either be a scalar (single) value or a table, but for *database scalar function mapping* and *computed columns* (see section 8.3), the function must return a scalar value of the correct type.

I think the DbFunction feature is useful, especially when you want to improve the performance of an EF Core query. For instance, in section 13.2, on performance tuning, you'll use DbFunction to bring a 60% performance improvement to one part of the book list query.

The steps to using a UDF in EF Core are as follows:

1. Configuration:
   a. Define a method (must be static in EF Core 2.0, but can be static or an instance in EF Core 2.1 onward) that has the correct name, input parameters, and output type that matches the definition of your UDF. This acts as a reference to your UDF.
   b. Declare the method in the application's DbContext, or in a separate class.
   c. Add the EF Core configuration commands to map your static UDF reference method to a call to your UDF code in the database.
2. Database setup: Manually add your UDF code to the database by using some form of SQL command.
3. Usage: Now you can use the static UDF reference in a query. EF Core will convert that method into a call to your UDF code in the database.

With that process in mind, let's detail the three stages: configuration, database setup, and usage.

8.2.1 Configuring a scalar user-defined function

The configuration consists of defining a static method to represent your UDF and then registering that method with EF Core at configuration time. For this example, you're going to produce a UDF, called `AverageVotes`, that works out the average review votes for a book. It takes in the primary key of the book you want to calculate for and returns a nullable double value—`null` if no reviews exist, or the average value of the review votes if there are any reviews.

Figure 8.1 shows the method that will represent the `AverageVotes` UDF in your software, with rules for forming this method. Note that the software method should never actually be called, which is why it throws an exception if it is.

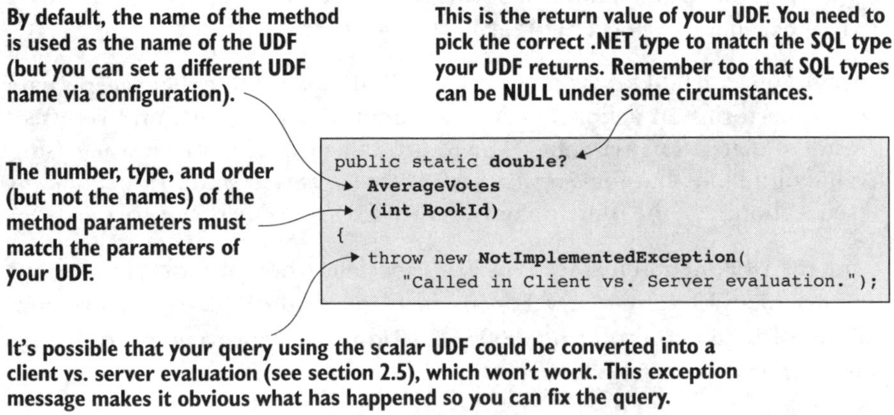

By default, the name of the method is used as the name of the UDF (but you can set a different UDF name via configuration).

This is the return value of your UDF. You need to pick the correct .NET type to match the SQL type your UDF returns. Remember too that SQL types can be NULL under some circumstances.

The number, type, and order (but not the names) of the method parameters must match the parameters of your UDF.

```
public static double?
    AverageVotes
    (int BookId)
{
    throw new NotImplementedException(
        "Called in Client vs. Server evaluation.");
```

It's possible that your query using the scalar UDF could be converted into a client vs. server evaluation (see section 2.5), which won't work. This exception message makes it obvious what has happened so you can fix the query.

Figure 8.1   An example static method that will represent your UDF inside your EF Core code. The captions highlight the parts that EF Core will use to map any calls to your UDF code, and the rules that you need to follow when building your own method to map to your UDF.

You can register your static UDF representation method with EF Core in one of two ways: by using either the DbFunction attribute or the Fluent API. You can use the DbFunction attribute if you place the method representing the UDF inside your application's DbContext. In this example of this approach, the DbFunction attribute and the static method are in bold.

Listing 8.3   Using a `DbFunction` attribute with a static method inside DbContext

Defines the method as being a representation of your UDF. The DbFunction can be used without any parameters, but here it's setting the schema because EF Core 2.0 didn't set the default schema property (fixed in 2.1).

```
public class Chapter08EfCoreContext : DbContext
{
    public DbSet<Book> Books { get; set; }
    //... other code removed for clarity

    public Chapter08EfCoreContext(
        DbContextOptions<Chapter08EfCoreContext> options)
        : base(options) {}
```

The return value, the method name, and the number, type, and order of the method parameters must match your UDF code.

```
    [DbFunction(Schema = "dbo")]
    public static double? AverageVotes(int id)
    {
        throw new NotImplementedException(
            "Called in Client vs. Server evaluation.");
    }
```

If your query that uses the scalar UDF is converted into a client vs. server evaluation, this software method will be executed client-side. NotImplementedException will be called if that happens; you can then decide what you want to do about it.

```
    protected override void
        OnModelCreating(ModelBuilder modelBuilder)
    {
        //... no Fluent API needed
    }
}
```

If you use DbFunction, you don't need any Fluent API to register the static method.

The other approach is to use the Fluent API to register the method as a UDF representation. The advantage of this is you can place the method in any class, which makes sense if you have a lot of UDFs. This listing shows the Fluent API approach for the same method, AverageVotes, but it's defined in a class called MyUdfMethods, as shown in figure 8.1.

Listing 8.4   Registering your static method representing your UDF using Fluent API

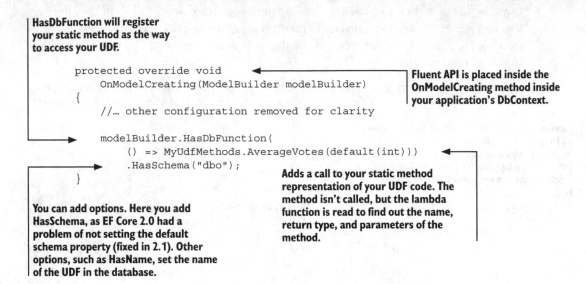

HasDbFunction will register
your static method as the way
to access your UDF.

```
protected override void
    OnModelCreating(ModelBuilder modelBuilder)
{
    //… other configuration removed for clarity

    modelBuilder.HasDbFunction(
        () => MyUdfMethods.AverageVotes(default(int)))
        .HasSchema("dbo");
}
```

Fluent API is placed inside the
OnModelCreating method inside
your application's DbContext.

Adds a call to your static method
representation of your UDF code. The
method isn't called, but the lambda
function is read to find out the name,
return type, and parameters of the
method.

You can add options. Here you add
HasSchema, as EF Core 2.0 had a
problem of not setting the default
schema property (fixed in 2.1). Other
options, such as HasName, set the name
of the UDF in the database.

After you've used either of these configuration approaches, EF Core knows how to access your UDF in a query.

8.2.2   *Adding your UDF code to the database*

Before you can use the UDF you've configured, you need to get your UDF code into the database. A UDF is normally a set of SQL commands that run on the database, so you need to add your UDF code to the database manually. Chapter 11, which is about database migrations, discusses ways of combining any SQL setup, such as adding a UDF, into your database migrations.

Next, you'll work through a simple example, more applicable to unit testing than production usage, showing what a UDF looks like and how to add it to a database. This listing uses the EF Core ExecuteSqlCommand command to add the SQL code that defines the AverageVotes UDF.

Listing 8.5   Adding your UDF to the database via the ExecuteSqlCommand method

Uses EF Core's ExecuteSqlCommand
method to add the UDF into the database

Captures the name of the static method that
represents your UDF and uses it as the name
of the UDF you add to the database

```
public const string UdfAverageVotes =
    nameof(MyUdfMethods.AverageVotes);

context.Database.ExecuteSqlCommand(
    $"CREATE FUNCTION {UdfAverageVotes} (@bookId int)" +
    @"  RETURNS float
    AS
    BEGIN
```

The SQL code that
follows adds a UDF to an
SQL server database.

```
DECLARE @result AS float
SELECT @result = AVG(CAST([NumStars] AS float))
    FROM dbo.Review AS r
    WHERE @bookId = r.BookId
RETURN @result
END");
```

This code should be executed when a new database is created. As I said, chapter 11 gives more details on how to do this properly in a production environment.

8.2.3 *Using a registered scalar UDF in your database queries*

Having registered the UDF as mapped to your static method, you're ready to use this in a database query. You can use this method as a return variable, or as part of the query filter or sorting. Here's a code snippet that returns information about a book, including the average review votes:

```
var bookAndVotes = context.Books.Select(x => new Dto
{
    BookId = x.BookId,
    Title = x.Title,
    AveVotes = MyUdfMethods.AverageVotes(x.BookId)
}).ToList();
```

This produces the following SQL code to run on the database, with the UDF call in bold:

```
SELECT [b].[BookId], [b].[Title],
[dbo].AverageVotes([b].[BookId]) AS [AveVotes]
FROM [Books] AS [b]
```

> **NOTE** EF Core can calculate the average without using a UDF via the LINQ command `x.Reviews.Average(q => q.NumStars)`. The calculation of the average votes is a running theme in this book, so you use it in the `AverageVotes` UDF example too.

UDFs can be used in any part of an EF Core query, either as return values, or for sorting or filtering. Here's another example, where you return only books whose average review is 2.5 or better:

```
var books = context.Books
    .Where(x =>
        MyUdfMethods.AverageVotes(x.BookId) >= 2.5)
.ToList();
```

8.3 *Computed column—a dynamically calculated column value*

Another useful SQL-side feature is a computed column, as it too can move some of the calculation over to the database. A *computed column* is a column whose value is calculated when you read the column, possibly by using other columns in the same row. For instance, the SQL computed column containing `[TotalPrice] AS (NumBook *`

`BookPrice`) would dynamically calculate the total price for that order. The result can be returned or used for sorting, filtering, and so on.

> **EF6** You can use computed columns in EF6.x, but EF6.x can't create them for you, so you have to add them via a direct SQL command. EF Core now provides a configuration method to define computed columns so that when EF Core creates or migrates a database, it'll add the computed column.

This example provides another take on the private date-of-birth backing fields in chapter 6, where you wanted to hide the exact date. In this example, you obscure the date of birth by using a computed column to return just the year of the person's birth. You declare the property in the normal way in the class, as shown in the following listing.

Listing 8.6 `Person` **entity class with computed column property** `YearOfBirth`

```
public class Person
{
    private DateTime _dateOfBirth;

    public int PersonId { get; set; }
    public string Name { get; set; }
    public int YearOfBirth { get; private set; }
    ...
```

The column that you'll set up as computed. You give it a private setter, as it's a read-only property.

Then you need to configure the column. The only way to do this is via the Fluent API. This listing shows this being done in bold, along with the backing field that the computed column accesses.

Listing 8.7 **Configuring a computed column**

```
protected override void OnModelCreating
    (ModelBuilder modelBuilder)
{
    modelBuilder.Entity<Person>()
        .Property<DateTime>("DateOfBirth")
        .HasField("_dateOfBirth")

    modelBuilder.Entity<Person>()
        .Property(p => p.YearOfBirth)
        .HasComputedColumnSql(
            "DatePart(yyyy, [DateOfBirth])");
}
```

Configures the backing field, with the column name DateOfBirth

Configures the property as a computed column and provides the SQL code that the database server will run

Figure 8.2 shows what happens when you update the Person table. EF Core knows that the table contains a computed column, so reads the value back after an add or update.

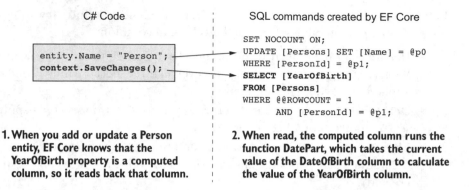

1. When you add or update a Person entity, EF Core knows that the YearOfBirth property is a computed column, so it reads back that column.

2. When read, the computed column runs the function DatePart, which takes the current value of the DateOfBirth column to calculate the value of the YearOfBirth column.

Figure 8.2   Because EF Core knows that `YearOfBirth` is a computed column, it'll read back the value of that column into the entity that took part in an addition or update to the row. When you read a computed column, the database server runs the SQL code to recalculate the value to return.

Computed columns can be quite useful for several reasons. First, the value of the column is calculated using the SQL code associated with the column, so the column's value is always up-to-date when you access it. Second, some calculations can be done more efficiently in SQL, such as some string concatenations. You can also call system or UDFs (see section 8.2), with columns as parameters, which gives you a wide range of features.

The disadvantage of computed columns is that each read causes a recalculation of the value. For simple calculations, the compute time will be minimal, but if you call a UDF that accesses the database, the time taken to read the data from the database can increase.

8.4   Setting a default value for a database column

When you first create a .NET type, it has a *default value* for an int, it's 0; for a string, it's null, and so on. Sometimes it's useful to set a different default value for a property; if you asked someone their favorite color, but they didn't reply, you could provide the default string not given instead of the normal null value.

You could set the default value in .NET by using the C# 6.0 autoproperty initializer feature with code such as this:

```
public string Answer { get; set; } = "not given";
```

EF Core provides three ways to set a default value for database columns, which go deeper than the C# 6.0 autoproperty initializer feature:

- A constant value is added to the column definition, and the database server applies that when a new row is added.
- An SQL fragment (a small, self-contained piece of SQL) is added to the column definition, and the database server applies that when a new row is added.
- A value is dynamically created by your code every time a new entity is added to the database—the entity's State is set to Added. This uses EF Core's ValueGenerator class.

Before exploring the pros and cons of each approach, let's define a few things that all the EF Core's default value-setting methods have in common:

- Defaults can be applied to properties, backing fields, and shadow properties. We'll use the generic term *column* to cover all three, because they all end up being applied to a column in the database.
- Default values—such as int, string, DateTime, GUID, and so on—apply only to scalar (nonrelational) columns.
- EF Core will apply a new default value only if the property contains the CLR default value appropriate to its type (it has the value it was given when it was first created).
- EF Core's default value methods work at the entity instance level, not the class level. The defaults won't be applied until you've called SaveChanges, or in the case of the value generator, when you use the Add command to add the entity.

Just to be clear: default values happen only on new rows added to the database. They don't apply to updates. Now you'll look at the three ways of setting a default value, starting with the simplest method, HasDefaultValue.

> **EF6** These three methods for setting a default value are new to EF Core. EF6.x has no equivalent commands.

8.4.1 Adding a constant as a default constraint

With EF Core, you can, via the Fluent API only, add a new SQL default constraint to a column definition in the database. The following code sets a default date of 1 January 2000 to the column DateOfBirth in the SQL table called People:

```
protected override void OnModelCreating
    (ModelBuilder modelBuilder)
{
    modelBuilder.Entity<DefaultTest>()
        .Property("DateOfBirth")
        .HasDefaultValue(new DateTime(2000,1,1));
    ...
}
```

The SQL code that EF Core produces, if it's asked to create/migrate an SQL Server database, looks like the following SQL snippet, with the default constraint in bold:

```
CREATE TABLE [Defaults] (
    [Id] int NOT NULL IDENTITY,
    -- other columns left out
    [DateOfBirth] datetime2 NOT NULL
            DEFAULT '2000-01-01T00:00:00.000',
    CONSTRAINT [PK_Defaults] PRIMARY KEY ([Id])
);
```

If the column in a new entity has the CLR default value, EF Core doesn't provide a value for that column in the SQL INSERT, which means the database server will apply the default constraint of the column definition to provide a value to insert in the new row.

This feature doesn't add a lot over using the C# 6.0 autoproperty initializer if the database is accessed only by EF Core. But if your application, or another application, uses direct SQL commands, this feature can be useful, as the defaults will apply to any access to the database. The downside over the C# 6.0 autoproperty initializer is that the default value is set in the entity class only after the entity has been written to the database, but EF core will read the value back when SaveChanges is called.

8.4.2 Adding an SQL fragment as a default constraint

The SQL syntax of a default constraint allows the call of a function to get the new default value, which allows interesting possibilities. For instance, you can call a system function that returns the current date/time, which for SQL Server is getdate or getutcdate. This function is executed at the time that the new row is added to the table, which means you can automatically capture the exact time that the row was inserted.

The following code shows you how to configure this using EF Core's Fluent API:

```
protected override void
    OnModelCreating(ModelBuilder modelBuilder)
{
    modelBuilder.Entity<DefaultTest>()
        .Property(x => x.CreatedOn)
        .HasDefaultValueSql("getutcdate()");
    …
}
```

The SQL commands to create the table look the same as the previous example, where you provided a constant value, but now it holds the system function surrounded by brackets. If you want to use this column to track when the row was added, you need to make sure the .NET property isn't set by code (it remains at the default value). You do this by using a property with a private setter. The following code snippet shows a property with a private setter and creates a simple tracking value that automatically tells you when the row was first inserted into the database:

```
public DateTime CreatedOn {get; private set;}
```

This is a useful feature. In addition to accessing system functions such as getutcdate, you can place your own SQL UDFs in a default constraint. There's a limit to the SQL commands that you can place—for instance, you can't reference another column in the default constraint, but it can provide useful features over the use of the C# 6.0 autoproperty initializer.

8.4.3 Creating a value generator to generate a default value dynamically

The third and last method to add a default value isn't executed in the database, but inside EF Core's logic. EF Core allows the class that inherits from the class Value-Generator or ValueGenerator<T> to be configured as a value generator for a property or backing field. This class will be asked for a default value if both of the following statements are true:

- The entity's State is set to Added; the entity is deemed to be a new entity to be added to the database.
- The property hasn't already been set; its value is at the .NET type's default value.

As an example, the next listing shows a simple value generator that creates a unique string by using the Name property in the entity plus a unique number to create a value for the property OrderId.

Listing 8.8   A value generator producing a unique string with the Name property

Called when you Add the entity to the DbContext.

Your value generator needs to inherit from EF Core's ValueGenerator<T>.

```
public class OrderIdValueGenerator
    : ValueGenerator<string>
{
    public override bool
        GeneratesTemporaryValues => false;

    public override string Next
        (EntityEntry entry)
    {
        var name = entry.
            Property(nameof(DefaultEntity.Name))
                .CurrentValue;
        var uniqueNum = DateTime.UtcNow.Ticks;
        return $"{name}-{uniqueNum}";
    }
}
```

Set this to false if you want your value to be written to the database.

Gives you access to the entity that the value generator creates a value for. You can access its properties, etc.

Selects the property called Name and gets its current value

You need to return a value of the type you've defined as T in the inherited ValueGenerator<T>.

This is the code to configure the use of a value generator:

```
protected override void
    OnModelCreating(ModelBuilder modelBuilder)
{
    modelBuilder.Entity<DefaultTest>()
        .Property(p => p.OrderId)
        .HasValueGenerator((p, e) =>
            new OrderIdValueGenerator());
    …
}
```

Note that the value generator's Next method is called when you Add the entity via context.Add(newEntity), but before the data is written to the database. Any database-provided values, such as the primary key using SQL IDENTITY, won't be set when the Next method is called.

NOTE   There's a NextAsync version too, if you need to implement an async version; for instance, if you need to access the database while generating the default value. In that case, you need to use the `AddAsync` method when adding the entity to the database.

The value generator is a specialized feature with limited applications, but one that's worth knowing about. The next chapter shows you how to intercept writes to the database to add tracking or other information, which is more work but provides more capabilities than the value generator.

8.5 Sequences—providing numbers in a strict order

Sequences in a database are a way to produce numbers in a strict order with no gaps—for instance, 1,2,3,4. Key values created by the SQL `IDENTITY` command aren't guaranteed to be in sequence; for instance, they might go 1,2,10,11. Sequences are useful when you want a guaranteed known sequence, such as for an order number for purchases.

The way sequences are implemented differs between database servers, but in general, a sequence isn't assigned to a specific table or column, but to a schema. Every time a column wants a value from the sequence, it asks for it. EF Core can set up a sequence and then, by using the `HasDefaultValueSql` method, the value of a column can be set to the next in the sequence.

The following listing shows an `Order` entity class that has an `OrderNo` that uses a sequence. The `HasDefaultValueSql` SQL fragment is for an SQL Server database, and will be different for other database servers.

Listing 8.9 The DbContext with the Fluent API configuration and the `Order` class

```
class MyContext : DbContext
{
    public DbSet<Order> Orders { get; set; }

    protected override void OnModelCreating
        (ModelBuilder modelBuilder)
    {
        modelBuilder.HasSequence<int>(
                "OrderNumbers", "shared")
            .StartsAt(1000)
            .IncrementsBy(5);

        modelBuilder.Entity<Order>()
            .Property(o => o.OrderNo)
            .HasDefaultValueSql(
                "NEXT VALUE FOR shared.OrderNumbers");
    }
}

public class Order
{
    public int OrderId { get; set; }
    public int OrderNo { get; set; }
}
```

Creates a sequence OrderNumber in the schema "shared". If no schema is provided, it'll use the default schema.

These are optional, and allow you to control the sequence start and increment. The default is start at 1 and increment by 1.

A column can access the sequence number via a default constraint. Each time the **NEXT VALUE** command is called, the sequence is incremented. The SQL shown is for an SQL Server database and will be different for other database providers.

EF6 This is a new feature in EF Core, with no corresponding feature in EF6.

8.6   *Marking database-generated properties*

When working with an existing database, you may need to tell EF Core about specific columns that are handled differently from what EF Core expects. If your existing database has a computed column that you didn't set up using EF Core's Fluent API (see section 8.2), EF Core needs to be told the column is computed so it handles the column properly.

I should say straightaway that marking columns in this way isn't the norm, because EF can work out the column attributes itself based on the configuration commands you've provided. You don't need any of the features in this section if you use EF Core to:

- Create or migrate the database.
- Reverse-engineer your database. (EF Core reads your database schema and generates your entity classes and application DbContext.)

If you want to use EF Core with an existing database without reverse-engineering (described in chapter 11), you need to tell EF Core about columns that don't conform to its normal conventions. The following sections will teach you how to mark three types of columns, starting with the most important type:

- Generated columns
- Columns added on insert
- "Normal" columns

EF6   EF6 has the same data annotation for setting the database-generated properties, but EF Core provides Fluent API versions too.

8.6.1   *Marking a column that's generated on an addition or update*

EF Core needs to know if a column's value is generated by the database, such as a computed column, if for no other reason than it's read-only. EF Core can't "guess" that the database sets a column's value, so you need to mark it as such. You can use Data Annotations or the Fluent API.

The data annotation for an add-or-update column is shown in the following code snippet. Here, EF Core is using the existing DatabaseGeneratedOption.Computed setting. The setting is called Computed because that's the most likely reason, but there are other ways that a database column can be updated on adding a new row or updating the row:

```
public class PersonWithAddUpdateAttibutes
{
    ...

    [DatabaseGenerated(DatabaseGeneratedOption.Computed)]
    public int YearOfBirth { get; set; }
}
```

This code snippet uses the Fluent API to set the add-or-update setting to the column:

```
protected override void OnModelCreating(ModelBuilder modelBuilder)
{
    modelBuilder.Entity<Person>()
        .Property(p => p.YearOfBirth)
        .ValueGeneratedOnAddOrUpdate();
    ...
}
```

8.6.2 *Marking a column's value as set on insert of a new row*

When a row is first inserted into the database, a column can be given a value in two common ways:

- By some form of key generation, of which SQL's IDENTITY command is the primary method. In these cases, the database creates a unique value to place in the column when a new row is inserted.
- Via an SQL default constraint, which provides a default value if no value is given in the INSERT command.

Taking the key generation case first, I'd say that EF Core normally knows via other methods whether the key is going to be generated. Section 6.3.5 talked about how EF Core can find a primary key, or you can define the primary key (section 6.8).

It's unusual to need to tell EF Core that a column's value is created via the IDENTITY command. EF Core requires a primary key of some form, and the database provider can work out from the key's type if it's one that the database server can create a unique value for. But if you do need to specify that the column value is created by identity, you can use Data annotations or the Fluent API. This shows the use of Data Annotations:

```
public class MyClass
{
    public int MyClassId { get; set;}
    ...
    [DatabaseGenerated(DatabaseGeneratedOption.Identity)]
    public int SecondaryKey { get; set;}
}
```

The second example does the same thing, but using the Fluent API. For this, you have a column with a default constraint, and the Fluent API code to set this is shown in the following code snippet:

```
protected override void OnModelCreating(ModelBuilder modelBuilder)
{
    modelBuilder.Entity<Person>()
        .Property("DateOfBirth")
        .ValueGeneratedOnAdd();

    ...
}
```

8.6.3   *Marking a column as "normal"*

In the last case, EF Core assumes that the column has some form of key generation applied to it, but you don't have/want a key generated. Although this rarely occurs, one case I know about is a primary key using a *GUID*, where your software supplies the value.

> **DEFINITION**   A *GUID* is a *globally unique identifier*, a 128-bit integer that can be used safely anywhere. It makes a good key value in a few cases. In one case, the software wants to define the key, normally because some other part of the software needs the key before the row is inserted. In another case, you have replicated databases with inserts into both/all databases, which makes creating a unique key more difficult.

Our tests show that if you use a GUID as a primary key, EF Core will automatically create a GUID value if you don't supply one (it uses a GUID value generator inside EF Core). You can turn this off with a data annotation:

```
public class MyClass
{
    [DatabaseGenerated(DatabaseGeneratedOption.None)]
    public GUID MyClassId { get; set;}
    ...
}
```

You can also do this by using the following Fluent API configuration:

```
protected override void OnModelCreating(ModelBuilder modelBuilder)
{
    modelBuilder.Entity<MyClass>()
        .Property("MyClassId")
        .ValueGeneratedNever();
    ...
}
```

8.7   *Handling simultaneous updates—concurrency conflicts*

Concurrency conflicts are a big topic, so let me start by explaining what simultaneous updates look like before explaining why they can be a problem and how you can handle them. Figure 8.3 shows an example of simultaneous updates to the PublishedOn column in a database. This happens because of two separate pieces of code running in parallel, which read the column and then update it.

By default, EF Core uses an Optimistic Concurrency pattern. In figure 8.3, this means that the first update is lost because it's overwritten by the second. Although this is often acceptable, in some cases overwriting someone else's update is a problem. The next sections explain unacceptable overwrites, known as *concurrency conflicts*, and how EF Core allows you to detect and fix such conflicts.

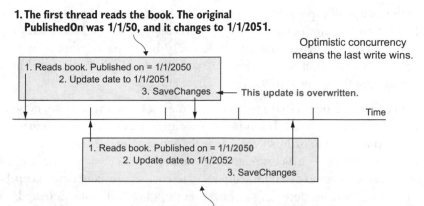

1. The first thread reads the book. The original PublishedOn was 1/1/50, and it changes to 1/1/2051.

Optimistic concurrency means the last write wins.

1. Reads book. Published on = 1/1/2050
2. Update date to 1/1/2051
3. SaveChanges ◄— This update is overwritten.

Time

1. Reads book. Published on = 1/1/2050
2. Update date to 1/1/2052
3. SaveChanges

2. The second thread reads the book and gets the original PublishedOn was 1/1/2050. It then changes the PublishedOn date to 1/1/2052, which overwrites the first task's update.

Figure 8.3   Two pieces of code (say, on a web application) that are running in parallel and make a near-simultaneous update of the same column (in this case, the publication date of the same book). By default, EF Core allows the second write to win, and the first write is lost. This is called optimistic concurrency, but the "last write win" rule may not be useful in all cases.

8.7.1   Why do concurrency conflicts matter?

If you think about it, a setting can be overwritten anyway. For instance, you could set the publication date of a book to 1/1/2020, and tomorrow you could change it to 1/1/2040, so why are concurrency conflicts such a big deal?

In some cases concurrent conflicts do matter. For instance, in financial transactions, you can imagine that the purity and auditing of data is going to be important, so you might want to guard against concurrency changes. Another concurrent conflict exists in the example in section 7.10, where you calculated the average book review votes. In that case, if two people added reviews at the same time, that recalculation would be incorrect, so you need to detect and fix that conflict if that example is going to be robust.

Other human-level concurrent conflicts can occur. Instead of two tasks clashing on updates, two users looking at screens can clash, with the same default result—the second person to press the Submit button overwrites the update the first person thought they had done (section 8.7.4 covers the details).

Sometimes you get around concurrency conflicts by design, by creating applications such that dangerous concurrent updates can't happen. For instance, in an e-commerce website that I designed, I had an order-processing system that used background tasks, which could've caused concurrent conflicts. I got around this potential problem by designing the order processing to remove the possibility of concurrent updates:

- I split the customer order information into an immutable order part that never changed. This contains data, such as what was ordered and where should it be sent. After that order was created, it was never changed or deleted.

- For the changing parts of the order, which was the order status as it moved through the system, I created a separate table in which I added each new order status as it occurred, with the date and time (this approach is known as *event sourcing*). I could then get the latest order status by sorting them by date/time order and picking the status with the newest date and time.

This design approach meant that I never updated or deleted any order data, so concurrent conflicts couldn't happen. It did make handling a customer change to an order a bit more complicated, but orders were safe from concurrent conflict issues.

But when concurrent conflicts are an issue, and you can't design around it, EF Core provides several features to catch and allow you to correct any concurrent conflicts. EF Core provides two ways of detecting a concurrent update and, once detected, a way of getting at all the relevant data so you can implement code to fix the issue.

8.7.2   *EF Core's concurrency conflict–handling features*

EF Core's concurrency conflict-handling features consist of two ways that EF Core can detect a concurrency update, activated by adding one of the following to an entity class:

- A *concurrency token*, to mark a specific property/column in your entity class as one to check for a concurrency conflict.
- A *timestamp*, which marks a whole entity class/row as one to check for a concurrency conflict.

EF6   EF Core concurrency-handling features are the same as in EF6.x, but reimplemented in EF Core.

In both cases, when `SaveChanges` is called, EF Core produces database server code to check updates of any entities that contain concurrency tokens or timestamps. If that code detects that the concurrency tokens or timestamps have changed since it read the entity, it throws a `DbUpdateConcurrencyException` exception. At that point, you can use EF Core's features to inspect the differing versions of the data and apply your custom code to decide which of the concurrent updates wins.

Now you'll learn how to set up the two approaches, a concurrency token and then a timestamp, and how EF Core detects the change.

DETECTING A CONCURRENT CHANGE VIA CONCURRENCY TOKEN

The concurrency token approach allows you to configure one or more properties as a concurrency token. This tells EF Core to check that the current database value is the same as the value found when the tracked entity was loaded as part of the SQL `UPDATE` command sent to the database. That way, the update will fail if the loaded value and the current database value are different. Figure 8.4 shows an example of marking the `PublishedOn` property as a concurrency token, and then a concurrency conflict occurs.

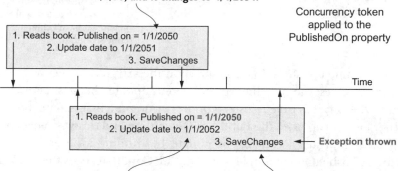

1. The first thread reads the book. The original PublishedOn was 1/1/50, and it changes to 1/1/2051.

1. Reads book. Published on = 1/1/2050
2. Update date to 1/1/2051
3. SaveChanges

Concurrency token applied to the PublishedOn property

Time

1. Reads book. Published on = 1/1/2050
2. Update date to 1/1/2052
3. SaveChanges ◄— Exception thrown

2. The second thread reads the book and gets the original PublishedOn was 1/1/2050. It then changes the PublishedOn date to 1/1/2052.

3. SaveChanges produces an UPDATE command that checks that the PublishedOn column value is still 1/1/2050. This fails because the PublishedOn column in the database has changed, so EF Core throws a DbUpdateConcurrencyException.

Figure 8.4   Two pieces of code—say, on a web application—that are running in parallel and make a near-simultaneous update of the `PublishedOn` column. Because you've marked the `PublishedOn` property as a concurrency token, EF Core uses a modified SQL `UPDATE` command that performs the update only if the database PublishedOn column is the same as it was when it read in the `Book` entity. If it isn't the same, the `UPDATE` fails and `SaveChanges` throws `DbUpdateConcurrencyException`.

To set this up, you add the `ConcurrencyCheck` data annotation to the `PublishedOn` property in our `ConcurrencyBook` entity class, shown here. EF Core finds this data annotation during configuration and marks the property as a concurrency token.

> **Listing 8.10   The `ConcurrencyBook` entity class, with a `PublishedOn` property**

```
public class ConcurrencyBook
{
    public int ConcurrencyBookId { get; set; }
    public string Title { get; set; }

    [ConcurrencyCheck]
    public DateTime PublishedOn { get; set; }

    public ConcurrencyAuthor Author { get; set; }
}
```

Tells EF Core that the PublishedOn property is a concurrency token, which means EF Core will check it hasn't changed when you update it

In this case, you've used the `ConcurrencyCheck` data annotation to define the property as a concurrency token, which has the benefit of making it clear to anyone looking at the code that the `PublishedOn` property has special handling. Alternatively, you can define a concurrency token via the Fluent API.

> **Listing 8.11   Setting a property as a concurrency token by using the Fluent API**

```
protected override void
    OnModelCreating(ModelBuilder modelBuilder)
{
```

The OnModelCreating method is where you place the configuration of the concurrency detection.

```
modelBuilder.Entity<ConcurrencyBook>()
    .Property(p => p.PublishedOn)
    .IsConcurrencyToken();

//… other configuration removed
}
```

Defines the PublishedOn property as a concurrency token, which means EF Core checks it hasn't changed when writing out an update

Now when the same update is done, as shown at the start of this section on handling simultaneous updates, the handling of the second update changes. Figure 8.4 shows that when SaveChanges is called, instead of overwriting the first update, it now detects that another task has updated the PublishedOn column and throws an exception.

Listing 8.12 simulates a concurrent update by running an SQL command that changes the PublishedOn column between the EF Core that reads the book and then updates the book. The SQL command represents another thread of the web application, or another application that has access to the same database, updating the PublishedOn column. In this case, a DbUpdateConcurrencyException exception is thrown when SaveChanges is called in the last line.

Listing 8.12 Simulating a concurrent update of the PublishedOn column

Simulates another thread/application, changing the PublishedOn column of the same book

Loads the first book in the database as a tracked entity

```
var firstBook = context.Books.First();

context.Database.ExecuteSqlCommand(
    "UPDATE dbo.Books SET PublishedOn = GETDATE()"+
    " WHERE ConcurrencyBookId = @p0",
    firstBook.ConcurrencyBookId);
firstBook.Title = Guid.NewGuid().ToString();
context.SaveChanges();
```

Changes the title in the book to cause EF Core to update the book

This SaveChanges will throw DbUpdateConcurrencyException.

The important thing to note is that only the property marked as a concurrency token is checked. If your SQL-simulated update changed, say, the Title property, which isn't marked as a concurrency token, no exception would be thrown.

You can see this in the SQL that EF Core produces to update the Title in this example, shown next. The SQL WHERE clause contains not only the primary key of the book to update, but also the PublishedOn column.

Listing 8.13 SQL code to update Book where PublishedOn is a concurrency token

```
SET NOCOUNT ON;
UPDATE [Books] SET [Title] = @p0
WHERE [ConcurrencyBookId] = @p1
      AND [PublishedOn] = @p2;
SELECT @@ROWCOUNT;
```

The test fails if the PublishedOn column has changed, which stops the update.

Returns the number of rows updated by this SQL command.

When EF Core runs this SQL command, the WHERE clause will find a valid row to update only if the PublishedOn column hasn't changed from the value EF Core read in from the database. EF Core then checks the number of rows that have been updated by the SQL command. If the number of rows updated is zero, EF Core raises DbUpdate-ConcurrencyException to say that a concurrency conflict exists; EF Core can catch a concurrency conflict caused by another task either changing the PublishedOn column or deleting the row, when this task does an update.

The good thing about using a concurrency token is that it works on any database, because it uses basic commands. The next way of detecting concurrency changes, called a *timestamp* by EF Core, relies on a database server-side feature, called *Row Version* in SQL server.

DETECTING A CONCURRENT CHANGE VIA TIMESTAMP

The second way of checking for concurrency conflicts is by using what EF Core calls a *timestamp*. This works differently than the concurrency token, as it uses a unique value provided by the database server that's changed whenever a row is inserted or updated. The whole entity is protected against concurrency changes, rather than specific properties/columns as with the concurrency token.

Figure 8.5 shows that when a row with a property/column marked as a *timestamp* is either inserted or updated, the database server will produce a new, unique value for that column. This has the effect of detecting an update to an entity/row whenever SaveChanges is called.

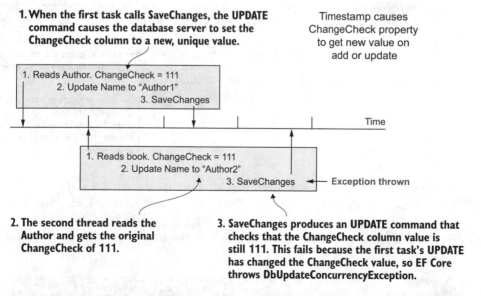

1. When the first task calls SaveChanges, the UPDATE command causes the database server to set the ChangeCheck column to a new, unique value.

Timestamp causes ChangeCheck property to get new value on add or update

1. Reads Author. ChangeCheck = 111
2. Update Name to "Author1"
3. SaveChanges

Time

1. Reads book. ChangeCheck = 111
2. Update Name to "Author2"
3. SaveChanges ◄— Exception thrown

2. The second thread reads the Author and gets the original ChangeCheck of 111.

3. SaveChanges produces an UPDATE command that checks that the ChangeCheck column value is still 111. This fails because the first task's UPDATE has changed the ChangeCheck value, so EF Core throws DbUpdateConcurrencyException.

Figure 8.5   Configuring a property as a timestamp means that the corresponding column in the table must be set to a database server type that will be set to a new, unique value every time an SQL INSERT or UPDATE command is applied to the row. (If you use EF Core to create your database, the database provider will ensure the correct column type.) Then, when EF Core does an update, it checks that the timestamp column has the same value as when the entity was read in. If the value is different, EF Core will throw an exception.

Each database server implements the timestamp feature in a slightly different way. I'm going to describe how SQL Server implements it, but section 14.1.3 describes some of the ways other databases handle this feature.

Listing 8.14 adds a `ChangeCheck` property, which will watch for any updates to the whole entity, to an entity class called `ConcurrencyAuthor`. In this case, the `ChangeCheck` property has a `Timestamp` data annotation. This tells EF Core to mark this as a special column that the database will update with a unique value. In the case of SQL Server, the database provider will set the column as an SQL Server `rowversion`; other databases have different approaches to implementing the `TimeStamp` column.

Listing 8.14   The `ConcurrencyAuthor` class, with the `ChangeCheck` property

```
public class ConcurrencyAuthor
{
    public int ConcurrencyAuthorId { get; set; }
    public string Name { get; set; }
    [Timestamp]
    public byte[] ChangeCheck { get; set; }
}
```

> Marks the **ChangeCheck** property as a timestamp. This causes the database server to mark it as an SQL ROWVERSION, and EF Core will check this when updating to see if this has changed.

Again, you use a data annotation, `Timestamp`, to mark the `ChangeCheck` property as a timestamp. This is my recommended way of configuring this, because it makes it obvious to anyone looking at the code that there's special concurrency handling of this entity. Alternatively, you can use the Fluent API to configure a timestamp.

Listing 8.15   Configuring a timestamp by using the Fluent API

```
protected override void
    OnModelCreating(ModelBuilder modelBuilder)
{
    modelBuilder.Entity<ConcurrencyAuthor>()
        .Property(p => p.ChangeCheck)
        .IsRowVersion();
}
```

> **OnModelCreating is where you place the configuration of the concurrency detection.**

> Defines an extra property called **ChangeCheck** that will be changed every time the row is created/updated. EF Core checks that it hasn't changed when it does an update.

Both configurations create a column in a table that the database server will automatically change whenever there's an `INSERT` or `UPDATE` to that table. For SQL Server database, the column type is set to `ROWVERSION`, as seen in the following listing. Other database servers can use different approaches, but they all provide a new, unique value on an `INSERT` or `UPDATE`.

Listing 8.16   The SQL to create the Authors table, with a `ROWVERSION` column

```
CREATE TABLE [dbo].[Authors] (
    [ConcurrencyAuthorId] INT  IDENTITY (1, 1),
    [ChangeCheck]         ROWVERSION NOT NULL,
    [Name]                NVARCHAR (MAX) NULL
);
```

> If the table is created by EF Core, it will set the column type to ROWVERSION if your property is of type byte[]. This column's value will be updated on each INSERT or UPDATE.

You simulate a concurrent change by using the code in listing 8.17. This consists of three steps:

1 You use EF Core to read in the Authors row that you want to update.
2 You use an SQL command to update the Authors table; this simulates another task updating the same Author that you have just read in. EF Core doesn't know anything about this change because raw SQL bypasses EF Core's tracking snapshot feature.
3 In the last two lines, you update the Author's name and call `SaveChanges`, which will cause a `DbUpdateConcurrencyException` to be thrown. This is because EF Core has found that the ChangeCheck column has changed from step 1.

Listing 8.17 Simulating a concurrent update of the `ConcurrentAuthor` entity

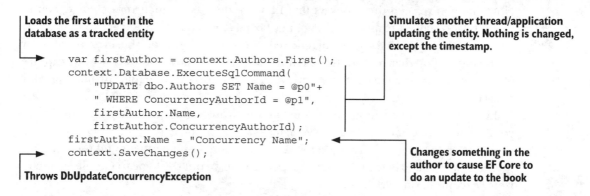

Loads the first author in the database as a tracked entity

Simulates another thread/application updating the entity. Nothing is changed, except the timestamp.

```
var firstAuthor = context.Authors.First();
context.Database.ExecuteSqlCommand(
    "UPDATE dbo.Authors SET Name = @p0"+
    " WHERE ConcurrencyAuthorId = @p1",
    firstAuthor.Name,
    firstAuthor.ConcurrencyAuthorId);
firstAuthor.Name = "Concurrency Name";
context.SaveChanges();
```

Throws DbUpdateConcurrencyException

Changes something in the author to cause EF Core to do an update to the book

This code is like the previous case, where you used a `concurrency token`. The difference is that the timestamp detects an update of the row via the unique value in the property/column called ChangeCheck. You can see this in the following listing, where you show the SQL that EF Core produces to update the row with the check on the timestamp property, ChangeCheck.

Listing 8.18 The SQL code to update the author's name, with `ChangeCheck` check

```
SET NOCOUNT ON;
UPDATE [Authors] SET [Name] = @p0
WHERE [ConcurrencyAuthorId] = @p1
    AND [ChangeCheck] = @p2;
SELECT [ChangeCheck]
FROM [Authors]
WHERE @@ROWCOUNT = 1
    AND [ConcurrencyAuthorId] = @p1;
```

The check that the ChangeCheck column is the same as the value EF Core read in

Because the update will change the ChangeCheck column, EF Core needs to read it back so its in-memory copy is correct.

Checks that one row was updated in the last command. If not, it won't return the ChangeCheck value and EF Core will know that a concurrent change has taken place.

The UPDATE part checks that the ChangeCheck column is the same value as the copy it found when it first read the entity, and if it is, it executes the update. The second part returns the new ChangeCheck column that the database server has created after the current update, but only if the UPDATE was executed. If no value is returned for the ChangeCheck property, EF Core knows that a concurrency conflict has happened and it will throw DbUpdateConcurrencyException.

Choosing between the two approaches, concurrency token or timestamp, depends on your business rules. The concurrency token approach provides a specific protection of the property/properties you place it on, and will be triggered only if a property marked as a concurrency token is changed. The timestamp approach catches any update to that entity.

8.7.3 *Handling a DbUpdateConcurrencyException*

Now that you've seen the two ways that EF Core detects a concurrent change, you're ready to look at an example of catching DbUpdateConcurrencyException. The way you write your code to fix a concurrency conflict depends on your business reasons for capturing it. For that reason, this example is going to show you only how to capture DbUpdateConcurrencyException, and what data you have available for making your decisions.

Listing 8.19 shows the method you call after you've updated the Book entity with your change. This method, BookSaveChangesWithChecks, calls SaveChanges and captures any DbUpdateConcurrencyException exception if one happens and uses another method called HandleBookConcurrency, where you've put the logic to handle a concurrency exception on a Book entity.

> **Listing 8.19   The method you call to save changes that trap concurrency conflicts**

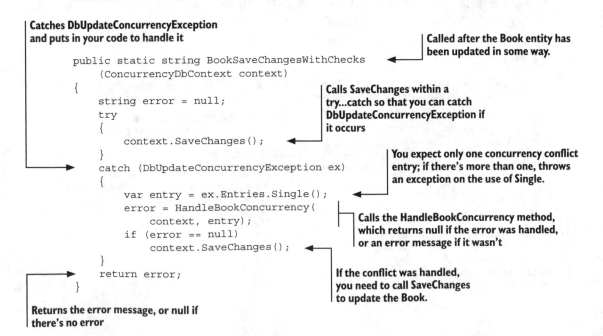

Catches DbUpdateConcurrencyException
and puts in your code to handle it

Called after the Book entity has
been updated in some way.

```
public static string BookSaveChangesWithChecks
    (ConcurrencyDbContext context)
{
    string error = null;
    try
    {
        context.SaveChanges();
    }
    catch (DbUpdateConcurrencyException ex)
    {
        var entry = ex.Entries.Single();
        error = HandleBookConcurrency(
            context, entry);
        if (error == null)
            context.SaveChanges();
    }
    return error;
}
```

Calls SaveChanges within a
try...catch so that you can catch
DbUpdateConcurrencyException if
it occurs

You expect only one concurrency conflict
entry; if there's more than one, throws
an exception on the use of Single.

Calls the HandleBookConcurrency method,
which returns null if the error was handled,
or an error message if it wasn't

If the conflict was handled,
you need to call SaveChanges
to update the Book.

Returns the error message, or null if
there's no error

The `BookSaveChangesWithChecks` method returns a string, which is `null` if successful or an error message if it can't handle this concurrency conflict. (In this example, you handle an update conflict, but you return an error message on a delete conflict—see the `HandleBookConcurrency` method in listing 8.15.) Note that you must call the `SaveChanges` method again, but only if you've fixed the concurrency problem. Otherwise, it'll keep looping around with the same exception.

The `HandleBookConcurrency` method handles a `Book` entity update concurrency conflict. You have at your disposal three versions of the database data, shown in table 8.1. In this example, you're looking at the `PublishedOn` property, which is protected by a concurrency token. The table columns are in time order, with the newest on the left. I've also highlighted in bold the columns that are different from the version read at the start of our update code in listing 8.15.

Table 8.1 The three versions of the data when the concurrency update exception occurs

Column names	1. The version you read before the update	2. What someone else wrote to the database	3. What you wanted to write out
ConcurrencyBookId	1	1	1
Title	Default Title	Default Title	**Changed title**
PublishedOn	2014/1/1	**2016/2/8**	2014/1/1

The following listing shows the content of your `HandleBookConcurrency` method used in the listing 8.19. The code names some of the variables starting with `version1`, `version2`, or `version3`. These correspond to the three versions of the data, as listed in table 8.1.

Listing 8.20 Handling a concurrent update on the book

```
private static string HandleBookConcurrency(      ◄─── Takes in the application DbContext and
    ConcurrencyDbContext context,                      the ChangeTracking entry from the
    EntityEntry entry)                                 exception's Entities property.
{
    var book = entry.Entity
        as ConcurrencyBook;          Handles only ConcurrencyBook, so
    if (book == null)    ◄───        throws an exception if the entry isn't
        throw new NotSupportedException(   of type Book.
"Don't know how to handle concurrency conflicts for " +
            entry.Metadata.Name);
                                                   Entity must be read as NoTracking;
    var databaseEntity =                           otherwise, it'll interfere with the
        context.Books.AsNoTracking()      ◄─────── same entity you're trying to write.
            .SingleOrDefault(p => p.ConcurrencyBookId
                == book.ConcurrencyBookId);
    if (databaseEntity == null)  ◄───
```

You want to get the data that someone else wrote into the database after your read.

Concurrency conflict method doesn't handle the case where the book was deleted, so it returns a user-friendly error message.

You get the TEntity version of the entity, which has all the tracking information.

You go through all the properties in the book entity to reset the Original values so that the exception doesn't happen again.

```
        return "Unable to save changes.The book was deleted by another
    user.";

    var version2Entity = context.Entry(databaseEntity);

    foreach (var property in entry.Metadata.GetProperties())
    {
        var version1_original = entry
            .Property(property.Name).OriginalValue;
```

Holds the version of the property at the time you did the tracked read of the book.

Holds the version of the property as written to the database by someone else.

```
        var version2_someoneElse = version2Entity
            .Property(property.Name).CurrentValue;
        var version3_whatIWanted = entry
            .Property(property.Name).CurrentValue;
```

Holds the version of the property that you wanted to set it to in your update.

```
        // TODO: Logic to decide which value should be written to database
        if (property.Name ==
            nameof(ConcurrencyBook.PublishedOn))
        {
            entry.Property(property.Name).CurrentValue
                = new DateTime(2050, 5, 5);
        }
```

Your code to fix the concurrency issue goes here. You set the PublishedOn property to a specific value so you can check it in your unit test.

```
        entry.Property(property.Name).OriginalValue =
            version2Entity.Property(property.Name)
                .CurrentValue;
    }
    return null;
}
```

You return null to say you handled this concurrency issue.

Here you set the OriginalValue to the value that someone else set it to. This handles using concurrency tokens or a timestamp.

The main part you need to change is the section starting with the comment // TODO. You should put your code to handle the concurrent update there. The code you put in sets a specific date so that your unit test can check that your code worked, but what you put there depends on the business rules in your application.

Note that your HandleBookConcurrency method also detects that a concurrency conflict caused by the original Book entity has been deleted. In that case, when your concurrency-handling method tries to reread the actual row in the database using the Book's primary key, it won't find that row and will return null. Your current implementation doesn't handle that case and returns an error message to show the user.

8.7.4   *The disconnected concurrent update issue*

In applications such as a website, another concurrency update scenario can occur that encompasses the user-interaction part of the system. The examples so far covered simultaneous code updates, but if you bring in the human factor, the problem is more likely, and possibly more business relevant.

For instance, figure 8.6 shows employee John Doe getting a pay raise being set by both John's boss and by Human Resources. Now the time between each person seeing the figure and deciding what to do is measured in minutes instead of milliseconds, but if you don't do anything about it, you can have another *concurrency conflict*, with potentially the wrong salary set.

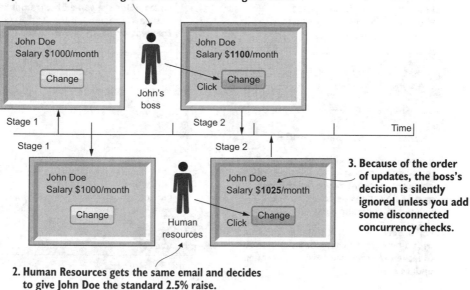

1. John Doe's boss gets an email saying it's time to review John's salary. The boss gives him a 10% raise for good work.

2. Human Resources gets the same email and decides to give John Doe the standard 2.5% raise.

3. Because of the order of updates, the boss's decision is silently ignored unless you add some disconnected concurrency checks.

Figure 8.6   A concurrency problem, now running in human time. John Doe's salary review is due, and two people, John's boss and a Human Resources employee, try to update his salary at the same time. Unless you add concurrency checks, the boss's update, which came first, is silently ignored, which most likely isn't the correct business outcome.

Although this looks very much like the concurrency conflicts example in section 8.7.2, the change is in the way a disconnected concurrency conflict is found. To handle a disconnected update, the original value of the property you're protecting (in this case, the `Salary`) must be passed from the first stage of the disconnect to the second stage. Then your second stage must use that original `Salary` in the concurrency-conflict check during the update part of the process.

Also, the way a concurrency conflict is dealt with is often different. Typically, in a human user case, the decision on what should happen is given back to the user. If a conflict occurs, the user is presented with a new screen indicating what happened and is given a choice on what should be done. This changes the code that handles DbUpdate-ConcurrencyException into more of a diagnostic role rather than code that fixes the problem.

If a concurrency conflict exists, the user is presented with a new screen with an error message indicating what happened. The user is then invited to accept the current state, or apply the update, knowing that this overrides the last user's update.

Figure 8.7 shows what happens when the user clicks the Change button after setting the new salary. As you can see, the original salary, which was displayed to the user on the first screen, is sent back with the other data and used in the concurrency check when the Salary is updated (see the UpdateSalary method in listing 8.16).

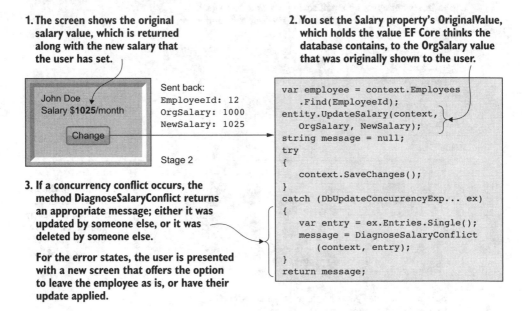

1. The screen shows the original salary value, which is returned along with the new salary that the user has set.

2. You set the Salary property's OriginalValue, which holds the value EF Core thinks the database contains, to the OrgSalary value that was originally shown to the user.

```
Sent back:
EmployeeId: 12
OrgSalary: 1000
NewSalary: 1025
```
Stage 2

```
var employee = context.Employees
    .Find(EmployeeId);
entity.UpdateSalary(context,
    OrgSalary, NewSalary);
string message = null;
try
{
    context.SaveChanges();
}
catch (DbUpdateConcurrencyExp... ex)
{
    var entry = ex.Entries.Single();
    message = DiagnoseSalaryConflict
        (context, entry);
}
return message;
```

3. If a concurrency conflict occurs, the method DiagnoseSalaryConflict returns an appropriate message; either it was updated by someone else, or it was deleted by someone else.

For the error states, the user is presented with a new screen that offers the option to leave the employee as is, or have their update applied.

Figure 8.7   After the user has changed the salary and clicked the Change button, the new salary and the original salary values are sent back to the web application. It then calls the UpdateSalary **method, shown in listing 8.16, that both updates the salary and sets the original value expected in the database when it does the update. If a concurrency conflict is found, a new screen with an appropriate error message is shown to the user, who can then accept the existing database state, or apply their own update to the employee.**

Listing 8.21 shows the entity class used for this example, with the Salary property set as a concurrency token. You also create a method called UpdateSalary that contains the code you need to execute in order to update the Salary property in such a way that DbUpdateConcurrencyException will be thrown if the Salary value has changed from the value originally shown on the user's screen.

Listing 8.21 Entity class used to hold an employee's salary with concurrency check

```
public class Employee
{
    public int EmployeeId { get; set; }

    public string Name { get; set; }

    [ConcurrencyCheck]
    public int Salary { get; set; }

    public void UpdateSalary
        (DbContext context,
         int orgSalary, int newSalary)
    {
        Salary = newSalary;
        context.Entry(this).Property(p => p.Salary)
            .OriginalValue = orgSalary;
    }
}
```

Salary property set as a concurrency token by the ConcurrencyCheck attribute.

Updates the Salary in a disconnected state

Sets the Salary to the new value

Sets the OriginalValue, which holds the data read from the database, to the original value that was shown to the user in the first part of the update

After applying the UpdateSalary method to the Employee entity of the person whose salary you want to change, you call SaveChanges within a try...catch block to update the Employee. If SaveChanges raises DbUpdateConcurrencyException, the job of the DiagnoseSalaryConflict method shown in the following listing isn't to fix the conflict, but to create an appropriate error message so the user can decide what to do.

Listing 8.22 Returns different errors for update or delete concurrency conflicts

```
private string DiagnoseSalaryConflict(
    ConcurrencyDbContext context,
    EntityEntry entry)
{
    var employee = entry.Entity
        as Employee;
    if (employee == null)
        throw new NotSupportedException(
"Don't know how to handle concurrency conflicts for " +
            entry.Metadata.Name);

    var databaseEntity =
        context.Employees.AsNoTracking()
            .SingleOrDefault(p =>
                p.EmployeeId == employee.EmployeeId);

    if (databaseEntity == null)
        return
```

Called if a DbUpdateConcurrencyException occurs. Its job isn't to fix the problem, but form an error message and provide options for fixing the problem.

If the entity that failed wasn't an Employee, you throw an exception, as this code can't handle that.

You want to get the data that someone else wrote into the database after your read.

You check whether this was a delete conflict—the employee was deleted because the user attempted to update it.

Must be read as NoTracking; otherwise, it'll interfere with the same entity you're trying to write.

```
        $"The Employee {employee.Name} was deleted by another user. " +
        $"Click Add button to add back with salary of {employee.Salary}" +
        " or Cancel to leave deleted.";

            return
        $"The Employee {employee.Name}'s salary was set to " +
        $"{databaseEntity.Salary} by another user. " +
        $"Click Update to use your new salary of {employee.Salary}" +
        $" or Cancel to leave the salary at {databaseEntity.Salary}.";
        }
```

Error message to display to the user, with two choices on how to carry on . . .

. . . otherwise, it must be an update conflict, so you return a different error message with the two choices for this case.

Listing 8.23 shows two methods, one for the update conflict case and one for the delete conflict. These methods are called depending on which sort of concurrency conflict was found (update or delete), and only if the user wants to apply an update to Employee.

The update conflict can be handled using the same UpdateSalary method as used for the normal update, but the orgSalary parameter is now the salary value as read back when the DbUpdateConcurrencyException was raised. The FixDeleteSalary method is used when the concurrent user deletes the Employee and the current user wants to add the Employee back with their new salary value.

Listing 8.23   Two methods to handle update and delete conflicts

```
public class Employee
{
    public int EmployeeId { get; set; }

    public string Name { get; set; }

    [ConcurrencyCheck]
    public int Salary { get; set; }

    public void UpdateSalary
        (DbContext context,
         int orgSalary, int newSalary)
    {
        Salary = newSalary;
        context.Entry(this).Property(p => p.Salary)
            .OriginalValue = orgSalary;
    }

    public static void FixDeletedSalary
    (DbContext context,
        Employee employee)
    {
```

Set as a concurrency token by the ConcurrencyCheck attribute

The same method used to update the Salary can be used for the Update conflict, but this time it's given the original value as found when the DbUpdateConcurrencyException occurred

Sets the Salary to the new value

Sets the OriginalValue, which is now the value that the database contained when the DbUpdateConcurrency Exception occurred

Handles the Delete concurrency conflict.

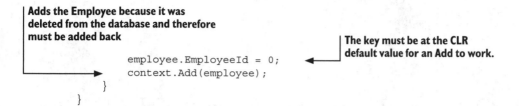

Adds the Employee because it was deleted from the database and therefore must be added back

The key must be at the CLR default value for an Add to work.

```
        employee.EmployeeId = 0;
        context.Add(employee);
    }
}
```

NOTE These disconnected concurrency-conflict examples use a concurrency token, but they work equally well with a timestamp. To use a timestamp instead of passing the `Salary` concurrency token used in these examples, you'd pass the timestamp and set the timestamp's original value before any update.

Summary

- A collection navigational property can be turned into a backing field, which allows you more control over how software can add or remove elements from the collection.
- You can register an SQL user-defined function (UDF) with EF Core and then use it in any database query.
- A column can be configured as an SQL computed column, including specifying the SQL fragment that should be used in the computation.
- There are three ways to provide a default value for a property/column in an entity; these go beyond what setting a default value via .NET could achieve.
- EF Core's `HasSequence` method allows a known, predictable sequence provided by the database server to be applied to a column in a table.
- When the database is created/migrated outside EF Core, EF Core provides configuration commands to mark columns that behave differently than the norm.
- EF Core provides concurrency tokens and timestamps to detect a concurrency conflict.
- When a concurrency conflict is detected, EF Core throws `DbUpdateConcurrency-Exception` and then allows you to implement code to handle the conflict.

For readers who are familiar with EF6:

- The three default value methods, the `HasSequence` method, and the setting of a computed column aren't available in EF6.x.
- EF Core's handling of a concurrency conflict is identical to the way EF6.x handles a concurrency conflict, but Microsoft suggests a few minor changes in how the `DbUpdateConcurrencyException` should be handled.

Going deeper into the DbContext

9

This chapter covers

- How EF Core detects changes to an entity

- Using change tracking to build an audit trail

- Using raw SQL commands from EF Core

- Inspecting EF Core's database model

- Using EF Core's database connection resiliency

So far in this book, you've seen a wide range of EF Core commands available to you. This chapter digs deeper into the properties and methods available in the application's DbContext. In some cases, I provide a more detailed explanation of commands in chapter 3, such as the Add, Update, and Delete methods. I also introduce methods that haven't been covered, such as Attach and TrackGraph, that give you options on how to change the database data.

The EF Core's DbContext class has a wide range of methods and features. After dealing with the methods and properties relating to adding, updating, or deleting data, you'll explore numerous other topics. We'll start with an overview of the three properties in the DbContext class, with pointers to coverage of their related features.

9.1　*Overview of the DbContext class's properties*

The DbContext class has only three properties:

- ChangeTracker—This provides access to EF Core's *change tracking* code. You used this in chapter 3 to run data validation before SaveChanges, and you'll spend quite a bit of time looking at how this works in this chapter, starting with the next section. Quite a few of DbContext's methods work with the ChangeTracker, and you'll learn about those in this chapter.
  - Database—This property provides access to three main groups of features:
  - Transaction control, covered in section 4.6.2
  - Database creation/migration, covered in chapter 11
  - Raw SQL commands, covered in section 9.5
- Model—This provides access to the database model that EF Core uses when connecting to or creating a database. Section 9.6 covers this topic.

Section 9.7 covers one other topic, which is database connection resiliency.

9.2　*Understanding how EF Core tracks changes*

EF Core uses a property called State that's attached to all tracked entities. The State property holds the information about what you want to happen to that entity when you call the application's DbContext method, SaveChanges.

> **DEFINITION**　As you may remember from chapter 2, *tracked entities* are entity instances that have been read in from the database using a query that didn't include the AsNo-Tracking method. Alternatively, after an entity instance has been used as a parameter to EF Core methods, such as Add, Update, or Delete, then it becomes tracked.

This State property, an enum of type EntityState, is normally set by the change tracking feature inside EF Core, and, in this section, you're going to explore all the ways the State can be set.

Chapter 3 gave you a brief introduction to State but skipped many of its features, especially related to relationships, as well as extra commands, which this section covers. The following list, repeated from chapter 3, lists possible values of the State property, which is accessed via the EF command context.Entry(myEntity).State:

- Added—The entity doesn't yet exist in the database. SaveChanges will insert it.
- Unchanged—The entity exists in the database and hasn't been modified on the client. SaveChanges will ignore it.
- Modified—The entity exists in the database and has been modified on the client. SaveChanges will update it.
- Deleted—The entity exists in the database but should be deleted. SaveChanges will delete it.
- Detached—The entity you provided isn't tracked. SaveChanges doesn't see it.

Figure 9.1 shows the change of State of the entity instance, without any relationships, as it's added, modified, and deleted from the database. This gives a good overview of the values that the State of an entity can have.

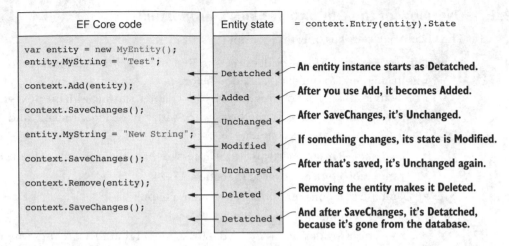

Figure 9.1 **The code on the left uses all the standard ways of creating, updating, and deleting data in a database. The right column, Entity state, shows the EF Core** `state` **of the entity as it moves through each of these stages.**

When you have an entity in the `Modified` state, another per property `boolean` flag, called `IsModified`, comes into play. This identifies which of the properties, both scalar and navigational, have changed in the entity. This `IsModified` property for a scalar property is accessed via

```
context.Entry(entity).Property("PropertyName").IsModified,
```

and the `IsModified` property for navigational properties is accessed via

```
context.Entry(entity).Navigation("PropertyName").IsModified
```

These provide a per property/backing field/shadow property flag to define what has changed if the entity's `State` is set to `Modified`.

9.3 Details on every command that changes an entity's State

Figure 9.1 covers a simple entity, but when relationships are involved, the `State` settings get more complex. The following subsections present each command that can change the `State` of an entity and its relationships.

> **EF6** EF Core's approach to tracking entity changes has gone through a significant upgrade, based on lessons learned from EF6.x. In addition to having new commands, the way some commands work has changed too. I recommend "Change default graph behavior of Add/Attach/etc.," by Rowan Miller, plus the follow-up thread on the EF Core Git issues site (https://github.com/aspnet/EntityFramework/issues/4424).

EF Core's approach has been finely tuned, based on feedback from the previous versions of EF (EF6.x and EF Core 1.x), to set the `State` of related entities to the most "natural" `State` setting based on certain criteria. To give you an example, if you use the `Add` method to add a new entity to the database, EF Core will decide whether the relationship entity should be set to the Added or Modified state, depending on whether EF Core is tracking the entity. Generally, this results in the right decisions for most Add calls, but knowing how EF Core decides how to set the State helps you when your needs are outside the normal usage.

The following subsections use the MyEntity entity class with its optional one-to-one relationship and its one-to-many relationship to the ManyEntity entity class collection, as shown in figure 9.2. Each subsection covers a method or approach that changes the State of the entity and its relationships. You'll see a table for each EF Core method showing the State and IsModified flags for the main entity, MyEntity, and its optional relationship to the OneEntity entity class.

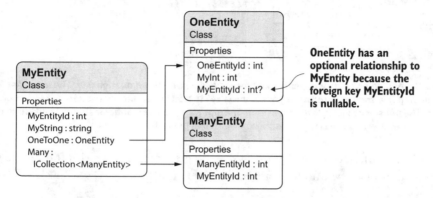

Figure 9.2   The examples that follow use these entity classes. OneEntity **is an optional one-to-one relationship, because the foreign key back to** MyEntity **is nullable.** OneEntity **can exist in the database without being linked to** MyEntity **(its foreign key will be** null**). The** ManyEntity **entity class provides the** Add **command—creating a new entity/row in the database**

9.3.1   The Add command–inserting a new row in the database

The Add/AddRange methods are used to create a new entity in the database by setting the given entity's State to Added. Section 3.2 covered the Add method. If the added entity has any relationships, the value of the State of each relationship entity depends on whether that relationship entity is tracked:

- *Not tracked*—The relationship entity is assumed to be new, and its State is set to Added.
- *Is tracked*—The relationship entity is assumed to be in the database. The State of the relationship entity depends on whether a foreign key needs to be set in it. If the relationship entity contains a foreign key that needs to be set, its State will be set to Modified, or left at its current State if it doesn't need to be modified.

Figure 9.3 shows an example of both the *not tracked* and the *is tracked* cases. The overall effect of these rules means that if you add a new entity with any navigational entities attached, then, when you call SaveChanges, EF Core will correctly create any new relational entities for instances you just created, or add a reference to any existing entities if you read them in from the database.

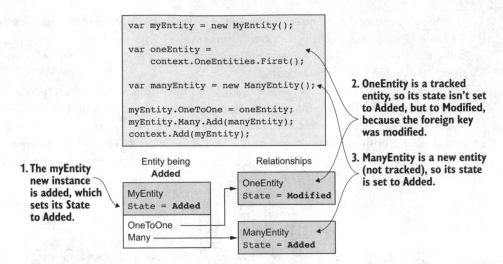

Figure 9.3   Adding an entity with both an *is tracked* and a *not tracked* relationship. The *is tracked* case is shown in step 2: a tracked `OneEntity` instance is set to `Modified` because a foreign key in that entity was set. The *not tracked* case is shown in step 3: a new `ManyEntity` entity instance is added to the `myEntity`'s entity instance `Many` collection navigational property.

Table 9.1 gives three examples of using the `Add` method, starting with the simple scalar and then adding a new, and then an existing, relationship.

Table 9.1   Examples of using the `Add` method, with and without relationships

EF Core code	Entity's state	IsModified == true

```var entity = new MyEntity();```
```entity.MyString = "Test";```
```context.Add(entity);```
	entity: Added	

```var entity = new MyEntity();```
```var oneToOne = new OneEntity();```
```entity.OneToOne = oneToOne;```
```context.Add(entity);```
	entity: Added
	oneToOne: Added	

```var entity = new MyEntity();```
```var oneToOne =```
```   context.OneEntities```
```   .First();```
```entity.OneToOne = oneToOne;```
```context.Add(entity);```
	entity: Added
	oneToOne:
	Modified
		entity.OneToOne
		oneToOne.
		MyEntityId
		
		See Note

NOTE The third example works for only a tracked, optional relationship—a relationship that has a nullable foreign key that's already in the database. For EF Core to track the changes, it needs to set the `IsModified` flag on the `OneToOne` navigational property in the `MyEntity` class, and change the foreign-key property of the `OneEntity` to the primary key of the `MyEntity` class.

NOTE `AddAsync`/`AddRangeAsync` methods are available as well, but are rarely needed. These async methods are there for entities that use a value generator (see section 8.1.3) or a sequence generator (see section 8.2). Both key generators have an `Async` option for value generation, which will be called if you use the `AddAsync`/`AddRangeAsync` methods.

9.3.2   *The Remove command—deleting a row from the database*

The `Remove/RemoveRange` methods delete the entity from the database by setting the given entity's `State` to `Deleted`. Section 3.5 covered the `Remove` method.

If the removed entity has any relationships, the value of the `State` for each relationship entity depends on whether that relationship entity's primary key is generated by the database and is set (its value isn't the default value for the key's .NET type):

- *Database-generated key and not the default value*—EF Core will assume that the relationship entity is already in the database and will set the `State` to either `Unchanged` or `Modified`, depending on whether anything needs changing.
- *Not a database-generated key, or the key is the default value*—EF Core assumes that the relationship entity is new and sets its `State` to `Added`.

This last bullet point may seem odd. Why is EF Core adding entities when you're trying to delete them? This is because at this stage, EF Core is looking at only the `State` of the entity here, and EF Core must have a plan to handle the possibility of new entities, and setting the `State` to `Added` is the most logical decision. But the `State` isn't the only thing that affects what happens to a relationship when the principal entity's `State` is set to `Deleted`. EF Core, and possibly the database, will separately apply the cascade delete settings that are applied to the relationships. A new relationship's `State` might be set to `Added` for *change tracking*, but then be deleted by the cascade delete settings (section 7.7.1 covered cascade delete settings).

Figure 9.4 shows an example of both cases: the database-generated key that's not the default value, and the key that's not generated by the database or is the default value.

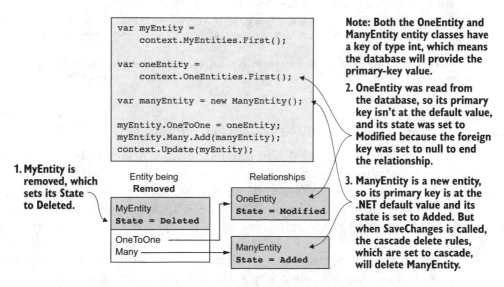

Figure 9.4   Updating an entity with both a Db generated key and not default value and a Not Db generated key, or key is default value relationship. The "Db generated key and not default value" case is shown in step 2. The "Not Db generated key, or key is default value" case is shown in step 3.

Table 9.2 shows the `State` and `IsModified` flags after the `DetectChanges` method has run, which happens when your code calls the `SaveChanges` method. The table shows the results for various arrangements on relationships.

Table 9.2 Examples of using the `Remove` method, with and without relationships

EF Core code	Entity's state	IsModified == true

`var entity =`
`  context.MyEntities.First();`
`context.Remove(entity);`
	entity: Deleted	

`var entity =`
`  context.MyEntities`
`  .AsNoTracking.First();`
`context.Remove(entity);`
	entity: Deleted	See Note 1

`var entity =`
`  context.MyEntities`
`  .Include(x => x.OneToOne)`
`  .First();`
`context.Remove(entity);`
	entity: Deleted
	OneToOne: Unchanged
		See Note 2

`var entity =`
`  context.MyEntities.First();`
`var oneToOne =`
`  context.OneEntities`
`  .First();`
`entity.OneToOne = oneToOne;`
`context.Remove(entity);`
	entity: Deleted
	oneToOne: Modified
		entity.OneToOne
		oneToOne.
		MyEntityId
		
		See Note 3

NOTE 1 You can delete an untracked entity. EF Core looks for a nondefault primary key.

NOTE 2 A `State` of `Unchanged` for the dependent entity `OneEntity` seems incorrect, but the cascade delete rules, which you can set, are applied by `SaveChanges`, which handles what happens to the dependent entity. See sections 7.4.4 and 7.7.1 for more on this.

NOTE 3 This is a deletion of a principal entity with an optional dependent. What happens here is that `OneEntity` isn't deleted, but its foreign key, `MyEntityId`, is set to `null`. See sections 7.4.4 and 7.7.1 for more on this.

9.3.3   *Modifying a tracked entity—EF Core's DetectChanges*

As you've seen in chapter 3 and throughout this book, the default way to modify an entity is to update a property/backing field/shadow property, and EF Core's `DetectChanges` method will detect the change. `DetectChanges` does this by using the tracking snapshot held inside the current application's DbContext. Figure 1.8 describes this, but figure 9.5 gives you a more in-depth look at the process of detecting changes.

Table 9.3 shows the `State` and `IsModified` flags after the `DetectChanges` method has run, which happens when your code calls the `SaveChanges` method. The table shows the results for various configurations of the entity and its `OneToOne` navigational property.

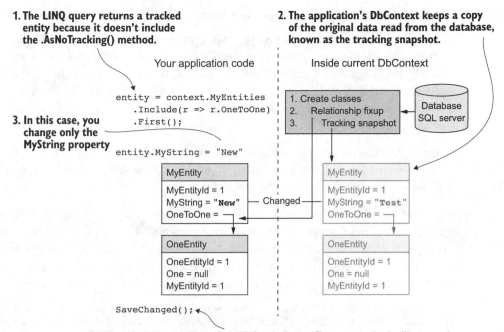

1. The LINQ query returns a tracked entity because it doesn't include the .AsNoTracking() method.

2. The application's DbContext keeps a copy of the original data read from the database, known as the tracking snapshot.

Your application code

Inside current DbContext

```
entity = context.MyEntities
    .Include(r => r.OneToOne)
    .First();
```

3. In this case, you change only the MyString property

```
entity.MyString = "New"
```

1. Create classes
2. Relationship fixup
3. Tracking snapshot

Database SQL server

MyEntity

MyEntityId = 1
MyString = **"New"** ── Changed
OneToOne =

MyEntity

MyEntityId = 1
MyString = **"Test"**
OneToOne =

OneEntity

OneEntityId = 1
One = null
MyEntityId = 1

OneEntity

OneEntityId = 1
One = null
MyEntityId = 1

```
SaveChanged();
```

4. When SaveChanged is called, EF Core's DetectChanges method will run and compare an entity with a State of Unchanged with the tracking snapshot to see if anything is modified. It will also set the IsModified flag on those properties that are different.

Figure 9.5 The default way that EF Core finds whether anything has been changed. EF Core holds a tracking snapshot of any entities loaded as tracked entities—any query that doesn't include the `AsNoTracking` method. When `SaveChanges` is called, EF Core, by default, runs the `DetectChanges` method, which compares tracked entities with the tracking snapshot and sets the `State` of the entities that have been modified to `Modified`.

Table 9.3 Examples of modifying an entity, with and without relationships

EF Core code	Entity's state	IsModified == true

`var entity =`
`  context.MyEntities`
`  .First();`
`entity.MyString = "Changed";`
	entity: Modified	entity.MyString

`var entity =`
`  context.MyEntities`
`  .First();`
`var oneToOne = new OneEntity();`
`entity.OneToOne = oneToOne;`
	entity: Unchanged
	OneToOne: Added	

`var entity =`
`  context.MyEntities`
`  .First();`
`var oneToOne =`
`  context.OneEntities`
`  .First();`
`entity.OneToOne = oneToOne;`
	entity: Unchanged
	oneToOne: Modified
		entity.OneToOne
		oneToOne.MyEntityId

9.3.4 *INotifyPropertyChanged entities—a different way of tracking changes*

In some applications, you may have a large number of tracked entities loaded. When executing mathematical modeling or building artificial intelligence applications, for instance, holding a lot of data in memory may be the only way to achieve the level of performance that you require. If you want to update that data, then when you call SaveChanges, which in turn calls DetectChanges, DetectChanges can take a long time to compare every loaded entity with its tracking snapshot.

> **NOTE** An unscientific test of loading 1,000 Book entities, with their Author-Links, Authors, and Reviews, and then timing how long SaveChanges took to run, gave an answer of more than a second.

For this reason, EF Core provides another way to track changes, by using INotifyProp-ertyChanged. This requires you to send an event to EF Core every time you change a property. The following listing shows the NotifyEntity class, which has the same relationship types as the MyEntity shown in figure 9.2, but uses INotifyPropertyChanged and ObservableHashSet to raise events every time the properties are changed.

Listing 9.1   `NotifyEntity` using `NotificationEntity` class for events

```
public class NotifyEntity : NotificationEntity
{
    private int _id;
    private string _myString;
    private NotifyOne _oneToOne;

    public int Id
    {
        get => _id;
        set => SetWithNotify(value, ref _id);
    }

    public string MyString
    {
        get => _myString;
        set => SetWithNotify(value, ref _myString);
    }

    public NotifyOne OneToOne
    {
        get => _oneToOne;
        set => SetWithNotify(value, ref _oneToOne);
    }

    public ICollection<NotifyMany>
        Collection { get; }
        = new ObservableHashSet<NotifyMany>();
}
```

Each noncollection property must have a backing field.

If a noncollection property is changed, you need to raise a PropertyChanged event, which you do via the inherited method SetWithNotify.

You can use any Observable collection, but for performance reasons, EF Core prefers ObservableHashSet<T>.

Any collection navigational property must be an Observable collection, so you need to predefine that Observable collection.

The `NotificationEntity` helper class, which contains the `SetWithNotify` method used by the `NotifyEntity`, is shown here.

Listing 9.2 `NotificationEntity` **helper class that** `NotifyEntity` **inherits**

Automatically gets the propertyName by using System.Runtime.CompilerServices

Only if the field and the value are different do you set the field and raise the event.

```
public class NotificationEntity : INotifyPropertyChanged
{
    public event PropertyChangedEventHandler PropertyChanged;

    protected void SetWithNotify<T>(T value, ref T field,
        [CallerMemberName] string propertyName = "")
    {
        if (!Object.Equals(field, value))
        {
            field = value;
            PropertyChanged?.Invoke(this,
                new PropertyChangedEventArgs(propertyName));
        }
    }
}
```

Sets the field to the new value

... with the name of the property

Invokes the PropertyChanged event, but using ?. to stop the method from failing when the new entity is created and the PropertyChangedEventHandler hasn't been filled in by EF Core...

After you've defined your entity class in the right way, you need to configure the EF Core tracking strategy to `ChangedNotifications`. To set this up for one entity class, you use the Fluent API command.

Listing 9.3 **Setting the tracking strategy for one entity to** `ChangedNotifications`

```
protected override void OnModelCreating(ModelBuilder modelBuilder)
{
    modelBuilder
      .Entity<NotifyEntity>()
      .HasChangeTrackingStrategy(
          ChangeTrackingStrategy.ChangedNotifications);
}
```

Alternatively, to set the tracking strategy for *all* the entity classes, you leave out the `Entity<T>` part:

```
modelBuilder
  .HasChangeTrackingStrategy(
      ChangeTrackingStrategy.ChangedNotifications);
```

I've described one of the three available settings of `ChangeTrackingStrategy`. The `ChangedNotifications` setting means that EF Core still takes a tracking snapshot (needed for features like concurrency checking), but the `DetectChanges` method doesn't use the tracking snapshot to detect changes. The `SaveChanges` method executes quickly for entities that have a tracking strategy of `ChangedNotifications`, even if there are lots of tracked entities loaded.

Another setting, `ChangingAndChangedNotifications`, does away with the need for taking a tracking snapshot, but requires you to implement another interface called `INotifyPropertyChanging`. This requires the `NotificationEntry` class to issue an event before a property is changed so that EF Core knows what the original value was before the change. The changes to `NotificationEntry` require two property events, changing and changed. This listing shows a variant called `Notification2Entry`, which has the second event added.

> **Listing 9.4   `Notification2Entry` with two property events**

```
public class Notification2Entry :
    INotifyPropertyChanged,
    INotifyPropertyChanging            ◄── Adds the extra interface,
{                                           INotifyPropertyChanging

    public event PropertyChangedEventHandler PropertyChanged;
    public event PropertyChangingEventHandler PropertyChanging;

    protected void SetWithNotify<T>(T value, ref T field,
        [CallerMemberName] string propertyName = "")
    {
        if (!Object.Equals(field, value))
        {                                       ◄── Triggers an event before
            PropertyChanging?.Invoke(this,           the property is changed
                new PropertyChangingEventArgs(propertyName));
            field = value; //
            PropertyChanged?.Invoke(this,
                new PropertyChangedEventArgs(propertyName));
        }
    }
}
```

A third option for the `ChangeTrackingStrategy` is `ChangingAndChangedNotificationsWithOriginalValues`. This version works the same as `ChangingAndChangedNotifications` but does take a tracking snapshot of the entity when it's loaded. This is useful if you need to access the original values—for instance, when your entity needs concurrency-conflict handling (covered in chapter 8).

9.3.5   *The Update method—telling EF Core that everything has changed*

The `Update/UpdateRange` methods aren't the normal way of updating an entity. You typically do that by changing a property and calling `SaveChanges`, which I've just described. The `Update` method is useful if you want to update all the data in the database for an entity instance. The Update method is normally applied to untracked entities—say, from an external source. (Figure 3.3 showed an example.)

The Update method tells EF Core to update all the properties/columns in this entity by setting the given entity's State to Modified, and sets the IsModified property to true on all nonrelational properties, including the foreign key, in the entity class. This means the row in the database will have all its columns updated.

Like the Remove method, the value of the State for each relationship of the updated entity depends on whether the relationship entity's primary key is generated by the database and is set (its value isn't the default value for the key's .NET type):

- *Database-generated key and not the default value*—In this case, EF Core will assume that the relationship entity is already in the database and will set the State to Modified if a foreign key needs to be set; otherwise, the State will be Unchanged.
- *Not database-generated key, or the key is the default value*—In this case, EF Core will assume that the relationship entity is new and set its State to Added.

Figure 9.6 shows an example of both cases.

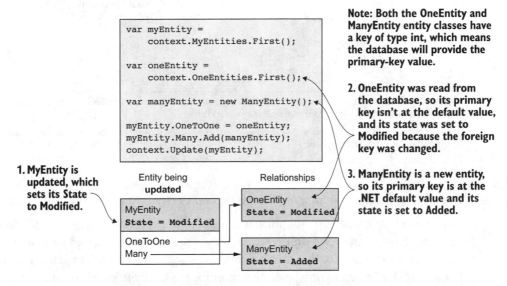

Figure 9.6   The updating of an entity with both a Db generated key and not default value and a Not Db generated key, or key is default value relationship. The Db generated key and not default value case is shown in step 2: a tracked OneEntity instance is set to Modified because a foreign key in that entity was set. The Not Db generated key, or key is default value case is shown in step 3: a new ManyEntity entity instance is added to the myEntity's entity instance Many collection navigational property.

Table 9.4 shows the State and IsModified flags after the DetectChanges method has run, which happens when your code calls the SaveChanges method. The table shows the results for various configurations of the entity and its OneToOne navigational property after the Update method has been called.

Table 9.4   Examples of using the Update method, with and without relationships

EF Core code	Entity's State	IsModified == true
`var entity = new MyEntity();` `context.Update(entity);`	`entity: Added`	

`var entity =`
`    context.MyEntities`
`    .AsNoTracking.First();`
`context.Update(entity);`
	`entity: Modified`	`entity.MyString`
		
		See Note 1

`var entity = context.MyEntities`
`    .Include(x => x.OneToOne)`
`    .First();`
`context.Update(entity);`
	`entity: Modified`
	`OneToOne: Unchanged`
		`entity.MyString`
		
		See Note 1

`var entity = context`
`    .MyEntities.Single();`
`entity.OneToOne =`
`    new OneEntity();`
`context.Update(entity);`
	`entity: Modified`
	`OneToOne: Added`
		`entity.MyString`
		
		See Note 1 and Note 2

`var entity =`
`    context.MyEntities.First();`
`var oneToOne =`
`    context.OneEntities`
`    .First();`
`entity.OneToOne = oneToOne;`
`context.Update(entity);`
	`entity: Modified`
	`oneToOne: Modified`
		`entity.MyString`
		`entity.OneToOne`
		`oneToOne.MyEntityId`

NOTE 1—The `MyString` property is the only nonprimary key, non-navigational property in this entity class. If there were more such properties, they too would have their `IsModified` flag set to `true`.

NOTE 2—The `OneEntity` entity is new, with a database-generated primary key of type `int`, which is at the default value of 0, so this entity is added rather than modified.

9.3.6   *The Attach method—changing an untracked entity into a tracked entity*

The `Attach/AttachRange` methods are useful when you have a whole entity instance but it's not being tracked. After you attach the entity, it's tracked, and EF Core assumes that its content matches the current database state. This could be useful in a disconnected state, where an entity's whole content is passed from one instance of the application's DbContext to another, different context. You can `Attach` the entity, and it becomes a normal tracked entity, without the cost of loading it from the database. The `Attach` method does this by setting the entity's `State` to `Unchanged`.

As with the `Remove` and `Update` methods, what happens to the relationships of the updated entity depends on whether the relationship entity's primary key is generated by the database and is set (its value isn't the default value for the key's .NET type):

- *Database-generated key and not the default value*—EF Core will assume that the relationship entity is already in the database and will set the `State` to `Unchanged`.
- *Not a database-generated key, or the key is the default value*—EF Core will assume that the relationship entity is new and set its `State` to `Added`.

This behavior works well at reconstituting entities with relationships that have been serialized and then deserialized to an entity, but only if it's being written back to the same database, as the foreign keys need to match.

> **WARNING** Serialized and then deserialized to an entity with shadow properties needs special handling with the `Attach` method. The shadow properties aren't part of the class, so they'll be lost in any serialization. Therefore, you must save/restore any shadow properties, especially foreign keys, after the `Attach` method has been called.

Table 9.5 shows the `State` and `IsModified` flags after the `DetectChanges` method has run, which happens when your code calls the `SaveChanges` method. The table shows various configurations of the entity and its `OneToOne` navigational property after the `Attach` method has been called.

Table 9.5 Examples of using the `Attach` method, with and without relationships

EF Core code	Entity's State	Notes
`var entity = new MyEntity();` `context.Attach(entity);`	entity: Added	

`var entity =`
`    context.MyEntities`
`    .AsNoTracking().First();`
`context.Attach(entity);`
	entity: Unchanged	

`var entity =`
`    context.MyEntities`
`    .AsNoTracking().First();`
`entity.OneToOne =`
`    new OneEntity();`
`context.Attach(entity);`
	entity: Unchanged
	OneToOne: Added
		The relationship is established because the `OneToOne` entity `State` is set to `Added`.

`var entity =`
`    context.MyEntities`
`    .AsNoTracking().First();`
`var oneToOne =`
`    context.OneEntities`
`    .First();`
`entity.OneToOne = oneToOne;`
`context.Attach(entity);`
	entity: Unchanged
	oneToOne: Unchanged
		The relationship isn't changed because both entities are in `State` Unchanged.

9.3.7 Setting the State of an entity directly

Another way to set the `State` of an entity is to set it manually to whatever state you want. This direct setting of an entity's `State` is useful when an entity has many relationships and you need to specifically decide which state you want each relationship to have. The next section shows a good example of this.

Because the entity's `State` is read/write, you can set it. In the following code snippet, the `myEntity` instance's `State` is set to `Added`:

```
context.Entry(myEntity).State = EntityState.Added;
```

You can also set the `IsModified` flag on the property in an entity. The following code snippet sets the `MyString` property's `IsModified` flag to `true` and the entity's `State` to `Modified`:

```
var entity = new MyEntity();
context.Entry(entity).Property("MyString").IsModified = true;
```

> **NOTE**   If the entity wasn't tracked before you set the `State`, it'll be tracked afterward.

9.3.8   *TrackGraph—handling disconnected updates with relationships*

The `TrackGraph` method is useful if you have an untracked entity with relationships and you need to set the correct `State` for each entity. The `TrackGraph` method will traverse all the relational links in the entity, calling an action you supplied on each entity it finds. This is useful if you have a group of linked entities coming from a disconnected state (say via some form of serialization) and you want to change only part of the data you've loaded.

> **EF6**   The `TrackGraph` method is a welcome addition to EF Core. There's no equivalent command in EF6.x.

Let's expand on the simple example of a RESTful API in chapter 3, in which an author's `Name` property was updated. In that case, the external system sent back only the `Author` entity data. In this example, the external system will send back the whole book, with all its relationships, but still wants you to update only the author's `Name` property.

Although you could still use the `Update` command to do this, it'd be inefficient because it'd update every table and column in the book's relationships instead of just the authors' names. This is where EF Core's `ChangeTracker.TrackGraph` method provides a better approach. Figure 9.7 shows an external system that returns all the data relating to a `Book` entity, but by using `TrackGraph`, you can set the `States` in such a way that only the author's `Name` property gets updated.

`TrackGraph` traverses the entity provided as its first parameter and any entities that are reachable by traversing its navigation properties. The traversal is recursive, so the navigation properties of any discovered entities will also be scanned. The `Action` method you provide as the second parameter is called for each discovered entity and can set the `State` that each entity should be tracked in. If the visited entity's `State` isn't set, the entity remains in the `State` of `Disconnected` (the entity isn't being tracked by EF Core). Also, `TrackGraph` will ignore any entities it visits that are currently being tracked.

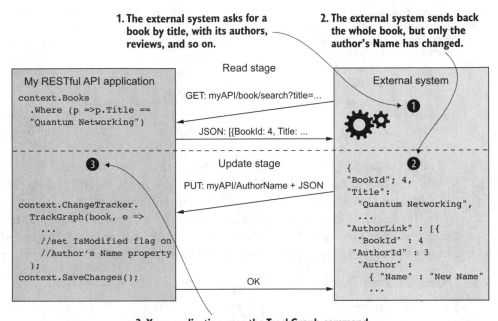

1. The external system asks for a book by title, with its authors, reviews, and so on.

2. The external system sends back the whole book, but only the author's Name has changed.

3. Your application uses the TrackGraph command to update only the author's Name property.

Figure 9.7 An external system that asks for a specific book and gets the JSON containing the book and all its relationships. When the external system wants to update the authors' names, it sends back *all* the original JSON, with the changed names, but tells your application that it needs only the authors' names changed. Your application uses EF Core's `ChangeTracker.TrackGraph` method to set all the classes to state `Unchanged`, but sets the `IsModified` flag on the `Name` property in the `Author` entity class.

Listing 9.5 shows the code you'd need to traverse a Book entity instance, which you've reconstituted from a JSON copy (it isn't a tracked entity). The TrackGraph method will call your lambda Action method, given as the second parameter, for every entity, starting with the Book entity instance and then working through all the relational navigational property's entity instances it can reach.

Listing 9.5 Using `TrackGraph` to set each entity's `State` and `IsModified` flags

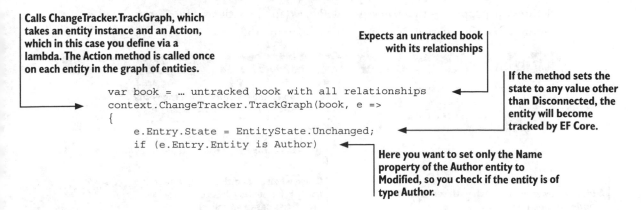

Calls ChangeTracker.TrackGraph, which takes an entity instance and an Action, which in this case you define via a lambda. The Action method is called once on each entity in the graph of entities.

Expects an untracked book with its relationships

If the method sets the state to any value other than Disconnected, the entity will become tracked by EF Core.

```
var book = … untracked book with all relationships
context.ChangeTracker.TrackGraph(book, e =>
{
    e.Entry.State = EntityState.Unchanged;
    if (e.Entry.Entity is Author)
```

Here you want to set only the Name property of the Author entity to Modified, so you check if the entity is of type Author.

Calls SaveChanges, which finds that only the Name property of the Author entity has been marked as changed; creates the optimal SQL to update the Name column in the Authors table.

Sets the IsModified flag on the Name property. This also sets the State of the entity to Modified.

```
        {
            e.Entry.Property("Name").IsModified = true;
        }
    });
    context.SaveChanges();
```

The result of running this code is that only the `Author` entity instance's `State` is set to `Modified`, whereas the `State` of all the other entity types is set to `Unchanged`. In addition, the `IsModified` flag is set only on the `Author` entity class's `Name` property.

In this example, the difference between using an `Updated` method and using the `TrackGraph` code in listing 9.5 is about 20 updates to columns (19 of them needlessly) with the `Updated` method, against one column being updated by the `TrackGraph` code.

9.4   *Using ChangeTracker to detect changes*

You've learned how to set the `State` of an entity, but now you'll see how `ChangeTracker` can be used to find out what has changed, and use this information in some way. Here are some of the possible uses of detecting what's about to be changed in the database:

- Automatically add extra information to an entity—for instance, adding the time when an entity was added or updated
- Produce a history audit trail of each time a specific entity type is changed
- Add security checks to see whether the current user is allowed to update that particular entity type

The basic approach is to override the `SaveChanges/SaveChangesAsync` methods inside your application's DbContext and execute a method before the base `SaveChanges/SaveChangesAsync` is called. That method can use `ChangeTracker.Entries` to obtain a list of all the entities that have changed, and what `State` they're in. What you do with this information is up to you, but next is an example that logs the last time the entity was added or updated.

The following listing provides an interface you can add to any entity class. This defines the properties that you want filled in when the entity is added or updated, and a method that can be used to set the properties to the right values.

Listing 9.6   The `IWhen` interface defining two properties and method for logging

```
public interface IWhen
{
    DateTime CreatedOn { get; }
    DateTime UpdatedOn { get; }

    void SetWhen(bool add);
}
```

Holds the datetime when the entity was first added to the database

Holds the datetime when the entity was last updated

Called when an addition or update to the entity is found. Its job is to update the properties based on the add flag.

Added to any entity class when the entity is added or updated.

The following listing shows an entity class called AutoWhenEntity that inherits the IWhen interface that you'll detect when your modified SaveChanges method is called (see listing 9.8). The SetWhen method, which you'll call in your modified SaveChanges method, sets the UpdatedOn property, and the CreatedOn property if needed, to the current time.

Listing 9.7   AutoWhenEntity automatically sets the datetime of a change

Required by the IWhen interface. They have private setters to stop software from changing them, but they still allow EF Core to fill them in when the entity is loaded.

Entity class inherits the interface IWhen, which means any addition/update of the entity is logged.

```
public class AutoWhenEntity : IWhen
{
    public int AutoWhenEntityId { get; set; }

    public string MyString { get; set; }

    public DateTime CreatedOn { get; private set; }
    public DateTime UpdatedOn { get; private set; }

    public void SetWhen (bool add)
    {
        var time = DateTime.UtcNow;
        if (add)
        {
            CreatedOn = time;
        }
        UpdatedOn = time;
    }
}
```

Required by the IWhen interface. Its job is to set the two IWhen properties appropriately.

Obtains the current time so that an addition will have the same values in both the Created and Updated properties

You always set the Updated properties.

If it's an add, you set the Created properties.

The next step is to override all versions of the SaveChanges method inside your application's DbContext and then precede the call to the base SaveChanges with a call to your HandleWhen method. This method looks for entities with a State of Added or Modified, and inherits the IWhen interface. If you find an entity(s) that fits that criteria, you call the entity's SetWhen method to set the two properties to the correct values. The following listing shows your application's DbContext, called Chapter09DbContext, which implements that code. (To keep the code shorter, you'll override only one of the four possible SaveChanges methods. Normally, you'd override all four versions of the SaveChanges/SaveChangesAsync methods.)

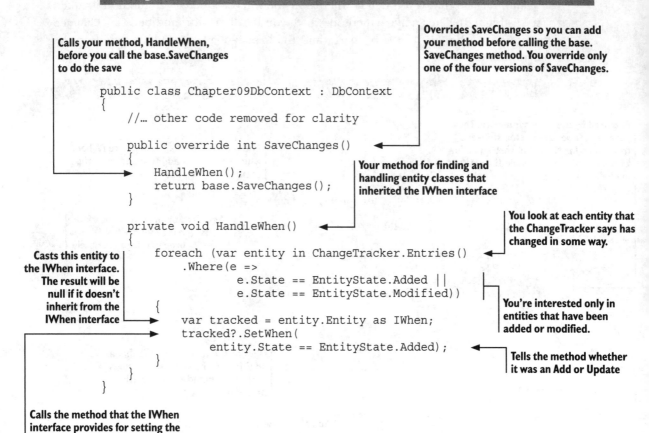

Listing 9.8   Your DbContext looks for added or modified `IWhen` entities

Calls your method, HandleWhen, before you call the base.SaveChanges to do the save

Overrides SaveChanges so you can add your method before calling the base. SaveChanges method. You override only one of the four versions of SaveChanges.

```
public class Chapter09DbContext : DbContext
{
    //… other code removed for clarity

    public override int SaveChanges()
    {
        HandleWhen();
        return base.SaveChanges();
    }

    private void HandleWhen()
    {
        foreach (var entity in ChangeTracker.Entries()
            .Where(e =>
                    e.State == EntityState.Added ||
                    e.State == EntityState.Modified))
        {
            var tracked = entity.Entity as IWhen;
            tracked?.SetWhen(
                entity.State == EntityState.Added);
        }
    }
}
```

Your method for finding and handling entity classes that inherited the IWhen interface

You look at each entity that the ChangeTracker says has changed in some way.

Casts this entity to the IWhen interface. The result will be null if it doesn't inherit from the IWhen interface

You're interested only in entities that have been added or modified.

Tells the method whether it was an Add or Update

Calls the method that the IWhen interface provides for setting the IWhen properties

This is only one example of using `ChangeTracker` to take actions based on the `State` of tracked entities, but it establishes the general approach. The possibilities are endless.

9.5   *Using raw SQL commands in EF Core*

EF Core has methods that allow raw SQL commands to be used, either as part of a LINQ query or a database write, such as an SQL UPDATE. These are useful when the query you want to perform can't be expressed using LINQ—for instance, if it calls an SQL stored procedure, or if using a LINQ query is resulting in inefficient SQL being sent to the database.

> **DEFINITION**   An SQL *stored procedure* is a set of SQL commands—which may or may not have parameters—that can be executed. They typically read and/or write to the database. The set of SQL commands is stored in the database as a stored procedure and given a name. The stored procedure can then be called as part of an SQL command.

There are several ways to include SQL commands in EF commands. This chapter covers:

- `FromSql` method, which allows you to use a raw SQL command in an EF Core query
- `ExecuteSqlCommand` method, which executes a nonquery command
- `Reload` command, used to refresh an EF Core–loaded entity that has been changed by an `ExecuteSqlCommand` method
- EF Core's `GetDbConnection` method, which provides low-level database access libraries to access the database directly

EF6 The commands in EF Core for SQL access are different from the way EF6.x provides SQL access to the database.

9.5.1 *FromSql—adding raw SQL to an EF Core query*

The `FromSql` method allows you to add raw SQL commands to a standard EF Core query. This allows you to include SQL commands that you wouldn't be able to call from EF Core, such as an SQL stored procedure. Here's an example of calling a stored procedure that returns only books that have an average review vote of the given value.

Listing 9.9   Using the `FromSql` method to add SQL into an EF Core query

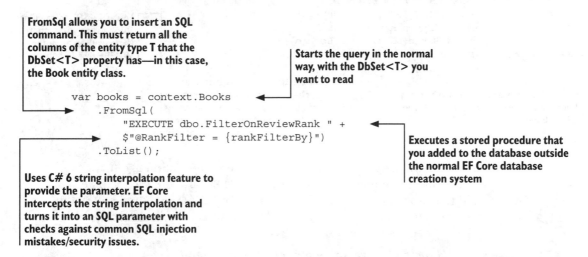

In the preceding code, you were querying an entity class property, which is all you could do up to EF Core 2.0. But from EF Core 2.1, you'll be able to use the `FromSql` method with a *query type*, which is a type that isn't an entity class (see appendix B, section B.1.5).

EF Core's SQL commands support the C# 6 string interpolation feature that allows you to place a variable name in the string, which EF Core will then check and turn into parameters. The parameters will be checked to stop SQL injection attacks. Using string interpolation makes it easier to see what the parameters are, especially in complex SQL commands that have multiple parameters.

> **WARNING** If you form the command string by using the C# 6 string interpolation feature outside the `FromSql` command, you lose the SQL injection attack detection built into the `FromSql` method.

The `FromSql` method has some limitations:

- The column names in the result set must match the column names that properties are mapped to.
- If you're loading to an entity class, the SQL query must return data for all properties of the entity type. This is because the entity will be tracked after the query.

You can use an `Include` method with the `FromSql` method, if you're querying an entity class and not executing a stored procedure. The following listing shows an example in which you call an SQL user-defined function (explained in section 8.1.2). In this case, you use the `Include` method to eager load the `Book`'s `Reviews` collection.

Listing 9.10   Using `FromSql` with `Include` to eager load other data

```
var books = context.Books
    .FromSql(
        "SELECT * FROM Books b WHERE " +
          "(SELECT AVG(CAST([NumStars] AS float)) " +
          "FROM dbo.Review AS r " +
          "WHERE b.BookId = r.BookId) >= {0}", 5)
    .Include(r => r.Reviews)
    .ToList();
```

You write SQL to calculate the average votes, then use that result in an outer **WHERE** test.

The Include method works with FromSql because you're not executing a stored procedure.

You use the normal SQL parameter check and substitution method of {0}, {2}, {3} etc. in the string and then provide extra parameters to the FromSql call.

> **WARNING** If you're using model-level query filters (see section 3.5.1), the SQL you can write has limitations—for instance, `ORDER BY` won't work. The way around this problem is to apply the `IgnoreQueryFilters` method before the `FromSql` command and re-create the model-level query filter in your SQL code.

9.5.2   *ExecuteSqlCommand—executing a nonquery command*

In addition to putting raw SQL commands in a query, you can execute nonquery SQL commands via EF Core's `ExecuteSqlCommand` method. Typical commands are SQL `UPDATE` or `DELETE` commands, but any nonquery SQL command can be called. Listing 9.11 shows an SQL `UPDATE` command, which takes two parameters.

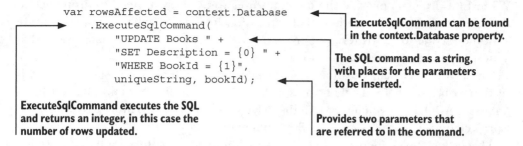

Listing 9.11   The `ExecuteSqlCommand` method executing an SQL UPDATE

```
var rowsAffected = context.Database
    .ExecuteSqlCommand(
        "UPDATE Books " +
        "SET Description = {0} " +
        "WHERE BookId = {1}",
        uniqueString, bookId);
```

ExecuteSqlCommand can be found in the context.Database property.

The SQL command as a string, with places for the parameters to be inserted.

ExecuteSqlCommand executes the SQL and returns an integer, in this case the number of rows updated.

Provides two parameters that are referred to in the command.

The `ExecuteSqlCommand` method returns an integer, which is useful for checking that the command was executed in the way you expected. In this example, you'd expect it to return 1 to show that it found a row in the `Books` table that had the primary key you provided and updated it.

9.5.3 Reload—useful after an ExecuteSqlCommand

If you have an entity loading and you use an `ExecuteSqlCommand` method to change the data on the database, your loaded entity is now out-of-date. That could cause you a problem later, because EF Core doesn't know the values have been changed. To fix this, EF Core has a method called `Reload`, which updates your entity by rereading the database.

In this listing, you load an entity, change its content via the `ExecuteSqlCommand` method, and then use the `Reload` method to make sure the entity's content matches what's in the database.

Listing 9.12   Using the `Reload` method to refresh the content of an existing entity

You now use ExecuteSqlCommand to change the Description column of that same Book entity. After this command has finished, the Book entity EF Core load is out-of-date.

Loads a Book entity in the normal way

```
var entity = context.Books.
    Single(x => x.Title == "Quantum Networking");
var uniqueString = Guid.NewGuid().ToString();

context.Database.ExecuteSqlCommand(
        "UPDATE Books " +
        "SET Description = {0} " +
        "WHERE BookId = {1}",
        uniqueString, entity.BookId);
context.Entry(entity).Reload();
```

By calling the Reload method, EF Core will reread that entity to make sure the local copy is up-to-date.

At the end of this code, the entity instance will match what's in the database.

9.5.4   *GetDbConnection—calling database access commands*

When EF Core can't provide the query features you want, you need to drop back to another database access method that can. A few low-level database libraries require a lot more code to be written, but provide more-direct access to the database so that almost anything you need can be done.

These low-level database libraries are normally database server-specific. In this section, you'll use a library that works with SQL Server called System.Data.SqlClient, known as ADO.NET, which is part of the .NET standard library. This bypasses all of EF Core's cleverness and uses standard SQL commands.

This listing shows the use of the ADO.NET library to execute an SQL SELECT command and then read the resulting data.

Listing 9.13   An example of using a low-level database access library with EF Core

You need to open the connection before you use it.

Asks EF Core for a DbConnection, which the low-level SqlClient library can use

```
var bookDtos = new List<RawSqlDto>();
var conn = context.Database.GetDbConnection();
try
{
    conn.Open();
    using (var command = conn.CreateCommand())
    {
        string query = "SELECT b.BookId, b.Title, " +
        "(SELECT AVG(CAST([NumStars] AS float)) " +
        "FROM dbo.Review AS r " +
            "WHERE b.BookId = r.BookId) AS AverageVotes " +
            "FROM Books b";
        command.CommandText = query;
```

Creates a DbCommand on that connection

Assigns your command to the DbCommand instance

The ADO.NET library transfers SQL directly to the database server; hence all the database accesses must be defined in SQL.

The ExecuteReader method sends the SQL command to the database server and then creates a reader to read the data that the server will return.

```
        using (DbDataReader reader = command.ExecuteReader())
        {
            while (reader.Read())
            {
                var row = new RawSqlDto
                {
                    BookId = reader.GetInt32(0),
                    Title = reader.GetString(1),
                    AverageVotes = reader.IsDBNull(2)
                        ? null
                        : (double?) reader.GetDouble(2)
                };
                bookDtos.Add(row);
            }
```

This tries to read the next row and returns true if it was successful.

You have to hand-code the conversion and copying of the data from the reader into your class. Have a look at Dapper for a slightly easier way to read data into a class.

```
        }
      }
    }
    finally
    {
        conn.Close();
    }
```

> When the read has finished, you
> need to close the connection to
> the database server.

As you can see, the code is longer than EF Core, but it does allow you to do almost anything with the database. At the same time, you get no help on handling relationships, tracking changes, and so on that EF Core provides—it's all on you to handle. Chapter 13 presents more examples of direct SQL database accesses, but using a more developer-friendly NuGet package called Dapper.

9.6　*Using Context.Model to access EF Core's view of the database*

The Model property on the application's DbContext provides access to the database information for each entity and its properties. You might use this if you want to find out the table name and column names of an entity so that you can build a raw SQL command using ADO.NET, or if you're building a tool to compare or build a database yourself.

> **EF6**　EF Core's Model property is a tremendous improvement over EF6.x's access to the model metadata. In EF Core, the IModel interface gives you access to all the database properties that EF Core uses. EF6.x's version is cumbersome and doesn't cover every aspect of the database.

The following listing uses the context.Model property to get the table name of the Book entity class.

> **Listing 9.14　Using the application's DbContext `Model` property to get a table name**

```
var eType = context.Model
    .FindEntityType(typeof(Book).FullName);
var bookTableName = eType
    .Relational().TableName;
```

In this case, the Book entity class's table name is Books (see section 6.10.1, on how EF Core defines the table name during configuration). The context.Model property has a rich interface allowing access to both the representation of the data in the database and information on the relationships between tables, and the last example just scratches the surface. The next example is more complex and shows more of what the Model property and its IEntityType classes contain.

9.6.1　*Using the Model property to build a fast database wipe method*

To help with our unit-test library, you'll implement a method that wipes all the data from all the tables in the database by using raw SQL commands. This is useful in unit testing, because it's much quicker than the EF Core alternative of using the EnsureDeleted method followed by the EnsureCreated method; in section 15.5.3, you'll use this approach to create a CreateEmptyViaWipe method for use in unit testing.

This isn't a trivial problem, because the order in which you can delete rows depends on the cascade delete settings of relationships. In chapter 4, you defined how a book order was held, and you set up the cascade delete settings such that once a Book entity was referred to by a LineItem entity in an order, that specific Book entity (row) couldn't be deleted. If you want to wipe that database, you need to delete all the LineItem table rows before you delete the Books table rows.

Figure 9.8 shows an example of a database with relationships between the various entities/tables. You assume that all the cascade delete settings are set to Restrict, which means you must delete in the order shown.

1. The diagram represents a set of entities with navigational links shown as arrows. If the cascade delete setting on each link is set to Restrict, then the order in which you can delete all the entities in a table matters. Dependents must be deleted first.

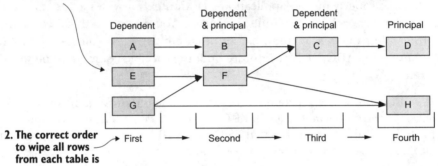

2. The correct order to wipe all rows from each table is

Figure 9.8   Each rectangle represents a table in the database that you want to delete all rows from. Because of the foreign-key links—which may have a cascade delete setting that precludes deleting a row because another row points to it with a foreign key—the order in which you delete rows from a table matters. The row at the bottom defines the correct order for deleting all the rows from a table.

This example is a useful piece of code, but here you want to concentrate on how the Model property can be used to obtain the information you need to implement your GetTableNamesInOrderForWipe method. The code is long, so the following listing shows only the first part of the code, in which all the accesses to the Model and its IEntityType information are used.

Listing 9.15   The extraction of the IEntityType information

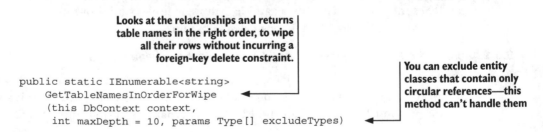

Looks at the relationships and returns table names in the right order, to wipe all their rows without incurring a foreign-key delete constraint.

You can exclude entity classes that contain only circular references—this method can't handle them

```
public static IEnumerable<string>
    GetTableNamesInOrderForWipe
    (this DbContext context,
     int maxDepth = 10, params Type[] excludeTypes)
```

Gets the IEntityType for all the entities, other than those that were excluded. This contains the information on how each table is built, with its relationships.

Contains a check for the hierarchical case in which an entity refers to itself; if the delete behavior of this foreign key is set to restrict, you can't delete all the rows in one go.

```
{
    var allEntities = context.Model
        .GetEntityTypes()
        .Where(x => !excludeTypes.Contains(x.ClrType))
        .ToList();

    ThrowExceptionIfCannotWipeSelfRef(allEntities);

    var principalsDict = allEntities
        .SelectMany(x => x.GetForeignKeys()
            .Select(y => y.PrincipalEntityType))
                .Distinct()
        .ToDictionary(k => k, v =>
            v.GetForeignKeys()
                .Where(y => y.PrincipalEntityType != v)
                .Select(y => y.PrincipalEntityType).ToList());

    var result = allEntities
        .Where(x => !principalsDict.ContainsKey(x))
        .ToList();

    ///… more code left out as it doesn't use Model so much
```

... puts them in a dictionary, with the IEntityType being the key

Extracts all principal entities from the entities you're considering ...

Removes any self-reference links, as these are automatically handled...

...and extracts the PrincipalEntityType at the value part of the dictionary

Starts the list of entities to delete by putting all the dependent entities first, as you must delete the rows in these tables first, and the order doesn't matter

NOTE You can find all the code for the GetTableNamesInOrderForWipe method at http://mng.bz/07vz.

Listing 9.16 shows how to use the GetTableNamesInOrderForWipe method and EF Core's ExecuteSqlCommand method to wipe all the data from the database; by that, I mean deleting all the rows in all the tables in the database that the given application's DbContext is linked to.

Listing 9.16 Wiping all data from the tables in the application's DbContext

```
foreach (var tableName in
    context.GetTableNamesInOrderForWipe())
{
    var commandString = $"DELETE FROM {tableName}";
    context.Database
        .ExecuteSqlCommand(commandString);
}
```

Returns the table names to wipe in the correct order to minimize the likelihood of foreign-key delete constraints returning an error

You must form the command string outside the ExecuteSqlCommand; EF Core will reject this string because it could be an SQL injection attack.

Executes the SQL command, which quickly deletes all the rows in that table

9.7   *Handling database connection problems*

With relational database servers, especially in the cloud, a database access can fail because the connection times out, or certain transient errors occur. EF Core has an execution strategy feature that allows you to define what should happen when a time-out occurs, how many time-outs are allowed, and so on. Providing an execution strategy can make your application less likely to fail due to connection problems, or internal errors that are transient.

> **EF6**   EF Core's execution strategy is an improvement on the EF6.x execution strategy, as EF Core can handle retries in a transaction.

The SQL Server database provider includes an execution strategy that's specifically tailored to SQL Server (including SQL Azure). It's aware of the exception types that can be retried and has sensible defaults for maximum retries, delay between retries, and so on. This listing shows how to apply this to the setup of SQL Server, with the execution strategy shown in bold.

> **Listing 9.17   Setting up a DbContext with the standard SQL execution strategy**

```
var connection = @"Server=(localdb)\mssqllocaldb;Database=… etc.";
var optionsBuilder =
    new DbContextOptionsBuilder<EfCoreContext>();

optionsBuilder.UseSqlServer(connection,
    option => option.EnableRetryOnFailure());
var options = optionsBuilder.Options;

using (var context = new EfCoreContext(options))
{
    … normal code to use the context
```

Normal EF Core queries or SaveChanges calls will automatically be retried without your doing anything. Each query and each call to SaveChanges will be retried as a unit if a transient failure occurs. But database transactions do need a little more work.

9.7.1   *Handling database transactions with EF Core's execution strategy*

Because of the way that an execution strategy works, you need to adapt any code that uses a database transaction (in which you have multiple calls to SaveChanges within an isolated transaction—see section 4.6.2 for information how transactions work). The execution strategy works by rolling back the whole transaction if a transient failure occurs, and then replaying each operation in the transaction again; each query and each call to SaveChanges will be retried as a unit.

In order for all the operations in the transaction to be retried, the execution strategy must be in control of the transaction code. This listing shows both the addition of the SQL Server EnableRetryOnFailure execution strategy, and the use of that execution strategy (in bold) with a transaction. The transaction code is written such that if a retry is needed, the whole transaction is run again from the start.

Listing 9.18 Writing transactions when you've configured an execution strategy

```
var connection = @"Server=(localdb)\mssqllocaldb;Database=… etc.";
var optionsBuilder =
    new DbContextOptionsBuilder<EfCoreContext>();

optionsBuilder.UseSqlServer(connection,
    option => option.EnableRetryOnFailure());
var options = optionsBuilder.Options
using (var context = new Chapter09DbContext(options))
{
    var strategy = context.Database
        .CreateExecutionStrategy();
    strategy.Execute(() =>
    {
        try
        {
            using (var transaction = context
                .Database.BeginTransaction())
            {
                context.Add(new MyEntity());
                context.SaveChanges();
                context.Add(new MyEntity());
                context.SaveChanges();
                transaction.Commit();
            }
        }
        catch (Exception e)
        {
            //Error handling to go here
            throw;
        }
    });
}
```

Configures the database to use the SQL execution strategy. This means you have to handle transactions differently.

Creates an IExecutionStrategy instance, which uses the execution strategy you configured the DbContext with

The important thing is to make the whole transaction code into an Action method it can call.

The rest of the transaction setup and running your code is the same.

WARNING The code in listing 9.18 is *safe* when it comes to a retry; by *safe*, I mean that the code will work properly. But in some cases, such as when data outside the execution strategy retry action is altered, the retry could cause problems. An obvious example is an `int count = 0` variable defined outside the scope of the retry action that's incremented inside the action. In this case, the value of the `count` variable would be incremented again if there was a retry. Bear this in mind when you design transactions if you're using the execution strategy retry facility.

9.7.2 Altering or writing your own execution strategy

In some cases, you might need to change the execution strategy for your database. If there's an existing execution strategy for your database provider (for instance, SQL Server), then there are options you can change, such as the number of retries, or the SQL errors that you know can be retried.

If you want to write your own execution strategy, you need to implement a class that inherits the interface IExecutionStrategy. I recommend you look at the EF Core internal class called SqlServerExecutionStrategy as a template. This can be found in the EF Core GitHub repo under the EFCore.SqlServer package in the directory Storage/Internal.

After you've written your own execution strategy class, you can configure it into your database by using the ExecuteStrategy method in the options, as shown here in bold.

Listing 9.19   Configuring your own execution strategy into your DbContext

```
var connection = this.GetUniqueDatabaseConnectionString();
var optionsBuilder =
    new DbContextOptionsBuilder<Chapter09DbContext>();

optionsBuilder.UseSqlServer(connection,
    options => options.ExecutionStrategy(
        p => new MyExecutionStrategy()));

using (var context = new Chapter09DbContext(optionsBuilder.Options))
{
    … etc.
```

Summary

- You can use EF Core's entity State property, with a little help from a per property IsModified flag, to define what will happen to the data when you call SaveChanges.
- You can affect the State of an entity and its relationships in several ways. You can use the methods Add, Remove, Update, Attach, and TrackGraph; set the State directly; and use two ways of tracking modifications.
- With EF Core's ChangeTracker, you can explore the State of all the entities that have changed.
- You can use several EF Core methods that allow you to use raw SQL command strings in your database accesses.
- You can access information about the database structure via the Model property.
- EF Core contains a system that allows you to provide a retry capability if there are connection or transient errors.

For readers who are familiar with EF6:

- The ways that the entity State is set has changed in EF Core to be more "natural," based on lessons learned from EF6.x.
- In EF6.x, the methods such as Add, Remove, and Update are found only in the DbSet<T> properties. In EF Core, those same methods are available via the application's DbContext as well, which makes the code shorter.
- EF Core introduces a new method called TrackGraph, which will traverse a graph of linked entities and call your code to set each entity's State to the value you require.

- The way you use raw SQL commands in EF Core is different from the way it's done in EF6.x.
- EF Core's `Model` property is a tremendous improvement over EF6.x's access to the model metadata. Now you can access every aspect of the database model.
- EF Core's execution strategy is an improvement on the EF6.x execution strategy, as EF Core can handle retries in a database transaction.

Part 3

Using Entity Framework Core in real-world applications

In my experience, you don't really know something until you need to use it for a real job. I might have read books containing great recipes and watched inspiring cooking videos, but it isn't until I have to cook an important meal that I know whether I've learned what I've seen. Part 3 is a bit like that: you've read a lot about EF Core in the previous chapters, so now I'll help you take that knowledge and implement more-complex issues, such as database migration and performance tuning, in EF Core.

Part 3 starts with tips and techniques in chapter 10. I think every developer has a software architect inside them and, even if you have the smallest of jobs in a project, you should be thinking about the best way to build your part. I introduce patterns and techniques that you can study to help you perfect your own patterns for your project. Some topics, such as domain-driven design, need multiple books to cover, but my aim is to give you an overview so you can decide whether looking at that topic in more detail is worthwhile.

Chapter 11 is about how to migrate/change a database structure, a task that became critical to me when I was designing and building a 24/7 e-commerce site. Trying to build a system in which you can change the database structure on a live site is a daunting job, especially if you might have paying customers using the site while you're applying the changes. I look at the overall problem of changing the database structure and the three ways you can approach this safely.

Chapters 12 and 13 are all about performance tuning EF Core database accesses. My philosophy is "Get your EF code working, but be ready to make it faster if you need to." Chapter 12 looks at what needs performance tuning, how to detect performance issues, all the things that you can do to improve your EF Core code. In chapter 13, you'll follow a worked example of performance tuning; I'll take you through three stages of performance tuning, two of which go beyond what EF Core can do on its own.

Chapter 14 starts by looking at the issues that arise when using various database types with EF Core. It goes on to describe a hybrid SQL/NoSQL application that's designed for situations that need to quickly handle millions of rows of data and many thousands of simultaneous users. You'll also look at extensibility features designed into EF Core, as well as EF Core's services and how to replace them or co-opt them for your own use.

Chapter 15 covers unit-testing applications that use EF Core for its database access. Unit testing when a database is involved needs careful thought, especially if you don't want the unit test to run slowly. I share several techniques and approaches, and I provide a NuGet package called EfCore.TestSupport I built that contains setup methods to help you unit-test EF Core applications safely and quickly.

Useful software patterns for EF Core applications

This chapter covers

- Applying the separation-of-concerns principle
- Using a LINQ mapper to speed up development
- Using a domain-driven-design approach to EF Core
- Splitting your database across multiple DbContexts
- Building error-handling for database errors

This chapter introduces techniques, patterns, and packages to help you become a more productive developer. I find that I become a better developer by taking a pattern or design principle that looks promising, using it in a project, reviewing how that went, and improving the pattern in the next project. This chapter shares techniques I've used and perfected over many years as well as some that I've only just starting looking at now that EF Core has been released.

The techniques in this chapter aren't the only ones you could use, and not all the approaches I describe will be applicable to your needs, but they're a good mix of techniques to consider. Like me, you won't know if an approach is useful until you've used it in a real-world project, but you have to start somewhere. I hope this chapter gets you thinking, so enjoy the journey.

10.1 *Another look at the separation-of-concerns principle*

Section 5.5.2 covered the software design principle called *separation of concerns* (SoC). This design principle states that a software system should be decomposed into parts that overlap in functionality as little as possible. SoC is linked to two other principles:

- *Low coupling*—You want each component in your application to be as self-contained as possible.
- *High cohesion*—Each project in your application should have code that provides similar or strongly related functions.

Figure 10.1 (taken from chapter 5) shows the SoC principle applied to our book app.

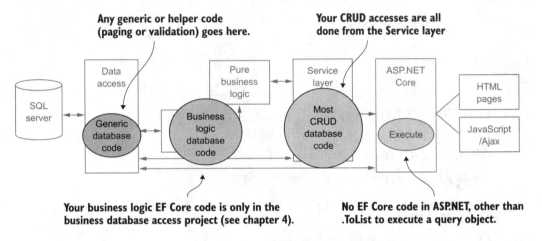

Figure 10.1   The application of the software design principle called separation of concerns to our layered architecture. Your EF Core code lives in two primary places: any database access that your business logic needs can be found in your BizDbAccess project, and the CRUD database accesses are all in the Service layer.

By arranging your software code as shown in figure 10.1, you place each piece of database code in an appropriately named class whose job it is to execute the database access, and nothing more. This isolates the database access code and makes it easier to test. In addition, the code is grouped into two main areas in our application; *high cohesion* makes the code easier to find when you need to refactor or performance tune the database access code. I'll introduce new approaches in this chapter that will further improve the SoC beyond what you see in figure 10.1.

In our example web application, you'll use a layered architecture because it's simple to understand while being close to what might be used in a real-world application. But you could use other architectures (such as microservices, event-driven, CQRS architecture), but in all cases the SoC principle would still be applicable.

10.2   Using patterns to speed development of database access

Over the years, I've learned from software giants such as Martin Fowler and Eric Evans, and developed my own patterns and supporting libraries for building applications. These patterns make me quicker at developing each application, and make testing and performance tuning easier. This section covers using Eric Evan's domain-driven design (DDD) and Martin Fowler's Service layer (figure 10.2).

I normally form these patterns by reviewing what I've done and looking for parts I could improve or turn into patterns or libraries. Chapter 4 described one pattern for business logic, my interpretation of DDD, and in section 10.4.2 you'll enhance the business logic further by applying additional DDD techniques.

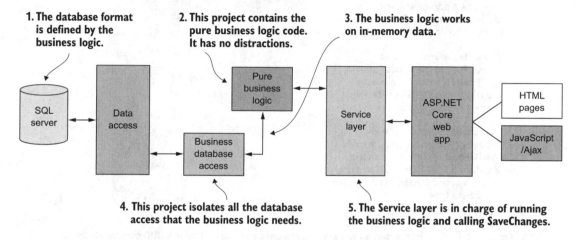

1. The database format is defined by the business logic.

2. This project contains the pure business logic code. It has no distractions.

3. The business logic works on in-memory data.

4. This project isolates all the database access that the business logic needs.

5. The Service layer is in charge of running the business logic and calling SaveChanges.

Figure 10.2   My implementation of the DDD pattern for handling business logic with EF Core. This also uses the SoC approach, with low coupling between the business logic and the database access. You can find a detailed description of the five steps in chapter 4, and in section 10.4 I extend the design to move some of the business logic inside the entity classes.

You'll use another pattern in the book app. This pattern, which I developed for my own web application development work, allows you to quickly build the CRUD database access code that's needed in most web applications. Figure 10.3 pulls out the four key attributes that allow you to develop a robust, testable application quickly.

This review/improve cycle works well for me, and I recommend you try it too. I review each project/subproject I work on and decide what worked well, what didn't work well, and what was repetitive. I especially look for patterns I can create to improve future coding. That way, the simple things will get easier to develop, which allows me to put my time into the complex parts that need my serious effort. Patterns make me quicker, because I know ahead of time what I'm going to write. The right pattern makes my code more robust, because I've thought through what could go wrong. The patterns you develop with experience will be different from mine, and, like me, you might need a few attempts to get something that works well. In the end, defining a set of good patterns can make you a much more efficient developer.

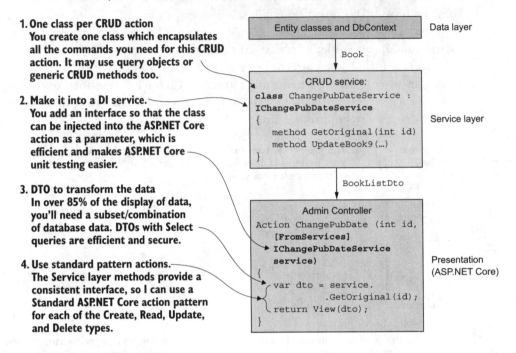

1. One class per CRUD action
You create one class which encapsulates all the commands you need for this **CRUD** action. It may use query objects or generic **CRUD** methods too.

2. Make it into a DI service.
You add an interface so that the class can be injected into the **ASP.NET Core** action as a parameter, which is efficient and makes **ASP.NET Core** unit testing easier.

3. DTO to transform the data
In over 85% of the display of data, you'll need a subset/combination of database data. DTOs with Select queries are efficient and secure.

4. Use standard pattern actions.
The Service layer methods provide a consistent interface, so I can use a Standard **ASP.NET Core** action pattern for each of the Create, Read, Update, and Delete types.

Figure 10.3 Four key patterns I've developed to speed up the writing of CRUD commands using the EF Core framework inside an ASP.NET Core application. Your pattern might be different, but developing your own pattern will make you quicker and less error-prone.

10.3 *Speed up query development—use a LINQ mapper*

Over the years, I've built many applications, and I noticed that a large percentage (>85%) of the database queries I built needed to extract data from multiple entities, just like the book list query in chapter 2. The most efficient way to achieve this, both in performance and speed of development, was to use EF Core's `Select` method to pick the exact properties from an entity class and map the related data into a DTO.

Although writing a LINQ `Select` statement to map to a DTO isn't hard, it's time-consuming, can be error-prone, and most important, it's boring! The answer to writing a LINQ `Select` statement quickly and accurately is to use an *object-to-object mapper* (I refer to this as a *mapper* from now on), with certain characteristics, to automatically build the `Select` statement.

> **DEFINITION** An *object-to-object mapper* is a piece of software that transfers data from one object (class), including any nested object, to another object. A mapper can work out the mapping between the two objects in several ways; the most useful ones do so automatically.

To be able to use a mapper with EF Core, the mapper library must support `IQueryable` mapping; the mapper must be able to produce a LINQ query capable of copying the data from one `IQueryable` source to another. Quite a few mappers support `IQueryable`, but the best known, and possibly best supported, mapper that handles `IQueryable` mapping is AutoMapper (see https://github.com/Automapper/Automapper).

I've used AutoMapper for several years and found it to provide a comprehensive and configurable package. It has recently been tuned to be faster at building object-to-object maps. To give you an example of how the mapping works, you'll map the `Book` entity class to a `BookDto` class. Figure 10.4 shows the ways that the mapper builds a `Select` query.

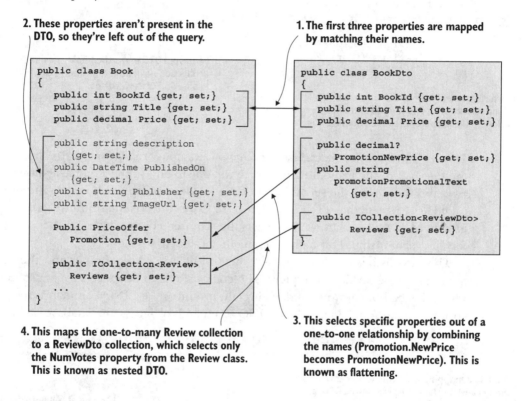

2. These properties aren't present in the DTO, so they're left out of the query.

1. The first three properties are mapped by matching their names.

```
public class Book
{
    public int BookId {get; set;}
    public string Title {get; set;}
    public decimal Price {get; set;}

    public string description
        {get; set;}
    public DateTime PublishedOn
        {get; set;}
    public string Publisher {get; set;}
    public string ImageUrl {get; set;}

    Public PriceOffer
        Promotion {get; set;}

    public ICollection<Review>
        Reviews {get; set;}
    ...
}
```

```
public class BookDto
{
    public int BookId {get; set;}
    public string Title {get; set;}
    public decimal Price {get; set;}

    public decimal?
        PromotionNewPrice {get; set;}
    public string
        promotionPromotionalText
        {get; set;}

    public ICollection<ReviewDto>
        Reviews {get; set;}
}
```

4. This maps the one-to-many Review collection to a ReviewDto collection, which selects only the NumVotes property from the Review class. This is known as nested DTO.

3. This selects specific properties out of a one-to-one relationship by combining the names (Promotion.NewPrice becomes PromotionNewPrice). This is known as flattening.

Figure 10.4 Four ways that AutoMapper maps the `Book` entity class to the `BookDto` class. The default convention is to map via similar names, including handling relationships by having a name equivalent to the property access, but without the dot. For instance, the DTO property `PromotionNewPrice` is mapped to the `Promotion.NewPrice` property in the source. Mappings also can be nested; a collection in the entity class can be mapped to a collection with a DTO.

Listing 10.1 shows the `BookDto` class, which holds only those properties you want to copy, thereby minimizing the number of columns that are read back. This code also includes flattening and nested DTOs to select specific properties from navigational properties.

Listing 10.1   The `BookDto` class, with the properties you want to copy

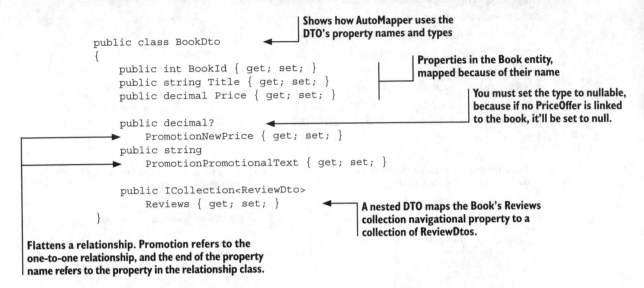

Shows how AutoMapper uses the DTO's property names and types

```
public class BookDto
{
    public int BookId { get; set; }
    public string Title { get; set; }
    public decimal Price { get; set; }

    public decimal?
        PromotionNewPrice { get; set; }
    public string
        PromotionPromotionalText { get; set; }

    public ICollection<ReviewDto>
        Reviews { get; set; }
}
```

Properties in the Book entity, mapped because of their name

You must set the type to nullable, because if no PriceOffer is linked to the book, it'll be set to null.

A nested DTO maps the Book's Reviews collection navigational property to a collection of ReviewDtos.

Flattens a relationship. Promotion refers to the one-to-one relationship, and the end of the property name refers to the property in the relationship class.

The DTO property `PromotionNewPrice` is an example of *flattening*. AutoMapper maps the first half of the name, `Promotion`, to the one-to-one `Promotion` navigational property, and then maps the second part of the DTO property, `NewPrice`, to the property called `NewPrice` in the `PriceOffer` entity. EF Core converts the resulting `Select` query into an SQL `INNER JOIN`, which selects the required column by using the foreign key for that relationship. This makes for an efficient data access query.

The next listing builds the `Select` method by using AutoMapper and then uses a query to create an EF Core query. The code uses AutoMapper's `ProjectTo` method which, instead of copying the data directly, produces the LINQ commands needed to copy that data. You then use those LINQ commands to access the database via EF Core.

Listing 10.2   Setting up your mapping, and using `ProjectTo` to build the query

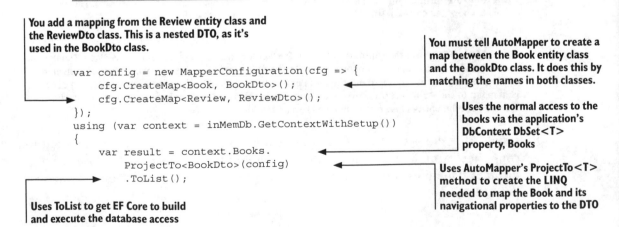

You add a mapping from the Review entity class and the ReviewDto class. This is a nested DTO, as it's used in the BookDto class.

```
var config = new MapperConfiguration(cfg => {
    cfg.CreateMap<Book, BookDto>();
    cfg.CreateMap<Review, ReviewDto>();
});
using (var context = inMemDb.GetContextWithSetup())
{
    var result = context.Books.
        ProjectTo<BookDto>(config)
        .ToList();
```

You must tell AutoMapper to create a map between the Book entity class and the BookDto class. It does this by matching the names in both classes.

Uses the normal access to the books via the application's DbContext DbSet<T> property, Books

Uses AutoMapper's ProjectTo<T> method to create the LINQ needed to map the Book and its navigational properties to the DTO

Uses ToList to get EF Core to build and execute the database access

It's much quicker to build Select queries by using AutoMapper than the hand-coded way shown next, especially if you have more properties to copy. It's also a lot less boring.

> **Listing 10.3   A hand-coded Select query to do the same job as the mapper version**

```
using (var context = inMemDb.GetContextWithSetup())
{
    var result = context.Books.
        Select(p => new BookDto
        {
            BookId = p.BookId,
            Title = p.Title,
            Price = p.Price,
            PromotionNewPrice = p.Promotion == null
                ? (decimal?)null
                : p.Promotion.NewPrice,
            PromotionPromotionalText = p.Promotion == null
                ? null
                : p.Promotion.PromotionalText,
            Reviews = p.Reviews
                .Select(x => new ReviewDto
                {
                    NumStars = x.NumStars
                })
                .ToList()
        })
        .ToList();
```

AutoMapper has many features, including allowing the developer to include custom LINQ mapping for mappings that are too complex for AutoMapper to automatically map. Nearly all Select queries can be built with the help of AutoMapper.

NOTE The range of features and settings of AutoMapper can take some time to get used to. A good start is https://github.com/AutoMapper/AutoMapper/wiki/Getting-started.

Using AutoMapper with dependency injection

If you're using AutoMapper in an application that uses DI, such as ASP.NET Core, you need to use AutoMapper's AutoMapper.Extensions.Microsoft.DependencyInjection NuGet package. This finds your mapping by looking for classes that inherit from AutoMapper's Profile class, and then provides the config you need to do the mapping. You can find information on how to do this in Jimmy Bogard's blog post, http://mng.bz/14nL. You can find a simpler explanation of DI in ASP.NET Core from Stack Overflow at https://stackoverflow.com/a/40275196/1434764.

10.4 *Domain-driven-design database repository*

Another design concept for accessing a database that's worth considering is the domain-driven-design (DDD) entity and repository. This comes from Eric Evans' seminal book, *Domain-Driven Design*, which I referred to in chapter 4 when looking at business logic. Evans' book puts the business domain-relation problems at the heart of software design and implementation.

Evans describes a database access design, referred to as a *DDD repository*, that centralizes the reading and writing of a group of related business objects to a persistent store. In his book, Evans lists four main advantages of a DDD repository:

- They present the client with a simple model for obtaining persistent objects (classes) and managing their lifecycle.
- They decouple applications and domain (business) design from persistence technology, multiple database strategies, or even multiple data sources.
- They communicate design decisions about object access.
- They allow easy substitution of a dummy implementation for use in testing.

When it comes to the implementation of a DDD design, a few key design principles are applied to database accesses:

- To reduce the mental complexity, entities are grouped into what DDD calls a *root entity* and *aggregates*. *Aggregates* are entities that are so closely aligned with the root entity that the only way you can access them is via the root entity.

  Our Book entity is a good example of a root/aggregates entity: the Book class is the root entity; and the Review, PriceOffer, and BookAuthor linking tables, and the Author classes, are aggregates. The idea is you can access the aggregates only via the root entity.

- Setting the entity's data is done not by directly setting an entity's property, but via methods that reflect the business goal you're trying to achieve. For instance, when you want to update the publication date for a book, instead of setting the PublishedOn property in the Book entity, you must go through a method with an appropriate business name, such as ChangePublicationDate(newDate).

- You use a repository pattern to "decouple applications and domain (business) design from persistence technology" (as noted in the list of advantages). In our implementation, shown next, you'll create a DDD repository in the Data layer in such a way that the software layers that need to access the database never use any EF Core code, but only go through the appropriate DDD repository.

Figure 10.5 compares the original, non-DDD design with the DDD repository and the original design for the ChangePubDateService action (shown in figure 10.3).

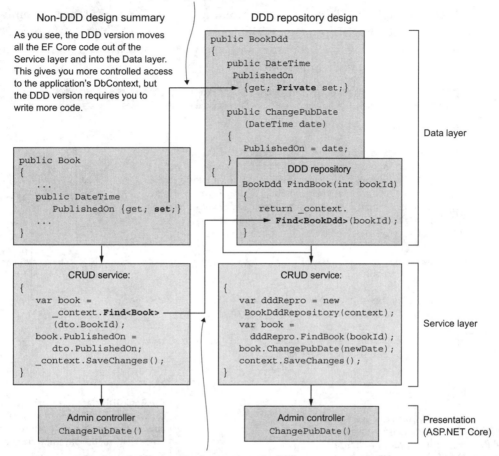

Figure 10.5 **Comparing the non-DDD design for updating the book's publication date in the book app (left) with the DDD design (right). The code required for the update has the same parts, but the DDD version moves all the EF Core code into the Data layer. If you also "hide" the application's DbContext in the DDD version, you can ensure that the developer can access the database only via the DDD repository.**

The DDD concepts include so many details that I can't hope to cover them all here, but let me show you two examples:

- An implementation of a DDD Book entity with aggregates and a DDD repository.
- The refactoring of the order-processing business logic to take account of the new constructors used by the DDD entity classes.

10.4.1 *Example Book DDD entity and repository*

In this example, you'll create a BookDdd entity class that's a copy of the Book entity class, but set up using DDD principles. The BookDdd entity is split into two listings. The following listing shows the properties and constructors, and listing 10.5 shows the DDD business-oriented setting methods.

> **Listing 10.4   Part 1 of the BookDdd class showing properties and constructors**

```
public class BookDdd
{
    public int BookId { get; private set; }
    public string Title { get; private set; }
    public string Description { get; private set; }
    public DateTime PublishedOn { get; private set; }
    public string Publisher { get; private set; }
    public decimal Price { get; private set; }
    public string ImageUrl { get; private set; }

    //------------------------------------------------
    //relationships

    public PriceOfferDdd Promotion { get; private set; }
    public IEnumerable<ReviewDdd> Reviews
        => _reviews?.ToList();
    public IEnumerable<BookAuthorDdd> AuthorsLink
        => _authorsLink?.ToList();

    //------------------------------------------------
    //ctors

    private BookDdd() { }

    public BookDdd(string title, string description,
        DateTime publishedOn, string publisher,
        decimal price, string imageUrl,
        IReadOnlyList<AuthorDdd> authors)
    {
        if (string.IsNullOrWhiteSpace(title))
          throw new
          ArgumentNullException(nameof(title));
        Title = title;
        Description = description;
        PublishedOn = publishedOn;
        Publisher = publisher;
        Price = price;
        ImageUrl = imageUrl;
```

All the properties now have private setters so that you can set properties only via the DDD repository methods.

Collection navigational properties are IEnumerable<T>, which doesn't have the Add and Remove methods; you can change them only via the DDD repository methods.

The BookDDD class has a private, no-parameter constructor for EF Core to use. This stops any code outside this entity class from creating a BookDDD other than via the parameterized constructor.

The developer uses this constructor to create BookDdd. This takes all the parameters it needs to create a book, including the Author(s).

Allows you to add a few system checks, such as the book title not being empty.

If a new BookDDD is created, the _reviews collection
is initialized. This allows ReviewDDD to be added to
a new BookDDD before being written to the database.

Allows you to add a few
system checks, such as the
book title not being empty.

```
        _reviews = new HashSet<ReviewDdd>();

        if (authors == null || authors.Count < 1)
            throw new ArgumentException(
                "You must have at least one Author for a book",
                nameof(authors));
        _authorsLink = new HashSet<BookAuthorDdd>(
            authors.Select(a =>
            new BookAuthorDdd
            {
                Book = this,
                Author = a
            }));
    }
```

The caller doesn't have to
worry about setting up the
BookAuthorDdd linking
table, as you do it inside
the constructor.

You can see that all the properties now have private setters, and the one-to-many nav-igational properties are now IEnumerable<T>, so you can't Add or Remove items to/from the collection. This forces all updates to properties to be done via methods that are business-oriented (you'll see these in listing 10.5).

Notice also that you add a parameterless constructor with a private access modi-fier. This stops any code outside the Data layer from creating the BookDdd entity other than via the public constructor, which requires various parameters to create a BookDdd instance. EF Core does need a parameterless constructor, but can use a private access constructor.

The following listing shows part 2 of the BookDdd entity class, in which you add several methods that update the BookDdd entity instance. These methods, which have names that represent the business need they're providing, allow the developer to modify the BookDdd entity and its relationships, or, in DDD terms, its aggregates.

> **Listing 10.5   Part 2 of the** BookDdd **class with the create/update methods**

Updates the book's PublishedOn date.
The property has a private setter.

```
public class BookDdd
{
    //… see previous listing for properties and the constructors

    public void ChangePubDate(DateTime newDate)
    {
        PublishedOn = newDate;
    }

    private HashSet<ReviewDdd> _reviews;
    private HashSet<BookAuthorDdd> _authorsLink;
```

Uses backing fields to hold the two collection
navigational properties. These are null unless the
property is loaded, or a new BookDDD instance is
created by the constructor that takes all the
parameters needed to set up the entity.

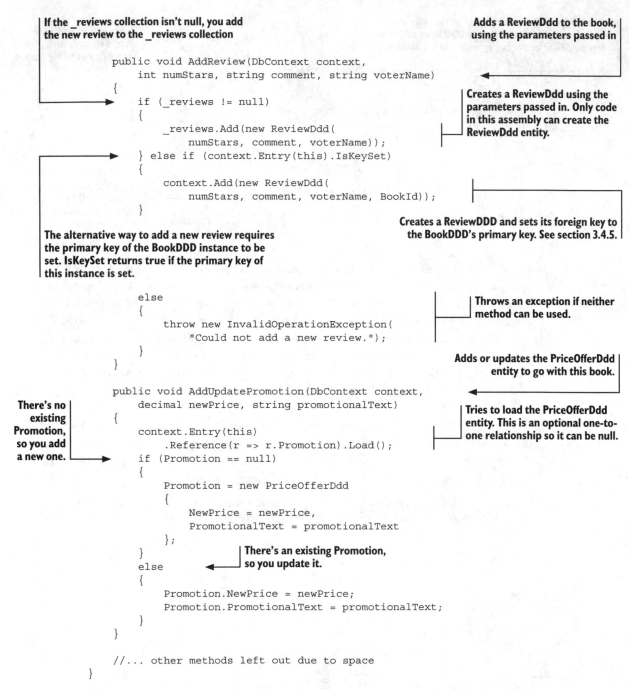

If the _reviews collection isn't null, you add the new review to the _reviews collection

Adds a ReviewDdd to the book, using the parameters passed in

```
public void AddReview(DbContext context,
    int numStars, string comment, string voterName)
{
    if (_reviews != null)
    {
        _reviews.Add(new ReviewDdd(
            numStars, comment, voterName));
    } else if (context.Entry(this).IsKeySet)
    {
        context.Add(new ReviewDdd(
            numStars, comment, voterName, BookId));
    }
```

Creates a ReviewDdd using the parameters passed in. Only code in this assembly can create the ReviewDdd entity.

Creates a ReviewDDD and sets its foreign key to the BookDDD's primary key. See section 3.4.5.

The alternative way to add a new review requires the primary key of the BookDDD instance to be set. IsKeySet returns true if the primary key of this instance is set.

```
    else
    {
        throw new InvalidOperationException(
            "Could not add a new review.");
    }
}
```

Throws an exception if neither method can be used.

Adds or updates the PriceOfferDdd entity to go with this book.

```
public void AddUpdatePromotion(DbContext context,
    decimal newPrice, string promotionalText)
{
    context.Entry(this)
        .Reference(r => r.Promotion).Load();
    if (Promotion == null)
    {
        Promotion = new PriceOfferDdd
        {
            NewPrice = newPrice,
            PromotionalText = promotionalText
        };
    }
    else
    {
        Promotion.NewPrice = newPrice;
        Promotion.PromotionalText = promotionalText;
    }
}
```

There's no existing Promotion, so you add a new one.

Tries to load the PriceOfferDdd entity. This is an optional one-to-one relationship so it can be null.

There's an existing Promotion, so you update it.

```
//... other methods left out due to space
}
```

The other class you create in the Data layer is the DDD repository itself, which is shown in listing 10.6. This contains methods to create (add), find, and delete a Book entity instance, plus a method called GetBookList that provides a similar, but not identical, functionality as the original ListBooksService class described in section 2.8.

Listing 10.6 The `BookDddRepository` class that provides a DDD repository

```
public class BookDddRepository
{
    private readonly Chapter10DbContext _context;

    public BookDddRepository(Chapter10DbContext context)
    {
        _context = context;
    }

    public void AddBook(BookDdd book)
    {
        _context.Add(book);
    }

    public BookDdd FindBook(int bookId)
    {
        return _context.Find<BookDdd>(bookId);
    }

    public bool DeleteBook(int bookId)
    {
        var book = FindBook(bookId);
        if (book == null)
            return false;
        _context.Remove(book);
        return true;
    }

    public IQueryable<BookDdd> GetBookList(
        DddSortFilterPageOptions options)
    {
        var booksQuery = _context.Books
            .AsNoTracking()
            .OrderBooksBy(options.OrderByOptions)
            .FilterBooksBy(options.FilterBy,
                options.FilterValue);

        options.SetupRestOfDto(booksQuery);

        return booksQuery.Page(options.PageNum - 1,
            options.PageSize);
    }
}
```

Creates the repository by passing in the applications's DbContext

Adds the book to the context

Finds an existing book by using its primary key

Tries to delete the book with the given primary key. It returns true if it finds a book to delete, or false if it doesn't.

The DDD equivalent to the ListBooksService class, but it passes back IQueryable<BookDdd> rather than IQueryable<BoolListDto> that the original verision did.

Copies of the query objects in the original, non-DDD design.

Most of the DDD repository code contains the methods that contain the EF Core code, which, in our original design, was located in separate classes in the Service layer. For instance, the EF Core commands found in the non-DDD designed `ChangePubDate-Service` class are now brought inside the `Book` entity class.

The biggest change is the `GetBookList` method. It delivers an `IQueryable<BookDdd>` result rather than the `IQueryable<BookListDto>` that the non-DDD design provides. The DDD repository `GetBookList` method returns `IQueryable<BookDdd>` because the

SoC principle says that the frontend design, which needs a `BookListDto` result, shouldn't influence the Data layer or the business layer. Therefore, the `GetBookList` method returns `IQueryable<BookDdd>`. You must add a select query object in the Service layer to convert the `GetBookList` method output to the `IQueryable<BookListDto>` result that the ASP.NET Core presentation layer needs.

Listing 10.7 executes the change of the `PublishedOn` property in a disconnected state. This code uses a combination of `BookDddRepository` and a method in the `BookDdd` entity to set the new published date for a book. Also, EF Core's `SaveChanges` must be called outside `BookDddRepository`, because the `SaveChanges` call must come at the end of any sequence of database commands.

> **Listing 10.7   How `BookDdd` and `BookDddRepository` update a book's publish date**

```
var dddRepro = new BookDddRepository(context);
var book = dddRepro.FindBook(bookId);
book.ChangePubDate(newDate);
context.SaveChanges();
```

This code would most likely be placed in a class in the Service layer and called in the same way that the original `ChangePubDateService` class's `UpdateBook` method (see listing 3.8 in chapter 3) was used.

10.4.2   *How the DDD design changes the business logic design*

Section 4.3 described a non-DDD approach to handing business logic, as it was a good starting point. But the DDD approach can bring significant benefits to writing your business logic. The DDD version you create in this section still applies the five rules presented in chapter 4, but with much of the business logic now handled by the constructors of the entity classes involved in the business logic. This makes the business logic much simpler, and "locks down" the entities so that a developer must use the proscribed public constructor to create a new instance of the entity.

As an example, you're going to rework the entity classes and business logic for creating a customer's order for books in the book app. You'll write new versions of the `Order` and `LineItem` entity classes, and refactor the business logic code in the `PlaceOrderAction` class. The new classes will all end with Ddd so that you can compare the new DDD design with the original design. You start by writing the `LineItemDdd` and `OrderDdd` entity classes, which will differ from the non-DDD version in the following ways:

- The properties in the `LineItemDdd` and `OrderDdd` entity classes are read-only to outside code; the properties setting has `private` or `internal` access modifiers, so that only the entity classes can set them.
- The only way to create an instance of the DDD entity classes `LineItemsDdd` and `OrderDdd` is via their public constructor. This constructor requires specific parameters, which it uses to build an instance of the entity in the approved form.
- Data validation, and some extra checks in the entity's public constructors, catch any possible errors in the customer's order before it's written to the database.

The next listing shows the `LineItemDdd` entity class, but focuses on the constructors: one private, parameterless constructor for EF Core, and a second public constructor used to create a `LineItemDdd` entity instance for a customer's order.

Listing 10.8 The `LineItemDdd` entity class showing the constructors

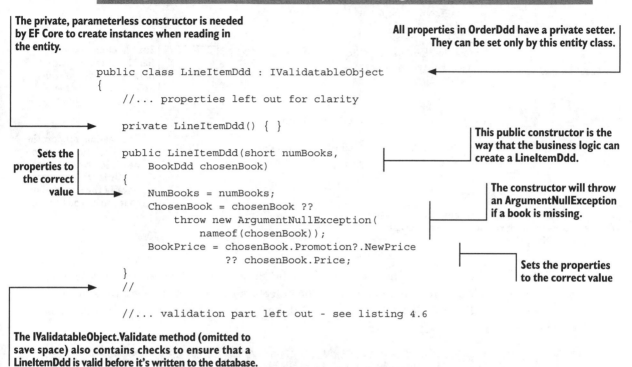

The private, parameterless constructor is needed by EF Core to create instances when reading in the entity.

All properties in OrderDdd have a private setter. They can be set only by this entity class.

```
public class LineItemDdd : IValidatableObject
{
    //... properties left out for clarity

    private LineItemDdd() { }

    public LineItemDdd(short numBooks,
        BookDdd chosenBook)
    {
        NumBooks = numBooks;
        ChosenBook = chosenBook ??
            throw new ArgumentNullException(
                nameof(chosenBook));
        BookPrice = chosenBook.Promotion?.NewPrice
                ?? chosenBook.Price;
    }
//

    //... validation part left out - see listing 4.6
```

Sets the properties to the correct value

This public constructor is the way that the business logic can create a LineItemDdd.

The constructor will throw an ArgumentNullException if a book is missing.

Sets the properties to the correct value

The IValidatableObject.Validate method (omitted to save space) also contains checks to ensure that a LineItemDdd is valid before it's written to the database.

The `OrderDdd` entity class's constructor, shown next, takes the customer's name, plus a collection of `ListItemDdds` to produce a valid order. The `OrderDdd` entity class's `LineItems` navigational collection property is handled by a backing field, so that the `LineItems` property can't be changed after the `OrderDdd` entity class is created.

Listing 10.9 The `OrderDdd` entity class, focusing on the constructors

```
public class OrderDdd
{
    private HashSet<LineItemDdd> _lineItems;

    //... properties left out for clarity

    private OrderDdd() {}

    public OrderDdd(string customerName,
        IEnumerable<LineItemDdd> lineItems,
```

All properties in OrderDdd have a private setter. They can be set only by this entity class.

EF Core needs the private, parameterless constructor to create instances when reading in the entity.

The public constructor is the way that the business logic can create an OrderDdd.

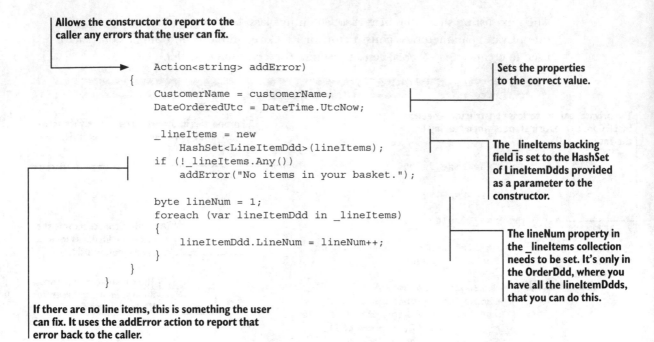

**Allows the constructor to report to the
caller any errors that the user can fix.**

```
         Action<string> addError)
     {
         CustomerName = customerName;
         DateOrderedUtc = DateTime.UtcNow;

         _lineItems = new
             HashSet<LineItemDdd>(lineItems);
         if (!_lineItems.Any())
             addError("No items in your basket.");

         byte lineNum = 1;
         foreach (var lineItemDdd in _lineItems)
         {
             lineItemDdd.LineNum = lineNum++;
         }
     }
 }
```

**Sets the properties
to the correct value.**

**The _lineItems backing
field is set to the HashSet
of LineItemDdds provided
as a parameter to the
constructor.**

**The lineNum property in
the _lineItems collection
needs to be set. It's only in
the OrderDdd, where you
have all the lineItemDdds,
that you can do this.**

**If there are no line items, this is something the user
can fix. It uses the addError action to report that
error back to the caller.**

Having moved the order creation code into the entity classes, the code required in the
business logic class reduces dramatically. The PlaceOrderAction class, shown in listing 4.2,
is refactored to use the DDD entities; and the new business logic class, shown here, is
called PlaceOrderActionDdd.

Listing 10.10   The `PlaceOrderActionDdd` class that creates an order

```
public class PlaceOrderActionDdd :
    BizActionErrors,
    IBizAction<PlaceOrderInDto, OrderDdd>
{
    private readonly IPlaceOrderDbAccessDdd _dbAccess;

    public PlaceOrderActionDdd(IPlaceOrderDbAccessDdd dbAccess)
    {
        _dbAccess = dbAccess;
    }

    public OrderDdd Action(PlaceOrderInDto dto)
    {
        if (!dto.AcceptTAndCs)
        {
            AddError(
"You must accept the T&Cs to place an order.");
            return null;
        }
```

**Now the lineItem tests are
either in the constructor or
in the data validation parts**

**Same call as the
original non-DDD**

**Same test as the
original non-DDD**

**Now the lineItem tests are either in the
constructor or in the data validation parts**

```
var lineItems = dto.LineItems.Select(
    x => new LineItemDdd(x.NumBooks,
        _dbAccess.GetBookWithPromotion
            (x.BookId)));
var order = new OrderDdd(
    dto.UserId.ToString(),
    lineItems,
    s => AddError(s));

if (!HasErrors)
    _dbAccess.Add(order);

return HasErrors ? null : order;
    }
}
```

**The OrderDdd
constructor builds the
order. The constructor
and the data validation
parts handle the error
checking.**

**The OrderDdd constructor reports
errors back to the business logic
via an action parameter**

**Same ending as the
original non-DDD**

The `PlaceOrderActionDdd` version is much shorter than the non-DDD version: 35
lines of code in `PlaceOrderActionDdd`, compared with 83 for the `PlaceOrderAction`
version. Also, an order is much less likely to be built incorrectly when using the DDD
version, because the entity classes control, and check, how the order is built.

10.4.3 *Impressions from building this DDD design*

I've been using DDD design principles for some time and find them helpful; see chapter 4 for my first take on DDD in business logic, which I expanded upon in the previous
section. I did look at creating a DDD entity with aggregates in EF6.x, but there were
limitations on controlling access to collection navigational properties. But now, with EF
Core's capability to have navigational properties using backing fields (see section 7.10),
building a DDD entity with controlled access via methods is possible—which is exciting.

Having built this DDD entity/repository design and the modified business logic
code, I have some views on what works and what doesn't. But because I haven't yet
used a DDD design in a real project, these are only my first impressions. I'm going to
describe aspects of the design, and you can make your own decision on whether a DDD
design would help with your specific application. Here are what I think are the good
and bad parts of using a DDD approach.

THE GOOD PARTS OF USING A DDD APPROACH WITH EF CORE

First, let's consider the good parts:

- *Using specific constructors to create entity instances works well.* Section 10.4.2 shows that
  moving the code for building a valid entity class into the class's constructor pro-
  motes simpler business logic. Also, making the entity class properties read-only
  reduces the likelihood of a developer incorrectly interpreting how a class should
  be initialized or updated.
- *Using business-oriented methods to change the entity is clearer.* The act of making all the
  properties have a private setter and then having to use meaningful named methods to change the properties is positive. For instance, the `BookDdd` constructor

shown in listing 10.4 hides the creation of the many-to-many linking table, which is nice. Also, the other methods in part 2 (see listing 10.5) are clear and concise and express what you're doing.

- *Altering the aggregates via business-oriented methods works well too.* Hiding some of the code relating to altering the BookDdd's aggregate entities (the Review, PriceOffer, and BookAuthor linking tables) and the OrderDdd's LineItems property had a good feel about it too. The method's name more clearly indicates what's going on, and the methods hide some of the complexities of updating these aggregates.

THE BAD PARTS OF USING A DDD APPROACH WITH EF CORE

And now for the bad parts:

- *The DDD repository can cause performance issues.* I noticed a subtle but important issue about creating the DDD repository in the Data layer. Because of SoC, I didn't let the frontend design/needs affect my DDD repository. The DDD repository can return only entity classes, or other business classes, available at the Data layer. In many cases, these classes won't match what the frontend layer needs, and further code will be needed in the Service layer to add a LINQ Select method to map the data to a DTO.

  For instance, the DDD repository method GetBookList returns an IQueryable<BookDdd> result instead of the original, non-DDD design, which returns IQueryable<BookListDto>. You therefore must add a Select query object to the IQueryable<BookDdd> result in the Service layer to turn it into what the frontend wants—BookListDto. This can preclude some SQL optimizations that EF Core could achieve because some columns will be accessed in different levels in the LINQ statements.

- *The DDD CRUD code requires more code to be written.* If you look at figure 10.5, you can see that the DDD CRUD implementation has more code in it compared to our initial, non-DDD design. The plus side is the DDD CRUD code is DRY (don't repeat yourself), as the methods only exist once in the entity class.

  In small applications, the extra development effort might not be worth the improvement in SoC. But in large, multideveloper projects, the discipline of the DDD design would help hide the database code from other developers working on higher layers and therefore would warrant the extra code.

I could say a lot more about our DDD repository/entity implementation, but I hope the code and my comments will help you to understand how you might use DDD design principles with EF Core. In the end, the architecture you use must fit the business need, the project type, and the people on the project. Now that you've been introduced to one implementation of the DDD pattern for database access, you can decide whether you want to consider a DDD approach in more detail.

> **NOTE** You might be interested in an article I wrote called "Creating Domain-Driven Design entity classes with Entity Framework Core" where I compare and contrast the standard way of creating entity classes with the DDD-styled entity classes: http://mng.bz/1iJW.

10.5 Is the Repository pattern useful with Entity Framework?

I said in section 10.4.3 that the DDD repository had some problems. These problems aren't limited to a DDD repository, but can occur in many Repository patterns when working with EF Core.

> **DEFINITION** Martin Fowler's website states that a *Repository pattern* "mediates between the domain (business) and data mapping layers using a collection-like interface for accessing domain objects." The idea of a repository is that it takes data from the generalized database access library (DAL) and delivers an interface that's better matched to the business needs (see https://martinfowler .com/eaaCatalog/repository.html).

My view, and the view of others such as Rob Conery and Jimmy Bogard, is that EF Core provides an interface that's already a form of repository. That isn't to say you can't add useful things to EF Core, such as using query objects (see chapter 2), but a full-blown repository on top of EF Core is normally overkill and, in some cases, can cause problems.

I'm not saying repositories are all bad. In chapter 4, you effectively produced a mini Repository pattern to isolate the EF Core code from your business logic (see section 4.4.4). That sort of repository is what I call an *EF repository*; you're not hiding EF Core, but putting all the EF Core commands for that business need in one place. This leads me to talk about Repository patterns that I'd steer away from.

10.5.1 Some forms of Repository patterns to avoid

These are the forms of repository that try to hide the DAL in such a way that one DAL could be replaced by another DAL without any need for change to the higher code. For instance, you could create a general repository that uses EF Core underneath, but then replace the EF Core library with another DAL such as Dapper or NHibernate. My experience is that such repositories are hard to write correctly and difficult to maintain.

The problem with a DAL-hiding repository is that you stop thinking about how EF Core works, and assume that the repository method you call "does what it says on the box." The classic example of where a DAL-hiding repository is both inefficient and can be misleading is with an update of data.

A DAL-hiding repository must provide an Update method, because that's the typical database action you want to do. But how should this Update method work? You know that EF Core can detect updates by using tracked entities, but the DAL-hiding repository must ignore all aspects of tracked entities, because they're DAL-specific. Therefore, the DAL-hiding repository implementation would normally call EF Core's Update method, which is inefficient because it updates all the columns in the table. Also, EF Core's Update method has certain rules for handling navigational properties, and the DAL-hiding repository can't easily hide that from you.

I believe the idea that a DAL-hiding repository would allow you to change from, say, EF Core to even another high-level O/RM (say, NHibernate) is a fallacy. There are just too many nuances in these powerful DALs that make changing a big job. I think it's better to embrace whatever DAL you've chosen (hopefully, EF Core) and work out how to use it to the best of your ability.

10.6   *Splitting a database across multiple DbContexts*

The SoC principle can also be applied to the database and its tables. Splitting database tables across multiple DbContexts based on their business grouping can be a useful approach, especially in large systems. In DDD terms, each DbContext is called a *bounded context*.

> **DEFINITION**   A large business (domain) problem can be broken into small groups called *bounded contexts,* which hold a subset of the business objects that are related. This concept is central to DDD and goes way beyond splitting a database among multiple DbContexts, but it's still a good term to apply to this section (see https://martinfowler.com/bliki/BoundedContext.html).

Figure 10.6 shows an example of such a splitting using an extended version of the book app into three DbContexts: `BookContext`, `OrderContext`, and `CustomerContext`, which cover displaying books, handling orders for books, and holding the customer's details, respectively.

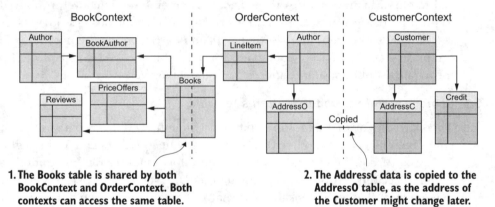

1. **The Books table is shared by both BookContext and OrderContext. Both contexts can access the same table.**

2. **The AddressC data is copied to the AddressO table, as the address of the Customer might change later.**

Figure 10.6   Access to a database can be split into business groups, or in DDD terms, bounded contexts. Here you see two ways of linking between contexts. First, you can share access to the same table, as shown between `BookContext` and `OrderContext`. Second, you can send over the data from one context to the other, as shown by the customer address being copied when an order is taken, as the customer may change the address later.

Let's start by creating a bounded context. Then you'll learn how the application can communicate between two bounded contexts.

10.6.1   *Creating DbContexts that contain only a subset of entities/tables*

When creating a DbContext for a bounded context that doesn't include all the entities in an application, you need to consider how the entities/tables are linked, and whether you want to retain these links. Let's look at two examples, starting with the simplest.

In the first example, the `BookContext` bounded context is focused on the `Book` entity class and its aggregate entities, and as such is self-contained (it doesn't have any links outside its context). The creation of the `BookContext` DbContext is straightforward, as you can see.

Listing 10.11 The `BookContext` class covers the `Book` entity and aggregates

Defines three of the five tables in the database: Books, Authors, and PriceOffers. The other two tables, Review and BookAuthor, are found via navigational links from the other tables.

```
public class BookContext : DbContext
{
    public DbSet<Book> Books { get; set; }
    public DbSet<Author> Authors { get; set; }
    public DbSet<PriceOffer> PriceOffers { get; set; }

    public BookContext(
        DbContextOptions<BookContext> options)
        : base(options) { }

    protected override void
        OnModelCreating(ModelBuilder modelBuilder)
    {
        modelBuilder.ApplyConfiguration(
            new BookConfig());
        modelBuilder.ApplyConfiguration(
            new BookAuthorConfig());
        modelBuilder.ApplyConfiguration(
            new PriceOfferConfig());
    }
}
```

Moves the Fluent API configuration of various entity classes to separate configuration classes that implement the IEntityTypeConfiguration<T> interface

The second example is the `OrderContext`, which is different in that you want it to include the `Book` entity, but not the entities that the book links to via navigational properties. In this case, you need to tell EF Core that you don't want the entities `Review`, `PriceOffer`, `Author`, or `BookAuthor` included in the DbContext. You do this by using the Fluent API method, `Ignore<T>`, shown here.

Listing 10.12 `OrderContext` class includes `Book` but not its aggregates

```
public class OrderContext : DbContext
{
    public DbSet<Book> Books { get; set; }
    public DbSet<Order> Orders { get; set; }
    public DbSet<AddressO> Addresses { get; set; }

    public OrderContext(
        DbContextOptions<OrderContext> options)
        : base(options) { }
```

Includes the DbSet<Book> property to make sure the name of the table is set.

```
    protected override void
        OnModelCreating(ModelBuilder modelBuilder)
    {
        modelBuilder.ApplyConfiguration(new BookConfig());
        modelBuilder.ApplyConfiguration( new LineItemConfig());

        modelBuilder.Ignore<Review>();
        modelBuilder.Ignore<PriceOffer>();
        modelBuilder.Ignore<Author>();
        modelBuilder.Ignore<BookAuthor>();
    }
}
```

> Uses the Fluent API Ignore<T> method to stop these entities/tables from being included in the DbContext

> **NOTE**   In EF Core 2.1, you have the ability to create read-only classes, known as *query types* (see appendix B). It would be appropriate to configure the Book entity as a query type in the OrderContext because that context treats the Book entity as a read-only entity.

I haven't shown CustomerContext because it doesn't introduce any new concepts that you haven't seen in the BookContext example. It doesn't refer to entities that are outside its context, so it's simple to set up.

10.6.2 Passing data between bounded contexts

Although each bounded context should be as self-contained as possible, in some situations information needs to be passed between bounded contexts. This is a big topic, so as an introduction, I cover only two ways to pass data from one bounded context to another.

> **NOTE**   If you want to research this topic in more detail, "Strategies for Integrating Bounded Contexts" by Philip Brown gives a good overview of many ways to communicate between bounded contexts; see http://mng.bz/96Bg.

SHARED KERNEL—SHARING A TABLE(S) BETWEEN BOUNDED CONTEXTS

Your BookContext and OrderContext both access the Books table in the database. BookContext uses the Books table a lot and oversees changes to it, but the OrderContext's LineItem entity refers to the Book entity, as it needs a reference to the book that someone has bought. Sharing the Books table between the contexts works well in this case, because when the order is placed, the OrderContext needs only a read-only reference to the book.

> **NOTE**   The PlaceOrderAction business logic, covered in chapter 4, needs access to the optional PriceOffer class to work out the price. You could share that table too, but OrderContext shouldn't be involved in setting the price, so that isn't a good option. You therefore would arrange the actual price shown onscreen to be returned with each order (with security to stop fraud).

One advantage of the shared kernel approach is that it's simple to set up, especially when one bounded context is read-only. The other advantage is that the database, which is designed to handle multiple accesses, manages the connection. The disadvantage is that both bounded contexts are tightly linked through an entity/table, which means that any changes affect both sides, which starts to break down the separation between the two bounded contexts.

CUSTOMER/SUPPLIER—BEING SENT DATA FROM ANOTHER BOUNDED CONTEXT

In the second part of our bounded context example, you'll propose a situation in which `OrderContext` needs a delivery address, which is obtained from `CustomerContext`. In this case, you'll use another approach in which `CustomerContext` provides a copy of the delivery address, read from table AddressC. `OrderContext` then writes this copy into its own table, AddressO.

Copying the data works well in this situation, because the customer could change addresses, but you want an old order to still show the original delivery address. The advantages of copying the data are that the communication is one-way and final: one bounded context sends the data to another bounded context, which then holds its own copy.

The disadvantage of copying is that it doesn't work for data that might change. If the customer changes their email address, the order-processing system needs to know straight away so that it can send the confirmation emails to the correct place. For that, you'd need another approach using events passing, which Julie Lerman covers in an article at https://msdn.microsoft.com/magazine/dn802601.

10.7 *Data validation and error-handling patterns*

If you fill in a form on an app and get an error, which you fix, and then you get another error, you'll get frustrated, especially if the site should have told you about both errors in the first place. Nowadays, users expect good feedback on *all* the errors so that you can fix them in one go. Most of that comes at the frontend of your application code, but the database access code has a part to play in this situation. We'll cover the area of error detection and error feedback when using EF Core in an application.

We'll look at three areas:

- Making sure data validation is available on your entity classes and DTOs
- Ensuring that your business logic returns a full list of errors
- Turning database server errors into user-friendly feedback

10.7.1 *Data validation to your entity classes makes for better error feedback*

Because EF Core is aimed at being higher performing and lightweight, it assumes that a higher level, such as ASP.NET Core, will validate the data. But for the higher layer to be able to validate input to an entity class, you must put the appropriate data validations on each entity class. Otherwise, you could be writing bad data to your database.

EF6: Developers who are used to EF6.x need to watch out for changes in data validations in EF Core. EF6.x validates data being written to the database, whereas EF Core doesn't. Section 4.6.1 shows how to validate data upon calling `SaveChanges`.

In section 6.12.2, I recommended that you use data validations, such as `Required` and `MaxLength(256)`, rather than using the Fluent API when configuring the database. This is because higher levels that apply validation can use these data validations to check input. In addition, I recommend adding data validations that EF Core doesn't use, such as `EmailAddress`, or inheriting the `IValidatableObject` interface, to your entity classes so that if your entity class is used in an input form at the frontend, the validation rules are there to provide a comprehensive set of error checks.

The other point is about DTOs. When you build a DTO, you want to replicate any data annotations you have on your entity class into the DTO. Otherwise, you'll miss these validation checks. As I said, I use DTOs a lot, and I generally create each DTO by copying over the properties and any associated data validations to the DTO. That way, the validations set in the entity class will still be applied even if you use a DTO for input.

> **TIP** If you use data validations that have a constant in them, such as `MaxLength(256)`, I recommend replacing the constant value with a .NET constant; for instance, `MaxLength(MyConstants.TitleMaxLength)`. By using this approach, any changes to the constant will affect the entity class and the DTO.

10.7.2 *Business logic should contain checks and return a list of all errors*

Your business logic often includes a range of checks to ensure that the data it has received is acceptable. I classify these into two main types:

- *User correctable errors*—Data provided by users that isn't correct—for instance, the user hasn't ticked the T&C's box on the order.
- *Unrecoverable system errors*—These suggest a software/system error, and the code shouldn't continue.

Let's explore each of these in turn.

USER-CORRECTABLE ERRORS—GIVE THE USER GOOD, COMPREHENSIVE FEEDBACK

My business logic always checks its input, because the business logic is at the center of what my system is doing and it's the right place to write/check any business rules. If I can catch errors early via some form of validation on the input form, so much the better for the user, but I personally (re)test the input inside my business logic too, as you can't be too careful.

> **TIP** Section 4.6.1 shows how to add validation to the writing of entities to the database. This may allow you to move some of the business checks to data validation or `IValidatableObject` methods.

The second point is that you accumulate all the errors you can find, and return them to the user in one go; that's being courteous to your user. Because of this user requirement, you don't use .NET exceptions to report errors, but instead return a list of all the errors, if possible with the name of the property that caused the error, so that it can be highlighted properly to the user.

> **NOTE** Views vary on the best way to handle errors. Some people say exceptions are the best way, and some say passing back error messages is the best way. I've tried most options, and they all have their advantages and disadvantages, but I personally use exceptions only for system/coding errors that can't be fixed by the user. The main point is that you want to give a great experience to your user, which means providing a list of *all* the error messages if there's something the user can fix.

UNRECOVERABLE SYSTEM ERRORS WHERE CONTINUING ISN'T ADVISABLE

EF Core can produce a range of exceptions if it finds something that it deems is incorrect. In my experience, the EF Core exception error messages are good at pointing the developer to the problem, but they're definitely not user-friendly. So, for most EF Core exceptions, you'll let them bubble up, and the frontend system will need to provide a generic "Sorry, there was a system error" message to the user.

Some specific EF Core exceptions, such as `DbUpdateConcurrencyException`, are useful to handle, because they occur only if you've enabled some form of concurrency conflict test (see section 8.5). In addition, some database-related exceptions are useful to capture, because they allow you to provide better error feedback to your users. The following is an example.

10.7.3 *Catching database server errors and providing user-friendly feedback*

EF Core will pass on errors found by the database server when it's writing to the database. Relational databases provide a lot of error checking, mostly in the form of constraints. Some database checks, such as ensuring that each entry in a unique index is unique, can be properly done only by the database. I have developed a system for capturing certain database errors and reporting them to the user.

Although you could catch a database error and show its native error message to the user, you don't do that because database errors are normally not user-friendly and, more important, could reveal something about your database structure, which is a possible security breach. My solution, which I've used in a few projects, is to build a system that catches specific database errors and then provides a user-friendly error message.

Any solution that traps database errors is going to be database server–specific, because the way errors are reported is different for each type of database server. In this example, you'll see how to capture the insert of a duplicate entry in a unique index for a SQL Server database. Figure 10.7 shows the process.

```
Configuration code in OnModelCreating

modelBuilder.Entity<MyClass>()
  .HasIndex(p => p.UniqueString)
  .IsUnique().HasName(
  "UniqueError_MyClass_MyProperty");
```

1. **You add a unique index with a constraint name to a set format, starting with a unique name, followed by class and property name, for instance: UniqueError_MyClass_MyProperty**

```
public ValidationResult
   SaveChangesWithSqlChecks()
{
   try
   {
      _context.SaveChanges();
   }
   catch (DbUpdateException e)
   {
      var error = CheckHandleError(e);
      if (error != null)
      {
         return error;
      }
      throw;
   }
   return null;
}
```

2. **Your method SaveChangesWithChecking calls SaveChanges, but traps any DbUpdateException.**

3. **If any exceptions are found, call a method registered in your dictionary with the same number as the SQL error number.**

Dictionary<int, Func...>

2016	UniqueError(sqlError, entites)
2627	UniqueError(sqlError, entites)
...	...

4. **If your method finds the expected constraint format, it returns a user-friendly error message; otherwise, it returns null.**

Figure 10.7   You add a unique index and set its constraint name to a set format. You then use a class for registering SQL error formatters based on the SQL error number that they handle. `SaveChangesWithSqlChecks` catches any `DbUpdateExceptions` and, if the SQL error number is found in the dictionary, it calls the associated SQL error formatter, which returns a user-friendly error message if it finds the constraint format it expected. Otherwise, it returns `null`, and the original error is rethrown.

This listing shows the class containing the `SaveChangesWithSqlChecks` method, which you use to capture any exception and to see whether any error formatter has been assigned to that SQL error number.

Listing 10.13   Class providing a version of `SaveChanges` with formatted SQL errors

Provides a dictionary of all the SQL errors to
format, plus a method to do that formatting.

```
public class SaveChangesSqlCheck
{
    private readonly DbContext _context;
    private readonly Dictionary<int, FormatSqlException> _sqlMethodDict;

    public SaveChangesWithSqlChecks(DbContext context,
        Dictionary<int, FormatSqlException> sqlMethodDict)
```

The method you call to do SaveChanges, but also capture and format the SQL errors you've registered

```
        {
            _context = context
                ?? throw new ArgumentNullException(nameof(context));
            _sqlMethodDict = sqlMethodDict
                ?? throw new ArgumentNullException(nameof(sqlMethodDict));
        }

        public ValidationResult SaveChangesWithSqlChecks()
        {
            try
            {
                _context.SaveChanges();
            }
            catch (DbUpdateException e)
            {
                var error = CheckHandleError(e);
                if (error != null)
                {
                    return error;
                }
                throw;
            }
            return null;
        }

        private ValidationResult CheckHandleError
            (DbUpdateException e)
        {
            var sqlEx = e.InnerException as SqlException;

            if (sqlEx != null
                && _sqlMethodDict
                    .ContainsKey(sqlEx.Number))
            {
                return
                    _sqlMethodDict[sqlEx.Number]
                        (sqlEx, e.Entries);
            }
            return null;
        }
    }
```

Catches the DbUpdateException to see if you have a formatter for that SQL error

Calls SaveChanges inside a try...catch block

Returns a ValidationError if it can format the error, or null if it can't

Manages to format the error, so return that

Doesn't manage to format the error, so you rethrow the original error

If it gets to here, there were no errors, so it returns null to show that

Private method handles the lookup and calling of any error formatters that have been registered.

Tries to convert InnerException to SqlException. It'll be null if InnerException is null, or the InnerException wasn't of type SqlException.

Passes only if InnerException was an SqlException, and your dictionary contains a method to format the error message

...otherwise, you return null to say you couldn't format the error.

Calls that formatting method, which has a predefined signature, and returns its result...

This listing shows how to set up the `SaveChangesSqlCheck` class by entering a directory of SQL errors with a method to format that error.

Listing 10.14   Setting up, then calling the `SaveChangesWithSqlChecks` method

Creates the SaveChangesSqlCheck class with its two parameters

Provides a dictionary with keys of 2601 and 2627, a violation of unique index, both paired with a method that can format that exception into a user-friendly format

```
var checker = new SaveChangesSqlCheck(
    context, new Dictionary<int, FormatSqlException>
{
    [2601] = SqlErrorFormatters.UniqueErrorFormatter,
    [2627] = SqlErrorFormatters.UniqueErrorFormatter
});
var unique = Guid.NewGuid().ToString();

context.Add(new MyUnique() { UniqueString = unique });
var error = checker.SaveChangesWithSqlChecks();
```

Calls SaveChangesWithSqlChecks, which returns null if there was no error, or a ValidationResult if there was a formatted error to show the user

Listing 10.15 shows the `UniqueErrorFormatter` method that you wrote to handle a unique validation error. It looks for a constraint name in the defined format shown in figure 10.7. If the constraint name doesn't fit that format, the method assumes that the unique validation error wasn't one that you as the developer wanted to report to the user, so it returns null to signal that the original exception should be rethrown. Otherwise, it returns a user-friendly error message that you construct from the constraint name and extract the duplicate value from the SQL error message.

Listing 10.15   Decoding the SQL error and returning a user-friendly message

SqlException is passed in, as this holds the information you need to decode the error

```
private static readonly Regex UniqueConstraintRegex =
    new Regex("'UniqueError_([a-zA-Z0-9]*)_([a-zA-Z0-9]*)'",
        RegexOptions.Compiled);

public static ValidationResult UniqueErrorFormatter
    (SqlException ex,
     IReadOnlyList<EntityEntry> entitiesNotSaved)
{
    var message = ex.Errors[0].Message;
    var matches = UniqueConstraintRegex
        .Matches(message);

    if (matches.Count == 0)
        return null;
```

Creates a method to handle the unique SQL error

The caller provides the entities not saved by default. You don't use this in this case.

If there's no match, this isn't an exception that the method is designed to handle. You return null to report that you couldn't handle the exception.

Uses Regex to check that the constraint name matches what you expect, and to extract the entity class name and the property name from the constraint

You know the format of the SQL violation "unique index" error, so you try to extract the duplicate value from the error message.

Forms the first part of the user-friendly message

```
var returnError = "Cannot have a duplicate "+
    matches[0].Groups[2].Value + " in " +
    matches[0].Groups[1].Value + ".";
```

Adds the information about the duplicate value

```
var openingBadValue = message.IndexOf("(");
if (openingBadValue > 0)
{
    var dupPart = message.Substring(openingBadValue + 1,
        message.Length - openingBadValue - 3);
    returnError += $" Duplicate value was '{dupPart}'.";
}

return new ValidationResult(returnError,
    new[] { matches[0].Groups[2].Value });
}
```

Sends back the property that the error related to, in case this can be used to highlight the offending property on the input form

Returns the user-friendly error message in ValidationResult

This approach allows you to provide better error feedback to your users, while not revealing anything about your application's database type and structure, which could be a security risk.

Summary

- Using the separation-of-concerns(SoC) software principle can help you build robust, refactorable, testable applications.
- Developing your own software patterns can help you develop applications quickly, but with a good design. You may need a few iterations to develop a pattern that works well, but that's OK.
- Using a LINQ mapper can speed up the building of the many CRUD database accesses that a typical application needs.
- Building a domain-driven design (DDD) database repository can offer a much more business-focused access to the database, but some other Repository patterns should be avoided.
- Splitting the EF Core access to your database into separate business-oriented groupings, referred to in DDD as bounded contexts, can improve separation of concerns.
- You should think about data validation and how to return user-friendly error messages when dealing with the EF Core entities and the database.

For readers who are familiar with EF6:

- EF Core is better than EF6.x at allowing a domain-driven design, with its root/aggregate entities, because you can control access to one-to-many collections.

Handling
database migrations

This chapter covers

- Using EF Core's migration to update a database

- Building a DbContext from an existing database

- Changing a database by using SQL command scripts

- Applying updates to your production database

This chapter covers the three ways of changing the structure of a database. The structure of the database is called the *database schema*—the tables, columns, constraints, and so on that make up a database. Creating and updating a database schema can seem simple because EF Core provides a method called `Migrate` to do it all for you; you create your entity classes and add a bit of configuration, and EF Core builds you a nice, shiny database.

The problem is that EF Core's `Migrate` method hides a whole series of database migration issues that might not be immediately apparent; for example, moving data from one entity class to another entity class can cause loss of data when applying a database schema change. Getting a database change wrong on a database that has live data in it is a scary problem.

I've split the chapter into two distinct parts. Part 1 describes all the ways to update a database's schema when working with EF Core. Part 2 presents the issues around a database schema change, starting with simple changes and working up to the much more complex situations requiring real care to ensure that data isn't lost.

11.1 Part 1—EF Core methods to change the database schema

Using EF Core to access a database assumes that the database schema and the application's entity classes and DbContext "match." The EF Core view of the database structure, known as EF Core's *database model*, needs to match the actual database schema; otherwise, problems will occur when EF Core accesses the database. EF Core builds this database model by looking at the entity classes and the application's DbContext. This database model is available via the Model property on the application's DbContext.

> **NOTE** The word *match* in the preceding paragraph is a complex concept. Using EF Core's Migrate method will produce an exact match between the database schema and EF Core's Model property. But in some cases, the match doesn't have to be perfect. Your database may have features that EF Core doesn't include in its Model—for instance, SQL stored procedures. The match also doesn't have to be perfect when EF Core accesses only part of a database (see section 10.6 on splitting a database across multiple DbContexts).

There are four ways to ensure that a match exists between EF Core's database model and the actual database schema. This chapter covers the first three, and chapter 15 covers the last one. They are:

- *Code-first*—The standard way to create or update a database schema is by using your entity classes and the application's DbContext as the template for your database. Section 11.2 covers this topic.
- *Database-first*—EF Core has a command that inspects an existing database and creates the various entity classes and the application's DbContext to match that database. Section 11.3 covers this topic.
- *SQL-first*—You can change a database's schema by using SQL commands, known as an *SQL change script*. These are typically applied to your database by using a database migration/deployment tool. Section 11.4 covers this topic.
- *Database.EnsureCreated method*—EF Core's Database.EnsureCreated method is useful only for unit testing because it has no provision for updating the database schema later. Chapter 15 refers to the Database.EnsureCreated method.

11.1.1 A view of what databases need updating

Before I describe how to update a database's schema, let's look at the databases that can be involved in an application being developed. Figure 11.1 shows a possible arrangement of a multiperson development team, with development, testing, pre-production, and production.

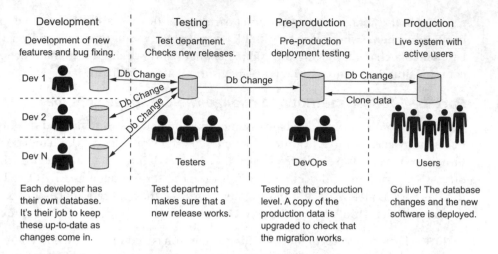

Figure 11.1   Various databases can be used in an application's development, all of which will need database schema changes applied to them. The terms *development*, *testing*, *pre-production*, and *production* refer to different parts of the development, testing, and deployment of an application and any associated database schema changes.

Not all development projects have all these stages, and some have more or different stages. Also, this figure assumes that only one database is being used in production, but you may have multiple copies of the same database. The permutations are endless. This chapter refers to the *development* and the *production* databases, but be aware that database schema updates may be needed on other databases as well.

11.2   *Code-first: using EF Core's migrations*

EF Core's migration feature is the standard way to create and update a database from EF Core. This approach is known as *code-first*, because your application's code is used to define the database schema. It's the easiest approach for software developers, because it uses the entity classes and DbContext in your application as the template for the database. You don't need to learn SQL language to create and change the application's database. But EF Core's migration feature does have some limitations, which I cover as I describe its use.

> **EF6**   EF Core's migration feature looks the same as EF6.x's migration from the outside, but a lot of changes are underneath. Automatic migrations have been removed, which simplifies the internals. The migration files produced by EF Core are different too, as they make combining migrations from different developers easier when working on a multiperson development (see https://msdn.microsoft.com/en-us/magazine/mt614250.aspx).

The migration process has two stages:

1   *Create a migration*—By running a command, EF Core will build a set of migration code, which is added to your application. You need to run this "create a migration" stage after each change to your EF configuration or entity classes, which means you'll end up with multiple migrations in your application.

2 *Apply migrations*—The migrations created in step 1 are applied to a database either via code in your application or via a manual command. You need to apply a new migration to each database that needs updating; for instance, your development database and your production database.

I describe the first stage in section 11.2.1 and the second stage in section 11.2.2.

11.2.1 Stage 1: creating a migration—building the code for migration

When you change the database aspect of your EF Core code, you need to create a new migration. Typical changes that affect the EF Core database model include:

- Changing the properties in one of your entity classes; for instance, changing a property name or adding a new property.
- Changing some aspects of your EF Core configuration; for instance, changing the way a relationship is defined.
- Changing the DbSet<T> properties in your application's DbContext; for instance, adding a new DbSet<T> property or changing the name of a DbSet<T> property.

TIP I tend to "batch up" any changes that affect the database and run unit tests on them before I build migration. This catches any errors before I go through the longer process of creating and applying a migration to my application.

NOTE A new feature called *.NET Core Global tools* is being added to .NET Core 2.1 (see appendix B). This is likely to provide a new way to call the design-time tools described in this chapter. Please look out for Microsoft's documentation after EF Core 2.1 is released.

You can access the command for building a migration either via Visual Studio or via a command line on your computer:

- From the Package Manager Console (PMC) inside Visual Studio, the command is

```
Add-Migration MyMigration [options]
```

To use this migration command, you need to install one extra EF Core NuGet package, called `Microsoft.EntityFrameworkCore.Tools`, in your application's startup project. This command has lots of options; which you can find at http://mng.bz/lm6J.

- From your development system, for instance, via a command in the Windows command prompt, the command is

```
dotnet ef migrations add MyMigration [options]
```

This command requires that you installed the .NET Core SDK. If you're running the command on the development system where you built your application, that .NET Core SDK will have already been installed. This command has lots of options, which you can find at http://mng.bz/454w.

NOTE Describing all the command-line migration options would take up too much space and push out the important information on approaches to database changes. But you can check out the links to Microsoft's detailed information on these commands. For a more complete description of the Add-Migration command, see section 2.2.3.

HOW THE MIGRATION TOOLS OBTAIN A COPY OF YOUR APPLICATION'S DBCONTEXT

The migration commands try to create an instance of the application's DbContext via a parameterless constructor. If your application's DbContext is built for an ASP.NET Core application, it doesn't have a parameterless constructor; when you try to use a migration command, you'll get the error message "No parameterless constructor was found."

The way around this is to create a class that implements the IDesignTimeDbContext-Factory<T> interface, which is there specifically to help the design-time commands such as Add-Migration. This class, located in the same project as your application's DbContext, provides a method that will create a fully configured instance of the application's DbContext. Here's the IDesignTimeDbContextFactory<T> class in our book app.

Listing 11.1   The `IDesignTimeDbContextFactory<T>` class from our book app

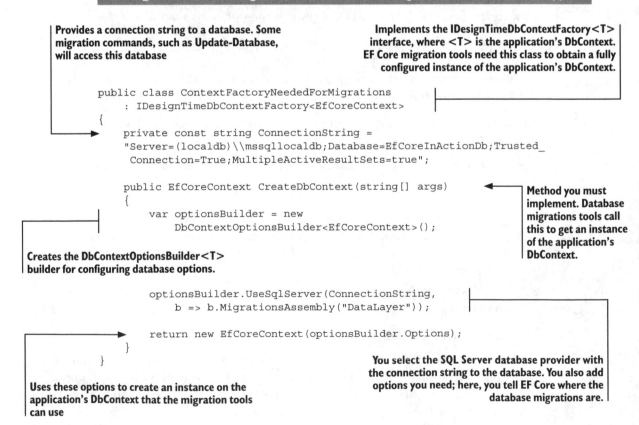

Provides a connection string to a database. Some migration commands, such as Update-Database, will access this database

Implements the IDesignTimeDbContextFactory<T> interface, where <T> is the application's DbContext. EF Core migration tools need this class to obtain a fully configured instance of the application's DbContext.

```
public class ContextFactoryNeededForMigrations
    : IDesignTimeDbContextFactory<EfCoreContext>
{
    private const string ConnectionString =
    "Server=(localdb)\\mssqllocaldb;Database=EfCoreInActionDb;Trusted_
     Connection=True;MultipleActiveResultSets=true";

    public EfCoreContext CreateDbContext(string[] args)
    {
        var optionsBuilder = new
            DbContextOptionsBuilder<EfCoreContext>();

        optionsBuilder.UseSqlServer(ConnectionString,
            b => b.MigrationsAssembly("DataLayer"));

        return new EfCoreContext(optionsBuilder.Options);
    }
}
```

Method you must implement. Database migrations tools call this to get an instance of the application's DbContext.

Creates the DbContextOptionsBuilder<T> builder for configuring database options.

Uses these options to create an instance on the application's DbContext that the migration tools can use

You select the SQL Server database provider with the connection string to the database. You also add options you need; here, you tell EF Core where the database migrations are.

WHAT HAPPENS WHEN YOU CALL THE ADD-MIGRATION COMMAND?

Figure 11.2 shows what happens when you call the Add-Migration command. It uses the application's DbContext's method, Database.Model, introduced in section 9.6.

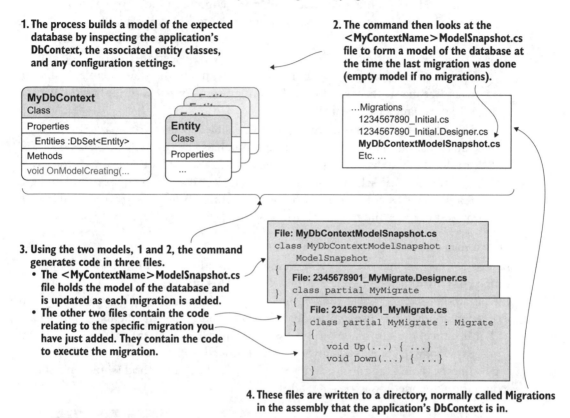

The process kicked off by the Add-Migration MyMigrate command

1. The process builds a model of the expected database by inspecting the application's DbContext, the associated entity classes, and any configuration settings.

MyDbContext
Class

Properties

Entities :DbSet<Entity>

Methods

void OnModelCreating(...

Entity
Class

Properties

...

2. The command then looks at the <MyContextName>ModelSnapshot.cs file to form a model of the database at the time the last migration was done (empty model if no migrations).

...Migrations
1234567890_Initial.cs
1234567890_Initial.Designer.cs
MyDbContextModelSnapshot.cs
Etc. ...

3. Using the two models, 1 and 2, the command generates code in three files.
- **The <MyContextName>ModelSnapshot.cs file holds the model of the database and is updated as each migration is added.**
- **The other two files contain the code relating to the specific migration you have just added. They contain the code to execute the migration.**

File: MyDbContextModelSnapshot.cs
```
class MyDbContextModelSnapshot :
    ModelSnapshot
{
}
```

File: 2345678901_MyMigrate.Designer.cs
```
class partial MyMigrate
{
}
```

File: 2345678901_MyMigrate.cs
```
class partial MyMigrate : Migrate
{
    void Up(...) { ...}
    void Down(...) { ...}
}
```

4. These files are written to a directory, normally called Migrations in the assembly that the application's DbContext is in.

Figure 11.2 Running the Add-Migration command to create a new EF Core migration. The command compares two models of the database. One comes from our current application, with its DbContext, entity classes, and EF Core configuration; and the other is from the <MyContextName>ModelSnapshot.cs file (which is empty if this is your first migration). By comparing these two models, EF Core can create code that will update the database schema to match EF Core's current database model.

Three new files are added to your application as a result of running the Add-Migration command. By default, these files are written to a directory called Migrations in the project that contains your application's DbContext. They contain the commands that are used in the second stage of applying migrations to a database.

Using EF Core's migrations to change a database is the easy option. EF Core builds a migration file that the database provider can convert into the relevant commands to change the database schema. But this approach has limitations:

- If your migration includes moving data from one table to another, EF Core can't build code to do that. The Add-Migration command warns you with a "… may result in the loss of data" message if the migration removes a table or a column. Sections 11.5.2 and 11.5.3 cover how to handle a possible data loss scenario.
- If you have multiple application DbContexts (see section 10.6) and you share a table, the migrations can fail if a change occurs to the shared table. You need to either manually correct one of the migrations or use a script-based database schema change (see section 11.4.1).
- EF Core doesn't allow you to define every possible aspect of a database. For instance, you can't add a column CHECK constraint such as Age int CHECK (Age>=18). For this level of database control, you need to use a script-based approach to changing the database schema (see section 11.4). But if you only want to add an SQL feature such as stored procedures or user-defined functions, you can do that with migrations (see the next section).

ADDING YOUR OWN MIGRATION CODE TO A MIGRATION

Figure 11.2 shows that the Add-Migration command creates numerous files, one of which contains the code to change the schema. This file has an Up method which, via the parameter of type MigrationBuilder, provides access to a broad range of methods to execute that you can use to introduce your own changes to the database schema.

For instance, the MigrationBuilder parameter includes an Sql method, which you can use to run SQL code to add an SQL stored procedure to your database. The following listing shows an example of adding SQL code via the Sql method (shown in bold) to a migration's Up method in order to add a stored procedure.

Listing 11.2   Using an SQL method to add code to an Up migration

```
protected override void Up
   (MigrationBuilder migrationBuilder)
{
    migrationBuilder.CreateTable(
        name: "CustomerAndAddresses",
        … other code left out
    );

    migrationBuilder.Sql(
        @"CREATE PROC dbo.MyStoredProc
        @Name nvarchar(1000)
        AS
        SELECT * FROM dbo.CustomerAndAddresses
        WHERE Name = @Name");
}
```

NOTE   For more examples of using the Sql method in a migration file, see section 11.5.2, where you'll add more commands to copy data.

If you add code into the Up method in a migration, you might want to add an Sql method containing code in the Down method to drop (delete) MyStoredProc. This is useful if you decide the migration doesn't work; then, when you remove that migration (see section 11.2.3), the extra SQL features you added manually will also be removed from your development database.

MIGRATIONS ARE DATABASE-PROVIDER-SPECIFIC

The first thing to understand is that EF Core migrations are built for the database type your application's DbContext is configured for. If your application's DbContext uses the SQL Server database provider, it creates migrations for an SQL Server database, and those migrations won't work for another database type (for instance, on a MySQL database).

If you decide to change the database type your application is going to work with, you need to delete all the existing migrations and create a new migration for the new database type. That's what you have to do when you change the book app from working with an SQL Server database to a MySQL database in section 14.1.2.

It's unusual for an application to run with different databases on different hosts. This would mean that your application's DbContext and its migrations must work with more than one database type (for instance, SQL Server and MySQL). If you must do this, you'll need to manually combine the different migration files into one migration file that the application can use. This is possible through the ActiveProvider property, which holds the name of the database provider that's currently being used. Listing 11.3 shows the use of the ActiveProvider property in an if statement (shown in bold) to select the correct configuration commands for the database type being migrated.

> **WARNING** I don't recommend using different database types with an application, such as running one instance using SQL Server and another instance using MySQL. First, each database server works in a slightly different way. EF Core can hide (almost) all of these differences, but section 14.1.3 covers subtle variations between database servers and how they might introduce bugs into your application. Second, EF Core migrations are going to be difficult and cumbersome.

Listing 11.3 Using `ActiveProvider` to handle different database server types

```
protected override void Up(MigrationBuilder migrationBuilder)
{

    if (ActiveProvider ==
      "Microsoft.EntityFrameworkCore.SqlServer")     ◀──
    {
        //... code to configure the SQL Server
    }
    else
    {
        //... code to configure the MySQL tables
    }
}
```

This test will be true only if the database being migrated is using the SqlServer database provider. This allows you to change the migration code applied depending on the database server type.

The other way isn't to use EF Core migrations but to use an SQL script-based migration approach (see section 11.4).

> **Warning: some databases don't support all EF Core migration commands**
>
> Each database has its own capabilities on what sort of database schema changes you can make. For instance, the SQLite database has significant limitations on what changes you can apply to the database schema, such as not being able to rename a column in a table or add/remove a foreign key (see http://mng.bz/wuNO).
>
> SQLite is a rather extreme example, but if you're using a non-Microsoft-supplied database provider, you should check the commands that the database provides for changing its schema and the database provider's supports of EF Core's `MigrationBuilder`.

11.2.2 Stage 2: applying migrations—updating a database schema

After you've created a migration, or even several migrations, you need to apply them to each of the databases associated with your application (for instance, your development database and your production database). You can apply each migration to the database in four main ways:

- Outputting the migration as an SQL change script, and applying it to a database
- Calling the `Database.Migrate` method from your main application
- Calling the `Database.Migrate` method from a special application just to execute the migration
- Using one of the command-line methods to execute the migration

NOTE   Microsoft recommends that you use only the first option for production databases: outputting an SQL change script and then applying it to the database. That's because the `Database.Migrate` method has limitations, such as not supporting multiple, parallel versions of the `Database.Migrate` method running at the same time, which I detail later.

EF Core's migration uses a table called __EFMigrationsHistories, which holds a list of all the migrations applied to that database. If an entry is found for a migration on the database being updated, that migration won't be applied again.

Each migration is applied within an SQL transaction, which means that the whole migration either succeeds or fails, so your database isn't left in an indeterminate state. If you have multiple migrations to apply, they're applied in the order they were created. If one migration fails, it and any following migrations aren't applied.

EF6   In EF6.x, migrations were automatically installed, based on the database initializer. EF Core doesn't do that. Migrations are applied only if you explicitly include code to call the `Database.Migrate` method or use a command-line method.

OUTPUTTING THE MIGRATION AS AN SQL CHANGE SCRIPT

This is the most robust, but also the most difficult, way of applying a migration to a database. It's Microsoft's recommended way to update a production database, because it works in all setups. There are two stages to the process.

> **NOTE** For software developers not used to using SQL change scripts, this approach can be a bit intimidating, and they may prefer using the `Database.Migrate` method (described after this SQL change script section). The `Database.Migrate` migration approach will work fine if you understand and abide by its limitations.

First, you need to output the SQL changes script after you create an EF Core migration. You use one of the command-line migration commands to create an SQL change script. Both command types take two optional arguments:

- `From`—The name of the first migration you want included in the SQL change script; for instance, `AddColToMyTable`. The number 0 indicates the initial empty database, which is the default if this argument is left out.
- `To`—The last migration you want included in the SQL change script. If you leave out this argument, the code references the last migration.

The two versions of the commands are as follows:

- From the PMC inside Visual Studio, the command is

```
Script-Migration [From] [To] [options]
```

    See http://mng.bz/lm6J for more information.

- From your development system, for instance, via a command in the Windows command prompt, the command is

```
dotnet ef migrations script [From] [To] [options]
```

    See http://mng.bz/454w for more information.

The script output by these commands is written either to a new window in Visual Studio (PMC) or to the screen (command line).

The second stage is applying that SQL change script to the database. You must copy the code output by the `Script-Migration` command and put it into a .sql file, using some form of naming convention to make sure it'll be applied in the correct order (see section 11.4). These scripts will contain the same code to check/update the migration history file so that an SQL change script is applied only once to a database.

Then you should apply the SQL change scripts to the database, as explained in section 11.4.

RUNNING THE MIGRATE COMMAND AS PART OF YOUR APPLICATION

The easiest way to update a database associated with your application is to include code in the startup of that application to apply any outstanding migrations. The effect is that any outstanding migrations are applied to the database it's connected to whenever your application starts. The advantage is you can't forget to do the migration, but some disadvantages exist, which I mention at the end.

Section 5.9.2 showed how to apply a migration on the startup of an ASP.NET Core application. You can apply a similar approach with other application types. The following listing shows an example for a console application, which executes the `Migrate` method every time it starts. If the database is up-to-date, the `Migrate` method does nothing.

> **Listing 11.4   Running the `Migrate` command during startup of a console application**

```
class Program
{
    static void Main(string[] args)
    {
        using (var context = new EfCoreContext())
        {
            context.Database.Migrate();
        }
        //... then start the rest of my code
    }
}
```

Setup of the appliction's DbContext is done by overriding the OnConfiguring method, so you don't need to provide any connection string of the database provider here.

Calling the Migrate method applies any outstanding migrations to the database it's attached to. If no outstanding migrations exist, it does nothing.

The advantage of using the `Database.Migrate` method is simplicity. This method ensures that any database that it connects to is migrated to the correct level before using it. This is the only approach that makes all migrations, breaking and nonbreaking changes (see section 11.5), in one stage. This works across all your databases, including the production database (with some caveats). But there are a few disadvantages:

- If a migration fails, your application won't start. A migration can fail for several reasons; for example, if you drop a table that other rows refer to via a required foreign key. In a production environment, a failed migration can mean your application is down, and it isn't always easy to diagnose the problem.
- The `Database.Migrate` method isn't designed to handle multiple copies of `Database.Migrate` running at the same time. This could happen if you're running multiple instances of your application, say, in a cloud web application with scaling. If this could happen in your application, you can either use the alternative method defined next or use an SQL change script approach, as defined in section 11.4.

ALTERNATIVE: RUNNING MIGRATE IN A STANDALONE MIGRATION APPLICATION

Instead of running the migration as part of your startup code, you can create a standalone application to apply a migration to your databases. For instance, you could add a console application project to your solution that uses your application's DbContext and calls the `context.Database.Migrate` method when it's run, possibly taking the database connection string as a parameter.

This approach has advantages over calling the `Migrate` method in the application's startup:

- If the migration fails, you get good feedback, because the code can report any errors to the local console.
- It overcomes the problem that the `Migrate` method isn't thread-safe, because you run only one instance of the application that's applying the migration.

The disadvantage of this approach is that it works only if your migration is *safe*, in what I call a *nonbreaking change*: the database schema change doesn't affect the parts of the database that the current live version of your application is running. You can add new columns, tables, and relationships (within reason—see section 11.5.1 for more detail) for example, but you can't remove any columns, tables, or relationships that the previous version uses. Section 11.5 covers applying database changes.

RUNNING MIGRATE BY CALLING A COMMAND-LINE METHOD

Just as you created the migration via the command line, you can also manually apply a migration to your development database. But updating the production database in this way has limitations, depending on whether you used `IDesignTimeDbContextFactory<T>` with a fixed connection string in your application.

NOTE See section 11.2.1 for details on the software you need to install to be able to run either of these commands.

You can access the command for updating a database either via Visual Studio or via a command line on your computer:

- From the PMC inside Visual Studio, the command is

```
Update-Database [options]
```

  By default, this applies the last migration to your development database. This command has lots of options, which you can find at http://mng.bz/lm6J.

- From your development system, for instance, via a command in the Windows command prompt, the command is

```
dotnet ef database update [options]
```

  As with the PMC version, this applies the last migration to your development database. This command has lots of options, which you can find at http://mng.bz/454w.

11.2.3 Undoing a migration—Remove-Migration or update command

After you've applied a migration to a database, you might decide it doesn't fit your needs. If this happens, you can use the command-line tools to undo any migration. You shouldn't need this command if you unit test your new database configuration before applying a migration, but if you need to undo a migration, you have a command to do that.

TIME-SAVER   I've never needed the command to undo a migration. A quick survey of EF users at a recent talk revealed that none of them had ever used this command either.

Two commands can be used to remove a migration. They work by using the Down version of the migration code created in stage 1 to undo the changes to the database. The commands take options, which allow you to define the project where your application's DbContext is, and so on (see links to the documentation in section 11.2.2).

- From the PMC inside Visual Studio

  The Remove-Migration command removes the last migration you created:

```
Remove-Migration [options]
```

  To remove all migrations down to a specific migration:

```
Update-Database MyMigration [options]
```

  The Update-Database command takes your database back to the state as defined by the migration name given.

- From your development system; for instance, via a command in the Windows command prompt

  To remove the last migration you created:

```
dotnet ef migrations remove [options]
```

  To remove all migrations down to a specific migration:

```
dotnet ef database update MyMigration [options]
```

  As with the PMC version, the dotnet ef database update version takes your database back to the state as defined by the migration name given.

The limitation of these commands is the same as the application of a migration via a command line: it'll work for your development database, but problems could arise with other databases such as production.

11.3   *Database-first: creating a DbContext from a database*

EF Core's code-first approach works by using your software as the template for the database you want to create/update. But in some cases, you'll want to build an application that accesses an existing database via EF Core code. For this, you need to apply the opposite of migrations and allow EF Core to produce your entity classes and application's DbContext by using your existing database as the template. This is known as *database-first*, also referred to as *reverse engineering a database*. Figure 11.3 shows this process.

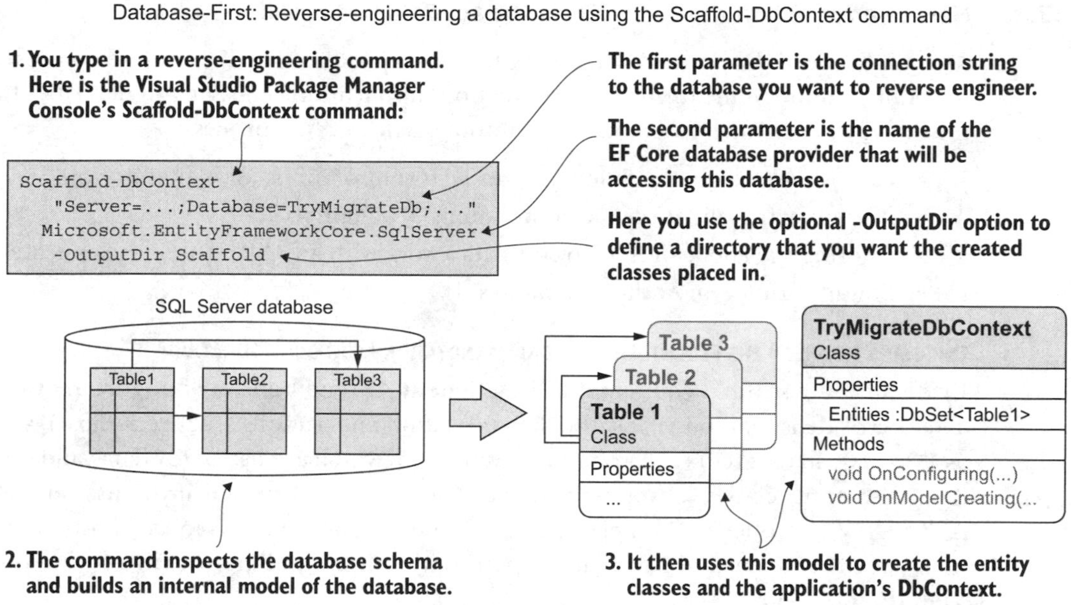

Database-First: Reverse-engineering a database using the Scaffold-DbContext command

1. You type in a reverse-engineering command. Here is the Visual Studio Package Manager Console's Scaffold-DbContext command:

The first parameter is the connection string to the database you want to reverse engineer.

The second parameter is the name of the EF Core database provider that will be accessing this database.

Here you use the optional -OutputDir option to define a directory that you want the created classes placed in.

```
Scaffold-DbContext
    "Server=...;Database=TryMigrateDb;..."
 Microsoft.EntityFrameworkCore.SqlServer
    -OutputDir Scaffold
```

2. The command inspects the database schema and builds an internal model of the database.

3. It then uses this model to create the entity classes and the application's DbContext.

Figure 11.3 Typical use of EF Core's reverse-engineering command, which inspects the database found via the database connection string and then generates the entity classes and the application's DbContext to match the database. It uses the foreign-key database relationships to build a fully defined relationship between the entity classes.

Reverse-engineering a database is done via command-line interfaces, like the migration commands. The two commands are as follows:

- From the PMC inside Visual Studio, the command is

```
Scaffold-DbContext [Connection] [Provider] [options]
```

The first argument, [Connection], is a connection string that points to the database you want to reverse-engineer. The second argument, [Provider], is the name of the EF Core database provider that you want to access the database with; for instance, Microsoft.EntityFrameworkCore.SqlServer. A series of other options can be found at http://mng.bz/lm6J.

- From your development system, via a command at the Windows command prompt, the command is

```
dotnet ef dbcontext scaffold [Connection] [Provider] [options]
```

The first two arguments, [Connection] and [Provider], are the same as in the PMC command. The options are similar too; you can find the full list at https://mng.bz/454w.

11.3.1 *How to alter or edit the output from the scaffold command*

The application's DbContext and the entity classes produced by the scaffold command may not be quite in the form you need for your application. This section describes the four ways you can alter or enhance the output of the scaffold process:

- Choosing between the Fluent API and data annotations for configuration
- Adding extra validation data annotations to an entity class
- Altering the application's DbContext to work with an ASP.NET Core application
- Singularizing your entity class names

CHOOSING BETWEEN THE FLUENT API AND DATA ANNOTATIONS FOR CONFIGURATION

By default, the scaffold command will use Fluent API methods to configure EF Core. The downside is that you've lost the data validation annotations (see section 6.4), such as [StringLength(100)], [Required], and so on, which are useful for data validation if you use entity classes for input in your UI/presentation layer. Or if you use separate ASP.NET ViewModel or DTO classes, having the data annotations in the entity classes makes it easier to cut and paste the properties with their validation attributes into your ViewModel/DTO classes.

By including the -DataAnnotations (Visual Studio 2017) or -d (.NET Core CLI) option to the scaffold command, the scaffolder will use data annotations rather than Fluent API wherever possible to configure EF Core.

ADDING EXTRA DATA VALIDATION ANNOTATIONS TO AN ENTITY CLASS

You may want to add extra data validation annotations, such as [EmailAddress], for the UI/presentation layer. Because the scaffolding process creates the entity classes as partial classes, there's a way to add extra data validation annotations to a property in a partial entity class without needing to edit the original class.

Let me give you an example. Here, the scaffolding has created a class called Users with a property called Email:

```
public partial class Users
{
    public int UserId { get; set; }
    [StringLength(100)]
    public string Email { get; set; }
    //… other parts left out
}
```

Listing 11.5 shows how to use the ASP.NET Core ModelMetadataType attribute to add the extra data validation attribute EmailAddress to the property Email.

Listing 11.5 Adding a data validation attribute to the partial class, `Users`

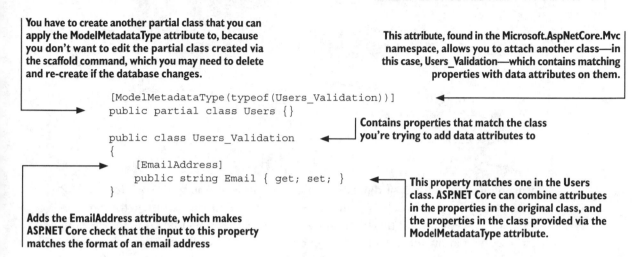

You have to create another partial class that you can apply the ModelMetadataType attribute to, because you don't want to edit the partial class created via the scaffold command, which you may need to delete and re-create if the database changes.

This attribute, found in the Microsoft.AspNetCore.Mvc namespace, allows you to attach another class—in this case, Users_Validation—which contains matching properties with data attributes on them.

```
[ModelMetadataType(typeof(Users_Validation))]
public partial class Users {}

public class Users_Validation
{
    [EmailAddress]
    public string Email { get; set; }
}
```

Contains properties that match the class you're trying to add data attributes to

This property matches one in the Users class. ASP.NET Core can combine attributes in the properties in the original class, and the properties in the class provided via the ModelMetadataType attribute.

Adds the EmailAddress attribute, which makes ASP.NET Core check that the input to this property matches the format of an email address

WARNING The `ModelMetadataType` attribute works only for ASP.NET Core, so other validation systems, such as the `Validator` class used to validate data written to the database in section 4.6.1, won't pick up extra data validation attributes added this way.

ALTERING THE APPLICATION'S DBCONTEXT TO WORK WITH AN ASP.NET CORE APPLICATION

The scaffold command will create an application's DbContext, which uses the `OnConfiguring` method to set the database options. It uses the database provider and connection string you used when you ran the scaffold command to build the database options inside the `OnConfiguring` method. This listing shows an example of the application's DbContext that the scaffold command would create, if you told it you wanted the application's DbContext class to be called `MyDbContext`.

Listing 11.6 Format of the application's DbContext output by the scaffold command

```
public partial class MyDbContext : DbContext
{
    //… DbSet<T> properties left out

    protected override void OnConfiguring(
        DbContextOptionsBuilder optionsBuilder)//
    {
        if (!optionsBuilder.IsConfigured)
        {
#warning To protect potentially sensitive …
```

Creates a partial class that inherits from EF Core's DbContext class.

Overrides the OnConfiguring method to configure the database options by using the information you provided in the scaffold command

Adds a warning because the connection string may contain authorization information that you don't want made public.

If you configure the database options via a constructor, the "if" test will fail and the configuration won't be changed by this method.

Uses the database provider name you provided and inserts the correct Use method for that database provider.

```
                        optionsBuilder.UseSqlServer(
                            @"Server=(localdb)\... etc."
        }
    }

    protected override void OnModelCreating
        (ModelBuilder modelBuilder)
    {
        //... configuration code left out
    }
}
```

Uses the connection string you provided as the connection string that the application's DbContext should use.

The problem is, this form of database option setting isn't going to work for an ASP .NET Core application, which provides the database options via a constructor parameter. But you can get around this by creating another partial class that contains the constructor with a parameter of type `DbContextOptions<T>`. This listing shows the partial class you'd write to add the parameterized constructor to the application's DbContext that the scaffold command created in listing 11.6.

Listing 11.7   The new class to make the application DbContext work with ASP.NET Core

Creates another partial class with the same name as the application's DbContext that the scaffold command produced

Adds the single-parameter constructor that the ASP.NET Core application needs to work with the application's DbContext that was created by the scaffold command

```
public partial class MyDbContext
{
    public MyDbContext (
        DbContextOptions<MyDbContext> options)
        : base(options) {}
}
```

The new database options provided via the parameterized constructor will replace the configuration in the `OnConfiguring` method. This works because the `OnConfiguring` code output by the scaffold command first checks to see whether the database options have already been set. If they've been set, then the `OnConfiguring` method doesn't run its code to set the database options.

> **TIP** You create partial classes to add data annotations or provide the parametrized constructor for ASP.NET Core because you don't want to edit the code that the scaffold command produced. This is because all your edits would be lost if you had to run the scaffold command again. I also suggest you don't place your partial classes in the same directory that the scaffolder writes to, because sometimes you might want to delete the whole directory created by the scaffold command before running the scaffolder again.

SINGULARIZING YOUR ENTITY CLASS NAMES

By default, the scaffold command creates entity classes with the same name as the table it's mapped to. If a table is called Books, the entity class that the scaffolder outputs will also be called Books.

If you like your entity class names to be singular, you can inject code to override the scaffold command's normal operation. This listing shows the two classes you provide that will produce entity class names by singularizing the table name the entity is mapped to.

> Listing 11.8 Injecting your own class to singularize the entity class names

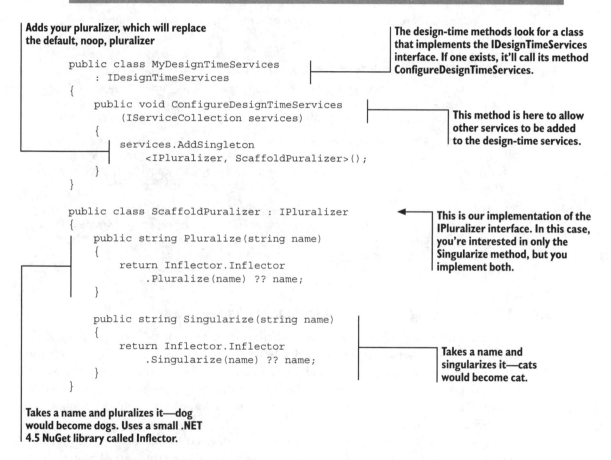

Adds your pluralizer, which will replace the default, noop, pluralizer

The design-time methods look for a class that implements the IDesignTimeServices interface. If one exists, it'll call its method ConfigureDesignTimeServices.

```
public class MyDesignTimeServices
    : IDesignTimeServices
{
    public void ConfigureDesignTimeServices
        (IServiceCollection services)
    {
        services.AddSingleton
            <IPluralizer, ScaffoldPuralizer>();
    }
}

public class ScaffoldPuralizer : IPluralizer
{
    public string Pluralize(string name)
    {
        return Inflector.Inflector
            .Pluralize(name) ?? name;
    }

    public string Singularize(string name)
    {
        return Inflector.Inflector
            .Singularize(name) ?? name;
    }
}
```

This method is here to allow other services to be added to the design-time services.

This is our implementation of the IPluralizer interface. In this case, you're interested in only the Singularize method, but you implement both.

Takes a name and singularizes it—cats would become cat.

Takes a name and pluralizes it—dog would become dogs. Uses a small .NET 4.5 NuGet library called Inflector.

11.3.2 The limitations of the reverse-engineering feature

The reverse-engineering feature is a great tool for working with existing databases. It adds the entity classes and an application's DbContext that you need to access the existing database you provided to the scaffold command. This approach has a few limitations/downsides, but they're small:

- If you change the existing database schema after running the scaffold command, you need to delete the entity classes and the application's DbContext and run the scaffold command again. This gets a bit tedious if you have lots of changes to the database, at which point the script update approach (section 11.4) may make more sense.

- The scaffolding fully defines the relationships between each entity. The scaffolding produces entity classes that have navigational properties going each way, which may not be as "clean" as the entity classes you'd have written. See section 7.2, which covers minimizing the navigational properties based on the business need.

Look out for the Update Model from Database feature

The plan is for EF Core to gain a feature called Update Model from Database (EF Core GitHub issue #831) in EF Core version 2.2 or later. This feature will significantly help developers who have an existing database with a schema that changes regularly.

The problem with the reverse-engineering feature (section 11.3) is that if the database's schema is changed, you have to run the whole reverse-engineering process again. If the schema changes a lot, this can become tedious. The Update Model from Database feature will make handling database schema changes much easier and quicker.

This feature will be a design-time command that updates the application's DbContext and/or entity classes to match the schema in the attached database. This will help developers using the reverse-engineering feature, and possibly developers for whom the database schema is updated using SQL change scripts (see section 11.4).

11.4   *SQL-first: using SQL change scripts to change the schema*

The last way to manage your database schema change is to produce *SQL change scripts* and then apply them to any of your databases. These scripts contain SQL commands that update the schema of your database. This is more of a traditional approach to handling database schema updates and gives you much better control over the database features and the schema update. But you need some knowledge of SQL commands to understand what these scripts do.

The complication with this approach is that you need to make sure that your SQL change scripts produce a database that matches what EF Core thinks the database looks like; otherwise, EF Core won't work properly with the database. I've found three ways of building the SQL scripts so that I can confirm that they match EF Core's database model:

- Using EF Core's migration script feature to produce SQL change scripts for each of your migrations. Section 11.2.1 covered the first part of this.

- Using an SQL comparison tool to build an SQL change script by comparing your existing database with a database created by EF Core.
- Using the tool `EfSchemaCompare` to check that the SQL change scripts you've created produce a database that matches EF Core's database model.

By using one or a combination of these approaches, you can produce an SQL change script. These scripts need to be applied in order, just as migrations do. I name each script starting with `Script` and then a number; for instance, `Script02 - add date col to MyEntities.sql`. This way, I can sort the SQL change scripts by name so that they can be applied in the right order.

> **TIP** If you're working in a multiperson project, you need a process to allocate a script number, or you can use a timestamp in the filename, so that the scripts are applied in the right order.

Figure 11.4 shows an example of applying SQL change scripts to a database.

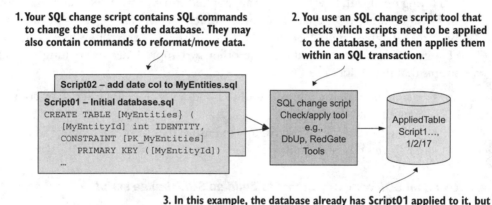

1. Your SQL change script contains SQL commands to change the schema of the database. They may also contain commands to reformat/move data.

2. You use an SQL change script tool that checks which scripts need to be applied to the database, and then applies them within an SQL transaction.

Script02 – add date col to MyEntities.sql

Script01 – Initial database.sql
```
CREATE TABLE [MyEntities} (
    [MyEntityId] int IDENTITY,
    CONSTRAINT [PK_MyEntities]
        PRIMARY KEY ([MyEntityId])
    …
```

SQL change script
Check/apply tool
e.g.,
DbUp, RedGate
Tools

AppliedTable
Script1…,
1/2/17

3. In this example, the database already has Script01 applied to it, but needs Script02 applied to get the database to the required state.

Figure 11.4   The process of applying SQL change scripts is normally handled by a tool that checks a table in the database to see what scripts have already been applied to the database. It then applies any missing scripts to the database.

You can apply an SQL change script to the database (step 2 in figure 11.4) in multiple ways, ranging from manually applying them in Microsoft's SQL Server Management Studio to using open source and commercial tools that check which change scripts have already been applied and applying only new change scripts. The important issues are as follows:

- You must apply the SQL change scripts to your database in the correct order.
- You must apply an SQL change script only once to a database.

- Each database schema change should be applied within an SQL transaction. This ensures that either the whole schema change is applied or your database is left in its original stage.
- If an SQL change script fails, all subsequent scripts shouldn't be applied.

Several packages meet these four criteria. Here are two:

- DbUp (http://dbup.github.io/), an open source NuGet package that will apply SQL change scripts.
- Redgate has commercially available tools that have more features than DbUp (see www.red-gate.com/products/sql-development/readyroll/).

Some packages, such as Redgate's offerings, can be run manually or as part of a software deployment tool. DbUp is a software package, so you can build whatever you like. I've used DbUp to create a console application, which I can either trigger manually or use in an automated software deployment.

Having dealt with how the scripts are applied to a database, let's focus on the critical issues of creating SQL change scripts in which the database schema changes match EF Core's database model. Section 11.2.1 has already covered how to produce an SQL change script from a migration. The other two approaches to creating SQL change scripts that match EF Core's model are as follows:

- Using an SQL comparison tool to build an SQL change script by comparing a new and old database
- Using the `EfSchemaCompare` tool to ensure that your SQL change script matches EF Core's database model

11.4.1 *Using an SQL comparison tool to build an SQL change script*

One method to automatically create an SQL change script is to compare two databases: your original database and a new database created by EF Core after you've updated the EF Core configuration. Comparing these two databases shows the differences, and you can create a script that will change your original database to the same schema as the newly EF Core–generated database.

Thankfully, many SQL comparison tools produce an SQL change script for you automatically. One is available for SQL Server in Visual Studio 2017 (any version), called *SQL Server Object Explorer*, found in the Data Storage and Processing workload in the Visual Studio installer.

Figure 11.5 shows how to compare the database in chapter 2 with the changes in chapter 4, where you add `Order` and `LineItem` entity classes, and get an SQL change script by using SQL Server Object Explorer inside Visual Studio.

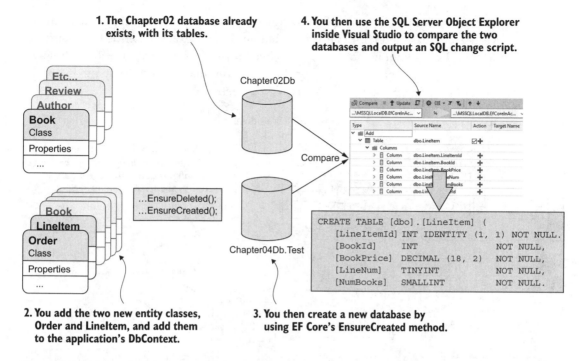

1. The Chapter02 database already exists, with its tables.

4. You then use the SQL Server Object Explorer inside Visual Studio to compare the two databases and output an SQL change script.

```
CREATE TABLE [dbo].[LineItem] (
    [LineItemId] INT IDENTITY (1, 1) NOT NULL,
    [BookId]     INT              NOT NULL,
    [BookPrice]  DECIMAL (18, 2)  NOT NULL,
    [LineNum]    TINYINT          NOT NULL,
    [NumBooks]   SMALLINT         NOT NULL,
```

2. You add the two new entity classes, Order and LineItem, and add them to the application's DbContext.

3. You then create a new database by using EF Core's EnsureCreated method.

Figure 11.5 The process of building an SQL change script by comparing two databases. The important point is that the second database is created by EF Core, so you know it matches the current EF Core model. In this example, you use the SQL Server Object Explorer feature inside Visual Studio to compare the two databases and build an SQL change script that will migrate the Chapter02 database to the correct level for the software changes added in chapter 4.

11.4.2 Using EfSchemaCompare to check your SQL matches EF Core's model

In the second approach, you write the SQL change scripts yourself and then use a tool called EfSchemaCompare to ensure that your changes match EF Core's database model. This is attractive to developers who want to define the database in ways that EF Core can't. For instance, this approach allows you to set more-rigorous CHECK constraints on columns, add stored procedures or user-defined functions, add seed data, and so on via SQL scripts.

The only disadvantage for a software developer is that you need to know enough SQL to be able to write/edit the SQL change scripts. This might put off some developers, but it's not as bad as you think because you can look at the SQL EF Core outputs to create a database and then tweak that SQL with your changes. Section 15.8.1 shows how to do that. Also, plenty of online help is available for SQL commands, such as Stack Overflow, which I find invaluable.

The main problem in writing SQL change scripts is making sure they exactly match EF Core's database model. I can testify that getting an exact match is hard, and not something I'd attempt without a tool to check my scripts. Figure 11.6 shows how the `EfSchemaCompare` tool solves that problem by automating the comparison of the updated database against EF Core's database model.

The SQL-first approach uses a tool to compare EF Core's database model with the database schema.

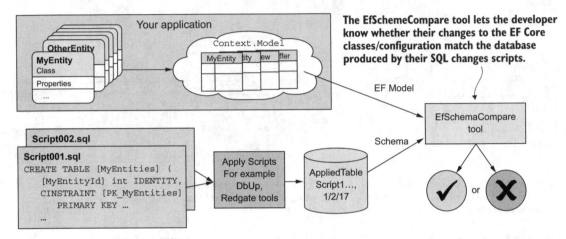

Figure 11.6   The `EfSchemaCompare` tool compares EF Core's model of the database, which it forms by looking at the entity classes and the application's DbContext configuration, with the actual database schema. It will output human-readable error messages if it finds a difference.

I chose the SQL-first approach, and I built the tool called `EfSchemaCompare` after becoming cautious about using EF's database migrations in a production environment. The `EfSchemaCompare` tool is available in my EfCore.TestSupport package (see https://github.com/JonPSmith/EfCore.TestSupport/wiki/9.-EfSchemaCompare). With this tool, I create unit tests that check my development database, and more important, my production database, to see whether the EF Core's database model has drifted away from the actual database schema.

The process for using the SQL-first approach is to change your entity classes and/or the EF Core configuration of your application, and build an SQL change script that will alter the database schema. Then you can apply your SQL change script to a database in development, and run the `EfSchemaCompare` tool to check whether the new database and the EF Core's model of the database match. If they don't match, the tool outputs a series of error messages that highlight the differences so you can fix them.

NOTE   Section 15.9 provides examples of using the `EfSchemaCompare` tool.

11.5   *Part 2—Issues around a database schema change*

Now that you understand the three approaches to updating a database's schema (sections 11.2 to 11.4), you're ready to focus on the application of database schema changes. This section includes information about not losing data in the production database, because that's valuable to clients and their users; losing or corrupting that data is a job-limiting event that I don't think any of us want to have.

Let's start with a simple update and then progress to more-complex update scenarios. They're as follows:

- *Nonbreaking schema change*—Adding a new table or column that's used in only the new application version. This shouldn't cause a problem to the currently running application, because it won't be accessing those changed parts of the database. You can apply the database schema change while the existing software version is running (with some caveats).

- *Breaking schema change*—If your schema change involves changes to the tables, columns, constraints, and so on, I refer to this as a *breaking schema change*. Your currently running application will throw exceptions when accessing the modified database, because the database doesn't match its database model. You can update a database with a breaking schema change in two ways:

  - *Can stop the application*—You stop your running application, and apply the database change and any data copying before loading and running your new application that matches the changed database.

  - *Can't stop the application*—If you want to apply a breaking schema change while providing continuous service to your users, you need a more complex approach. I describe how you can achieve this type of schema update without interrupting your users, but it's much more complex than the preceding approach.

TIP When I'm in the development stage and haven't released to production yet, I may find that a breaking database schema change just isn't worth handling, so I delete (drop) the whole development database and start again.

The following sections describe these scenarios and how to handle them.

11.5.1 Applying nonbreaking changes while the current app is running

When I'm developing a new application with a new database, I tend to grow the database schema as the project progresses; for instance, by adding new tables that the previous version of the software doesn't know about. I call these *nonbreaking changes*, because they don't cause any currently running application to fail, as the parts of the database it uses haven't changed.

With nonbreaking changes, the modifications to a database schema can be applied using any of the previous methods described, and at any time—even to the production database while the old software is running. But you need to be sure that your changes don't affect the old tables. For instance, adding a new table can often require you to add columns to existing tables (say, a foreign key to link to a new table). This can work, but you need to be careful. Here are some issues to consider:

- If you're adding a new scalar property to an existing table, the old application won't set it. That's OK, because SQL will give it a default value—but what default do you want it to have? You can control that by setting an SQL default value for the column (see section 8.1.1).

- If you're adding a new foreign-key column to an existing table, you need to make that foreign key nullable and have the correct cascade delete settings. That allows the old application to add a new row in that table without the foreign-key constraint reporting an error.

TIP   Testing a (supposedly) nonbreaking database change that alters columns in existing tables is highly recommended, especially if going to a production database.

11.5.2 *Applying breaking database changes by stopping the application*

Breaking changes are those that change the database schema in a way that the old application will fail. Your database change affects the current tables, columns, constraints, and so on that the currently running application uses. My example of a breaking database schema change is described in section 11.2.2, where you split one entity class called `CustomerAndAddress` into two entity classes, `Customer` and `Address`.

This example of splitting one table into two has the added problem that, without manual intervention, you'd lose data. If you deleted the old CustomerAndAddresses table and created the two new tables, Customers and Addresses, you'd lose any data that was in the original CustomerAndAddresses table. This section describes the first approach to changing the database schema without losing data, but at the cost that you'll stop your application from accessing its database.

The simplest way to stop your application from accessing its database is to stop the application itself. Your users might not be happy with you, but it makes updating your database schema and copying data much easier.

> **Things to consider when stopping an application for a database update**
>
> You need to consider what will happen if you abruptly stop an application. It could cause users to lose data that's irretrievable, or on an e-commerce site, a user could lose their order. For this reason, a warning, or *soft stop*, should be considered.
>
> I had this problem on an e-commerce system I was building, and I developed a "down for maintenance" approach. This provided an onscreen warning to users indicating when the site would close. During the closing, I show a "this site is down for maintenance" page. You can read about this at http://mng.bz/mXkN.
>
> Another way to softly stop your application is to provide read-only access to the database. You disable every method that could update the database. The application is still reading the database, so you can't change the existing database structures, but this does allow you to add new tables and safely copy data into them. After you've loaded the new application, you can apply another database schema update to remove the database parts that are no longer needed.
>
> Section 11.5.3 describes how to apply a breaking database schema change while providing continuous service to your users. This is the ultimate solution for the users, but comes at a price of a much more complex database update process.

Stopping your current application means that you can change the database in a way that the previously running application wouldn't like; for instance, you can delete or rename tables, columns, constraints, and so on. Stopping the application makes the database schema change into a simpler, one-stage database change. Figure 11.7 shows an example of splitting the CustomerAndAddresses table into two tables, Customers and Addresses, with a "before" view of the database on the left, and an "after" view of the database on the right.

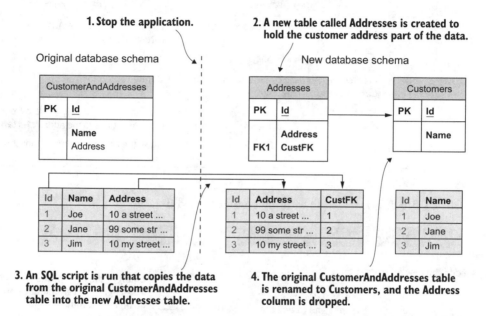

1. Stop the application.

2. A new table called Addresses is created to hold the customer address part of the data.

3. An SQL script is run that copies the data from the original CustomerAndAddresses table into the new Addresses table.

4. The original CustomerAndAddresses table is renamed to Customers, and the Address column is dropped.

Figure 11.7 The steps in changing a database schema that requires data to be copied to ensure no loss of data. In this case, the application software is stopped while the database schema change is applied and data is copied to the new Addresses table. When that has finished, the new application software can start.

You can update the database schema and copy the data in two ways:

- Use EF Core's `Migrate` method, with hand-coded changes to the Migrate file.
- Use SQL change scripts that combine schema changes with data copying.

I describe each of these next, using the example of splitting the CustomerAndAddresses table into two tables, Customers and Addresses, as shown in figure 11.7.

USING EF CORE'S MIGRATE METHOD TO UPDATE THE DATABASE SCHEMA

For this example, you can use EF Core's `Migrate` method, but you need to edit the migration heavily because the standard migration code produced by the EF Core's `Add-Migration` command lacks the code to copy the data.

When you run the `Add-Migration` command after you've deleted the Customer-AndAddresses table and added the two tables, Customers and Addresses, you get a warning message that the migration "...may result in the loss of data." EF Core can't work out what code is needed to fix this, so you need to go in and change the code inside the Migrate file. Table 11.1 shows the differences between EF Core's migration code and your improved migration code.

Table 11.1 Differences in the standard EF Core migration code produced by the `Add-Migration` command and your improvements to that migration code to not lose data

Step	EF Core migration	Improved migration
1.	Drops the CustomerAndAddresses table	Renames the CustomerAndAddresses table to Customers so the data is preserved
2.	Creates the Customers table	- Not needed -
3.	Creates the Addresses table and links to the Customers table, plus index	- Same -
4.	- End -	Copies the Address column data from the Customers table to the Addresses table
5.		Drops the Address column from the Customers table

Here's the migration code with the changes listed in table 11.1.

Listing 11.9 The changed `Up` method to change the database and not lose data

EF Core adds the new Addresses table.

Changes the code produced by EF Core's Add-Migration command to produce the changes you want

```
protected override void Up
    (MigrationBuilder migrationBuilder)
{
    migrationBuilder.RenameTable(
        name: "CustomerAndAddresses",
        newName: "Customers");

    migrationBuilder.CreateTable(
        name: "Addresses",
        … code removed to shorten the code
        … the code builds the Addresses table
        });

    migrationBuilder.CreateIndex(
        name: "IX_Addresses_CustFK",
        table: "Addresses",
        column: "CustFK",
        unique: true);

    migrationBuilder.Sql(
        @"INSERT INTO [dbo].[Addresses]
            ([Address], [CustFK])
        SELECT Address, Id
```

EF Core would drop the CustomerAndAddresses table and create a new Customers table, but to save data, you rename the CustomerAndAddresses table to Customers

Copies the Address part of the renamed CustomerAndAddresses table to the Addresses table

```
        FROM [dbo].[Customers]");

    migrationBuilder.DropColumn(          ◄──── Drops the Address column from the renamed
        name: "Address",                        CustomerAndAddresses so it now acts like the
        table: "Customers");                    Customers table that EF Core expects
}
```

If you're running only one instance of the application, and you call the `Migrate` method in the startup of your application, this type of update works well. This is because the act of deploying the new application will stop the old version, the database will be updated during the startup of your new version, and then the application will start working. This is likely to provide the shortest downtime of your application, but remember my comment in section 11.2.2: if a migration fails during the startup of your production system, it can be hard to diagnose.

USING SQL CHANGE SCRIPTS TO UPDATE THE DATABASE SCHEMA

The other way to apply a database schema change with data copying is by using an SQL change script. As explained in section 11.4, you can use various methods to create a script, but if you need to copy data, you have to write that part of the code yourself. SQL scripts provide the most complete control of the database schema via SQL commands.

This listing shows the content of an SQL change script that would apply the database schema changes and data copying as shown in figure 11.7.

Listing 11.10 SQL change script to change the database schema and retain the data

Renames the CustomerAndAddresses table to
Customers now, as you want the Addresses table to
have a foreign-key relationship to the Customers table

```
    EXEC sp_rename N'CustomerAndAddresses', N'Customers';
    GO

    CREATE TABLE [Addresses] (          ◄──┘ Creates the new Addresses table ...
        [Id] int NOT NULL IDENTITY,
        [Address] nvarchar(max),
        [CustFK] int NOT NULL,
        CONSTRAINT [PK_Addresses] PRIMARY KEY ([Id]),
        CONSTRAINT [FK_Addresses_Customers_CustFK]
            FOREIGN KEY ([CustFK])
            REFERENCES [Customers] ([Id])
            ON DELETE CASCADE
    );
    GO

    CREATE UNIQUE INDEX [IX_Addresses_CustFK]          ... with a unique index
        ON [Addresses] ([CustFK]);          ◄──┘     for the foreign key
    GO

    INSERT INTO [dbo].[Addresses]          ◄──── Copies the Address part of the renamed
        ([Address], [CustFK])                    CustomerAndAddresses table to the
                                                 Addresses table
```

```
SELECT Address, Id
FROM [dbo].[Customers];
GO

ALTER TABLE [Customers] DROP COLUMN [Address];
GO
```

◄── **Drops the Address column from the Customers table, as the data has been copied**

For breaking changes like this example, you need to stop the old version of software, apply your SQL change script, and then deploy/start your new application. That way, the database schema will be in the correct state for each version. The disadvantage is that your application is down (not responding to users) for longer than the EF Core's migrations approach, but it's easier to debug if it goes wrong.

11.5.3 Handling breaking database changes when you can't stop the app

The most complicated situation occurs when you want to provide continuous service to your users, even during a breaking database schema change. For instance, applications providing critical services such as credit card payment, banking, or other 24/7 services can't afford any downtime. Also, many large e-commerce websites don't want to lose a customer, so they also plan on running 24/7.

Figure 11.8 shows how Microsoft Azure web hosting can provide continuous service during software updates. Azure has *deployment slots*, which you can use to start a new version of the application, known as *warming up* your application, so that it's ready to take over from the current live application. After you swap the deployment slots, your new code immediately takes over handling any HTTP requests.

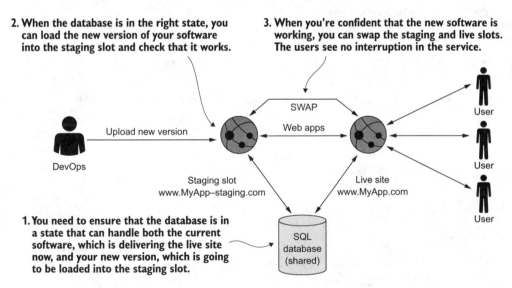

2. When the database is in the right state, you can load the new version of your software into the staging slot and check that it works.

3. When you're confident that the new software is working, you can swap the staging and live slots. The users see no interruption in the service.

1. You need to ensure that the database is in a state that can handle both the current software, which is delivering the live site now, and your new version, which is going to be loaded into the staging slot.

Figure 11.8   Azure provides a continuous service to the user when deploying a new version of the software. In Azure, you have a deployment slot, often called staging, where you can run up your new application ready to take the load. When you're happy with how it's working, you can swap the deployment slots, and your new code will take over. The important point from the EF Core/database perspective is that the database must be in a state that both your current and new software can use.

The issue I want to cover in this continuous service example is that the two software versions—the current live application and the new application in staging—must both be able to work with the same database. The solution is a more complex operation, consisting of multiple schema changes and an interim software release.

As an example of this continuous service approach, let's look at the splitting of the table CustomerAndAddresses into the two tables, described in section 11.5.2. This time, you'll produce the same update, but for a continuous service application. Figure 11.9 shows the stages that you must go through to migrate from a single CustomerAndAddresses table to separate Customers and Addresses tables. Your particular database schema change will be different from this example, but your changes should follow the same, five-stage approach.

Figure 11.9 shows exactly which software versions are running (at the top) and when the three SQL change scripts are run (at the bottom). This shows how careful you need to be to ensure that there's never a time when the database and the application software version(s) accessing that database are incompatible. You can see the two points where two versions of the software are running in parallel—the original and the interim software after Script01 has run, and the interim and final software after Script02 has run to copy the data.

It would be great to just copy the data from the CustomerAndAddresses table into new Customers and Addresses tables, but until you know that the original software has gone, there's always a chance (albeit small) that that software could add another entry after the copy has finished. You can't take the risk of missing data, so the interim software needs to be running as it's designed to write any new data to both the old and the new tables.

NOTE I don't list the SQL change scripts shown in figure 11.9 because they would fill quite a few pages. You can find these scripts at http://mng.bz/Bbth; you can find the unit tests that go with these scripts at http://mng.bz/g4Mv. I've also created two DbContexts, `Chapter11ContinuousInterimDb` and `Chapter11ContinuousFinalDb`, which show how the two application DbContexts differ (and help check that the code in this book works!).

This continuous service example could be implemented in other ways. Here are some other options:

- Use a more sophisticated SQL arrangement with SQL views and triggers to update the tables. See http://mng.bz/0vxk.
- Use a more EF Core approach, and move some of the updating and copying out of the SQL change scripts.
- Don't change the database at all, but use a DDD repository approach, as explained in section 10.4, to "hide" the suboptimal database structure.

I think you'll agree that the database schema change example for a continuous service application is a lot harder than the same example in which you can stop the application to do an update (see section 11.5.2). You need to think hard before you propose a change to a continuous service application's entity classes/EF configuration that would cause a data-moving database schema change. What might be easy in software can have big implications in the production database.

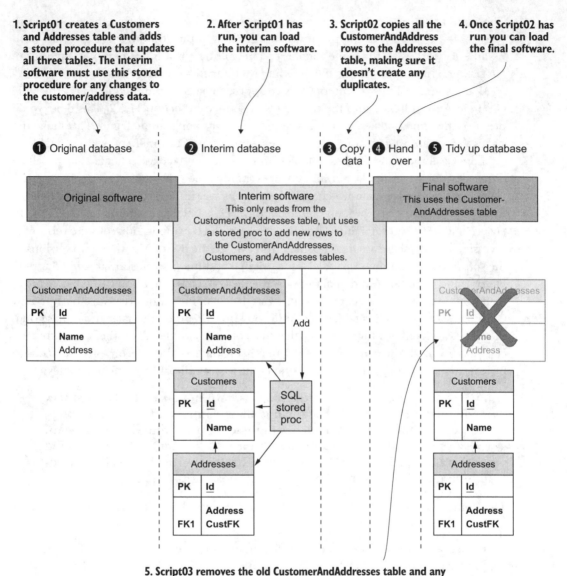

1. **Script01 creates a Customers and Addresses table and adds a stored procedure that updates all three tables. The interim software must use this stored procedure for any changes to the customer/address data.**

2. **After Script01 has run, you can load the interim software.**

3. **Script02 copies all the CustomerAndAddress rows to the Addresses table, making sure it doesn't create any duplicates.**

4. **Once Script02 has run you can load the final software.**

1 Original database   **2** Interim database   **3** Copy data   **4** Hand over   **5** Tidy up database

Original software

Interim software
This only reads from the CustomerAndAddresses table, but uses a stored proc to add new rows to the CustomerAndAddresses, Customers, and Addresses tables.

Final software
This uses the Customer-AndAddresses table

CustomerAndAddresses

PK	Id
	Name
	Address

CustomerAndAddresses

PK	Id
	Name
	Address

Add

SQL stored proc

Customers

PK	Id
	Name

Addresses

PK	Id
FK1	Address / CustFK

CustomerAndAddresses

PK	Id
	Name
	Address

Customers

PK	Id
	Name

Addresses

PK	Id
FK1	Address / CustFK

5. **Script03 removes the old CustomerAndAddresses table and any interim columns/procedures that are no longer needed.**

Figure 11.9 The five stages of changing a database when you want to supply a continuous service to your users. The three software versions—original, interim, and final—overlap to provide a continuous service. The interim software needs to read data from the original database structure because the original software is running in parallel, but the interim software calls an SQL stored procedure to do any updates; this ensures all three tables are updated. After that's in place, you can copy the data without missing any new customer and address information that's added.

Summary

- The easiest way to change a database schema is to use EF Core's migration feature, but that feature has limitations when dealing with more-complex applications. Using the migration feature is the *code-first* approach.
- You can use EF Core's scaffold command to get EF Core to work with an existing database. This is known as the *database-first* approach.
- You can change the database schema via direct SQL commands. I refer to this as the *SQL-first* approach. The trick is to make sure that your schema changes match EF Core's model of the database, which the `EfSchemaCompare` tool helps with.
- Updating a production database is a serious undertaking, especially if data could be lost in the process.
- Updating a database while providing continuous service to your users requires a complex, five-stage update procedure if you're changing something that the old application relies on.

For readers who are familiar with EF6:

- EF Core provides similar migration features to EF6.x, but has different commands.
- EF Core's migration feature is significantly changed and improved.
- There's no automatic migration—you control when a migration happens.
- It's easier to combine migrations in a multiperson team.

EF Core
performance tuning

This chapter is the first of two covering performance tuning your database accesses. Covering what, where, and how to improve your EF Core database code, this chapter is divided into three parts:

- *Part 1*—Understanding performance, the difference between speed and scalability, deciding what to performance tune, and determining the costs of performance tuning.
- *Part 2*—Techniques you can use to find performance issues and the use of EF Core's logging to help you spot problems.
- *Part 3*—A whole range of database access patterns, both good and bad, to help you diagnose and fix many EF Core performance issues.

In chapter 13, you'll apply the approaches shown in this chapter to the book app's book list query. You'll start by tuning EF Core code and then progress to more-complex techniques, such as using raw SQL commands to squeeze the best performance out of the database accesses.

12.1 Part 1—Deciding which performance issues to fix

Before describing how to find and fix performance issues, I want to provide an overview of the subject of performance. Although you can ignore performance at the start of a project, some concepts might help you later, when someone says, "The application is too slow—fix it."

When people talk about an application's *performance*, they're normally thinking about how fast an application deals with requests; for instance, how long it takes an API to return a specific request, or how long a human user has to wait when searching for a specific book. I call this part of the application's performance *speed*, and use terms such as *fast* and *slow*.

The other aspect is what happens to the speed of your application when it has lots of simultaneous requests. For instance, a fast website with a few users might become slow when it has many simultaneous users. This is referred to as the *scalability* of the application—the ability of the application to feel fast even when it has a high load of users. Scalability is often measured via *throughput*—the number of requests an application can handle per second.

12.1.1 "Don't performance tune too early" doesn't mean you stop thinking

Pretty much everyone says you shouldn't performance tune early; the number one goal is to get your application working properly first. A saying attributed to Kent Beck is "Make it Work. Make it Right. Make it Fast," which gets across the progressive steps in building an application, with performance tuning coming last. I totally agree, but with three caveats:

- Make sure any software patterns you use don't contain inherent performance problems. Otherwise, you'll be building in inefficiencies from day one. (See section 12.4.)
- Don't write code that makes it hard to find and fix performance problems. For instance, if you mix your database access code in with other code, such as front-end code, performance changes can get messy and are difficult to test. (See section 12.4.6.)
- Don't pick the wrong architecture. Nowadays, the scalability of web applications is easier to improve by running multiple instances of the web application. But if you have an application that needs high scalability in its database accesses, a Command and Query Responsibility Segregation (CQRS) architecture might help.

It's often hard to predict what performance problems you're going to hit, so waiting until your application is starting to take shape is sensible. But a bit of up-front thought can save you a lot of pain later if you find your application is too slow.

12.1.2 How do you decide what's slow and needs performance tuning?

The problem with terms such as *fast, slow,* and *high load* is that they can be subjective. You might think your application is fast, but your marketing department may think it's slow. Sticking with subjective views of an application's performance isn't going to help, so the key question is, does the speed matter in this case, and how fast should it be?

You should remember that in human-facing applications, it's not just the raw speed that matters, but the *user's expectations* of how fast a certain feature should be. For instance, Google's search has shown how blindingly fast a search can be, and we therefore expect all searches to be fast. Conversely, paying for an online purchase, with the need to fill in your address, credit card number, and so on isn't something that we expect to be fast (although too slow, and we'll give up!).

When thinking about what needs to be performance tuned, you need to be selective; otherwise, you're in for a lot of work for little gain. For example, I developed a small e-commerce site that had a little more than 100 different queries and updates to 20 database tables. More than 60% of the database accesses were on the admin side, some of which were rarely used. For the paying user, maybe 10% of the database accesses affected them. That analysis helped me to decide where to put my effort.

Figure 12.1 shows what happens when you apply the same analysis of the user's expectations against the speed of the database access for the book app. This analysis covers the book listing/search, the placing of an order, and the few admin commands ranging from updating the publication date of a book (fast) to wiping and re-inputting all the books (very slow).

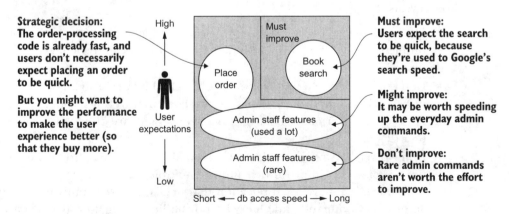

Figure 12.1 Various features from the book app graded with the user's expectations of speed on the vertical access, and the actual complexity/speed of the database access part of the feature. The type of user and user expectations have a big impact on what needs performance tuning.

After you've done some analysis of your application, you should get a list of features that are worthy of performance tuning. But before you start, you need clear metrics to work from:

- *Define the feature*—What's the exact query/command that needs improving, and under what circumstances is it slow (for instance, how many concurrent users)?
- *Get timings*—How long does it take now, and how fast does it need to be?
- *Cost of fix*—How much is the improvement worth? When should you stop?
- *Prove it still works*—Do you have a way to confirm that the feature is working properly before you start the performance tuning and that it still works after the performance change?

TIP You can find a useful article on general performance tuning at http://mng.bz/8oZ5.

12.1.3 *The cost of finding and fixing performance issues*

Before diving into finding and fixing performance issues, I want to point out that there's a cost to performance tuning your application. It takes development time and effort to find, improve, and retest an application's performance. As figure 12.1 illustrates, you need to be picky about what you plan to improve.

A couple of years ago, I wrote an article, "The Compromise Between Development Time and Performance in Data-Driven ASP.NET MVC," in which I measured the gain in performance in an EF6.x database access against the time it took me to achieve that improvement. Figure 12.2 shows the results of that work. I started with an existing EF Core query (1 on the horizontal scale) and then applied two steps (2 and 3) of improvement, still using EF6.x, and then I estimated the time it would take to write a raw SQL version (4 on the horizontal scale).

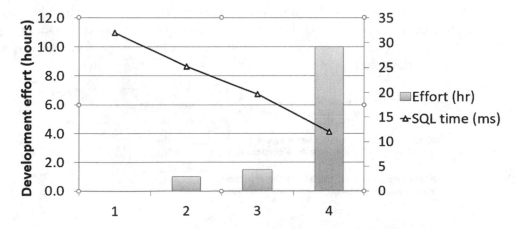

Figure 12.2 The trade-off between database performance and development effort for three stages of improvement of an EF database access. Development time is shown as a bar chart (hours—left scale), and the speed of the database access is shown as a line (milliseconds—right scale). An almost exponential increase occurs in development effort against an almost linear reduction on the database access time.

NOTE You can find the original article, "The Compromise Between Development Time and Performance in Data-Driven ASP.NET MVC," at http://mng .bz/n5EJ.

The point of figure 12.2 is to show that extreme performance improvements aren't easy. I had an exponential increase in development effort against an almost linear reduction on the database access time. Therefore, it's worth thinking about the problem holistically. Although it might be that the database access is slow, the solution might come from changing other parts of the application. For instance, for web/ mobile applications, you have a few other possibilities:

- *HTTP caching*—This allows you to remember a request in memory and return a copy if the same URL is presented, thus saving any need to access the database. Caching takes work to get it right, but it can have a big effect on perceived performance.
- *Scaling up/out*—Cloud hosting allows you to pay for more powerful host computers (known as *scaling up* in Azure) and/or running more instances of the web application (known as *scaling out* in Azure). This might solve a lot of small performance problems quickly, especially if it's a scalability problem.

I'm not suggesting sloppy programming. I certainly try to show good practices in this book. But by choosing EF Core over writing direct SQL commands, you've already opted for quicker development time against (possibly) slower database access times. In the end, it's always about effort against reward, so you should only performance tune parts of your application that really need the extra speed or scalability.

12.2   *Part 2—Techniques for diagnosing a performance issue*

In part 1, you decided which parts of your application need improving and how much improvement you want. The next step is to find the code involved in the slow feature and diagnose the problem.

This book is about EF Core, so you'll concentrate on the database code, but those database accesses rarely exist on their own. You need to drill down through your application to find the database code that's hitting the application's performance. Figure 12.3 shows a three-step approach I use to pinpoint performance bottlenecks.

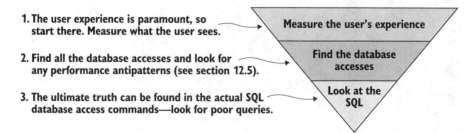

1. The user experience is paramount, so start there. Measure what the user sees.   **Measure the user's experience**

2. Find all the database accesses and look for any performance antipatterns (see section 12.5).   **Find the database accesses**

3. The ultimate truth can be found in the actual SQL database access commands—look for poor queries.   **Look at the SQL**

Figure 12.3   Finding database performance issues requires you to start with what the user sees and then drill down to the database code. After finding the database code, you check that it uses the optimal strategies outlined in this chapter. If this doesn't improve the situation, you need to look at the actual SQL commands sent to the database and consider ways to improve them.

You'll explore each of these stages in more detail in the next three subsections.

12.2.1 Stage 1: get a good overview—measuring the user's experience

Before you go digging to find a performance problem, you need to think about the user's experience, because this is what matters. You might improve the speed of a database access by 500%, but if it's a small part of the whole picture, it won't help much.

First, you need to find a tool measuring how long a specific request/feature takes. What you use will depend on the type of application you're using. Here's a list of free tools that are available for looking at the overall time a request takes:

- For Windows applications, you can use the Performance Profiler in Visual Studio.
- For websites, you can use Google Chrome browser in developer mode to obtain timings. There are other ways of doing this, such as Glimpse (see http://getglimpse.com/).
- For the ASP.NET Core Web API, you can use Azure Application Insights locally in debug mode.

NOTE Plenty of other commercial (paid for) tools are available for testing and profiling all manner of systems. I've listed at least one free version for each of the main types of applications.

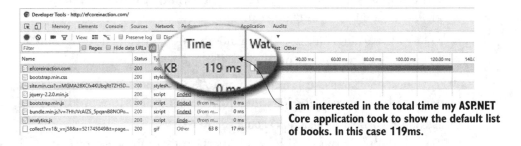

Figure 12.4   Using the Google Chrome browser in development mode to find out how long the book app takes to display 54 books when using EF Core 1.1, before you start any performance tuning

Figure 12.4 shows the timeline for the book app (using EF Core 1.1 and before any performance tuning) as measured by the Google browser, Chrome, in developer mode (F12). It shows only one timing. You should take timings for a range of sort/filter combinations to get an overview of where the performance issues exist in the book list feature. See the next chapter for an example of timings for multiple sort/filter combinations.

WARNING Measuring the time it takes for ASP.NET Core to execute a command in debug mode can give misleading figures, because some slow logging methods may be enabled. These can add significant extra time to each HTTP request. I recommend testing your software in Release mode to get more representative figures.

12.2.2   Stage 2: find all the database code involved in the feature you're tuning

Having identified the part of the application you want to performance tune, you need to locate all the database access code involved in that feature. After you've found the database code, run your eye over the code, looking for performance antipatterns (see section 12.4). This is a quick way to find and fix issues. It's not foolproof, but after a while, you get a feel for what might be causing a problem.

For example, when you look at the listing of books in your book app, various parts jump out as possible performance bottlenecks:

- Calculating the average review votes, including sorting and filtering on the average votes. That needs a database-side calculation to be fast.
- Sorting on the actual price. The problem is that the price changes depending on whether the `Book` entity has a `PriceOffer` entity attached to it, so you can't use a simple index.

My user experience timing shows that sorting or filtering on average votes was slow, but it wasn't until I had looked at the EF Core logging output, which I cover next, that I saw the problems.

12.2.3   Stage 3: inspecting the SQL code to find poor performance

The ultimate source of database access performance is the SQL code. Even if you don't know the SQL language well, EF Core logging has two features that help you diagnose the problem. The EF Core logging can

- Provide warnings on LINQ commands that EF Core can't directly translate to SQL
- List the SQL sent to the database, with the time that query took

I'll cover how you can use this information to look for performance issues, but first let me describe how to access the logging information that EF Core produces.

ACCESSING THE LOGGING INFORMATION PRODUCED BY EF CORE

.NET Core defines a standard logging interface that any piece of code can use. EF Core produces a substantial amount of logging output, which is normally collected by the application it's running in. Logging information is categorized by a `LogLevel`, which ranges from the most detailed information at the `Trace` (0) level, right up to `Critical` (5). In production, you'd limit the output to `Warning` (3) and above, but when running in debug mode, you might output any logs from the `Debug` (1) level and above.

You need to supply a logging provider to capture any logging and make it available for you to look at. Logging is so useful that most applications include code to set up the logging providers. For instance, in an ASP.NET Core application, a logging provider(s) is configured during startup (see http://mng.bz/KH6W).

If you want to capture logging information inside your unit tests, you need to link a logging provider into EF Core's `ILoggerFactory`. Because you're using the xUnit unit tests library (see https://xunit.github.io/), you can't use a normal logging provider such as `Console`, as xUnit runs tests in parallel. You'll therefore write a simple logger that returns a list of logging information produced by EF Core.

> **TIP** I provide a prebuilt logging tool in my EfCore.TestSupport library that goes with chapter 15; see section 15.8 for more on capturing EF Core's logs in your unit tests.

This listing shows how to add your own logging provider such that any EF Core logging from this context will be sent to your logger. This allows you to capture the logging output in your unit test and output it to the test screen.

> **Listing 12.1   Capturing EF Core's logging output in a unit test**

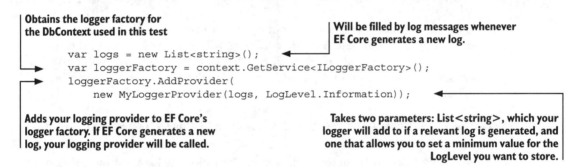

Obtains the logger factory for the DbContext used in this test

Will be filled by log messages whenever EF Core generates a new log.

```
var logs = new List<string>();
var loggerFactory = context.GetService<ILoggerFactory>();
loggerFactory.AddProvider(
    new MyLoggerProvider(logs, LogLevel.Information));
```

Adds your logging provider to EF Core's logger factory. If EF Core generates a new log, your logging provider will be called.

Takes two parameters: List<string>, which your logger will add to if a relevant log is generated, and one that allows you to set a minimum value for the LogLevel you want to store.

Having covered how to capture EF Core's logging, now you'll see how to use this information to find performance issues.

USING EF CORE LOGGING TO DETECT SUBOPTIMAL LINQ QUERIES

EF Core will alert you to possible suboptimal LINQ commands by logging a warning of state `QueryClientEvaluationWarning`, indicating that EF Core couldn't translate the LINQ command into a corresponding SQL command. It'll produce this warning only the first time EF Core translates the LINQ command, so it'll see the warning only once after your application starts (or every time in a unit test).

In this example, when you start the project under version 1.0 of EF Core and run your Book listing query, you get a `QueryClientEvaluationWarning`. This tells you that EF Core couldn't convert the LINQ `Average` method into an SQL `AVE` (average) command (this was fixed in version 2 of EF Core). The average review votes are calculated by reading all the `Review` entity class's `Votes` properties for each book and calculating the average vote in software. That was obviously a performance bottleneck.

For extra protection, you can get EF Core to throw an exception if EF Core logs a
QueryClientEvaluationWarning. To do this, you use the ConfigureWarning method
when building the options to set up the application's DbContext. The following listing shows how you might alter the ASP.NET Core configuration such that EF Core will
throw an exception on QueryClientEvaluationWarning.

Listing 12.2   ASP.NET Core application DbContext with ConfigureWarnings

```
var connection = Configuration
    .GetConnectionString("DefaultConnection");
services.AddDbContext<EfCoreContext>(options => options.
    UseSqlServer(connection,
    b => b.MigrationsAssembly("DataLayer"))
    .ConfigureWarnings(warnings =>
        warnings.Throw(
            RelationalEventId
            .QueryClientEvaluationWarning)));
```

Allows you to define
what happens on a
log of LogLevel
Warning.

You want EF Core to throw an
exception if the EventId of the log
is QueryClientEvaluationWarning.

TIP   Personally I don't cause an exception in my live application as I would
rather it run slowly than fail. But I do configure this exception in my unit test.
The EfCore.TestSupport library used in chapter 15 will, by default, enable the
throwing of an exception on a QueryClientEvaluationWarning, but it can be
turned off—see section 15.8.

EXTRACTING THE SQL COMMANDS SENT TO THE DATABASE VIA EF CORE'S LOGGING OUTPUT

If you set the log level to Information, you'll get a complete list of the SQL commands
generated by EF Core and sent to the database. The following listing shows an example
of an Information message containing the SQL code.

Listing 12.3   An Information log showing the SQL command sent to the database

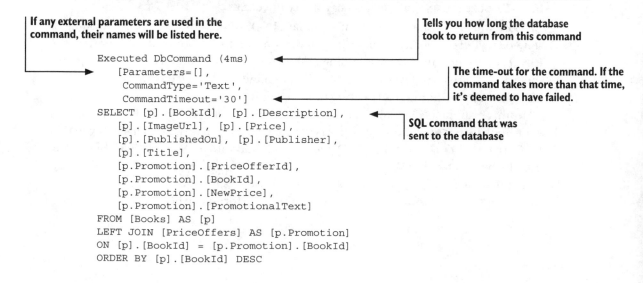

If any external parameters are used in the
command, their names will be listed here.

Tells you how long the database
took to return from this command

```
Executed DbCommand (4ms)
    [Parameters=[],
     CommandType='Text',
     CommandTimeout='30']
SELECT [p].[BookId], [p].[Description],
    [p].[ImageUrl], [p].[Price],
    [p].[PublishedOn], [p].[Publisher],
    [p].[Title],
    [p.Promotion].[PriceOfferId],
    [p.Promotion].[BookId],
    [p.Promotion].[NewPrice],
    [p.Promotion].[PromotionalText]
FROM [Books] AS [p]
LEFT JOIN [PriceOffers] AS [p.Promotion]
ON [p].[BookId] = [p.Promotion].[BookId]
ORDER BY [p].[BookId] DESC
```

The time-out for the command. If the
command takes more than that time,
it's deemed to have failed.

SQL command that was
sent to the database

One LINQ database access command can produce multiple information logs like this, because EF Core may split your LINQ command into multiple SQL commands. For instance, the LINQ query `context.Books.Include(r => r.Reviews).First()` produces two information logs because EF Core knows that loading the `Book` entity and the `Reviews` collection separately is (normally) more efficient.

For those of you who are more aware of the SQL language, you can copy the SQL code from the logging output and run it in some form of query analyzer. Microsoft SQL Server Management Studio (SSMS) allows you to run a query and look at its execution plan, which tells you what each part of the query is made up of and the relative cost of each part. Other databases have a query analyzer, such as MySQL Query Analyzer and the PostgreSQL plprofiler.

12.2.4 Techniques for finding database scalability issues

In the introduction, I talked about the scalability of the application—the ability of the application to still feel fast even when it has a high load of users. Testing for scalability issues is much harder than finding speed issues, because it requires a test setup that can generate a lot of users all accessing the database at the same time.

For ASP.NET web applications, I've used the Apache HTTP server benchmarking tool, ab (https://httpd.apache.org/docs/2.4/programs/ab.html), to measure scalability. This tool can produce multiple HTTP requests at the same time, and measure how long the site takes to respond. I used ab to test a simple website, but I didn't get great results because I couldn't produce enough requests to overload the site (see this article I wrote on async/await and using ab: http://mng.bz/13b6).

Andrew Lock, the author of *ASP.NET Core in Action* (Manning, 2018), pointed me to the ASP.NET site on benchmarking, which recommends another load generation tool called wrt (https://github.com/aspnet/benchmarks#generating-load). The document also describes the system that the ASP.NET team built for benchmarking, which uses a series of powerful computers and a dedicated, high-bandwidth network.

Nowadays, the cloud seems to be the way to go for load testing. Many online load-testing tools are available that can (at a price) spin up multiple test instances to produce high levels of demand to your site.

12.3 Part 3—Techniques for fixing performance issues

The rest of this chapter provides a list of good and bad EF Core patterns for database access. These are here both to teach you what can help or hurt performance, and to act as a reference when hunting for database performance issues. This section consists of four parts:

- *Good EF Core patterns*—These look at "apply always" patterns that you might like to adopt. They aren't foolproof but give your application a good start.
- *Poor database patterns*—These are EF Core code *antipatterns*, or patterns you shouldn't adopt, because they tend to produce poor-performing SQL commands.

- *Poor software patterns*—These are EF Core code antipatterns that make your software run more slowly.
- *Scalability patterns*—These are techniques that help your database handle lots of database accesses.

Chapter 13 walks you through an example of the performance tuning approaches shown in this chapter. Chapter 13 starts with tuning the EF Core commands in your book app, but then goes into deeper techniques such as replacing EF Core code with direct SQL and changing the database structure to provide better performance.

12.4   *Using good patterns makes your application perform well*

Although I'm not a fan of early performance tuning, I do look at the performance aspects of any patterns I adopt. It's silly to create a pattern that's going to "bake in" poor performance right from the start. Many of the patterns and practices described in this book do have some effect on performance, or make performance tuning easier. Here's a list of the patterns that help with performance issues that I always apply right from the start of a project:

- Using `Select` loading to load only the columns you need
- Using paging and/or filtering of searches to reduce the rows you load
- A warning that using lazy loading will affect database performance
- Always adding the `AsNoTracking` method to read-only queries
- Using the async version of EF Core commands to improve scalability
- Ensuring that your database access code is isolated/decoupled, so it's ready for performance tuning

12.4.1   *Using Select loading to load only the columns you need*

In section 2.4, you learned about the three ways of loading related data, one of which was to use the LINQ `Select` command. For database queries that require information from multiple tables, the `Select` method often provides the most efficient database access code for queries (see section 12.5.1 on minimizing database accesses). Figure 12.5 illustrates this process.

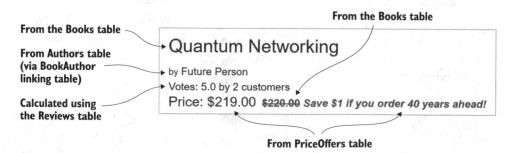

Figure 12.5   `Select` queries provide the best-performing database access, in which the final result consists of a mixture of columns from multiple tables.

Creating a `Select` query with a DTO does take more effort than using eager loading with the `Include` method (see section 2.4.1), but benefits exist beyond higher database access performance, such as reducing coupling between layers.

> **TIP** Section 10.3 describes how an object-to-object mapper, such as AutoMapper, can automate the building of a `Select` query for you, and thus speed up your development.

12.4.2 Using paging and/or filtering of searches to reduce the rows you load

Because EF Core's queries use LINQ commands, you can sometimes forget that one query can pull in thousands or millions of rows. A query that works fine on your development system, which might have only a few rows in a table, may then perform terribly on your production system that has a much larger set of data.

You need to apply commands that will limit the amount of data returned to the user. Typical approaches are as follows:

- *Paging*—You return a limited set of data to the user (say, 10 rows) and provide the user with commands to step through the "pages" of data (see section 2.7.3).
- *Filtering*—If you have a lot of data, a user will normally appreciate a search feature, which will return a subset of the data (see section 2.7.2).

Remember not to write open-ended queries, such as `context.Books.ToList()`, because you might be shocked when it runs on your production system, especially if you're writing code for Amazon's book site.

12.4.3 A warning that using lazy loading will affect database performance

Lazy loading (see the sidebar in section 2.4.3) is a technique that allows relationships to be loaded when read. This feature is in EF6.x, and now added to EF Core in version 2.1. The problem is, lazy loading has a detrimental effect on the performance of your database accesses, and after you've used lazy loading in your application, replacing it can require quite a bit of work.

This is one of the instances where you bake in poor performance, and you might regret it. When I understood the effects of lazy loading in EF6.x, I didn't use it anymore. Sure, it can make development easier in some cases, but each lazy load is going to add another database access. Considering that the first performance antipattern I list is "Not minimizing the number of calls to the database" (section 12.5.1), then if you have too many lazy loaded, your query is going to be slow.

> **NOTE** I've found that lazy loading is often used when a developer adopts a Repository pattern on top of EF Core. See my article about why this isn't best way to get good performance: http://mng.bz/5VH2.

12.4.4 Always adding the AsNoTracking method to read-only queries

If you're reading in entity classes directly and you aren't going to update them, including the `AsNoTracking` method in your query is worthwhile. It tells EF Core not to create a tracking snapshot of the entities loaded, which saves a bit of time and memory usage. This is an example of a query in which the `AsNoTracking` method, in bold, will improve performance.

Listing 12.4   Using the `AsNoTracking` method to improve the performance of a query

```
var result = context.Books            Returns a Book entity class and a
    .Include(r => r.Reviews)          collection of Review entity classes.
    .AsNoTracking()
    .ToList();                        Adding the AsNoTracking method tells
                                      EF Core not to create a tracking snapshot,
                                      which saves time and memory usage.
```

If you use a `Select` query in which the result maps to a DTO, and that DTO doesn't contain any entity classes, you don't need to add the `AsNoTracking` method. But if your DTO contains an entity class inside it, adding the `AsNoTracking` method will help.

12.4.5 Using the async version of EF Core commands to improve scalability

Microsoft's recommended practice for ASP.NET applications is to use async commands wherever possible (section 5.10 explains async/await). This improves the scalability of your website by releasing a thread while the command is waiting for the database to respond; this freed-up thread can run another user's request.

Although I agree with Microsoft's blanket "Use async everywhere" statement, a more case-by-case use of the async database commands may be correct in some circumstances for performance-critical systems. Section 12.7.2 covers this in more detail, as you learn about the trade-offs between async's scalability versus its speed.

12.4.6 Ensuring that your database access code is isolated/decoupled

As I said earlier, I recommend that you get your EF Core code working first, without any performance tuning—but you should be ready to make that code faster if you need to later. To achieve this, the code must

- *Be in a clearly defined place (isolated).* This allows you to find the database code that's affecting performance.
- *Contain only the database access code (decoupled).* My advice is to not mix your database access code with other parts of the application, such as the UI or API. That way, your database access code can be changed without worrying about other, nondatabase issues.

Throughout this book, you've seen lots of examples of this approach. Chapter 2 introduced the Query Object pattern (see section 2.6.1), and chapter 4 showed the use of a separate project to hold the database access code for the business logic (see section 4.4.4). These patterns make performance tuning your database access code easier, as you have a clearly defined section of code to work on.

12.5 Performance antipatterns—database access

The previous patterns are ones that are worth using all the time, but you'll still bump into issues requiring you to tune up your LINQ. EF doesn't always produce the best-performing SQL commands: sometimes it's because EF didn't come up with a good SQL translation, and sometimes it's because the LINQ code you wrote isn't as efficient as you thought it was.

This section presents some of the performance antipatterns that affect the time it takes to get data to/from the database. I use the negative antipattern terms, as that's what you're looking for—places where the code can be improved. Here's a list of potential problems, followed by how to fix them, with the ones you're more likely to hit coming first:

- Not minimizing the number of calls to the database
- Calling `SaveChanges` multiple times
- Allowing too much of a data query to be moved into the software side
- Not replacing suboptimal SQL translations with user-defined functions
- Not precompiling queries that are used frequently
- Expecting EF Core to build the best SQL database commands
- Not using the `Find` method when the entity might be already loaded
- Missing indexes from a property that you want to search on
- Mismatching column data types

12.5.1 Not minimizing the number of calls to the database

If you're reading an entity from the database with its related data, you have four ways of loading that data: eager loading, explicit loading, select loading, and lazy loading (lazy loading was introduced in EF Core 2.1). Although they all achieve the same result, their performance differs quite a lot. The main difference comes down to the number of separate database accesses they make; the more separate database accesses you do, the longer your database access will take.

You'll build a test to use eager loading, explicit loading, and select loading to load the `Book` entity class and all its relationships. Table 12.1 shows the number of SQL commands, the number of database accesses, the time the access took, and the percentage difference from the eager-loading time.

Table 12.1   Comparing relationship-loading techniques—the more database accesses, the longer your code takes to finish

Three ways of loading data with their relationships	Number of SQL commands	Number of DB accesses	Time (ms)/%
Select loading, for example: `Books.Select(p=>new {x.BookId...`	4	1	3.4 ms/80%
Eager loading, for example: `Books.Include(p => p.Reviews)`	3	1	4.3 ms/100%
Explicit loading, for example: `Collection(c=>c.Reviews).Load()`	6	6	**29.2 ms/680%**

The table speaks for itself: multiple accesses to the database cost. In the explicit-loading case (item 3 in the table), the database access code does six database accesses and is over six times slower than the other two approaches, which use only one database access.

So, the rule is, try to create one LINQ query that gets all the data you need in one go. Select queries are the best performing if you need only specific properties; otherwise, eager loading, with its Include method, is better if you want the entity with its relationships.

NOTE   In a performance issue called the *N + 1 query problem*, one query that returns a collection of *N* items produces a single database query, followed by *N* extra queries—one for each item. EF Core suffers with this issue when using a Select query that contains a collection, as you'll see in section 13.2. This has been improved in EF Core 2.1 (see https://github.com/aspnet/EntityFrameworkCore/issues/9282).

12.5.2   Calling SaveChanges multiple times

If you have lots of information to add to the database, you have two options:

1   *Add one entity and call* SaveChanges. For example, if you're saving 10 entities, you call the Add method followed by a call to the SaveChanges method, 10 times.

2   *Add all the entity instances and call* SaveChanges *at the end.* For example, to save 10 entities, call Add 10 times (or even better, one call to AddRange) followed by one call to SaveChanges at the end.

Option 2, in which you call SaveChanges only once, is a lot faster, as you can see in table 12.2. This is because EF Core will "batch" multiple data writes on database servers that allow this approach, such as SQL Server. This means it'll generate SQL code that's more efficient at writing multiple items to the database. Table 12.2 shows the difference in time for the two ways of writing out 100 new entities to an SQL Server database on my development system.

Table 12.2. A comparison of calling `SaveChanges` after adding each entity, and adding all the entities and then calling `SaveChanges` at the end. Calling `SaveChanges` at the end is about four to six times faster.

One at a time	All at once (batched on an SQL Server)

```for (int i = 0; i < 100; i++)```
```{```
   ```context.Add(new MyEntity());```
   ```context.SaveChanges();```
```}```
	```for (int i = 0; i < 100; i++)```
	```{```
	   ```context.Add(new MyEntity());```
	```}```
	```context.SaveChanges();```

Total time = 160 ms (±40 ms)	Total time = 30 ms (±15 ms)

NOTE One reviewer commented that there was a huge variation in the results I show. Well, welcome to the problem of performance measurement and tuning! My experience is that getting good software performance figures takes effort. In my performance tests, I normally measure one try, followed by multiple tries. I also run the tests multiple times to see if there's much variation; in this case, there was a lot of variation.

The difference between the two ways of saving multiple entities is large: calling `SaveChanges` every time (left side) is four to six times slower than calling `SaveChanges` once (right side). This batching capability applies to inserting, updating, and deleting data in the database. For a more detailed look at this this, see http://mng.bz/ksHg.

NOTE It's also not good practice to call `SaveChanges` after each change, because what happens if something goes wrong halfway through? The recommendation is to do all your additions, updates, and removals and then call `SaveChanges` at the end. That way, you know that either all your changes were applied to the database, or, if there was an error, none of the changes will have been applied to the database.

12.5.3 Allowing too much of a data query to be moved into the software side

It's all too easy to write LINQ code that will move part of the database evaluation out of the database and into the software, often with a big impact on performance. Let's start with a simple example.

Listing 12.5 Two LINQ commands that would have different performance times

```
context.Books.Where(p => p.Price > 40).ToList();
context.Books.ToList().Where(p => p.Price > 40);
```

This query would perform well, as the Where part would be executed in the database.

This query would perform badly, as all the books would be returned (which takes time), and then the Where part would be executed in software.

Although most people would immediately spot the mistake in listing 12.5, it's possible for code like this to be hidden in some way. In particular, the *client vs. server evaluation* feature (see section 2.5) makes it much easier to write code that calls software-only methods, such as `string.Join`, `ToString`, and so on, that then moves part of the query into the software. Mostly, this has little effect on performance, as it's applied to the returned data, but sometimes it'll affect performance, possibly badly.

For example, the query in listing 12.6 uses `string.Join` to concatenate all the authors into a comma-delimited string called `AuthorsString`. That's fine, as that can be done when all the data is returned (see figure 2.7). But you then use that `AuthorsString` property to order the books returned from the database, which hits the performance of this query.

Listing 12.6   An example of a poor-performing client vs. server evaluation

```
var books = context.Books
    .Select(p => new
    {
        p.BookId,
        p.Title,
        AuthorsString = string.Join(", ",
            p.AuthorsLink
            .OrderBy(q => q.Order)
            .Select(q => q.Author.Name)),
    }
    ).OrderBy(p => p.AuthorsString).ToList();
```

> `string.Join` isn't translated into SQL by EF Core, so this must be evaluated in software after the data is returned from the database.

> You ask for the data to be sorted by a value that's created in software, so EF Core calculates that value and then rereads the database to execute the OrderBy command.

The result of running this code is that EF Core produces SQL code that reads all the books, and then reads each row individually, twice—definitely not an optimal database access!

Thankfully, this is one of the situations in which EF Core will log a `QueryClientEvaluationWarning` warning (see section 12.2.3). This means you should be able to spot this type of problem. The solution is to change your code to remove this sort of problem, or use a user-defined function (see next section) or other raw SQL commands to move the calculation into the database.

12.5.4   *Not replacing suboptimal SQL translations with user-defined functions*

Section 12.2.3 already talked about a suboptimal translation of LINQ to SQL; in version 1 of EF Core, the LINQ `Average` method doesn't get translated into an SQL `AVG` command. In that sort of case, you'll get a `QueryClientEvaluationWarning` warning, but what can you do about it?

One way around this problem is to create an SQL *user-defined function* (UDF) containing the optimal SQL code, and then include that in your query. This requires an understanding of the SQL language and extra work to add the UDF to the database, but it does allow you to get around any suboptimal SQL that EF Core produces.

Although the translation of LINQ `Average` to SQL `AVG` is fixed in version 2 of EF, it's still a helpful example of the process of replacing suboptimal SQL translations, so I use it in listings 12.7 and 12.8. This replaces the suboptimal SQL code by providing a UDF to work out the average review votes that uses the optimal SQL command, `AVG`.

The following listing shows the SQL change script that can add a UDF to your database (see section 11.5.2 with listings 11.4 and 11.5 on how to add an SQL command to a database schema change). This contains the code to calculate the average of the review votes.

Listing 12.7   SQL change script with a UDF containing optimal code for averaging

```
CREATE FUNCTION udf_AverageVotes (@id int)        udf_AverageVotes takes the primary key of
RETURNS float                                      the FixSubOptimalSql entity referenced by
AS                                                 the Ch12Reviews' foreign key.
BEGIN
DECLARE @result AS float
SELECT @result = AVG(CAST([NumStars] AS float))
    FROM dbo.Ch12Review AS r
    WHERE @bookId = r.Ch12BookId
RETURN @result            Returns the result, which can be
END                       null if no Ch12Reviews are linked
                          to the FixSubOptimalSql entity
```

Here you use the SQL command AVG, which is the optimal SQL command for this.

You then use this UDF in a computed column called `AverageVotes`, which you add to the `Ch12Book` entity class. When the `AverageVotes` is read by EF Core, the computed column is executed, and calls the `udf_AverageVotes` UDF to calculate the average within the SQL database. The configuration to set this up is shown next. (See section 8.3 for more on computed columns.)

Listing 12.8   Configuring a computed column to call the `udf_AverageVotes` UDF

```
protected override void OnModelCreating
    (ModelBuilder modelBuilder)
{
    modelBuilder.Entity<Ch12Book>()         The AverageVotes column will contain
        .Property(p => p.AverageVotes)      the computed value when it's loaded.
        .HasComputedColumnSql(
            "dbo.udf_AverageVotes([Ch12BookId])");
}
                                            udf_AverageVotes UDF takes an input of the
udf_AverageVotes UDF must be in the database  primary key of the Ch12Book entity class.
before this HasComputedColumnSql configuration
method is called.
```

NOTE   There are other ways to get around this problem, and chapter 13 shows two alternatives.

12.5.5 *Not precompiling queries that are used frequently*

When you first use an EF Core query, it's compiled and cached, so if it's used again, the compiled query can be found in the cache, which saves compiling the query again. But there's a cost to this cache lookup, which the EF Core method `EF.CompiledQuery` can bypass.

The `EF.CompiledQuery` method allows you to hold the compiled query in a static variable, which removes the cache lookup part.

Listing 12.9   Creating a compiled query and holding it in a static variable

```
private static Func<EfCoreContext, int, Book>
    _compiledQuerySimple =
    EF.CompileQuery(
        (EfCoreContext context, int i) =>
        context.Books
            .Skip(i)
            .First()
    );
```

You define a static function to hold your compiled query. In this case, the function with two inputs and the type of the returned query.

You define the query to hold as compiled.

Expects a DbContext, one or two parameters to use in your query, and the returned result, either an entity class or IEnumerable<TEntity>.

Compiling a query in this way has limitations. First, the query returns a class, or an `IEnumerable<T>` result, so you can't chain query objects as you've done in the book query in chapter 2. Second, the query can't be dynamic; the LINQ commands provided to the `EF.CompiledQuery` method can't change. In chapter 2, for example, you built a book filter query object that dynamically chose whether to filter on votes, publication date, or no filter; that wouldn't work in a compiled query.

The `EF.CompiledQuery` method is for taking a specific query and compiling it. In the case of the book query, you'd need to build a separate compiled query for each filter and sort option to allow each one to be compiled; for instance:

- Query books, no filter, no sort
- Query books, filter on votes, no sort
- Query books, filter on votes, sort on votes
- Query books, filter on votes, soft on publication date

So, the `EF.CompiledQuery` method is useful, but it's best to apply it when the query you want to performance tune is stable. This is because it may take some work to reformat your query into the correct form to fit the `EF.CompiledQuery` method.

12.5.6 *Expecting EF Core to build the best SQL database commands*

EF Core makes development quick and easy, and for simple queries, EF Core generates quite efficient SQL commands. But in some cases it won't create the best SQL and you might need to replace it with hand-coded SQL commands sent to the database by the ADO.NET or Dapper libraries. Three things could hit performance:

- Is your LINQ code efficient? There are often many ways to write a LINQ query, but some will perform better than others on the database. Chapter 3 shows one such case, in which you can update a relationship via the principal entity in section 3.4.3, but I then show you a quicker way using foreign keys in section 3.5.4.
- EF Core doesn't always produce the SQL commands that take advantage of all the features of a particular database type. EF Core's translation of LINQ queries, which uses a calculated property in two places, isn't optimal for SQL Server. For instance, the code in this listing calculates the ReviewCount property twice.

Listing 12.10 An example of using a calculated value twice in an EF Core query

```
var books = context.Books.Select(b => new
    {
        b.BookId,
        ReviewCount = b.Reviews.Count
    }).OrderBy(x => x.ReviewCount)
    .ToList();
```

Calculates the number of reviews

Recalculates the number of reviews again for the OrderBy.

It's possible to create an SQL command that would produce the same output as listing 12.10, but would calculate the ReviewCount only once. This SQL command would be quicker than EF Core's version at the time of writing (version 2.0).

- EF Core has software-side performance issues also. It takes longer than the Dapper library to create and fill an entity class instance when reading in data. These software-side issues are much smaller than any suboptimal SQL-related issues, but they can add up in certain situations.

NOTE Chapter 13 provides a worked example of progressively improving the main book listing query to show what can be done to improve or replace EF Core commands.

12.5.7 *Not using the Find method when an entity might be already loaded*

The EF Core Find method finds and loads an entity based on its primary key. For instance, context.Find<Book>(1) loads the Book entity instance whose primary key is 1. The special feature of the Find method is if the entity is already loaded into the context, then it's returned without querying the database. This makes the Find method much faster when the entity might already be loaded.

Therefore, it's worth using the Find method anytime you need to find/load an entity by using its primary key. The only downside is that you can't use eager loading; use the Include method to load a relationship when using the Find method.

12.5.8 *Missing indexes from a property that you want to search on*

If you plan to search a large amount of data on a property that isn't a key (EF Core adds an index automatically to primary, foreign, or alternate keys), adding an index to that property will improve the search and sort performance. It's easy to add an index to a property; see section 6.9.

There's a performance cost to having an index on a property, especially if the data is changed a lot, as the database must update the index. Indexes work best for tables that don't change much and have many rows.

12.5.9 *Mismatching column data types*

If the type that EF Core has for a table column differs from the actual column type, you won't get an error under some circumstances; instead, the database server will translate the data between the two types, but at a performance cost. This shouldn't happen if you follow the recommended ways of creating and updating a database's schema, covered in chapter 12. But if it does happen, it can be a difficult performance problem to find.

I've never had this problem, but Ben Emmett of Redgate has a detailed description of what happens if a NVARCHAR/VARCHAR type difference exists between EF Core's database model and the actual database schema. See the "Mismatched data types" section in his article at http://mng.bz/H2rR. (Ben's article is about performance tuning EF6.x, so many of his other performance comments don't apply to EF Core.)

12.6 *Performance antipatterns—software*

Now that you've learned about performance antipatterns that apply to the database, let's look at performance antipatterns that apply to the software side. These performance issues take more compute time to run than they need to, thus they slow your application. I've listed the problems with the most likely one first:

- Making DetectChanges work too hard
- Startup issue: using one large DbContext

12.6.1 *Making DetectChanges work too hard*

Every time you call SaveChanges, it runs by default a method inside your application's DbContext called DetectChanges to see whether any of the tracked entities have been updated (see section 9.3.3 for more details). The time DetectChanges takes to run depends on how many tracked entities are loaded—the number of entities that you read in without the AsNoTracking method and that don't implement the INotifyPropertyChanged interface (see section 9.3.4).

If you read 1,000 tracked entities and call SaveChanges, the DetectChanges method would need to check all 1,000 entities to find whether any have changed. That can take some time; one of the unit tests in chapter 9 showed that calling `SaveChanges` with 1,000 `Book` entities, with their `Review` and `Author` entity relationships, took over 2 seconds to run.

This sort of problem has various solutions, depending on the design of your application. Here are ways to solve this sort of performance issue:

- Do you need all these tracked entities loaded? If `SaveChanges` is taking a long time, did you forget to use the `AsNoTracking` method when you read all the entities?

- Can you break up a big insert into smaller batches? I did this in chapter 13 where I built a class to create large test data sets for performance tests. My initial implementation took 7 minutes for 100,000 books, but by splitting up the database write into multiple writes of small groups of <500 books, then the time came down to 2 minutes.

- When you need a lot of entities loaded that are ready to be modified, consider changing your entity classes over to using the `INotifyPropertyChanged` change tracking strategy. This requires extra coding of your entity classes to add the `INotifyPropertyChanged` and configure the entity class's change tracking strategy (see section 9.34). The result is that your entities will report any changes to EF Core and `DetectChanges` doesn't have to scan your loaded entities for changes.

12.6.2 *Startup issue: using one large DbContext*

The first time you create your application's DbContext, it'll take some time, maybe several seconds. There are many reasons for this, but part of it is that EF Core needs to scan all the entity classes in the application's DbContext to configure itself and build a model of the database you want to access. Normally, this isn't a big problem, because after your application is running, the configuration and database model information is cached by EF Core. But if your application is constantly being started and stopped—say, in a serverless architecture (see https://martinfowler.com/articles/serverless.html)—this startup time could matter.

You can help speed up the building of the first application's DbContext by reducing the number of entity classes it includes. The only reasonable way to do that is to produce multiple application DbContexts, with each one covering a subset of the tables in the database. Section 10.6 covered splitting a database across multiple DbContexts based on the DDD approach of *bounded contexts*. Figure 12.6 shows a cut-down version of this diagram, illustrating how a large database could be split across multiple applications' DbContexts.

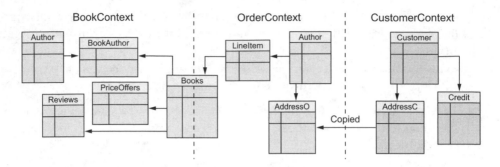

Figure 12.6   A large database can be split into multiple applications' DbContexts. In this case, the database is split along business lines. If you need to minimize application startup costs, you could create specific DbContexts for each application that contain only the entities that application needs to access.

Figure 12.6 splits the database across different applications' DbContexts based on the *business domains*, which might be an appropriate split for some applications. If you're building small, self-contained applications, such as in a serverless architecture or a microservices architecture (see https://martinfowler.com/articles/microservices.html), you could build an application's DbContext, including only the entities/tables specific to each application.

12.7   *Performance patterns—scalability of database accesses*

Scalability of an application (the number of simultaneous accesses that the application can handle) is a big topic. Even when limiting the scope to database access scalability, you still have a lot of things to think about. Scalability issues can't typically be tracked down to a poorly written piece of code, because scalability is more about design. This section covers

- Using pooling to reduce the cost of creating a new application's DbContext
- Using async/await to aid scalability, but with little effect on overall speed
- Helping your database scalability by making your queries as simple as possible
- Picking the right architecture for applications that need high scalability

12.7.1   *Using pooling to reduce the cost of a new application's DbContext*

If you're building an ASP.NET Core application, EF Core provides a method called `AddDbContextPool<T>` that replaces the normal `AddDbContext<T>` method. The `AddDbContextPool<T>` method uses an internal pool of an application's DbContext instances, which it can reuse. This speeds up your application's response time in cases where you have lots of short requests.

This is simple to use, and this listing shows an updated registration of the `EfCoreContext` context in the book app.

Listing 12.11   Using `AddDbContextPool` to register the application's DbContext

You're using an SQL Server database, but pooling works with any database provider.

You register your application DbContext by using the AddDbContextPool<T>.

```
services.AddDbContextPool<EfCoreContext>(
    options => options.UseSqlServer(connection,
    b => b.MigrationsAssembly("DataLayer")));
```

Because you're using migrations in a layered architecture, you need to tell the database provider which assembly the migration code is in.

Whether it makes a significant difference to the scalability of your application depends on the type of concurrent traffic you have. But you should get at least a small improvement in speed, as the `AddDbContextPool<T>` method will be quicker at returning a fresh application's DbContext instances.

12.7.2 Async/await—adding scalability, with small effect on speed

In section 12.4.5, I said you should use the async versions of the database access methods in an application that must handle multiple simultaneous requests. This is because async/await releases a thread to allow other requests to be handled while the async part is waiting for the database to respond (see figure 5.7). But using an async method instead of the normal, synchronous method does add a small overhead to each call. Table 12.3 gives performance figures for a few types of database access.

Table 12.3   Performance for types of database access of the normal, sync version, and async version on a database containing 1,000 books. Sync and async times are in milliseconds.

Type of database access	DB trips	Sync	Async	Async/sync%
Read book: book only, simple load	1	0.14	0.47	236%
Read book: eager-load book and relationships	3	1.38	3.76	172%
Read book: explicit-load book and relationships	6	54.00	53.00	-2%
Read book: book only, sort, filter, and take	1	1.72	1.95	13%

From this table, you can make the following observations:

- If the SQL database command is simple, and therefore quick (see the first entry in the table), using async/await costs a lot. The async method doesn't give you much back in scalability, as the command is quick, and the cost of async/await is high compared to the short time the command takes. But it's a quick command, so if it's async, it's not the end of the world.

- If the SQL database command is complex and takes some time, using async/await is worth it. You gain a thread for all the time you're waiting for the database, and the cost of async/await is small in comparison to the database wait.

NOTE   I wrote an article some time ago covering async/await and its features, scalability, and speed issues in more detail. You can find it at http://mng.bz/13b6.

12.7.3 *Helping your database scalability by making your queries simple*

Creating SQL commands that have a low "cost" on the database server (meaning, are easy to execute and return a minimal amount of data) minimizes the load on the database. Performance tuning your key queries to be simple and return only the data needed, not only improves the speed of your application, but also helps with the scalability of your database.

12.7.4 *Picking the right architecture for applications that need high scalability*

Section 5.2 detailed how a web application can have multiple instances to provide more scalability. That's helpful for the software/compute performance, but if all the web application instances are accessing just one database, then it doesn't necessarily help the database scalability.

Although software/compute performance is normally the bottleneck on scalability, for applications that make high demands on the database, extra instances of the web application won't help much. At this point, you need to be thinking about other architectures. This topic is beyond the scope of this book, but I recommend you look at architectures that split the read-only database accesses from the write database access, such as the CQRS architecture.

Because most applications read the database more than they write to the database, the CQRS architecture can help with database performance. In addition, by splitting out the read-only queries to a NoSQL database, you can make the replication of the read-only databases easier, which gives you more database bandwidth. I implement just such an architecture using a CQRS approach in section 14.4, with impressive performance gains.

Summary

- Don't performance tune too early; get your application to work properly first. But try to design your application so that if you need to performance tune later, it's easier to find and fix your database code.
- Performance tuning isn't free, so you need to decide what performance issues are worth the development effort to fix.

- EF Core's logger output can help you identify database access code that has performance issues.
- Make sure any standard patterns or techniques you use in writing your application perform well. Otherwise, you'll "bake in" performance issues from day one.
- Avoid, or fix, any database performance antipatterns (database accesses that don't perform well).
- If scalability is an issue, try simple improvements, but high scalability may need a fundamental rethinking of the application's architecture.

For readers who are familiar with EF6:

- Some of the EF6.x performance issues, such as using the `AddRange` method over repeated `Add` method calls, have been fixed.
- Some performance tweaks in EF6.x have been lost. In EF Core 2.0, the LINQ `GroupBy` method doesn't convert into an SQL `GROUP BY` command, but this is available in version 2.1.
- EF Core has new, potential performance problems, such as the client vs. server evaluation feature, allowing you to produce nonoptimal SQL code.

A worked example
of performance tuning

This chapter covers

- Ensuring that your LINQ query translates into good SQL
- Using EF Core's DbFunction to improve a query
- Building high-performance queries via raw SQL
- Using cached values to improve performance
- Trading development effort for performance gains

Section 12.1.2 showed that the book list query needs to have great performance, so this chapter is about performance-tuning that query. The query has already avoided nearly all the performance issues mentioned in chapter 12, so you must go beyond the normal changes to make any further improvements. This chapter takes you through a series of performance-tuning steps, starting with EF Core–focused approaches and then branching out to more-extreme changes to get the best performance possible.

The aim is to show you how to tackle performance-tuning an application, and the amount of effort needed to get that next level in performance. You may never need some of the extreme performance-tuning techniques covered here, but at least you'll know that better performance is possible if you need it.

This chapter is divided into four distinct parts for improving the performance of the book list query:

- Working with EF Core–built queries
- Part 1a— Making sure a single query performs as well as possible
- Part 1b—Performance-tuning the existing EF Core query by adding a DbFunction
- Part 2—Replacing the EF Core book query code with a SQL-based OR/M called Dapper
- Part 3—Changing the database structure to make it easier for EF Core to query it

At the end of this chapter, you'll look at the scalability issue: the number of concurrent users your website can handle. You'll also learn about a different database architecture that provides better scalability.

Because your performance issues will be different from the ones found in the book app, parts 1a to 3 cover generic issues, such as making sure your query is translated properly, or what to do if you want to write your own SQL. At the end of each part, I give you performance-tuning takeaways that might help when you need to make your own application run faster.

13.1 *Part 1a—Making sure a single query performs well*

In this part, you're going to do all you can to get the book app's list query running as fast as possible, while still using EF Core for the query. As you'll see, EF Core can produce excellent SQL code if you write LINQ queries in the correct form for EF Core. It's also true that EF Core can produce terrible SQL code if you don't write your LINQ queries with EF Core and the database in mind.

Your starting point is the book list query described in chapter 2. This query already has most of the features I recommended in chapter 12: using a `Select` query, minimizing database accesses, paging to minimize the data loaded, and so on. It turns out that most things perform well, although you do have one issue that highlights a generic problem—see section 13.1.2. But first, let's see the challenges involved in displaying one book.

13.1.1 *Analyzing the book list query to see potential performance issues*

First, you want to ensure that displaying the information on one book is fast. Some items, such as the book title, are straightforward, but as you can see in figure 13.1, parts of the book information take a bit more time to calculate. The aim of this section is to ensure that they're as fast as they can be, just using EF Core.

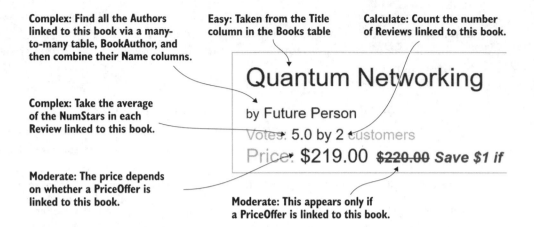

Complex: Find all the Authors linked to this book via a many-to-many table, BookAuthor, and then combine their Name columns.

Easy: Taken from the Title column in the Books table

Calculate: Count the number of Reviews linked to this book.

Complex: Take the average of the NumStars in each Review linked to this book.

Moderate: The price depends on whether a PriceOffer is linked to this book.

Moderate: This appears only if a PriceOffer is linked to this book.

Figure 13.1   The level of difficulty in displaying each part of one single book listing. As you can see, all but one of the displayed data items need some form of calculation to get the right value.

To create the book list display, you created a class called `BookListDto`, which contains all the elements needed for display. In section 2.6.1, you created the `BookListDto` class as well as the `MapBookToDto` method that contains the LINQ commands to fill in that class. The following listing shows the code in the `MapBookToDto` method, the starting point for our performance tuning.

Listing 13.1   The `MapBookToDto` method that fills the `BookListDto` class

```
public static IQueryable<BookListDto>
    MapBookToDto(this IQueryable<Book> books)
{
    return books.Select(p => new BookListDto
    {
        BookId = p.BookId,
        Title = p.Title,
        Price = p.Price,
        PublishedOn = p.PublishedOn,
        ActualPrice = p.Promotion == null
                ? p.Price
                : p.Promotion.NewPrice,
        PromotionPromotionalText =
                p.Promotion == null
                    ? null
                    : p.Promotion.PromotionalText,
        AuthorNamesOrdered = p.AuthorsLink
            .OrderBy(q => q.Order)
            .Select(q => q.Author.Name),
        ReviewsCount = p.Reviews.Count,
        ReviewsAverageVotes =
            p.Reviews.Select(y => (double?)y.NumStars).Average()
    });
}
```

It took me some time to get the LINQ in the `MapBookToDto` method right, and in this part and part 1b I'll talk you through the problems I had. Hopefully, knowing the process I went through will help you tackle any problems of your own. Let's start with the problem of client-side calculations.

13.1.2 *Turning the book's Votes display into a client-side calculation*

I always knew that calculating the average of all the customer reviews for a book was going to be a challenge. I also knew that SQL has a handy `AVG` command that would help a lot with performance. My problem was writing the LINQ code such that EF Core would properly translate my use of the LINQ's `Average` method into the SQL `AVG` command. That turned out to be a challenge.

First, let me explain that any part of a LINQ sequence that EF Core can't properly translate into SQL will, by default, be converted to a client-side calculation by using the client vs. server evaluation feature (see section 2.5). This feature is great for quick development, because it'll make almost any valid LINQ query work. But when it comes to performance, having that client vs. server evaluation run part of your query in software instead of in the database can be bad news for performance!

> **EF6** If you produced LINQ code that couldn't be translated into SQL when using EF6.x, it threw an exception. EF Core is much more tolerant, and, via the client vs. server evaluation feature, it'll handle LINQ queries that EF6.x wouldn't touch.

Table 13.1 shows my attempts to get the correct format for the LINQ, with indicating that it didn't translate to the SQL AVG command, and indicating that it did. It took me a while to get this right, and I got the correct answer only by raising an issue on the EF Core GitHub issues page. (Thanks to Andrew Peters on the EF Core team for providing the right answer.)

Table 13.1 My attempts at getting the right LINQ code for calling the SQL AVG command

LINQ code	OK?
`double? AveVotes = b.Reviews.Select(y => y.NumStars).Average();`	✗
`double? AveVotes = b.Reviews.Count == 0 ? null :` `    (double?)b.Reviews.Select(y => y.NumStars).Average();`	✗
`double? AveVotes = b.Reviews.Select(y =>` `    (double?)y.NumStars).Average()`	✔

After I was shown the right format, it made sense, but I didn't see it immediately! The first two examples in table 13.1 end up as client vs. server evaluations, which are slow. Only the last row has the correct form for the LINQ query to be translated into the following SQL code:

```
SELECT AVG(CAST([y].[NumStars] AS float))
FROM [Review] AS [y]
WHERE [b].[BookId] = [y].[BookId]
```

How I measured the performance—my test environment

Throughout this chapter, I'll show you timing, in milliseconds, and here I'll explain how I got these figures. I followed my own advice in section 12.2.1 by concentrating on what the user experiences. Therefore, my timings were taken by using the Chrome browser (see figure 12.4) from the running book app. I took multiple readings and show the average of those readings.

I did all my testing on my development PC, using the book app running in debug mode. This ASP.NET Core application had only in-memory logging, but also had application insights running, which slows the overall application. For comparison, accessing the About page, which has no database accesses in it, typically takes 11 ms to load, so the database accesses are always going to be slower than that.

Note also that the 10-book display includes about 3 ms of sending the HTML to my browser (called *content download* by Chrome), whereas the 100-book display includes somewhere between 15 to 18 ms of sending HTML to my browser. It still affects the user, but it's not something that EF Core can do anything about. These content download overheads are included in all the 10-book and 100-book performance figures in this chapter. I recommend Alan Hume's *Progressive Web Apps* (Manning, 2017) on reducing the content download overheads.

The effect of getting the correct translation of LINQ into SQL is significant, as you can see in table 13.2.

Table 13.2   Comparing the performance of client vs. server evaluation of the average votes with SQL's AVG command

How the average review values were calculated	10 books	100 books
Average review votes evaluated client-side, in software via client vs. server evaluation	64 ms	410 ms
Average review votes evaluated server-side, in the database using SQL AVG command	54 ms	230 ms
How much faster SQL AVG is over client vs. server	15%	40%

Getting the SQL right for calculating the average votes has an even more massive effect on sorting or filtering of books based on average votes—think about how slow it would be to calculate in software the average votes of 100,000 books!

The takeaways from this example are twofold:

- You should check your logs for the `QueryClientEvaluationWarning` warning, which says that the client vs. server evaluation has moved a part of your query to the client-side (software). An alternative is to get EF Core to raise an exception if `QueryClientEvaluationWarning` is logged.
- Even knowing that part of your LINQ code is being run client-side, finding the right form can still take some effort. But it's worth the effort.

TIP I recommend not configuring your application to throw an exception on poor SQL translations, as a slow application is often better than a broken application. I do enable the throwing of an exception on `QueryClientEvaluationWarning` in my unit tests. See section 15.8.

13.2 Part 1b—Improving the query by adding a DbFunction

You need to create a comma-delimited list of the authors' names to show in the book list display. To form this combined name, EF Core must pick out the `Name` property from each `Author` entity class that's linked to the `Book` entity via the many-to-many `BookAuthor` entity class. See figure 13.2 for a view of the database and the actions needed to form the combined authors string.

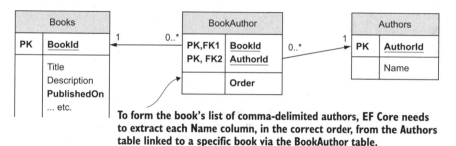

To form the book's list of comma-delimited authors, EF Core needs to extract each Name column, in the correct order, from the Authors table linked to a specific book via the BookAuthor table.

Figure 13.2 The many-to-many relationship between a `Book` **and an** `Author`**. To generate the list of authors of a book, you have to extract the** `Name` **property from each** `Author` **class in the order defined by the** `Order` **property in the BookAuthor linking table.**

EF Core produces an efficient piece of SQL code to do this, but it returns the resultant collections as a separate database access (each individual collection is returned as a separate database access). This is known as the *N + 1 query problem*, which I note in section 12.5.1. This particular performance issue is fixed in EF Core 2.1, but uses two database accesses in this case. The solution you'll use in this section executes the query using only one database access.

We know that not minimizing the calls to the database is the top issue in database performance antipatterns (see section 12.5.1). So, you need to reduce the number of database accesses required to produce the list of authors of a book in order to improve performance. EF Core 2.1's improvement to the *N + 1* query problem would go a long way to fixing this particular problem, but the approach you use in this section can be used in other cases where you need to inject your own custom SQL into an existing LINQ query.

In this case, you know something that EF Core doesn't know—that you want to concatenate the names into a comma-delimited string—and it turns out you can do that concatenation in the database. You can return a single string in the main query, thus removing all the extra database accesses EF Core needs to return the collections. As you'll see, this makes a significant difference in the performance of displaying multiple books.

To achieve this, you need to insert your own piece of SQL into EF Core's SQL. The easiest way to do this is by using an SQL UDF to find and combine the authors' names. The code for the UDF, called `AuthorsStringUdf`, is here.

Listing 13.2   `AuthorsStringUdf` **SQL code for combining authors' names**

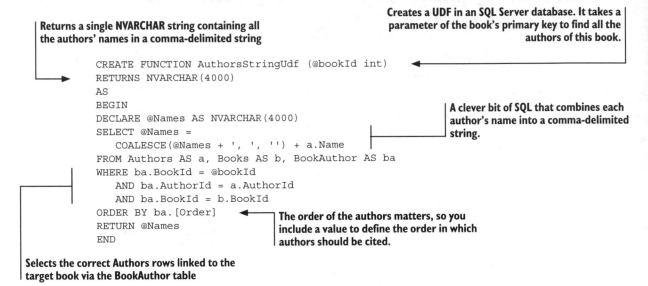

Returns a single NVARCHAR string containing all the authors' names in a comma-delimited string

Creates a UDF in an SQL Server database. It takes a parameter of the book's primary key to find all the authors of this book.

```
CREATE FUNCTION AuthorsStringUdf (@bookId int)
RETURNS NVARCHAR(4000)
AS
BEGIN
DECLARE @Names AS NVARCHAR(4000)
SELECT @Names =
    COALESCE(@Names + ', ', '') + a.Name
FROM Authors AS a, Books AS b, BookAuthor AS ba
WHERE ba.BookId = @bookId
    AND ba.AuthorId = a.AuthorId
    AND ba.BookId = b.BookId
ORDER BY ba.[Order]
RETURN @Names
END
```

A clever bit of SQL that combines each author's name into a comma-delimited string.

The order of the authors matters, so you include a value to define the order in which authors should be cited.

Selects the correct Authors rows linked to the target book via the BookAuthor table

Thanks to Stack Overflow for the tip about combining each author's name into a comma-delimited string (https://stackoverflow.com/a/194887/1434764).

NOTE   You need to add this UDF into your database for this to work. Chapter 11 explores the whole area of including SQL in your database migrations.

To use this UDF, you need to register it with EF Core, and the DbFunction described in section 8.2 is the best way to do this. You then alter your `BookListDtoSelect` query object to call this UDF instead of the client vs. server code shown in section 2.5.1. This listing shows the new code in bold.

Listing 13.3   Modified `MapBookToDto` **method showing how the UDF is called**

```
public static IQueryable<BookListDto>
    MapBookToDto(this IQueryable<Book> books)
{
    return books.Select(p => new BookListDto
    {
        BookId = p.BookId,
        //… other property setting removed for clarity
        AuthorsOrdered =
            UdfDefinitions.AuthorsStringUdf(p.BookId)
    });
}
```

Having registered the AuthorsStringUdf with EF Core, and ensured that the AuthorsStringUdf UDF was added to the database as part of the migration, you can then call the UDF within a query.

Table 13.3 compares the query produced by EF Core 2.0, which has the "N + 1" query problem and causes multiple database accesses, against the use of a UDF to combine the authors' names in the database into a single string. The speed improvement shown in the table isn't primarily because the database is quicker at combining the authors' names into a string, but because the number of database accesses is reduced.

Table 13.3   Comparing the performance of the standard EF Core 2.0 query with a query that uses a UDF to return a comma-delimited list of author's names

Parts	10 books Time	10 books #DB access	100 books Time	100 books #DB access.
1a. Returning collection of authors' names and combining in software	48 ms	12	230 ms	102
1b. Using UDF to combine authors' names in the database and returning a single string within the main query	34 ms	2	94 ms	2
How much faster using the UDF is	30%		60%	

Here are the takeaways from this example:

- You sometimes have specific information that can suggest shortcuts that EF Core can't be expected to see. This may allow you to spot areas where you could write better SQL than EF Core could.
- Try to minimize the number of database accesses, as each one adds overhead. As you can see in this example, the extra database accesses had a significant detrimental effect on the performance of this query.
- The DbFunction feature of EF Core (see section 8.2) is a great tool for adding your own SQL into a query. You need to add the UDF you write to the database before it's called, which takes a bit more work, but the gain in performance might be worth all that effort.

13.2.1 *Looking at the updated query*

Before moving on to improving the sorting and filtering, it's instructive to see the SQL command produced from our improved `MapBookToDto` method, shown in figure 13.3. The important thing to realize is that EF Core produces all that code by translating your LINQ commands inside the `MapBookToDto` method. The only place you intervene is in writing SQL inside `AuthorsStringUdf` and then adding a call to that UDF in the `MapBookToDto` method (see listing 13.3 for the change to `MapBookToDto`).

Overall, I think EF Core did a great job on the SQL. The other nice thing about EF Core is that it produces SQL in a format and style that's close to the way an SQL programmer would write it (see section 15.8 on capturing that SQL via logging). This makes it much easier to understand what the SQL is doing.

Now we're ready to move from the query to sorting and filtering, as that brings up bigger issues that'll take a bit more work.

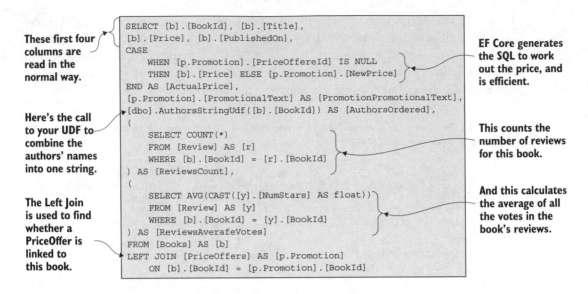

These first four columns are read in the normal way.

Here's the call to your UDF to combine the authors' names into one string.

The Left Join is used to find whether a PriceOffer is linked to this book.

EF Core generates the SQL to work out the price, and is efficient.

This counts the number of reviews for this book.

And this calculates the average of all the votes in the book's reviews.

```
SELECT [b].[BookId], [b].[Title],
[b].[Price], [b].[PublishedOn],
CASE
    WHEN [p.Promotion].[PriceOffereId] IS NULL
    THEN [b].[Price] ELSE [p.Promotion].[NewPrice]
END AS [ActualPrice],
[p.Promotion].[PromotionalText] AS [PromotionPromotionalText],
[dbo].AuthorsStringUdf([b].[BookId]) AS [AuthorsOrdered],
(
    SELECT COUNT(*)
    FROM [Review] AS [r]
    WHERE [b].[BookId] = [r].[BookId]
) AS [ReviewsCount],
(
    SELECT AVG(CAST([y].[NumStars] AS float))
    FROM [Review] AS [y]
    WHERE [b].[BookId] = [y].[BookId]
) AS [ReviewsAverafeVotes]
FROM [Books] AS [b]
LEFT JOIN [PriceOffers] AS [p.Promotion]
    ON [b].[BookId] = [p.Promotion].[BookId]
```

Figure 13.3   As a result of applying your two performance improvements, EF Core now produces a main query that returns all the book information in one go. EF Core produces 90% of the SQL code from your LINQ query. You have to improve only one area by using a UDF to concatenate the authors' names so that string can be returned in this one query.

13.2.2   *Ensuring that the query sorting and filtering are performing well*

Right from the start, I designed the book query's sort-and-filter feature to contain different levels of difficulty, because I knew I wanted to cover performance tuning in detail. Sorting and filtering a few books is no challenge and doesn't represent real-world problems, so for this chapter you'll build a tool to generate any amount of book test data. That way, I can show you where performance starts to drop and what you can do about it. I recommend anyone who wants to performance-tune to get a known, large data set to help with performance testing.

For this section, you'll use 100,000 books as your testing environment. You'll also ensure that the data has a range of associated data; for instance, you'll produce books with a set of reviews ranging from 0 to 12 reviews. Table 13.4 shows the number of rows for each table in the database.

NOTE   I like my test data to look real, so I've recycled a set of about 400 book titles, authors, and publication dates taken from Manning's book site. I find that using test data that looks like real data makes the testing more focused on the performance issues.

Table 13.4 The test data used for running the sorting and filtering tests

Table names ->	Books	Review	BookAuthor	Authors	PriceOffers
Number of rows	100,000	549,984	188,235	580	14,286

You'll then create a series of sorting/filtering tests, starting with simple queries and then increasing in difficulty. These provide a good platform to test the performance of the book list query. Here are your four tests:

- *Easy (default sort/page)*—For paging to work, you need to sort on something, so you use the primary key, which has an index.
- *Moderate (sort on PublishedOn)*—You add an index to this property, but by default it wouldn't have an index. You want to see the effect on the sorting performance of adding an index to this property.
- *Hard (sort by average votes)*—The average votes value is dynamically computed by averaging all the votes from all the book's reviews. There are over a half-million reviews to consider, so that's a challenge.
- *Double hard (filter by average votes, sort by price)*—This is a double whammy. Both the price and the average votes are dynamically computed, so it's interesting to see what happens here.

You'll also test with a page size of 10 books and 100 books to see whether that affects the sorting/filtering performance, with the results shown in table 13.5.

Table 13.5 The results of four sorting/filtering tests with both a 10 and 100 on a database containing 100,000 books and associated entities for the part 1b version of the query

Test scenario	10 books	100 books	Comment
Easy—default sort/page	30 ms	80 ms	
Moderate—sort on `PublishedOn`	ix = 30 ms no ix = 95 ms	ix = 80 ms no ix = 150 ms	You show the figures with an index (`ix = NN ms`) and without an index (`no ix = NN ms`).
Hard—sort by average votes	500 ms	530 ms	Long, but it has to process over a half-million reviews to do that.
Double hard—filter by average votes (four or more), sort by price	440 ms	490 ms	More work, but fewer books to sort. If you filter on votes 1 or more, it goes to 1.3 seconds!

The first two timings, especially with the index on the `PublishedOn` column, are acceptable, but the other two are a little longer than you'd like.

Personally, I'm impressed that the sort on the average votes is as fast as it is, because it had to process over a half-million reviews to do that. For your application, this may well be good enough performance, in which case you can stop. I'm sure you have plenty of other things to do.

But in this case, I've deemed that 500 ms is slow, as is the "filter by votes, sort by price" case, so you need to do something about these. You can't add indexes because the values are dynamically calculated, and there isn't a simple change to the SQL that will help. But I do have a plan, which I describe in part 3 of this chapter.

Looking at the SQL code, you can see places to improve it. For example, EF Core doesn't use the average votes calculated in the SELECT query in the sort or filter, but EF Core repeats the calculation again for the sort (see an example of this problem in section 12.5.6). This is a small thing, but in part 2 of this chapter, which is on replacing the EF Core queries with SQL queries, you'll correct that, and you can see whether the extra development effort is worth the performance gain.

Here are the takeaways from this section:

- *Get the query for a single instance performing well before worrying about anything else.* I'm glad I persevered and got the average votes to run on the database in part 1a; just think how long a sort on the average votes of 100,000 books would take if the average was being executed in software!

- *Take the time to write code to generate large, deterministic datasets for performance tuning—it will pay off in the long run.* Also, producing test data that looks real helps make the testing more appropriate, and it helps if you're demonstrating performance to the customer.

- *Don't forget to apply an index to a property that you're going to do lots of sorts or filtering on (see section 12.5.8).* But be warned: indexes increase the time it takes to insert or update an entity.

13.3　*Part 2—Converting EF Core commands to SQL queries*

As a developer of database access code, your "get out of jail free card" is to drop down into SQL to get around anything that EF Core can't do or doesn't do well. I ended the last section saying there's one place you could improve the SQL that EF Core produces from the LINQ, so let's see if hand-tuning the SQL helps. To help with this, you're going to use a package called Dapper.

13.3.1　*Introducing Dapper*

Dapper (https://github.com/StackExchange/Dapper) is a NuGet package, available on .NET and .NET Core, that executes SQL code and then copies the results back to .NET classes. It uses ADO.NET underneath, so it can work with any databases that ADO.NET supports, such as SQL Server, SQLite, Oracle, MySQL, PostgreSQL, and others. It's well-known and has been downloaded over a million times.

Getting Dapper to work with EF Core is easy, because Dapper matches database columns to the names of properties in the same way as EF Core's By Convention configuration. Also, EF Core can provide the correct type of database connection that Dapper needs via its Database.GetDbConnection method. Here's an example of using Dapper to read all the rows in the Books table into a collection of Book entity classes. The Dapper part is in bold.

Listing 13.4 Using Dapper with EF Core to read the Books table

You need to get a DbConnection for EF Core, as that's what Dapper needs to access the database.

Use the application's DbContext to run the Dapper query.

```
var books = context.Database
    .GetDbConnection()
    .Query<Book>("SELECT * FROM Books");
```

The Dapper call executes the SQL code provided in the first parameter, and Dapper then maps the results to the class type you supplied, in this case, Book.

Although you could do the same thing with EF Core's `FromSql` method (see section 9.5.1), the advantage of Dapper is that it'll work with any class, whereas `FromSql` maps only to an entity class. You can use Dapper with your `BooksListDto` class, but you can't use `FromSql` to do that.

> **NOTE** A lot of people, including me, have been asking for "Support for ad hoc mapping of arbitrary types" (issue #1862 in the EF Core GitHub). This will come in the form of *query types* in EF Core 2.1 (see appendix B), but Dapper also fulfills that role admirably.

What Dapper doesn't do is handle any of the relationships that you set up in EF Core (the navigational properties, such as the `Reviews` property in the `Book` entity class). Dapper executes SQL commands—it's up to you to handle relationships at the SQL level by returning primary keys and setting foreign keys.

This means Dapper is great for replacing `Select`-type EF Core queries, such as the book list you're trying to performance-tune. But using Dapper to write out a new `Book` entity with its `Reviews`, `BookAuthor`, `Author`, and `PriceOffer` entities would require a lot more code than EF Core would.

Thankfully, it's often the `Select` queries you want to improve, so let's see if you can make the book query any faster by using your hand-tuned SQL, executed by Dapper.

13.3.2 Rewriting MapBookToDto and associated EF queries using Dapper

The book list query implemented in chapter 2 is split into four separate query objects: `MapBookToDto`, `OrderBooksBy`, `FilterBooksBy`, and a generic paging method. That means each part is easy to understand and can be separately tested. Duplicating this query in Dapper requires you to sacrifice the elegance of query objects and move to a design that combines snippets of SQL to create the query. But sometimes that's what you need to do to squeeze out the best performance. Figure 13.4 shows how the Dapper version of the book list query dynamically builds the SQL command.

Building an SQL query from its parts: filter, count/select, sort, and paging

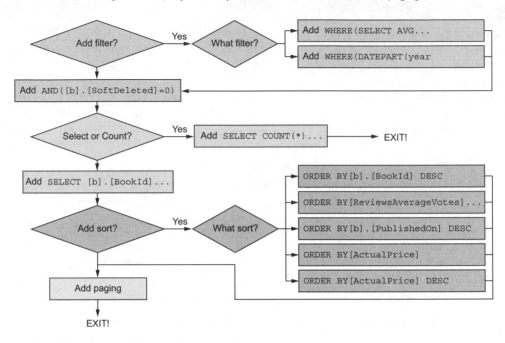

Figure 13.4   The Dapper code consists of a series of string concatenations to produce the final SQL query. It's not as elegant as the EF Core version, with its four query objects, but when you're performance tuning, you often must accept some loss of "cleanness" from your original code to achieve the performance you need.

Listing 13.5 shows the method called `BookListQuery` that'll execute the book list query by using the sort, filter, and paging options the user has requested. The listing also shows the `BuildQueryString` that does the string concatenations shown in figure 13.4. To save space, I've left out all the rest of the code for creating the SQL. You can find the full code on GitHub at http://mng.bz/z1gE.

Listing 13.5   Top-level methods for building and executing the book list query

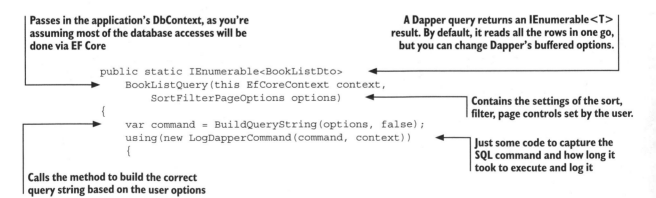

Passes in the application's DbContext, as you're assuming most of the database accesses will be done via EF Core

A Dapper query returns an IEnumerable<T> result. By default, it reads all the rows in one go, but you can change Dapper's buffered options.

```
public static IEnumerable<BookListDto>
    BookListQuery(this EfCoreContext context,
        SortFilterPageOptions options)
{
    var command = BuildQueryString(options, false);
    using(new LogDapperCommand(command, context))
    {
```

Contains the settings of the sort, filter, page controls set by the user.

Just some code to capture the SQL command and how long it took to execute and log it

Calls the method to build the correct query string based on the user options

Takes the SQL command string and an anonymous class with the variable data.

Gets the type of connection that Dapper needs from the application's DbContext

```
        return context.Database.GetDbConnection()
            .Query<BookListDto>(command, new
            {
                pageSize = options.PageSize,
                skipRows = options.PageSize
                    * (options.PageNum - 1),
                filterVal = options.FilterValue
            });
    }
}
```

Combines the parts of the SQL query. Takes in the sort, filter, page options and a boolean if the query is just counting the number of rows.

```
    private static string BuildQueryString
        (SortFilterPageOptions options, bool justCount)
    {
        var selectOptTop = FormSelectPart(options, justCount);
```

Forms the Select part: if it's just for counting, it returns "SELECT COUNT(*) FROM [Books] AS b"; otherwise, it includes all the columns, calculated values, and so on.

Builds the filter, starting with "WHERE ([b].[SoftDeleted] = 0)" and filling in the rest depending on the options

```
        var filter = FormFilter(options);
        if (justCount)
            return selectOptTop + filter;
```

If it's only a count, you return the SELECT and WHERE parts, because paging needs to total number of rows available.

```
        var sort = FormSort(options);
        var optOffset = FormOffsetEnd(options);
```

For paging, add an OFFSET value.

```
        return selectOptTop + filter
            + sort + optOffset + "\n";
    }
```

Returns the complete SQL command

Adds a sort of the form "ORDER BY [b].[PublishedOn] DESC" or similar

This might seem like a lot of work, but because you have access to the SQL that EF Core produces, which is already pretty good, it doesn't take too long. It took me less than a day to add Dapper, write the Dapper version of the book query, write tests, and convert the ASP.NET application to use the Dapper version.

You make two changes to the SQL command that Dapper uses from the SQL that EF Core has produced for the book list query:

- The initial count of the books includes a LEFT JOIN on the PriceOffer table, which you know it doesn't need, so you remove it. It turns out that makes no difference; the execution plan is the same for either form.
- You know from the tests that EF Core repeats (at the time of this writing) the calculation of a value, such as the average votes, in the ORDER BY part of the SQL. You know that in SQL Server you can refer to a calculated column in ORDER BY (but not in WHERE), so you alter the SQL to do that.

Having rerun the four tests in section 13.2.1, the only changes are on the sort of your average votes. Table 13.6 compares your part 1b EF Core query with your part 2, improved SQL version, with the change in sort by average votes in bold.

Table 13.6   The results of the four sorting/filtering tests on a database containing 100,000 books and associated entities

Test scenario	Part 1b—EF Core	Part 2—SQL	Comment
Easy—default sort/page	10 = 30 ms 100 = 80 ms	10 = 30 ms 100 = 85 ms	No real change, within normal variations
Moderate—sort on `PublishedOn`	10 = 30 ms 100 = 80 ms	10 = 30 ms 100 = 90 ms	No real change, within normal variations
Hard—sort by average votes	**10 = 500 ms** **100 = 530 ms**	**10 = 325 ms** **100 = 390 ms**	**Improved SQL is about 40% faster than EF Core**
Double hard—filter by average votes (four or more), sort by price	10 = 440 ms 100 = 490 ms	10 = 455 ms 100 = 520 ms	No real change, within normal variations

NOTE I checked the execution plans in Microsoft's SQL Server Management Studio for the sort on price in EF Core's SQL and this simplified SQL in Dapper. This confirmed that both versions produce identical execution plans. The only improvement from referencing a calculated value is in the sort on average votes.

I find these results interesting, as the Dapper GitHub site states that it's ten times faster or more than EF (most likely EF6.x), which didn't show up in these results. I tried a simple "read one book row" test, and yes, in that case Dapper is about seven times faster than EF Core. That makes sense, because EF Core has several things to do on loading, including relational fix up, whereas Dapper only executes the SQL. But when it comes to large or complex queries for which the database execution is the limiting factor, the performance depends on the quality of the SQL produced, and not the software-side of the library.

Small accesses don't normally need performance tuning, because they're quick anyway. So, the question is, "Was all that effort to swap to SQL worth it?" Before you decide, read part 3, where you'll try another approach that takes more work but improves performance much more than the hand-tuned SQL does.

Here are the takeaways from this section:

- It's the SQL translation that matters. If something is slow, have a look at the SQL found in the logs.
- Swapping to Dapper isn't hard, especially if you capture the SQL that EF Core produces and use it as a template for your SQL. If you see a query in which EF Core is producing suboptimal SQL code, and you can produce better SQL, then consider swapping that query over to Dapper. Dapper takes less compute time to run the query, but this gain is very minor once the SQL is longer than a few milliseconds. It's only worth swapping to Dapper if you have some SQL that is better than the SQL that EF Core produces.

13.4 Part 3—Modifying the database to increase performance

As you've seen, if you can add an SQL index to a property, as you did with the
`PublishedOn` property, then any sort or filter is fast. The problem is, the average votes
and the price both need to be calculated on the fly, so they can't have an index, which
means your application's performance suffers. This section shows you a way to precalculate these values so an index can be added. Overall, the changes in part 3 provide
a significant boost in performance, but they also come with significant issues that you
need to solve. Let me explain.

A well-designed database has only one copy of a piece of data. Having two copies
could mean that those pieces of data can get out of step. This is why your default query
calculates the average votes every time, as someone might have just added a new review
to a book and so changed its average votes value. I'm sure you've heard the software
term *caching*, in which a calculation that takes a long time is calculated once, and used
again and again. Well, you want to cache some data in your database, but the problem
is, what happens when your cached value gets out-of-date?

The good news is, EF Core has excellent tools to help you keep a cached value in the
database up-to-date. The bad news is, doing this requires extra development work, and
you must think carefully to make sure the cache doesn't get out of step with the database's calculated value. This extra work and complexity is the price you pay if you want
to improve your application's intrinsic performance.

In the rest of part 3, you'll cache three precalculated values by using three techniques, each tuned to the specifics of the cached value(s). Here are the ways you'll
create cached values:

- *Adding ActualPrice and OrgPrice properties.* You change the way a promotion is
  added to the book and fold the `PriceOffer` entity class into the `Book` entity class.
  See section 13.4.1.
- *Adding AverageVotes and ReviewsCount properties.* You still keep the `Review` entity
  class, but you ensure that reviews can be added/removed only via the `Book` entity
  class. This allows you to calculate the average votes and the number of votes
  whenever the book's reviews change. See section 13.4.2.
- *Adding an AuthorsString property.* You move the adding of authors into the `Book`
  entity class's constructor so that you can precalculate the comma-delimited
  authors string. See section 13.4.3.

13.4.1 Creating an ActualPrice property—changing the promotion process

In parts 1a, 1b, and 2, the price of a book relies on whether a `PriceOffer` is linked to
a book: if a `PriceOffer` is present, the `NewPrice` property in the `PriceOffer` overrides
the `Price` property in the `Book` entity class. The nice feature of this approach is that
these actions are transparent: you add/remove a `PriceOffer` to a book to add/remove
a price promotion. See figure 13.5.

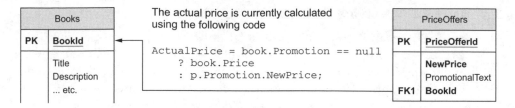

Figure 13.5   The `Price` property in the `Book` can be overridden if a `PriceOffer` is linked to a Book. In part 3, you'll remove the `PriceOffer` entity from the database and add three properties to the `Book` entity class—`OrgPrice`, `ActualPrice`, and `PromotionalText`—to take over from the `PriceOffer` entity.

But to improve performance, you want to do away with the `PriceOffer` entity and move the data normally held in the `PriceOffer` entity class into the `Book` entity class. This requires changing the form that the promotion takes, and you'd use three properties in the `Book` entity class:

- `OrgPrice`—The recommended retail price of the book, which is used if there isn't a promotion on the book.
- `ActualPrice`—Set to either the `OrgPrice` or a promotional price.
- `PromotionalText`—Holds the text that should be shown when a promotional price is in place, for example, "50% off today."

This change is fine, but for me it makes the process of adding or removing a price promotion less obvious. For that reason, you'll create an `AddPromotion` method and `RemovePromotion` method to the `Book` entity class that adds or removes a price promotion, respectively. This makes it crystal clear what's going on and leaves the logic inside the `Book` entity.

In addition, you set the `OrgPrice`, `ActualPrice`, and `PromotionalText` property setters to `private`. This ensures that the only way the price can be changed is via the `AddPromotion` and `RemovePromotion` methods.

> **Listing 13.6   The changes to the `Book` entity class to handle price promotions**

```
public class Book
{
    //… other properties removed for clarity

    public decimal OrgPrice { get; private set; }
    public decimal ActualPrice { get; private set; }
    [MaxLength(PromotionalTextLength)]
    public string PromotionalText { get; private set; }

    //This ctor is needed for EF Core
    private Book()
    {
    }

    public Book( //… other params removed for clarity
```

The properties that control the price all have a private setter so that only the Book entity can change their values.

The only public way to create a Book entity is now via this constructor.

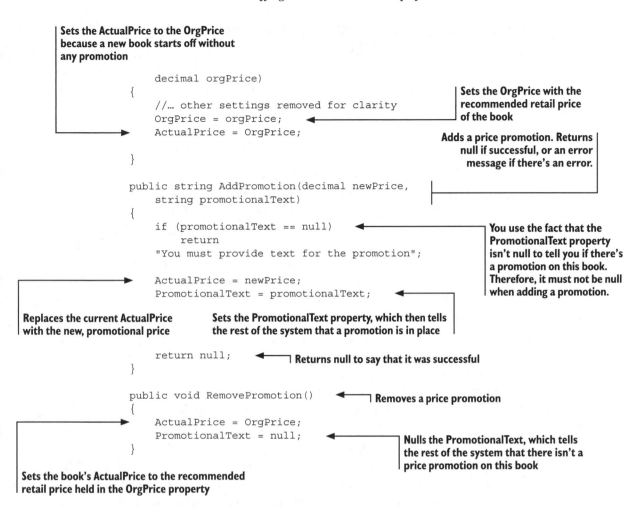

Sets the ActualPrice to the OrgPrice because a new book starts off without any promotion

```
        decimal orgPrice)
    {
        //… other settings removed for clarity
        OrgPrice = orgPrice;
        ActualPrice = OrgPrice;

    }

    public string AddPromotion(decimal newPrice,
        string promotionalText)
    {
        if (promotionalText == null)
            return
        "You must provide text for the promotion";

        ActualPrice = newPrice;
        PromotionalText = promotionalText;

        return null;
    }

    public void RemovePromotion()
    {
        ActualPrice = OrgPrice;
        PromotionalText = null;
    }
```

Sets the OrgPrice with the recommended retail price of the book

Adds a price promotion. Returns null if successful, or an error message if there's an error.

You use the fact that the PromotionalText property isn't null to tell you if there's a promotion on this book. Therefore, it must not be null when adding a promotion.

Replaces the current ActualPrice with the new, promotional price

Sets the PromotionalText property, which then tells the rest of the system that a promotion is in place

Returns null to say that it was successful

Removes a price promotion

Nulls the PromotionalText, which tells the rest of the system that there isn't a price promotion on this book

Sets the book's ActualPrice to the recommended retail price held in the OrgPrice property

As you can see, this change requires you to "lock down" more of the Book entity: you remove features, such as being able to change the price via its setter, so that you must use the new, prescribed path (you saw this in section 10.4 which covered DDD entity classes). In this case, you provide clearly named methods for handling the adding and removing of a price promotion, and change the access modifiers on the price properties so that only the designated methods can change the promotion state.

This "locking down" is important in multiperson projects, because it ensures that another developer doesn't, inadvertently, bypass your approach and therefore introduce a bug. I'd lock down my design even if I were the only developer on this project, because it's so easy for me to forget what I did if I come back a year later and need to add a new feature in the same area.

The result of all this is that one property, ActualPrice, holds the price at which the customers can buy the book. You can add an index to this column, so the sort on price will be much faster. The "sort on price" is now the same speed as the sort on the book's published date. (You can see the full results at the end of part 3.)

13.4.2 *Caching the book review values, and not letting them get out-of-date*

In parts 1a, 1b, and 2, the average votes value was dynamically calculated by looking at which Review entities were linked to each Book entity. This works fine but requires the SQL server to process over a half-million Reviews rows to sort or filter on the average votes value. In this section, you'll add two properties to the Book entity class:

- AverageVotes—Holds the average votes of all the Reviews linked to this Book
- ReviewsCount—Holds the number of Reviews linked to this Book

As with the price promotion example just covered, you add two new methods, called AddReview and RemoveReview, to the Book entity to add/remove a review, respectively, on the Book. You still need to keep the Review entities so that users can look at the Review's comments on a book. But that makes this caching implementation much more complicated than the price promotion example, because you'll have two versions of the "truth": what your cached values say, and what the actual Review rows in the database say. You must take extra steps to make sure your cached values stay up-to-date. The first part is to "lock down" the adding, removing, or changing of a review. The two parts of the problem are as follows:

1 You still need the Reviews property, which sets up the one-to-many relationship between a Book entity and its Review entities. But you must ensure that Review entities can't be added or removed from the Reviews property; all additions or removals must go through the AddReview and RemoveReview methods.

   You need to lock down the Review entity class by changing its properties to have private setters. You also stop any methods outside the DataLayer from being able to create a Review entity instance by adding an internal access modifier to its constructors.

2 Because the AverageVotes and ReviewsCount properties are cached values, the possibility exists of a concurrent addition or removal of a review, which could invalidate the cached values.

The next two subsections cover each of these in turn.

> **NOTE** To save time, I haven't implemented the capability to see the individual reviews on a book, nor have I given a user the ability to edit their review in the book app. But my performance-tuning code does handle those features if they're ever added.

ENSURING ADD/REMOVE OF REVIEWS TO A BOOK MUST GO THROUGH YOUR ACCESS METHODS

EF Core has a great feature called *backing fields* (see section 6.15), which allows you to better control access to an entity's property. In this case, you want to control access to the Reviews navigational property and, because it's a collection, you want to remove the capability to add or remove instances from the collection. This you can do by using the IEnumerable<Review> type for your Reviews property, with a backing field behind it.

Figure 13.6 shows the various parts in the Book entity class and the Review entity class, with the AddReview method that does all the work.

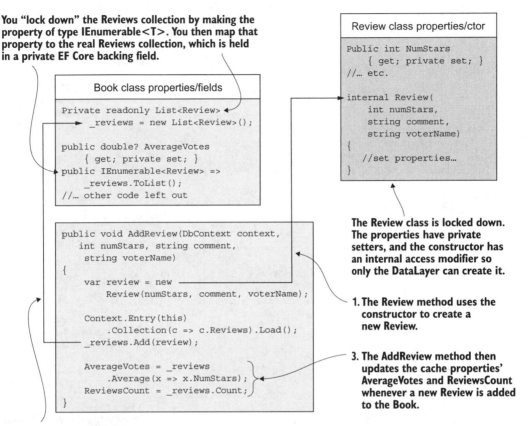

You "lock down" the Reviews collection by making the property of type IEnumerable<T>. You then map that property to the real Reviews collection, which is held in a private EF Core backing field.

Book class properties/fields

```
Private readonly List<Review>
    _reviews = new List<Review>();

public double? AverageVotes
    { get; private set; }
public IEnumerable<Review> =>
    _reviews.ToList();
//... other code left out
```

Review class properties/ctor

```
Public int NumStars
    { get; private set; }
//... etc.

internal Review(
    int numStars,
    string comment,
    string voterName)
{
    //set properties...
}
```

The Review class is locked down. The properties have private setters, and the constructor has an internal access modifier so only the DataLayer can create it.

```
public void AddReview(DbContext context,
    int numStars, string comment,
    string voterName)
{
    var review = new
        Review(numStars, comment, voterName);

    Context.Entry(this)
        .Collection(c => c.Reviews).Load();
    _reviews.Add(review);

    AverageVotes = _reviews
        .Average(x => x.NumStars);
    ReviewsCount = _reviews.Count;
}
```

1. The Review method uses the constructor to create a new Review.

3. The AddReview method then updates the cache properties' AverageVotes and ReviewsCount whenever a new Review is added to the Book.

2. The AddReview method adds the new Review to the backing field collection.

Figure 13.6 The Book entity class (top left) and the Review entity class (top right) are "locked down." The properties that the class doesn't want anyone else to change have private setters, and the Reviews navigational collection is of type IEnumerable<T> to stop adding or removing reviews from the collection. The AddReview method (bottom) in the Book entity class is the only way a developer can add a new Review. When a new Review is added, the method also recalculates the cache properties, AverageVotes and ReviewsCount.

Listing 13.7 shows the Book entity with the various changes:

- You change the way to handle reviews, with a backing field to hold the collection and the public Reviews property now of type IEnumerable<Review>.
- You add two properties, AverageVotes and ReviewCount, to hold the cached values. Both properties have private setters to stop them from being changed accidentally.
- You add two methods, AddReview and RemoveReview, that update the backing field _reviews and at the same time recalculate the AverageVotes and Review-Count cache properties.

Listing 13.7   The Book entity class focusing on the new Review-handling code

Adds a [ConcurrencyCheck] attribute to this property

Adds a backing field, which is a list. You then tell EF Core to use this for all reads and writes.

```
public class Book
{
    private readonly List<Review> _reviews
        = new List<Review>();

    //… other properties removed for clarity
    [ConcurrencyCheck]
    public int ReviewsCount { get; private set; }
    [ConcurrencyCheck]
    public double? AverageVotes { get; private set; }
```

Holds a precalculated average of the reviews and the number of reviews for this book. It's read-only so it can't be changed outside this class.

Adds a method to allow a new review to be added to the _reviews collection

```
    public IEnumerable<Review> Reviews =>
        _reviews.ToList();

    //… other ctors and methods removed for clarity

    public void AddReview(DbContext context,
        int numStars, string comment,
        string voterName)
    {
        context.Entry(this)
            .Collection(c => c.Reviews).Load();
        var review = new
            Review(numStars, comment, voterName);
        _reviews.Add(review);
        AverageVotes = _reviews
            .Average(x => x.NumStars);
        ReviewsCount = _reviews.Count;
    }
```

Returns a copy of the reviews that were loaded. By taking a copy, no one can alter the list by casting IEnumerable<T> to List<T>.

Makes sure the backing field, _reviews, has the reviews for this book loaded

Recalculates the average votes and number of reviews for this book

Creates a review using the data given and then adds the new review to the backing field _reviews. This updates the database on the call to SaveChanges.

Adds a method to remove a review from the _reviews collection

```
    public void RemoveReview(DbContext context,
        Review review)
    {
        context.Entry(this)
            .Collection(c => c.Reviews).Load();

        _reviews.Remove(review);
        AverageVotes = _reviews.Any()
            ? _reviews.Average(x => x.NumStars)
```

Removes the review from the list. This updates the database on the call to SaveChanges

Makes sure the backing field, _reviews, has the reviews for this book loaded

If there are reviews, you recalculate the average votes for the book

```
          : (double?)null;
        ReviewsCount = _reviews.Count;
    }
}
```

To ensure that the backing field, _reviews, is updated when the reviews are loaded, you need to add some configuration, as shown here (the configuration syntax may change in EF Core 2.1):

```
public class BookConfig : IEntityTypeConfiguration<Book>
{
    public void Configure
        (EntityTypeBuilder<Book> entity)
    {

        //… other configrations removed for clarity
        entity.Metadata
            .FindNavigation(nameof(Book.Reviews))
            .SetPropertyAccessMode
            (PropertyAccessMode.Field);
    }
}
```

The final stage is locking down the Review entity class so no one outside the DataLayer can create or change a review. This listing shows the Review entity class with private setters, and all constructors having an internal access modifier.

Listing 13.8 Review **class showing private setters and internal constructors**

```
public class Review
{
    public const int NameLength = 100;

    public int ReviewId { get; private set; }
    [MaxLength(NameLength)]
    Public string VoterName { get; private set; }
    Public int NumStars { get; private set; }
    Public string Comment { get; private set; }

    //-----------------------------------------
    //Relationships

    public int BookId { get; private set; }

    private Review() { }

    internal Review(int numStars,
        string comment, string voterName)
    {
        NumStars = numStars;
        Comment = comment;
        VoterName = voterName;
    }
}
```

All the Review class's properties have a private setter to stop anyone from altering the Review, therefore invalidating the cached values.

You must create a parameterless constructor for EF Core. You add a private access modifier to it so only EF Core can create a Review using this constructor.

The result of all this is that the only way to add, update, or remove a `Review` entity from a `Book` entity is via `AddReview` and `RemoveReview`. The cached values can't become out-of-date by a developer directly manipulating the `Reviews` property or a `Review` entity instance.

ENSURING THAT A CONCURRENT UPDATE OF A BOOK'S REVIEWS DOESN'T INVALIDATE THE CACHED VALUES

As I stated before, concurrent adding or removing of a review could invalidate the cached values. That's because a small window of time exists between the loading of the current reviews linked to a book and the saving of the new review collection and the associated cached values. In that time window, another `Review` could be added/removed from the same book by another user, which would make the cached values out of step with the database. The solution to this problem is to use EF Core's concurrency conflict feature (see section 8.7) when saving a `Review` addition/removal.

Listing 13.9 shows the modified `AddReviewToBook` method in the `AddReviewService` class, which the ASP.NET Core's `AddBookReview` action uses to allow a user to add a review to a book. At the end of this listing, you'll see the important call to the specialized `SaveChangesWithReviewCheck` method (in bold) that ensures the cached values are correct even if a simultaneous addition/removal occurs of another `Review` on this `Book`.

> **Listing 13.9 Calling `SaveChangesWithReviewCheck` after a review update**

```
public class AddReviewService : IAddReviewService
{
    private readonly EfCoreContext _context;

    public AddReviewService(EfCoreContext context)
    {
        _context = context;
    }

    //… other methods removed for clarity

    public void AddReviewToBook(int bookId,
        int numStars, string comment, string voterName)
    {
        var book = _context.Books.Find(bookId);
        book.AddReview(_context,
            numStars, comment, voterName);
        _context.SaveChangesWithReviewCheck();
    }
}
```

ASP.NET Core action calls this method to add a new review to a book

Finds the book that the user wants to add a review to

Calls a special version of SaveChanges, which checks if the AverageVotes or ReviewsCounts are different from the values it obtained when it loaded the Book entity

Calls the AddReview method in the Book instance loaded

Listing 13.10 shows the `SaveChangesWithReviewCheck` method, which executes the `SaveChanges` method and catches situations in which another concurrent `AddReview` or `RemoveReview` has changed the cached values. In this case, the method recalculates both cached values and retries `SaveChanges` (see section 8.7 for more detail on how concurrency handling is done).

Listing 13.10 `SaveChangesWithReviewCheck` **method to fix invalidated cached values**

Calls the normal SaveChanges method within a try/catch block. If it works, it returns. If there's a DbUpdateConcurrencyException, it'll enter the "catch" part and execute code to fix the problem.

```
public static class SaveChangesBookFixer
{
    public static int SaveChangesWithReviewCheck
        (this EfCoreContext context)
    {
        try
        {
            return context.SaveChanges();
        }
        catch (DbUpdateConcurrencyException ex)
        {
            var entityToFix = ex.Entries
                .SingleOrDefault(x => x.Entity is Book);
            if (entityToFix == null)
                throw;



            if ( FixReviewCachedValues(context, entityToFix))
                return context.SaveChangesWithReviewCheck ();
        }
        return 0;
    }
    private static bool FixReviewCachedValues(
        EfCoreContext context,
        EntityEntry entry)
    {
        var book = (Book) entry.Entity;

        var actualReviews = book.Reviews
            .Where(x =>
                context.Entry(x).State == EntityState.Added)
            .Union(context.Set<Review>().AsNoTracking()
                .Where(x => x.BookId == book.BookId))
            .ToList();

        var databaseEntity =
            context.Books.AsNoTracking()
            .SingleOrDefault(p => p.BookId == book.BookId);
```

Method automatically handles any concurrency issues.

Handles only Book entities, so you filter those out.

If the entity isn't a book, you rethrow the exception because you can't handle it.

You expect only one Book concurrency issue, so you check that's the case.

Calls your private method to handle this book concurrency issue. If it returns true, it has updated the book entity.

If someone deletes the book you were updating, you leave that as is and return 0 to say nothing was updated.

You cast the entity to a book so that you can access the properties you know.

Gets the combination of the reviews in the database and any new reviews being added. That's what the cached values must match.

Need to load the current values for the book entity in the database. You need that later to stop EF Core from seeing a concurrency error again.

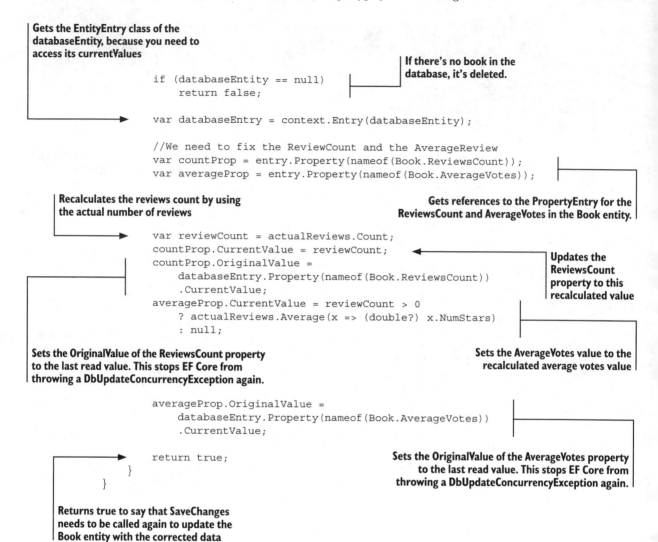

Gets the EntityEntry class of the databaseEntity, because you need to access its currentValues

If there's no book in the database, it's deleted.

```
if (databaseEntity == null)
    return false;

var databaseEntry = context.Entry(databaseEntity);

//We need to fix the ReviewCount and the AverageReview
var countProp = entry.Property(nameof(Book.ReviewsCount));
var averageProp = entry.Property(nameof(Book.AverageVotes));
```

Gets references to the PropertyEntry for the ReviewsCount and AverageVotes in the Book entity.

Recalculates the reviews count by using the actual number of reviews

```
var reviewCount = actualReviews.Count;
countProp.CurrentValue = reviewCount;
countProp.OriginalValue =
    databaseEntry.Property(nameof(Book.ReviewsCount))
    .CurrentValue;
averageProp.CurrentValue = reviewCount > 0
    ? actualReviews.Average(x => (double?) x.NumStars)
    : null;
```

Updates the ReviewsCount property to this recalculated value

Sets the OriginalValue of the ReviewsCount property to the last read value. This stops EF Core from throwing a DbUpdateConcurrencyException again.

Sets the AverageVotes value to the recalculated average votes value

```
averageProp.OriginalValue =
    databaseEntry.Property(nameof(Book.AverageVotes))
    .CurrentValue;

return true;
    }
}
```

Sets the OriginalValue of the AverageVotes property to the last read value. This stops EF Core from throwing a DbUpdateConcurrencyException again.

Returns true to say that SaveChanges needs to be called again to update the Book entity with the corrected data

Yes, this is complex, but that's because you need to handle all combinations of adding/ removing in memory and in the database. The result is the SaveChangesWithReview-Check method will automatically correct the AverageVotes and ReviewsCount cache properties if a concurrent update makes them incorrect.

The other benefit of using EF Core's ConcurrencyCheck on the two cache properties is, if you forget to use the specialized SaveChangesWithReviewCheck method and use the normal SaveChanges, EF Core will throw a DbUpdateConcurrencyException instead of letting the cached values be incorrectly written out.

Having done all this, you have two columns, AverageVotes and ReviewsCount, in the Books table that you can add an index to. This makes a significant difference in the "sort on votes" feature. Now it's as fast as the sort on the book's published date (full results shown at the end of part 3).

13.4.3　*Calculating AuthorsString when a book is first created*

The final cached part is precalculating the AuthorsString property instead of using the AuthorsStringUdf UDF to build the string dynamically. This doesn't help on searching or sorting, but it does remove a small amount of time that AuthorsStringUdf takes to combine the book authors' names. This should knock off a few milliseconds in displaying the book info.

You make a simple decision here to precalculate the comma-delimited string of author names when the Book entity is first created and added to the database. You also make the Author entity's Name property have an internal setter, and the BookAuthor entity's foreign keys and linking entities to have private setters. This stops the authors of a book from being changed, and the name of an author in the Author entity from being changed.

This level of restriction may be unacceptable, but these are the sorts of decisions you need to make. The more restricted you can be, the simpler your cached values will be to create and maintain. As you saw with adding/removing Review entities to a Book entity, you had to write quite a bit of code to handle all the options. In this case, you lock down the features the application could offer to allow you to produce simpler caching. This listing shows the modifications to the Book entity to do this.

> **Listing 13.11**　Book **entity class—calculating the** AuthorsString **on construction**

Holds the precalculated comma-delimited list of authors' names.

```
public class Book
{
    private readonly List<BookAuthor>
        _bookAuthors = new List<BookAuthor>();

    //… other properties removed for clarity

    public string AuthorsString
        { get; private set; }

    public IEnumerable<BookAuthor>
        AuthorsLink => _bookAuthors.ToList();

    private Book () {}

    public Book(
        //… other params removed for clarity
```

Uses a backing field to hold the _bookAuthors list

Access to the AuthorList is via an IEnumerable<Author> property so that no one can add or remove items from the collection.

The public Book constructor allows other projects to create a Book.

EF Core needs a parameterless constructor. You add a private access modifier to it so only EF Core can create a Review using this constructor.

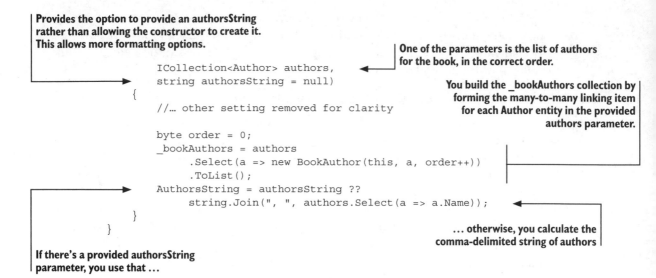

Provides the option to provide an authorsString
rather than allowing the constructor to create it.
This allows more formatting options.

One of the parameters is the list of authors
for the book, in the correct order.

```
        ICollection<Author> authors,
        string authorsString = null)
    {
        //... other setting removed for clarity

        byte order = 0;
        _bookAuthors = authors
            .Select(a => new BookAuthor(this, a, order++))
            .ToList();
        AuthorsString = authorsString ??
            string.Join(", ", authors.Select(a => a.Name));
    }
}
```

You build the _bookAuthors collection by
forming the many-to-many linking item
for each Author entity in the provided
authors parameter.

... otherwise, you calculate the
comma-delimited string of authors

If there's a provided authorsString
parameter, you use that ...

You can set various configuration values, but you should get the idea from listing 12.3 that you calculate the AuthorsString when the Book entity instance is first created, and you set the access modifiers on the other involved classes, such as the Author and BookAuthor entity classes, to restrict access outside the DataLayer.

As a result, you have the precalculated, comma-delimited string of authors' names stored in the AuthorsString property. Therefore, you don't need to use the Authors-StringUdf UDF every time you display the information about a book, but you can access the AuthorString property.

13.4.4 Analyzing the changes—Is the performance gain worth the effort?

In subsections 13.4.1 to 13.4.3, you saw three ways of producing precalculated values to improve performance. They took quite a bit of work, and you might ask yourself whether the gain in performance is worth that level of effort.

Let's start with the performance gains. Table 13.7 shows the improvements compared to part 2, the improved SQL version.

Table 13.7   The timing for the four tests for part 3 (cached values) with the improvement over part 2 (improved SQL version).

Test	10 books	Improvement	100 books	Improvement
All books	30 ms	no improvement	80 ms	No improvement
Sort by publication dates	30 ms	no improvement	80 ms	No improvement
Sort by votes	30 ms	**12 times better**	80 ms	**5 times better**
Sort by price, filter by 4+ votes	30 ms	**12 times better**	80 ms	**5 times better**

Here are some notes on performance:

- I tried a half-million books: the 10-book time was 85 ms, and the 100-book time was 150 ms. For this number of books, the database server is starting to be a limiting factor.
- In parts 1a, 1b, and 2 the "sort by price, filtered by +1 votes" timings were all over a second in length. But this part 3 implementation still comes in at 30 ms.
- You took the SQL produced by EF Core in part 3 and used Dapper to execute it, but there was no further performance improvement, so it wasn't worth doing.

The standout improvements of part 3 are the last two items in the table (see bold results in previous table): sort by votes and sort by price, filter by 4+ votes. These now execute in the same time as the ordinary book display, which is ordered on the `Book`'s primary key, and the sort by publication date. This makes sense, because the value it's sorting or filtering on is a property, and you add indexes to those properties.

This also shows that the precalculation of the `AuthorsString` had little or no effect. I was initially surprised, but when I thought about it, the `AuthorsString` is used only in the display of the information and not in any sort or filter.

This leads me to the following conclusions on the value of the changes:

- The `ActualPrice` change is well worth it, for performance and features.

  This change improves the performance, and it improves the application structure. Before this change, you had to remember to add code to calculate the correct price everywhere you needed it. Now you can just reference the `Actual-Price` property to get the correct price for the book in question. That's a win-win.

- The `AverageVotes`/`ReviewCount` changes are a lot of work but provide great performance.

  The changes to produce cached `AverageVotes` and `ReviewCount` values are complex, but the sorting and filtering performance is brilliant. Although the underlying code is complicated, the methods `AddReview` and `RemoveReview` are easy to understand and use. Sorting and filtering on the average votes of a book are important features that users need, so I'd definitely do this again.

- The `AuthorsString` isn't worth it: no performance gain, with complex rules.

  To make `AuthorsString` easy to calculate, you apply a lot of rules, which limits what the application can do, for no measurable gain in performance. In a real-life application, you'd remove this change, because it reduces the inherent features of your application. For instance, without this change, you could update the `Name` property in the `Author` entity, and that new name would appear in all the books that the author is involved in.

Here are the takeaways from part 3:

- Precalculating and caching values that the database takes a long time to calculate has two benefits: the value is available instantly, and you can have an SQL index added to that cached property.

- Using cached values is at the extreme end of the spectrum of performance tuning because, if done incorrectly, it can produce hard-to-find issues and a cached value that can become out-of-date.
- To stop a developer from bypassing your caching code, you must "lock down" accesses to the cached values and the database values that are used to calculate the cached values. Otherwise, someone (even you) might forget what you did and write code that invalidates your caching feature.
- Restricting some features in your application may make building and maintaining a cached value simpler. But at the same time, you need to decide whether that's going to be a problem later.
- If you can't change the database structure to avoid concurrency issues, as you did in the ActualPrice property (section 13.4.1), you'll need to add concurrency checking and fixing code, as you did in section 13.4.2.

13.5 Comparing parts 1a, 1b, 2, and 3

In summary, you've taken a specific query in our book app and seen how much you could improve it. Let's start with an overview chart of the gains in performance. Figure 13.7 shows the performance gains over the four parts for two different, but difficult, query types: displaying 100 books, sorted on average votes; and displaying 100 books sorted on primary key.

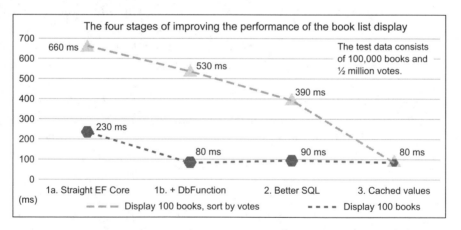

Figure 13.7   Two of the hardest queries: the display of 100 books, sorted on votes, and the display of 100 books. Although the Straight EF Core version looks poor compared to the others, just remember that to sort on votes, it needs to average over a half-million votes.

This graph gives a great overview, but what it doesn't convey is that the part 3 performance improvements make all the 10-book displays, or any sort or filter, come in at around 30 ms. Because the 10-book display is the default, the site is now really fast. Also, the 30 ms is the time for the ASP.NET page to display, which includes other overhead outside the database access—in fact, the database accesses are between 10 ms and 15 ms.

Although the improvements in performance are undeniable, there are other factors to consider:

- How much effort did each stage take?
- Were there any problems or adverse effects to the application?

Table 13.8 gives my answers to these questions.

Table 13.8 The amount of effort needed to create each stage

Part	Effort	Comments
1a Straight EF Core	Few days	Finding the correct format for the LINQ average wasn't easy. I had to ask the EF Core team via EF Core's GitHub issue page. But after I got this right, EF Core produced great SQL code.
1b + DbFunction	Half day	Very easy. I like the DbFunction a lot, and in this case, it made a significant improvement to the performance.
2 Better SQL	One day	Fairly easy, as I copied the SQL code that EF Core produces and tweaked the bit that my experiments said would help. But useful only if you can come up with some better SQL; the difference in speed of Dapper over EF Core helps on only small, quick database accesses, which you don't need to performance-tune anyway!
3 Cached values	Three days	Definitely hard work, but also a fantastic result. Other than the cached `AuthorsString` (which I'd remove in a real application), I think the performance changes to the code don't hinder future development of the application at all. But it does add a lot of complexity to the application, which isn't ideal.

Overall, I'm pleased with the process. EF Core produces great SQL code from the get-go, but only because you made sure your LINQ queries were written in a way that's sympathetic to how EF Core works. The methods and approaches introduced in the first five chapters are a good starting point. As I said in chapter 12, make sure your standard patterns for queries work well; otherwise, you'll be building inefficiencies into your application right from the start. Even so, you had to persevere with the LINQ `Average` method to get EF Core to translate that to SQL.

But, at some point, you'll need more performance than EF Core can give you, and I think I've shown that you can do plenty of things to improve performance. Using EF Core to develop your database access code should mean you get your application up and working more quickly, leaving plenty of time to tune up the parts that matter in your application.

NOTE Section 14.2 goes to an even higher level of performance by changing the overall architecture of the database query.

13.6   *Database scalability—what can you do to improve that?*

The performance tuning covered in parts 1 to 3 is all about speed: how fast you can return the result to the user. The other aspect is *scalability*: handling large numbers of concurrent users. To end this chapter, let's look at database scalability.

I talk about database scalability because although this book is about EF Core, the overall scalability of a website is normally the limiting factor. That scalability is the overall time that the website, including the database access, takes—which is what you've been measuring using Chrome. It turns out that for simple book list queries, such as displaying 10 books, the database part isn't the main cost. For instance, even in part 1a, the EF Core query for 10 books takes 8 ms, and the overall time is 45 ms—this means most of the time is spent in the ASP.NET Core application. So, the first thing to try for better scalability is to improve ASP.NET Core's scalability, which is easy to do by running multiple instances of your web application.

The other thing about database scalability is, the simpler you make the database accesses, the more concurrent accesses the database can handle. The part 3 solution, in which the worst database access time is 15 ms, provides much better database scalability than the other versions.

I've already given you suggestions in section 12.7, one of which is using async/await. For small queries, async/await has overhead, but for queries such as the book list (which take a long time), async/await is well worth it. I produced an async version of part 2, which at its worst is only 5% slower than the sync version; in longer-running queries, async/await adds less than 1% overhead. Use async/await on your big queries, because you'll gain scalability while the application is waiting for the database to return.

But some large applications will have high concurrent database accesses, and you need a way out of this. The first, and easiest, approach is to pay for a more powerful database. If that isn't going to cut it, here are some ideas to consider:

- *Split your data over multiple databases—sharding your data*. If your data is segregated in some way (for instance, if you have a financial application used by many small businesses), you could spread each business's data on a different database. This is called *sharding* (see http://mng.bz/9Ck3).
- *Split your database reads from your writes—the CQRS architecture*. A Command Query Responsibility Segregation (CQRS) architecture (see https://martinfowler.com/bliki/CQRS.html) splits the database reads from the database writes. This allows you to optimize your reads, and possibly use a separate database, or multiple read-only databases, on the CQRS read side.
- *Mixing NoSQL and SQL databases—polyglot persistence*. In part 3, you started to make the Book entity look like a complete definition of a book, like a JSON structure would hold. With a CQRS architecture, you could have used a relational database to handle any writes, but on any write you could build a JSON version of the book and write it to a read-side NoSQL database or multiple databases. This might provide a higher read performance. This idea is one form of a polyglot

persistence (see https://martinfowler.com/bliki/PolyglotPersistence.html). See section 14.2, where you'll implement a mixed SQL/NoSQL application to gain even more performance.

Summary

- If you build your LINQ queries in a way that matches the EF Core approach, EF Core will reward you by producing excellent SQL code.
- Check that your queries don't produce a `QueryClientEvaluationWarning` warning indicating that the client vs. server evaluation feature will evaluate the values in software. This is a sign that you have an inefficient query.
- You can use EF Core's DbFunction feature to inject a piece of SQL code held in an SQL user-defined function (UDF) into a LINQ query. This allows you to tweak part of an EF Core query that's run on the database server.
- If a database query is slow, check the SQL code that EF Core is producing. You can obtain the SQL code by looking at the Information logged messages that EF Core produces.
- If you feel you can produce better SQL for a query than EF Core is producing, you can use EF Core 2.1's *query types* in a `FromSql` method call, or use Dapper to execute your SQL query.
- If all other performance-tuning approaches don't provide the performance you need, consider altering the database structure, including adding properties to hold cached values. But be warned: you need to be careful how you do this.

For readers who are familiar with EF6:

- EF6.x doesn't have EF Core's DbFunction feature, which makes calling a UDF so easy.
- EF6.x doesn't have EF Core's backing fields feature (and the `IEnumerable<T>` navigational collection feature—see section 8.1) that allows you to stop a developer from adding/removing entries to a navigational collection.

Different database types and EF Core services

This chapter covers

- Looking at different database server types
- Using the CQRS architecture with EF Core
- Understanding how the `SaveChanges` method sets keys
- Using EF Core's internal services
- Accessing EF Core's command-line services

This chapter starts with the differences you might encounter in the range of relational databases that EF Core supports. To bring this to life, you'll convert our book app from using SQL Server to the MySQL database to see what changes. I make that application available in the Git repo branch Chapter14MySql.

You'll then look at the Command Query Responsibility Segregation (CQRS) architecture discussed at the end of the preceding chapter (see section 13.6). We'll spend quite a bit of time on this, as it's a useful architecture and its implementation highlights advanced features inside EF Core. You'll also add a NoSQL database to the mix to end up with a high-performance version of our original book-selling site application. It might not challenge Amazon, but it's still pretty fast for a single-instance

ASP.NET Core application. This application is available on the book's Git repo branch Chapter14 as well as on a live site at http://cqrsravendb.efcoreinaction.com/.

The end of this chapter goes deeper into EF Core and looks at its internal services and what you can do with them. The EF Core team has designed these services to allow you to alter the way EF Core works inside. This is advanced stuff, but it's worth knowing about in case your project could benefit from it.

14.1 What differences do other database server types bring?

In most of this book, you've used an SQL Server database, but what happens if you want to use a different type of database server? EF Core has multiple database providers that access a range of database servers, and that list will grow over time. So, the question is, does anything change with different database types and providers?

You'll tackle this wide-ranging question with a worked example: you'll convert our book app from using an SQL Server database to a MySQL database. Typically, you don't change databases of an application; you just have to get your application working with the database of your choice. But it's instructive to see what changes when you swap database types, because it gives you an idea of the sorts of issues you may encounter when using different database types.

To make the example a bit harder, you'll convert the performance-tuned version of the book app (see section 13.2), which has an SQL UDF in it. That brings in the complication of raw SQL code that you add to the database outside EF Core, and this does create some issues.

I've chosen a MySQL database because it's a well-known database with a community version that's available under the GPL license on many platforms. You can run the application locally by downloading a MySQL server; I give full details on how to do that next. Following that, this section covers the following topics:

- First steps: creating an instance of our application's DbContext for a MySQL database
- What you have to do to convert the book app from SQL Server to MySQL
- A general look at other database server types and the differences they may bring

---

How to run the MySQL version of the example book-selling site locally

If you want to run the MySQL version of the book app, you need a local MySQL database server. Here are the steps you need to follow to run the Chapter14MySql branch of the Git repo:

1　Download a copy of the MySQL Community database server.
2　Go to https://dev.mysql.com/downloads/ and select the MySQL Community edition.
3　Click the MySQL Community Server and then select the correct installer for your development system. MySQL works across many operating systems.

Note: I recommend this video showing the steps on how to download and install the community version of the MySQL database: www.youtube.com/watch?v=fwQyZz6cNGU.

(continued)

4   Install the MySQL Community database server.

I chose the custom installation, and selected the server and the MySQL Workbench. The Workbench is like Microsoft's SQL Server Management Studio and allows you to inspect the databases and then delete them when you've finished.

5   Configure the community MySQL database server.

6   After the MySQL Community server is installed, you need to configure the server. During the configuration stage, I left all the settings at their default values. The only specific item you need to set is a user in the MySQL User Account section, with a username of `mysqladmin` and a password of `mysqladmin`.

7   I use `mysqladmin` for the username and password in the connection strings already in the Chapter14MySql application. If you want to use a different username/password, you need to update the connection strings in the appsetting.json file.

After this, you can run the Chapter14MySql application via Visual Studio 2017 (press F5), or VS Code (Debug > Net Core launch (web)), or type `dotnet run` on a console terminal in the EfCoreInAction project directory.

I use the MySQL EF Core database provider Pomelo.EntityFrameworkCore.MySql in my application. There's another MySQL database provider, MySql.Data.EntityFrameworkCore, but when I was building my application, that database provider didn't support EF Core 2.0; it's worth checking out, though.

14.1.1 Creating an instance of the application's DbContext for MySQL

The first thing you need is to be able to create an instance of the application's DbContext that accesses a MySQL database rather than an SQL Server database. Section 2.2.2 showed how to create an instance of the application's DbContext with SQL Server, and this listing shows the same code, but with the changes needed to use a MySQL database shown in bold. In this case I show the connection string as a constant, but in the ASP.NET Core-based book app you would need to update the connection string in the appsetting.json/appsettings.Development.json file.

Listing 14.1   Creating an instance of the DbContext to access the database

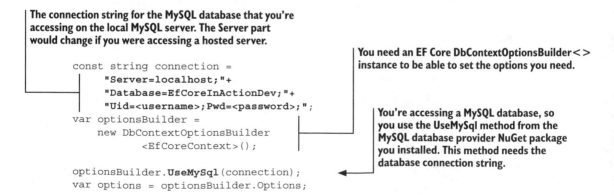

```
using (var context = new EfCoreContext(options))
{
    var bookCount = context.Books.Count();
    //... etc.
```

Uses DbContext to find out how
many books are in the database

Creates the EfCoreContext using the options you've set
up. DbContext should be disposed of after you've
finished your data access.

As you can see, there aren't a lot of changes—just the connection string and changing the `UseSqlServer` method to the `UseMySql` method. You have to install the EF Core MySQL database provider NuGet package Pomelo.EntityFrameworkCore.MySql to get access to the `UseMySql` method, and a MySQL database.

14.1.2 *What you have to do to convert the SQL Server application to MySQL*

Although the changes to create an instance of the application's DbContext are small, other changes are necessary to make the application work. This section lists all the changes required to make the Chapter13-Part1 branch version of the book app, which used SQL Server, now work with MySQL. I've split these into significant changes and housekeeping changes.

SIGNIFICANT CHANGES NEEDED TO CONVERT FROM CHAPTER13-PART1 VERSION TO USE MYSQL

The significant changes required in the Chapter13-Part1 application are related to migrations and the raw SQL in the application, as detailed here:

1 Rerun the `Add-Migration` command for the MySQL database provider.

In chapters 2 and 4, you added database migrations to the book app application (see section 11.2). These migrations are built for an SQL Server database, not a MySQL database, so you must change them.

First, you update the class called `ContextFactoryNeededForMigrations` in the DataLayer to MySQL. You change the connection string to point to your local MySQL database and replace the `UseSqlServer` method with the `UseMySql` method. That requires you to add the MySQL database provider package to the DataLayer project. You need to do that because the command-line migration tools use this class to obtain an instance of the application's DbContext.

After deleting the old migration files, you run the `Add-Migration/dotnet ef migrations add` command to build a new set of migration files using the MySQL database provider.

2 Change the raw SQL in places where the MySQL format is different from SQL Server.

In section 13.2, you added a UDF called `AuthorsStringUdf` to your database to improve the performance of building the comma-delimited list of authors of a book. That UDF is written for an SQL Server database, and, although MySQL supports UDFs, the syntax of a UDF is different. You converted the

`AuthorsStringUdf` UDF to the MySQL format successfully, but unfortunately, the `COALESCE` string-combining trick that you used doesn't work on MySQL. You therefore have to remove the UDF and go back to the LINQ-based approach to combine the author names.

This is a typical problem when you change database server types and have raw SQL commands. The EF Core's database provider translates LINQ or EF Core commands into the correct format for the database type, but any raw SQL commands you write need checking to ensure they work on the new database type. But even with the EF Core–produced SQL, problems can arise, as the next point shows.

3   Fix any type mapping between .NET and the database that has changed.

When you converted from an SQL server database to a MySQL database, the LINQ query that calculates the average review votes (see section 13.1.2) threw an exception. It turns out that the returned type of the SQL `AVG` command on MySQL is a nullable `decimal`, rather than the nullable `double` in SQL Server. To overcomes this, you need to change the `BookListDto`'s `AverageReviewVotes` property .NET type to `decimal?` to match the way MySQL works.

Other, more subtle type differences exist between database servers. For instance, MySQL stores all strings in Unicode (16-bits), MySQL's `DATETIME` default precision is slightly lower than SQL Server's `DATETIME2` precision, and so on. One of my unit tests broke because of the difference in the `DateTime` precision, but everything else worked fine. In bigger applications, other problems could arise from these small changes.

THE SMALL, HOUSEKEEPING CHANGES NEEDED TO SWAP TO MYSQL DATABASE PROVIDER

You need to make minor changes to make the Chapter13-Part1 application work with the MySQL database provider. They're trivial, but the application isn't going to work without them.

The first change is to the `DefaultConnection` string in ASP.NET Core's appsetting.json file. When running the application locally for development, the connection string must be in the correct format to access the local MySQL database (see listing 14.1). If you deploy the application to a web host, you need to provide the correct connection string during the publish process to access the hosted MySQL database (see section 5.4.1).

You also need to alter ASP.NET Core's `ConfigureServices` method in the `Startup` class, where the application's DbContext is registered as a service. You replace the `UseSqlServer` method with the `UseMySql` method. That requires you to add the MySQL database provider package to your ASP.NET Core project.

14.1.3 *Looking at other database server types and differences*

The two key issues when looking at a database to use with EF Core are as follows:

- Does the database have the features you need?
- Does EF Core have a database provider that properly supports that database?

Looking at the database features first, mostly minor differences exist in SQL syntax or features. The SQLite database has the biggest number of feature limitations (it does have the suffix *lite*), but most other database servers provide good coverage of all SQL features that EF Core uses.

> **NOTE** If you're interested in SQLite, you can learn about the limitations of the SQLite database in chapter 15 (see table 15.2), which covers using SQLite in-memory databases for quicker unit testing.

Typical of a minor database difference is MySQL's requirement that the EF Core's concurrency timestamp (see section 8.7.2) must be of the .NET type `DateTime`, rather than the `byte[]` in SQL Server, whereas a PostgreSQL database uses a column called `xmin` (see http://mng.bz/5zB9). I'm sure that lots of subtle EF Core issues exist in various databases, because each database server works in a slightly different way.

> **TIP** Most of the Microsoft documentation, and mine, uses SQL Server as the primary example. Most other database providers publish documentation highlighting any differences from the standard EF Core setup. You can find links to this documentation via the EF Core's database providers' list (see https://docs .microsoft.com/en-us/ef/core/providers/).

The quality of the EF Core database provider and the level of support it provides is also another part of the equation. Writing a database provider for EF Core is a nontrivial task, and the SQL Server database provider written by the EF Core team is the gold standard. You should test any database provider to ensure that it works for you. When I started using the Pomelo.EntityFrameworkCore.MySql database provider, I found a problem, and when I raised an issue on the Pomelo Foundation EF Core GitHub issue page, I got a workaround in 24 hours—which I thought was a good result.

> **NOTE** Although talking about various databases is important for EF Core, I don't cover running an EF Core application on different platforms, such as Linux, macOS, and so on. That topic is a .NET Core issue, and I recommend Dustin Metzgar's *.NET Core in Action* (Manning, 2018), which covers this in detail.

14.1.4 Summarizing EF Core's ability to work with multiple database types

Doing this database swap, plus a bit of work with PostgreSQL, shows me that EF Core and its database providers do an excellent job of handling various database types. The only problems I had during the conversion from SQL Server to MySQL were the differences in how each database server worked. EF Core can also produce database migrations specifically for each database type (see section 11.2.1, subsection "Migrations are database-provider specific"), which is another help for developers who don't know the SQL language well.

14.2   *Developing a CQRS architecture application with EF Core*

Having talked about various databases, I now want to talk about a solution that combines a relational database handled by EF Core with a NoSQL database. This comes about from my suggestion in section 13.6 that a CQRS architecture using a polyglot database structure would provide better scalability performance.

> **DEFINITION**   A *CQRS architecture* segregates operations that read data from operations that update data, by using separate interfaces. This can maximize performance, scalability, and security, and supports the evolution of the system over time through higher flexibility. See http://mng.bz/Ix8D.

> **DEFINITION**   A *polyglot database structure* uses a combination of storage types; for instance, relational databases, NoSQL databases, and flat files. The idea is that each database type has its strengths and weaknesses, and by using two or more, you can obtain a better overall system. See http://mng.bz/6r1W.

The CQRS architecture acknowledges that the read side of an application is different from the write side. Reads are often complicated, drawing in data from multiple places, whereas the write side is often much simpler. You can see in the example application that listing the books is complex, but adding a review is fairly trivial. Separating the code for each part can help you focus on the specific features of each part; this is another application of the SoC software principle.

In chapter 13, you produced the performance version, in which you cached values (see section 13.4). It struck me then that the final query didn't access any relationships and could be stored in a simpler database, such as a NoSQL database. In this example, you'll use a *polyglot* database structure, with a mixture of SQL and NoSQL databases, for the following reasons:

- Using an SQL write-side database makes sense because business applications often use relational data. Think about a real book-selling site: it would have a *lot* of complex, linked data to handle business aspects such as suppliers, inventory, pricing, orders, payment, delivery, tracking, audits, and so on. I think a relational/SQL database with its superior level of data integrity is the right choice for many business problems.
- But those relationships and some aspects of an SQL database, such as the need to dynamically calculate some values, can make it slow at retrieving data. So, a NoSQL database with precalculated values such as the "average review votes" can improve performance considerably over an SQL database. This is what Mateusz Stasch calls "a legitimate cache" in his article at http://mng.bz/A7eC.

The result of these design inputs means you'll develop what I refer to as a *two-database CQRS architecture,* as shown in figure 14.1.

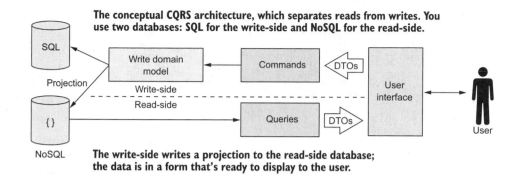

Figure 14.1   A conceptual view of a CQRS architecture with an SQL database for the write side, and a NoSQL database for the read side. A write takes a bit more work because it writes to two databases— the normal SQL database and the new NoSQL read-side database. In this arrangement, the read-side database is writing in the exact format needed by the user, so reads are fast.

Using two databases is a logical step with the CQRS architecture. It brings potential performance gains for reads, but a performance cost on writes. This makes the two-database CQRS architecture appropriate when your business application has more reads of the data than writes. Many business applications have more reads than writes (e-commerce applications are a good example), so this architecture fits our book app well.

14.2.1   Implementation of a two-database CQRS architecture application

You want to move only the book list view data to the read-side database, and not do this for the order-processing part, because only the book list view has a performance issue. It turns out that although adding CQRS does require a fair amount of work, it's simple to apply the CQRS architecture to only part of our application. Figure 14.2 shows the design of our changed book application, with the book list implemented as a two-database CQRS part.

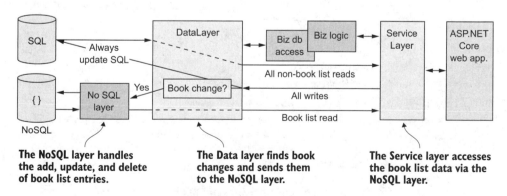

Figure 14.2   To implement the CQRS architecture for the book list, you inspect every write to see whether it'll change the book list data. That's best done by the DataLayer, where you can use the EF Core change tracker to see what's being added, updated, or deleted. If it'll change the book list data, you ask the NoSQL layer to update the database.

Figure 14.2 shows different lines between the ServiceLayer and the DataLayer to illustrate the different routes that data takes through the system, but the lines are notional. The ServiceLayer and BusinessLayer continue to work in the same way, and it's the DataLayer's job to split out any writes that will change the book list view. You do this by overriding the `SaveChanges` method(s) inside the application's DbContext and adding code to work out whether the book list view has changed. If this new code detects a book list view change, it sends a request to the new NoSQL layer to update the NoSQL database.

The other part to change is the `BookListService` class in the ServiceLayer. This class handles the book list, and you change it to access the NoSQL database instead of the SQL database. I selected the RavenDB NoSQL database, which has a community version of its database server that you can run locally. There's also a .NET package that supports LINQ commands, so the LINQ built for EF Core works directly with RavenDB.

I don't cover the RavenDB database access code because it's outside the scope of this book. Visit https://ravendb.net/ for documentation, or the GitHub documentation site at https://github.com/ravendb/docs/, which includes sample code.

NOTE   Thanks to Oren Eini (Twitter @ayende) for his help with using the RavenDB database. Oren is the main force behind the RavenDB NoSQL database and contacted me after one of my articles. He provided support and guidance that were helpful.

How to run the SQL Server and RavenDB CQRS application locally

If you want to run the two-database CQRS application locally, you need a local copy of a RavenDB server. Here are the extra steps you need to follow to run the CQRS application in the Chapter14 branch of the Git repo:

1   Go to the https://ravendb.net/ site; click Buy; and request a license for the free, community version of the RavenDB server. Please read the terms and conditions at https://ravendb.net/terms.

2   Click Download and click the .zip package to download a .NET version of RavenDB to run locally. The Chapter14 EfCoreInAction code uses the 3.5.4 RavenDB Client; if the RavenDB server is of a different version (version 4 is now out), you should update the RavenDB Client NuGet package across the solution.

Note: If you aren't developing on a Windows platform, you can use a hosted RavenDB database instead. I went to www.ravenhq.com and found a package called Experimental, which was free. You can create a database on there and use that in the CQRS application. You need to copy the connection string into the EfCoreInAction appsetting.json file. There's also a Docker container version of RavenDB; see http://mng.bz/CaE4.

3   Unzip the RavenDB .zip package and click the Start.cmd file. This starts the RavenDB server. It should also start a RavenDB database screen in your browser on localhost:8080.

(continued)

4   In the RavenDB database screen on your browser, create a database by clicking the + New Resource button. Name the database `EfCoreInAction-Develop-ment`. You don't need to set any other settings.

5   Now select the Git repo branch Chapter14, which contains the two-database CQRS version of our book app.

6   You can run the CQRS application via Visual Studio 2017 (press F5), or VS Code (Debug > Net Core launch (web)), or type `dotnet run` on a console terminal in the EfCoreInAction project directory.

7   The example site starts with no books in it. You need to click the Admin button and select Generate Books to create test data. Try 100 books as a start. You can always add more books later. After you've created those books, you're good to go.

NOTE   You can see a live version of the two-database CQRS book app at http://cqrsravendb.efcoreinaction.com/. This site has 250,000 books in its database. This site uses a hosted RavenDB database courtesy of www.ravenhq.com (thanks to Jonathan Matheus at RavenHQ for organizing that). The RavenDB hosting I'm using is the simplest/cheapest, so the performance of the live site won't match the performance figures given in this chapter.

In addition to being a high-performance combination, the implementation of this architecture reveals advanced aspects of the way EF Core works. The following are the points covered in the next few subsections:

- How the parts of this CQRS solution interact with each other.
- Finding the book view changes—part 1, finding the correct State and primary key.
- Finding the book view changes—part 2, building the correct `State`.
- Why the CQRS solution is less likely to have out-of-date cached values.

14.2.2 *How the parts of the CQRS solution interact with each other*

When updating an existing application for performance reasons, you need to be careful not to break the application in the process. The book-selling site isn't that complicated, but you still need to be careful when you modify the application over to a CQRS architecture. You therefore want a design that minimizes the changes and isolates the new parts.

I came up with a design that keeps all the NoSQL/RavenDB parts separate. In this final design, the EF Core doesn't know, or care, what database is being used for the read-side part of the CQRS system. This makes the update simpler, plus offers the possibility of changing the NoSQL database used. I like RavenDB, with its support of LINQ, but EF Core version 2.1 previews Azure's NoSQL database, Cosmos, which might be an interesting alternative.

Keeping as much of the new database code in the NoSqlDataLayer, and using interfaces, keeps the impact of the changes to a minimum. Figure 14.3 shows how to hide the NoSQL code behind interfaces to keep that code isolated. You use dependency injection to provide both the DataLayer and the ServiceLayer with methods that allow access to the database.

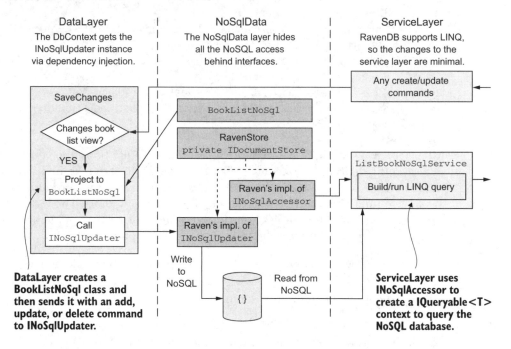

Figure 14.3 **Internals of the NoSqlDataLayer are hidden from the DataLayer and ServiceLayer. The DataLayer and ServiceLayer work with the `BookListNoSql` class, which maps to the book list view, and several interfaces. The aim is to make it easy to add the CQRS read-side database with minimal impact on the existing application. It also allows you to change the read-side database server with minimal refactoring to the code outside the NoSqlDataLayer.**

The changes from the existing, SQL-based book app are as follows:

1. New code is added to the DataLayer by overriding the `SaveChanges` methods. This detects when a change to the database means a certain book list view needs to be updated.
2. The whole of the NoSqlData project is new. It contains all the RavenDB code.
3. Minor changes are made to `ListBookService` to use RavenDB.

The core of this NoSQL implementation is a class I call `RavenStore` (see listing 14.2). RavenDB requires a single instance of the RavenDB's `IDocumentStore`, which is set up on the application's start. This `RavenStore` class provides two methods: one for the DataLayer to get a class for writing to the read-side database, and one for the ServiceLayer to get a class to allow reading of the read-side database.

Listing 14.2 `RavenStore`, with methods to create, read, and write accessors

The primary class to access the RavenDB store.

Defines the two creator methods: CreateNoSqlUpdater and CreateNoSqlAccessor.

```
public class RavenStore :
    INoSqlCreators
{
    public const string RavenEventIdStart
        = "EfCoreInAction.NoSql.RavenDb";
    private readonly DocumentStore _store;
    private readonly ILogger _logger;

    public RavenStore(string connectionString,
        ILogger logger)
    {
        if (string.IsNullOrEmpty(connectionString))
            return;
        _logger = logger;

        var store = new DocumentStore();
        store.ParseConnectionString(connectionString);
        store.Initialize();
```

You use this EventId name when logging accesses. It allows the logging display to mark these as database accesses.

The RavenStore needs the RavenDB connection string and a logger.

To stop the application from throwing an exception on startup if there's no connection string, you leave the store as null. You can throw a better exception later.

RavenDB commands to initialize the database

```
        //Add indexes if not already present
        new BookById().Execute(store);
        new BookByActualPrice().Execute(store);
        new BookByVotes().Execute(store);

        _store = store;
    }

    public INoSqlUpdater CreateNoSqlUpdater()
    {
        return new RavenUpdater(_store, _logger);
    }

    public INoSqlAccessor CreateNoSqlAccessor()
    {
        return new RavenBookAccesser(_store, _logger);
    }
}
```

Ensures that the indexes the application needs have been created

Saves the store ready for the calls to the Create methods

Returns a class that matches the INoSqlUpdater interface. It contains methods to create, update, and delete a BookListNoSql item.

Returns a class that matches the INoSqlAccessor interface. It has a method to create a context (session in RavenDB terms) and then gain LINQ access to the BookListNoSql items.

The `INoSqlCreators` interface is used by the DataLayer to get the method to update the read-side database, and by the ServiceLayer to gain access to the read-side for querying. You need to register a single `RavenStore` instance with ASP.NET Core's dependency injection service as the service to be accessed via the `INoSqlCreators` interface. The following listing shows the section of code in the `ConfigureServices` method in the Startup class that registers the RavenStore as a singleton, which provides the service INoSqlCreators.

Reads the connection string for the RavenDB from the appsettings.json file in the ASP.NET Core application

Registers the RavenStore class as a singleton that's accessed via the INoSqlCreators interface

You need to provide a logger to the RavenStore, along with the RavenDB connection string. You do this in a factory method.

```
var ravenDbConnection =
    Configuration.GetConnectionString
        ("RavenDbConnection");
services.AddSingleton<INoSqlCreators>(ctr =>
{
    var logger = ctr.GetService<ILogger<RavenStore>>();
    return new RavenStore(ravenDbConnection, logger);
});
```

The listing shows part of the Raven implementation of the INoSqlUpdater interface, which the DataLayer would use to update the read-side database. This gives you some idea of how this works.

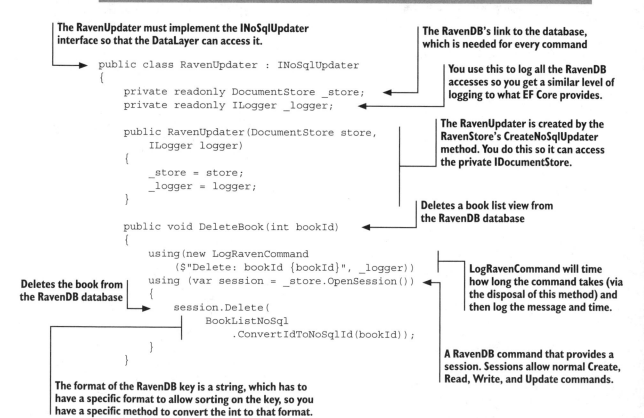

The RavenUpdater must implement the INoSqlUpdater interface so that the DataLayer can access it.

The RavenDB's link to the database, which is needed for every command

You use this to log all the RavenDB accesses so you get a similar level of logging to what EF Core provides.

```
public class RavenUpdater : INoSqlUpdater
{
    private readonly DocumentStore _store;
    private readonly ILogger _logger;

    public RavenUpdater(DocumentStore store,
        ILogger logger)
    {
        _store = store;
        _logger = logger;
    }

    public void DeleteBook(int bookId)
    {
        using(new LogRavenCommand
            ($"Delete: bookId {bookId}", _logger))
        using (var session = _store.OpenSession())
        {
            session.Delete(
                BookListNoSql
                    .ConvertIdToNoSqlId(bookId));
        }
    }
}
```

The RavenUpdater is created by the RavenStore's CreateNoSqlUpdater method. You do this so it can access the private IDocumentStore.

Deletes a book list view from the RavenDB database

Deletes the book from the RavenDB database

LogRavenCommand will time how long the command takes (via the disposal of this method) and then log the message and time.

A RavenDB command that provides a session. Sessions allow normal Create, Read, Write, and Update commands.

The format of the RavenDB key is a string, which has to have a specific format to allow sorting on the key, so you have a specific method to convert the int to that format.

```
public void CreateNewBook(BookListNoSql book)          ◀── Creates a new book list entry
{                                                            in the RavenDB database
    using (new LogRavenCommand
        ($"Create: bookId {book.GetIdAsInt()}",
            _logger))
    using (var bulkInsert = _store.BulkInsert())
    {
        bulkInsert.Store(book);
    }
}
//The UpdateBook and BulkLoad methods are left out to save space
```

For this command, Oren Eini suggested using the BulkInsert, as it's slightly quicker.

LogRavenCommand will time how long the command takes (via the disposal of this method) and then log the message and time.

Now that you've seen the code that'll update the read-side database, the other major part of the CQRS implementation is in how the DataLayer detects changes to the SQL database, which will alter the NoSQL book list view. I describe this next.

14.2.3 Finding book view changes—Part 1, finding the correct state and key

As explained in section 14.2.2, you override the SaveChange methods (sync and async) in the application's DbContext and add code to find changes that will affect the book list view. This turns out to be quite complex; I solved it only by understanding how EF Core works underneath. I think this learning is useful outside the CQRS situation, so in this section I explain how EF Core handles the setting of the foreign keys by looking at the navigational properties.

For this example, you'll add a new Book entity instance, with one new Review entity instance attached to it via the Book's Reviews navigational property. This is the simplest example that shows all the stages that EF Core goes through. Table 14.1 shows the value of the State of the Book entity in the Book's State column after the code in column 1 has run. The other two columns, Book's BookId and Review's BookId, show the value of BookId property of the Book entity, and BookId of the Review entity, respectively, after the code in column 1 has run.

Now, you might be wondering about the large negative value that appears after stage 2, the Add stage in table 14.1. What has happened here is that the Add method has looked at the Book entity's navigational properties to see whether there are any changes in its relationships. EF Core finds that a new Review entity is assigned to the Book entity, so it wants to set the foreign key. In this case, the Book entity hasn't yet been written to the database, so it uses a negative key to represent that relationship. The negative key is unique within the current tracked entities and tells the SaveChanges method which new entities are linked.

In stage 3, in which the SaveChanges method is called, these negative keys link the Book entity and the Review entity. This causes EF Core to output SQL code that first INSERTs the Book entity into the Books table, returning its primary key as normal, followed by an INSERT of the Review entity, including a BookId value taken from the Book entity.

Table 14.1   How EF Core tracks relationships when adding new entities to the database. EF Core's `Add` **method uses negative key values to define the relationships. These negative keys are replaced with the real key value after the entities have been written to the database.**

The three stages in the code	Book's State	Book's BookId	Review's BookId

1. Create instances
 	
`var review = new Review`
`    {NumStars = 5};`
 	
`var book = new Book`
`    {Title = "New book"};`
 	
`book.Reviews = new`
`    List<Review> {review};`
	Detached	0	0

2. `Add` stage `context.Add(book);`	Added	–2147482643	–2147482643
3. `SaveChanges` stage `context.SaveChanges();`	Unchanged	1	1

The problem is, if you wait until after the call to the `SaveChanges` method to get the correct key values, the `State` of the entities will have been cleared. You need a two-stage process, as shown in this listing. In the first part of the process, you capture the `State` and the relationships; and in the second part, you capture the primary key of any `Book` entities.

Listing 14.5   The code inside one of the overridden `SaveChanges`

You must override all the SaveChanges methods (sync and async) to make sure you capture all updates to the database.

This stage is all about detecting the State of all the tracked entities before they get cleared by the call to the base SaveChanges.

```
public override int SaveChanges()
{
    var detectedChanges = BookChangeInfo
        .FindBookChanges(ChangeTracker.Entries());

    var result = base.SaveChanges();

    var booksChanged = BookChange
        .FindChangedBooks(detectedChanges);
    var updater = new ApplyChangeToNoSql
        (this, _updater);
    updater.UpdateNoSql(booksChanged);
    return result;
}
```

Now you can call the base SaveChanges, as you have all the `State` information.

Multiple changes may have been made to a single Book. This stage combines them so you send only one update to the NoSQL database.

Applies any updates to the NoSQL database

The DataLayer oversees the projection of the SQL database into the form that the NoSQL database needs it in. The NoSQL provides an updater method, via the constructor, which will do the update.

Now, let's look inside the `BookChangeInfo` class and the `FindChangedBooks` method, as it's interesting to see the steps required to get the `State` and the `BookId` in the correct form.

14.2.4 Finding the book view changes—Part 2, building the correct State

The preceding section showed you how the `State` property was correct before the call to the `SaveChanges` method, but the `BookId` wouldn't be correct for a new `Book` until after that method call. Obviously, you need to do something before and after the `SaveChanges` method call. This section shows those steps.

Listing 14.5 showed the overridden `SaveChanges` method, with the extra code before and after the call to the base `SaveChanges` method. Now you'll look at what's happening before and after the base `SaveChanges` method call.

BEFORE THE BASE SAVECHANGES METHOD CALL—GET THE STATE AND RELATIONSHIPS

Any change to a relationship in the `Book` entity class could affect the book list view. You therefore mark the `Book` entity and all its relationship entities with an `interface`, as shown in this code snippet:

```
public interface IBookId
{
    int BookId { get; }
}
```

You apply the `IBookId` interface `Book` entity, any entity class that has a foreign-key relationship with the `Book` entity (the `Review`, `PriceOffer`, and `BookAuthor` entities). This allows you to detect when a command changes any of these entities, which in turn will affect the book list view. After you find any change, you decode that change into a series of `BookChangeInfo` instances. The `BookChangeInfo` class holds the `State` before the `SaveChanges` method is called, and the `BookId` that refers to the `Book` entity it changes. This may be a negative value, as shown in table 14.1, or the real `BookId` for an update, but either way you can use it to find all the entities that are linked to a single `Book` entity.

Listing 14.6 shows how the `BookChangeInfo` class works out the correct `State` for the book list view. Working out the right `State` from the `Book` entity's perspective is complex—for instance, a new `Book` entity should set the `State` to `Added`—but a new `Review` should only set the `State` to `Modified`, because the new `Review` only modifies the book list view.

Listing 14.6 The `BookChangeInfo` class and how it decides on the correct `State`

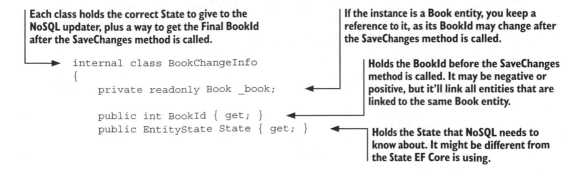

Each class holds the correct State to give to the NoSQL updater, plus a way to get the Final BookId after the SaveChanges method is called.

If the instance is a Book entity, you keep a reference to it, as its BookId may change after the SaveChanges method is called.

Holds the BookId before the SaveChanges method is called. It may be negative or positive, but it'll link all entities that are linked to the same Book entity.

Holds the State that NoSQL needs to know about. It might be different from the State EF Core is using.

```
internal class BookChangeInfo
{
    private readonly Book _book;

    public int BookId { get; }
    public EntityState State { get; }
```

Can be used after the SaveChanges method call to access the correct BookId.

Takes in the BookId provided by the IBookId interface and the entity itself.

```
public int FinalBookId => _book?.BookId ?? BookId;

private BookChangeInfo(int bookId,
    EntityEntry entity)
{
    BookId = bookId;
    _book = entity.Entity as Book;
```

Takes a copy of the entity if it's of type Book. The Book entity always takes precedence in any update.

If the entity is of type Book, you need to handle the SoftDeleted state, as that affects whether you want a book list view for that book.

You find the SoftDeleted property, as you need to see whether this property was changed.

```
    if (_book != null)
    {
        var softDeletedProp = entity.Property(
            nameof(_book.SoftDeleted));

        if (softDeletedProp.IsModified)
        {
            State = _book.SoftDeleted
                ? EntityState.Deleted
                : EntityState.Added;
        }
        else if (entity.State ==
            EntityState.Deleted)
        {
            State = _book.SoftDeleted
                ? EntityState.Unchanged
                : EntityState.Deleted;
        }
        else
        {
            State = _book.SoftDeleted
                ? EntityState.Unchanged
                : entity.State;
        }
    }
    else
    {
        State = EntityState.Modified;
    }
}
```

If the SoftDeleted property has changed, it defines whether the book list contains this book.

If the Book is deleted, you don't want to delete it again if it is already excluded via the SoftDeleted property...

...otherwise, the Book's State will be used, unless the Book is already SoftDeleted.

If it's a linked entity that has changed, this can cause only an update of the book list view.

That might seem like a lot of work to decide on the final State, but because you're using the SoftDeleted property to hide a Book entity (see section 3.5.1), you need to honor that in the NoSQL database. If a Book entity's SoftDeleted property is set to true, you must delete it from book list NoSQL database. Listing 14.6 must correctly handle all the combinations to ensure that it doesn't try to delete an already soft-deleted book from the NoSQL database.

AFTER THE BASE SAVECHANGES METHOD CALL—BUILD A LIST OF BOOKS THAT NEED UPDATING

Now, let's look at how to use this information after the SaveChanges method has been called. You take the BookChangeInfo information, which may include multiple updates to the same Book entity, and coalesce them down to a one-change-per-book list. The trick is to make sure the type of change is correct for the read-side database. This listing shows the BookChange class, with its static method that produces the final update information.

> **Listing 14.7** The BookChange class with its static FindChangedBooks method

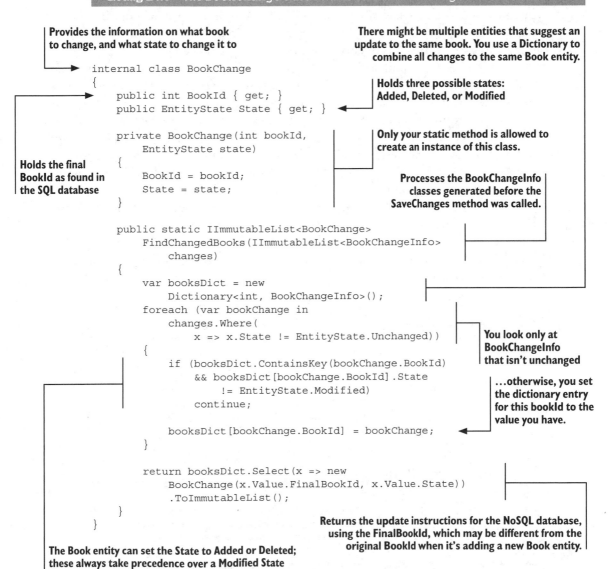

Provides the information on what book to change, and what state to change it to

There might be multiple entities that suggest an update to the same book. You use a Dictionary to combine all changes to the same Book entity.

Holds three possible states: Added, Deleted, or Modified

Only your static method is allowed to create an instance of this class.

Holds the final BookId as found in the SQL database

Processes the BookChangeInfo classes generated before the SaveChanges method was called.

You look only at BookChangeInfo that isn't unchanged

...otherwise, you set the dictionary entry for this bookId to the value you have.

Returns the update instructions for the NoSQL database, using the FinalBookId, which may be different from the original BookId when it's adding a new Book entity.

The Book entity can set the State to Added or Deleted; these always take precedence over a Modified State that other related entities might provide...

```csharp
internal class BookChange
{
    public int BookId { get; }
    public EntityState State { get; }

    private BookChange(int bookId,
        EntityState state)
    {
        BookId = bookId;
        State = state;
    }

    public static IImmutableList<BookChange>
        FindChangedBooks(IImmutableList<BookChangeInfo>
            changes)
    {
        var booksDict = new
            Dictionary<int, BookChangeInfo>();
        foreach (var bookChange in
            changes.Where(
                x => x.State != EntityState.Unchanged))
        {
            if (booksDict.ContainsKey(bookChange.BookId)
                && booksDict[bookChange.BookId].State
                    != EntityState.Modified)
                continue;

            booksDict[bookChange.BookId] = bookChange;
        }

        return booksDict.Select(x => new
            BookChange(x.Value.FinalBookId, x.Value.State))
            .ToImmutableList();
    }
}
```

The result of this is a list of `BookChange` classes, which conveys the `BookId` of the book list view to change, and the `State` it should be changed to. You make this class as small as possible, because in a real system, you might want to save the information in the database, or send it to a background job to process. That would allow you to improve on the performance of the write, but more important, to provide retry and error-checking facilities in case the NoSQL database access fails.

14.2.5 Why the CQRS solution is less likely to have out-of-date cached values

When you create any system in which you cache values, the key issue is to make sure that the cached values stay in step with the calculated values. Applications that handle lots of simultaneous updates can produce situations in which a cached value gets out of step. This is one form of a concurrency issue (see section 8.7).

In section 13.4, you built a version of our application that stored various values, such as the average book's review votes (what I refer to as *cached-values SQL* from now on). In that version, you use EF Core's concurrency detection to find and fix a possible concurrency issue around simultaneous `Reviews` being added to a `Book`. That works, but you need to correctly identify that this is a potential problem and then write code to handle it. But it's better if the design avoids potential concurrency issues, as you did with the `ActualPrice` in the cached-values SQL solution (section 13.4.1). The CQRS solution does that, by removing any concurrency issues right from the start.

Figure 14.4 shows the difference in how the cached-values SQL solution (section 13.4) and the CQRS solution handle the "two simultaneous reviews" problem. Each makes sure that the calculated values are up-to-date, but I believe the CQRS approach is much better because it designs around the problem instead of having special code to handle the problem.

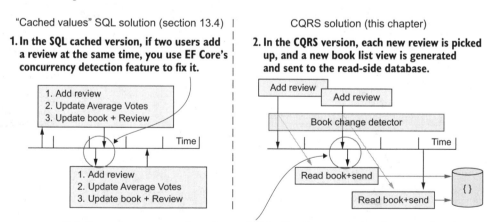

This figure shows a case where the read of the Book's current state happens after the second Add review. But this out-of-sequence update doesn't matter, as all that happens is the read-side database would be updated slightly early with the final, correct value.

Figure 14.4   On the left, the cached-values SQL performance-tuning implementation developed in section 13.4 fixes the problem of two simultaneous reviews being added, by using EF Core's concurrent detection and handling feature. On the right, the CQRS architecture handles the same problem by design; it doesn't need any special handling to cope with this problem.

Unlike the cached-values SQL solution, in which you had to consider each cached value separately and devise a different solution for each, the CQRS design handles all potential problems in one go; it effectively designs them out. In addition, the CQRS architecture helps with the overall design of the system, which is why I think CQRS architecture is worthy of consideration for systems that have more reads of data than writes.

14.2.6 Is the two-database CQRS architecture worth the effort?

Implementing this two-database CQRS architecture isn't simple and took me over a week to develop, which is long for me. Admittedly, the main part is learning a new database approach, but there are also some complex EF Core parts to write to. So, is it worth the effort? I'll answer that question in terms of three distinct aspects:

- Is the improvement in read-side performance worth the extra effort to convert the application?
- Is the drop in the performance of any book-related database write acceptable to gain the extra read-side performance?
- Does the extra effort, complexity, and robustness warrant the read-side performance that the CQRS architecture brings?

THE DIFFERENCES IN READ-SIDE PERFORMANCE BETWEEN THE NON-CQRS AND CQRS SOLUTIONS

First, let's compare the performance of the CQRS solution against the "best-SQL" solution—the part 2 version (see section 13.3) in which SQL had to calculate the average vote every time the book list was displayed. Figure 14.5 shows the performance of the CQRS solution against the part 2 version for the following database content:

- 100,000 books, which have ½ million book reviews
- 250,000 books, which have 1.4 million book reviews
- 500,000 books, which have 2.7 million book reviews

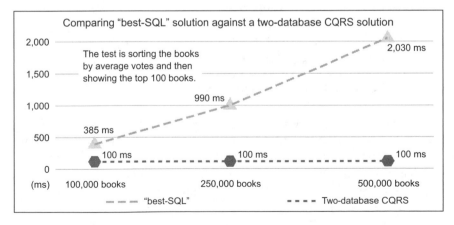

Figure 14.5 The time it takes to sort all the books by the average review votes and then show the 100 top books. The graph compares the "best-SQL" solution (see section 13.3) of the book app against the two-database CQRS solution.

> ### How I measured the performance—the test environment
>
> The performance testing is done the same way as in chapter 13 (see sidebar in section 13.1.2): I measured the time it takes for the request to complete in the Chrome browser.
>
> The SQL database and the RavenDB database were running locally on my development machine. There are variations in the measured figures, so I discarded the first access, which could be slow, and took the average of several repeated requests.

Clearly, the performance of this two-database CQRS solution is much better than the "best-SQL" solution from section 13.3. No user wants to wait two seconds for the books to be sorted. The SQL version is slow because it must dynamically calculate the average votes every time. The CQRS solution, in which the book list view contains a precalculated average votes value with an index, is obviously much faster.

But to provide a fair comparison, you need to compare the CQRS solution against the part 3 solution (see section 13.4), in which you add cached values to your SQL database (the cached-values SQL solution). In this case, the difference is much smaller; see figure 14.6.

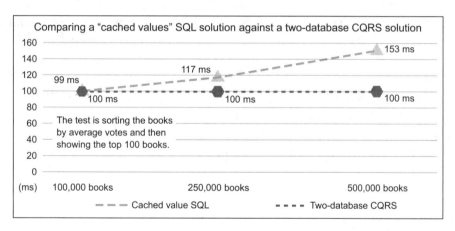

Figure 14.6   The time it takes to sort all the books by the average review votes and then show the 100 top books. This graph compares the "cached values SQL" version (see section 13.4) of the book app against the two-database CQRS solution.

Figure 14.6 shows that the cached value with its index is the main reason that the CQRS solution is quicker. When using a CQRS solution to improve performance, the primary goal must be to store the exact data that the user wants to see or sort and/or filter on what I call *a precalculated view*. If you're not going to build a precalculated view, but just access the same database as before, you won't gain much in terms of performance. The precalculated view is the main performance multiplier.

Looking beyond the precalculated view issue, figure 14.6 also shows that the RavenDB database, with its simpler database structure, has better performance as the number of books in the database increases. This brings us to another side of performance: scalability.

Scalability determines how many simultaneous users an application can handle while still providing good performance (see chapter 12, especially section 12.7). Because NoSQL databases such as RavenDB are dealing with a single entry containing all the information, a read or write is simpler than in the SQL case. In general, this makes NoSQL databases easier to duplicate (to have multiple databases all containing the same data).

The effect of having multiple databases on scalability can be significant. Not only can you spread database access across multiple databases, but you can locate databases geographically around the world to provide shorter access times.

To summarize on performance:

- The CQRS architecture solution provides better performance than a noncached SQL version, when its read-side database holds a precalculated view of the book list. This precalculated view makes the handling of sorting, filtering, and viewing a book much faster.
- Using a NoSQL database, which has a simpler, single-entry view, for the read-side database does have performance benefits, especially around scalability, over an SQL database.

IS THE DROP IN THE PERFORMANCE OF ANY BOOK-RELATED DATABASE WRITE ACCEPTABLE?

I said previously that a two-database CQRS architecture is going to be slower on writes, because it must write to two databases. I've measured this in my solution and there's an effect, but it's pretty small. Table 14.2 shows one common case, which is a user adding a review to a book, and the difference in write time.

Table 14.2 The difference in the time taken for the ASP.NET action to return after adding a new review to a book

Solution type	Total time	Notes
Cached-values SQL	13 ms	Simple addition of `Review` entity to the database and a recalculation of the cached values.
Two-database CQRS	35 ms	The extra time is mainly around writing to the NoSQL database. I measured the RavenDB update as taking 25 ms, which is quite long compared to an SQL write.

In my mind, a function that takes less than 50 ms to return to the user isn't worth performance tuning. But in applications with more-complex updates, this time might get too long. But there are plenty of ways to handle this; for instance, you could pass the update a background task to be executed so that the application returns immediately to the user. The only downside of that approach is the user may be shown out-of-date data, which could be confusing. These are the design trade-offs you must think through.

THE DIFFERENCES IN SOFTWARE IMPLEMENTATION BETWEEN NON-CQRS AND CQRS SOLUTIONS

This section compares the cached-values SQL solution in section 13.4 and the two-database CQRS solution in this chapter. Both solutions take extra work to build, and make the software structure more complex. Table 14.3 compares the development effort, complexity, and robustness of the two designs.

Table 14.3   Comparing the cached-values SQL solution in section 13.4 and the two-database CQRS solution against three software criteria

Solution type	Effort	Complexity	Robustness
Cached-values SQL	~ 3 days	Same	Good
Two-database CQRS	~ 8 days	Same	Very good

In terms of development effort, the CQRS implementation takes longer to create than the cached-values SQL solution. Part of that is learning about RavenDB's philosophy and software package, and part of it is coming up with a clever design to separate the NoSQL code from the rest of the application. But I think this is still within a sensible development cost, considering you're performance-tuning an existing, SQL-only, EF Core application (but some managers may not agree with me!).

The CQRS design is more complex than the original EF Core design in chapter 5, but I accept some additional complexity whenever I apply performance tuning. But the cached-values SQL solution also added complexity, just in other places. Their complexity is different: the CQRS design has complex interfaces to hide things, the cached-values SQL solution has complex concurrency handling code. Overall, I think the CQRS design and the cached-values SQL solution are comparable in the extra complexity they add to the book app.

The big, positive difference is in the robustness of the CQRS design. I rate it above the cached-values SQL solution because it designs out the concurrency issues that the cached-values SQL solution has. You don't need any explicit code to handle concurrency in my CQRS solution. That's a big plus.

To summarize the differences in implementation:

- The CQRS is superior to the cached-values SQL solution (see section 13.4) because the design doesn't need special handling of concurrency issues.
- Changing the book app over to a CQRS architecture adds complexity to the code, but no more than the cached-values SQL solution does.
- The CQRS implementation takes longer (about eight days) to develop than the cached-values SQL solution (about three days). But, in my opinion, it's worth the extra effort.

14.3 Accessing and changing EF Core services

> **TIME-SAVER** This section discusses advanced features within EF Core that aren't useful in everyday use of EF Core. If you're new to EF Core, you might want to skip this section for now.

Now let's look at a completely different area of EF Core: its internal services. EF Core is built in a modular way, with most of the key parts of its code linked by dependency injection (see section 5.3). The EF Core team has made these services available for developers to use for their own uses; you can override some of the services if you want to change the way EF Core works.

Using or overriding the EF Core services is an advanced feature, but it can be useful when you need to customize EF Core behavior, or to save you from writing code that EF Core has already implemented. This section covers the following:

- How and why you might use an EF Core's service in your own code
- How and why you might override one of EF Core's internal services

14.3.1 Accessing an EF Core service to help in your own application

EF Core has more than 50 services that you could gain access to. Most aren't that useful, but a few might help with a project you're working on. One part of EF Core I'm interested in is its mapping of entity classes to SQL tables. In previous applications I wrote with EF6.x, I had to have a table of how EF mapped .NET types to database types. With EF Core, you can tap into its relational mapping service and obtain that information directly from the EF Core code.

To do this, you need to access the database provider mapping service via the `IRelationalTypeMapper` interface. This service provides methods that can map a .NET type, with any EF Core configurations or attributes, to an SQL type, and from an SQL type to a .NET type. Listing 14.8 shows how to obtain an instance of the SQL-type-to-.NET-type mapper that EF Core uses for an SQL Server database. In this case, you give it the SQL type, and it tells you the information about the .NET type, including information you'd need to configure EF Core to match that SQL Server type.

> **Listing 14.8 Determining how EF Core would map an SQL type to a .NET type**

The mapping depends on the database provider you're using. In this case, you're using an SQL Server.

You must create an instance of the application's DbContext to access the services.

```
//… other setup code left out
optionsBuilder.UseSqlServer(connection);
using (var context = new EfCoreContext(optionsBuilder.Options))
{
    var service = context.GetService<IRelationalTypeMapper>();
    var netTypeInfo = service.FindMapping("varchar(20)");
```

You use the GetService<T> method to get the IRelationalMapper; this will be mapped to the database provider's mapper.

You can use this service to find the mapping from an SQL type to a .NET type.

```
netTypeInfo.ClrType.ShouldEqual(typeof(string));
netTypeInfo.IsUnicode.ShouldBeFalse();
netTypeInfo.Size.ShouldEqual(20);
}
```

**Unit test checks that verify that
the .NET version would be a string**

**Unit test checks that confirm the EF Core
configuration parts needed to property-map
a string to the specific SQL type**

There are other services, but many are even more specific to EF Core and therefore not that useful outside EF Core itself. But the next section shows how you can replace an EF Core service with your own custom variant, which opens interesting possibilities.

> **TIP** If you want to see all the services that EF Core makes available, there isn't a simple method to call. But if you write the code var service = context.GetService <IServiceScopeFactory>(); and use the debugger to look at the nonpublic members, you can see the list of all services.

14.3.2 Replacing an EF Core service with your own modified service

Wouldn't it be great if you could change how the internals of EF Core work? For instance, you could modify the IModelValidator service to check that the database table names adhere to your specific project rules. Or you could apply a new property-ty-naming convention to set the correct SQL varchar/nvarchar type by overriding the IRelationalTypeMapper service.

Even if you could replace them, some of these services are complicated; for instance, the RelationalModelValidator class has 11 methods. So it would be a nightmare if you had to re-create all that code, and you might have to change your code when a new EF Core version comes out. Thankfully the EF Core team has thought about developers wanting to alter or extend EF Core internal services.

The EF Core development team has built all the EF Core internal services with over-ridable methods. You can inherit the appropriate class and then just override the specific method you want to change, with the option of calling the base method if you need to. This makes it much easier to build a customer service, although you still need to understand what you're doing.

For this example, you're going to override part of the EF Core SqlServerType-Mapper class, which has 20 parts that can be overridden. Writing all those parts would be an impossible job, but you can override just the one you want to change and leave the rest alone, as shown in figure 14.7.

You're going to override the FindMapping(IProperty property) method to add your own By Convention rule to EF Core's configuration stage. The new rule will allow you to configure the SQL storage of certain string properties as a non-Unicode (8-bit) string to save space (normally, string properties are held in 16-bit Unicode characters in SQL Server). The new rule is as follows: if a string property name ends with Ascii, it should be stored using SQL Server's varchar type (8-bit chars) rather than the normal string mapping to SQL Server's nvarchar type (16-bit chars).

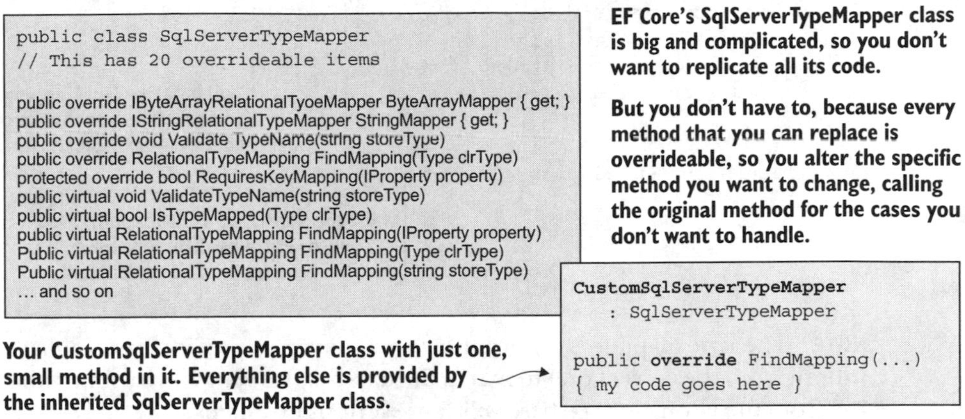

```
public class SqlServerTypeMapper
// This has 20 overrideable items

public override IByteArrayRelationalTypeMapper ByteArrayMapper { get; }
public override IStringRelationalTypeMapper StringMapper { get; }
public override void ValidateTypeName(string storeType)
public override RelationalTypeMapping FindMapping(Type clrType)
protected override bool RequiresKeyMapping(IProperty property)
public virtual void ValidateTypeName(string storeType)
public virtual bool IsTypeMapped(Type clrType)
public virtual RelationalTypeMapping FindMapping(IProperty property)
Public virtual RelationalTypeMapping FindMapping(Type clrType)
Public virtual RelationalTypeMapping FindMapping(string storeType)
... and so on
```

EF Core's SqlServerTypeMapper class is big and complicated, so you don't want to replicate all its code.

But you don't have to, because every method that you can replace is overrideable, so you alter the specific method you want to change, calling the original method for the cases you don't want to handle.

```
CustomSqlServerTypeMapper
    : SqlServerTypeMapper

public override FindMapping(...)
{ my code goes here }
```

Your CustomSqlServerTypeMapper class with just one, small method in it. Everything else is provided by the inherited SqlServerTypeMapper class.

Figure 14.7 A tiny change to one of EF Core's key services can be achieved by inheriting the service you want to change and then overriding just the method that you want to change. You can even call the original method for the cases you don't want to change.

The first step is to create a custom type mapper, which is shown in the following listing. You override the .NET-type-to-SQL-type mapping method, in which you add the new code.

Listing 14.9 The custom SQL Server type-mapping class

Creates a custom type mapper by inheriting the SqlServer type mapper

You need to add a constructor that passes the dependencies it needs to the inherited class.

```
public class CustomSqlServerTypeMapper
    : SqlServerTypeMapper
{
    public CustomSqlServerTypeMapper(
        RelationalTypeMapperDependencies dependencies)
        : base(dependencies) {}
```

You override only the FindMapping method that deals with .NET type to SQL type. All the other mapping methods you leave as is.

Gets the mapping that the SQLl Server database provider would normally do. This gives you information you can use.

```
    public override RelationalTypeMapping
        FindMapping(IProperty property)
    {
        var currentMapping = base.FindMapping(property);
        if (property.ClrType == typeof(string)
            && property.Name.EndsWith("Ascii"))
        {
            var size = currentMapping.Size == null
                ? "max"
                : currentMapping.Size.ToString();
```

You insert the new rule here. If the property is of .NET type string and the property name ends with Ascii, you want to set it as an SQL varchar instead of the normal SQL nvarchar.

You work out the size part of SQL type string—either the size provided, or max if the size is null.

```
        return new StringTypeMapping(
            $"varchar({size})",
            DbType.AnsiString, true,
            currentMapping.Size);
    }

    return currentMapping;
    }
}
```

Builds **StringTypeMapping** with the various parts set to a varchar type column—an 8-bit character string

If the property didn't fit the new rule, you want the normal EF Core mapping. You therefore return the SQL type mapping that the base method has calculated.

NOTE   The type mapper is different for every database provider, so you have to inherit from the correct one to match the database server you're using. Inheriting from the wrong service base will cause serious problems.

The second step is to alter the configuration options sent to the application's DbContext when you create a new instance. Listing 14.10 shows the alteration of the ASP.NET Core's ConfigureServices method in the Startup class, which registers the application's DbContext, plus its options, with ASP.NET Core's dependency injection module. The new line of code is shown in bold.

> **Listing 14.10   Registering the custom type mapper to replace the normal mapper**

The normal code registers the **EFCoreContext** class, which is the application's DbContext, and its options with ASP.NET Core dependency injection module

The new code that replaces the normal relational type mapper with the modified type mapper

```
var connection = Configuration
    .GetConnectionString("DefaultConnection");
services.AddDbContext<EfCoreContext>(
    options => options.UseSqlServer(connection,
        b => b.MigrationsAssembly("DataLayer"))
        .ReplaceService<IRelationalTypeMapper,
        CustomSqlServerTypeMapper>()
    );
```

NOTE   You must specify the interface for service as the first part of the generic ReplaceService<IService, TImplementation> method.

14.4   *Accessing command-line tools from software*

EF Core provides a series of command-line tools to allow you to migrate your database or reverse-engineer a database (see chapter 11 for more details). These are known as *design-time services*, because these services are normally run by typing a command into the PMC in Visual Studio or the command prompt on your system. But you can access them via software, which can be useful if you want to automate something or exploit a tool for your own use.

> **WARNING**   This code accesses internal parts of the EF Core system, which may change with no warning when a new release of EF Core comes out.

As an example, you'll tap into the EF Core's reverse-engineering tool design-time service and use it to get data that allows you to list the schema of a database referred to by a connection string.

14.4.1 *How to access EF Core design-time services*

To access EF Core design-time services, you need to re-create the setup that EF Core uses when you call commands such as Add-Migration or dotnet ef dbcontext scaffold. This is a bit complicated, and thanks to Erik Ejlskov Jensen (http://erikej.blogspot .co.uk/) for helping me with this.

Listing 14.11 shows the code to create the scaffolding (also known as *reverse-engineering*) service that's used to produce the entity classes and application's DbContext from an existing database (see section 11.3). For this to compile, you need to include the NuGet packages for the database providers that you want to access the design-time services; for instance, Microsoft.EntityFrameworkCore.SqlServer to access the SQL Server services.

> **Listing 14.11** Building and returning the scaffolder design-time service

Uses an enum to select which database provider's design services you want to use. You also have a method (not shown) that will select the correct enum based on the current DbContext.

Just like the command-line versions, the design-time commands can return errors or warnings. They're placed in these lists.

```
public enum DatabaseProviders { SqlServer, MySql }

public class DesignTimeProvider
{
    private readonly List<string> _errors
        = new List<string>();
    private readonly List<string> _warnings
        = new List<string>();

    public ImmutableList<string> Errors =>
        _errors.ToImmutableList();
    public ImmutableList<string> Warnings =>
        _warnings.ToImmutableList();

    public ServiceProvider GetScaffolderService
        (DatabaseProviders databaseProvider,
        bool addPrualizer = true)
    {
        var reporter = new OperationReporter(
            new OperationReportHandler(
                m => _errors.Add(m),
                m => _warnings.Add(m)));

        // Add base services for scaffolding
        var serviceCollection =
            new ServiceCollection()
            .AddScaffolding(reporter)
            .AddSingleton<IOperationReporter,
                OperationReporter>()
            .AddSingleton<IOperationReportHandler,
                OperationReportHandler>();
```

You provide the Errors and Warnings as immutable lists.

Returns the design services for the chosen type of database provider. The addPluralizer parameter adds/leaves out a pluralizer used to make classes singular and tables plural.

All this code is required to create the scaffolder design-time service.

```
if (addPrualizer)
    serviceCollection.AddSingleton
        <IPluralizer, ScaffoldPuralizer>();

switch (databaseProvider)
{
    case DatabaseProviders.SqlServer:
    {
        var designProvider =
            new SqlServerDesignTimeServices();
        designProvider.
            ConfigureDesignTimeServices(
                serviceCollection);
        return serviceCollection
            .BuildServiceProvider();
    }
    case DatabaseProviders.MySql:
    {
        var designProvider =
            new MySqlDesignTimeServices();
        designProvider.
            ConfigureDesignTimeServices(
                serviceCollection);
        return serviceCollection
            .BuildServiceProvider();
    }
    default:
        throw new ArgumentOutOfRangeException(
            nameof(databaseProvider),
            databaseProvider, null);
    }
}
}
```

You optionally add a pluralizer.

In this case, you support only two types of database providers: SQL Server and MySQL

Creates the SQL Server design-time service for the loaded SQL Server database provider NuGet package

Creates the MySQL design-time service for the loaded MySQL database provider NuGet package

Adds the services the scaffolder needs and returns the built service

You can use other design-time services, such as the migration tools, but those services will need a different setup. The best way to find out what's required is to look at the EF Core source at https://github.com/aspnet/EntityFrameworkCore.

14.4.2 How to use design-time services to build the EfSchemaCompare tool

Section 11.4.2 introduced the EfSchemaCompare tool I created to help with database migrations. This uses the design-time scaffolding service to read in the schema of the database you want to inspect. Using the scaffolding service replaces a large amount of ADO.NET code I had to write when I built the EF6.x version of the EfSchemaCompare tool. And because the scaffolding service is provided by the database provider, my new EfSchemaCompare tool can work with any relational database that EF Core supports.

This listing shows how to use one of the available scaffolding services to get information on the schema of the database.

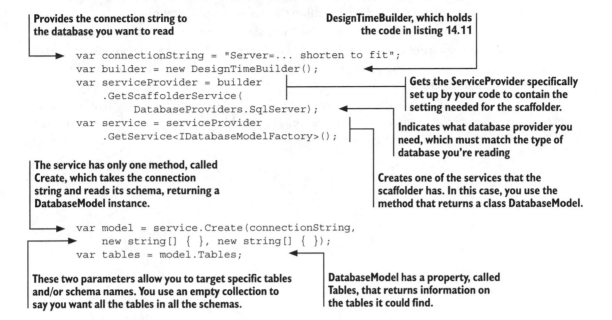

Listing 14.12 Using the design-time service in your code to read a database's schema

Provides the connection string to
the database you want to read

DesignTimeBuilder, which holds
the code in listing 14.11

```
var connectionString = "Server=... shorten to fit";
var builder = new DesignTimeBuilder();
var serviceProvider = builder
    .GetScaffolderService(
        DatabaseProviders.SqlServer);
var service = serviceProvider
    .GetService<IDatabaseModelFactory>();
```

Gets the ServiceProvider specifically
set up by your code to contain the
setting needed for the scaffolder.

Indicates what database provider you
need, which must match the type of
database you're reading

The service has only one method, called
Create, which takes the connection
string and reads its schema, returning a
DatabaseModel instance.

Creates one of the services that the
scaffolder has. In this case, you use the
method that returns a class DatabaseModel.

```
var model = service.Create(connectionString,
    new string[] { }, new string[] { });
var tables = model.Tables;
```

These two parameters allow you to target specific tables
and/or schema names. You use an empty collection to
say you want all the tables in all the schemas.

DatabaseModel has a property, called
Tables, that returns information on
the tables it could find.

From this code, EfSchemaCompare can use the data to compare with EF Core's `Model` property, which contains a model of what the database should look like based on the entity classes and EF Core configuration.

Using this design-time service provides three things to help build the EfSchema-Compare tool:

- It removes the need to write a lot of complicated ADO.NET code to read in a database's schema and convert it to a useful form.
- It provides a solution that would work with any relational database supported by EF Core.
- If new features appear in EF Core, it's more likely that the design-time service will upgrade too, thus reducing the amount of refactoring required to support that new feature.

Summary

- The main differences between each database type are the EF Core database provider, the `UseXXX` method (for instance `UseMySql`), and the connection string.
- Features and syntax differ slightly among the various database types. You need to read the documentation relevant to the database type and its EF Core provider.
- The CQRS architecture with different read-side and write-side databases can improve performance, especially if you use a NoSQL database as the read-side database.

- When tracking changes to an entity, the `State` of an entity is correct before the call to the `SaveChanges` method, but the primary and foreign keys of a new entity will be correct only after the call to the `SaveChanges` method.
- You can access EF Core internal services via the `context.GetService<T>` method.
- You can replace an EF Core internal service by using the `ReplaceService <IService, TImplemenation>` method at the time that you configure the application's DbContext.
- You can access the EF Core design-line services, such as `Add-Migration` or `Scaffold` commands, via software. This could save you time when developing a tool to work with EF Core.

Unit testing
EF Core applications

15

This chapter covers

- Simulating a database for unit testing

- Using an in-memory database for unit testing

- Using real databases for unit testing

- Unit testing a disconnected state update

- Capturing logging information while unit testing

This chapter is about unit testing applications that use EF Core for database access. You'll learn what unit-testing approaches are available and how to choose the correct tools for your specific needs. I also describe numerous methods and techniques to make your unit testing both comprehensive and efficient.

Unit testing is a big subject, with whole books dedicated to the topic. I focus on the narrow, but important, area of unit-testing applications that use EF Core for database accesses. To make this chapter focused, I don't explain the basics of unit testing, but leap right in. I therefore recommend anyone new to unit testing to skip this chapter, or come back to it after you've read up on the subject. This chapter won't make any sense without that background, and I don't want to discourage you from unit testing because I make it look too hard.

TIP   To learn more about unit testing, have a look at https://msdn.microsoft .com/en-us/library/hh694602.aspx. For much more in-depth coverage of unit testing, I recommend Roy Osherove's *The Art of Unit Testing: with Examples in C#, Second Edition* (Manning, 2013), http://mng.bz/1f92.

OK, if you're still with me, I assume you know what unit testing is and have at least written some unit tests. I'm not going to cover the differences between unit tests and integration tests, or acceptance tests, and so on. I'm also not here to persuade you that unit tests are useful; I assume you're convinced of their usefulness and want to learn the tips and techniques for unit testing an EF Core application.

Still with me? Good, because I think unit testing is useful and I use it a lot. I have more than 500 in the EfCoreInAction Git repo. But that doesn't mean I want to spend a lot of time writing unit tests. I want to be as efficient as I can at writing the unit tests, and I seek to be efficient in two areas, depicted in figure 15.1:

- *Fast to develop*—I'll introduce tools and techniques to help you write unit tests quickly for applications that use EF Core.
- *Fast to run*—I want my unit tests to run as quickly as possible, because a quick test-debug cycle makes developing and refactoring an application a much nicer experience.

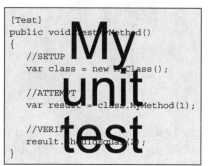

Figure 15.1   **I believe wholeheartedly in unit tests, but that doesn't mean I want to spend a lot of time developing or running them. My approach is to try to be efficient at using unit tests, and that splits into developing quickly and not having to hang around while they run.**

15.1   *Introduction—our unit test setup*

Before I start explaining the techniques, I need to introduce you to our unit test setup; otherwise, the examples won't make any sense. I use a fairly standard approach, but as you'll see, I've also created tools to help with the EF Core and database side of unit testing. Figure 15.2 shows a unit test with some of the features/methods covered in the chapter.

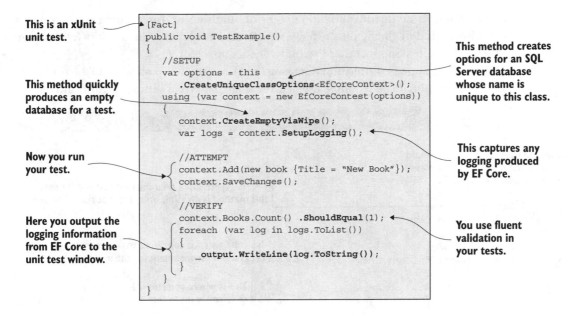

This is an xUnit unit test.

This method quickly produces an empty database for a test.

Now you run your test.

Here you output the logging information from EF Core to the unit test window.

This method creates options for an SQL Server database whose name is unique to this class.

This captures any logging produced by EF Core.

You use fluent validation in your tests.

```
[Fact]
public void TestExample()
{
    //SETUP
    var options = this
        .CreateUniqueClassOptions<EfCoreContext>();
    using (var context = new EfCoreContest(options))
    {
        context.CreateEmptyViaWipe();
        var logs = context.SetupLogging();

        //ATTEMPT
        context.Add(new book {Title = "New Book"});
        context.SaveChanges();

        //VERIFY
        context.Books.Count() .ShouldEqual(1);
        foreach (var log in logs.ToList())
        {
            _output.WriteLine(log.ToString());
        }
    }
}
```

Figure 15.2 This gives you a flavor of some of the unit-test features covered in this chapter. Some of these methods are also available in a NuGet package called **EfCore.TestSupport**.

This section covers

- The test environment you'll be using—the xUnit unit test library
- A NuGet package I created to help with unit testing EF Core applications

15.1.1 *The test environment—the xUnit unit test library*

I'm using the xUnit unit test library (see https://xunit.github.io/) because Microsoft supports it well. xUnit is also quicker than some other unit test frameworks, such as NUnit (which I used to use), because xUnit can run unit test classes in parallel. This has downsides, which I show you how to get around, but it does mean you can run your complete unit test suite a lot quicker.

I also use *fluent validation*—see row 1 in table 15.1. I find the fluent validation style much easier to work with than the assert method approach; it's slightly shorter, and IntelliSense can suggest the fluent validation methods that are appropriate.

Table 15.1 Two approaches to checking that two books were loaded by the previous query that was under test

Type	Example code
Fluent validation style	`books.Count().ShouldEqual(2);`
Assert method style	`Assert.Equal(2, books.Count());`

You can find these fluent validation extension methods at http://mng.bz/6mu6, but I've also included them, plus a few extra fluent validations, in the NuGet package called EfCore.TestSupport that I've built. See section 15.1.2.

This listing shows a simple unit test using the xUnit unit test package and the fluent validation extensions. This example uses a three-stage pattern of setup, attempt, and verify.

Listing 15.1   **A simple example of an xUnit unit test method**

The method must be public. It should
return void, or, if you're running async
methods, it should return a Task.

The [Fact] attribute tells the unit test runner that
this method is an xUnit unit test that should be run.

```
[Fact]
public void DemoTest()
{
    //SETUP
    const int someValue = 1;

    //ATTEMPT
    var result = someValue * 2;

    //VERIFY
    result.ShouldEqual(2);
}
```

Typically, you put code here that sets up the
data and/or environment for the unit test.

This is where you run the
code you want to test.

Here is where you put the test(s) to check
that the result of your test is correct.

I use JetBrain's ReSharper (see www.jetbrains.com/resharper/) to run my unit tests inside Visual Studio 2017, but that costs money. You can run your unit tests using Visual Studio's built-in Test Explorer, found under the Test menu item.

If you're using Visual Studio Code (VS Code), the test runner is built in. You need to set up the `build` and `test` tasks in the VS Code tasks.json file, which allows you to run all the tests via the Task > Test command. You can also run all the tests from the command line by typing `dotnet test` while in the Test directory of your application. Individual unit tests can be run by selecting the class containing the test and clicking the | run test | debug test | markers over each test method.

> **NOTE** Visual Studio 2017 Enterprise offers *live unit testing*: it will automatically rerun the unit tests associated with the code you're writing. Other commercial tools, such as dotCover, NCrunch, and NCover, have similar features. You might also like to look at "The Rise of Test Impact Analysis," an article describing an approach to speeding up the testing phase; see http://mng.bz/66tg.

15.1.2 *A library I've created to help with unit testing EF Core applications*

I learned a lot about unit testing EF Core applications as I built the software that goes with this book. If I had to do it again, I'd organize my unit tests differently. I therefore decided to build a unit test library by rearranging and improving my original unit test code. This library is available as an open source NuGet package called EfCore.TestSupport (see www.nuget.org/packages/EfCore.TestSupport/).

This chapter uses many of the methods in the EfCore.TestSupport library, but I don't detail their signatures as I do in the EfCore.TestSupport Git repo at https://github .com/JonPSmith/EfCore.TestSupport. But I'll be explaining the how and why of unit testing by using some of the methods from my EfCore.TestSupport library and showing some of the code I developed too.

15.2 *Simulating the database when testing EF Core applications*

If you unit test your application and it includes accesses to a database, you have several approaches to simulating the database. Over the years, I've tried many approaches to simulating the database in a unit test, ranging from mimicking, or *mocking*, the DbContext (not easy!) through to using real databases. This chapter covers some of those approaches and a few new tactics that EF Core offers.

> **DEFINITION** *Mocking* simulates the features of another object. For instance, if you access the database via an interface, you can *mock* the database's access code by creating a class that matches that interface. This *mock* can then provide test data without accessing a database.

Early consideration on how to unit test with a database can save you a lot of pain later, especially if you're using EF Core. As I said in section 15.1.2, I had to change my unit testing as I progressed with the code in this book, and things got messy toward the end. But that isn't new; in some of my projects, I later regretted my early decisions on how to unit test, as they start to fall apart at the project grows. Although some rework of early unit tests is inevitable, you want to minimize this, as it slows you down.

So, let's start by looking at your options for simulating the database and how you might select the right options for your project.

15.2.1 *The options you have for simulating the database*

You can simulate a database in EF Core in many ways, and I list the four mains ones in this section. These options range in complexity, speed, and which features they support. Typically, you might use a mixture of these options in unit testing an application.

USING AN IN-MEMORY DATABASE DESIGNED FOR UNIT TESTING

EF Core has an InMemory database designed specifically for unit testing. You can also use an SQLite in-memory database, which provides more relational checks.

- Pros: Quick to run, builds fresh database every time.
- Cons: In-memory databases don't support advanced SQL features such as UDFs, computed columns, and so on.

USING A "REAL" DATABASE OF THE SAME TYPE AS YOUR APPLICATION USES

You can create a database, or databases, of the same type as your application (say, SQL Server or MySQL) for running your unit tests.

- Pros: Perfect match to your application. Handles any SQL feature that you could use in your application.
- Cons: Can be slow to create. If using xUnit in parallel, you need a separate database for each unit test class.

MOCKING A DATABASE REPOSITORY PATTERN

Chapter 4 described building business logic with a DbAccess part, which acts as a Rrepository pattern to access the database. This is easy to mock.

- Pros: Fast, total control over what data comes in and out.
- Cons: Can be used in only specific areas. More code to write.

MOCKING YOUR APPLICATION'S DBCONTEXT

You could try to mock EF Core's DbContext. I mention this only for completeness; I don't recommend trying this, other than in simple access cases.

- Pros: Fast.
- Cons: Hard to mock EF Core's DbContext successfully.

You'll likely need to use a database in a lot of your unit tests, which means choosing between the first two options: using an in-memory or "real" database. The next section talks about how you choose.

15.2.2 *Choosing between an in-memory or real database for unit testing*

I didn't get this decision quite right at the start of building the EfCoreInAction code base. I started out with EF Core's InMemory database, quickly swapped to an SQLite in-memory database, and then had problems later when I started using SQL UDFs, as some of my early unit tests broke. The simple lesson here is, if you're going to build an application that uses features that the SQLite server can't handle, you need to use a "real" database. Otherwise, you can use an in-memory database.

If you're building an application that uses the SQL features listed in table 15.2, you can't use an SQLite in-memory database for unit testing. (The EF InMemory database provider has even more limitations.)

Table 15.2   The SQL features that EF Core can control, but that aren't going to work with SQLite—either because SQLite doesn't support the feature, or because SQLite uses a different format from SQL Server, MySQL, and so on.

SQL feature	See section	SQLite support?
Different schemas	6.11.2	Not supported
SQL sequences	8.5	Not supported
SQL computed columns	8.3	Different format than SQL Server
SQL user-defined functions (UDFs)	8.2	Different format than SQL Server
SQL fragment default value	8.4.2	Different format than SQL Server

If you decide you can use an in-memory database, you can use either of these:

- EF Core's InMemory database
- SQLite with an in-memory database

I highly recommend the SQLite in-memory option, because SQLite is a true relational database, whereas EF Core's InMemory database provider isn't a real relational database. EF Core's InMemory database won't pick up on data that would break referential integrity, such as foreign keys that don't match the appropriate primary key. About the only good thing about EF Core's InMemory is that it's about 40% faster on setup than SQLite (but slower in execution), but both are fast at setup anyway. I cover using SQLite in-memory in the next section.

> **NOTE** If you want to use EF Core's InMemory database, I provide the code to do that in my EfCore.TestSupport library. See http://mng.bz/94tj for an example of a unit test that uses an InMemory database provider. You can find my InMemory options setup code at http://mng.bz/f4tt.

15.3 Getting your application's DbContext ready for unit testing

Before you can unit test your application's DbContext with a database, you need to ensure that you can alter at least the database name. Otherwise, you can't provide a database that your unit tests can use to read and write to. The technique you use to do this depends on how the application's DbContext expects the options to be set. The two approaches that EF Core provides for setting the options are as follows:

- The application's DbContext expects the options to be provided via its constructor. This is the recommended approach for ASP.NET Core applications.
- The application's DbContext sets the options internally in the `OnConfiguring` method. This is the recommended approach for all other types of applications.

The technique you use to define the database differs in the two cases.

15.3.1 The application's DbContext options are provided via its constructor

This form of option setting is perfect for using with unit tests and doesn't need any changes to the application's DbContext. Providing the options via the application's DbContext constructor gives you total control over the options; you can change the database connection string, the type of database provider it uses, and so on.

This listing shows the format of an application's DbContext that uses a constructor to obtain its options. The constructor is shown in bold.

Listing 15.2   An application DbContext that uses a constructor for option setting

```
public class EfCoreContext : DbContext
{
    public DbSet<Book> Books { get; set; }
    public DbSet<Author> Authors { get; set; }
    public DbSet<PriceOffer> PriceOffers { get; set; }

    public EfCoreContext(
        DbContextOptions<EfCoreContext> options)
        : base(options) {}

    //… rest of the class left out
}
```

For this type of application's DbContext, the unit test can create the options and then provide them as a parameter in the application's DbContext constructor. The next listing shows an example of creating an instance of your application's DbContext in a unit test that will access an SQL Server database, with a specific connection string.

Listing 15.3   Creating a DbContext by providing the options via a constructor

You need to create the DbContextOptionsBuilder<T>
class to build the options.

Holds the connection string for
the SQL Server database

```
const string connectionString
    = "Server= … content removed as too long to show";
var builder = new
    DbContextOptionsBuilder<EfCoreContext>();
builder.UseSqlServer(connectionString);
var options = builder.Options;
using (var context = new EfCoreContext(options))
{
    //… unit test starts here
```

Defines that you want
to use the SQL Server
database provider

Builds the final DbContextOptions<EfCoreContext>
options that the application's DbContext needs

Allows you to create an instance
for your unit tests

15.3.2   *Setting an application's DbContext options via OnConfiguring*

This form isn't immediately ready for unit testing and requires you to modify your application's DbContext before you can use it in unit testing. But before you change the application's DbContext, I want to show you the normal arrangement of using the OnConfiguring method to set the options; the OnConfiguring method is in bold.

Listing 15.4 A DbContext that uses the `OnConfiguring` method to set options

```
public class DbContextOnConfiguring : DbContext
{
    private const string connectionString
        = "Server=(localdb)\\... shortened to fit";

    protected override void OnConfiguring(
        DbContextOptionsBuilder optionsBuilder)
    {
        optionsBuilder.UseSqlServer(connectionString);
        base.OnConfiguring(optionsBuilder);
    }
    // … other code removed
}
```

Microsoft's recommended way to change a DbContext that uses the `OnConfiguring` method to set up the options is shown next. As you'll see, this adds the same sort of constructor setup as ASP.NET Core uses, while making sure the `OnConfiguring` method still works in the normal application.

Listing 15.5 An altered DbContext allows the connection string to be set by the unit test

```
public class DbContextOnConfiguring : DbContext
{
    private const string ConnectionString
        = "Server=(localdb)\\ … shortened to fit";

    protected override void OnConfiguring(
        DbContextOptionsBuilder optionsBuilder)
    {
        if (!optionsBuilder.IsConfigured)
        {
            optionsBuilder
                .UseSqlServer(ConnectionString);
        }
    }

    public DbContextOnConfiguring(
        DbContextOptions<DbContextOnConfiguring>
        options)
        : base(options) { }

    public DbContextOnConfiguring() { }
    // … other code removed
}
```

Changes the OnConfigured method to run its normal setup code only if the options aren't already configured

Adds the same constructor-based options settings that the ASP.NET Core version has, which allows you to set any options you want

Adds a public, parameterless constructor so that this DbContext works normally with the application

To use this modified form, you can provide options in the same way you did with the ASP.NET Core version.

Listing 15.6   A unit test provides a different connection string to the DbContext

Sets up the options you want to use

Holds the connection string for the
database to be used for the unit test

```
const string connectionString
    = "Server=(localdb)\\... shortened to fit";
var builder = new
    DbContextOptionsBuilder
        <DbContextOnConfiguring>();
builder.UseSqlServer(connectionString);
var options = builder.Options;
using (var context = new
    DbContextOnConfiguring(options)
{
    //... unit test starts here
```

Provides the options to the DbContext
via a new, one-parameter constructor

Now you're good to go for unit testing.

15.4   *Simulating a database—using an in-memory database*

SQLite has a useful option for creating an in-memory database. This option allows a
unit test to create a new database in-memory, which means it's isolated from any other
database. The database lives in the SQLite connection.

To make an SQLite database be in-memory, you need to set `DataSource` to `":memory:"`,
as shown here. This listing comes from the `SQLiteInMemory.CreateOptions` method in
my EfCore.TestSupport library.

Listing 15.7   Creating `DbContextOptions<T>` for in-memory SQLite database

Creates an SQLite connection string with
the DataSource set to ":memory:"

By default, it throws an exception if a
QueryClientEvaluationWarning is logged
(see section 15.8). You can turn this off by
providing a value of false as a parameter.

```
public static DbContextOptions<T> CreateOptions<T>
    (bool throwOnClientServerWarning = true)
    where T : DbContext
{
    var connectionStringBuilder =
        new SqliteConnectionStringBuilder
            { DataSource = ":memory:" };
    var connectionString =
        connectionStringBuilder.ToString();
    var connection =
        new SqliteConnection(connectionString);
    connection.Open();

    // create in-memory context
    var builder =
```

Turns the SQLiteConnectionStringBuilder
into a string

Forms an SQLite connection
using the connection string

You must open the SQLite connection. If you
don't, the in-memory database doesn't work.

Calls a general method used on all your option builders. If throwOnClientServerWarning is true, it configures the warning to throw on a QueryClientEvaluationWarning being logged.

Builds DbContextOptions<T> with the SQLite database provider and the open connection

```
        new DbContextOptionsBuilder<T>();
    builder.UseSqlite(connection);
    builder.ApplyOtherOptionSettings
        (throwOnClientServerWarning);

    return builder.Options;
}
```

Returns the DbContextOptions<T> to use in the creation of your application's DbContext

You can then use the `SQLiteInMemory.CreateOptions` method in one of your unit tests, as shown in the next listing. You should note the line `context.Database.Ensure-Created()`. This is the main method provided by EF Core to create the database with the correct schema (the databases tables, columns, and so on) based on the application's DbContext.

Listing 15.8 Using an SQLite, in-memory database in an xUnit unit test

Uses that option to create your application's DbContext

```
    [Fact]
    public void TestSQLiteOk()
    {
        //SETUP
        var options = SQLiteInMemory
            .CreateOptions<EfCoreContext>();
        using (var context = new EfCoreContext(options))
        {
            context.Database.EnsureCreated();

            //ATTEMPT
            context.SeedDatabaseFourBooks();

            //VERIFY
            context.Books.Count().ShouldEqual(4);
        }
    }
```

Calls your SQLiteInMemory.CreateOptions to provide an in-memory database. It has an optional boolean parameter called throwOnClientServerWarning, which defaults to true; see section 15.8.

You must call context.Database. EnsureCreated, a special method that creates a database using your application's DbContext and entity classes.

Checks that your SeedDatabaseFourBooks worked, and added four books to the database

Runs a test method you've written that adds four test books to the database

> **WARNING** If you are working with .NET 4.7 then you need to call `SQLitePCL`
> `.Batteries_V2.Init()` before every use of the SQLite database. See the issue
> raised by Tomás López at https://github.com/JonPSmith/EfCore.TestSupport/
> issues/6. Another crucial point is that the in-memory database is held in the
> connection. You can create multiple instances of the application's DbContext,
> and they'll all access the same database. This is useful when writing tests for
> checking disconnected state updates, covered in section 15.6.

15.5   *Using a real database in your unit tests*

Although using an in-memory database for unit testing is great, sometimes you need to use a real database—possibly because you use a feature that the in-memory databases don't support, or maybe because you want to look at the SQL produced for performance tuning. When this happens, handling a real database is a bit more complicated. The issues you'll look at in this section are as follows:

- Setting up a real database for unit testing—connection string options
- Running unit tests in parallel—uniquely named databases
- Speeding up the database creation stage of a unit test
- Handling databases that have added extra SQL code

When you have unit tests that check some of the advanced SQL features that EF Core supports, such as computed columns and sequences (see chapter 8), you need a real database. If you're also interested in the SQL that EF Core produces, then again, you'll use an SQL Server database. Because of these requirements, the EfCore.TestSupport library contains several useful tools for handling real databases.

All the following examples use an SQL Server database, but the approach works equally well with other database types.

15.5.1   *How to set up a real database for unit testing*

For an SQL Server database, you need a connection string. You could define a connection string as a constant and use that, but as you'll see, that isn't as flexible as you'd want. You'll mimic what ASP.NET Core does, and add a simple appsettings.json file that holds the connection string, and use some of the ASP.NET Core packages to access the connection string in our application. The appsettings.json file looks something like this:

```
{
  "ConnectionStrings": {
    "UnitTestConnection": "Server=(localdb)\\mssqllocaldb;Database=... etc"
  }
}
```

The following listing shows the `GetConfiguration` method from my EfCore.Test-Support library. This loads an appsettings.json file from the top-level directory of the assembly that calls this method, which would be the assembly in which you're running your unit tests.

> Listing 15.9   `GetConfiguration` method allowing access to the appsettings.json file

In the TestSupport library, a method returns the absolute path of the calling assembly's top-level directory. That's the assembly that you're running your tests in.

Returns IConfigurationRoot, from which you can use methods, such as GetConnectionString("ConnectionName"), to access the configuration information

```
public static IConfigurationRoot GetConfiguration()
{
    var callingProjectPath =
        TestData.GetCallingAssemblyTopLevelDir();
```

Calls the Build method, which returns the IConfigurationRoot type

Uses ASP.NET Core's ConfigurationBuilder to read that appsettings.json file. It's optional, so no error is thrown if the configuration file doesn't exist.

```
var builder = new ConfigurationBuilder()
    .SetBasePath(callingProjectPath)
    .AddJsonFile("appsettings.json", optional: true);
return builder.Build();
}
```

You can use the `GetConfigration` method to access the connection string, and then use this to create an SQLServer DbContext, as shown in this code snippet:

```
var config = AppSettings.GetConfiguration();
config.GetConnectionString("UnitTestConnection");
var builder = new DbContextOptionsBuilder<EfCoreContext>();
builder.UseSqlServer(connectionString);
using (var context = new EfCoreContext(builder.Options))
{
    … etc.
```

You'll build a range of methods that do this, and add extra magic to sort out the issues around running your unit tests in parallel, which is the default execution policy of xUnit. The following section explains these extra methods.

15.5.2 *Running unit tests in parallel—uniquely named databases*

You'll use xUnit, which runs each class of unit tests in parallel. If all your unit tests access one database, it'd be difficult to know what test was doing what. Good unit tests need a known starting point and should return a known result, so you need to overcome the problem of using one database for all unit tests.

Our solution (which is also used by many others) is to have separately named databases for each unit test class, or possibly each unit test method. You'll create two methods that produce an SQL Server `DbContextOptions<T>` result in which the database name is unique to a test class or method. Figure 15.3 shows the two methods: the first one creates a database with a name unique to this class, and the second one produces a database with a name that's unique to that class and method.

> **NOTE** The database name must end with *Test*. This is a safety measure, because in section 15.5.3 you'll provide a method that can delete all the databases that start with the database name in your appsettings.json file. Forcing the database name to end in *Test* makes it much less likely that that method will delete a production database.

The result of using either of these classes is that each test class or method has its own uniquely named database. Running all the unit tests in parallel won't end up with different test classes writing to the same database.

> **TIP** xUnit runs each test class in parallel; but within a class, it runs each test serially. Because of this, I normally use a class-unique database. I use a class-and-method-unique database when I want a new, empty database for a specific test method.

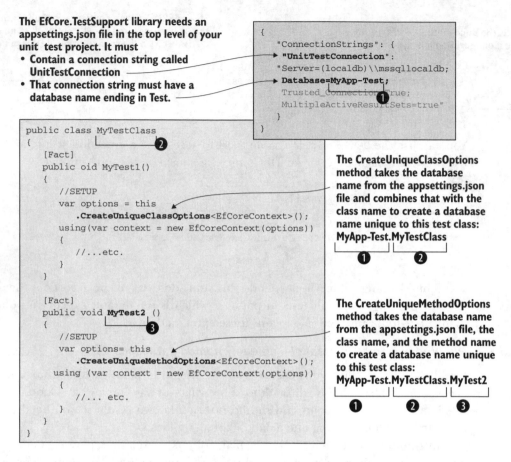

The EfCore.TestSupport library needs an appsettings.json file in the top level of your unit test project. It must
- Contain a connection string called **UnitTestConnection**
- That connection string must have a database name ending in Test.

```
{
   "ConnectionStrings": {
      "UnitTestConnection":
      "Server=(localdb)\\mssqllocaldb;
      Database=MyApp-Test;
      Trusted_Connection=true;
      MultipleActiveResultSets=true"
   }
}
```

```
public class MyTestClass
{
   [Fact]
   public oid MyTest1()
   {
      //SETUP
      var options = this
         .CreateUniqueClassOptions<EfCoreContext>();
      using(var context = new EfCoreContext(options))
      {
         //...etc.
      }
   }

   [Fact]
   public void MyTest2 ()
   {
      //SETUP
      var options= this
         .CreateUniqueMethodOptions<EfCoreContext>();
      using (var context = new EfCoreContext(options))
      {
         //... etc.
      }
   }
}
```

The CreateUniqueClassOptions method takes the database name from the appsettings.json file and combines that with the class name to create a database name unique to this test class: **MyApp-Test.MyTestClass**

The CreateUniqueMethodOptions method takes the database name from the appsettings.json file, the class name, and the method name to create a database name unique to this test class: **MyApp-Test.MyTestClass.MyTest2**

Figure 15.3   Two methods that set up the database options for an SQL Server database, but alter the database name to be either class-unique, or class-and-method-unique. When you run multiple unit test classes, they'll have their own databases, which means they won't interfere with each other.

This listing shows the code inside the CreateUniqueClassOptions extension method. It encapsulates all the settings of the DbContext options to save you from having to include them in every unit test.

Listing 15.10   CreateUniqueClassOptions extension method with a helper

It's expected that the object instance provided will be "this"—the class in which the unit test is running.

Returns options for an SQL Server database with a name starting with the database name in the original connection string in the appsettings.json file, but with the name of the class of the instance provided in the first parameter.

```
public static DbContextOptions<T>
   CreateUniqueClassOptions<T>(
      this object callingClass,
```

Throws an exception if QueryClientEvaluationWarning is logged. You can turn this off by setting it to false if you don't want that to happen.

Calls a private method shared between this method and the CreateUniqueMethodOptions options

```
        bool throwOnClientServerWarning = true)
    where T : DbContext
{
    return CreateOptionWithDatabaseName<T>
        (callingClass, throwOnClientServerWarning);
}
```

Builds the SQL Server part of the options, with the correct database name

```
    private static DbContextOptions<T>
        CreateOptionWithDatabaseName<T>(
            object callingClass,
            bool throwOnClientServerWarning,
            string callingMember = null)
        where T : DbContext
    {
        var connectionString = callingClass
            .GetUniqueDatabaseConnectionString(
                callingMember);
        var builder =
            new DbContextOptionsBuilder<T>();
        builder.UseSqlServer(connectionString);
        builder.ApplyOtherOptionSettings(
            throwOnClientServerWarning);

        return builder.Options;
    }
```

These parameters are passed from CreateUniqueClassOptions. For CreateUniqueClassOptions, the calling method is left as null.

Returns the connection string from the appsetting.json file, but with the database name modified with the callingClass's type name as a suffix

Sets up OptionsBuilder and creates an SQL Server database provider with the connection string

Returns the DbContextOptions<T> to configure the application's DbContext

Calls a general method used on all your option builders. This enables sensitive logging and throwOnClientServerWarning if a QueryClientEvaluationWarning is logged.

xUnit's parallel running feature brings some constraints. For instance, the use of static variables to carry information causes problems, as different tests may set a static variable to different values in parallel. That's why running in parallel wasn't viable in .NET 4.x, which used statics for things such as the user information (`Thread.CurrentPrincipal`). Thankfully .NET Core doesn't use static variables, but uses dependency injection for all variables, so running your code in parallel isn't a problem. If you use static variables in your code, you should either turn off parallel running in xUnit or use NUnit, which runs unit tests serially.

15.5.3　Tips on how to speed up the database creation stage of a unit test

The preceding section showed how to create unique databases for your tests, but you still have the problem of making sure that its schema is up-to-date and it's empty of data when you rerun a test. There's an easy way to do this, but it takes a long time (on my PC it takes 10 seconds). This section covers the approaches and tools I've built to try to speed this up.

Let's start with the foolproof, but slow, method. The following listing shows Microsoft's recommended way of creating an empty database with the correct schema.

Listing 15.11   **The foolproof way to create a database that's up-to-date and empty**

```
[Fact]
public void TestExampleSqlDatabaseOk()
{
    //SETUP
    var options = this
        .CreateUniqueClassOptions<EfCoreContext>();
    using (var context = new EfCoreContext(options))
    {
        context.Database.EnsureDeleted();        ◄───── Deletes the currect
        context.Database.EnsureCreated();        ◄──┐   database (if present)
        //… rest of test removed                    └── Creates a new database, using the configuration
                                                        inside your application's DbContext
```

That works every time, and you're welcome to use it. But if you're debugging a method by using a unit test that uses this approach, you'll have a 10-second or so wait before the database is ready for the test. I find that frustrating, so I've come up with another approach.

> **NOTE** How long `EnsureDeleted`/`EnsureCreated` takes depends on the database. On my development PC, a delete/create of an SQL Server database takes about 10 seconds, but a MySQL database takes only 1 second.

My approach isn't as foolproof as the `EnsureDeleted`/`EnsureCreated` approach, but typically takes only about 100 ms. I've created a method called `CreateEmptyViaWipe` that wipes the database instead of deleting and re-creating it. I use the `WipeAllDataFromDatabase` method created in section 9.6.1 to wipe the database, coupled with a call to `Database.EnsureCreated` to make sure the database exists in the first place. The following listing shows an example of this approach.

Listing 15.12   **Using `CreateEmptyViaWipe` to get an empty database quickly**

```
[Fact]
public void TestExampleSqlDatabaseOk()            This ensures the database exists. If it does
{                                                 exist, it uses the WipeAllDataFromDatabase
    //SETUP                                        method to wipe all the data from the database.
    var options = this
        .CreateUniqueClassOptions<EfCoreContext>();
    using (var context = new EfCoreContext(options))
    {
        context.CreateEmptyViaWipe();        ◄─────────┘
        //… rest of test removed
```

The CreateEmptyViaWipe method has two limitations:

- The "wipe database" part can't handle circular references in the entity classes. For instance, if class A links to B, which links back to A, then the method will throw an exception. There are ways around this, but you must write code to handle that.
- It saves time by creating the database only once, at the start. If you change the application's DbContext configuration, or alter the entity classes, the database won't be in the correct format, and your tests will fail.

This last point could be a showstopper, but I have a way around it. I've created a method that will delete all the unit test databases, so the next time you run a test, it'll create a new database using the new application's DbContext configuration. After a change that will affect my database schema, I run this method to delete all the test databases; on the next run of a unit test, it creates a fresh database with the correct schema.

To help with support methods like this "delete all unit test databases," I created unit commands (instead of unit tests). *Unit commands* are methods that you can run by using the unit test runner, but aren't normal unit tests and shouldn't be run normally. Therefore, I place all my unit command methods in a directory, called UnitCommands, which is separate from the normal unit tests. I also decorate each unit command method with a RunnableInDebugOnly attribute, so that they aren't accidentally run if I run all my unit tests. The RunnableInDebugOnly attribute is available in the EFCore.TestSupport library.

Listing 15.13 shows the unit command called DeleteAllTestDatabasesOk, which does just that: it deletes all the databases that start with the default connection string.

> **WARNING** You *must* ensure that your unit test connection string in your test project's appsettings.json file is unique, because it'll delete *all* database files that start with that name. That's why the EfCore.TestSupport library insists that the database name ends with *Test*, as it makes it much less likely that a production database will have that name.

Listing 15.13 The unit command that deletes all the test databases

This has the format of a unit test: it's a public method that returns void.

Makes sure the unit command isn't run by accident when the main unit tests are run. You must manually run this method in debug mode.

```
[RunnableInDebugOnly]
public void DeleteAllTestDatabasesOk()
{
    var numDeleted = DatabaseTidyHelper
        .DeleteAllUnitTestDatabases();
    _output.WriteLine(
        "This deleted {0} databases.", numDeleted);
}
```

Writes out how many databases were deleted by this method

Calls the DeleteAllUnitTestDatabases method from your EcCore.TestSupport library. This returns the number of databases that it deleted.

15.5.4 *How to handle databases in which you've added extra SQL code*

One problem I came across in unit testing occurred when my database had extra SQL commands that EF Core doesn't add. For instance, if I use a UDF in my code, I need to add it to my unit test database manually because EF Core's `context.Database.EnsureCreated` method won't have added that. I have three ways around this:

- For simple SQL, such as a UDF, I execute a script file as part of the startup.
- If you've added your SQL to the EF Core migration files (see section 11.2), you should call `context.Database.Migrate` instead of ....`EnsureCreated`.
- If you're using script-based migrations (see section 11.4), you should execute the scripts to build the database.

The last two items have a solution, which I detailed in the list, but the first item needs something to handle this. I created a method called `ExecuteScriptFileInTransaction` that executes the SQL inside an SQL script file on the database that the application's DbContext is connected to. The format of the script is in a Microsoft SQL Server Management Studio format: a set of SQL commands, each ending with a single line containing the SQL command `GO`. This shows an SQL change script file that adds a UDF to a database.

> **Listing 15.14   An example SQL script file with `GO` at the end of each SQL command**

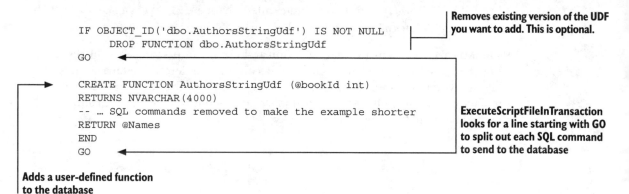

```
IF OBJECT_ID('dbo.AuthorsStringUdf') IS NOT NULL
    DROP FUNCTION dbo.AuthorsStringUdf
GO
```
Removes existing version of the UDF you want to add. This is optional.

```
CREATE FUNCTION AuthorsStringUdf (@bookId int)
RETURNS NVARCHAR(4000)
-- … SQL commands removed to make the example shorter
RETURN @Names
END
GO
```
ExecuteScriptFileInTransaction looks for a line starting with GO to split out each SQL command to send to the database

Adds a user-defined function to the database

The EfCore.TestSupport library contains an extension method called `ExecuteScript-FileInTransaction`, which can apply a script like this to a database. This listing shows a typical way to apply this script to a unit test database.

> **Listing 15.15   An example of applying an SQL script to a unit test database**

```
[Fact]
public void TestApplyScriptExampleOk()
{
    var options = this
        .CreateUniqueClassOptions<EfCoreContext>();
    var filepath = TestData.GetFilePath(
        "AddUserDefinedFunctions.sql");
    using (var context = new EfCoreContext(options))
```
Gets the file path of the SQL script file via your TestData's GetFilePath method

A new database was created, so you need to apply your script to the database by using the ExecuteScriptFileInTransaction method.

Uses your CreateEmptyViaWipe to ensure the database is empty. This returns true if a new database was created.

```
        {
            if (context.CreateEmptyViaWipe())
            {
                context
                    .ExecuteScriptFileInTransaction(
                    filepath);
            }
            //… the rest of the unit test left out
        }
    }
```

In this example, you execute the SQL script file only if the database was created, which you can do because the CreateEmptyViaWipe method returns true only if a new database was created.

15.6 *Unit testing a disconnected state update properly*

Before moving on from using databases in unit tests, I want to talk about the issues of simulating the disconnected state in a unit test (see section 3.4 for more on the disconnected state and updates). The disconnected state happens when an update is done in a web application consisting of two HTTP requests, as listed here:

1 In the first HTTP request, the web application reads data from the database and sends it to the user for inspection.

2 The user then changes the data and clicks the Submit button to send the data back to the web application to update the database. This is done in a new HTTP request, so a new instance of the application's DbContext is created to handle the database update.

You must be careful how you write unit tests that check a disconnected state update. To test this properly, you need to use two separate instances of the application's DbContext: one to set up the database ready for the test, and a second to run the test. The reason for this is that the setting up of the database leaves tracked data inside the application's DbContext. The state of the application's DbContext isn't the same as what the method under test would encounter in your web application. Sometimes it doesn't matter, but sometimes it does—which can lead to subtle bugs being missed.

Let me give you an example that illustrates the problem. Say you want to test the following code snippet, which should add a new review to a book:

```
var book = context.Books.Last();
book.Reviews.Add( new Review{NumStars = 5});
context.SaveChanges();
```

The problem is, it has a bug. The code should have Include(b => b.Reviews) added to the first line to ensure that the current reviews are loaded first.

In the first unit test, which is incorrect, you don't properly simulate the disconnected state because you set up the database in the same application's DbContext as you run your test. When the code under test loads the Book entity, EF Core applies the relational fix-up stage. This stage is clever and will try to link up all the entities it's tracking, which means the Book entity that was just loaded picks up the Reviews from the setup stage. That isn't what would happen in your disconnected state, and has the effect of incorrectly saying that the code worked.

Listing 15.16   An INCORRECT simulation of a disconnected state, with the wrong result!

Reads in the last book from your test set,
which you know has two reviews

```
public void INCORRECTtestOfDisconnectedState()
{
    //SETUP
    var options = SQLiteInMemory
        .CreateOptions<EfCoreContext>();
    using (var context = new EfCoreContext(options))
    {
        context.Database.EnsureCreated();
        context.SeedDatabaseFourBooks();

        //ATTEMPT
        var book = context.Books.Last();
        book.Reviews.Add( new Review{NumStars = 5});
        context.SaveChanges();

        //VERIFY
        //THIS IS INCORRECT!!!!!
        context.Books.Last().Reviews
            .Count.ShouldEqual(3);
    }
}
```

Sets up the test database with
test data consisting of four books

Adds another review to the
book. This shouldn't work,
but it does because the seed
data is still being tracked by
the DbContext instance.

Saves it to the database

Checks that you have three reviews,
which works, but the unit test should
have FAILED with an exception earlier

So let's see the correct way of testing a disconnected state update. The following listing uses two instances of the application's DbContext: one to set up the database and one to run the test. The result is that the unit test correctly simulates in the disconnected update, and in so doing, the test fails because an exception is thrown as the Reviews collection is null.

Listing 15.17   Two separate DbContext instances with the same in-memory database

```
[Fact]
public void CorrectTestOfDisconnectedState()
{
    //SETUP
    var options = SQLiteInMemory
        .CreateOptions<EfCoreContext>();
    using (var context = new EfCoreContext(options))
    {
        context.Database.EnsureCreated();
        context.SeedDatabaseFourBooks();
    }
```

Creates the in-memory SQLite options in
the same way as the preceding example

Creates the first instance of
the application's DbContext

Sets up the test database with test data
consisting of four books, but this time in
a separate DbContext instance

Closes that last instance and opens a new instance of the application's DbContext. The new instance doesn't have any tracked entities that could alter how the test runs.

Reads in the last book from your test set, which you know has two reviews

```
using (var context = new EfCoreContext(options))
{
    //ATTEMPT
    var book = context.Books.Last();
    book.Reviews.Add( new Review{NumStars = 5});

    //… rest of unit test left out, as has errored
}
}
```

When you try to add the new Review, EF Core throws a NullReferenceException because the Book's Review collection isn't loaded, and is therefore null.

I recommend that you use the two-instance approach when testing any create, update, or delete operation that's done with a disconnect between the first and second part of the command.

15.7 *Mocking a database repository pattern*

Moving away from using an actual database, let's look at the third item in the list in section 15.2.1, where I suggested that one way to simulate the database was to *mock* the database Repository pattern. In my business logic I use separate database access code (the Repository pattern) to isolate the database access from the business logic. This allows me to mock the repositories and avoid using a database. I find that mocking gives me much better control over the data into, and out of, the method I'm testing.

This next example is taken from my unit tests in the EfCoreInAction repo; here, you want to test the PlaceOrderAction's method developed in chapter 4. The PlaceOrder-Action class's constructor requires one parameter of type IPlaceOrderDbAccess, which is normally the PlaceOrderDbAccess class that handles the database accesses.

But for testing, you replace the PlaceOrderDbAccess class with our test class, our *mock*, that implements the same IPlaceOrderDbAccess interface. This mock class allows you to control what the PlaceOrderAction class can read from the database, and capture what it attempts to write to the database. The following listing shows a unit test that uses this mock, which captures the order that the PlaceOrderAction's method produces so that you can check that the user's ID was set properly.

Listing 15.18 The unit test providing a mock instance to the BizLogic

```
[Fact]
public void ExampleOfMockingOk()
{
    //SETUP
    var lineItems = new List<OrderLineItem>
    {
        new OrderLineItem {BookId = 1, NumBooks = 4}
    };
    var userId = Guid.NewGuid();
```

Creates the input to the PlaceOrderAction method

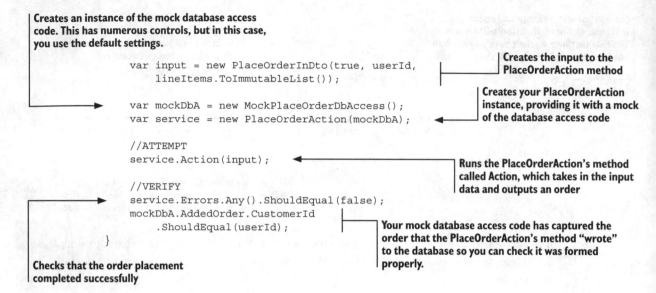

Creates an instance of the mock database access code. This has numerous controls, but in this case, you use the default settings.

Creates the input to the PlaceOrderAction method

Creates your PlaceOrderAction instance, providing it with a mock of the database access code

```
var input = new PlaceOrderInDto(true, userId,
    lineItems.ToImmutableList());

var mockDbA = new MockPlaceOrderDbAccess();
var service = new PlaceOrderAction(mockDbA);

//ATTEMPT
service.Action(input);

//VERIFY
service.Errors.Any().ShouldEqual(false);
mockDbA.AddedOrder.CustomerId
    .ShouldEqual(userId);
}
```

Runs the PlaceOrderAction's method called Action, which takes in the input data and outputs an order

Your mock database access code has captured the order that the PlaceOrderAction's method "wrote" to the database so you can check it was formed properly.

Checks that the order placement completed successfully

The mocked class, MockPlaceOrderDbAccess, doesn't access the database, but it has properties or methods that you can use to control every part of the reading of data from the database. This class also captures anything the PlaceOrderAction's method tries to write to the database, so you can check that too. This shows the mock database class, MockPlaceOrderDbAccess.

> **Listing 15.19 The mock database access code used for unit testing**

Holds the dummy books that the mock uses. Can be useful if the test wants to compare the output with the dummy database.

Mock MockPlaceOrderDbAccess implements the IPlaceOrderDbAccess, which allows it to replace the normal PlaceOrderDbAccess class.

```
public class MockPlaceOrderDbAccess
    : IPlaceOrderDbAccess
{
    public ImmutableList<Book> DummyBooks
        { get; private set; }

    public Order AddedOrder { get; private set; }

    public MockPlaceOrderDbAccess(
        bool createLastInFuture = false,
        int? promoPriceFirstBook = null)
    {
        var numBooks = createLastInFuture
            ? DateTime.UtcNow.Year -
                EfTestData.DummyBookStartDate.Year + 2
            : 10;
```

Will contain the Order built by the PlaceOrderAction's method

In this case, you set up the mock via its constructor.

Allows you to check that it won't accept an order for a book that hasn't yet been published.

Allows you to add a PriceOffer to the first book so you can check that the correct price is recorded on the order.

Works out how to create enough books such that the last one isn't published yet

Adds a PriceOffer to the first book, if required

Creates dummy books by using one of the unit test data generators

```
            var books = EfTestData.CreateDummyBooks
                (numBooks, createLastInFuture);
            if (promotionPriceForFirstBook != null)
                books.First().Promotion = new PriceOffer
                {
                    NewPrice = (int) promoPriceFirstBook,
                    PromotionalText = "Unit Test"
                };
            DummyBooks = books.ToImmutableList();
        }

        public IDictionary<int, Book>
            FindBooksByIdsWithPriceOffers
            (IEnumerable<int> bookIds)
        {
            return DummyBooks.AsQueryable()
                .Where(x => bookIds.Contains(x.BookId))
                .ToDictionary(key => key.BookId);
        }

        public void Add(Order newOrder)
        {
            AddedOrder = newOrder;
        }
    }
```

Called to get the books that the input selected. It uses the DummyBooks generated in the constructor.

Called by the PlaceOrderAction's method to write the Order to the database. In this case, you capture it so the unit test can inspect it.

Similar code to the original, but in this case it reads from the DummyBooks, not the database

This mock may look a bit complicated and hard to write, but because you copied the real `PlaceOrderDbAccess` class and then edited it, the job wasn't that hard. Some libraries, such as Moq (see www.nuget.org/packages/Moq), help with mock classes, but in this case, it's more efficient to write the code yourself.

Because business logic can be complex, often with complex validation rules, I find mocking a useful approach to replacing the database access. The mock provides a lot more control over the database access, and you can more easily simulate various error conditions.

15.8 Capturing EF Core logging information in unit testing

I've found the logging output of EF Core invaluable for seeing what SQL code EF Core translates my queries to, or the SQL commands it outputs to create the schema in a database. I have a couple of tools in my EfCore.TestSupport library to help you capture and check the logs produced by EF Core.

> **WARNING** A change in EF Core 2.0 seems to have produced a "bleed" between what should be separate logging contexts. I've seen a logging message from unit test A appear in logs of unit test B when running all the unit tests in parallel. This shouldn't be a problem if you're simply listing the logs, but be aware that this can happen.

The first thing I added was an optional parameter to all the methods that produced options—the `EfInMemory` and `SQLiteInMemory` static methods and the `SqlServerHelpers` extension methods. This optional parameter, called `throwOnClientServerWarning`, is set to `true` by default, which means EF Core will throw an exception if `Query-ClientEvaluationWarning` is logged. Any suboptimal SQL being produced in any of your queries will cause an exception in the unit test. The following listing shows this in action.

Listing 15.20   The `CreateOptions` method will throw an exception on poor SQL

xUnit's assert for catching exceptions. If no exception happens, it raises a unit test error.

By default, the optional throwOnClientServerWarning parameter is set to true, which means an exception will be thrown by EF Core if a QueryClientEvaluationWarning is logged. You can turn this off by providing a parameter of false.

```
[Fact]
public void TestQueryClientEvaluationThrowException()
{
    //SETUP
    var options = SQLiteInMemory
        .CreateOptions<EfCoreContext>();
    using (var context = new EfCoreContext(options))
    {
        context.Database.EnsureCreated();

        //ATTEMPT
        var ex = Assert.Throws<InvalidOperationException>(
            () => context.Books.Select(x =>
            new ClientSeverTestDto
            {
                ClientSideProp = x.Price.ToString("C")
            }).OrderBy(x => x.ClientSideProp)
            .ToList());

        //… rest of test left out
    }
}
```

The query that logs QueryClientEvaluationWarning

The part of the query that causes QueryClientEvaluationWarning to be logged

If you're only interested in seeing the logging, or you want to look for a specific logged item, you need to use the extension method `SetupLogging`. This provides a list of logs, which your log provider will add to when EF Core generates a new log. This listing captures the logs and lists them to the unit test runner's window at the end of the unit test.

Listing 15.21   Capturing EF Core's logging and outputting it to the unit test console

In xUnit, which runs in parallel, you need to use the ITestOutputHelper to output to the unit test runner.

The ITestOutputHelper is injected by the xUnit test runner.

```
private readonly ITestOutputHelper _output;

public TestEfLogging(ITestOutputHelper output)
```

```
{
    _output = output;
}


[Fact]
public void TestEfCoreLoggingExample()
{
    //SETUP
    var options = SQLiteInMemory
        .CreateOptions<EfCoreContext>();
    using (var context = new EfCoreContext(options))
    {
        context.Database.EnsureCreated();
        context.SeedDatabaseFourBooks();
        var logs = context.SetupLogging();

        //ATTEMPT
        var books = context.Books.ToList();

        //VERIFY
        foreach (var log in logs.ToList())
        {
            _output.WriteLine(log.ToString());
        }
    }
}
```

> Sets up the logging, which returns a reference to a list of LogOutput classes. This contains separate properties for the LogLevel, EventId, Message, and so on.

> The query that you want to log

> Adds a ToList method on the end of the logs. This stops the unit test from failing if there's bleed from another unit test running in parallel

> Outputs each log to the unit test runner window

The position where you call the SetupLogging method defines what you'll log. In this example, you'd log only the book query, but if you moved the setup of the logging before the context.Database.EnsureCreated call, then you'd log how the database was created.

The logs returned are a list of LogOutput classes, which you create to hold the log information. Listing 15.21 simply lists them out, but the LogOutput class has full information on each log, as shown in the following listing. This allows you to filter logs or to look for a specific log in your unit tests as appropriate.

Listing 15.22 The LogOutput class, with the properties available to test against

```
public class LogOutput
{
    private const string EfCoreEventIdStartWith
        = "Microsoft.EntityFrameworkCore";




    public LogLevel LogLevel { get; }
    public EventId EventId { get; }
    public string Message { get; }

    public string EfEventIdLastName =>
```

> Holds each log captured from EF Core

> Uses this string to identify logs that were produced by EF Core

> Holds the EventId—useful because EF Core 2.0 has named events

> Holds what LogLevel the log was reported at; for instance, Information, Warning, Error

> The logged message

> Returns the last part of the name, but only if it's an EF Core log. Useful, as it's a quick way to identify specific events.

The constructor for the class

Gets either the last part of the EF Core eventid name, or null if not EF Core

```
        EventId.Name?.StartsWith(
                EfCoreEventIdStartWith) == true
            ? EventId.Name.Split('.').Last()
            : null;

    internal LogOutput(LogLevel logLevel,
        EventId eventId, string message)
    {
        LogLevel = logLevel;
        EventId = eventId;
        Message = message;
    }

    public override string ToString()
    {
        return
            $"{LogLevel},{EfEventIdLastName}: " +
            Message;
    }
}
```

Typically, you'll show the logs as text, so the ToString method returns a useful string.

15.8.1 *Using logging to help you build SQL change scripts*

Chapter 11 described a way to update the database by using SQL change scripts that you write yourself (see section 11.4.2). The scripts need to produce a database that matches EF Core's view of the database, and one way to help you write these scripts is to capture the SQL commands that EF Core produces to create the database. You can use logging to do that. This listing shows the unit test code that will capture the SQL commands that EF Core uses to create a new database.

Listing 15.23   Capturing the SQL commands EF Core uses to create a database

```
[RunnableInDebugOnly]
public void CaptureSqlEfCoreCreatesDatabase()
{
    //SETUP
    var options = this.
        CreateUniqueClassOptions<BookContext>();
    using (var context = new BookContext(options))
    {
        var logs = context.SetupLogging();

        //ATTEMPT
        context.Database.EnsureDeleted();
        context.Database.EnsureCreated();

        //VERIFY
        foreach (var log in logs.ToList())
        {
            _output.WriteLine(log.Message);
        }
    }
}
```

You don't need this to run every time, so you add the RunnableInDebugOnly attribute so it isn't run in the normal unit test run.

Sets up the logging before the database is created

This combination ensures a new database is created that matches the current EF Core's database Model.

Outputs only the Message part of the logging, so you can cut and paste the SQL out of the logged data

The log messages are output to the unit test runner window. Here's an example of the type of output you'd see.

Listing 15.24 **An example of the SQL code captured when EF Core creates a database**

```
Executed DbCommand (86ms) [Parameters=[], CommandType='Text',
    CommandTimeout='60']
CREATE DATABASE [EfCore.TestSupport-Test_TestEfLogging];
Executed DbCommand (30ms) [Parameters=[], CommandType='Text',
    CommandTimeout='60']
IF SERVERPROPERTY('EngineEdition') <> 5 EXEC(N'ALTER DATABASE [EfCore.
    TestSupport-Test_TestEfLogging] SET READ_COMMITTED_SNAPSHOT ON;');
Executed DbCommand (5ms) [Parameters=[], CommandType='Text',
    CommandTimeout='30']
CREATE TABLE [Authors] (
    [AuthorId] int NOT NULL IDENTITY,
    [Name] nvarchar(100) NOT NULL,
    CONSTRAINT [PK_Authors] PRIMARY KEY ([AuthorId])
);
Executed DbCommand (0ms) [Parameters=[], CommandType='Text',
    CommandTimeout='30']
CREATE TABLE [Books] (
    [BookId] int NOT NULL IDENTITY,
    [Description] nvarchar(max) NULL,
    [ImageUrl] varchar(512) NULL,
    [Price] decimal(9,2) NOT NULL,
    [PublishedOn] date NOT NULL,
    … etc.
… the rest of the code left out
```

You should ignore the first parts that delete/create the database, and extract the parts that create the tables (shown as bold). You then extract the specific parts you need for the SQL change script. If you were adding a new table called Authors, you'd extract just that part of the SQL that does that. For more-complex changes, such as adding a new column to an existing table, the captured SQL will give you the names and types you need to use in an ALTER TABLE SQL command.

15.9 *Using the EfSchemaCompare tool in your unit tests*

Section 11.4.2 explained how the EfSchemaCompare tool, which is part of the EfCore. TestSupport library, can be used when you want to use the SQL-first approach to database migrations. The EfSchemaCompare tool compares a database with the current model of the database that EF Core creates based on your entity classes and EF Core configuration.

I generally include the EfSchemaCompare tool in my normal unit test so that if a change occurs between my current database and EF Core's database Model, I'm alerted immediately (the EfSchemaCompare tool is quick, so it doesn't slow my unit testing). The following listing shows an arrangement in which you're comparing the development database you use for running your application with the current software. You'll be alerted if a difference exists; say, when you merge in another developer's changes.

Listing 15.25   Checking that the development database matches the EF Core config

Creates an instance of your application's DbContext, which will contain the latest entity classes and EF Core configuration

```
[Fact]
public void CompareDatabaseViaConnectionName()
{
    //SETUP
    const string connectionStringName =
        "BookOrderConnection";
    //... left out option building part to save space
    using (var context = new MyContext(options))
    {
        var comparer = new CompareEfSql();

        //ATTEMPT
        bool hasErrors = comparer.CompareEfWithDb
            (connectionStringName, context);

        //VERIFY
        hasErrors.ShouldBeFalse(comparer.GetAllErrors);
    }
}
```

Adds BookOrderConnection to your unit test's appsettings.json file. Points to your development database.

Creates CompareEfSql. It can have various configurations set, but in this case, you use the default settings.

The hasErrors variable will be true if there were differences. If there are, the ShouldBeFalse fluent assert will fail and output the string given in the parameter. The comparer.GetAllErrors property returns a string, with each difference on a separate line.

Uses the version of the CompareEfWithDb method that takes a connection string, or a connection string name.

If differences exist, the unit test will fail and output human-readable error messages that show you the differences. There are three types of differences, detailed here:

- DIFFERENT: MyEntity->Property 'MyString', nullability. Expected = NOT NULL, found = NULL
  This says it found a difference in one aspect of a column—in this case, its nullability.

- NOT IN DATABASE: Entity 'LineItem', table name. Expected = LineItems
  This says the table LineItems that the entity class called LineItem maps to wasn't found in the database.

- EXTRA IN DATABASE: MyEntity->PrimaryKey 'PK_MyEntites', column name. Found = MyEntityId
  This tells you that a column called MyEntityId, which is (part of) a primary key, was found in the database but wasn't in EF Core's list of primary-key properties in the entity MyEntity.

Using these, you can alter either your SQL change script or your entity classes and EF Core configuration to make them match. If the error is in your SQL change scripts, you need to edit them and re-create the database again.

TIP If you have a production pipeline, you can add the EfSchemaCompare tool to ensure that the DbContext in the application you're about to deploy matches the production database.

15.9.1 *Features and options for the EfSchemaCompare tool*

This isn't the first time I've written an EfSchemaCompare tool. I built one for EF6.x. Therefore, I knew what worked and what didn't work in the old, EF6.x version, and I was able (with the great help from EF Core) to build a much better tool. Here's a list of the features of the EfSchemaCompare tool:

- It has almost complete coverage of all the EF Core features, including the various table-mapping features: table per hierarchy, table splitting, and owned types. For a list of limitations, see http://mng.bz/79hZ.
- It can handle multiple applications' DbContexts, known as *bounded contexts* (see section 10.6) mapped to one database. See http://mng.bz/o2Ip for more information.
- You can find the database in two ways when calling the `CompareEfWithDb` method:
  - If you provide only an application's DbContext, it'll get the connection string from the (first) application's DbContext.
  - If you provide a string as the first parameter, it'll look for a connection string of that name in the appsettings.json file. If a connection string of that name isn't found, it'll assume the string is a connection string and use that to access the database.

In addition, the `CompareEfSql` class constructor can take an optional parameter of the `CompareEfSqlConfig` class. This provides the following options:

- You can exclude tables in the database from being scanned. This is useful if you have tables that EF Core doesn't access, as it stops the comparison, outputting an `EXTRA IN DATABASE` error for those tables.
- Because of my experience, I know that the `EfSchemaCompare` tool can output errors that I'm not bothered about—say, an extra index that's found in the database but not in my code. These cause a unit test failure, which isn't what I want. I've added two methods, `AddIgnoreCompareLog` and `IgnoreTheseErrors`, which provide two ways of suppressing unwanted difference errors.

NOTE The full documentation of these options can be found at http://mng .bz/7cb8.

Summary

- The best way to simulate a database in unit tests depends on what advanced SQL features you use.
- Using in-memory databases to simulate a database makes your unit tests run faster, but in-memory databases don't support all the features available in a real database.

- A DbContext designed to work with an ASP.NET Core application is ready for unit testing, but any application's DbContext that uses the `OnConfiguring` method to set options needs to be modified to allow unit testing.
- If you're using a real database with the xUnit test runner, which runs each test class in parallel, then you need to provide separate databases for each unit test class.
- Testing a disconnected state update requires using two separate instances of the application's DbContext—one to set up the database and one to test the update method.
- When you have a repository pattern for accessing the database, such as in business logic as described in section 4.4.3, mocking that repository gives you fast and comprehensive control of the data for unit testing.
- The logging information output by EF Core can be useful. It can show you the SQL that EF Core produces, and allows you to catch possible suboptimal SQL problems.
- You can obtain access to the SQL commands that EF Core uses to create a database, which can be useful if you're using the SQL-first database migration approach (see section 11.4.2).
- The EfSchemaCompare tool provides a way to ensure that the EF Core's database `Model` of your application matches the database you're using. The same tool also helps you find those differences and correct them by providing human-readable difference messages.

For readers who are familiar with EF6.x:

- EF Core provides in-memory database techniques that can speed up the unit testing of EF Core database code.
- The two EF Core methods `context.Database.EnsureDeleted` and `context.Database.EnsureCreated` are useful methods for creating empty databases, but they're quite slow.

appendix A
A brief introduction to LINQ

This appendix covers

- An introduction to the LINQ language
- Data manipulation commands in LINQ
- An introduction to the `IQueryable<T>` .NET type
- How EF Core translates LINQ to database commands
- The three parts of an EF Core LINQ query

This appendix is for anyone who is new to Microsoft's Language Integrated Query, or LINQ, feature or anyone who wants a quick recap on how LINQ works. The LINQ language bridges the gap between the world of objects and the world of data, and is used by EF Core to build database queries. Understanding the LINQ language is key to using EF Core to access a database.

This appendix starts with the two syntaxes you can use to write LINQ code. You'll also learn the types of commands available in LINQ, with examples of how those commands can manipulate collections of in-memory data.

You'll then explore the related .NET type, `IQueryable<T>`, which holds LINQ code in a form that can be executed later. This allows developers to split complex queries into separate parts and dynamically change the LINQ query. The `IQueryable<T>`

451

type also allows EF Core to translate the LINQ code into commands that can be run on the database server.

Finally, you'll learn what an EF Core query, with its LINQ part, looks like.

A.1   *An introduction to the LINQ language*

You can manipulate collections of data by using LINQ's methods to sort, filter, select, and so on. These collections can be in-memory data (such as an array of integers, XML data, JSON data) and of course on databases, via libraries such as EF Core. The LINQ feature is available in Microsoft's languages C#, F#, and Visual Basic; by using LINQ's functional programming approach, you can create readable code.

> **TIP**   If you haven't come across functional programming, it's worth a look. Have a look at http://mng.bz/97CY or, for a more in-depth, .NET-focused book, have a look at Enrico Buonanno's *Functional Programming in C#* (Manning, 2017).

A.1.1   *The two ways you can write LINQ queries*

LINQ has two syntaxes for writing LINQ queries: the *method* syntax and the *query* syntax. This section presents the two syntaxes and points out which syntax is used in this book. You'll write the same LINQ query, a filter, and a sort of an array of integers in both syntaxes.

The following listing uses what is known as the LINQ *method*, or *lambda*, syntax. This code is a simple LINQ statement. Even if you haven't seen LINQ before, the names of the LINQ methods, such as `Where` and `OrderBy`, provide a good clue to what's going on.

Listing A.1   Your first look at the LINQ language, using the method/lambda syntax

Applies LINQ commands and returns a new array of integers

Creates an array of integers from 0 to 5, but in a random order

```
int[] nums = new[] {1, 5, 4, 2, 3, 0};

int[] result = nums
    .Where(x => x > 3)
    .OrderBy(x => x)
    .ToArray();
```

Filters out all the integers 3 and below

Orders the numbers

Turns the query back into an array. The result is an array of ints { 4, 5 }.

The *lambda* name comes from lambda syntax, introduced in C# 3. The lambda syntax allows you to write a method without all the standard method definition syntax. The `x => x > 3` part inside the `Where` method is equivalent to the following method:

```
private bool AnonymousFunc(int x)
{
    return x > 3;
}
```

As you can see, the lambda syntax can save a significant amount of typing. I use lambdas in all of my EF Core queries and in lots of other code I wrote for this book.

Listing A.2 shows the other way of writing LINQ code, called the *query* syntax. This code achieves the same result as in listing A.1 but returns a slightly different result type.

Listing A.2 Your first look at the LINQ language, using the query syntax

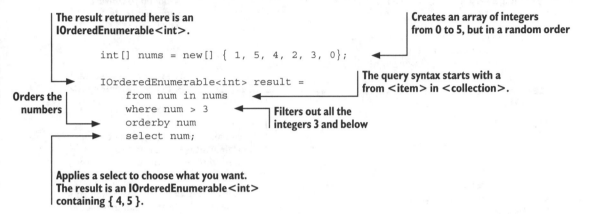

The result returned here is an
IOrderedEnumerable<int>.

Creates an array of integers
from 0 to 5, but in a random order

```
int[] nums = new[] { 1, 5, 4, 2, 3, 0};

IOrderedEnumerable<int> result =
    from num in nums
    where num > 3
    orderby num
    select num;
```

Orders the numbers

The query syntax starts with a
from <item> in <collection>.

Filters out all the
integers 3 and below

Applies a select to choose what you want.
The result is an IOrderedEnumerable<int>
containing { 4, 5 }.

You can use either syntax—the choice is up to you. Personally, I use the method syntax because it's slightly less typing, and I like the way that commands are chained together, one after the other. The rest of the examples in this book use the method syntax.

Before I leave the topic of the LINQ syntax, I want to introduce the concept of precalculating values in a LINQ query. The query syntax has a feature specifically to handle this: the `let` keyword. This allows you to calculate a value once and then use that value multiple times in the query, which makes the query more efficient. This listing shows code that converts an integer value to its word/string equivalent and then uses that string in both the sort and filter part of the query.

Listing A.3 Using the `let` keyword in a LINQ query syntax

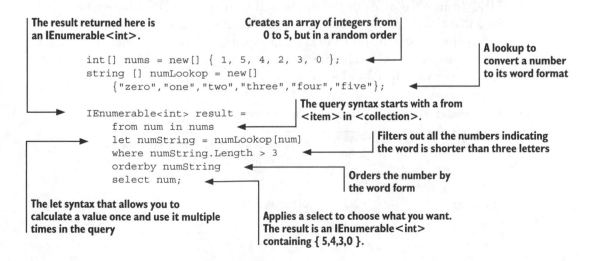

The result returned here is
an IEnumerable<int>.

Creates an array of integers from
0 to 5, but in a random order

A lookup to
convert a number
to its word format

```
int[] nums = new[] { 1, 5, 4, 2, 3, 0 };
string [] numLookop = new[]
    {"zero","one","two","three","four","five"};

IEnumerable<int> result =
    from num in nums
    let numString = numLookop[num]
    where numString.Length > 3
    orderby numString
    select num;
```

The query syntax starts with a from
<item> in <collection>.

Filters out all the numbers indicating
the word is shorter than three letters

Orders the number by
the word form

The let syntax that allows you to
calculate a value once and use it multiple
times in the query

Applies a select to choose what you want.
The result is an IEnumerable<int>
containing { 5,4,3,0 }.

The equivalent in the method syntax is to use the LINQ `Select` operator earlier in the query, as shown in listing A.4 (section A.2 provides more details about the LINQ `Select` operator).

Listing A.4   Using the LINQ `Select` operator to hold a calculated value

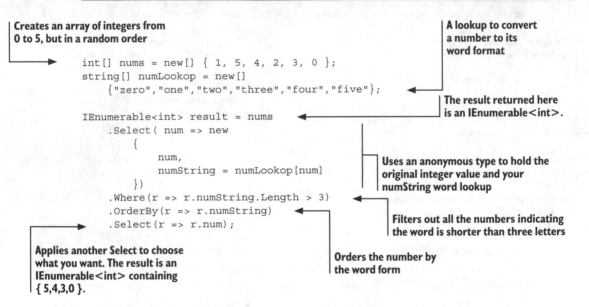

Creates an array of integers from 0 to 5, but in a random order

A lookup to convert a number to its word format

```
int[] nums = new[] { 1, 5, 4, 2, 3, 0 };
string[] numLookop = new[]
    {"zero","one","two","three","four","five"};

IEnumerable<int> result = nums
    .Select( num => new
        {
            num,
            numString = numLookop[num]
        })
    .Where(r => r.numString.Length > 3)
    .OrderBy(r => r.numString)
    .Select(r => r.num);
```

The result returned here is an IEnumerable<int>.

Uses an anonymous type to hold the original integer value and your numString word lookup

Filters out all the numbers indicating the word is shorter than three letters

Applies another Select to choose what you want. The result is an IEnumerable<int> containing { 5,4,3,0 }.

Orders the number by the word form

EF6   EF6.x used the `let` or the `Select` as a hint to precalculate a value only once in the database. EF Core 2.0 doesn't have that performance feature, so it recalculates every occurrence of a value. It's possible that this performance feature will be added to EF Core in the future.

A.1.2   The data operations you can do with LINQ

The LINQ feature has many methods, referred to as *operators*. Most have names and functions that clearly indicate what's going on. Table A.1 lists some of the more common LINQ operators; similar operators are grouped to help you see where they might be used. The list is not exhaustive; the aim is to show you some of the more common operators to give you a feel for what LINQ can do.

Table A.1   Examples of LINQ operators, grouped by their purpose

Group	Some examples (not all operators shown)
Sorting	`OrderBy, OrderByDescending, Reverse`
Filtering	`Where`
Select element	`First, FirstOrDefault`
Projection	`Select`

Group	Some examples (not all operators shown)
Aggregation	`Max, Min, Sum, Count, Average`
Partition	`Skip, Take`
Boolean tests	`Any, All, Contains`

NOTE You can get a full list of the LINQ operators at http://mng.bz/rP11. But be warned: EF Core can't translate some of the more complex operators to a database access command that will run on the database server. Because of the EF Core feature called client vs. server evaluation (see section 2.5), you can use any LINQ command in an EF Core query, although some won't be fast.

Listing A.1 showed a sorting and filtering example. Later in this appendix, I'll show you a few more examples so you can see some of the other LINQ operators in action. First, you need to define a new class called `Review` with data to help with the examples, as shown here.

Listing A.5 A `Review` class and a `ReviewsList` variable containing two reviews

```
class Review
{
    public string VoterName { get; set; }
    public int NumStars { get; set; }
    public string Comment { get; set; }
}

List<Review> ReviewsList = new List<Review>
{
    new Review
    {
        VoterName = "Jack",
        NumStars = 5,
        Comment = "A great book!"
    },
    new Review
    {
        VoterName = "Jill",
        NumStars = 1,
        Comment = "I hated it!"
    }
};
```

The `ReviewsList` field in LINQ code is shown in table A.2. This should give you a feel for how various LINQ operators work.

Table A.2 Four usages of LINQ on the ReviewsList field as data. The result of each LINQ operator is shown in the Result Value column.

LINQ Group	Code using LINQ operators	Result value

Projection	```string[] result = ReviewsList```
	``` .Select(p => p.VoterName)```
	``` .ToArray();```
		```string[]{"Jack", "Jill"}```

Aggregation	```double result = ReviewsList``` ``` .Average(p => p.NumStars);```	3 (average of 5 and 1)
Select element	```string result = ReviewsList``` ``` .First().VoterName;```	"Jack" (first voter)
Boolean test	```bool result = ReviewsList``` ``` .Any(p => p.NumStars == 1);```	true (Jill voted 1)

A.2   *Introduction to IQueryable<T> type, and why it's useful*

Another important part of LINQ is the generic interface IQueryable<T>. LINQ is rather special, in that whatever set of LINQ operators you provide isn't executed straightaway but is held in a type called IQueryable<T>, awaiting a final command to execute it. This IQueryable<T> form has two benefits:

- You can split a complex LINQ query into separate parts by using the IQueryable<T> type.
- Instead of executing the IQueryable<T>'s internal form, EF Core can translate it into database access commands.

A.2.1   *Splitting up a complex LINQ query by using the IQueryable<T> type*

In the book, you'll learn about *query objects* (see section 2.6.1), and you'll build a complex book list query by chaining together three query objects. This works because of the IQueryable<T> type's ability to hold the code in a specialized form, called an *expression tree*, so that other LINQ operators can be appended to it.

As an example, you're going to improve the code from listing A.1 by adding your own method that contains the sorting part of the query. This allows you to alter the sort order of the final LINQ query. You'll create this method as an *extension method*, which allows you to chain the method in the same way as the LINQ's operators do (LINQ operators are extension methods).

> **DEFINITION** An *extension method* is a static method in a static class; the first parameter of the method has the keyword this in front of it. To allow chaining, the method must also return a type that other methods can use as an input.

The following listing shows the extension method MyOrder, which takes in an IQueryable<int> type as its first parameter and returns an IQueryable<int> result. It also has a second boolean parameter called ascending that sets the sort order to either ascending or descending, for the results.

Listing A.6   Your method encapsulates part of your LINQ code via IQueryable<int>

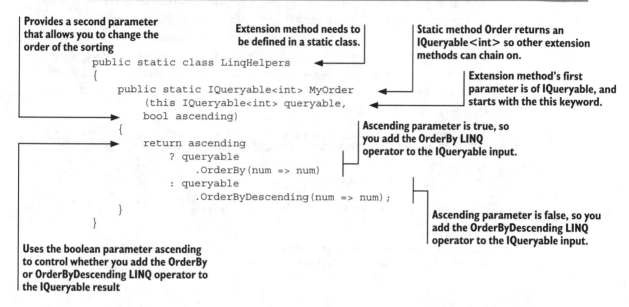

This listing uses this IQueryable<int> extension method to replace the OrderBy LINQ operator in the original code in listing A.1.

Listing A.7   Using the MyOrder IQueryable<int> method in LINQ code

Calls the MyOrder IQueryable<int>
method, with true. This gives you an
ascending sort of the data.

```
var numsQ = new[] { 1, 5, 4, 2, 3 }
    .AsQueryable();
```

Turns an array of integers
into a queryable object.

```
var result = numsQ
    .MyOrder(true)
    .Where(x => x > 3)
    .ToArray();
```

Filters out all the
numbers 3 and below

Executes the IQueryable and turns
the result into an array. The result
is an array of ints { 4, 5 }.

Using extension methods, such as the `MyOrder` example, provides two useful features:

- *It makes your LINQ code dynamic.* By changing the parameter into the MyOrder method, you can change the sort order of the final LINQ query. If you didn't have that parameter, you'd need two LINQ queries, one using OrderBy and one using OrderByDescending, and then have to pick which one you wanted to run by using an `if` statement. That isn't good software practice, as you'd be needlessly repeating some LINQ code, such as the `Where` part.
- *It allows you to split complex queries into a series of separate extension methods that you can chain together.* This makes it easier to build, test, and understand complex queries. In section 2.8, you split your book app book list query, which is rather complicated, into separate query objects. The following listing shows this again, with each query object highlighted in bold.

Listing A.8   The book list query with select, order, filter, and page query objects

```
public IQueryable<BookListDto> SortFilterPage
    (SortFilterPageOptions options)
{
    var booksQuery = _context.Books
        .AsNoTracking()
        .MapBookToDto()
        .OrderBooksBy(options.OrderByOptions)
        .FilterBooksBy(options.FilterBy,
                       options.FilterValue);

    options.SetupRestOfDto(booksQuery);

    return booksQuery.Page(options.PageNum-1,
                           options.PageSize);
}
```

The book list query uses both features I've mentioned. First, it allows you to dynamically change the sorting, filtering, and paging of the book list. Second, it hides some of the more complex code behind an aptly named method, which tells you what it's doing.

A.2.2   *How EF Core translates IQueryable<T> into database code*

EF Core translates your LINQ code into database code that can run on the database server. It can do this because the `IQueryable<T>` type holds all the LINQ code as an *expression tree*, which EF Core can translate into database access code. Figure A.1 shows what EF Core is doing behind the scenes when it translates a LINQ query into database access code.

EF Core provides many extra extension methods to extend the LINQ operators available to you. EF Core methods add to the LINQ expression tree, such as `Include`, `ThenInclude` (see section 2.4.1), and so on. Other EF methods provide async versions (see section 5.10) of the LINQ methods, such as `ToListAsync` and `LastAsync`.

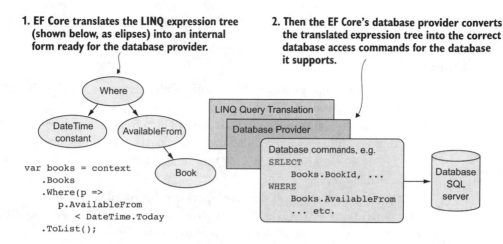

1. EF Core translates the LINQ expression tree (shown below, as elipses) into an internal form ready for the database provider.

2. Then the EF Core's database provider converts the translated expression tree into the correct database access commands for the database it supports.

```
var books = context
    .Books
    .Where(p =>
        p.AvailableFrom
            < DateTime.Today
    .ToList();
```

Figure A.1   Some book query code (bottom left) with its expression tree above it. EF Core takes the expression tree through two stages of translation before it ends up in the right form for the database that the application is targeting.

A.3   Querying an EF Core database by using LINQ

Using LINQ in an EF Core database query requires three parts, as shown in figure A.2. The query relies on an application's DbContext, which is described in section 2.2.1. This section concentrates on just the format of an EF Core database query, with the LINQ operators shown in bold.

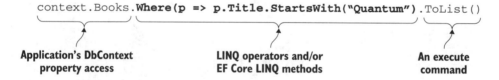

Figure A.2   An example database access, with the three parts

These three component parts of an EF Core database query are as follows:

- *Application's DbContext property access*—In your application's DbContext, you define a property by using a DbSet<T> type. This returns an IQueryable<T> data source to which you can add LINQ operators to create a database query.
- *LINQ operators and/or EF Core LINQ methods*—This is where your database LINQ query code goes.
- *The execute command*—Commands such as ToList and First trigger EF Core to translate the LINQ commands into database access commands that are run on the database server.

In chapter 2 and onward, you'll see much more complex queries, but they all use the three parts shown in figure A.2.

Summary

- The LINQ language provides data manipulation features for the C#, F#, and Visual Basic languages.
- The LINQ feature manipulates a collection of data by using methods, called *operators*, that sort, filter, select, project, aggregate, partition, and so on.
- The IQueryable<T> type holds LINQ commands in a specialized form called an *expression tree*.
- The IQueryable<T> type allows developers to split complex queries into separate parts. This allows a LINQ query to be dynamically changed by adding different LINQ operators to the end of the current expression tree.
- The IQueryable<T> type allows EF Core to translate the expression tree into database access code that runs on the database server.
- An EF Core database access consists of three parts:
  - The IQueryable<T> source from the application's DbContext.
  - The LINQ code that sorts, filters, selects, and so on that IQueryable<T> source.
  - A command that triggers the translation and execution of the LINQ query on the database.

appendix B
Early information on EF Core version 2.1

This appendix covers

- What does a 2.1 release of EF Core mean?
- The new features in EF Core 2.1
- The improvements in EF Core 2.1

All books need to be finished, and this book went into the print process phase before EF Core 2.1 was released. Thankfully, version 2.1 is a minor update, so it doesn't change the code in this book that much, but it does add new features and improvements. The changes are welcome, especially some of the new features; hence, I added this appendix and various EF Core 2.1 notes to the book before it went to print.

> **NOTE** You can find the latest information on EF Core 2.1 at https://docs .microsoft.com/en-us/ef/core/what-is-new/ef-core-2.1.

My evaluation of EF Core 2.1's new features is that they're well thought through and follow the overall architectural approach used in EF Core. It would be easy to quickly tack on a new feature that people are asking for, which would make the design of EF Core messy or hard to follow. But I don't see that happening. For instance, the new lazy-loading feature in version 2.1 has an implementation that uses the existing backing-fields feature, which makes it quite natural to use. Similarly, EF Core 2.1's new data-seeding implementation improves on EF6.x's data-seeding approach, which had some limitations.

This appendix gives you an overview of the new features and changes in EF Core 2.1 and how you might use them. I'll limit the information to the new feature changes with only a few code examples. The idea of this appendix is to alert you to the new features so you know about them when you are developing an application.

> **TIP** I recommend a video from Microsoft's Build 2018 conference on EF Core 2.1 given by Diego Vaga and Andrews Peters from the EF Core team. As well as explaining some of the new 2.1 features the video starts with the vision that drives the developer of EF Core. See www.youtube.cm/watch?v=k55kDH_ixrQ.

B.1   What does the 2.1 in the EF Core release number mean?

The .NET Core platform and the associated packages, such as ASP.NET Core and EF Core, are on a rolling improvement program. All the .NET Core packages use a *semantic versioning* approach for releases (see https://mng.bz/L2t1), with the version number made up of three parts: Major.Minor.Patch—for instance, 2.1.0. With a minor update, such as this step from EF Core 2.0 to 2.1, new features are added, but existing features/APIs aren't changed.

This book was written around EF Core 2.0. Because EF Core 2.1 is a minor release, everything in the book is still relevant for EF Core 2.1. But the new features in EF Core 2.1 do offer some new ways of working, so you'll find prerelease notes throughout this book on other options that might be available after EF Core 2.1 is released, and this appendix provides a list of the changes that have been pre-announced.

Clearly, things could change in EF Core 2.1 before release, with features added or removed. So don't treat this appendix and the EF Core 2.1 notes as the definitive truth, but more like signposts about new features that you might like to look up on the Microsoft EF Core documentation site—see https://docs.microsoft.com/en-gb/ef/core/what-is-new/ef-core-2.1.

B.2   Brand-new features

EF Core 2.1's features offer you new ways to use EF Core. Some, such as lazy loading and data seeding, have been a user-led request for EF6.x features to be included in EF Core. Other features, like the Azure Cosmos NoSQL database provider, continue the general improvement of EF Core. The new features are as follows:

- Lazy loading—loading relationships when you need them
- Parameters in entity class constructors
- Value conversion—defining the mapping of value types to the database
- Data seeding—adding initial data to a new/updated database

- Query types—using non-entity classes in read-only queries
- Including derived types when using table per hierarchy
- Linking to entity class state change events
- Supporting NoSQL—Cosmos NoSQL database provider (preview)

B.2.1 Lazy loading—loading relationships when you need them

Lazy loading is a way to load relationships only when you access that relationship. In chapter 2, I talked about the four ways of loading relationships in a query: eager loading, explicit loading, select loading, and lazy loading. Many EF6.x developers are used to lazy loading and find it useful, mainly because you can read in a relationship without needing a copy of the application's DbContext. There are two ways to use lazy loading:

1 Using the `LazyLoader` class with backing fields.
2 Using proxy classes by adding the keyword `virtual` to your relationships

USING THE LAZYLOADER CLASS WITH BACKING FIELDS

This listing shows how to use the `LazyLoader` service to load the navigational collection property `Many`, only if you read that property. The `ILazyLoader` service is injected via a private constructor on the entity class (see B.2.2).

Listing B.1 Using the `LazyLoader` class for lazy loading of navigational properties

Normal public constructor used by your code to obtain an instance of MyEntity

#A The LazyLoader class is used for any navigational properties that you want to lazy load.

```
public class MyEntity
{
    private readonly ILazyLoader _lazyLoader;

    private MyEntity(ILazyLoader lazyLoader)
    {
        LazyLoader = lazyLoader;
    }

    public MyEntity() {}

    private Collection<ManyEntity> _many =
        new Collection<ManyEntity>();

    //… other properties left out
    public Collection<ManyEntity> Many
    {
        get => _lazyLoader?.Load(this, ref _many);
        set => _many = value;
    }
}
```

The LazyLoader instance is injected by EF Core via the constructor. The constructor can be private.

The collection you want lazy loaded is set up as a backing field.

The collection navigational property is accessed via a getter and a setter.

An attempt to load the property triggers the lazy loader, which reads in the collection from the database. You need to provide a reference to the field for lazy loading to work.

The basic idea is that an EF Core's `LazyLoader` instance will be provided via an entity class constructor with a parameter (see section B.2.2). As you can see in listing B.1, the navigational property you want to lazy load must be set up as a backing field (see section 8.1). The property's getter accesses the backing field via a call to the `LazyLoader` service, which ensures that the navigation property is loaded on a read.

> **NOTE**   A look at the `LazyLoading` class in the EF Core GitHub repo shows that if the navigation property is loaded, it doesn't load it again, the same behavior as in EF6.x.

Using the backing-field approach for lazy loading is quite elegant, as you can choose how and when lazy loading is used. You also still have the option to allow access to the data only via methods and still use lazy loading if you want to.

USING PROXY CLASSES BY ADDING THE KEYWORD VIRTUAL TO YOUR RELATIONSHIPS

In EF6.x lazy loading was automatically enabled by adding the keyword `virtual` to a navigational property. EF Core provides the same approach but, unlike EF6.x, you do need to enable it.

> **EF6**   This approach is useful for developers porting EF6.x code to EF Core, as your entity classes will work the same.

Using this approach in EF Core requires you to add the NuGet package Microsoft.EntityFrameworkCore.Proxies to your application. You also need to enable lazy loading by applying the `UseLazyLoadingProxies` method when configuring your DbContext, as shown in this code snippet from an ASP.NET Core configuration

```
.AddDbContext<EfCoreContext>(
    b => b.UseLazyLoadingProxies()
        .UseSqlServer(myConnectionString));
```

Listing B.2 shows the Book entity class with the Reviews collection set up for lazy loading

Listing B.2 Using the `virtual` keyword to lazy loading navigational properties

```
public class MyEntity
{
    //… other properties left out
    public virtual Collection<ManyEntity>
        Many { get; set; }
}
```

> The virtual keyword, coupled with the Proxies NuGet package, means that the Many collection will be lazy loaded if read.

Clearly this is simpler to write than the `ILazyLoader` example, but it does require EF Core to create proxy classes for all entities that use lazy loading.

Comments on the lazy-loading feature and database performance

Many developers like lazy loading because it's simple to use, but I and others don't recommend using lazy loading at all. Why? Because each lazy loading requires a separate database access, and, as I said in section 12.5.1, each database access comes with a time cost. Lazy loading can significantly reduce the performance of your database accesses.

My impression is that many people need lazy loading because they're using a *Repository pattern* (see section 10.5) for their database accesses, which hides the EF Core code. The Repository pattern can make writing the database accesses easier, especially if you use lazy loading, but such repositories don't always produce well performing database access code. This means you might create a lot of your database access code quickly, but then find yourself caught up in serious performance-tuning issues later.

In this book, I use the *Query Object* pattern (see section 2.6) to produce tailored code for each query. I show in section 10.4 how to use a DDD approach to updating entities. Using these two approaches lets you build well-performing queries quickly, without resorting to lazy loading. See my article at http://mng.bz/5VH2 for a more detailed discussion on this topic.

B.2.2 Parameters in entity class constructors

Prior to version 2.1, EF Core used a parameterless constructor to create an instance of an entity class before filling in each property or field. EF Core 2.1 provides another way to create an entity class, using constructors that have parameters. There are two very different reasons for using constructors with parameters.

1 Binding the data read from the database to the properties
2 Injecting services into your entity class, for instance `ILazyLoader`

BINDING THE DATA READ FROM THE DATABASE TO THE PROPERTIES

EF Core 2.1 and above can create an instance of an entity class by using a parameterized constructor. If EF Core finds a parameterized constructor with parameter names and types that match those of mapped properties, it will use that constructor with values for those properties and won't set each property explicitly. Otherwise, it will use a parameterless constructor and set the properties directly.

> **NOTE** There are lots of subtle features in binding via parameterized constructors, such as that the navigational properties cannot be set via the constructor. I recommend you look at the latest EF Core documentation on this topic for more information—see https://mng.bz/MDpm .

INJECTING SERVICES INTO YOUR ENTITY CLASS

To make lazy loading work, you need to provide an instance of EF Core's `ILazyLoader` when the class is created. You need to have an entity class constructor that can take parameters. EF Core 2.1 can inject the following services when it creates an instance of an entity class:

- `ILazyLoader`. The lazy-loading service—see section B.2.1.
- `Action<object, string>`. This is a lazy-loading delegate; it will inject the lazy-loading service—see section B.2.1.

- `DbContext`. The current context instance, which can also be typed as your application's DbContext, for instance `EfCoreContext`.
- `IEntityType`. The EF Core metadata associated with this entity type

The first two are obviously used for lazy loading; the final two provide some interesting possibilities.

> **NOTE**   Again there as some subtle features, such as what happens if you attach an existing entity and you need the application's DbContext. Please look at the latest EF Core documentation for more information—see http://mng.bz/aM86.

B.2.3   Value conversion—defining the mapping of value types to the database

Before version 2.1, EF Core could only map scalar property types (see chapter 6) that are natively supported by the underlying database provider. Starting with EF Core 2.1, value conversions can be applied to transform the values obtained from columns before they're applied to properties, and vice versa. This provides several new features. You can do the following:

- Store `Enum` types as strings instead of as the enum value
- Provide a mapping for user-defined `structs` to the database
- Transform a property—for instance, transparently encrypting a property on save, and decrypting that same property on load

EF Core 2.1 provides several conversions that can be applied by convention, as well as an explicit configuration API that allows registering delegates for the conversions between columns and properties—see https://docs.microsoft.com/en-gb/ef/core/modeling/value-conversions for more information.

B.2.4   Data seeding—adding initial data to a new/updated database

Sometimes you might want to populate a new or updated database with initial data—for instance, a list of countries you can ship to. EF6.x had such a feature, which was run at startup, but it had limitations. EF Core 2.1 provides a better implementation of seeding that incorporates your initial data into the database migrations:

- The data is written out only if the migration needs to be applied to the database.
- Later database migrations can add, delete, or update data that was applied in previous migrations.

EF Core 2.1's data-seeding feature is associated with an entity type as part of the model configuration. The seeding configuration code is then turned into database migration code when you use the design-time method to add a new migration. See https://docs.microsoft.com/en-gb/ef/core/modeling/data-seeding for more information.

B.2.5 *Query types—using non-entity classes in read-only queries*

EF Core 2.1 introduces a feature called *query types,* which has several possible applications. Query types are .NET classes that can be mapped to the database, but unlike entity classes, query types are only for read-only queries (which is where the *query* part of its name comes from). Query types work in the same way as the DTOs described in section 2.6.1, in that query types contain the specific data needed by the frontend system.

EF Core 2.1 allows query types to be used in several places. For instance, you can do the following:

- Define a LINQ query in your configuration code, such that you can use that query type, via the Query<T> method, in a LINQ-based query.
- Use a query type in a FromSQL method. This allows you to write SQL that maps to a class that isn't an entity class.
- Map a query type to a database view. A database view is an SQL SELECT statement stored in the database and associated with a name.
- You can map a query type to a table that has no primary key. A relational table without a primary key is unusual, but they can occur. Before EF Core 2.1, you couldn't map to it, but now you can.

This feature makes select-type queries, which this book has shown can produce efficient database queries, into a first-class citizen. You can predefine a LINQ-based query, use an SQL-based query, or you can use a database view and define the SQL query in your database. See https://docs.microsoft.com/en-gb/ef/core/modeling/query-types for more information.

B.2.6 *Include derived types when using table per hierarchy*

When using a table-per-hierarchy (TPH) table mapping (see section 7.8.2), you might have a relationship in one of the inherited types. Say you have two types, PaymentCash and PaymentCard, and only the PaymentCard type has a relationship of type CardType. Before EF Core 2.1, you couldn't eager load this sort of relationship. But in EF Core 2.1, this has been fixed, and you can include relationships in one part of a TPH class. The following code snippet shows you one way of doing this

```
var orders = context.Payments.Include(p => ((CardType)p).Card)
```

B.2.7 *Ability to link to entity class state change events*

In section 9.4 we overrode the SaveChanges method in your application's DbContext to capture changes to entities and implement some of your own logic. The downside of that approach was you needed to override all four versions of the SaveChanges method to do that properly.

In EF Core 2.1 there is a new feature where you can link to entity state changes, which makes intercepting state changes much simpler to implement. In addition, there is a Tracked event which allows you to react to entities becoming tracked.

B.2.8   *Supporting NoSQL—Cosmos NoSQL Database provider (preview)*

From the start, EF Core was designed to handle SQL and NoSQL databases, but in the first releases, no NoSQL database providers were available. In EF Core 2.1, you'll find a preview version of a database provider for Azure's Cosmos NoSQL database. The idea is that you can use all the same tools and techniques you've used in EF Core on relational databases and apply them to NoSQL, nonrelational databases.

Personally, I'm pleased to see EF Core supporting NoSQL databases, because NoSQL databases have a role to play in modern applications. In section 14.2, I use a CQRS architecture with a NoSQL database handling the read-side to provide improved performance and scalability over an SQL-only implementation. Allowing EF Core to work with both SQL and NoSQL databases is a significant step forward.

> **NOTE**   The Cosmos database provider in EF Core 2.1 is a *preview* version and may well have limitations and/or bugs. This Cosmos database provider is there to expose and improve EF Core's current implementation of NoSQL databases. Also, it will act as a template to help other developers produce EF Core database providers for other NoSQL databases, such as MongoDB.

B.3   *Improvements to existing features*

This section lists changes in EF Core 2.1 that add to or modify existing features in EF Core. There's a slight overlap with the "new features" section, but I group these changes as improvements because in each case you could already use the feature in EF Core 2. But EF Core 2.1 brings better capabilities or performance to each feature. The items are as follows:

- LINQ `GroupBy` translation to SQL `GROUP BY` command
- Optimization of correlated subqueries—the $N + 1$ SQL query problem
- .NET Core global tools—installing design-time tools locally
- Column ordering in a database now follows entity-class property order
- `System.Transactions` support
- Specifying an owned type via an attribute

B.3.1   *LINQ GroupBy translation to SQL GROUP BY command*

One downside of EF Core before version 2.0 was that the LINQ `GroupBy` operator was evaluated in memory, whereas EF6.x translated it to the SQL `GROUP BY` command. In EF Core 2.1 and above, the common uses of the LINQ `GroupBy` operator are now converted to SQL. This is a welcome improvement, as some projects needed this feature.

B.3.2   *Optimization of correlated subqueries—*
the N + 1 SQL query problem

In section 13.2, I show that in EF Core 2.0, the loading of the Author's names collection for a book causes a new database access for each book. The book list query that reads in 10 books has 1 + 10 trips to the database: one for the book information of all 10 books, and then a single database access for each book's list of authors. This is known as the *N + 1 query problem.*

In EF Core 2.1, more work has gone into finding and fixing these $N + 1$ query problems. This should mean that any query that contains a collection should perform more quickly. To take advantage of this you need to add an execute method, such as `ToList`, to any subquery that loads a collection. For instance, to improve the performance of the book list `select` query in listing 2.10 you need to add the `ToList` method to the end of the subquery than reads in the Author's Name properties, as shown in bold in this code snippet.

```
public static IQueryable<BookListDto>
    MapBookToDto(this IQueryable<Book> books)
{
    return books.Select(p => new BookListDto
    {
        //… other parts of select removed
        AuthorsOrdered = string.Join(", ",
                p.AuthorsLink
                .OrderBy(q => q.Order)
                .Select(q => q.Author.Name).ToList()),
    });
}
```

According to the documentation this improvement turns the N + 1 into a 1 + 1 access, meaning the multiple accesses are reduced to just one access. Section 12.5.1 shows that each database access has a performance cost, so this improvement to N + 1 queries gives you a welcome performance boost with little effort.

B.3.3 *.NET Core global tools—installing design-time tools locally*

Microsoft has been looking at the design-time tools that various .NET Core libraries use, such as EF Core's migration commands, and developed a new way to handle design-time tools, called *global tools*. The idea behind .NET Core global tools is that you can install a tool from NuGet on your local machine and run that tool from any directory.

As a result, in EF Core 2.1, you will see the release of NuGet tools for handling database migrations. These new global tools are likely to be the same as the CLI tools, but will be independently loaded and will run without the `dotnet` prefix. The benefit is that the migration tools will be updateable in the normal NuGet way, and you won't need the tools in your .csprog file.

B.3.4 *Column ordering in database now follows entity-class property order*

Before EF Core 2.1, the order of the columns in the database was sorted alphabetically. Users have asked that the properties be declared in the same order as appear in the entity class, which EF Core 2.1 now implements.

B.3.5 *System.Transactions support*

EF Core 2.1 supports `System.Transactions` features and is linked to changes in .NET Core 2.1. This allows you to create an instance of your application's DbContext within an existing `TransactionScope`. This is an advanced feature and not many application's will need this.

B.3.6 *Specifying an owned type via an attribute*

In section 7.8.1 you created what EF Core calls an owned type class called `Address`, which could be added to entity class. You needed to use Fluent API to configure each use of the owned type `Address` class in an entity class.

In EF Core 2.1 there is a quicker way to do this. If you apply the `[Owned]` attribute to the class definition of your owned types, then EF Core will automatically configure any entity classes that uses that owned type.

Summary

- All .NET Core packages use sematic versioning, so the step from EF Core 2.0 to 2.1 is a minor release. Because EF Core 2.1 is a minor release, it doesn't change the content of this book. It only adds new features and improvements.
- In addition to this appendix on EF Core 2.1, you'll find notes in the chapters indicating where EF Core 2.1 offers new options over what's taught in those chapters.
- EF Core 2.1 has welcome improvements that EF6.x developers have been waiting for, such as lazy loading, LINQ `GroupBy` query translation to SQL, and data seeding.
- New features, such as a database provider for the NoSQL database Cosmos and value conversions, extend what you can do with EF Core.

index

V

W

X